SQL SERVER 2000

SQL Server 2000 Design & T-SQL Programming

MICHAEL **REILLY** & MICHELLE **POOLET**

Osborne/**McGraw-Hill**

Berkeley New York St. Louis San Francisco
Auckland Bogotá Hamburg London Madrid
Mexico City Milan Montreal New Delhi Panama City
Paris São Paulo Singapore Sydney
Tokyo Toronto

Osborne/**McGraw-Hill**
2600 Tenth Street
Berkeley, California 94710
U.S.A.

For information on translations or book distributors outside the U.S.A., or to arrange bulk purchase discounts for sales promotions, premiums, or fund-raisers, please contact Osborne/**McGraw-Hill** at the above address.

SQL Server 2000 Design & T-SQL Programming

1234567890 DOC DOC 01987654321

ISBN 0-07-212375-3

Publisher
Brandon A. Nordin
Vice President & Associate Publisher
Scott Rogers
Editorial Director
Wendy Rinaldi
Project Editors
Jenn Tust, Lisa Theobald
Acquisitions Editor
Tim Madrid
Technical Editor
Jessica Bonasso
Copy Editor
Lunaea Weatherstone
Proofreaders
Maggie Trapp, Linda Medoff
Indexer
Jack Lewis
Computer Designers
Roberta Steele, Jean Butterfield
Illustrators
Michael Mueller, Bob Hansen
Series Design
Peter F. Hancik
Cover Design
Greg Scott

This book was composed with Corel VENTURA™ Publisher.

To Philip Reilly,
Beloved father, father-in-law, and friend,
1924–2000

ABOUT THE AUTHORS

Michael D. Reilly, MA, MCSE, MCT, is a contributing editor and columnist for *SQL Server Magazine*. He is a co-founder and vice president of Mount Vernon Data Systems and a Microsoft Certified Trainer for SQL Server, Windows NT, and SMS.

Michelle A. Poolet, MCIS, MCP, is a contributing editor and columnist for *SQL Server Magazine*. She is faculty at the University of Denver, Extended Learning Division, and a course developer for both in-person and on-line courses. She is a co-founder and president of Mount Vernon Data Systems.

CONTENTS

ACKNOWLEDGMENTS

Thanks to Mike Otey, one of our co-authors at *SQL Server Magazine*, who introduced us to Osborne/McGraw-Hill and hence got us into this project. We'll find a way to repay you, Mike, you can be sure of that. Thanks to Wendy Rinaldi, our editorial director, who quickly discovered that the authors will agree to anything in exchange for a meal at a good Italian restaurant. Thanks to Monika Faltiss, Timothy Madrid, Jenn Tust, Lisa Theobald, and the entire team at Osborne, who kept pushing for us to deliver what we had apparently agreed upon one evening at an Italian restaurant in San Francisco. We appreciate the way that you improved the book but with a light editorial touch, so the authors are still responsible for what you see in the text.

Thanks to our technical editor, Jessica Bonasso, and Duncan the Corgi, who spent countless hours by the fireside reading manuscripts and making sure that we weren't telling any lies.

Thanks to Rusty and Molly, our collies, who reminded us that we needed to take a break from writing several times each day. They had to put up with some strange schedules and lots of late nights, but they remained good-natured about it all the way through.

—Michael Reilly and Michelle Poolet

INTRODUCTION

The purpose of this book is to offer guidance and encouragement to anyone who is embarking on a project to build a database in Microsoft SQL Server 2000. Whether you are starting from scratch or upsizing an existing desktop database, such as Microsoft Access, you will learn how SQL Server 2000 can help you construct a solid, reliable database that will meet your needs now and grow with your requirements in the future. The book starts with the design of the database, and it continues on with how to implement the design and the decisions that you have to make along the way.

WHO SHOULD READ THIS BOOK

Our intended audience includes the following groups. It is likely that you will belong to more than one of them.

- Database designers who want to know more about how to use the capabilities and features of SQL Server 2000 to build robust, easy-to-maintain applications.
- Programmers who want to learn more about the syntax of Transact-SQL and to learn how to leverage the functionality of this flexible programming language.
- Database administrators who want to find out more about what is going on "under the hood" of SQL Server 2000.
- Anyone studying for the Microsoft exams to become an MCDBA (Microsoft Certified Database Administrator), MCSE (Microsoft Certified Systems Engineer), or MCSD (Microsoft Certified Solution Developer). In particular, this book covers what you need to know to pass the exam for "Designing and Implementing Databases with Microsoft SQL Server 2000."

CHAPTER SUMMARY

Each of the 19 chapters in this book focuses on a distinctive topic that is used to plan, design, and implement a database. The book is divided into five parts that cover design, implementation, information retrieval, programming, and ancillary materials in the appendixes.

Part 1. Getting Started

Part 1 covers database design. It's all about gathering the business requirements and building the data models that precede a database implementation. In databases, good design is critical to good operations.

Chapter 1: Database Design

Chapter 1 is about data modeling and database design. We start with a discussion of relational databases, what they are, why they're different from other database management systems, and what they can be used for. Then we move into a discussion of Microsoft SQL Server—where it started, how it got to where it is today, and what it can do for you and your business. Then we introduce you to the Strawberry Smoooches™ Company, a little retail business that is used as a case study throughout this book. The Strawberry Smoooches Company sells a fruit drink at events such as state fairs and community gatherings. The company tracks various details of its business, and we're going to help by building the company a SQL Server 2000 database.

Chapter 2: Entity Relationship Modeling

Entity relationship modeling is a technique and a set of graphical languages that are used to create *data models*—abstractions of a database. The entity relationship diagrams incorporate the requirements you discovered and cataloged in Chapter 1. In the entity relationship diagram, you lay out the data components that will make up your database, identifying the client requirements in terms of database objects and attributes. We introduce the concept of entities and entity sets, and show how to define the attributes of your entities and select your primary identifying attribute. We talk about relationship cardinality and look at one-to-one, one-to-many, and many-to-many relationships. As we go into more detail about relationships, we look at binary, ternary, and recursive relationships, in the context of our entity relationship diagram. We examine type-subtype relationships, which will help us with entities such as employees and vendor contacts. We discuss strategies for subtyping and see how this impacts our entity-relationship modeling.

Chapter 3: Principles of Design

In Chapter 3 we look at the principles of database design. You'll want to pay special attention to this chapter because it contains the rules by which you can build a solid foundation for any database. We explain data normalization, which is a necessary—if sometimes confusing—part of the technique for insuring the integrity of the data in your database. Then we move on to the four rules of database integrity: the entity integrity rule, which says that every record in a database table must be uniquely identifiable; the referential integrity rule, which says no child record can exist if it doesn't have an associated parent; the domain integrity rule, which says that each column of a table shall have a well-defined meaning, to include datatype, data length, and a set or range of values; and the business integrity rule, which are those rules and regulations by which your business operates that can be enforced by the database management system. While we're on the subject of principles, in this chapter we cover the ethics of database design, something that is not usually covered in a book of this type but that is vitally important to you as a data modeler, database administrator, or database programmer. Among the many topics of concern in this area are information gathering and privacy, computer/database system security and privacy, overuse of the U.S. Social Security number, and the programmer's responsibility in this arena.

Chapter 4: Planning the Physical Implementation

In Chapter 4 we start with what a database table is: what it looks like, what it is used for, and why it is so important. Then we discuss the set of rules regarding how to map your entity-relationship diagram to a database table architecture, and we show you how it's done with the Strawberry Smooooches entity diagram. Up to this point, the requirements analysis and logical design steps have been almost completely vendor-neutral. Here we make the jump to a specific product platform and start translating our blueprints into a real plan for constructing an actual database using Microsoft SQL Server 2000. We create a physical design that's written to take advantage of the capabilities of SQL Server 2000.

In the process we identify primary and foreign keys for each of the tables. We discuss why we would choose one column over another, and what constitutes a good primary key. Then we talk about indexes, what they are and what they're used for and how to develop a plan for implementing them in your database. And we talk a little about constructive denormalization—why it's necessary at times and the associated costs.

Part 2. Implementation

Part 2 covers database implementation. It's all about how to create a database and how to create tables to hold the data. This part also includes discussions on SQL Server datatypes and data storage allocation.

Chapter 5: Implementing the Design

This chapter is about physical implementation of the design you developed in Part 1. We start with creating a database, the programming language commands, and all the command options. We take a side trip to look at database file structures and filegroups—what they look like in SQL Server and how they're used. We discuss RAID arrays, including when and how to use them to best advantage. Once you have a grasp of what the internal physical structure looks like, we introduce you to sizing databases (data and log files both), managing their growth, shrinking databases, and removing a database that is no longer needed. We also cover the different setable parameters in SQL Server and show you how to check and adjust them.

Chapter 6: Building Tables

Now that you have built your database, you need to create some tables to hold the data. One of the first things you need to know about is the datatype—that is, what are the datatypes supplied by SQL Server and how (and why) you can create your own. We take you through allocating space on your hard disk for the tables soon to be created and how that space is measured. Then you create tables; you also write code to add and drop columns from a table. The chapter teaches you how and when to use the identity property and the global unique identifier. Finally, we talk about the different ways of loading data into your newly created database.

Part 3. Information Retrieval

Part 3 covers information retrieval in the database. We start with simple SELECT statements and quickly work up to complex aggregate functions, subqueries, and views. We also cover data modification statements. The programming fun begins in this section.

Chapter 7: Data Retrieval

Modeling the database and implementing the design involves lots of hard work. The fun is in querying the database, and that is how this chapter begins. We take you on a walking tour of the Query Analyzer Window and show you how to run a query. Then we go over the SELECT statement, the most-used command in the SQL language. We talk about how to do arithmetic calculations and calculations involving dates and times. We discuss how to write queries that retrieve specific rows, using various operators and range-of-value language. We cover writing queries that do inexact matching, mostly done on character strings. We show you techniques for formatting the output results for easier-to-read, more informative reports. We wind up the chapter with a discussion of query caching—where does the SQL Server stash the query when it's in memory?

Chapter 8: Joins: Combining Data from Multiple Tables

Occasionally, a database query involves a single table; but more than likely the information comes from a combination of tables, joined together to provide the information you need to do your job. In this chapter we talk about all the different kinds of joins: inner, outer, cross, self, and multi-table joins. Then we discuss ways of combining data that are done at a system level: union operations, merge joins, and hash joins.

Chapter 9: Summarizing Data and Reporting

Detail reports can be very interesting, but a good share of the reports you write will be summary reports. In this chapter we study the code that will allow you to write these summary reports; aggregate data (summing, averaging, etc.); group by common values; limit the results returned to a set of rows with specific criteria; use the COMPUTE BY statement, the ROLLUP, and the CUBE functions; and retrieve the uppermost number of rows from a query. We also talk about when it's appropriate to use these functions, and when it's not.

Chapter 10: Data Modification

According to some reports, 85 percent of user activity in the average database environment is querying for data. However, the other 15 percent (more or less) of the user activity is very important: it's managing the data and making changes when necessary. In this chapter we look at how to add a single row to a table, how to delete rows from a table, and how to change a row that's already in a table.

Chapter 11: Subqueries

There are several different kinds of multi-table queries, so you don't have to use a JOIN each time you want to extract information from a combination of several different tables. The subquery is a multi-table query that can be used in lieu of the JOIN, albeit with certain constraints. In this chapter we look at these constraints. We define the simple subquery and the correlated, or complex, subquery. We look at what they are and what they do. We look at how to write a query that will perform an existence test on data. We also discuss each of the data modification statements (INSERT, UPDATE, DELETE) and see how to use a subquery in each of these to simplify the task of data management.

Chapter 12: Views

A view is an individualized "picture" into the database, custom created for one person or group. In this chapter we look at views—what they are, how to write them, why to write them, and what to do with them once you've got them written. We also look at the new features in SQL Server 2000—indexed views and partitioned views, and what benefit they might be to you.

Part 4. Programming for Performance

Part 4 covers programming techniques with an eye to maximizing performance. We cover transaction processing, implicit and distributed transactions, locking protocols and transaction isolation levels, data integrity enforcement, indexes and indexing schemes, stored procedures, triggers, and replication design issues.

Chapter 13: Introduction to Transactions

Writing SQL code is fun, but it's also serious work. You need to know how to write your code to retain the integrity of the data in your database. In this chapter we introduce the concept of a transaction—what it is and how it works. There is certain language in Transact SQL (T-SQL) that controls transactions, COMMIT, and ROLLBACK, and this chapter discusses how these work. We look briefly at locking and how it's handled in SQL Server. We look at the transaction log and see what part it plays in this scenario. And finally we talk about nesting transactions and distributing transactions across multiple servers.

Chapter 14: Locking

Locking schemes are critical to the functioning of any database management system. In this chapter we talk about the type of locking used by SQL Server and the potential problems addressed by these locking schemes. We talk about how to detect locking problems by using the SQL Profiler. We also cover setting SQL Server lock options, and the transaction isolation levels and how to adjust them.

Chapter 15: Data Integrity

A database management system must safeguard the integrity of data stored in its file system. In this chapter we investigate techniques that we can use to assure that integrity. We look at constraints, define them, and see what they can do. We analyze the various constraints that we can code into the database: primary and foreign key constraints, unique constraints, and check and default constraints. We discover how to enable and disable these constraints, and when it's appropriate to do so. We look at the differences between constraints, rules, triggers, and cascading triggers, and when you should use each.

Chapter 16: Indexes

Without an accompanying index, finding a random fact in a book would be a tedious, if not impossible, task. Indexes in database management systems play a very similar role, and in this chapter we look at database indexes—what they do and how they do it. We discuss when to use and when not to use an index, and how to find out which indexes are being used in a query. We look at file clustering and what part indexes play in this, and we compare clustered files to heaps. We discuss unique indexes and see how they relate to unique constraints. An index doesn't have to be composed of single-word terms, so we create composite indexes and covering indexes. We talk about fill factors and pad indexes, and we learn how to gather operational statistics on indexes. We generate index fragmentation reports, and we drop and rebuild indexes. Finally, we look at something new in SQL Server 2000: indexing materialized views.

Chapter 17: Stored Procedures

Stored procedures are the lifeblood of a relational database management system. With stored procedures (compiled programs) you can do synchronous access management to data stored in the database. In this chapter we look at how to use stored procedures, and then we do some serious study of stored procedures. We learn how to create a stored procedure and how that procedure is stored in the database's memory, or procedure cache. We discuss how to parameterize a stored procedure. We alter a stored procedure and drop it when we no longer need it. We cover how to pass parameters to stored procedures and then how to handle returning data to a calling procedure. We look at the recompile option and when it's appropriate to use this feature. We discuss how to handle error messages in stored procedure code. Then we look at extended stored procedures, remote stored procedures, and security issues surrounding stored procedures. We define a remote query and discuss the downside of a distributed transaction. Then we set up linked servers and query them. We discuss how a stored procedure works when executed on linked servers, and see how updates/deletes function on linked servers.

Chapter 18: Triggers

Triggers are the automated, or asynchronous, counterpart to stored procedures. In this chapter we investigate triggers—how and when to use them. We see how to create, alter, and drop a trigger. We look inside a trigger at the so-called "virtual tables" named Inserted and Deleted. We see how triggers can be used to enforce foreign key, or referential, integrity and how you can write a trigger to control cascading changes (updates and deletes) in related tables. We look at nesting triggers—when you want to use them and when not to use them. There is such a thing as a recursive trigger; this chapter deals with what it is and how it works, and it helps you determine whether this is really what you want to use. Lastly, we touch on the performance issues associated with the use of triggers.

Chapter 19: Distributed Data and Replication

No man is an island, and no corporate database can stand alone—at least not for long. In this chapter we look at distributed data and replication. We talk about log shipping, data transformation services, remote queries, and distributed transactions. Then we take a look at SQL Server replication, starting with terminology, mechanisms, and partitioning schemes for the data that you plan to replicate. Then we discuss the four basic replication schemes: snapshot, transactional, merge, and replication with immediate updating subscribers. Finally we investigate various replication topologies, with case studies to illustrate each arrangement of publisher and subscribers. We wind up this chapter with security issues in replication and a table of guidelines for distributing data.

Part 5. Data Models and Recommended Readings

Part 5 is the appendix section. Each appendix contains either a data model, a bibliography list, code to create the Strawberry Smoooches Company database, or even a recipe for a Strawberry Smooochie.

Appendix A: A Recipe for Strawberry Smoooches

This appendix gives you the recipe for the original Strawberry Smooochie, complements of the president of the Strawberry Smoooches Company, Beverly Diederich.

Appendix B: The Strawberry Smoooches Company Conceptual Data Model

This appendix contains the conceptual data model for the Strawberry Smoooches Company, as created with Microsoft Visio 2000. A conceptual model represents the concepts, foundations, and business rules of a company.

Appendix C: The Strawberry Smoooches Company Logical Data Model

Appendix C contains the logical data model for the Strawberry Smoooches Company. The logical data model is a detailed representation of the reality of the business requirements, and like the entity model, it is vendor neutral.

Appendix D: The Strawberry Smoooches Database Physical Model

Appendix D contains the physical model for the Strawberry Smoooches database. The physical model is a representation of the company, crafted to take advantage of the features of SQL Server 2000.

Appendix E: The Strawberry Smoooches Database: DDL and Data

This appendix contains the SQL script to create and populate the Strawberry Smoooches Company database.

Appendix F: Bibliography and Recommended Readings

Here you can read about books that are our full-time companions—that we think you may enjoy reading.

HOW THIS BOOK HELPS WITH MICROSOFT CERTIFICATION

If you are interested in the various Microsoft certifications, you may be thinking about taking the exam for "Designing and Implementing Databases with Microsoft SQL Server 2000." This exam is an elective for both the MCSE and MCSD certifications. It is also a requirement, or core exam, for the MCDBA certification.

As we write this book, the SQL Server 2000 exams are available only in beta edition. However, judging from our experience with the SQL Server 7.0 exams, some questions on the exam are not covered in the Microsoft official courses—or in their self-paced training kits. The topics of these questions cover the basics of good database design, including fundamentals of normalization and entity-relationship modeling. The reason that they are not covered in the Microsoft courses is because knowledge of these areas are actually prerequisites for the classes—specifically, the SQL Server Administration and the SQL Server Design Implementation classes. If you plan to attend those classes, read the sections of this book on design and modeling before you go; they will help you to get the most out of the class.

The SQL Server exams have a reputation for being tough—they certainly test your understanding of the product and how it works, making it difficult to pass by simply studying "brain-dumps" of questions. Many of the questions on the exams are scenario-based and require that you understand the topic thoroughly. In fact, even the answers tend to be lengthy and very detailed. To select the correct answer, you need to understand why, not just how, to address the issue presented in the question.

In this book, we explain the "why" and then the "how"—or perhaps sometimes the other way around—but we will not leave you wondering "why did they do it that way?" As with any programming language, there are many ways to achieve the desired result, so what is in this book is certainly not the last word. However, working through the examples here will give you a feel for the kind of scenarios that you may encounter in the exams.

WEB SITE CONTENTS

At the Osborne Web site (**www.osborne.com**) you'll find the following materials:

- DDL (data definition language) in the form of T-SQL scripts that you can copy and paste into Enterprise Manager to create your own Strawberry database (these will work with either SQL Server 7 or SQL Server 2000)
- Strawberry data ready for loading into your Strawberry database, or a detached SQL Server 2000 Strawberry database, so you can circumvent the first two options and directly attach this database to your SQL Server 2000
- T-SQL code examples arranged in chapter order

PART I

Getting Started

CHAPTER 1

Database Design

SQL Server is a relational database management system (RDBMS). In a relational database, data is stored in tables, each of which contains information about an object in the database. A table is a two-dimensional grid consisting of rows and columns, sometimes referred to as records and fields. A column or field contains data about some attribute of the object, such as the name of a customer, the color of a product, or the date of a sale. A row or record represents one instance of the object, such as a customer, an invoice, or a product.

In a relational database, there is no structure imposed on the data by the database or the database software. All the structure comes from the relationships you define between the tables. The relationships describe how the objects in the database interact. The relational database provides a set of tools to help you safeguard and maintain these relationships. For example, once you have defined the relationship between customers and invoices, the database can prevent you from deleting a customer who has an outstanding invoice.

A relational database also safeguards your data by employing transaction logging. This means that whenever a change is made to data stored in the database, the change is first written to a transaction log. Only then is the change made to the actual data. If the system were to crash during the change, SQL Server can complete or cancel the change entirely by referring to the transaction log. The data will never be left in an inconsistent state. As you develop applications in SQL Server 2000, keep in mind that how you program can impact the performance of the transaction log. Transaction logging cannot be turned off—logging change is inherent to a relational database.

A BRIEF SUMMARY OF THE DEVELOPMENT OF THE RELATIONAL DATABASE

Relational databases are built upon theoretical work performed in the 1970s, much of which was done at the IBM San Jose Research Lab. The main figure in this research effort was Dr. E.F. Codd, who published a treatise entitled "A Relational Model of Data for Large Shared Data Banks." His work looks at databases from the point of view of mathematical set theory. In this framework, a table is a set of data, and a join is the intersection of two sets of data. Data is not managed by persistent file structures. Instead, it is managed by dynamic combinations and recombinations of subsets of the data. In other words, in this model, data is *independent* of file structures.

An associate of Dr. Codd, D.D. Chamberlain, developed an interpreter for the relational database query language in 1974–1975. It was called SEQUEL-XRM and was used only in the research and development departments of IBM. With SEQUEL-XRM, the researchers could implement Dr. Codd's set theory method of data management. Good news travels fast, and in 1979 an upstart database company with the presumptuous name of Oracle Corporation introduced to the marketplace the first commercial RDBMS based on the SQL language. Quickly realizing they were about to lose market share, IBM scoured their own facilities looking for a competitive product. They found one in SEQUEL-XRM. It took a few years, but in 1982 IBM introduced their first RDBMS, named SQL/DS, for the VM operating system. They followed in 1985 with their second RDBMS, DB2, which ran on their mainframe MVS operating system.

Fortunately, it is not necessary to have a Ph.D. in mathematics in order to build a sound relational database. You might need this level of experience if you started from scratch and built your own relational database management system, but with products such as SQL Server on the market, why reinvent the wheel? The relational database management systems now available are based on these industry-standard principles, and code embedded in the database engine enforces the rules and relationships. So all we have to do is tell the database what we want done, and let the code take over from there.

A relational database stores data in a format that is independent of the file system that is native to the computer's operating system. This may seem like an odd point to bring up, but if you look at the history of databases, the storage of the data used to be dictated by the file system. Because the data was stored and accessed in a hierarchical manner, older database architectures were hierarchical in nature. In a modern relational database, the writing of data to the file system is handled by the operating system. The database and its tables are independent of the file system.

SQL Server: Its Background and Origins

SQL Server traces its origins back to 1988. Microsoft and IBM were jointly developing a new operating system, OS/2. IBM had a database known as Database Manager (it eventually evolved into DB2 for OS/2), which they planned to package with an enhanced version of OS/2, but Microsoft had no similar product to bundle with their version of OS/2. Microsoft decided to team with Sybase, Inc., who were about to launch their own RDBMS. The way the deal worked, Microsoft would get a database product, and Sybase would receive royalties and gain exposure to Microsoft clients who would be running the new operating system. Sybase would market other versions of the product on different operating platforms. Microsoft also wanted to attract customers from the dBase market and worked a deal with Ashton-Tate, the producers of dBase, to endorse the new server product. So this new product's original name was Ashton-Tate/Microsoft SQL Server, with no mention in the name of Sybase, the company that actually wrote the code for the database management system. By 1990, Ashton-Tate was no longer a star in the software community. Also, dBase and SQL Server were based on totally different philosophies. Microsoft and Ashton-Tate parted ways.

SQL Server 1.1 was released in 1990 as a Microsoft product. Even then Microsoft did not see SQL Server as one of its primary products. They saw it more as a product they needed to have in order to promote sales of LAN Manager and OS/2. But SQL Server version 1.1 did represent a major step forward for Microsoft because it provided an interface for Windows 3.0–based clients. This gave SQL Server a much-needed boost in the developer community because of the graphical interfaces and the Windows APIs, and third-party developers began to produce applications based on SQL Server. Microsoft, in its usual manner, provided development tools and programming libraries to encourage third-party developers. Nevertheless, SQL Server was still essentially a Sybase product.

The next split, one of several in the history of SQL Server, was with IBM when Microsoft withdrew their support for OS/2. The split caused some problems for Microsoft's SQL Server group, as their product depended on an operating system produced by a rival. The solution eventually came in the form of SQL Server 4.2, released early in 1992. This version of SQL Server was the only truly jointly developed product, with both Microsoft and Sybase working on the code. This product met with reasonable success in the marketplace, and the next logical step for Microsoft was to develop SQL Server for Windows NT. In a bold move, they decided to drop the OS/2 version and gambled that the customer base would be willing to switch operating systems to get a better database product. Of course, customers who preferred not to switch could always adopt the Sybase version of SQL Server, which would continue to run on OS/2.

Even though SQL Server 4.2 was developed jointly, philosophical differences began to develop between Microsoft and Sybase. Microsoft believed, given that they were developing for only one platform, that certain tasks and functions should be handled by the operating system. For example, multiple thread handling should be done by the Windows NT operating system, in Microsoft's viewpoint. Sybase, on the other hand, was writing their code to run on various operating systems, not all of which understood the concept of multithreading. So from the Sybase point of view, it would make more sense to include multiple thread handling in the database code. Regardless of the philosophical differences, Microsoft's product was a success in the marketplace, justifying—at least to Microsoft—the decision to integrate the product very closely with the operating system. Of course, in order to do so, they had sacrificed portability. Sybase continued to develop their product for multiple platforms and operating systems. The split between the two companies was inevitable, and it came in early 1994.

The first all-Microsoft version of SQL Server was a big undertaking by any standard, as Microsoft began to realize the importance of having a powerful database in their product line. Version 6.0 was released in 1995, and reaction from both customers and reviewers was very positive. Microsoft's market share began to grow, and SQL Server started to become a major player in the corporate database arena, taking market share from companies such as Oracle and, of course, Sybase. Within a year, Microsoft had capitalized on the success of SQL Server 6.0, with the release of version 6.5. At the same time, they were making even more ambitious plans for the next version, which was yet another major step forward. SQL server 7.0 was released in January 1999, and once again was received with approval and, possibly more important, orders for the product. Although many companies had stated that they would wait for the release of a service pack before making the switch to version 7.0, the advantages of the new release quickly became apparent. Adoption of version 7.0 came more rapidly than many people had predicted, and when the service pack finally arrived, it was a relatively minor event.

Microsoft, once they have spotted a bandwagon, can never be accused of being half hearted about jumping on it. Almost before the shrink-wrap had cooled on version 7.0, there was an early beta of SQL Server 7.5. It very quickly became apparent that the changes being planned for this next release were so profound that they justified a change in the version number. Hence the latest release is version 8.0, although its "public" name is officially SQL Server 2000.

The authors have been actively involved with SQL Server since version 6.0. We feel that SQL Server is the best product Microsoft has ever produced, and one of the best software products we have seen. We are excited about the changes we see happening, although it does seem as if we are always in a learning (and upgrading) mode. We suspect that even before this book hits the shelves, there will be a package on its way to us from Microsoft containing a compact disc and a nondisclosure agreement for SQL Server 9.0 beta 1. But at least life with SQL Server is never dull. We look forward to the next version and wonder what new magic the SQL Server development team will have cooked up this time.

Where SQL Server Fits in the Enterprise

SQL Server is currently a very capable departmental database server. With the release of SQL Server 2000, it must also be considered a contender for enterprise-level databases. In our opinion, SQL Server 2000 could be a serious contender, except that it has one potential Achilles heel that must be considered: It runs on Windows NT and Windows 2000. Although we would feel comfortable trusting our critical data to SQL Server 2000, the same cannot be said of the underlying operating systems, at least at the time of this writing. Windows NT 4.0 is not as stable as we would like for an enterprise computing system. Windows 2000 appears to have promise, but we want to wait for a couple of service pack releases before feeling comfortable with an operating system where so much has changed—in effect, it is a completely new operating system. The new clustering technology in both Windows 2000 and SQL Server 2000 is good to have, but we would still like to see more attention given to stability and increasing the time between system restarts.

SQL Server 2000 also has a place as a database server driving Web applications for businesses ranging in size from small companies to large corporations. Many Web sites are running SQL Server as the database engine that serves up the Web pages you see on your computer screen.

As applications become larger and are required to support more users, SQL Server is also gaining in popularity in many companies as an alternative to Microsoft Access. Access works well as a personal database, or when it is supporting a few users, but starts to run out of steam as you add more users. As the number of users connecting to the Access database increases, so does the possibility of data corruption. It only takes one or two occurrences of the database becoming corrupted for the company to start looking at "upsizing" their Access databases, and one obvious migration path is to retain the familiar Access interface while storing the data in SQL Server.

SQL Server is also moving to the desktop, in a slightly different form. SQL Server is a server product, part of Microsoft's Back Office Suite, and it is meant to support multiple users. SQL Server doesn't offer a suite of front-end tools that would make it user friendly. But it is making its way onto desktop systems as the core engine underlying Microsoft Access 2000. The result of this change in Access is that SQL Server could be the product on which almost all of your databases run, from very small to very large.

Different Versions of SQL Server

SQL Server 2000 comes in several different levels, with different platforms and target audiences in mind. The Standard edition, which is what most of us mean when we talk about SQL Server 2000, runs on Windows NT Server or Windows 2000 Server. This edition offers the full functionality of the SQL Server 2000 product, including the Full Text Search capability, which is based on Microsoft's Index Server, and the Analytical Services, formerly known as OnLine Analytical Processing (OLAP) Services.

For less demanding applications, or perhaps in a development environment, there's the Desktop edition. This edition runs on Windows NT Workstation (or Server, if you choose) or Windows 2000 Professional and provides the same functionality as the Standard version, with the exception of the Full Text Search option—it's not part of the SQL Desktop installation. Just like the Standard edition, it runs on NT/2000 as a service, meaning that nobody has to be logged in for it to run—it can be configured to start up with the operating system—so you don't need to go through the trouble and expense of installing a server-level OS on your developer's computer. In most cases you don't need Windows NT/2000 Server just to run a development workstation.

If you are running very large databases on SQL Server 2000 and find you are constrained by the memory limits imposed by the operating system, think about investing in an upgrade to the Enterprise edition of the database and operating system products. SQL Server Enterprise edition can take advantage of the larger amount of memory made available by using the equivalent version of the operating system, either Windows NT Enterprise edition or Windows 2000 Advanced Server or DataCenter editions. Windows NT Standard edition can support up to 4GB of RAM, split evenly between the OS and applications. In the case of NT Enterprise edition, the split can be adjusted to provide up to 3GB for the applications (such as the database management system). Windows 2000 raises the bar even higher, because the Advanced Server and DataCenter editions can now support up to 64GB of RAM. SQL Server also benefits from having multiple CPUs available, and Windows 2000 has a totally new way of handling multiple CPUs. It will be able to make use of more than four CPUs (the "out-of-the-box" limit in Windows NT). The DataCenter edition of Windows 2000, in special versions obtained directly from the hardware manufacturers, can support up to 64 CPUs. Hopefully machines with this level of power will become available, boosting the scalability of SQL Server to new heights.

At the other end of the spectrum is the Microsoft SQL Server Desktop Engine. The MSDE is intended as an eventual replacement for the Microsoft Jet Database Engine, introduced in 1993 with MS Access 1.0. The MSDE *is* the SQL Server core executable. What this means is that your Access programs can now use a fully relational database engine, but with the familiar Access interface. The possibilities this opens up are amazing—now Access developers can program against the MSDE and have a very easy upsizing path, because the database engine is already SQL Server. In fact, there's an entire book waiting to be written on the use of MSDE in Access or with Visual Basic applications. This version of SQL Server is intended for use on Windows NT Workstation, Windows 2000 Professional, and Windows 95/98. As far as we know, it will run on Windows Millenium, the suggested replacement for Windows 98. But as Windows Millenium is aimed squarely at the home market with an emphasis on the Internet and entertainment, we really do not see businesses adopting it since Windows 2000 offers more of the features that matter in the workplace.

Platforms Supported

As mentioned, SQL Server 2000 runs on Windows NT and Window 2000. Normally under these operating systems it runs as a service, so it can start in the background as the operating system starts up. The databases will then be available to the clients even if nobody is logged on to the server. The ability to run the desktop edition on the Windows 95/98 platforms was introduced with SQL Server 7.0. Of course these operating systems do not understand applications running in the background as services. So, with Windows 95/98 you have to start the SQL Server executable as an application after you have logged on, or perhaps you might choose to put it in the startup group so it starts automatically. When you log off, the SQL Server shuts down, unlike Windows NT/2000. The intent of writing SQL Server to run on these consumer-oriented operating systems is to allow mobile users to take the database, or a subset of the database, with them on a portable computer. But keep in mind that the security features on Windows 95/98 are essentially nonexistent. Even if it means spending money on a more powerful laptop computer, you might want to look into using Windows 2000 Professional on your laptop. It offers far more security features, including the new NTFS file encryption.

DATA MODELING

When you start to build a database, you need to have a sound model. In this section, we will explore how to construct a data model and some of the issues associated with data modeling. A data model is a representation of reality, a way to graphically plot your data requirements. It's a visual model of what your database can look like when you get it implemented.

Data modeling is essential to building a good database. Before your database can support your business activities, it must be built from a good blueprint and a solid foundation. The data model is both the blueprint and the foundation. If the data model contains flaws, the database and any programs that use it will exhibit the flaws. If you start with a bad data model, there is no way to recover, no matter how clever your code.

The data model represents both reality and the data on which you run your business. Data modeling can be considered an art and a science, just like architecture or engineering. In fact, we use the term "architecture" to describe our database design, and just like with a building, there is a combination of functionality and style in a database. You'll find plenty of room for creative expression while you are designing and implementing your database within the capabilities of SQL Server 2000. Keep in mind, though, that one person's ideal, elegant solution may look like a disaster in the eyes of another database designer. For any given business scenario you are modeling, there will be many possible solutions. If an entity relationship diagram is constructed correctly, the argument is not which approach is right or wrong, but rather which is better or worse. In many cases in the corporate world, solutions are categorized as "my way" or "somebody else's way," which can translate to "my way" or "wrong," and discussions can become quite heated at times. Personal or corporate preference and experience often determine the look of the final model.

In this book, we are not going to recommend one methodology over another, nor is it our intention to compare the various methodologies. When appropriate, we have elected to use the common Crow's Foot notation, which you will find is supported in most computer-assisted software engineering (CASE) tools and software packages, including Visio V5 and V2000 Professional Editions. Visio recently became a division of Microsoft, thus it has a high level of integrateability with SQL Server. We hope they continue to develop the neat tools they offer for database modeling, since Visio, when compared to other CASE products, is one of the least expensive CASE software packages, has a relatively short learning curve, and is packed with powerful tools.

The Phases of Data Modeling

Our convention is to split the data modeling process into three parts or steps: the conceptual design phase, the logical design phase, and the physical design phase. Each of these phases involves the generation of an entity-relationship diagram (ERD), and each phase also describes a deeper level of understanding of the database.

The *conceptual design phase* describes the concept of the database. The conceptual ERD graphically represents the data and information needs of the business. It illustrates the concept of what the eventual database will look like, what kind of data will be stored in it, and what information can be extracted from the database. An important distinction to note is that the conceptual ERD represents what the database can do and will do, but not how it does it. Typically, the conceptual ERD will not show processes or activities related to the data. Where an architect uses a blueprint, the database designer uses an entity relationship diagram. Another important consideration is that the conceptual ERD should be vendor neutral and technology independent, meaning that it can be implemented in any database architecture, relational or not, from any vendor. The conceptual ERD does not take advantage of features specific to one product or one vendor.

Figure 1-1 is a conceptual ERD of the Strawberry Smoooches Company™, which we will use as an example throughout this book. The model contains entities (Person, Sale, Supply), attributes that describe the entities (PersonID, Product Code), and relationships that describe how one entity interacts with another. This is often referred to as a conceptual model, because it lays out the concept of the database, what it means, and what it's for. Most importantly, the conceptual model is totally technology and vendor independent. This conceptual model does not incorporate any features from anyone's database product.

The second phase of data modeling is the *logical design*. In the logical design, you begin to convert or map the conceptual ERD to a more complete set of entities that begin to resemble tables, as shown in Figure 1-2. In this phase, you also test to make sure the tables

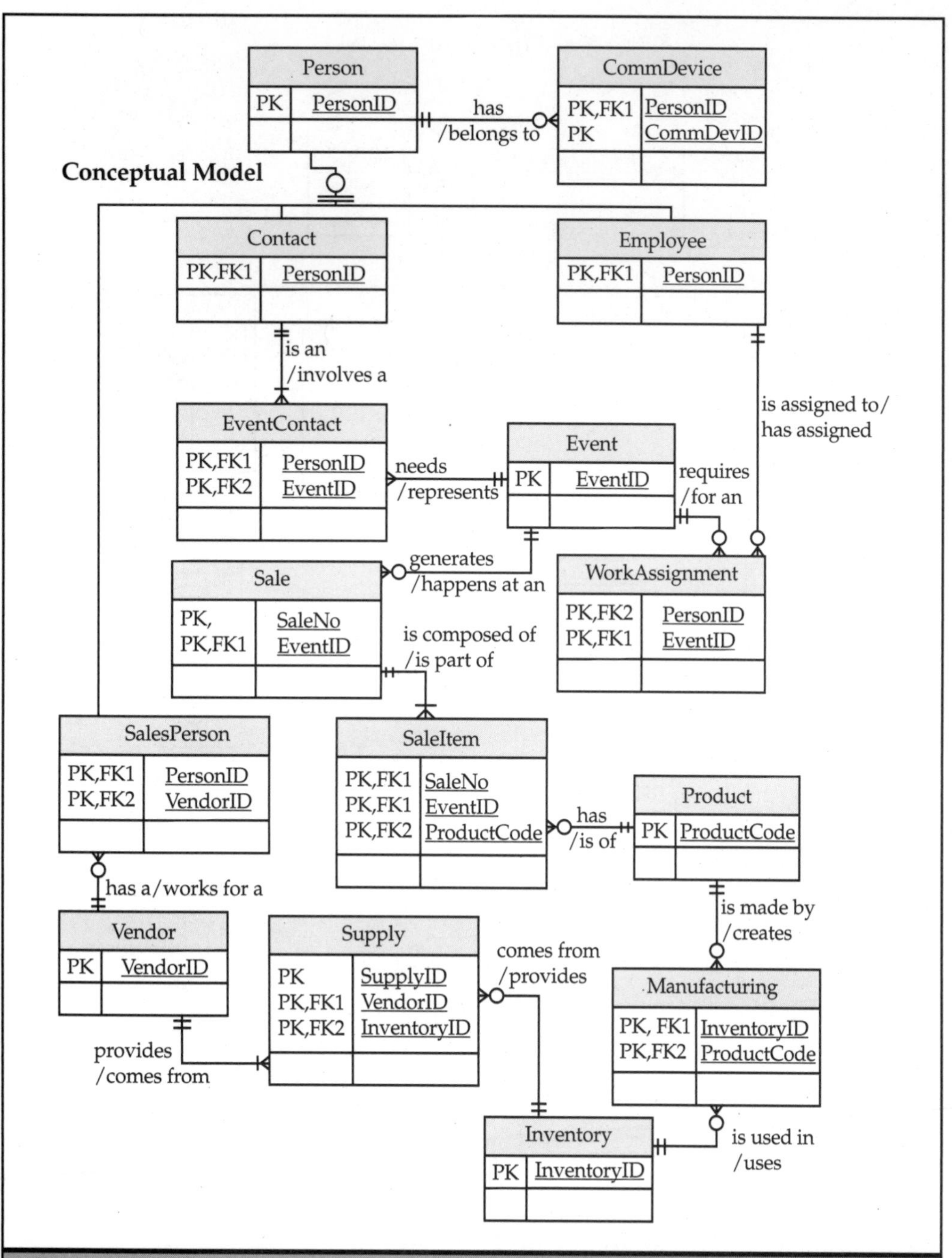

Figure 1-1. The Strawberry Smoooches™ Company conceptual model shows the concept of the database, what it is meant to represent, and how it will be laid out.

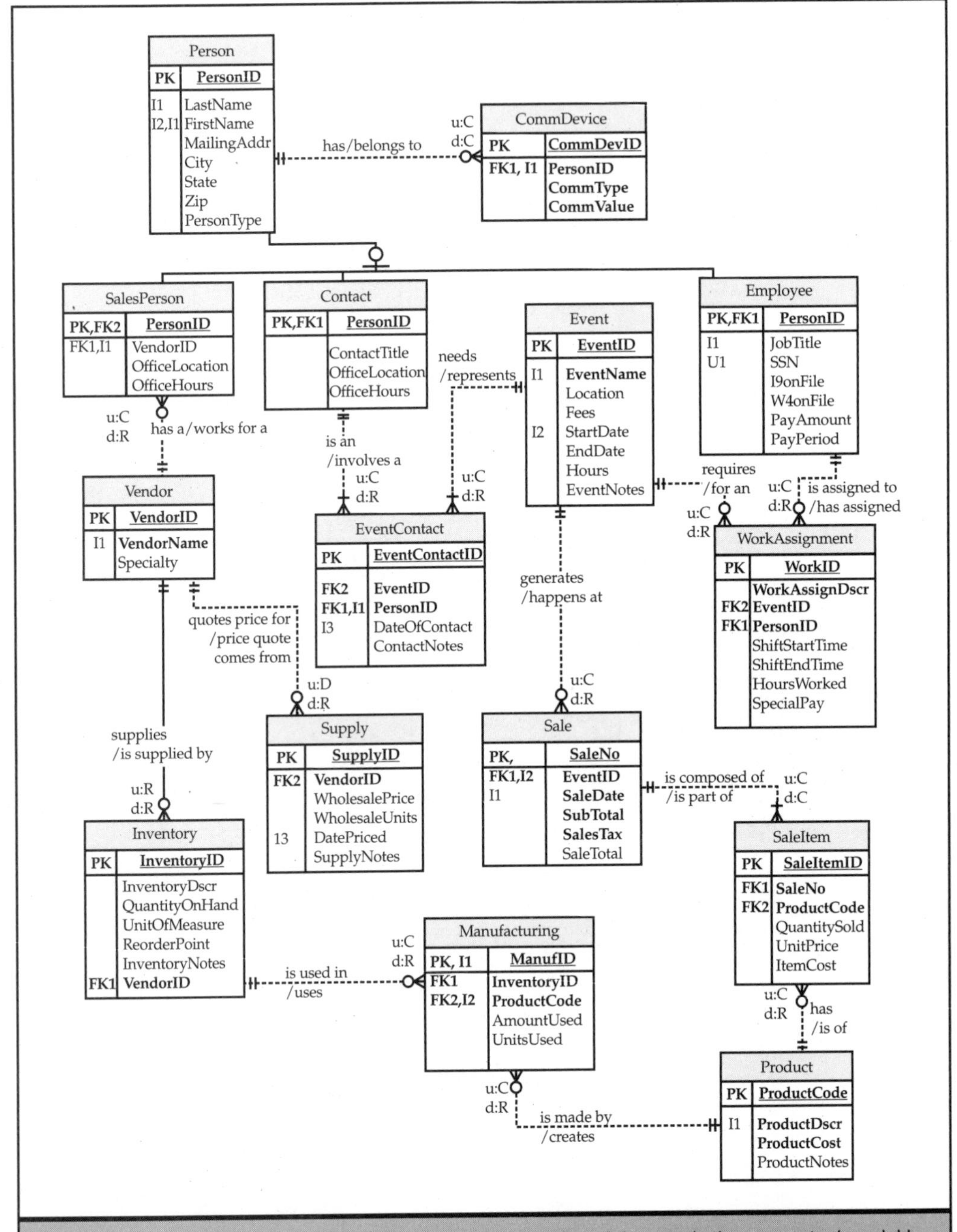

Figure 1-2. The Strawberry Smoooches Company logical model expands the conceptual model by including column names, primary and foreign keys, proposed indexes, and update and delete behaviors.

you designed are in third-normal form or better, and you make decisions on record modification behavior—for example, what will you do with a SalesPerson record when its associated master from table Person is deleted? We will discuss these issues in subsequent chapters. There are rules of normal form, first, second, and third, which you can step through that dictate how this mapping should be done. The logical design phase should also be technology and vendor independent.

The third phase of data modeling is the *physical design* phase, in which the logical model is converted to a specific product platform. Obviously, this phase is technology dependent. We will discuss this phase in more detail in upcoming chapters. Sometimes designers combine the physical design phase with the physical implementation phase, the result being a test database with a set of tables representing the database entities.

Some CASE tools do not distinguish between these three phases. Oracle Designer/2000 combines the conceptual design (phase one) and the logical design (phase two), calling it the logical model. Other tools (Visio, for instance) allow you more latitude to develop your own way of doing things. We feel that it's important not to skip any of these steps because in each phase you can check to make sure you are still on track for meeting the requirements for a successful database project.

Requirements Gathering

Before you jump in and start creating your data model, there is a step you must complete first, which is to perform a thorough requirements analysis. Requirements gathering allows you to answer the following questions:

- Why are you doing this project?
- What is this database supposed to do? What processes does it have to support?
- What kind of data do you need to capture?
- What kind of reports will you have to generate out of the database?
- How will the data be used—reads, writes—and at what level of activity?

Not only must you answer the question about why you are building the database, but you must also relate this to the overall goals and strategic plans for the corporation, the department, and the group with whom you are working. If they can express where they want to be in one, five, or ten years, you can design the ERD, keeping in mind possible future directions. You can make your design, and therefore your database, both expandable and extensible. This avoids the common situation of working on a database design and then finding it is obsolete before it is in production because the requirements and directions changed.

There are certain results you should expect from any requirements analysis:

- **Purpose** Why does the client want or need this new system?
- **Functionality** What is the client expecting this system to do for them?

- **Events** What does the client plan to do with the system once it is installed?
- **Outcomes** What are the long-term expectations for this system?

If these points are not clear from the requirements analysis, you should return to the client and interview them again. You need to know the purpose and reason for this data model; otherwise, the end product will not meet the expectations. Although we said that the conceptual model does not show processes or activities related to the data—in other words, it is not concerned with methods or activities—knowing how the data will be used will allow you to better analyze and define your database.

The Client's Perspective

Requirements analysis starts with you interviewing the clients. You have to ask lots of questions. Leave them in no doubt that you must understand the situation, the requirements, and their needs. If there's something you don't understand, all or part of the story seems to be missing, or the clients are using terminology in a way specific to their business that you don't understand, keep asking questions until it does become clear. You'll sometimes find that the confusion is not something you are imagining, but rather that your questions are exposing confusion that really exists within the organization and their processes. It is not unusual for an organization to not completely understand its own processes and procedures, especially where there has been a high turnover of staff. Often things are done in a certain way because somebody once did it that way, and nobody has ever thought to change it. Asking questions and demanding clarification will not only help you produce a better database, but it will also help the organization understand its own processes more thoroughly.

When this happens, don't be surprised if the organization takes a hard look at how it is conducting business and makes some changes. Hopefully, these changes, when combined with a new database around which to build the new processes, will result in increased productivity, and you will look like a hero. Meanwhile, you should be prepared to meet some resistance, as once the decision has been made to implement the database, people expect to see results immediately. They think they know what they want, and so they see no reason to keep answering questions. Make sure you talk both to the managers and to the people who will be using the database and actually doing the work. It's sometimes interesting to see the difference between the manager's idea of what the employees do all day and the employees' perspective.

Identifying the Entities

You can identify the entities in the database by reading through your requirements analysis and looking for descriptive nouns and verbs. A descriptive noun identifies an object or entity about which you want to capture information and store it in your database. A descriptive verb identifies actions and activities between two or more nouns and describes the interaction between the entities in your database. It often helps to do this as a work group, bringing together the data modelers and the clients or the subject matter experts.

You're looking for three specific sets of information when you review the requirements. You're trying to:

- Identify the major entities in your database
- Define the properties (attributes) that describe these entities
- Specify the relationships between the entities in your database

Identifying entities in this way really means you are identifying your metadata—descriptions of real data. You need to make sure you are identifying metadata rather than "real" data. For example, Figure 1-1 contains an entity called Person, which is described by a PersonID. PersonID is an attribute or property of Person; it helps describe a person. This is metadata. In the corresponding Strawberry Smoooches database, there will be a table called Person. This table will contain a list of people who are part of the Strawberry Smoooches organization, and each person will be assigned a unique PersonID to better identify them. This is real data. It's easy at times to confuse metadata with real data, so be careful to keep them separate in your mind.

Once construction of your entity relationship diagrams has begun, if you discover that you are asking more questions about how one entity relates to another, you need to go back and redo the requirements. You may need to perform the analysis in greater depth, possibly involving other people within the organization. The fundamental question to ask is, "Why are we doing this?" That will better define the database entities you need to track and the relationships between them.

INTRODUCTION TO STRAWBERRY SMOOOCHES

In the heartland of the United States, there is a small, family-owned business called the Strawberry Smoooches Company. This is the model around which this book is built. The Strawberry Smoooches Company is a seasonal concession that sells refreshments during outdoor festivals, mainly in the summer months. The company began operations in July 1998. It holds a food permit from the Department of Agriculture and a tax identification number from the state of Minnesota.

The Strawberry Smoooches Company is the creator of an all-natural, freshly blended fruit drink made with real strawberries. This fruit drink is made at an open-air, canopied concession stand, where customers can view the process of their drink being made from scratch. Strawberry Smoooches were presented at 13 events around Minnesota in 1998. Some of the events:

- Litchfield Watercade Festival
- New London Water Days
- SonShine Music Festival

- Wild Rice Days
- James J. Hill Days
- New Ulm Octoberfest

To ensure quality of the Strawberry Smooooches fruit drink, certain procedures have to be followed in the manufacture of the product. The inventory needed to produce a Strawberry Smooooches drink is whole strawberries, a measure of natural sweetener, crushed ice, and a fresh strawberry garnish for the glass. The Department of Agriculture set specific rules for the assembly of the drink and for the storage of all food inventory. Permission to make the Strawberry Smooooches beverage for the general public was granted in the form of a food permit, which must be renewed each year. In addition to the Strawberry Smooooches fruit drink, the concession stand also carries bottled water.

Non-food inventory is used to store ingredients, prepare the Strawberry Smooooches product, and present the drink. The drink itself is presented in a 16-ounce translucent glass, with a straw, a napkin, and a spoon on request. The drink is prepared using standard production equipment: commercial high-speed blenders, stainless steel serving utensils, stainless steel covered containers for the strawberries, a spouted container for the sweetener mixture, and a large container with a drain for the ice.

The concession stand is made up of a serving bench, the tented canopy, a washable floor mat for the serving area, six large ice chests with built-in drains, a table that holds the cleaning containers, six plastic water containers, four plastic containers for cleaning, a portable sink unit, and two plastic-lined trash containers.

The Strawberry Smooooches Company has a potential for growth, but without a means of organizing events, supplies, and personnel to staff the refreshment stands, it could be a bumpy, and perhaps costly, ride. The owners of the Strawberry Smooooches Company would like to be able to project future sales based on past events, better manage the inventory (a good part of the inventory is categorized as perishable items), and maximize the use and scheduling of their employees.

The data models for the Strawberry Smooooches database are contained in Appendix B.

The authors are grateful to the owner of the Strawberry Smooooches Company, Beverly Diederich of Litchfield, Minnesota, for allowing us to help her develop a plan for success using SQL Server.

CHAPTER 2

Entity Relationship Modeling

In the previous chapter, we talked about requirements gathering and how important this task is to a good database design. In this chapter, we'll talk about how to translate these requirements into a model of what the database will look like. In the process you'll learn about entity modeling and how to create entity-relationship diagrams, and then you'll create an entity model for the Strawberry Smooches™ Company.

INTRODUCTION TO ENTITY MODELING

A model is a representation of reality. An entity model is a representation of a database, which is in itself a representation of a corporation and its reality. Dr. Peter Chen first proposed the concept of an entity-relationship model back in 1976, so this technique of graphically representing a database is not a new one. Typically, the model consists of business entities, attributes that define each entity, relationships among entities, and implied business rules, which you discovered in the requirements-gathering phase of this project.

The entity model is to a database what a blueprint is to a house. The blueprint is created before the house is built and describes what the house will look like after it's built. A blueprint lays out each of the rooms in the house, and it shows how many windows and doors each room has. It shows how one room relates to another (the kitchen is adjacent to the dining room), and it implies traffic patterns through the house (to get from the garage to the living room you have to pass through the laundry room). A blueprint room is like an entity—the doors and windows are attributes, and the rooms relate to one another like the entity relationships. You get the analogy.

The entity model is also called a conceptual model because it represents the concept of a database and how the business will work with this database. The model shows what the database will look like, but it doesn't try to explain how it will work or how you can implement it. The model is vendor neutral—that is, it doesn't contain vendor-specific data types or index indicators, nor does it contain physical or logical constructs that would tie it to any vendor product. Different database management system products often have different schemes for internal file storage and data retrieval. Datatypes can vary from one vendor's product to another. Some vendors have strategies to enhance performance that you can incorporate into the physical model, but you wouldn't implement them at this stage of development.

The entity model is abstracted from physical reality. It is a very general statement of design, and that's intentional. The benefit to this approach is that an entity model can then be engineered forward into the logical and physical models for any vendor's database platform. For instance, you can take a single entity model and create two sets of logical and physical models—one physical model you could implement on Microsoft SQL Server, and another you could implement on Oracle 8*i*.

Like architecture or engineering, entity modeling is both an art and a science. There are software packages, called CASE (computer-assisted software engineering) tools that you can use to assist your design efforts. The vendors for these tools usually support the universally recognized system design methodologies: information engineering (IE) or the Information Systems Architecture (ISA), also known as the Zachman methodology. A methodology is a predefined way of doing something—a recipe, if you will. When you follow a methodology, you perform the tasks described by that methodology, in the order given. At the end, you have a viable systems design you can implement. In this book, we'll follow a variant of IE, something we call SPAD^3, the Single Person's Approach to Database Design and Development.

SPAD^3 was born out of necessity, because in our company we have only one data modeler who is responsible for all facets of database design. Other methodologies, especially ISA, require a team of modelers and developers for the methodology to work as it was intended. The IE and ISA methodologies address the entire system development, including (but not restricted to) backend servers, client-side software, and network middleware. As a design methodology, SPAD^3 is limited to database design and development. It can be used by itself, or it can be used in conjunction with IE. Briefly, SPAD^3 has five steps:

1. **Gather requirements** Create a process and/or data flow diagram.
2. **Create the conceptual design** Generate an entity relationship model.
3. **Create the logical design** Generate a logical data model.
4. **Create the physical design** Generate a physical data model, a data volume analysis model, a data use analysis model, a security matrix, a data retention plan, a disaster avoidance plan, a replication/distribution model.
5. **Implement the design** Create the database from the physical design documents.

We'll work through enough of the SPAD^3 methodology so you get the idea of how to do database design and development.

Within each methodology you can use any one of a number of notations to display the model. You can think of a notation as a stencil or template, a set of drawing objects you use to create your entity models. Some of the more popular notations are Object Role Modeling (ORM), Unified Modeling Language (UML), Entity Relationship Modeling (ERM), Martin ERD (entity-relationship design), Express-G, Chen ERD, and Bachman. Each of these notations have been developed over time to address specific operating environments (mainframe, distributed, client/server), different database architectures (relational, object, hierarchical, CODASYL), and different purposes (database design, application design, or entire systems design). We'll use the Crow's Foot subset of the ERM notation, which is widely supported by the CASE tools on the market.

Getting Started with Entity Modeling

Creating an entity model is not difficult. Each of the methodologies and notations ensure that you can work with well-defined procedures for representing the model objects. In a way, entity modeling is like programming, in that there are syntactical rules you must follow. In fact, we have heard people say that entity modeling is like a graphical programming language.

Entities and Entity Sets

An entity is something that has substance, about which you want to store data. An entity represents an object that exists, has properties, and is distinguishable from other objects. An entity will eventually become a table in the database. Figure 2-1 is an entity that represents the employees of the Strawberry Smoooches Company. It's a simple rectangle with a shaded header area. In the header area is the name of the entity—in this case, Employee. Below the header is the primary identifying attribute (PersonID in our example). Below that is where you'd see the non-key attributes (FirstName, LastName, HireDate). The left column below the shaded header is reserved to display attribute properties. As you can see, PersonID is a primary key (PK). FirstName and LastName are I1, and HireDate is I2. The "I" designation is for indexes (which we'll talk about later in the book). FirstName and LastName have been used to build a composite index on the combined string value of the first and last names—actually, the index is built on LastName+FirstName. HireDate was used to create a simple, single-column index, hence the I2 (second index built on the table) designation. If you created a single-column index on just FirstName, to the left of the FirstName attribute you'd see the designator I1,I3.

The CASE tool we use most often, Visio 2000, uses this shape and designator style for its version of the Entity Relationship and Object Relational notations. When modeling at this conceptual level it would be just as valid to create the Employee entity by hand—to simply draw a plain rectangle and write the entity name inside, as you'll see later in this chapter.

Employee is an entity class. It is a template for, and a model of, all occurrences or instances of Employee. An instance of the entity Employee would be a single employee in the Employee table of your database.

A collection of same-type entities is an entity set. In this case, all the Employee instances (all the employees who work for the Strawberry Smoooches Company) together

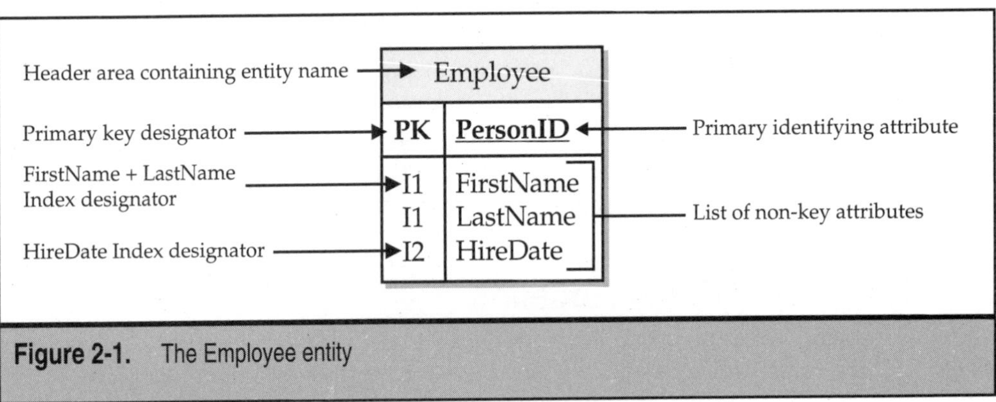

Figure 2-1. The Employee entity

form an entity set. Generally, we refer to the entity set, the instance, and the entity class as a plain, old-fashioned entity.

How do you know which entities to include in your model? In the last chapter, we talked about gathering requirements so you'd have a good understanding of the situation and the needs of the data users. Now you have to analyze these requirements, page by page, looking for words that describe business objects and business activities. The business objects might be identified by words like person, employee, product, marketing campaign, vendor, and inventory. Business activities have names like sales, manufacturing, shipping, and work assignments.

There are actually two different types of entities: noun-type entities and verb-type entities. The noun-type entities are the business objects, while the verb-types are the business activities. The verb-type entities often represent an interaction between two noun-type entities, as in employees who are assigned to work an event. In this example, Employee entities and Event entities interact with each other, and that interaction is represented by the WorkAssignment table. An employee is scheduled to work the Strawberry Smoooches booth at one or more events, while an event will require one or more employees to be present to work the booth.

Entity Groupings

While you're analyzing the requirements, you need to identify the functional modules within the business. Each company does many things, such as marketing and sales, manufacturing and production, and customer service. Each of these business units could be functional areas of the company, and each could have its own separate database or file system to handle the workload and data organization. Sometimes the functional modules track along with the way the organizational units are separated out, and sometimes they cross organizational unit boundaries. Human resource issues, for instance, is a functional module that occurs in nearly every unit of a company. The key when you're modeling for a corporate database is to recognize the autonomy of each of these functional modules while integrating each of the modules into the overall picture.

When you're modeling a database for a business, it's a good idea to gather together the entities that fall within a functional group. Even if this exercise is not a part of the formal presentations you have to make, it will help you better understand how the entities associate with one another. In Figure 2-2, you can see three such groups: the Person group, the Manufacturing group, and the Sale group.

Within each group, the entities are tightly interrelated. For instance, the Person group contains the entities Person, Sales_Person, Contact, Employee, and Comm_Device. A person can be a salesperson, and a salesperson is also a person. A person can be a contact (person); a contact (person) is also a person. A person can be an employee, and an employee is also a person. A person, a salesperson, a contact, or an employee can each have zero to many communication devices, while each communication device is related to a person, a salesperson, a contact, or an employee. The entities in the other two groups are similarly interrelated.

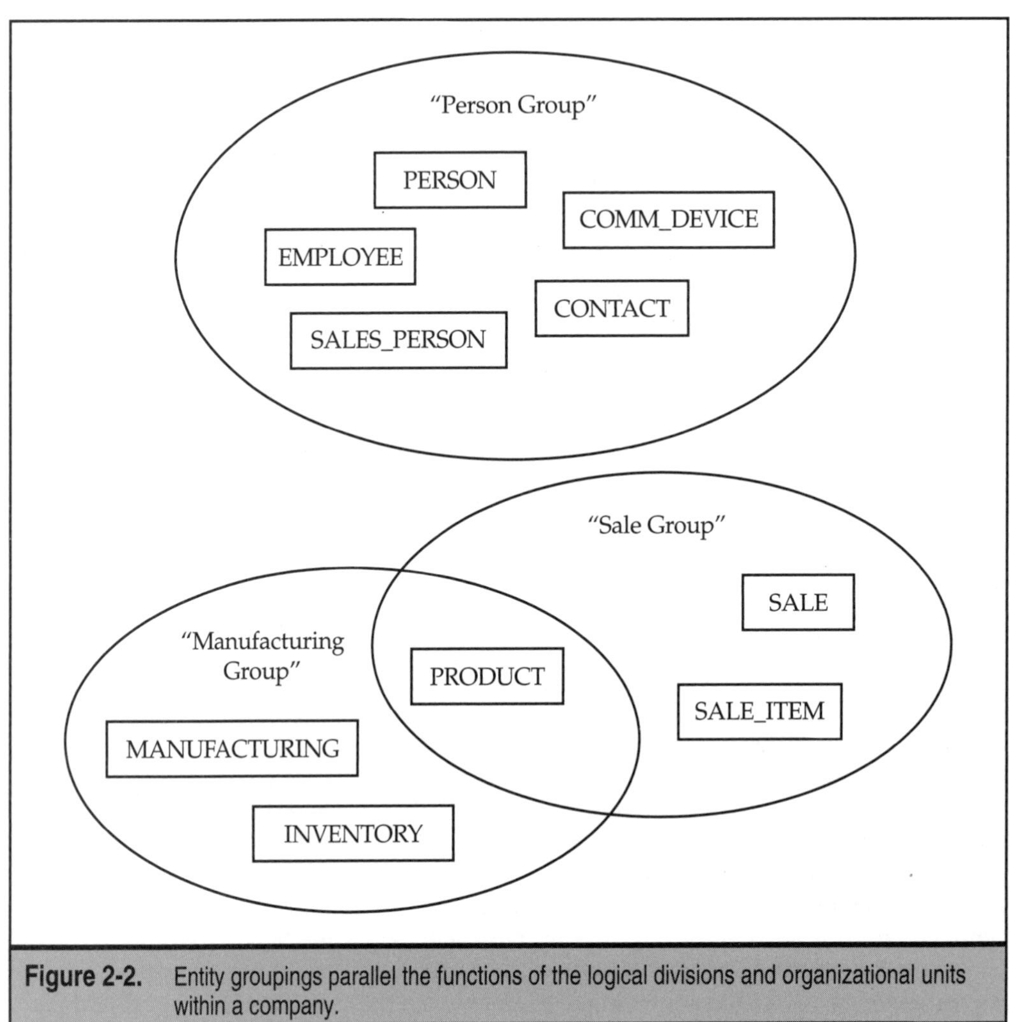

Figure 2-2. Entity groupings parallel the functions of the logical divisions and organizational units within a company.

Between groups you'll generally find a scarcity of interrelationships or no interrelationship at all, as between the Person group and the Sale group. Groups may overlap, as you can see in Figure 2-2, where the Sale and Manufacturing groups have an entity in common, the Product entity. Grouping these entities and resolving the relationships will help you understand the organization that much better.

There's a second reason for defining entity groups, and that's the possibility that the database platform you'll be implementing on will support defined schemas. A *schema* is a named group of related objects, such as tables, views, triggers, and stored procedures. If the DBMS supports schemas, there are things you can do, such as define security permissions on the schema, which are then inherited by the components of the schema. Microsoft SQL Server does have a CREATE SCHEMA statement, although it's mostly for compatibility with the ANSI-SQL standard. *Inside Microsoft SQL Server 7* (Soukup and Delaney, Microsoft Press, 1999) states that, "The SQL Server implementation of schema is essentially a check box feature providing conformance with the ANSI standard; it's not the preferred choice. Generally speaking, you'll want to use databases, not schemas."

Attributes

An entity has characteristics that describe the length, width, height, color, size, and so on of the entity. These characteristics are called *attributes*. Attributes come in two flavors: key and nonkey. A key attribute, such as PersonID, is instrumental in defining or referencing each instance of the entity it is part of. A nonkey attribute (Name, Address) simply defines and describes each instance of the entity.

There are three kinds of key attributes: the primary identifying attribute, the candidate key attribute, and the foreign key attribute.

The primary identifying attribute, also called the primary key attribute, is the unique identifier for each instance of an entity. Every entity should have a unique identifier, so that each instance of the entity can be retrieved by itself. We'll talk more about what makes a good primary key in the next section. In Figure 2-3 the primary key attribute, shown underlined, is PersonID.

A candidate key attribute is similar to a primary key attribute. Technically, an entity may contain more than one candidate for primary key, like the Person entity. Person has two candidates for primary key, PersonID and SSN. Based on such criteria as standards, tradition, or personal choice, one or another of the candidates is chosen as primary key. In this case, PersonID is the winner.

A foreign key attribute is an attribute of one entity that references the primary or candidate key attribute of another entity. The two entities form a parent-child, or one-to-many, relationship. The foreign key attribute is part of the child entity. In Figure 2-4, we've shown the dot-underlined foreign key attribute PersonID, which is part of the Comm_Device entity. Some methodologies discourage displaying the foreign key attribute; they maintain that the relationship between the entities *is* the foreign key. Technically they are right, but showing the foreign key attribute helps clarify the model for a lot of people.

There are two additional features on Figure 2-3, a composite attribute and a multi-valued attribute. The composite attribute Name is composed of FirstName and LastName. This is a technique you can use when you're conceptualizing the model and you're sure that you'll be storing a person's name, but you're not sure how it will be stored. A multi-valued attribute is one that will most likely have multiple occurrences, such as Phone. When you're just getting started with a project model, you might not know just how many or what type of phone numbers you'll need to store for each person. So you can represent phones, the plural, in this way. When you confirm that you'll need to store multiple phone numbers for each person, then you can convert the multi-valued attribute

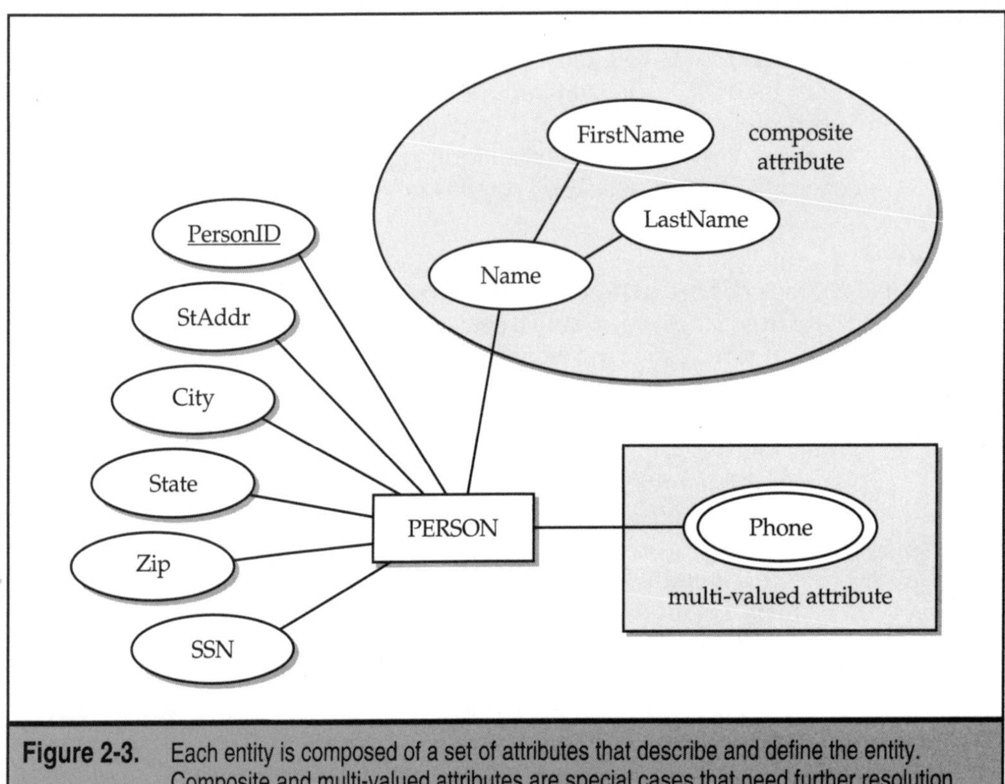

Figure 2-3. Each entity is composed of a set of attributes that describe and define the entity. Composite and multi-valued attributes are special cases that need further resolution.

into a child table, like the Comm_Device table in Figure 2-4, and associate the child table to the parent table (Person) with a foreign key.

These two techniques, the composite and the multi-valued attributes, should appear only on the conceptual model. By the time you've reached the next level, the logical model, you'll want to have resolved them into single attributes and a child table, respectively.

How do you tell an attribute from an entity? As you read through the requirements, you'll occasionally find an "entity" that has no characteristics and no attributes to describe it. What you're probably looking at is not an entity, but rather an attribute. When this happens, you need to analyze your requirements carefully to 1) confirm that this is, indeed, an attribute and not an entity; and 2) find an entity to associate the attribute to. This sounds obvious, but you cannot have a standalone attribute. Each attribute must be associated with an entity.

The Primary Identifying Attribute

As we mentioned earlier in this chapter, each entity has a primary identifying attribute, or primary key attribute, that uniquely identifies each instance of the entity. In Chapter 4

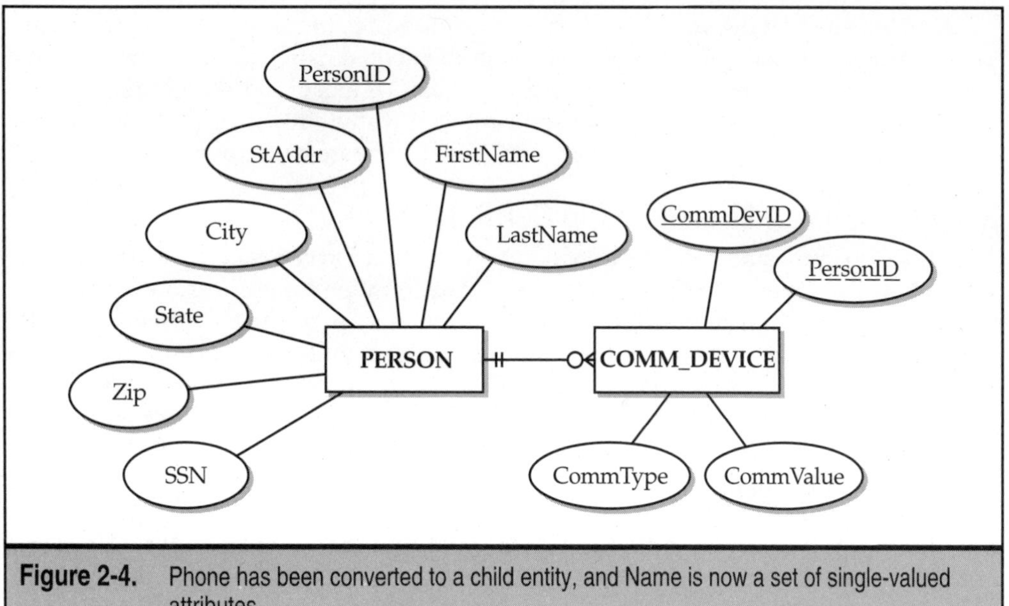

Figure 2-4. Phone has been converted to a child entity, and Name is now a set of single-valued attributes.

you'll forward-engineer the entity into a table; the primary identifying attribute will become the primary key. We also mentioned earlier that an entity may have several candidates for the primary identifying attribute, and for reasons as varied as corporate rules or personal preference, one of the candidates will be chosen to serve as primary key.

Not all candidates are created equal. Some are better than others, and a good candidate will have certain characteristics. These are

- **Brevity** Short is good. If you have to choose between two candidates that have the same data type, but one is shorter than the other (a char(4) versus a char(40), for instance), go with the shorter candidate.
- **Simplicity, unchangeable value** Stay away from complex character strings with embedded spaces, special characters, or differential capitalization. Don't use exponential number values or dates as a primary key. Don't choose values that will change over time.
- **Simple datatypes** Simple datatypes are the best, such as simple strings (codes, like FALL, WNTR, SPRG, SUMR) or integer numbers (1, 2, 3). Avoid floating point numbers or date/time datatypes; there's just too many machine instructions involved with interpreting these datatypes to make them a practical choice for primary key.

- **Non-identifying value** This may be your best bet for the primary identifying attribute. A non-identifying value is implemented in SQL Server as an identity property on a number data type or as a GUID (global unique identifier). It's meaningless—the value is not associated with anything other than the order of data entry into a table—so it probably won't change over time.

Relationships and Relationship Cardinality

A relationship in an entity model is a connection or association between two entities that describes how they interact with each other. Each relationship is an expression of a business rule, which is, as you recall, a policy or procedure that describes how the business operates. Within each modeling notation are rules about how you express these relationships. Figure 2-5 is an example of the typical one-to-many relationship expressed in the Crow's Foot notation, which is a widely used notation supported by many CASE software packages, including Visio 2000. This relationship is between Person and Comm_Device, and you read it as follows: from left to right, a Person may have zero or many communication devices, and from right to left, a CommDevice must belong to a person. Always read the relationship in both directions. You run the risk of not understanding a model if you look at things only from the one-to-many perspective; read the many-to-one rules, also, and get the full story.

So what do those little symbols at each end of the relationship line mean? Is it really necessary to use them? The answer to the second question is yes, you do have to use them in any model that means anything. What do the symbols mean? We've attempted to show, in Figure 2-6, a set of cardinality indicators (that's the proper term for these little symbols) and what they mean. If we were to substitute the cardinality indicators from Figure 2-6 for that in Figure 2-5 on the Comm_Device side, the relationships would read as follows, from the top:

—‖	A Person must have one and only one Comm_Device
—O+	A Person may have zero or one Comm_Device
—+<	A Person may have one or many Comm_Devices
—O<	A Person may have zero or many Comm_Devices

So you see, the cardinality indicator really does have meaning. Change the indicator and you change the relationship. Change the relationship and you change the way the company will be able to do business.

ERD EXAMPLES

Sometimes it helps to visualize these concepts if we look at a set of examples. Let's examine binary (two-way) relationships, ternary (three-way) relationships, and recursive (related-to-self) relationships. It'll help if you understand what a weak relationship is and how it differs from a strong relationship. Last, we'll review type-subtype relationships.

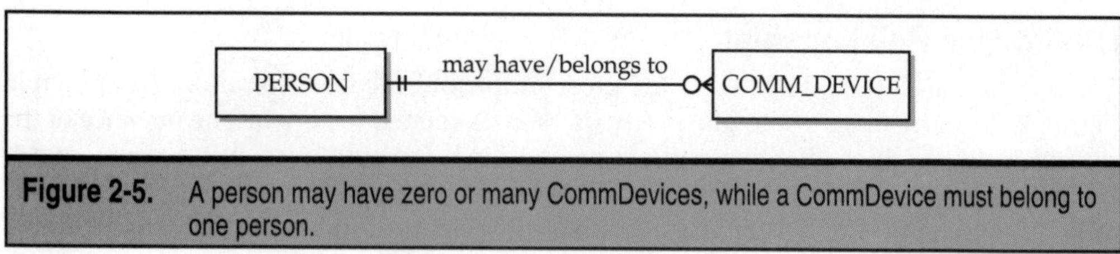

Figure 2-5. A person may have zero or many CommDevices, while a CommDevice must belong to one person.

Binary Relationships

So far in this chapter, we've been talking about binary relationships, the two-way, back-and-forth relationships that are the foundation of entity modeling and relational databases. Relationships come in three variations: one-to-one (1:1), one-to-many (1:M), and many-to-many (M:N), and each of these relationships is a binary relation—one entity related to a second entity, and the second entity related to the first. Each of these relationships, from the one-to-one to the one-to-many, and the one-to-many to the many-to-many, builds on the previous, adding more complexity to the relationship. Let's take a look at each of these three variants.

Before we do, let's make sure there's no confusion about how many-to-many relationships are represented. Traditionally, many-to-many relationships are designated as M:N, not M:M. M:M implies that you have the same number of instances on both sides of the relationship. For instance, if you expressed a many-to-many relationship as M:M, and you had five instances on one side of the relationship, you're implying that you also have five instances on the other side of the relationship. The designator M:N implies that you have some instances on one side of the relationship related to some instances on the other, but the number of instances is not necessarily the same.

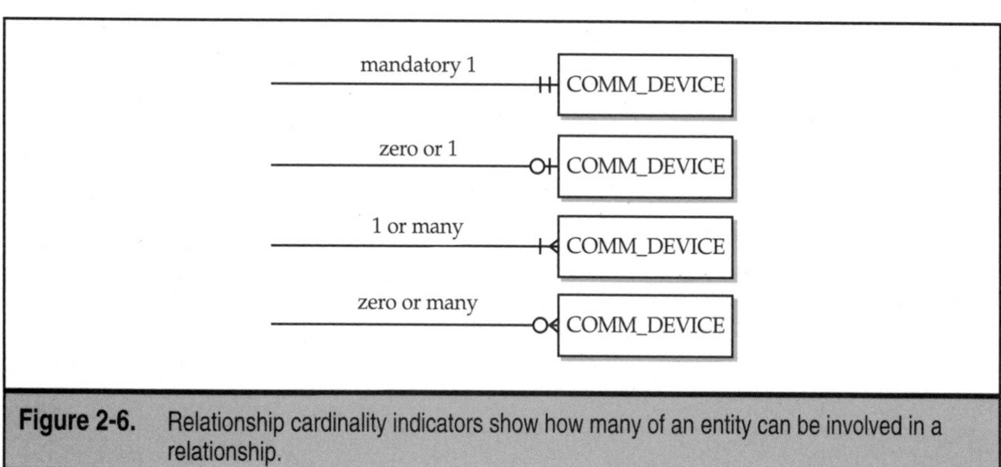

Figure 2-6. Relationship cardinality indicators show how many of an entity can be involved in a relationship.

One-to-One Relationships

The one-to-one (1:1) relationship is the most simple but the least common. As shown in Figure 2-7, one instance of the first entity (Person) is related to zero or one instance of the second entity (Employee). Simply put, a person can be an employee, but doesn't have to be—that's the "o" in the cardinality indicator near the Employee entity. An employee must be a person. The two entities will have the same primary identifying attribute, which in this case would be an identifier for the person. The names of the primary identifying attributes don't have to be the same from one entity to another, but the datatypes and lengths must be, and the meaning must also be the same. For instance, the entity Person might have a primary identifying attribute name of PersonID, and the entity Employee might have a primary identifying attribute name of EmployeeID. As long as the datatype and length of these two attributes are identical, and as long as they mean the same thing (a unique identifier for each instance of the entity), this is fine. However, we tend to use the same name for the primary identifying attributes of each of the entities in the one-to-one relationship. In fact, this might be a better technique to adopt if you don't already have standards that you're working with, because if both primary identifying attributes have the same name, there is no confusion about what they mean.

You're probably asking yourself, why would I want to use this one-to-one kind of relationship? We can think of several reasons:

- To separate little-used from often-used attributes to boost performance on data retrieval (shorter records, more per physical read, additional information in subsequent chapters).
- With regard to privacy/security issues, to separate everyday from sensitive data and limit access to the sensitive data by levying permissions on tables, not on columns.
- To split a long record that has exceeded the maximum byte length into two parts. SQL Server 6.x had an upper limit of about 1960 bytes per record. While that sounds plenty big enough, we have run into a couple of situations where the records needed to be longer than that. Your options then were to split the attributes into two sets and relate them one-to-one, or compromise on the data lengths of some of the attributes, or just not include some attributes in the record. The maximum length in bytes for SQL Server 7 and 2000 has increased to just under 8K bytes, so this is no longer a limitation.

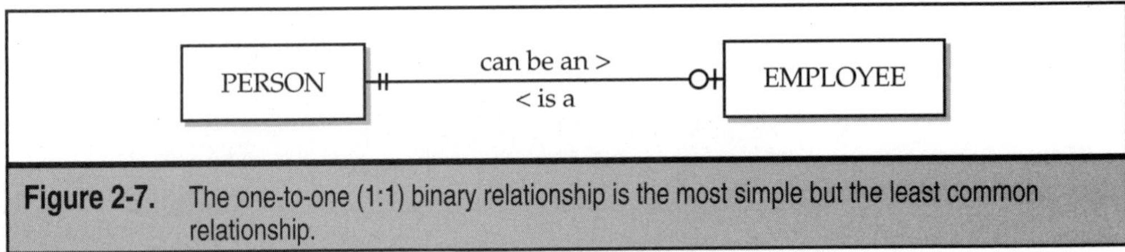

Figure 2-7. The one-to-one (1:1) binary relationship is the most simple but the least common relationship.

If there's one thing you should remember about one-to-one relationships, it's that the two entities involved will have the same primary key attribute.

One-to-Many Relationships

The one-to-many (1:M) relationship is the most common of the relationship types. As shown in Figure 2-8, one instance of the first entity (Employee) is related to zero or many instances of the second entity (Work_Assignment), and one instance of the second entity (Work_Assignment) is related only to one instance of the first entity (Employee). In other words, an employee can be given zero or many work assignments, and a work assignment can be given to an employee. The one-to-many relationship includes the definition of the one-to-one, and it extends its complexity by allowing an entity to be related not to just one but possibly many of a second entity. You'll need to take the primary identifying attribute of the first entity and make it a foreign key attribute of the second entity. In a relational database, this is how a relationship is expressed. For instance, the entity Employee might have a primary identifying attribute name of EmployeeID. The entity WorkAssignment would then have a foreign key attribute called EmployeeID, with a datatype and length the same as the EmployeeID in the Employee entity. The datatypes and lengths of these two EmployeeID attributes have to be the same, and they should mean the same thing (a unique identifier for each instance of Employee), so that when you combine the data from these two entities to get information, it makes sense.

If there's one thing you should remember about one-to-many relationships, it's that the primary key attribute of the entity on the "one" side of the equation will become a foreign key attribute on the "many" side.

Many-to-Many Relationships

The many-to-many (M:N) relationship is the most complex of the relationship types. As shown in Figure 2-9, one instance of the first entity (Employee) is related to zero or many instances of the second entity (Event), and one instance of the second entity (Event) is related to zero or many instances of the first entity (Employee). That is, an employee can work none to many events, while an event can have zero to many employees assigned to work it. In a relational database, it's not possible to express this kind of relationship directly, so you have to resolve the complexity by creating a new entity, called a gerund, associative, intersection, or join entity. Depending on which vendor environment you're working in, and which database platform you're developing on, this entity that cross-references two other entities will be known by one of these four names. Then you associate each of the two original noun-type entities (Employee and Event) with this verb-type

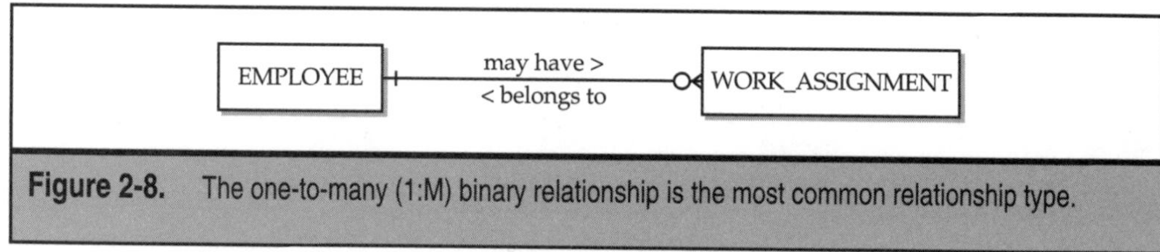

Figure 2-8. The one-to-many (1:M) binary relationship is the most common relationship type.

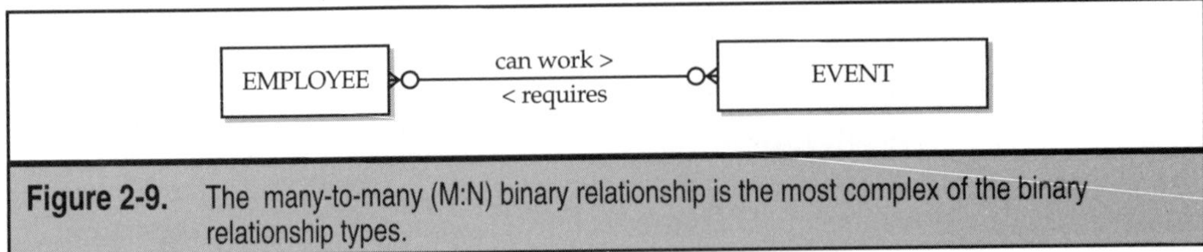

Figure 2-9. The many-to-many (M:N) binary relationship is the most complex of the binary relationship types.

gerund (Work_Assignment), using one-to-many relationships, as shown in Figure 2-10. A many-to-many relationship is always resolved by associating the two noun-type entities with the single verb-type entity as a pair of one-to-many relationships.

The term *gerund* means a verb that is behaving like a noun. The dictionary definition (Webster's New World) indicates that the gerund should end in an *–ing*, but for readability and understandability, we bend the rules and try to use noun-type words to describe this verb-type entity. Thus, the many-to-many relationship becomes a pair of one-to-many relationships, connected by a gerund, as shown in Figure 2-10. The rules for one-to-many behavior hold in this situation—the primary key attribute of the one becomes a foreign key attribute of the many. Thus, the gerund entity will always have more than one foreign key, one from each of the one-to-many relationships that it's involved in. For example, the gerund entity Work_Assignment would have two foreign key attributes, one from Employee (called EmployeeID), with a datatype and length the same as the EmployeeID in the Employee entity, and a second from Event (called EventID), with a datatype and length the same as the EventID in the Event entity. As before, the datatypes and lengths of these attribute sets have to be the same, and they should mean the same thing, so that when you combine the data from either pair of these three entities to get information, it makes sense.

If there's one thing you should remember about many-to-many relationships, it's that they must be resolved by the creation of a third, verb-type entity called a gerund. Each noun entity will relate to the gerund by a one-to-many relationship, and each primary key attribute becomes a foreign key in the gerund.

Ternary Relationships

A ternary relationship is a three-way relationship, as shown in Figure 2-11. Employees, customers, and events are all involved in the making of a sale. In this example, Sale is the gerund, the verb-type entity. In our example, a Sale involves someone buying (Cus-

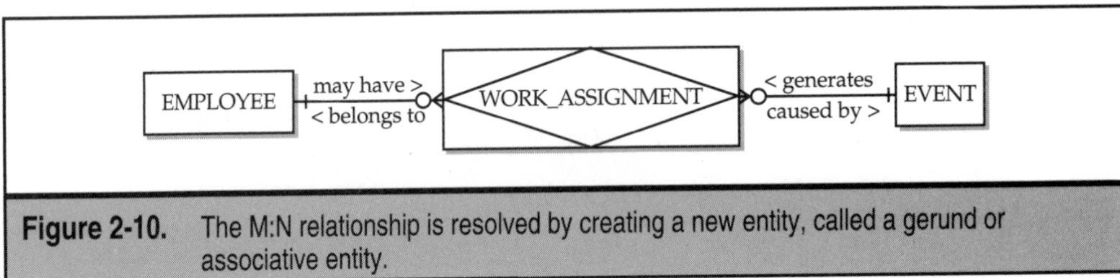

Figure 2-10. The M:N relationship is resolved by creating a new entity, called a gerund or associative entity.

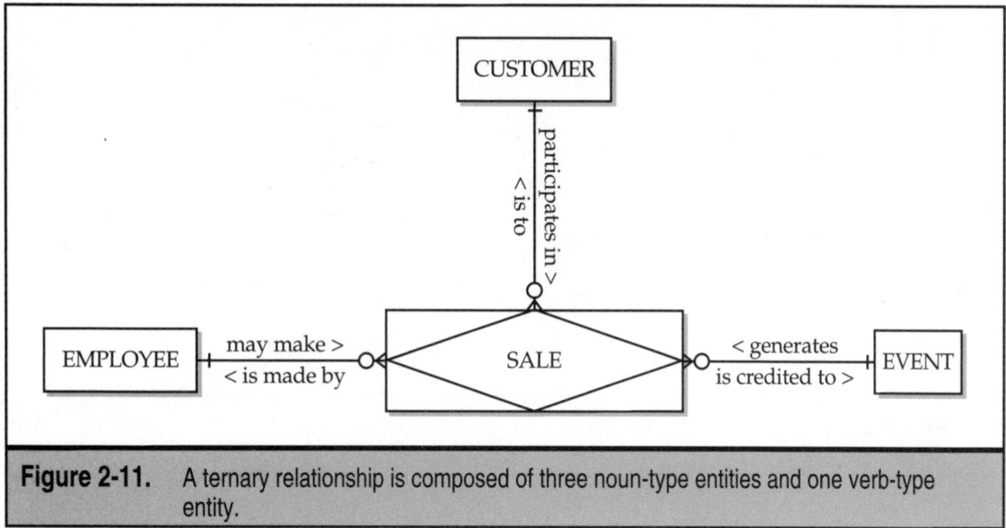

Figure 2-11. A ternary relationship is composed of three noun-type entities and one verb-type entity.

tomer), someone selling (Employee), and where this happened (Event)—thus the three-way relationship. Employee to Sale is one-to-many, as are Customer to Sale and Event to Sale. According to the rule established in the previous section, the primary key attribute of the one becomes a foreign key attribute of the many. Thus, Sale will have three foreign keys: EmployeeID from the Employee entity, CustomerID from the Customer entity, and EventID from the Event entity.

Recursive Relationships

A recursive relationship is one in which a single entity is related to itself. It's a binary relationship, except instead of having two different entities related to each other, you have one entity related to itself. Take a look at Figure 2-12. The entity Person is related to itself in a one-to-many fashion. Below the cardinality indicator on the "one" side you see the term "manager." Read this model like so: a Person manages zero or many Persons, and a Person is managed by one Person.

In this recursive model, all people are part of a single entity called Person, no matter what category they happen to be part of (employees, managers, students, teachers). The recursive relationship can also be many-to-many, as shown in Figure 2-13. This model says: a Person, an instructor, teaches many students, who are also people, and a Person, a student, is taught by many instructors, who are also people.

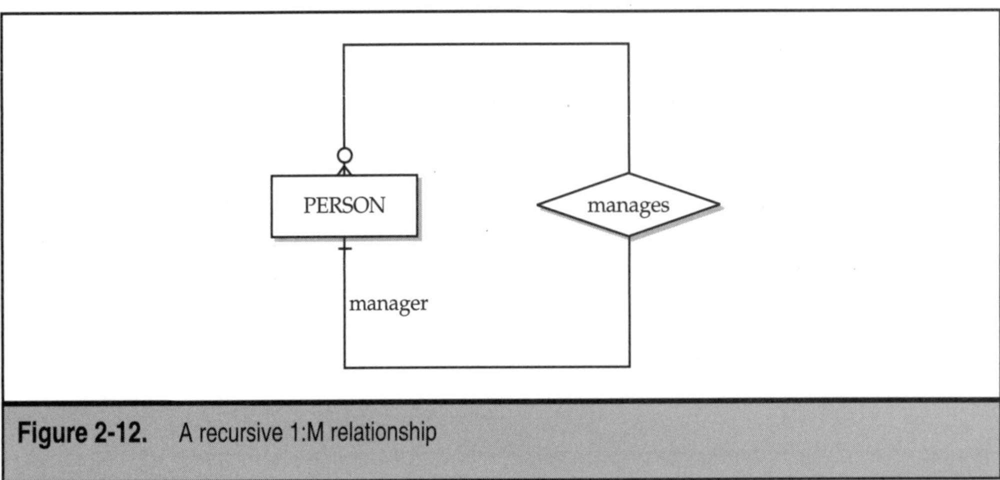

Figure 2-12. A recursive 1:M relationship

Weak Entities

One-to-many relationships are generally classified as dependent or independent. A dependent relationship has a "strong" entity on the parent side (the entity of the "one") and a "weak" entity on the child side (the entity of the "many"), like the arrangement in Figure 2-14. For each Sale (the strong entity, with attributes such as sale identifier, the date and time of the sale), there will be one or more Sale_Items (the weak entity, representing items that have been purchased as part of a sale). Each Sale_Item must be associated with a Sale. Under no circumstances do you want to have an instance of Sale_Item in your database without an associated Sale. The weak entity depends on its associated parent entity for its existence. Hence, Sale_Item is dependent on Sale.

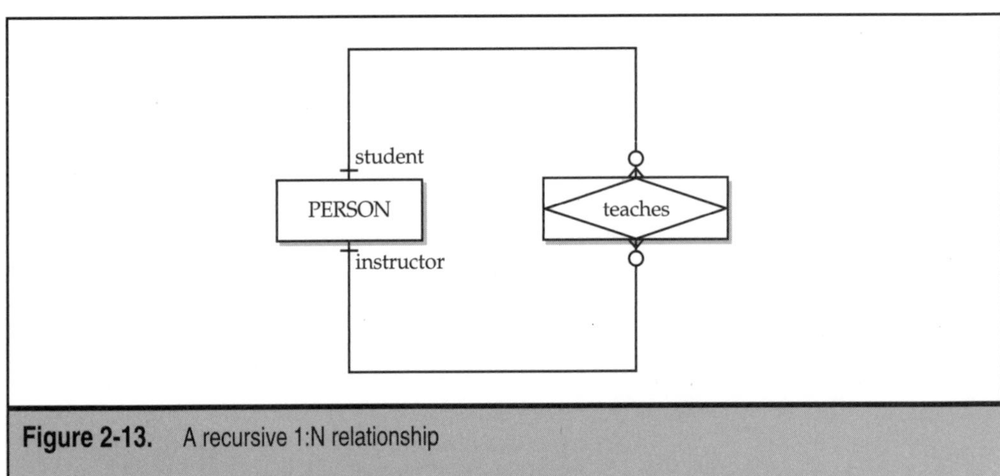

Figure 2-13. A recursive 1:N relationship

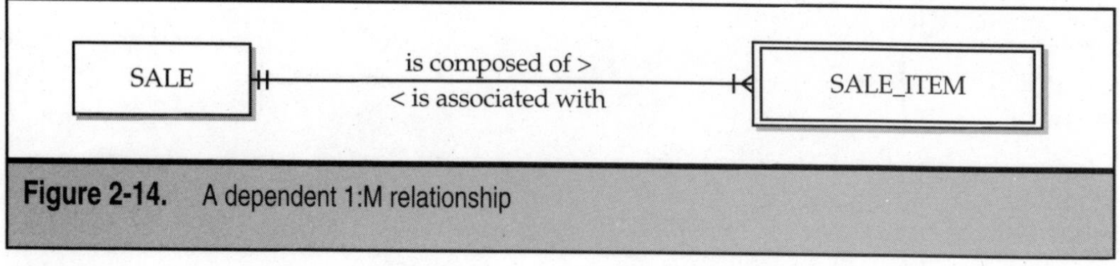

Figure 2-14. A dependent 1:M relationship

This dependent one-to-many relationship is the more common of the two types. If we had to guess, we would reckon that 80 to 90 percent of all one-to-many relationships are of the dependent type. Dependent relationships are those that lend themselves to being enforced, either through triggers or through declarative referential integrity (DRI) statements, which we will cover in the next chapter. Briefly, enforcing referential integrity in a one-to-many relationship means not allowing someone to insert a record into Sale_Item before an associated Sale record is already in place. It might also mean that if someone were to delete a Sale, all associated Sale_Items would be deleted also. Similarly, if for some reason the Sale identifying number (the primary key attribute) of a parent Sale instance had to be changed, you'd want that change repeated or cascaded to all child instances of Sale_Item.

The independent relationship is the opposite of the dependent. Here you have a relationship wherein the instances on the child side have some autonomy—they are not dependently linked to their associated parent. Figure 2-15 is an example of an independent one-to-many relationship, wherein a Vendor can provide zero or many Supplies, while a Supply can come from a Vendor. A Supply can exist without a Vendor of record. For instance, if the Strawberry Smoooches manager decided to stop by a local grocery store and buy boxes of straws, it would not be necessary to record Vendor information about that grocery store in the database. If the Strawberry Smoooches Company decided to stop doing business with a vendor and removed that vendor's record from the database, you don't want the record deletion cascading to Supplies and removing those supplies that this vendor previously sold you!

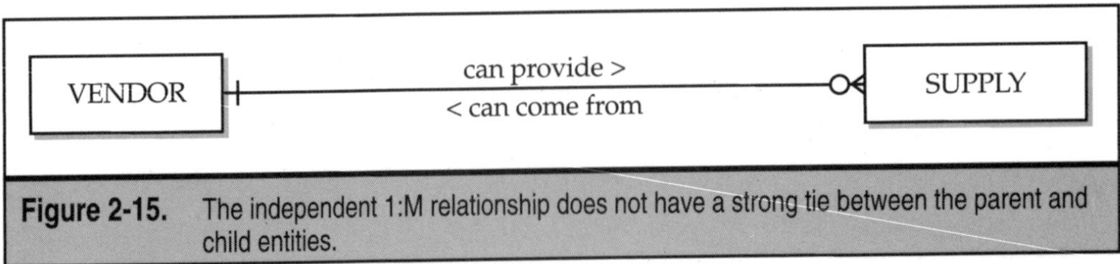

Figure 2-15. The independent 1:M relationship does not have a strong tie between the parent and child entities.

Type-Subtype Relationships

Earlier in this chapter, we mentioned that all categories of individuals are people, and in the section on recursive relationships we showed that all people can be represented by a single entity. There's another way to represent categories of people, and that's by using the type-subtype construct. Figure 2-16 is a representation of a type-subtype relationship that includes the different categories of Salesperson, Employee, and Contact (for a vendor). Each of these categories of individual is first and foremost a Person, and the Person attributes (name, address) modify each individual. This is the type entity. Each category of Person has attributes that are unique to that category, and those attributes belong to the subtype entity. Each of the subtype entities inherits the attributes of its type entity, so each category (Salesperson, Employee, and Contact) will inherit the name and address attributes of Person.

The relationships between the type and subtype entities are one-to-one. In Figure 2-16, the Person entity has a primary key attribute of PersonID, and so do all of the subtype entities. If you recall, according to the rules of the binary one-to-one relationship, both entities in the relationship have the same primary key attribute. This rule is extended in the type-subtype relationship to include all the entities.

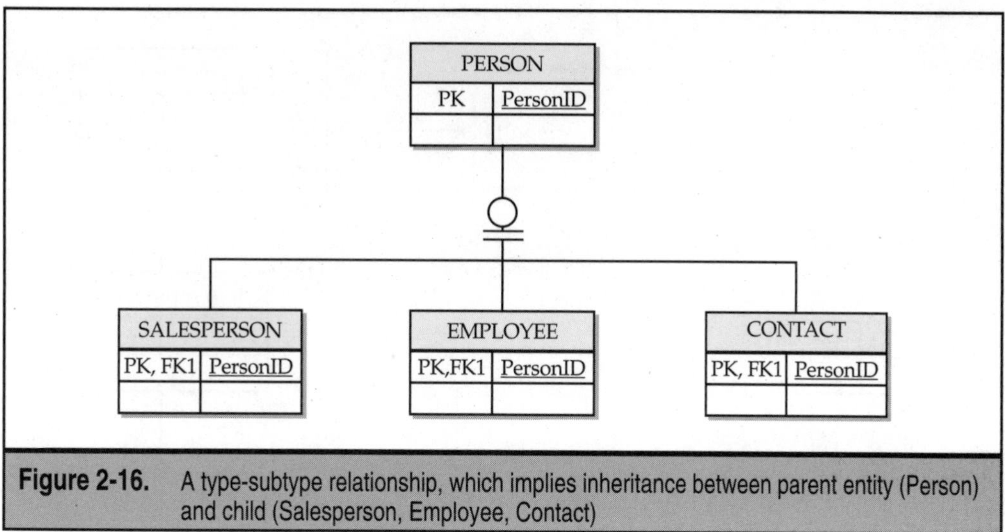

Figure 2-16. A type-subtype relationship, which implies inheritance between parent entity (Person) and child (Salesperson, Employee, Contact)

STRAWBERRY SMOOOCHES: THE ENTITY MODEL

Figure 2-17 is the entity-relationship model for the Strawberry Smooches Company. It was created with Microsoft Visio 2000, using the concepts we have discussed in this chapter combined with the notation provided by Visio 2000's ER source model. This model contains entities to cover person management, events management, inventory management, and manufacturing.

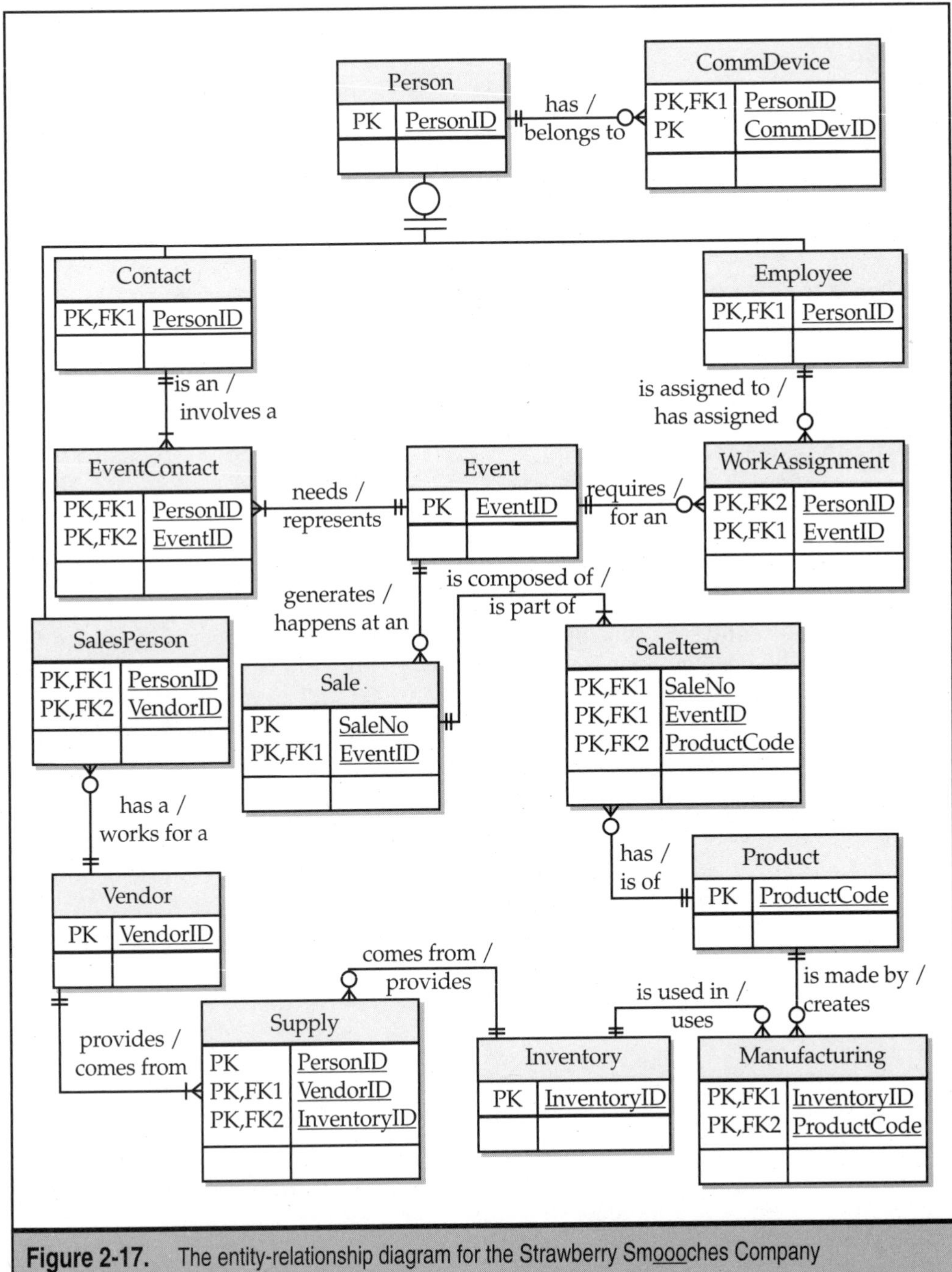

Figure 2-17. The entity-relationship diagram for the Strawberry Smoooches Company

CHAPTER 3

Principles of Design

Principles of database design have been developed over the years by both individuals (such as Dr. Peter Chen, who developed the Chen methodology and notation of entity modeling) and corporations (such as Oracle and its Designer/2000 software tool kit and methodology). By adhering to these principles, you will be following in the footsteps of others who have learned, often the hard way, what works and what does not. In this chapter, we will look at logical modeling and consider the rules of normalization, an important topic that tends to be overlooked in the rush to complete a project.

We might state the first principle of design as "Have a plan." Following your plan, you build your design. The second principle might be "Have a design in a form that can be shared." Whether it is on paper or in electronic form in a software tool such as Designer/2000, ERWin, or Visio, there must be a design that is accessible to everyone working on the database development team before coding begins. We have encountered databases where the only "design" is in someone's head. We have even been told "the design is too complex to document"—yet this company managed to implement the database and create applications that capture and report on the data. This is scary. It's like setting the framers and carpenters to work building a house, but without blueprints. So our third principle would be "Don't start coding until the design is in place." It's not necessary to have a 100-percent-final design, for it will change as the project evolves. But you need at least enough of a design to be able to diagram the entities in the database and the relationships among them, and to understand the various reports and data access methods that will be employed by the end-users.

In this chapter, we will look at some of the concepts you will use when designing your database. At this stage in the development cycle, the same concepts and principles can be applied to any database management system, relational or not.

LOGICAL MODELING

Logical modeling is the step that follows entity relationship modeling. Like entity modeling, logical modeling is a representation of the reality of your business requirements. Like the entity model, the logical model is vendor neutral. It's like a detailed blueprint of the database. You should be able to apply your logical model to any vendor's database platform.

The logical model differs from the entity model in that the entities and relationships are more completely defined in the logical model. In the entity model, you identified entities (which are analogous to tables), attributes that describe the entities, and relationships between the entities. For the logical model, you need to expand the definition of each of the attributes (which will become columns in the tables). You'll define properties such as generic datatypes and lengths, potential for nullability, and suitability for indexing, all of which we'll talk about in a moment. For each relationship, you'll define more precisely the rules that govern the behavior of data when you change a primary key value, as shown in Figure 3-1. Notice that, at the end of each of the relationships there are designators: u:C, u:R, d:C, d:R. The u: indicates behavior on update of the primary key, the d: on delete. The u:C and d:C indicate a cascade on update or delete of the primary key value. The u:R and d:R

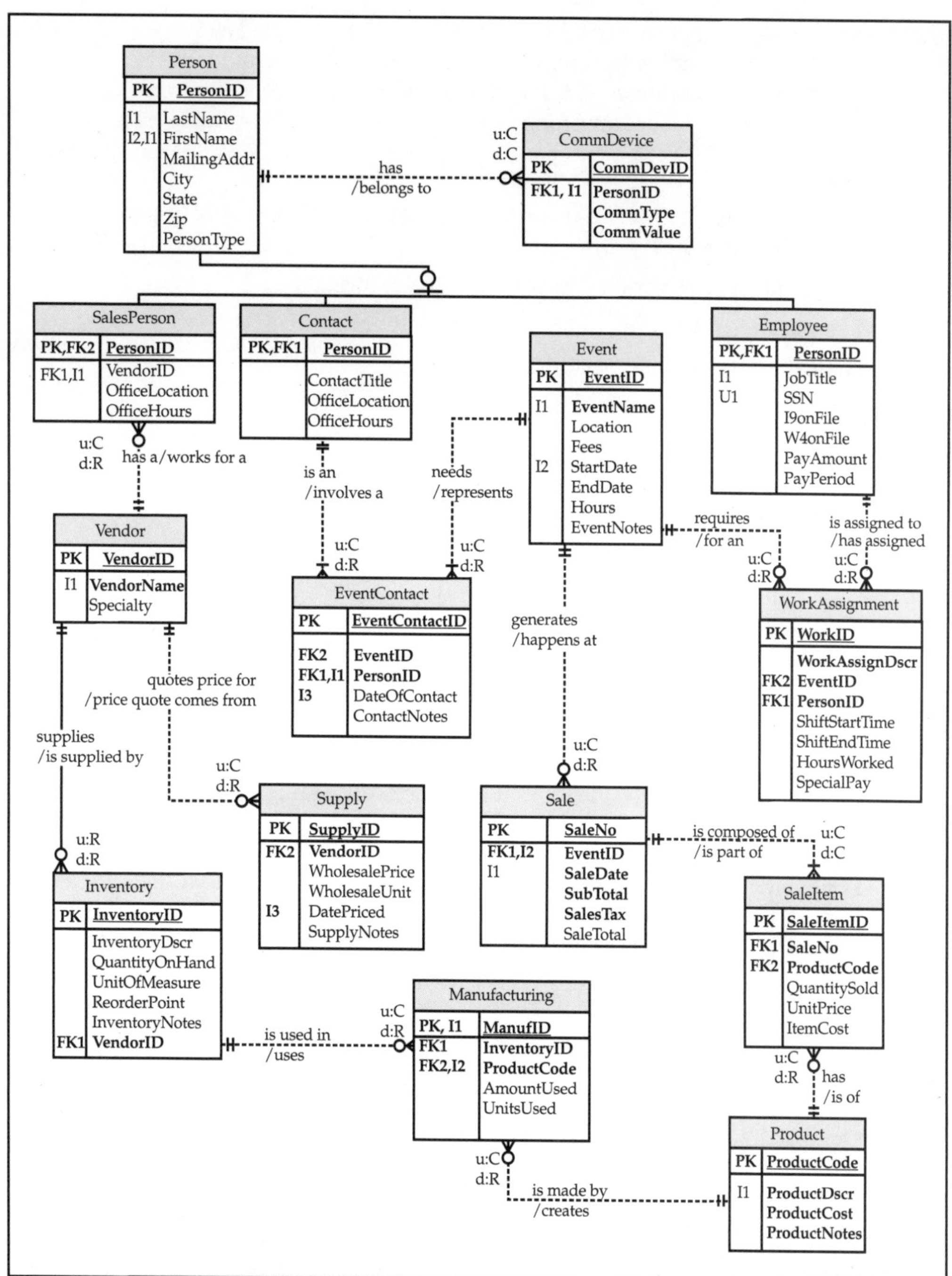

Figure 3-1. The Strawberry Smoooches Company logical model, showing behavior on update and delete operations

indicate a restrict—in other words, you won't be able to change the key value or delete the row in the parent table until you've removed related rows in the child table.

Generic datatypes are those that are considered portable—the kind that can be applied to any vendor's database environment. The most common portable datatypes are:

- **Text** Both fixed and variable length
- **Numeric** Signed integer, unsigned integer, auto-number, floating point, decimal, and money
- **Raw data** Fixed, variable, picture, and OLE object
- **Temporal** Timestamp, date, time, and datetime
- **Logical** True or false, yes or no, zero or one
- **Other** Row ID and object ID

Null is a condition of the data that means one of at least three things:

- The data value is not applicable (you don't have an email address)
- The data value is applicable but not available (you have an email address, but I don't know what it is)
- It's unknown if the data value is applicable (I don't know if you have an email address)

If a column is indicated as null, it means the data value can be omitted in the database. If a column is "not null," you need to include a value for this column when you insert a record into the table—the column must always have a value.

Indexing to a database is like the index in this book. We'll talk a lot more about indexing later, but simply put, an index is a copy of one or more columns of the data in a system-managed table, arranged in alphabetic order, which is used to facilitate data retrievals.

Rules of behavior in a database govern how a child record in a one-to-many relationship is handled when its associated parent record is removed from the database. If you remove a parent record, you need to determine what to do with the associated child records. Do you keep the child records as orphans without a parent, do you detach them from the old parent and reattached them to a new parent record, do you cascade the delete and get rid of all child records that belong to the deleted parent record, or do you prevent the parent record from being deleted at all? This determination of how a child record behaves is totally based on the requirements you gathered and your understanding of the data and its interrelationships.

Data Normalization

To normalize data, and ultimately your database, is to organize data into logical groupings based on meaning and functionality, with an eye toward easing the chore of data maintenance. Normalization is a process that is critical to the design, implementation, performance, and scalability of your database. You need to break down your data into subsets, each of which describes some object within the database or a relationship among those objects. You end up with many tables in a relational database, and you will have to join those tables in order to extract information. Typically, you would not store data about customers in the same table as the data about products. When a customer buys a product, that fact is recorded in the sales table. But how far do you go when breaking down or decomposing the data? The "Rules of Normalization" offer some guidance on whether your data has been split into tables correctly or if you may be heading for trouble by designing problems into your database.

The Rules of Normalization grew out of work by E.F. Codd and C.J. Date, working as consultants to IBM back in the 1980s, while they were developing the theories that became the foundation of today's relational databases. When your data meets the requirements of the First Rule of Normalization, it is said to be in "first normal form." It is common to normalize as far as third normal form. However, you should be aware of some of the pitfalls that can be avoided by keeping in mind the fourth and fifth normal forms. These will all be explained in the sections that follow.

The goals of normalization can be expressed as follows:

- Arranging data into logical groupings so the data in each normalized group describes some part of the whole database, usually a single entity or object within the database
- Minimizing the amount of data duplicated in the database
- Arranging the data so that when data is changed, the change has to be made in one place and one place only
- Allowing the data to be accessed and modified quickly and efficiently without risking the integrity of the data stored in the database

Some database designers express these goals using terms such as data integrity, referential integrity, or keyed database access. The difference is only in terminology; the methods used are the same.

In an ideal world, you would apply the Rules of Normalization before the database was built, as part of the design process. However, we all know that from time to time we have to maintain or modify applications and databases designed and built by others. You can apply these same rules to an existing database, which will help you decide whether it can be extended without too much trouble or will need a major reworking to meet the new requirements. It's no different from checking the foundation of a building to see if you can add an extra floor. If the foundation is solid, you can build up. If not, you will have to retro-engineer the structural components of the house or buy another.

Data normalization is absolutely essential when the database is going to be used for ongoing transactions. In the online transaction processing (OLTP) world, data modifications in the form of updates, inserts, and deletes are happening constantly and more or less at random throughout the data set. In this ever-changing environment, normalization is needed to make sure that the changes being made do not corrupt the data in any way. For example, one of the results of normalizing your data is that you would not store a field such as Year-to-Date Salary for an employee. You would calculate it from the current entries in the payroll tables. If you stored it in the database, you would have to remember to recompute the year-to-date salary every time you ran the payroll program. Granted, you can set up triggers to do this (which we will discuss later), but you would have to include this trigger in every possible change to the data to be totally sure this calculated value is reliable. Therefore, you generally don't store calculated data in an OLTP database.

The situation is quite different with a data warehouse. The purpose of the data warehouse is to store data for analysis, hence the term "online analytical processing" (OLAP). This data is, by definition, historical data and should not be changed without very good reason. The only major changes to a data warehouse will be the regular addition of new data, usually from OLTP databases, which is done by the database administrator (DBA) under very controlled conditions. Data warehouse users are not permitted to make changes to the data, only to query and analyze it. Many of the queries run against this data are looking for summary data (daily, weekly, or monthly sales totals) or comparing product sales between geographic areas or periods of time. Rather than summarize the data over and over again as similar queries are run, it is common to "preaggregate" the data by computing and storing the summarized data. You might store daily and weekly sales totals, for example, and then be able to compute monthly totals from the daily totals rapidly. In most data warehouses, the data is far from normalized. However, in this book we will be addressing the OLTP environment, so we are going to assume in later chapters that we are dealing with a normalized source database updated frequently by multiple users.

One of the fundamental precepts of database normalization is that the organization of data within the database by tables is very different from the way in which the users of the database expect to see the data. For example, a manager at a mail-order computer parts store is not likely to want to see a list of customers. You might use the list for a mass mailing of catalogs once a month, but you would not browse the list. What the managers want to see is which customers are placing orders and for what products. They might want to know on a specific sale who the customer was, what they bought, who the salesperson was, which items the customer purchased, what the total cost was, and how and when the items were shipped. This would involve pulling in data from several tables. This really is what you expect in a relational database, as the clients or end-users study not just the data but also the relationships between the data records.

Normalization and Business Standards

Before you jump in and start normalizing your database, you need to get some consensus within your company or with your client about what objects you need to track in your database. By this, we do not just mean a listing of objects—you need definitions. For example, many databases track customers. But what is a customer? To a high-level manager, a customer may be another company that purchases goods and services. To a customer service representative, it's the person at that company who calls and places the orders. To a salesperson, it may be a name on a business card, someone to whom he or she may make a sale in the future. Ask a salesperson what defines a "sale" and he will tell you that he played golf with a customer last week and the customer assured him he would be placing a huge order. Ask the production manager, and she will say that a sale is final only when the product actually ships. And the accounting department counts a sale as final only when the payment arrives. So you need to make sure that you have a consensus on what terms will mean in the database, and you should not assume that there is some standard definition for the objects and events you will be tracking.

The Rules of Normalization

Let's take a look at these Rules of Normalization and see how they can be applied to your databases. When you begin normalizing a database, you should start from the general and work toward the specific, applying tests as you go to make sure that you are in first, then second, and then third normal form. You cannot be in second normal form without also being in first normal form, and you can't be in third normal form without already being in second normal form. Database designers refer to this process as *decomposition*. Decomposition will remove the possibility of insert, update, and delete anomalies. It guarantees functional dependencies, removes transitive dependencies, and reduces non-key data redundancy. We will go into more detail about these terms as we decompose some example data into first, second, and then third normal form.

First Normal Form

A first normal form file is a "flat file," with no repeating groups, no array fields, and no multi-valued fields. A first normal form file typically contains data that is loosely related, such as that found in Table 3-1, which shows data about customers who have made purchases.

Sale#	CustomerName	CustomerAddress	Product	Cost	Salesperson
1027	John Jensen	47 Acacia Avenue Alamosa, CO 80444	Hard disk	$243	Jean
1028	Kathy Kimble	18 Alamosa Acres Santa Fe, NM 85038	Monitor	$449	Sam
1029	John Jensen	47 Acacia Avenue Alamosa, CO 80444	CD-ROM	$89	Sam

Table 3-1. A first normal form table contains atomic data, with no repeating groups. Primary key is underlined.

For a table to be in first normal form (1NF) the data has to be atomic with no repeating groups. By *atomic*, we mean that the data is broken down into the smallest possible units. Each cell of a table should hold only a single item of data. How do you define an item of data? A data item is an indivisible piece of information. What constitutes indivisibility? For instance, is a date a single data item? After all, a typical date is composed of a month, a day, and a year, right? Well, sort of. A more accurate description of a date is that the date has month, day, and year components (and in the case of SQL Server, time components—hour, minute, and second). If your requirements dictate that you store a date to mark an event, such as a sale or a paycheck, then not only do you want to store all of these components as a single item of data, but you also want to define this data item as a date or datetime datatype. Instances of this date are data items. On the other hand, if you need to store more general date information, such as the vintage year of a bottle of wine, then you need only store the year component of the date. In this case you'd define an integer datatype to hold the data, and then constrain the attribute with a check constraint to disallow any value less than 1700 or greater than 2020—a reasonable date range when you're talking about vintages of wine. In this case, the integer attribute "year" is a single data item.

When you arrange your data in first normal form, what you are really doing is identifying the various objects and entities in your database and trying to determine what is an entity and what is an attribute. Each table in the database represents one object, such as a customer, an invoice, or a product. Each column in the table represents one attribute describing that object, and each row in the table represents one instance of that object.

If your database has a table that contains two or more columns, and these columns contain the same kind of data (phone numbers, items purchased, and the like), you'd have a repeating group. In programming terminology, this is an *array*. If your database supports repeating groups (which it does not because it is a true relational database), you might encounter the following scenario: For a Sale table, you might have the customer information, the salesperson data, and a sale number. There would be multiple entries for the items ordered, the cost, and the quantity of each item ordered. If the client ordered five items, there would be five entries in the array. But then you have to decide how big to make the array. Do you allow for the client to order a maximum of five items, or ten, or twenty? At least you don't have the client information repeated for each item purchased!

There are other ways to achieve the same result without having to build an array, as you can see from Figure 3-2, taken from the Strawberry Smooches logical data model. The Sale table has an associated (1:M) SaleItem table. The Sale table contains a unique identifier for the table, a key column that relates the table to the Event that generated the sale, the date of the sale, and the amount of the sale. The SaleItem table is the child to Sale—it contains its own unique identifier, a key that relates it back to the parent table Sale; and then the product code, quantity sold, unit price, and item cost for each item purchased. With this normalized design, you can have from one to an unlimited number of SaleItems related to a Sale.

Also watch out for "hidden" arrays, such as telephone number. These days everyone has multiple phone numbers. As you start adding columns for home phone, work phone, fax, pager, cell phone, toll-free number, and so on, think about what you are doing. Is this

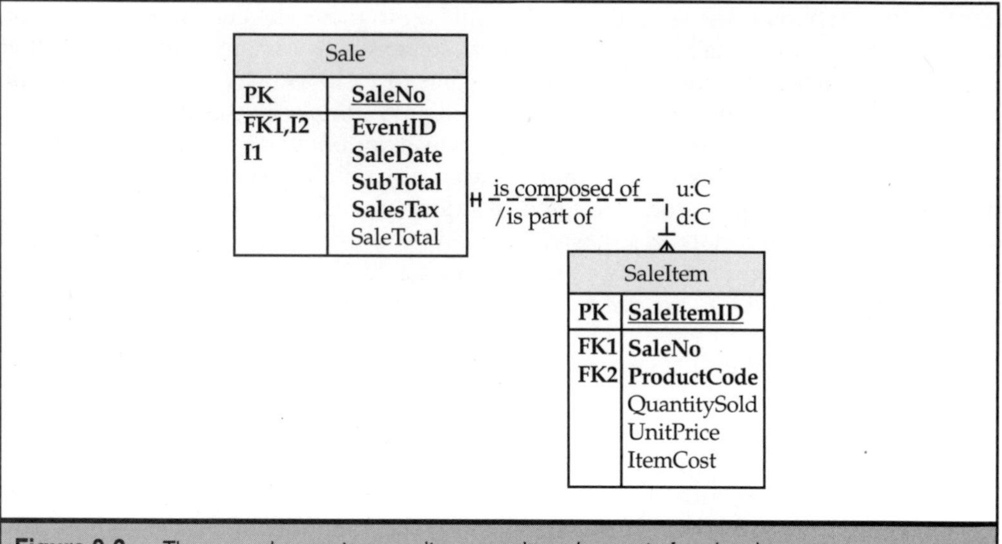

Figure 3-2. There may be one to many items purchased as part of each sale.

really a list of columns with unique meaning? Or is it really an array? We'll talk more on this topic later.

The primary key is a column or a combination of columns that are unique within the table—no duplicate values are allowed in a primary key. By having a primary key defined for the table, you know exactly to which row you are referring when you run a query or update that table. This is also called *entity integrity*—there is no confusion about which record or row is to be updated. The changes will be applied to the correct row, and only that row, and because there are no duplicate rows, the change will not have to be applied to multiple rows.

Table 3-1 is in first normal form. In it is recorded sales data, and for each sale, the product, the customer, and the salesperson. This is not unlike what you might find in a flat-file database, or even where the company had been using a spreadsheet to track data.

You can see the problems immediately. You have a duplicate record for one of your customers. If John Jensen calls and asks you to ship his order to his new address, you will have to make sure that you update all the sales records for this customer. You would also have a problem if you wanted to do targeted mailing to all of your customers in Alamosa, because the city name is part of the address. Yes, you can parse the address for "Alamosa," but then you might include your customer in Santa Fe, because the word Alamosa occurs in her address. To be more accurate, you could search on "Alamosa CO," but then you would also need to look for records with a comma after "Alamosa," or records with two or three spaces instead of one between the city name and the state code, and so on.

The first step in normalizing this table would be to move the customer information out of this table into a Customer table. There is currently no customer information that you can guarantee to be unique, so you would have to add a customer identifier to the new customers table. This is easy to do, by creating a column with the identity property. We'll discuss this in Chapter 6, but it will generate an automatically incrementing number for the column, and so is ideal for things like invoice number, purchase order number, membership number, and so on. The address definitely needs to be split out into columns for street address, city, state, zip/postal code, and country. While you are creating the customer table, it might be a good idea to include columns for telephone number and email address. Even if you are not tracking those data items now, you very likely will need to in the future.

Once the customer information has been moved to another table (as shown in Table 3-2), it is replaced in the Sales table with only the customer ID that was generated for each customer. With only that information, on any given sale, you can retrieve all the customer data.

Now what about the product information? You will definitely need a table in which to store information about your products, including such attributes as manufacturer, size, color, and price. Again, you will need a unique key to identify each product. You might use a product identifier, which is an auto-incrementing value. An alternative for retail products might be to use the UPC number, which accompanies the bar code. Or you might develop your own scheme of product codes (as we've done in the Strawberry Smoooches database). If you are selling books, the ISBN number might be a good choice, as long as all the books you will ever handle have ISBN numbers assigned. Whenever a product is sold, you would reference it by this identifier in the row in the Sales table. To complete the normalization, you would also have a table for your employees, and reference the employee in the sales record by some employee identifier. This would *not* be their Social Security number, because then too much confidential information would be available to anyone who could access the Employee table. The Windows NT login is a possible choice for identifier, as you know it is unique. Or you might follow the Customer example and generate an employee ID for each person. So now when a sale is entered into the database, the record looks like what you see in Table 3-3.

CustID	Customer Name	Street Address	City	State	Zip	Country
101	John Jensen	47 Acacia Avenue	Alamosa	CO	80444	USA
102	Kathy Kimble	18 Alamosa Acres	Santa Fe	NM	85038	USA

Table 3-2. The normalized Customer table contains only customer names and addresses.

SaleNo	CustomerID	ProductCode	Cost	Salesperson
1027	101	6573-3718	$243	Jean
1028	102	6228-1019	$449	Sam
1029	101	8494-8459	$89	Sam

Table 3-3. The normalized Sales table contains a customer ID that points to the customer who made the purchase.

How far you go with decomposing data items depends on how you will be using the data. For example, when you look at a telephone number, do you regard the area code as a separate data item from the exchange and number? If you often search by area codes, it might make sense to define it in a separate column. If you don't, then think about making the area code part of a more general telephone number field. You would probably split an address into its atomic components of street address, city, state, zip/postal code, and country, at least in the United States. Would you make the house number a separate item from the street name? Probably not, unless your users need to query and sort by street name.

Second Normal Form

Second normal form is often expressed as "There must be no partial key dependencies" in your tables. So what does that mean? First of all, you know there is a primary key in this table because it meets the requirements for first normal form. It must or you could not begin to put it into second normal form. Second, every other column must depend on the entire primary key, not just a part of it. That implies a multi-column primary key. 2NF is a condition of full functional dependency on the whole primary key; the primary key must determine the value of each of the non-key attributes.

Suppose that in your Sales table, you don't have a sale number. Instead, you have a sale date column, as shown in Table 3-4. You then would make a primary key of SaleDate+CustomerID+ProductCode. 1NF requires that a table have a primary key, so you selected this combination of columns as a composite key. The test for the data being in second normal form is to ask the question, "Does the primary key determine each of the non-key attributes?" The answer is no, because the cost of the product is determined by the ProductCode. It has nothing to do with the SaleDate or the CustomerID. Technically, this is a violation of the second normal form, and you should remove the Cost column. The cost of the product can be found by looking up the ProductCode in a Products table. In practice, you might actually include the cost in a table such as this. We'll explain why in the next chapter, but meanwhile, can you think of a reason for leaving the cost column in this table? Hint: It has nothing to do with performance issues.

SaleDate	CustomerID	ProductCode	Cost	Salesperson
6/01/2000	101	6573-3718	$243	Jean
6/01/2000	102	6228-1019	$449	Sam
6/02/2000	101	8494-8459	$89	Sam

Table 3-4. SaleDate, Customer ID, and ProductCode combine to form a composite primary key.

Third Normal Form

The third normal form requires that there be no transitive dependencies in the data. This means that every column in the table must have its value defined by the primary key, not by some other non-key column in the table. The column must not depend on the value in another column. For example, suppose you have an employee table such as that shown in Table 3-5. The columns in this table include employee ID, employee name, department, and manager. As you can see from the table, each employee in the sales department reports to Mary.

Suppose that Mary is promoted, and Alan takes over as manager of sales. Now you have to update all the employee records in the sales department to reflect the change in management. If you changed only some of the records, you would have inconsistent data. This condition is known as an *update anomaly*—where you have to make a change to data, but the change involves more than one record. In effect, you are storing the same information multiple times. It is also possible to introduce insert anomalies into your data. An insert anomaly happens when you can't add a new record because you're missing part of the primary key. If, in Table 3-5, you didn't have an Employee ID, but instead had a composite primary key of Name+Manager, you wouldn't be able to add a new employee record until you knew who that person's manager was going to be.

EmpID	Name	Department	Manager
1601	Mary	Sales	
1627	Dennis	Sales	Mary
1639	Cindy	Sales	Mary
1648	Thomas	Sales	Mary

Table 3-5. Each employee in the Sales Department reports to Mary, the manager.

You can also run into the problem of deletion anomalies. If you removed all the employees in Sales, how would you ever find out who had been the sales manager? A better way to organize this data would be to have a separate table showing the department and its manager. Tables 3-6 and 3-7 are a suggested solution to these anomalous situations. Table 3-6 contains data only on employees. Table 3-7 is all about departments.

Now you can see how easy it is to replace Mary with Alan. Only one row in the Department table (Table 3-7) needs to be updated, and the information about who is the manager of the sales department is stored only once, removing the possibility of inconsistent data. The original table included a transitive dependency. The Employee ID determined the department, and from the department you could determine who was the manager. The manager information did not depend on the primary key, the Employee ID, but rather it depended on another column that is not part of the primary key. By splitting the tables into the Employee table and the Department table, you have removed the transitive dependency. In practice, you would of course use the Employee ID, not the name, in the Manager column, but the principle remains the same.

Advanced Normal Forms

Most production systems are normalized to third normal form. Occasionally, though, you'll have to test for conditions beyond 3NF. Most often, if you're evaluating a "mature" database, one that has been in use for some time, you'll have to test for multi-valued dependencies—one-to-one or one-to-many relationships that occur *within a record*.

How does a table get into this state? The database might start life in 3NF, but then some new business requirement forces change. The change might involve capturing just one or two new data items. Instead of properly evaluating the impact of this change on the database design as a whole, most often because of time constraints, the DBA simply appends a field here, a column there, to tables where it "seems" to be a best fit. After several episodes of hurried appending here and there to accommodate changing requirements, you'll find that the tables are no longer in 3NF, but have developed multi-valued dependencies.

EmplD	Name	Department
1601	Mary	Sales
1627	Dennis	Sales
1639	Cindy	Sales
1648	Thomas	Sales
1651	Alan	Sales

Table 3-6. The updated Employee table contains only project member names and departments.

Department	Manager
Sales	Mary
Finance	Harold

Table 3-7. The updated Department table contains only departments and their managers.

Fourth Normal Form

Fourth normal form ensures that there are no independent multi-valued dependencies within a table. In other words, the columns that are part of the one-to-many or many-to-many relationship found in the record really are not intimately related. Consider, for example, Table 3-8, which lists Employees and Skills. The first two columns in this table are the Employee ID and the corresponding skill. These were the first two columns when this table was initially created. An employee may have more than one skill, so you can define a primary key of Employee ID+Skill. Now suppose that you add another column called Language, which shows the languages in which an employee is proficient.

This table modification made sense to you at the time you made it, but you have introduced a problem here. Look at employee 101. The implication is that this employee is proficient in French-language word processing, and is proficient in Spanish-language spreadsheets. By adding the extra column, you have implied a dependency between job skill and language proficiency that does not really exist. There are two solutions to this case. One possible solution is to make language a skill in its own right. Then you would add entries for employee 101 showing skill in both French and Spanish. To find an employee who can translate a Word document in French, you would join the table to itself,

Employee	Skill	Language
101	Word Processing	French
101	Spreadsheets	Spanish
102	Word Processing	Spanish
102	PowerPoint	
103	Spreadsheets	German
103	Databases	Swedish
104	Databases	Japanese

Table 3-8. This table is in violation of 4NF. There should not be any direct relationship between skills and languages.

Employee	Skill
101	Word Processing
101	Spreadsheets
102	Word Processing
102	PowerPoint
103	Spreadsheets
103	Databases
104	Databases

Table 3-9. The Employee-Skill table contains only employee and skill data.

looking for any employee ID where word processing skill is combined with skill in French. An alternative approach would be two separate tables, one for Skills and a second for Language, as shown by Tables 3-9 and 3-10. Then your search would be to simply join the two tables and find a match for word processors who are fluent in French.

The Fifth Normal Form

Fifth normal form ensures that there are no *dependent* multi-valued dependencies within a table. In other words, the columns that are part of the one-to-many or many-to-many relationship found within the record really *do* have a dependency of some sort. Suppose you have a table that shows who is working on which project, like Table 3-11. The columns in this table include Employee ID, Project Code, and Project Manager ID.

Employee	Language
101	French
101	Spanish
102	Spanish
103	German
103	Swedish
104	Japanese

Table 3-10. The Employee-Language table contains only employee and language data.

Employee	Project	Project Manager ID
101	A	103
102	A	103
103	A	103
104	B	105
105	B	105

Table 3-11. The Project Assignment table is in violation of 5NF; it contains a dependent multi-valued dependency.

This table has update and deletion anomalies. If Project Manager ID 103 gets a promotion and is replaced by Manager ID 200, this change will involve modifying more than one row in the table. If employees 104 and 105 leave the company and the rows are deleted, you've lost all record of Project Code B and who was the project manager, at least in this table.

You can decompose this table into two to eliminate the anomalies, as shown by Tables 3-12 and 3-13. The first table contains Employee ID and Project Manager ID, showing who reports to whom. The second table includes columns for Project Manager ID and Project Code, showing who is in charge of which project. At this point all seems to be well. When you recombine the two tables to get a project assignment report, you get back the same set of rows as Table 3-11, which is what you want. But as soon as you add another project, project C, which is assigned to manager 103, and then recombine the tables to get your report, you find there's a problem. Now it appears that employees 102 and 101 are also assigned to project C. This is not correct.

Employee	Project Manager ID
101	103
102	103
103	110
104	105
105	110

Table 3-12. A logical but incorrect decomposition from the Project Assignment table, the Employee-Project Manager table.

Project Manager ID	Project
103	A
105	B
103	C

Table 3-13. Another incorrect decomposition from the Project Assignment table, the Projects-Project Manager table.

The correct way to decompose the Project Assignment table is shown by Tables 3-14 and 3-15. Table 3-14 now contains Employee ID and Project Code, showing which employees are assigned to which projects. Table 3-15 contains the Project Code and the Project Manager ID for that project. From these two tables, you can easily determine who is working on which project, and who is in charge. When you add project C to Table 3-15, headed off by manager 103, you have not implied that any other employees are assigned this project yet. You can assign employees to the project using Table 3-14. In fact, this pair of tables gives you more flexibility than the original Project Assignment table, because now any employee can manage a project, and any employee can be assigned to a project. You also don't lose information because of update and deletion anomalies.

Employee	Project
101	A
102	A
103	A
104	B
105	B

Table 3-14. The correct decomposition of the Employee-Assignment table, showing which employees are assigned to which projects.

Project	Project Manager ID
A	103
B	105
C	103

Table 3-15. The correct decomposition of the Project-Manager table, showing which projects are managed by which manager.

Normalization, Performance, and Security

It is reasonable, you might even say obvious, that when you normalize and then have to recombine (join) tables back together to get the information you need, you'll pay a performance penalty. The more tables in a join, the more complex the queries become. Sometimes database designers will split data from a single table in third normal form into several smaller tables. Why would they do this? The relationships between the new tables are all one-to-one, so why not put all the data in one table?

One reason is performance. Yes, joining the tables involves some performance overhead, but think about what is stored in these tables. Is all of the data, all of the columns, normally read at the same time? Or do most of your queries only return a subset of the data? If the answer is "a subset," consider dividing the columns and moving the infrequently used data to another table. By moving the infrequently used data to another table you reduce the size of the data row in the main table. That means you can fit more rows on a single page, so you have to read in fewer pages to retrieve the data. Fewer pages means less I/O and better performance most of the time, with a small penalty on the few occasions when you have to retrieve all of the data.

Another frequent reason for splitting the data into multiple tables, beyond what is required for normalization, is privacy and security. You may elect to store confidential data in a separate table, with much tighter security permissions than the normal data. For example, in an employee table, there may be data such as name, department, and telephone extension. In a related table, with a one-to-one relationship, you might store Social Security number, salary, performance rating, and other information that should be kept confidential. When necessary, you join the tables together for the people who need access. Another reasonable approach would be to store all the data in one table and allow access to the data only through a set of views. The views would have differing permissions depending on who needs access to which data. The separate table approach reduces the risk of accidentally making the whole table available to unauthorized users, at the cost of having to write joins for the authorized users. The single table approach requires more complex view definitions and maintenance, as you would have to enumerate each of the columns to which different users should have access. Actually, some developers prefer the latter technique, as they like to keep tight control on exactly which columns they permit in each view. The decision as to which way to go could be based on performance issues as discussed above.

In earlier versions of SQL Server, there were tighter limits on the page size and hence the total number of bytes per row. The page size was 2K (2048 bytes), with a practical limit of 1962 bytes for user data storage. There was also a limit of 255 columns per table.

Because of these limits you might run into some older databases that have split data among two or more tables. Hopefully the split was on some logical boundary, such as confidential versus non-confidential data, so perhaps you just want to leave the tables as they are. But if you do decide to merge them to take advantage of the larger page size introduced in SQL Server 7.0, you will be able to justify the decision based on what you know about normalization. The SQL Server 7.0 page size is 8K, 8192 bytes, with the longest record size set at 8096 bytes and a maximum of 1024 columns.

You have probably heard of "denormalization," where database designers deliberately recombine tables and sometimes store calculated data in the database. This is done for performance reasons. You really cannot start this process until you have selected the platform and the database management software, because the various vendors have made different compromises in their code or have optimized certain database functions. So we will defer a discussion of denormalization until the next chapter, where we start building our physical model, based on SQL Server.

THE FOUR INTEGRITIES

One of the big selling points of a database in any organization is that the data is stored in one place, not scattered across many computers. True, the data may be replicated for many reasons, but there is only one master copy, from which all the replicates are automatically derived, and it is kept in one place. This makes for easier access to the data and reduces the chance of one copy being updated, without the changes being made to all the other copies. However, for this scheme to work, the master copy has to be kept in a consistent state, with no errors and no inconsistencies in the data. That is another big selling point of a database. The integrity of the data in the database *must* be maintained. Data integrity can be viewed as a combination of four integrities: entity integrity, referential integrity, domain integrity, and business integrity. If you apply each of these integrities properly, you can be assured that the DBMS will keep your data accurate and consistent.

Entity Integrity

The concept of entity integrity is fundamental to any database design and implementation. It requires that you can identify each row in a table, with no ambiguity. This type of integrity is enforced by defining a primary key, which consists of a column or a combination of columns that uniquely define each row contained in the table. In Figure 3-1, each of the entities has a primary key. For the Person table, it is PersonID. Every person who is entered into the database (specifically, into the Person table) is assigned a PersonID value that will distinguish him or her from every other person in the table. Because the value set of a primary key is by definition unique, there will be no duplicate values.

Setting a primary key instructs the database to enforce the concept of entity integrity. The rules of entity integrity are

- Rule one: No primary key can be null.
- Rule two: No change can be made that would make the primary key null.

These rules ensure that every row of data in a table will be accessible for data retrieval or updates. You can retrieve a single row of data just by specifying the value of its primary key.

We will talk more in later chapters about how SQL Server handles null, but for now, let us just state that a null in database terminology is not a space (for character/date datatypes), nor is it a zero value (for number datatypes). Null is a condition, and it can represent at least one of three different states:

- The data value is not applicable (the customer does not have a fax number).
- The data value is applicable but not available (the customer has a fax number, but you don't know what it is).
- It's unknown whether the data value is applicable (you don't know whether this customer has a fax number).

If you try to insert a new row that does not have a unique value for the primary key, you would be violating the first rule of entity integrity. And you should never make any changes to a primary key in an existing record so that it becomes null—that would violate the second rule of entity integrity.

You can ensure that users cannot perform either of these invalid operations in SQL Server by setting a primary key constraint on the table. A constraint is a rule or a limitation placed on the table, and this constraint is defined so that a column or combination of columns becomes the primary key and is not allowed to contain null values. Behind the scenes, the primary key constraint builds an index. The index is a unique index, and so it ensures that there can be no duplicate values in the primary key. The constraint can be created as part of the original CREATE TABLE statement, or it can be added later to an existing table. We will discuss constraints in more detail in Chapter 15, including the SQL syntax for creating the various types of constraints.

Referential Integrity

The second of the four database integrities is referential integrity. The rule of referential integrity states that the value of a foreign key must be within the domain (range of allowed values) of its related primary key, or it must be null. A foreign key is a column or combination of columns in a table that is used to establish a link from one table (typically the parent table) to another table (typically the child table). A foreign key is required for the implementation of a one-to-many relationship. The foreign key value in the child table column must have a corresponding entry in either the primary key column or a column with a unique index in the parent table. Such is the case in Figure 3-3, between the Person table and the CommDevice table. Each entry in CommDevice must relate to an entry in Person, because you don't want to have a phone number with no associated name from Person.

When you specify a foreign key, the database needs to know exactly which record in the other table is being referenced. The columns in each table should have the same datatype and length, and should of course have the same meaning.

Some foreign key columns can contain nulls, and some cannot. For example, the table SaleItem, which contains items purchased for each Sale, must contain a SaleNo identifier, which is a valid entry in the Sale table. Each Sale may have multiple line items, but any line item belongs to only one Sale. In this case, the one-to-many relationship is a dependent relationship. A relationship of this type should be enforced in the database. The preferred method would be to define a foreign key constraint when the tables are created, or possibly add a constraint after the tables have been created. Using a constraint like this is known as *declarative referential integrity (DRI)*. It is also possible to enforce such a relationship with triggers, but as we will see in a later chapter, that is a lot more coding and more work for the database. The DRI approach is faster than using triggers, because a constraint is an integral part of the table definition, so it is loaded into memory as the table is loaded. A trigger has to be read in when it is invoked, although chances are it will then remain in cache ready for the next time it's used. But the biggest factor is that a constraint prevents the problem from happening. For example, you cannot enter an item into the order details table unless there is already a corresponding entry in the orders table. If you were using a trigger, you could enter a record into the item detail table, but the trigger would then undo the changes as soon as it couldn't find a corresponding record in the orders table. This operation results in a higher overhead and performance loss for the database. We will return to this discussion of constraints versus triggers later in this chapter.

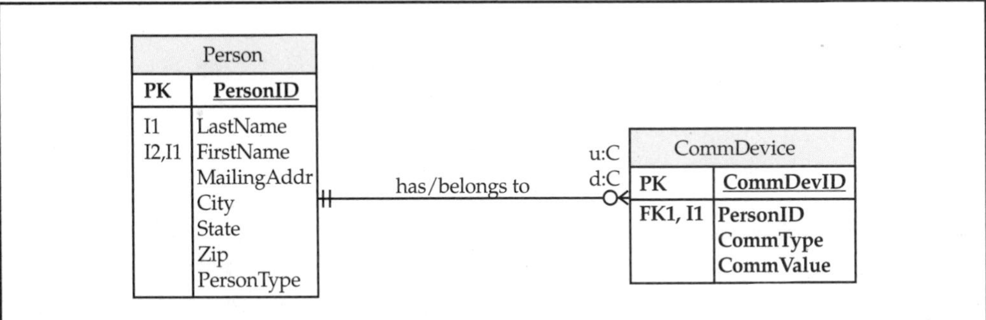

Figure 3-3. Each Person can have O:M communication devices, while each communication device must belong to a single person.

When the foreign key value can be null, you have an independent or non-identifying one-to-many relationship. This implies that a row can exist in the detail table without a related row in the master table. For example, you might have a customers table that includes a column for the name (or identifier) of the customer's assigned salesperson. If there is a value in the salesperson column, it would have to correspond to one of your salespeople, who would be listed in another table. But you might have some potential customers, perhaps people who have made enquiries about your product, who are in the database but do not yet have a sales rep assigned to them. Thus the salesperson identifier column for these people would be null. Your design would have to allow for a null in that column, and you would *not* enforce this relationship in the database.

Referential Integrity and Triggers

You can choose to implement your referential integrity checks with *triggers*. A trigger is a special type of stored procedure, which is compiled SQL code. Unlike a stored procedure, a trigger is not directly called by an application. Instead, a trigger is activated when a change is made to the table where the trigger is defined. Any update, insert, or delete operation on a table can activate a trigger. You can perform all sorts of complex cross-checking with triggers, going far beyond what is possible in a constraint. For example a constraint can verify that the item a customer wants to order is in fact an item you sell. The entry for the item in the SaleItem table is a foreign key reference to the corresponding item listed in the Product table. But that's as far as it can go. The constraint can reference another table, but it cannot query that table and return a result. Suppose you want to make sure the item is not only one you sell, but is also in stock. You can write the trigger to make sure that the quantity shown for that item is greater than zero. (The next step is, of course, to use the trigger to decrease the quantity in inventory, but we'll get to that when we discuss triggers in much more detail later in the book.) You can even do cross-database referential integrity checks with triggers, such as making sure that the new employee you are adding to the payroll database has already been entered into the list of employees in the personnel department database.

Referential Integrity and Cascading Updates

Prior to SQL Server 2000, there was no built-in cascading update or delete in SQL Server. A "cascading" update or delete would propagate changes through different tables in the database. For example, if you changed a Person identifier (PersonID), all of the records associated with that Person would also change to reflect the new PersonID. If you didn't do this, the detail records would no longer match the master record, and your data would be inconsistent. Access programmers have had this "cascade the change" feature for years, so why has it taken so long to show up in SQL Server? Like many powerful tools, cascade updates can do a lot of damage when they are used improperly. You have to be very careful with both cascade update and cascade delete. For example, let's suppose you delete a product you no longer sell from the Product table. Should all references to that product be deleted? With a cascade delete, it is possible to set this up. But just because it is possible does not mean it is a good idea. Cascading this delete would remove all reference to past sales of the product. The cascade effect might reach the accounting software records, and subsequently attempt to cascade those changes into accounts receivable! How would you generate reports of what customers are buying if you removed all references to this product out of their purchase records? Similar reasoning applies if you remove a person from your database—do you really want to delete all the information about this person's purchases? You may know you sold a certain volume of a product, but you will not be able to perform any analysis on who bought it, and where and when. In this second example, the best approach might be to remove any information that could positively identify a person, but retain the demographic information such as city, state, zip code, and sales activity data.

Cascade updates and cascade deletes certainly have their place, and the ability to implement them in SQL Server 2000 is welcome. What was in the past often accomplished with triggers can now be done more efficiently with these new tools. We'll talk more about them later in the book.

Domain Integrity

Each column in a table can have a defined set of values that are valid for that column. Limiting the values that may be entered into a column is also known as enforcing domain integrity. What you are doing is limiting the "domain" or range of values for a column that SQL Server will accept when the record is inserted or the column value is modified. The benefits are consistency across your database, and a reduction in data entry errors. For example, if you define the range of acceptable values for a customer's credit rating, you might limit the domain of values to "Poor," "Good," and "Excellent." The data entry personnel can then use only one of those three values, avoiding the risk of them inventing their own terms. Not only does it not look good on your reports to have different options ("OK," "terrible," and so on), it makes querying the column that much more difficult.

Enforcing domain integrity can be as basic as selecting a datatype for the column, and where appropriate, the length or size of the column. For example, you might define a date or datetime datatype for the employee's hire date. This ensures that a complete date, such as 06/06/2000, is entered, instead of just the year or the month and year only.

The ANSI SQL-89 standard defined a CREATE DOMAIN statement that is not supported by Transact-SQL. However, there's an alternative to the CREATE DOMAIN statement. The ANSI-SQL syntax allows you to create a domain by generating a user-defined datatype from an existing datatype, and then adding a check constraint to the column that would set the limits of the domain. (We will cover the syntax for constraints in Chapter 15.) In Transact-SQL, you can create user-defined datatypes, like ANSI-SQL can, but you cannot associate a constraint with this datatype. Your choices are to add a constraint to the column or add a rule to the datatype.

Constraints and Rules

There are two ways to impose limits on the data you enter into a column. Check constraints are supported by the ANSI-SQL standard, and Microsoft is encouraging their use whenever possible. Rules are not an ANSI standard, and thus are not the officially recommended method in SQL Server 7.0. We will discuss the pros and cons of rules and constraints, and how they are used, in Chapter 15. For now, let us just say that both methods allow you to limit the values that may be entered into a column. The permitted values may be entries in a list or may follow a specified pattern, as with telephone numbers that must be an area code followed by a seven-digit number (at least in the United States). Using either a check constraint or a rule will enforce domain integrity. You can write triggers to achieve the same result, but constraints and rules are usually easier to code and the performance is better than triggers. Constraints outperform triggers.

When you enforce referential integrity, you are also enforcing domain integrity. In any enforced one-to-many relationship, the domain of the foreign key is limited by the domain of its corresponding primary key in the parent table. If you create a table expressly for the purpose of restricting values in a column in another table, using referential integrity constructs, this list-of-values table is called a reference or lookup table. By intent, this is a dependent one-to-many relationship, as shown in Figure 3-4 with Product and SaleItem. The relationship between these two entities is one-to-many—Product to SaleItem. The list of ProductCodes in Product restricts the values that can be entered into the ProductCode column of SaleItem. Another example might be a list of the U.S. state codes or a chart of accounts for an accounting package. The reference table will have a one-to-many relationship with the table containing the data records, and this relationship will always be enforced by SQL Server.

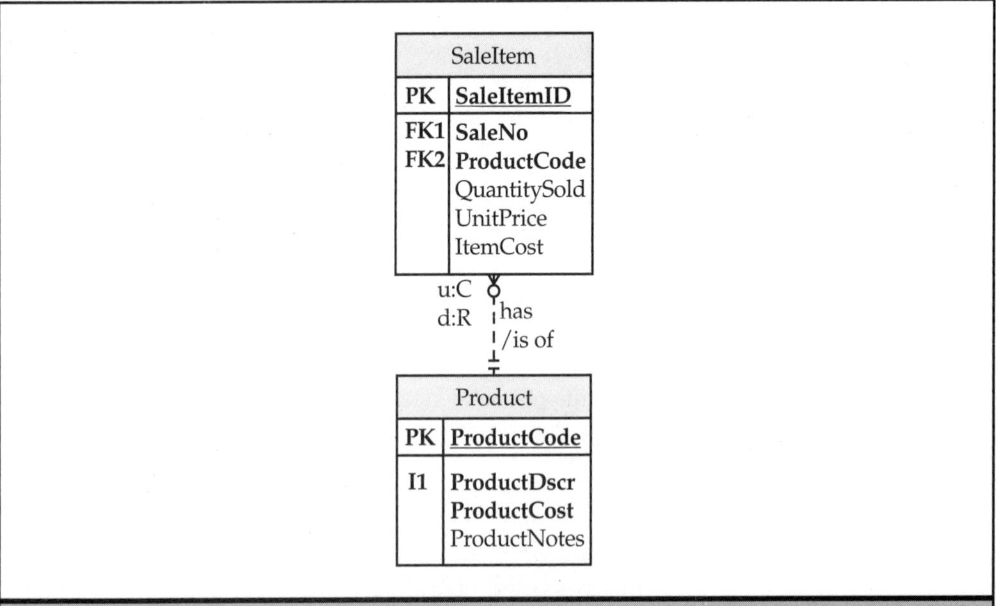

Figure 3-4. Each product description listed in the Product table can be purchased many times.

Business Integrity

The fourth database integrity is business integrity, sometimes called use integrity. This has nothing to do with being honest (although we do recommend that philosophy in business). You can restrict the data values entered into the database based on your business rules. Usually business integrity is made up of rules that do not fit into the other categories of entity, referential, or domain integrity. Occasionally the dividing line between domain integrity and business integrity gets blurred. For example, you may have a column in which you store state codes. The domain of allowed values is the list of the U.S. states, and perhaps also the Canadian and Mexican provinces. But you might place a business rule on your branch offices that says that the Atlanta office can insert and update data only in the customer table where the state code is GA.

Another example of a business rule: your data entry staff cannot place an order for an item that is not in stock. There's no technical reason why a column for quantity in stock should not contain a negative number, but in a business setting, a negative number means that you have accepted an order for an out-of-stock item. You have placed an order with your supplier and you hope the item will arrive in time to ship it out and still keep the customer happy. Perhaps you might decide that you don't want to accept orders for products that are not in stock. You could enforce this business rule with a trigger or a stored procedure. It's not possible to do this with a constraint because a constraint cannot cross table boundaries. A foreign key constraint could check to make sure that the product being ordered is one you sell because it has a valid product code from the products table. But you cannot, with a constraint, query the inventory table and find out how many products are in stock. Constraints cannot return data from another table, so you'll have to create a more complex business rule. The same logic would apply if you could not place an order that took the customer past his credit limit. The stored procedure that actually inserts the order record into the order table would have to check the customer table to determine the credit limit, the products table to find the price of the items being ordered, and possibly the accounts receivable table to find out how much the customer already owes you. This is a complex rule that currently can be done only with stored procedures or triggers, not with constraints.

We often think of business rules as preventing the user from doing certain things, but there are times when you can employ business rules to take some positive action. For example, you could encode a business rule, using triggers that would fire when the number of units in stock for any item fell below a threshold value. The triggers could then cause a notification to be sent, requesting that the item be reordered.

THE ETHICS OF DATABASE DESIGN

You may find it unusual that a programming book would talk about ethics. However, we firmly believe that a sense of ethics should be present in everything we do. Call us naïve if you want, but we are convinced that being ethical is just good business in the long run. The ethical, social, and moral impact of business is everyone's concern. Most companies do not have a department to take care of the ethical issues in their business. This job belongs to us all. If individuals are not aware of the implications of the work they do, then who will be? Rarely does a company set out to build a database to deliberately have a negative impact on anyone. But over time, information is made available to more and more people, with no safeguards to protect personal privacy or corporate security and liability, until the unfettered distribution of sensitive information becomes not just commonplace but is deemed necessary to getting the job done.

Information Gathering and Privacy Issues

When you start to plan which data to store in your database, your prime concern is usually how useful that information will be to the people using the database. But what about the people (your customers, employees, vendors, product suppliers) whose information will be stored in your database? Are they willing to supply the information in the first place? And if they do, will it be reliable? Some people may simply refuse to give out information, in the way that many people refuse to give their Social Security number to anyone who does not have a legal requirement for it. We'll talk more about Social Security numbers later in this chapter. For now, suffice it to say that identity theft is one of the fastest-growing crimes in the United States, and easy availability of private information like Social Security numbers is a big contributor to this situation.

Misinformation

There is a concept in the field of data warehousing known as "data lineage." The idea is that when you are making decisions based on data you have gathered, you may need to know where that data came from and how reliable it is. For example, suppose you want to find out how many of your customers have an income of more than $100,000 per year. If you are a credit card company, your customers would have supplied such information on the credit application. Because it is illegal to make false statements in order to obtain credit, you can trust that this information is fairly reliable. However, it might be out of date.

If you don't have access to reliable data like this, you might buy a list from a third party that specializes in selling this type of data. Much of the income data in this list may have come from sources such as the registration cards people fill out when they buy a new microwave or camera. Because there's no legal requirement to fill in correct information on these warranty cards, many people distort the truth. They might overstate their income in hopes of getting better deals from marketing companies who are looking for affluent customers. Or perhaps they understate their income so that they won't be bothered by sales pitches on the assumption that they have little disposable income. Maybe they just make up numbers and check boxes at random, in order to deliberately present an inconsistent profile. Whatever their motivation, you simply cannot trust this type of data. Decisions based on purchased data must take into account the possible unreliability of the data.

Security and Privacy

Privacy issues affect more than the confidentiality of information you store. You also have to consider the security issues. If the information you want to track could be regarded as in any way sensitive, you need to have some written policies in place about who gets to access that data. These policies will then have to be implemented in the database security model. You may have to track each and every time someone looks at the data. Or you may have to flag every time someone who is not supposed to see the data attempts to gain access to it. Auditing like this imposes an extra load on the system and can only have a negative impact on performance. You must also consider whether to store the confidential information in the same table as the open information or keep it in a separate table. In the first case, you would restrict access to the table and permit access to the appropriate columns through views, which adds a level of complexity to your design. But in the second case you may also have to provide views for the authorized users who need to see information from both tables but don't know how to write a join. It looks like you'll be creating views whichever way you go!

If you do store data that you know could be the target of unauthorized readers, consider the consequences of that information being made public or falling into the wrong hands. It is quite possible that the person or people affected by the release of this information will hold you or your company liable. If your company loses a big security-breach lawsuit, you know whose job is going to be on the line.

If your company is dealing with data from people who live only in the United States, where privacy concerns have taken a back seat to making a quick buck, you may be able to get away with gathering and storing information that in other countries would not be permitted. European companies, for example, have to work within much more strict rules about what information may be stored, including regulations about notifying people when data about them is collected and stored, and giving them the right to request a copy of the information and correct it if it is in error. The laws extend to placing limits on sharing or transmitting data to a non-secure server. Servers in the United States are presumed non-secure unless you can show otherwise. Some companies have taken the necessary steps to bring their servers into line with what is required by law in the EEC, and they can now do business internationally without fear of legal ramifications.

Why a Social Security Number Is a Poor Choice for a Primary Key

The use of a Social Security number (SSN) as a primary key, or as an identifier column, is not a good idea for many reasons. Let's look at the technical reasons before considering the legal implications and privacy issues.

SSN is an identifier unique to the United States. By using SSN as a primary key, you have laid the groundwork for a major complication as soon as you try to extend the database to cover your foreign affiliates. You will also have problems in the local database with workers who are on assignment in the United States from your overseas offices.

What is the format of SSN? It is usually three digits, a dash, two digits, a dash, and then four more digits. So you have to store it as character data, because of the dashes. You could remove the dashes and just store the numbers; many companies do. Also, if you tried to store the numbers in integer format, the leading zeros vanish. You would have to parse the numbers and reinsert the dashes for most reports and queries, because people are used to seeing SSN displayed in a specific format. So, given that SSN should be a character format, you should keep in mind that SQL Server handles integers faster than any other datatype, and decide to create an integer identifier as your primary key.

Note that we said, "should be a character format" for the SSN. There are SSNs that end with an alpha character, such as an "A" or "B." That's really going to mess you up if you chose to store SSN in an 11-character field, or even worse, an integer field. Where did these strange numbers come from? We have heard several explanations, but the most plausible seems to be that duplicate numbers were issued in the 1930s, and when the error was discovered, the holders of the duplicate numbers were told to add an "A" to the end of the SSN. We have also heard that when Social Security was first introduced, many women did not work outside of the home. When their husbands died, in order for them to continue receiving benefits, some number had to be used, and in order to preserve continuity, the Social Security Administration told them to use their husband's number with an "A" added on. Whatever the story, you cannot guarantee that SSN will be 11 characters. It's probably only a matter of time before we run out of numbers under the current scheme, just like we have with telephone numbers and IP addresses. Then the format will have to be lengthened.

Someone has proposed the scenario that, instead of lengthening the SSN, as the older SSN holders die off, the abandoned SSNs will be reused—reassigned to new people. If there's any truth to this, then the argument against SSN as a primary identifier is absolute. Under *no* circumstances should a primary key value *ever* be reused. A primary key value, once assigned, is never reassigned.

If your company has a legitimate need for storing SSN, such as in the employee and payroll databases, you will also want to ensure that the values stored are unique (even though, in the set of all SSNs, this may not be true). It would be quite reasonable to place a unique constraint on the SSN column for that purpose. You definitely cannot report tax data for two employees with the same SSN.

Legal Issues

It is quite possible that in the next few years we will see legislation passed that forbids the use and storing of Social Security numbers unless there is a legal requirement to do so, such as your bank reporting interest income to the IRS. We are seeing more awareness in the public sector (government) of the dangers of identity theft, and the problems caused by incomplete and often totally incorrect data being reported about people, usually without their knowledge. The law already forbids many federal government agencies from using SSN, with the obvious exception of the IRS and the Social Security Administration (and probably a few other security agencies as well). Unfortunately, the law does not yet apply to private industry, but it's only a matter of time. When that happens, you don't want to have to go back and totally re-architect your database design. Start planning now for the future and you will be minimally impacted when the laws change.

Privacy Issues

The Social Security number was never meant to be an all-purpose unique identifier. It's been forced into that role by many companies and organizations. There are obvious benefits from a marketing point of view to knowing everything about your customers—and there are obvious potential abuses when information from multiple sources can be collated. The use of one identifier makes it too easy for companies to track everything you do. Certainly, much of this information is supposed to be confidential. For example, following the revelation of the video viewing habits of a nominee for the U.S. Supreme Court, it is now illegal to divulge a person's videotape renting history. Nevertheless, a major video rental chain that shall remain nameless has a place on its application form for SSN. Ever stop to ask why? Ever stop and consider *not* complying?

Security Issues

Many organizations treat SSN as some sort of magic identifier. This reliance on SSN will lead to problems, as it is no longer a secure number. If you know a person's SSN, you can wreak havoc on their life. The problem is that a number that is no longer confidential is treated as if it were known only to two people on the planet: you and the person at the credit card company you just called to ask for an increase on the credit limit on your Plutonium Plus card. In fact, hundreds or thousands of people have access to your SSN, making it worthless as a secure identifier. If you are looking for a way to verify some fact about a person that only they know, you will have to look at public key/private key encryption schemes and certificates, or some as yet undeveloped scheme.

The Programmer's Responsibility in Ethical Programming

We believe that the database designer, the database administrator, and the database programmer all need to take some responsibility for the data stored on their databases. Remember, the information stored in your database may be used in many ways, far beyond what was originally in the specification. Sometimes, data is stored simply because it is available or might be useful, and then sooner or later, someone figures out a way to use it, perhaps without regard to the original reservations about storing the data in the first place. Perhaps a company with strict privacy policies is bought out by a company with a more freewheeling attitude about personal data and privacy. So we suggest that, as part of the design process, you ask some questions, including these:

- Why are we storing this data?
- How might it be used?
- How might it be misused?
- What level of security will it require?
- Will our customers be willing to supply this type of information?

And perhaps most of all, would you be willing to have this type of information about yourself stored in this database? And how would you feel if this information were made available to anyone in the company or even to the public?

At some point, the added costs of data storage, data maintenance, security, and auditing may make it less attractive to store certain kinds of data. So even if your management is not receptive to dropping some types of data from the requirements for ethical reasons, maybe you can persuade them to do so for cost reasons.

CHAPTER 4

Planning the Physical Implementation

Planning for the physical implementation and actually implementing the design are two different things entirely. Implementing the design is exciting because you're creating a real, live, working database. But before you can implement your design, you have one more stage of planning to work through, and that's the physical design.

THE PHYSICAL DESIGN

Like the conceptual and the logical designs we talked about in previous chapters, the physical design is a representation of reality. It is also a specification for implementing the database, much like an engineering blueprint is a specification for a house, a car, or an airplane. This time, however, the design is associated with a specific vendor's database product, and the specification is directly related to characteristics of a database management system. For the first time in the design process, you're acknowledging the product platform you're going to build on. You're going to exploit its strengths and attempt to compensate for its weaknesses. In this book, we're going to implement the design on Microsoft SQL Server 2000.

In general, the changes you'll make to your model are intended to help the resulting database function the very best it can in your environment. For SQL Server 2000, these include, but are not limited to

- Denormalizing the design
- Adding attributes to each entity that are not in the previous models
- Assigning vendor-specific datatypes to the attributes
- Creating surrogate primary identifiers to each entity
- Identifying candidate keys for additional foreign key references
- Evaluating declarative referential integrity
- Identifying the best attributes for indexing

Denormalize the Design

If you normalize your database to the absolute letter of the rules of normalization, you may end up with many small tables, each of which contains very specific but very limited data sets. When you want information, you'll have to combine some of these little tables—join them back together again. In future chapters, we'll look at a couple different ways of doing this.

Normalization carries with it a price tag. Well-normalized tables make for much easier data maintenance, in that when you make a change to a data value you generally have to make that change in only one place, one time. However, well-normalized tables make for awkward information retrieval. The additional level of complexity you've introduced for information retrieval may frustrate or even anger some of the other users of your database, especially the nontechnical data readers and data writers, who simply cannot understand why the data can't be stored the way that they picture it. Nontechnical users tend to think of data in a flat-file format, as a single record that contains everything they ever needed to know about a sale, for instance. Unfortunately, this will never do for database management and for maintaining data integrity.

You can hide some of this normalization complexity through views and stored procedures, which we'll address in upcoming chapters. The downside of this approach is that the database users will have to access data only by these views and stored procedures; they'll never have much success reading the data directly from the tables. While some database administrators applaud this concept (there is a school of thought that espouses keeping as much distance between data users and the database as possible), occasionally it would be nice if the data users could do their own data retrieval instead of having to depend on database programmers to build avenues of retrieval for them. This is especially true in smaller companies, where you might not have a large information technology staff.

Under certain circumstances you can recombine some of the normalized tables in a process known as denormalization. But what are you giving up when you denormalize? Sometimes you'll see very little impact from the denormalization process, but at other times you may find you've sacrificed the flexibility and future scalability of your database, and you may have even sacrificed performance. It all depends on how much you denormalize the data.

Let's look at a for-instance example. Figure 4-1 is your physical model. It is a fairly well-normalized model. However, your data users are not happy that you've separated the phones and email addresses (stored in the CommDevice table) from the people (stored in the Person table). They feel they should be able to pull up a person's record out of the database and see at a glance that person's phone number, email address, whatever—all in one record. Try as you might, you cannot convince them otherwise, so you decide to denormalize the design and combine these two tables. Immediately, you have a problem as to what kind of communication devices, means, and methods to record in this new, denormalized table.

In the normalized scheme (as represented by Figure 4-1), a person could have an unlimited number of phone numbers, email addresses, even home pages, because the relationship between tblPerson and tblCommDevice is one-to-many (1:M; one instance of tblPerson can be associated with many instances of tblCommDevice). You're trying to denormalize this relationship and recombine the two tables and still provide the flexibility that the normalized design gave, and you have some decisions to make, as shown in Figure 4-2, a representation of a table in second normal form (2NF). It contains information on a person (name and address, presumably the mailing address), and it also contains information on how to contact this person (varying phone numbers and email addresses). When you denormalize two tables that are in a 1:M relationship, you always have to set a limit on the number of "many" conditions you can represent in the denormalized table. In this case, you've chosen to provide a record of the person's home phone, work phone, cell phone, fax number, two email addresses, and a URL to their home page. Then, just in case something's not obvious, you've added room for comments.

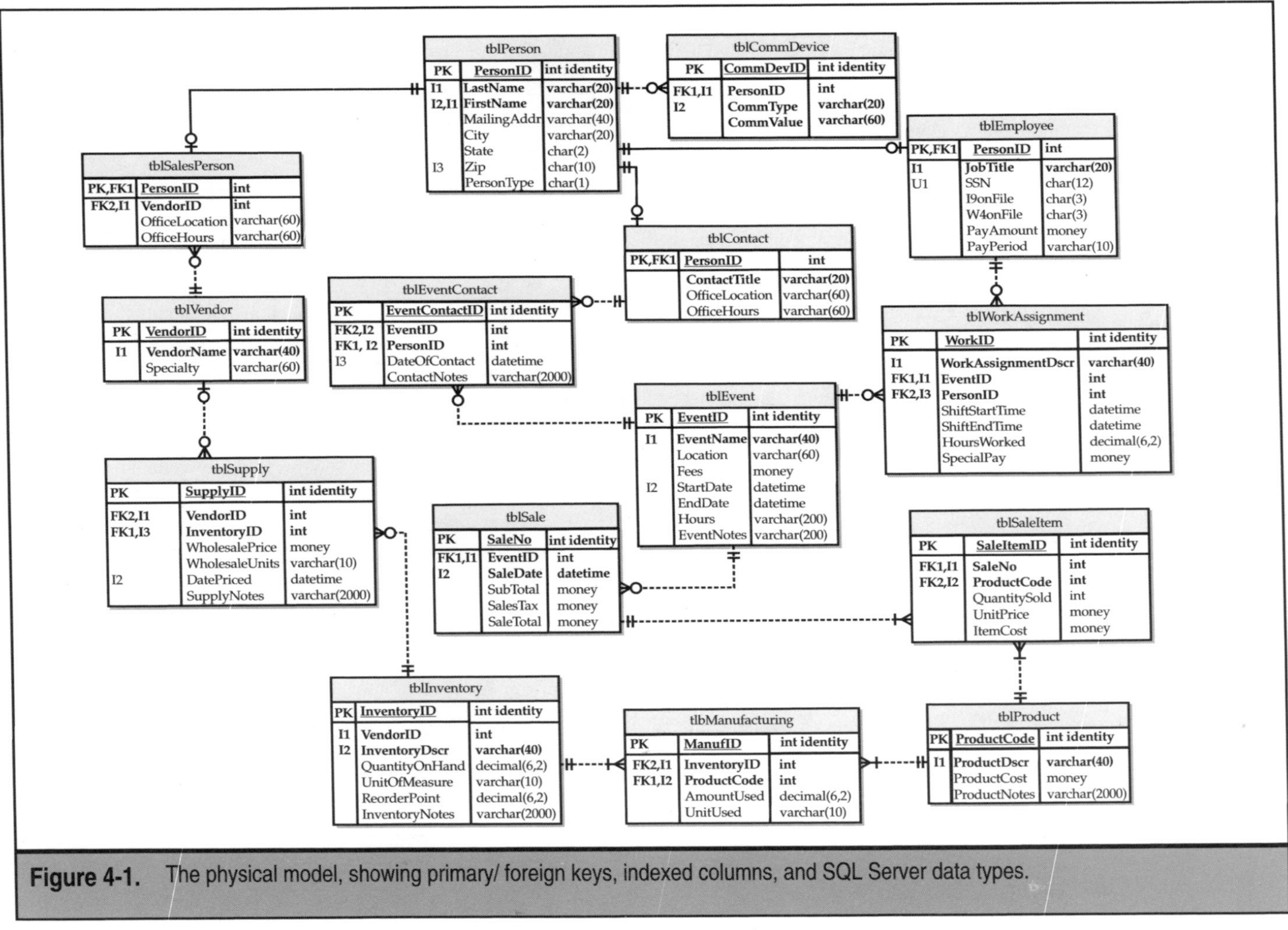

Figure 4-1. The physical model, showing primary/ foreign keys, indexed columns, and SQL Server data types.

tblPERSON-denormalized		
PK	PersonID	Int identity
I1	**LastName**	**varchar(20)**
I2,I1	**FirstName**	**varchar(20)**
	MailingAddr	varchar(40)
	City	varchar(20
	State	char(2)
I3	Zip	char(10)
	PersonType	char(1)
	HomePhone	char(10)
	WorkPhone	char(15)
	CellPhone	char(10)
	FaxPhone	char(10)
	Email-1	varchar(60)
	Email-2	varchar(60)
	HomePageURL	varchar(60)
	Comments	varchar(200)

Figure 4-2. A variation of the Person table, denormalized to include telephone and email columns in addition to the name and address columns

Will there ever be a problem with this table design? Let's start with these queries:

- Will every person stored in the database need to have all these phone numbers and so on recorded? Will this result in wasted storage space, having to deal with NULL when programming?
- How can you tell which is the day phone and which is the evening phone? (Some people work at night.)
- Is the fax machine located at the person's home or in his office? (What if that person has both?)
- How would you handle the person who has a third email address and insists that it be recorded in the database?
- Where would you store a person's digital pager number?
- When you get a change request that instructs you to change so-and-so's phone number to 505-111-5678, how do you know which number to change?

The problems with denormalized data are many, and this list is only a beginning. The denormalized table (Figure 4-2) is forcing you to make inaccurate decisions about where and how to store data. Adding a third email address is a prime example. (This argument also holds for storing a digital pager number.) In the normalized scheme (represented by Figure 4-1), you'd simply add another record to the CommDevice table, with a CommType value of "email, alternate #2" or whatever the person wanted the new email address to be known as. In the denormalized scheme (as represented by Figure 4-2), you have three options:

- Add a new column to the table, called email3.
- Put the third email address in the Comments field.
- Tell the person, "The database won't let me record a third email address for you."

Each of these three options is a less-than-ideal situation. Option one, adding a column to a table whenever you need to store something new, is bound to get you in trouble, and the trouble has a name: violation of fourth or fifth normal form (see Chapter 3). Eventually you'll end up renormalizing those tables, just to resolve the violations of 4NF or 5NF. Option two, putting data in a general-purpose Comments field, is always a dicey business. When you put data in a field for which it wasn't meant, your data integrity has been compromised. When the boss asks for a report that lists each person's phone numbers and email addresses, how are you going to do it? If you don't include the Comments field, you've left out information. If you do include it, you'll also include extraneous garbage that has nothing to do with phone numbers and email addresses. Either way you do it, you've compromised yourself and the perception of the database as a store of full-integrity data. Option three, tell the person that "the database won't let you do it," and you'll look like a fool to this customer or business associate. Any information technology professional knows that software is only a tool, and that the inhibiting factor is usually people related, not software related. This is especially true with database systems. Nontechnical people figure out pretty quickly who's in charge, the database or the database administrator, and this could compromise your relationships with your customers or business associates.

We can take the rest of the list point by point. First, will every person in the database need all these phone and email listings? Certainly not. From Figure 4-1 you can see that you have three distinctly different types of people: salespeople who represent your product vendors, event contact people with whom you work to schedule appearances at different events, and employees of your company. For a salesperson, you might want to store the home page URL, but you probably don't want to do that for an employee. Salespeople and event contact people will have work phone, fax phone, and cell phone numbers you'll want to capture, but you already know the work phone number of your employees. For your employees, you might want to capture home phone number and an email address, but only under rare circumstances would you need to store home phone numbers for salespeople or event contacts, as they tend to use pager or cell phone numbers for off-hours contacts. As a result of differing data requirements for the different types of people you're dealing with, you'll have a lot of "empty" space in the denormalized table (Figure 4-2) and a lot of fields that will be NULL. In future chapters we'll address how to handle NULLs, so for now let's just say that NULLs can occasionally be troublesome and can yield unexpected results in queries and reports if you don't know how to deal with them.

The normalized tables wouldn't have this problem at all. For each type of person, and for each type of contact method for that person, you create one record in tblCommDevice. So salespeople might have associated entries for work phones, cell phones, and fax machines, while each employee would most likely have entries for home phone and an email address.

Determining which phone, home or work, is the daytime phone would be quite tricky in the denormalized version of the table. As it is, you'd have to put a remark in the Comments field indicating which phone to use for daytime calling and—if this person is a night worker and a day sleeper—what would be the best time to call during the day. This doesn't sound terribly complex, but you have introduced another level of complexity into your database design. You're now relying on human behavior (making the appropriate entries under a specific set of circumstances) to sustain your data integrity and make sure the data in your database is correct. This is always a risky business and very prone to error. Modern database design methodology seeks to minimize the need for human interaction when maintaining data integrity. So how would you get around this problem?

In Figure 4-2, the denormalized design, you'd have a couple of options. You might add two new columns, DayPhone and EveningPhone, in addition to the HomePhone and WorkPhone. The implication here is that one phone number would have to be added to two columns. If 888-777-6666 is a person's work phone, but that person works at night, that number is also this person's EveningPhone, and you'd have to record it twice in the record. The alternative would be to modify the columns so you'd have four—DayWorkPhone, DayHomePhone, EveningWorkPhone, EveningHomePhone—and then you could enter 888-777-6666 in only one column, EveningWorkPhone.

Either suggestion is awkward and wasteful. In addition, now you're depending on the column header value (EveningWorkPhone) to give meaning and definition to the data in the column. Modern database design methodology seeks to minimize this kind of situation, because, should you port (export/import) the data from one database platform to another, you run the risk of losing the column headings and thus, the meaning of the numbers in the various columns. Ouch.

In Figure 4-1, the normalized design can be easily extended to accommodate a requirement for special notes about a phone number. Add one column to tblCommDevice, call it CommNotes, make it a varchar(50), and you've now given yourself the ability to add notes and comments about any special situation that might accompany a phone number, email address, or whatever. In addition, should you want to port this data to another database management system, you can do so without worrying about losing the column headings. Each record contains within itself a description of the type of communication method (CommType), the value string to make the connection (CommValue), and now any special notes or comments about this communication method (CommNotes). A normalized design is simple, easy to maintain, and easy to modify. This is what you give up when you denormalize. Where is the fax machine located, at home or at the office, has much the same arguments for both normalized and denormalized models.

How to modify data without clear and precise change requests will present challenges for both normalized and denormalized designs. The logical thing to do would be to contact the person making the change request and ask for more specific information, such as, "Is 505-111-5678 a home phone or a work phone or what?" If you're using the denormalized design, you're not going to have much option other than to record this incomplete change request in the Comments field of so-and-so's record, and just hope that your request for clarification doesn't fall through the cracks. Nevertheless, until you get this uncertainty straightened out, the new phone number will never appear on a report or listing unless you include the Comments field for each record—and we've already decided you don't want to do that. If you're using the normalized design, you can make a new record in tblCommDevice for old so-and-so, enter the new phone number in CommValue, type in "unknown" for CommType, and make a note in CommNotes regarding this incomplete change request, when you got it, and what you're doing about it. Then, when you run the report on phone numbers, the new phone number will be listed and the type will be unknown—but at least it will be in the list. Again, normalized beats denormalized for ease of data maintenance and maintaining data integrity.

Denormalization and Performance

In the last chapter, we talked about one-to-one (1:1) relationships and about queries that most often return only a subset of the data in a row. We suggested that you might want to consider moving the data least frequently used, or data that might be considered sensitive or confidential, to a secondary table and relate the two tables by building a relationship based on their common primary key. In other words, we suggested that you normalize your data based on frequency of access or on the user permissions needed to access the data. To recap: By splitting (normalizing) the data, you reduce the size of the row in the table for both data sets. That means when you're doing physical I/O, you can fit more rows of one table on a page, so you have to read in fewer pages to retrieve the data. Plus, you're retrieving data only on what you really want (person names and mailing addresses, for example) without having to drag all those extra bytes around during the I/O process. Fewer pages means less I/O and better performance most of the time, with a small penalty on the few occasions when you have to combine (join) the two tables to retrieve all of the data.

To illustrate this point, the maximum length of your normalized Person table is 113 bytes (plus 10 bytes of administrative overhead). The maximum length of your denormalized Person table is 538 byes (plus 10 bytes of overhead). Four times as many rows of the normalized Person data fits on a single page as the denormalized data. I/O processes (reading and writing) generally will be much faster with normalized data.

Time-Varying Data

Time-varying data is data whose value changes over time. Figure 4-3 is a portion of the physical model, which includes the tables Sale, SaleItem, and Product. These three tables together record a sale event. In the Sale table, you're recording the event indicator (EventID) and the date of the sale, so you know which event to associate this sale with. The Product table lists each of the products available for sale. The SaleItem table is where you record the individual items purchased that together make up a sale. Would you say that the SaleItem table is normalized? At first glance, you might be tempted to say yes, but the answer is no, because the cost of the product (UnitPrice) is actually determined by the ProductCost column in the Product table. So storing the cost of the product in two

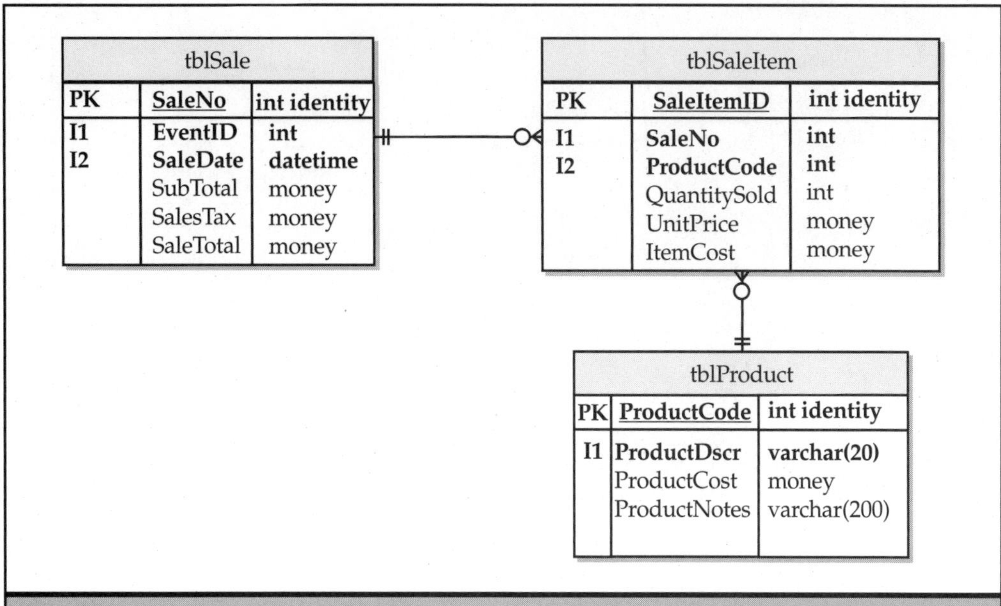

Figure 4-3. The Sale, SaleItem, and Product tables record a sale event; UnitPrice in the SaleItem table contains product cost.

places, first in the Product table (ProductCost) and again in the SaleItem table (UnitPrice), is a violation of third normal form (3NF). Why are you doing it, then? The answer is pretty simple: you want to capture the price of the item *at the time of the sale*.

The values stored in ProductCost will reflect the current selling price of each product. Product prices may fluctuate, depending on the cost of materials, the expense of manufacturing, and the public demand. At the end of the season, when you look at sale figures for the year, you want to know how much you sold each item for, not what the current price is. Time-varying data like this becomes a major concern for data warehouse applications, where it's more commonly referred to as "slowly changing dimensions." A data warehouse typically contains data collected over a much longer period of time than a data entry system does. On the other hand, data in the warehouse is not normalized, and it is routine to store both a history of the product cost and the unit price at the time of sale.

Time-varying data is a less common problem in transaction processing databases such as this order entry system, and when you encounter it there are a couple of ways to handle it. You can maintain third normal form by creating a PriceHistory table, as shown in Figure 4-4. PriceHistory is a detail table—it relates back to the Product table and records the variations on pricing for each product, either on a day basis or as price changes happen. The SaleItem table in this figure doesn't include UnitPrice or ItemCost. Instead, the PriceHistory table is related to the SaleItem table, and, by comparing the date of the sale (by relating SaleItem back to Sale) and the product code, you can determine the sale price of the item and then calculate the ItemCost. This is a complex solution, but it *is* the 3NF solution, and it will give you ultimate flexibility and control over your data.

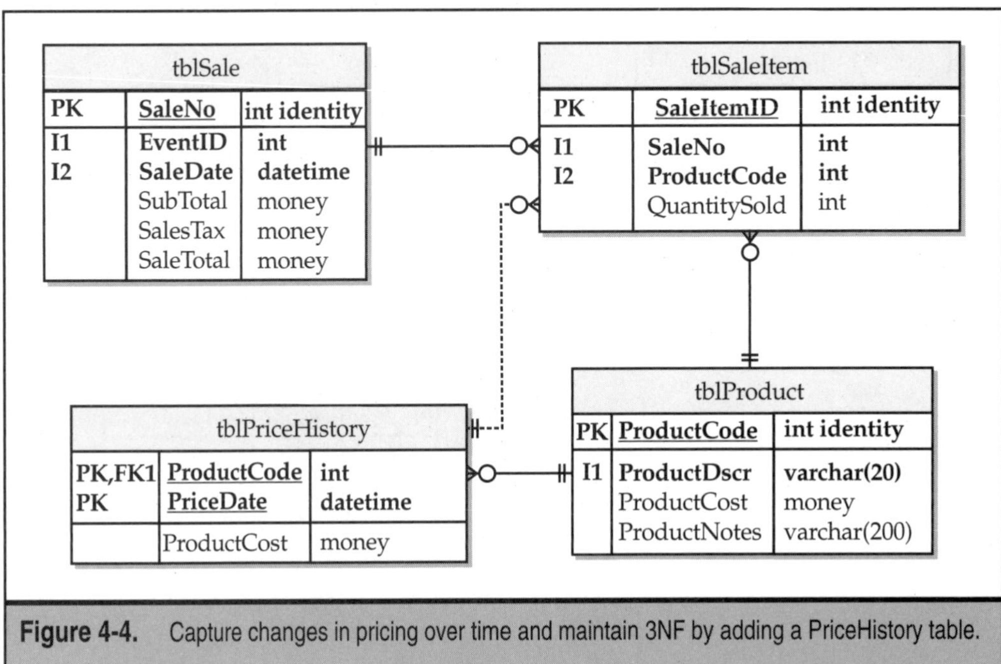

Figure 4-4. Capture changes in pricing over time and maintain 3NF by adding a PriceHistory table.

A more simple and slightly denormalized solution is to do as you did in Figure 4-3, to include the UnitPrice and ItemCost in the SaleItem table. These columns record the UnitPrice and ItemCost values as they were at the time of the sale. This answers the questions we raised in Chapter 3 about why these columns are in the SaleItem table. Like all denormalized models, you won't be able to extend or expand this model very easily. For instance, if you wanted to include a reason for a fluctuation in product prices, you could do so in the 3NF solution by including another column in the PriceHistory table to store the reason. But how would you record this information in your 2NF solution? The answer: you wouldn't.

Add Additional Attributes

One big difference between the physical model and conceptual/logical models is the sudden presence of attributes that appear to be either utilitarian in function or that are calculated values. Despite our admonition earlier in this book about relational databases not storing calculated values, sometimes, for performance reasons, you'll see exactly that. You'll see attributes like SaleTotal in the Sale table (refer to Figure 4-3) and ItemCost (which is determined by QuantitySold times UnitPrice) in the SaleItem table. These calculated values are a time and cost savings for the database management system. If, in your business, you need to be constantly calculating sale totals, it makes sense to store the calculated values in the records, rather than to ask the database to be constantly recalculating them on the fly as you retrieve the records.

The "utility attributes" are those that help clarify a situation or track events. Sometimes they're no more than single-byte flag fields, as in the Person table of Figure 4-1. Notice the PersonType attribute. This attribute's sole function is to store a single letter that indicates whether that person is a salesperson representing a vendor, a contact person for an event, or an employee. Other utility attributes are the threesome combination of RecordEntryDate, LastUpdate, and ByWhom, which we have not yet included in the model. These three tables do exactly what their names imply. All three are filled automatically by triggers firing after modification events. RecordEntryDate is auto-filled when the record is added. LastUpdate gets updated each time a change is made to the record (excluding the initial insert or a delete command). ByWhom gets filled in with the user's login ID on insert or on change. Now you can see who was the last person to mess with the records. None of these three utility attributes are included in your model; we'll modify this design and add them as table attributes later in the book.

Assign Vendor-Specific Datatypes

Vendor-specific datatypes are physical datatypes that are implemented by a specific vendor, such as the datatypes you see in the figures of this chapter. They differ from the portable datatypes that are sometimes used in logical models, in that a portable datatype is one that can be translated into any database vendor's set of physical datatypes without losing meaning, context, or value. The most common portable datatypes are

- **Text** Includes fixed length, variable length, and large length character datatypes
- **Numeric** Includes all signed integer, unsigned integer, autocounter, floating point, decimal, and money datatypes
- **Raw data** Includes fixed, variable, large length, picture, and OLE object datatypes
- **Temporal** Includes auto-timestamp, date, time, and datetime datatypes
- **Logical** Includes true or false, yes or no datatypes
- **Other** Includes row ID, object ID, and other or unknown datatypes

Create Surrogate Primary Keys

SQL Server 2000 (and preceding versions) can process numbers faster than it can process character data. Therefore, from a performance perspective, it is better to have keys, both primary and foreign, that are integer datatypes, rather than character or datetime datatypes.

You'll notice in the physical model that every entity has a primary key that is an integer datatype. As many as possible of these primary keys are also automatically incrementing values. Following the advice put forth in Chapter 2, the identity property ensures that you'll have a meaningless, unchanging, utterly simple primary key. Compare the physical model in this chapter to the conceptual data model presented in Chapter 2, and you'll see the difference right away. The conceptual data model illustrates ideal entity dependencies that result in identifying relations, composite primary keys, and strongly enforced referential integrity. By the time you arrive at the physical model in this chapter, you've backed out of most of the identifying relations, replaced composite primary keys with simple integer-identity datatypes, and reconsidered enforcement of nearly all referential integrity relationships.

When you're creating the physical model, you must place yourself in a production environment, and you must salt your model with a healthy dose of pragmatism. In a perfect world, each salesperson would represent one of your vendor companies. But in the real world, you might meet a salesperson before you ever start buying from the company he or she works for, and you might want to record that salesperson's name and phone number in your database before you get the particulars on the company. Also, salespeople change jobs, and often, if there's little to choose between with the companies, it's the salesperson you prefer to do business with. If you constrained the relationship between Vendor and SalesPerson, as indicated in the portion of the conceptual model represented by Figure 4-5, you wouldn't be able do this. You wouldn't be able to enter the salesperson's information in the SalesPerson table because her company's not already in your

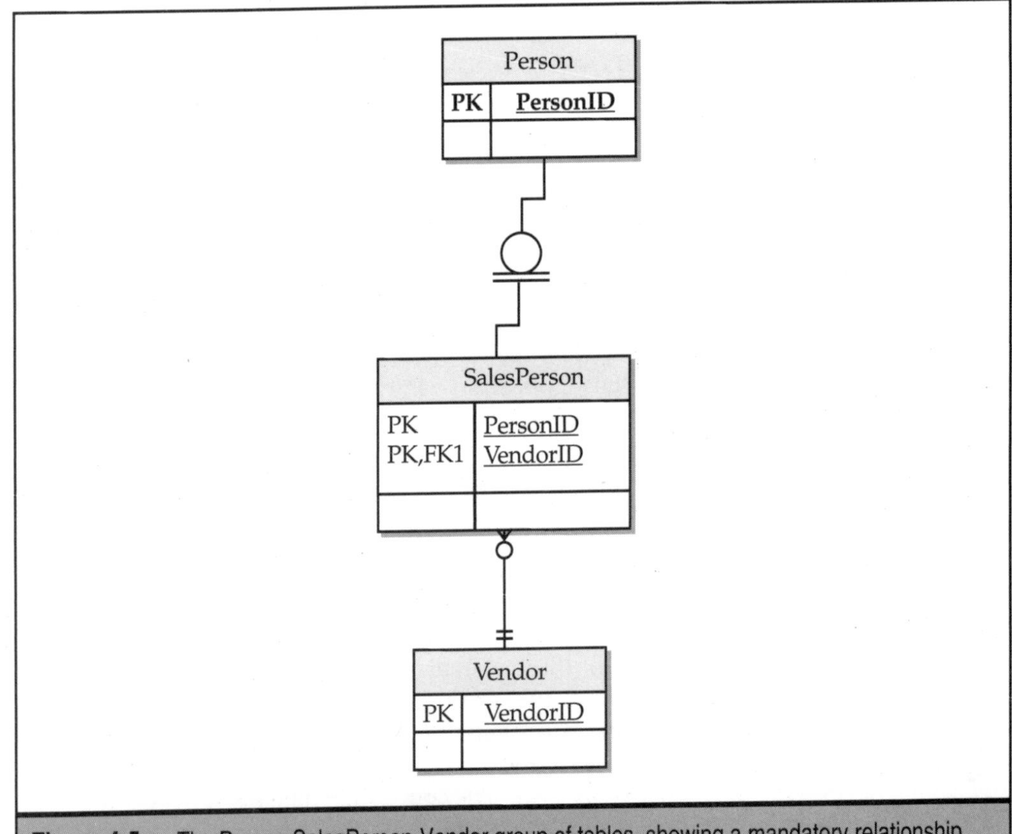

Figure 4-5. The Person-SalesPerson-Vendor group of tables, showing a mandatory relationship between Person and SalesPerson

database, and the primary key for the conceptual model version of SalesPerson is the composite PersonID plus VendorID. You can't add a record to a table until you have the entire primary key. Rather than restrict what you and your data users can do, you model your database to accommodate the imperfections of your world.

Identify Candidate Keys

SQL Server (all versions) has always been able to evaluate a query plan better if it can choose between multiple join strategies when combining tables. You can give SQL Server an extra boost if you identify the candidate keys and create additional foreign key relationships.

Unfortunately, your physical model doesn't contain a good example of a candidate key that is involved in a foreign key relationship. You'll have to extend the model as shown in Figure 4-6, where you have the Employee table from your physical model, and a new table, tblPayroll. The Payroll table is detail to the Employee table, as an employee (usually) collects one or more paychecks. The Employee table has two candidates for primary key: PersonID and SSN. Because of privacy, security, and integrity considerations (see Chapter 3 for a tirade on why you should not use SSN as primary key), you've chosen PersonID as the primary key for this table. But because SSN is a candidate, it too is underlain by a unique index (more on indexes later).

The other table in Figure 4-6 is the Payroll table. It has a primary key of PayrollID and foreign keys PersonID and SSN. This is a case where it is altogether proper to declare two foreign key constraints between the Employee table and the Payroll table. An employee may receive zero or many paychecks; a paycheck is issued for one and only one employee. You don't want a paycheck issued to a nonexistent employee, so you would reinforce the foreign key constraints between these two tables. In this case, you'd have one foreign key reference from tblPayroll back to tblEmployee on the PersonID column and a second reference on the column SSN. You also don't want a paycheck issued to a Social Security number that's not on file in your employee roster.

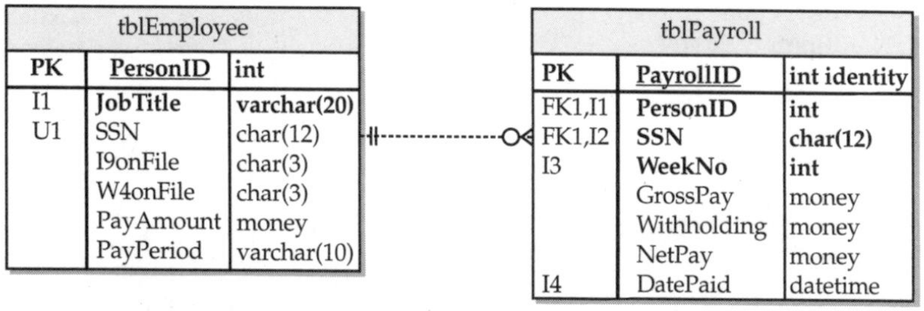

tblEmployee

PK	PersonID	int
I1	**JobTitle**	**varchar(20)**
U1	SSN	char(12)
	I9onFile	char(3)
	W4onFile	char(3)
	PayAmount	money
	PayPeriod	varchar(10)

tblPayroll

PK	PayrollID	int identity
FK1,I1	**PersonID**	**int**
FK1,I2	**SSN**	**char(12)**
I3	**WeekNo**	**int**
	GrossPay	money
	Withholding	money
	NetPay	money
I4	DatePaid	datetime

Figure 4-6. The Employee-Payroll table set

Creating a second foreign key reference between the two tables gives SQL Server options to evaluate when it's building its query plan in response to the weekly payroll program.

Evaluate Enforced Referential Integrity

We've already talked some about the wisdom and necessity of enforcing foreign key references. There is one situation you heartily want to avoid—the circular reference. There aren't any really good circular references in your physical model (of course), so we've shown one in Figure 4-7 that is outside your Strawberry Smoooches schema. This design is actually taken from a production database we encountered a few years ago. There are two tables in Figure 4-7, Customer and CustLocation, related 1:M. A customer—in this case a company identified by CustNo—may have more than one business location, while a CustLocation is used by only one customer. The relationship is strongly enforced, with referential integrity declared between Customer (CustNo) and CustLocation (CustNo).

However, notice in the Customer table an attribute called BillingSiteNo. Also notice that it's a foreign key to SiteNo in the CustLocation table. (SiteNo is the primary key of CustLocation.) If you were to enforce referential integrity between CustLocation (SiteNo) and Customer (BillingSiteNo), you would not be able to insert any new rows into either table! Obviously, this is not a condition you want to try to live with, so the lesser of the two relationships, CustLocation (SiteNo) to Customer (BillingSiteNo), cannot be enforced. There is a downside: now it is possible to insert into the Customer table a site number that doesn't exist in the CustLocation table.

This entire situation is a result of inadequate design. We've seen circular references in many production systems, and they're all a result of attempts to shortcut proper data modeling procedures.

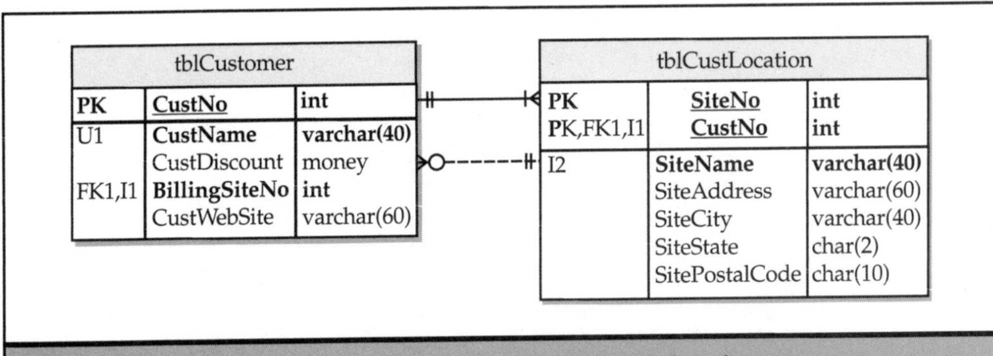

Figure 4-7. The Customer-CustLocation table set, showing a circular reference

Determine the Index Candidates

An index to a database is like an index in a book. You, as a reader of the book, use the index to find specific words or phrases buried in the text. A database uses an index to help it find specific records that have been requested by one of its data readers or data writers (users). The index structure is not a requirement of a relational database, but if you want any kind of performance in your production systems, you're going to want to create indexes.

An index can be constructed on one or more columns of a table, but it must be wholly contained within that table. The index pages are sorted by the values in the index column, and each index record contains a pointer to the data row it references. Data retrieval using an index can be substantially faster than scanning the entire table when SQL Server is looking for just a single record or two. The idea here is to give SQL Server as many options as you can so it can select the best query plan for executing data retrieval. Judiciously creating indexes can help SQL Server tremendously.

How many indexes do you want on a table? You can have up to 250 indexes on one table, each on a different column or combination of columns. The more indexes on a table, the more likely that there will be an index of value in resolving any given query. However, there's a tradeoff. Every time you add, delete, or update a row, you have to update all of the associated indexes. This turns what looks like a single-record modification operation into a multi-record update, and that can cause a lot of performance problems in a heavily loaded system. Here you have the classic conflict between the OLTP (OnLine Transaction Processing) people and the OLAP (OnLine Analytical Processing) people. The OLTP folks want as few indexes as possible—just what it takes to get the job done and no more. The OLAP crowd, on the other hand, wants to index everything (also called inverting the database). OLAP environments have no fixed set of production programs and often no idea what queries will be running on the data warehouse data set, so they need to index nearly everything.

So how do you determine which columns are good candidates for indexing? There are some rules you can religiously follow for indexing. Key columns—primary, foreign, and candidate—must be indexed. (Designated primary key columns automatically have a unique index built on them when the table is created.) Next, columns that will be used for sorting and grouping, like zip code or last name, had better be indexed or you'll wait all day for your query results. (Obviously, the length of time you wait for your query results depends on the size of your database, but you get the idea.) And finally, columns that will be used frequently to specify search criteria (the "where" clause of a T-SQL statement) need to be indexed. If you refer back to Figure 4-1, you'll see indicators in the left column of each of the entities, labeled I1, I2, and so forth. These are the columns to be indexed.

We'll talk a lot more about how to create indexes in Chapter 17.

MAPPING THE ERD TO A TABLE ARCHITECTURE

Now that you've carefully crafted a physical model, and checked it over twice, it's time to implement! If you've been fortunate enough to be able to use a CASE (Computer-Assisted Software Engineering) tool to assist you in your modeling tasks, here's where the payoff comes. A CASE tool such as ERWin, Designer/2000, or Visio can forward-engineer your physical model onto a database platform. Minimally, it will generate editable T-SQL scripts that you can check and then run in the Query Analyzer window to create your database and create the tables, columns, stored procedures, and other objects that make up a database.

We'll use Visio 2000 Enterprise to demonstrate how forward-engineering works. Visio 2000 has another nice forward-engineering feature: it will create the database for you, and as we walk you through this process, this is the option we'll use.

Figure 4-8 is a screenshot of your physical model in the Visio 2000 workspace. On the left is the drawing template—you can barely make out that it's an Entity Relationship

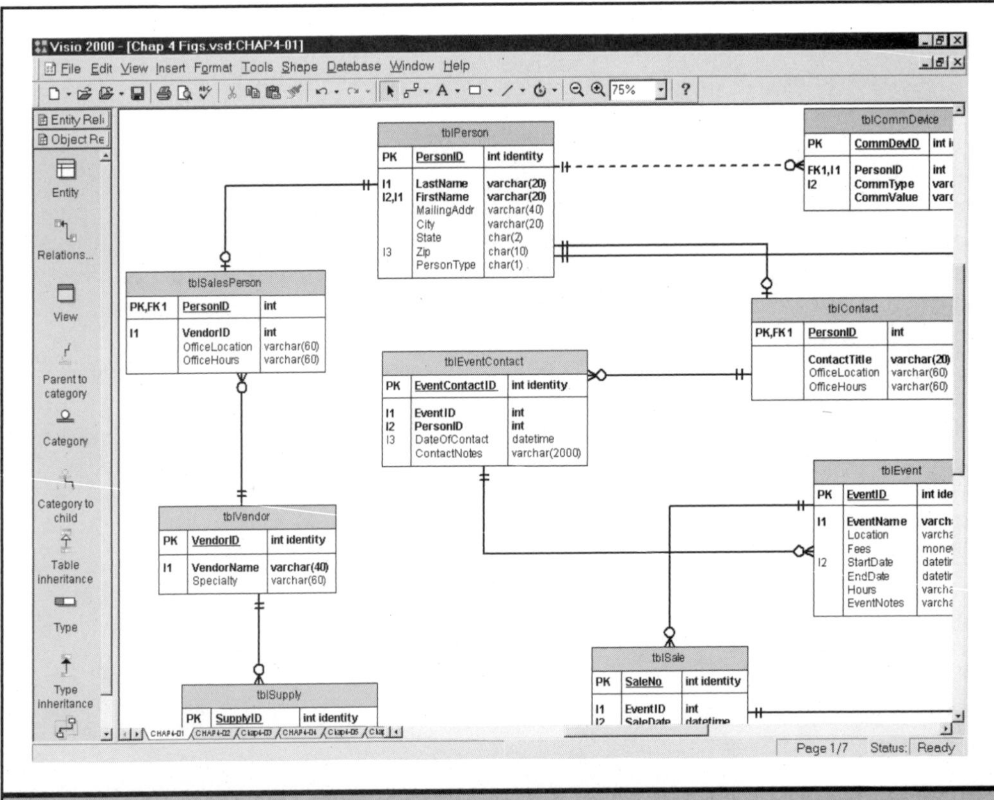

Figure 4-8. The Strawberry Smoooches Company physical model in a Visio 2000 workspace

Model drawing template. To forward-engineer a model, you have to have defined it as either an ER Source model or a Database Model Diagram. This is, obviously, an ER Source model. Before you can forward-engineer this model into the database, you need to run an error check on the model. The Visio error-check routines parse through the model, making sure you have defined everything correctly and completely. Figure 4-9 is such an error report, overlaid by the menu selections you have to choose to get this report generated. The error report specifies each object or object set that is out of compliance; you must fix these errors before you can forward-engineer.

Once you've got the errors resolved, you begin the forward-engineering process by choosing Database | Generate from the menu. The Generate Wizard then takes over and walks you through the process. As you can see in Figure 4-10, you're defining a data definition language (DDL) script that can be used to create the Strawberry Smooooches Company database, you're requesting to generate a new database, and you want to store the current database image in the model, so that the physical model becomes a living document—an ongoing record of changes and modifications that will be made to the database in the future.

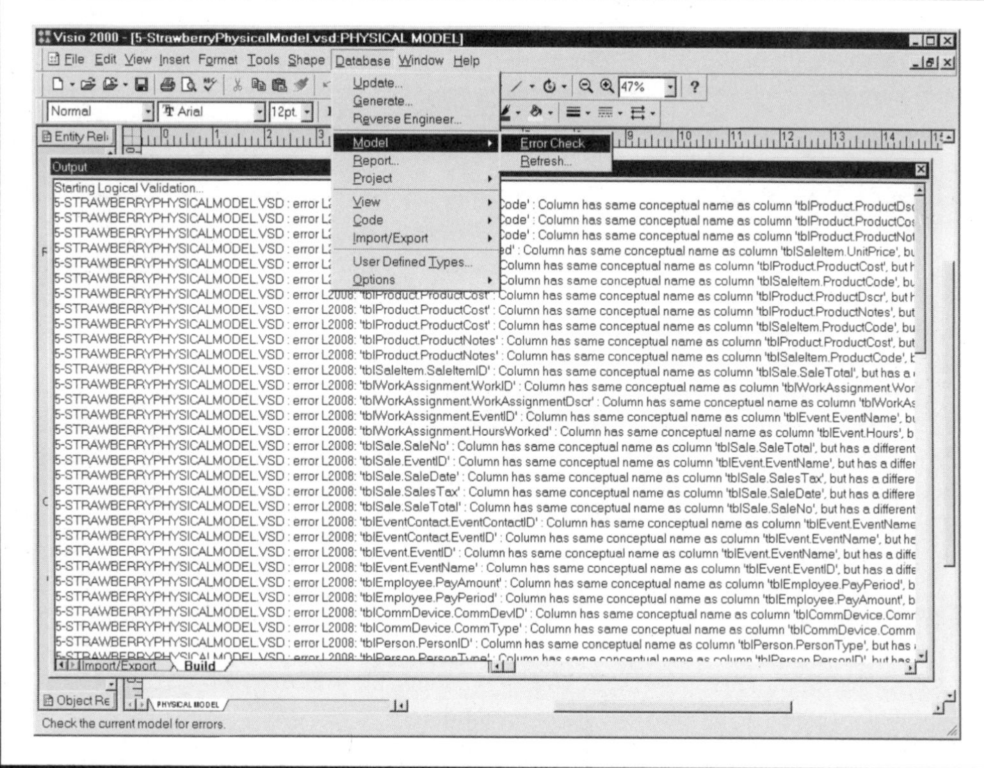

Figure 4-9. Choose Database | Model | Error Check to generate a report from the Visio 2000 model checker.

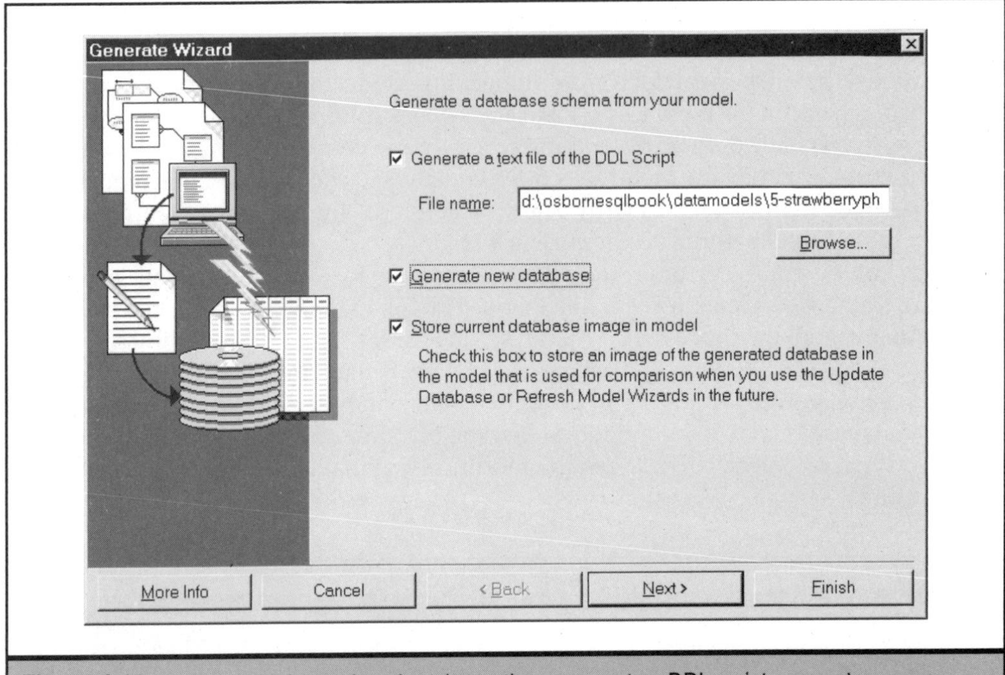

Figure 4-10. Visio 2000 forward-engineering options: generate a DDL script; generate a new database; store the current database image in the model for future synchronization; any combination of the three.

In Figure 4-11, you're establishing a connection with the SQL Server by specifying a data source name and a database name. At the time of writing, Visio 2000 did not support forward-engineering to SQL Server 2000 beta 2, so you're going to generate to a SQL 7 server called BlackDiamond. At this point, you're asked to log in. Even though you're logged into the network with administrative authority, Visio still requests that you provide your SQL Server login and password before it will generate the new database.

You get a final chance to review the tables that will be created in the database, as shown in Figure 4-12. If you change your mind about something, at this point you can still back up and modify the forward-engineer specifications. Then, a few clicks of the mouse later, you're informed that the wizard is ready to generate the database. Press Finish, and the wizard steps you through creating database files, both data and log, for the new database, as shown in Figure 4-13. You have to interact, doing things such as confirming the size, growth characteristics, and file group locations of the data and log files. When you press OK, the forward-engineering process finishes and you're given an opportunity to view the DDL script that was used to generate the database.

This is the easy way to create a database and the end result of all the hard work you've put into creating the physical model. In the next two chapters, we'll cover how to write code to create and modify databases and tables. You'll need to know how to do this, because, despite your very best efforts, you will undoubtedly overlook something in the modeling phases that will necessitate a correction to the living database.

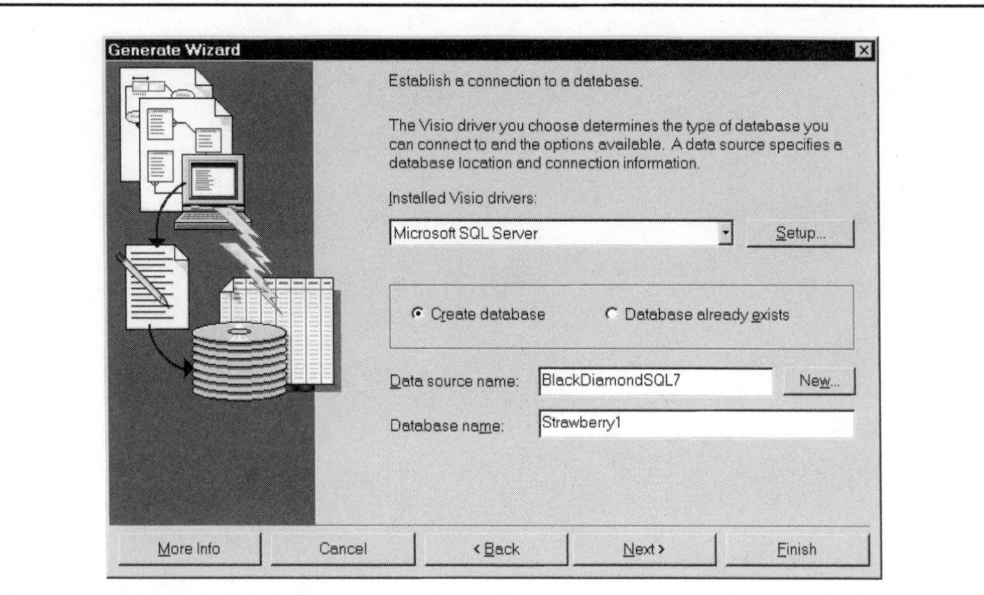

Figure 4-11. Establish a connection to the SQL Server you're going to forward-engineer to by specifying a data source name (DSN) and a database name.

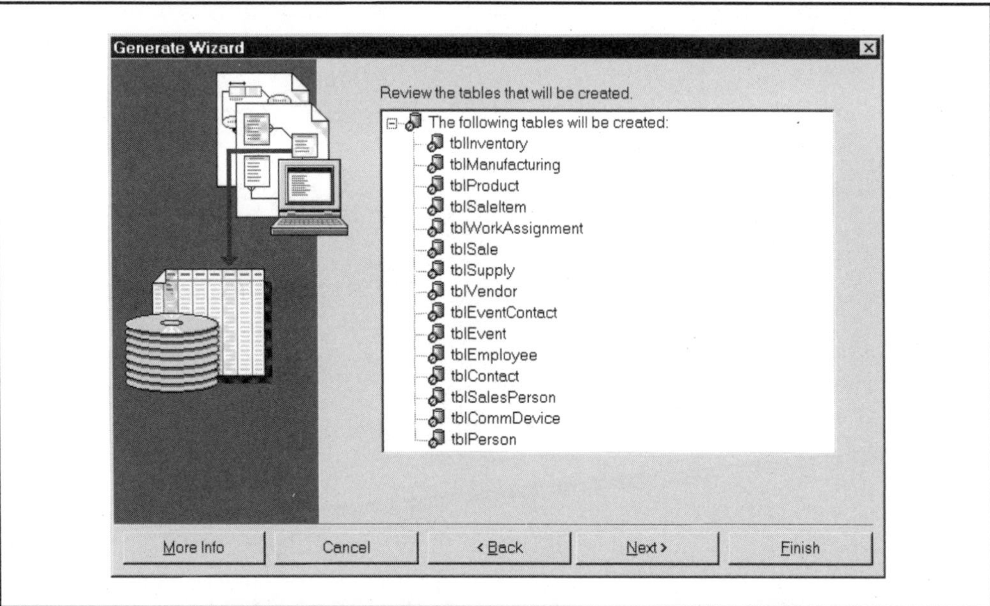

Figure 4-12. The final review of the tables that will be generated in the new database

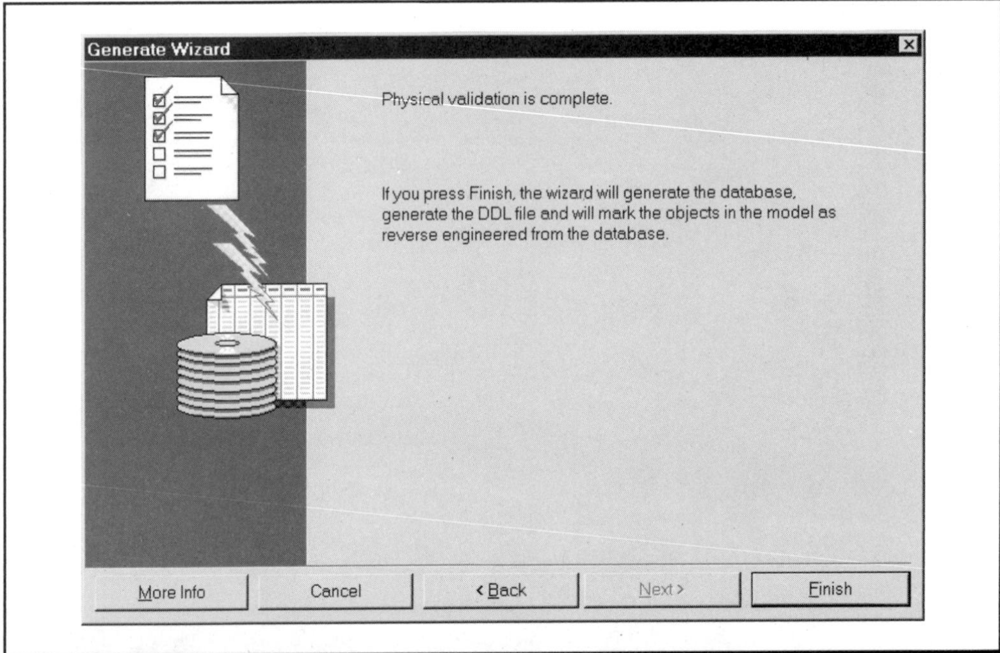

Figure 4-13. Once into execution mode, the Create Database Wizard takes over.

PART II

Implementation

CHAPTER 5

Implementing the Design

Now you are ready to start building your databases. In Chapter 4, we looked at building databases using a software tool such as Visio 2000 or ERWin. In this chapter, we will look at how you can create your databases without using a CASE tool, using just the tools provided with SQL Server.

CREATING DATABASES

In some companies, the task of creating databases is performed by the database administrator, rather than by the designer or developer. If this is true in your company, keep in mind that the DBA is still working from instructions received from the designer—at least we hope that is the case. In practice, the distinction between developers and database administrators is becoming less well defined than it was in the past. In smaller companies, one person often wears both hats.

In this chapter, we will look at how to create databases and consider strategies for placing the various components of the database on different disks, so it is less likely you will lose the log file and the data files at the same time. We will look at how you can use files and filegroups to optimize performance and also assist the administrator with backup strategies.

As with many operations in SQL Server, you can create databases using Enterprise Manager or you can use a script. This dual personality of SQL Server goes back to its heritage as an application that was developed for text-based operating systems, before it was implemented in a Microsoft Windows environment. The only available user interface was the command-line utility (isql). DBAs used this interface to run SQL commands or scripts. With the introduction of SQL Server 6.0, the graphical Enterprise Manager interface was added, but the scripts still work, and their capabilities have been enhanced and expanded. At first it might seem easier to build databases using the GUI, as shown in Figure 5-1, and indeed it is if you are just creating a quick test database. But when you want to create a second database and then a third, each of which might be similar to the first, perhaps on different server computers, then the GUI is less efficient. You will find it more efficient to have a script you can use to create these databases just by opening it in the Query Analyzer and running it. One other advantage to having a script is that it is documentation of the work you've done and the database objects you've created. If you are a GUI user who keeps detailed notes about what you did, you are part of a very small minority. It's even less likely that someone else could find those notes if you were out of the office. Consider using scripts to build your databases and storing the code scripts in a directory that is accessible to those who might need it. As with all code, once you've written the first script, most others are derivatives.

SQL Server Tools for Database Creation

In addition to the graphical point-and-click interface in Enterprise Manager, SQL Server does provide a script generation tool for tables, tasks, and other objects within the database. This is especially useful if you've created database objects using Enterprise Man-

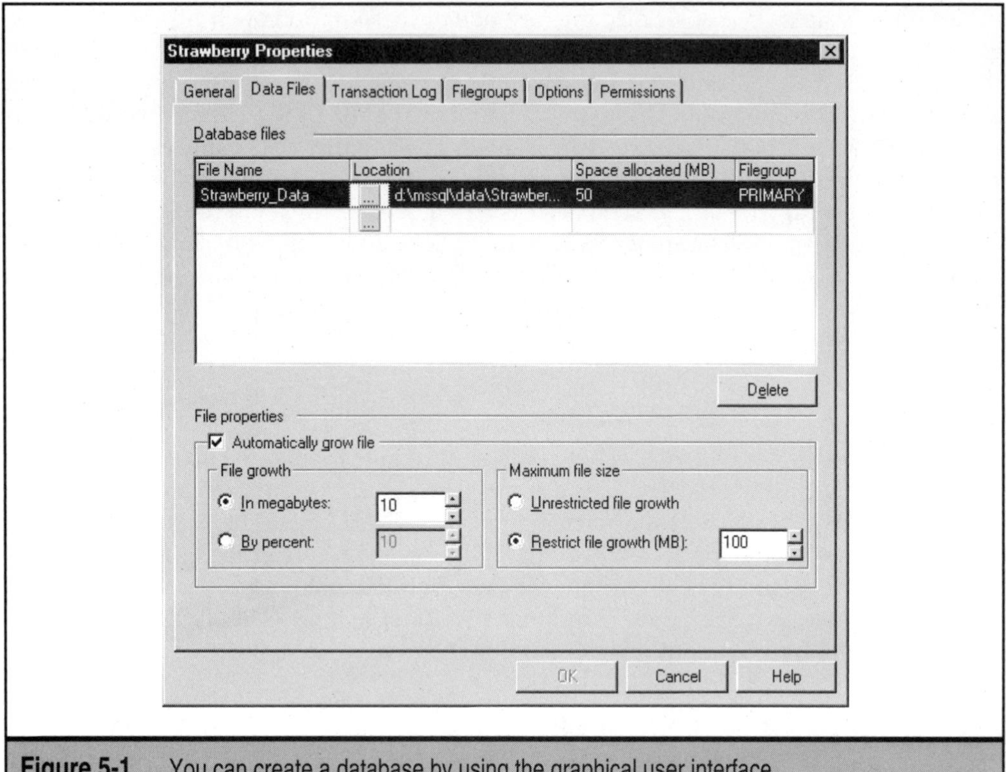

Figure 5-1. You can create a database by using the graphical user interface.

ager and now you want to document what you've done. To find this tool, select the database in the Enterprise Manager hierarchy, place your cursor over the yellow button next to Database in the right pane, and select Generate SQL Script from the menu that opens when you hover. Or right-click on the database name, select All Tasks, and then select the scripting option from the menu. A very welcome new addition to the scripting options is the ability to script the creation of the database itself, in addition to the tables and all the other objects. Once you have used the GUI to build your database, you can generate the database creation code script very easily. Also, it's a good way to teach yourself how to write SQL code.

Another neat tool new to version 2000 is a script template. Open up the Query Analyzer, and on the far left side of the toolbar you will see a icon for New Query with a drop-down arrow next to it. Click on this icon and it simply opens a new, blank query window. But click on the down arrow and you will see a list of object creation options, including Create Database, Create Index, Create Trigger, and Create Procedure. Expand the Create Database item and you will find options to create a basic database or create a database on multiple filegroups (which we'll talk about later in this chapter) and some other more complex options. Selecting any one of these options will fill the right pane with the script. All you have to do is substitute your own object names, as we will do shortly. This is a very useful tool. If we wanted to be picky, we would point out that the script uses the directory path where the default installation of SQL Server would be, not the directory where SQL Server really is located. This is a pity, especially as you can configure the default data location for your server so the file location is known. However, that's a minor complaint about an otherwise very helpful feature. On the Edit menu is the item Replace Template Parameters. Choosing this option gives you a small dialog box, where you can systematically go through each parameter in the template and supply your own values, as you can see in Figure 5-2. The SQL Server team is really trying hard to make life easier for you with these great tools.

Plan the Size of Your Database

In the next chapter, we will look at how data is stored in tables and discuss how you can figure out (roughly) how much disk space you'll need for your data. When you create the database, you will need to know approximately how big it needs to be, and you may want to allow some room for projected growth. SQL Server 7.0 introduced the capability of databases to grow automatically whenever they require more free space. You should use this feature more as a safety valve than as a routine method of allocating disk space, though. We'll talk more about this later in this chapter.

Modifying Your Model Database

Keep in mind that when SQL Server creates a database, it makes a copy of the model database to start with, and then expands it out to the size you requested. The implications are, first, that all databases will be at least as big as the model database (although it's really quite small, under 2MB) and, second, that anything in the model database will appear in

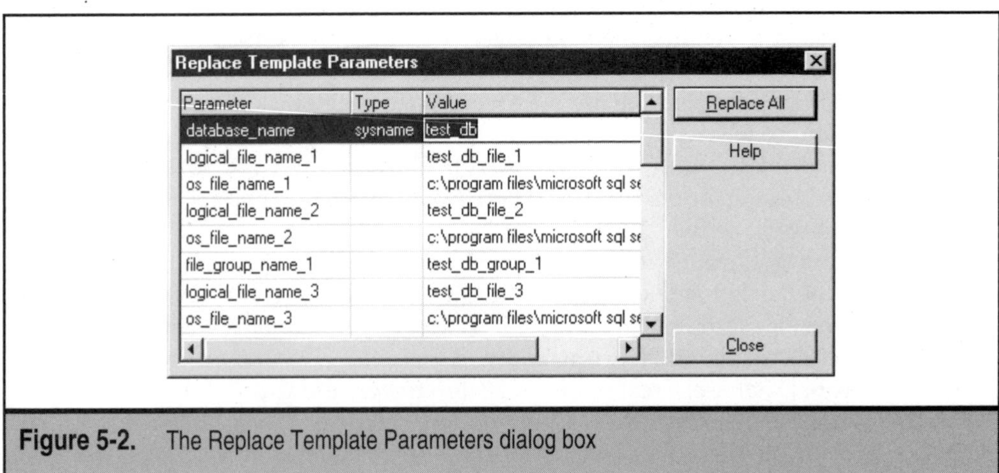

Figure 5-2. The Replace Template Parameters dialog box

all new databases created on this server from that point on. "Anything" includes tables, datatypes, rules, users, security settings, permissions, and so on. You can use this feature to your advantage if you want to standardize certain database settings companywide and you will be creating all databases from one server, working over the network. If you'll be creating databases on the servers they will reside on and you still want to standardize, you will have to make the same changes to every copy of the model database. Every installation of SQL Server in the company will have its own copy of the model database. You have to be careful: If you're creating a new database and the model database for that server is not synced (for whatever reason) with all the others, you could mess up the creation of a table or the setting of security parameters. For this reason, some designers prefer not to make changes to the model database. Instead, you can create standards by running a script immediately after any database is created, which adds all of the standard objects your programmers expect to find in a new database. This approach has the advantage of keeping all the standards in one place, easily editable. The script can be applied to existing databases if necessary, and you don't have to worry about backing up the model database. If you do elect to go with changes to the model, keep in mind that you'll need to keep it backed up just like your other system databases, because if you ever have to rebuild a SQL Server, the model database will revert to its original version.

Database Files

You'll also need to supply a name for your database, both a logical and a physical name for the data file and the log file. Each database has at least one data file, which is known as the *primary* data file and has a default extension of .mdf. Every database also has a separate log file, which has a default extension .ldf. A database can have multiple data files, and the additional files, known as *secondary* data files, have a default extension of .ndf. If necessary, you can add additional log files, still using the .ldf extension. You might find that you have to use multiple files if your database is large or you require a very large transaction log, because database files cannot span logical disks. Suppose you are planning a 100GB database. The biggest hard drives you can find are 40GB. The SQL Server solution is to spread your database among three logical disks, using one primary and two secondary files. The Windows NT/2000 solution is to create either a volume set or a RAID 0 or RAID 5 array, which looks to SQL Server like one logical drive, and place your database on that logical drive in one primary file. If the budget allows, you might even opt for a hardware RAID 5 array, which will give good performance. If the budget won't stretch to that, our preference would be to go with the SQL Server solution rather than incur the additional overhead of Windows NT/2000 software RAID arrays. It's true that software RAID 5 does give the protection of parity data, but you can protect your database in other ways with careful placement of data and logs on different physical disks.

If you add several files to your database, SQL Server sees these as one large allocation of space that it can use for tables and indexes. It fills up each file using an algorithm that looks at the free space within each file, and allocates extents (more on extents in the next chapter) proportionately. So if you start with a 4GB file and an 8GB file, SQL Server will allocate two extents from the 8GB file to every one on the 4GB file. Eventually, you will converge on equal space remaining on all the files.

RAID

RAID, Redundant Array of Inexpensive Disks, is a hardware configuration and technique for strong storage of data. A RAID configuration consists of a special disk controller—almost always SCSI or UltraWide SCSI—and an array of hard drives. RAID 5, the most popular of the RAID implementations, writes data in blocks, spread across all of the disks in the array. Reading the data may be faster, because multiple disk heads can read the data blocks simultaneously, with the controller assembling the blocks into the correct sequence. Redundancy in RAID 5 is provided by the addition of data parity information, which is also spread across the multiple disks, interleaved with the data. Parity information allows the controller to calculate the missing data should any one of the disks fail. If two or more disks fail, it's time to restore the database from a backup. RAID 0 also spreads the data across multiple disks, but with "zero" redundancy. It might be considered for read-only databases that can be easily re-created where performance is more important than redundancy. Windows NT and Windows 2000 can simulate a RAID controller in software, but the hardware solution is always better if the budget allows, because it involves less CPU overhead and provides "hot-swap" capabilities for changing out hard disks and for rebuilding the data on a disk.

Database Filegroups

Sometimes designers like to try to squeeze more performance out of their database by controlling the placement of tables and indexes on various physical disks. In SQL Server, you achieve this with *filegroups*. A filegroup is a logical, named grouping of database files. Each filegroup can contain one or more files, on one or more disks. The primary file (the .mdf file) is part of the primary filegroup. Its logical file name is PRIMARY.

There are three main reasons for using filegroups:

- You can specify which disk is used when creating the table and place some of the indexes on a different disk. When you retrieve the data, one set of disk heads is reading the index and returning pointers to the data rows. A second set of disk heads can then be busy retrieving the actual data records.
- Infrequently used data, or data that is relatively static, can be placed on a disk apart from the tables that are heavily modified.
- You have more flexibility in your backup strategies.

Placing data and indexes on different disks may bring a benefit only if you have one or more disk controllers that can handle multiple requests for data. Typically this would mean SCSI disks, which is what you'll find in most high-end database servers.

The second point, the separation of data, is worth considering if you have two groups of users with different requirements. Perhaps the data analysts are running complex queries on last month's sales, while your customer service people are taking orders over the phone and updating this month's sales. Although it would be preferable to move the data analysts to another server, that may just not be practical. At least this way you can reduce the disk contention as the two groups run their different queries against the data. When you do need to run a query that combines both sets of data—for example, to generate a sales report for the past three months—you can do so easily with the UNION operator (discussed in Chapter 8).

There are other benefits to using filegroups, including impacts on your backup strategy. As a designer you may not be involved in the daily backup tasks. But what happens when the administrator finds that the nightly backup takes eight hours, and the only time available is midnight to 5:00 am? Is there any way to design the database to help with this problem? Using filegroups is one way to partition the database so that the DBA can back up only selected filegroups each night. Suppose that you break your sales database into four filegroups: the primary filegroup contains the system files, reference tables, and so forth. A second filegroup holds sales data, the third is for customer information, and the last is allocated to the products table. The DBA backs up the whole database on the weekend. On Mondays, the backup covers the sales filegroup, on Tuesday the customers, and on Wednesday the products. The same three filegroups are backed up on Thursday, Friday, and Saturday. Each filegroup backup can be performed in the allocated time. The DBA is also backing up the transaction logs daily or possibly several times each day. This scheme works, and the DBA is happy, but there's an even better approach. Working with the DBA, you can show that the sales table is changing rapidly—thousands of sales per day. The customers table is changing, but only at the rate of a hundred or so new customers per day. And the products table changes even more slowly—a few new products each week, some price changes, but really this is a relatively stable table. So you come up with a backup plan for the six days that backs up the tables in a different order: sales, customers, sales, customers, sales, sales. The products table is backed up during the full database backup on the weekend. All the data and changes to this table originated within your company and can be re-created easily. Instead you focus on the safety of the customers and sales data, over which you have no control. If you lose a customer record, you can hardly expect the customer to call in again with their information—at least until their order does not show up.

The DBA will find another benefit to filegroups if there is a system problem and one of the hard disks crashes. Suppose it is the disk with the customers table, in the customer filegroup, which is lost. The restore process will go a lot faster because it is possible to restore just the one filegroup, which is obviously going to take less time than a full database restore. SQL Server has the option to restore the filegroup from a filegroup backup or from a full backup. Once it has restored the filegroup, it then goes through the transaction log backups, looking only for transactions that apply to that filegroup. When it is through applying these transactions, your database is back just the way it was before the crash.

Knowing which filegroups contain the most volatile data allows the DBA to watch those groups and periodically check to see whether they need more disk space. However, some

DBAs might prefer to simplify the issue and just allocate more space to the entire database. While an experienced DBA can take advantage of the benefits offered by filegroups, it may be confusing for someone with little or no experience with SQL Server. Keep in mind the level of expertise of the person who will be maintaining the databases—or you may end up doing it yourself!

Filegroups and BLOBs

As you will see in the next chapter, SQL Server stores certain types of data, such as BLOBs (binary large objects), apart from the normal rows of data. It also does this for text data, where you may be storing large amounts of text such as a legal document or the great American novel. If you try to store this type of data in the database rows, you will quickly run into the limit of 8,060 bytes per row. The same applies to image data, such as employee photos, images of products, or scanned documents. So SQL Server stores the binary or image data in a different set of pages. In the actual database row, it stores only a pointer or reference to these pages. Some database designers like to force the pages for the binary and image data to be on a different filegroup, away from the data records. If all the data is in one filegroup, as you add more and more data to the database, the file will fill up rapidly, but most of the pages will hold the binary or image data and only a few will hold normal row data. The pages containing the row data will be scattered throughout the pages of binary or image data, like raisins in a pudding, making data retrieval less efficient. This fragmentation will not happen if the data rows and the text or images pages are in different filegroups, as each will fill up its own filegroup in an orderly manner.

Filegroups vs. RAID Arrays

Although it is more effort to set up a database using filegroups, you may find some long-term benefits in doing so. On the other hand, if you are simply looking for performance, a hardware RAID array may be a better idea. The RAID array will give good throughput when retrieving large amounts of data, and having multiple disk heads to read the data can help when handling queries for specific data records from a large number of users. Using a RAID array avoids the design and maintenance complexities of filegroups. In fact, you can ignore filegroups completely. Don't even mention them when creating databases. The primary filegroup, built when you create the database, will be the only filegroup, and it will also be the default filegroup, so all your tables will be in the same filegroup.

The transaction log is always in its own filegroup. You can have several files dedicated to the log, but they will all belong to the same filegroup. If you install a RAID array, it is strongly recommended that you keep the transaction log off the RAID array. The best place for the log is on a separate physical disk or series of disks. The transaction log disk access is quite different from the manner in which the disk is accessed for data reads and data writes. Data access can involve retrieving records scattered throughout the database (random data reads) or many people each updating different records (random data writes), so it helps to have multiple disk heads, as in a RAID array, or at least disks with low random access times. Disk access time is a function of the rotational speed of the disk and how fast the heads can move across the disk from one record to another unrelated record. The transaction log is written sequentially, entry after entry, in a very steady progression from one disk sector to the next and is not at all random. It is read in the same sequential manner, whether for a backup or for the recovery process that SQL Server goes through each time it starts. What matters to the log is having a disk with good data throughput, rather than fast access times. A RAID array is not a good idea for a transaction log file, because SQL Server would be writing to one disk, then the next, and so on in sequence through the array. So there's no benefit from the multiple disk heads. Another reason for keeping the log off the RAID array is that there's not much point in incurring the overhead of calculating and storing parity information for data that is only read once or twice.

Even if you are not using a RAID array, you should still keep the log on its own physical disk to reduce the contention between data writes and log writes, and of course for safety. If you lose the data disk, you still have your backups and the transaction log to restore from.

Creating a Database

The syntax for creating a database is as follows (from SQL Books Online):

```
CREATE DATABASE database_name
[ ON [ PRIMARY ]
    [ < filespec > [ ,...n ] ]
    [ , < filegroup > [ ,...n ] ]
]
[ LOG ON { < filespec > [ ,...n ] } ]
[ COLLATE collation_name ]
[ FOR LOAD | FOR ATTACH ]

< filespec > ::=

( [ NAME = logical_file_name , ]
  FILENAME = 'os_file_name'
  [ , SIZE = size ]
  [ , MAXSIZE = { max_size | UNLIMITED } ]
  [ , FILEGROWTH = growth_increment ] ) [ ,...n ]

< filegroup > ::=

FILEGROUP filegroup_name < filespec > [ ,...n ]
```

For the Strawberry Smoooches database, you are going to build a database called Strawberry. You will use strawberry.mdf for the main database file, and strawberry.ldf for the log file. Your logical filenames will be strawberry_data and strawberry_log. You'll start with a 50MB database and a 10MB log, and allow for file growth, 10MB at a time for the database and 5MB for each increment on the transaction log file. At this point, you will put everything on the primary filegroup, which is also the default filegroup. The code will look like this:

```
USE MASTER
GO
CREATE DATABASE Strawberry
ON (NAME = Strawberry_Data ,
FILENAME = 'd:\mssql\data\Strawberry.mdf',
SIZE = 50 , MAXSIZE = 100, FILEGROWTH = 10)
LOG ON
(NAME = Strawberry_log,
FILENAME = 'd:\mssql\data\Strawberry.ldf',
SIZE = 10 , MAXSIZE = 20, FILEGROWTH = 5)
GO
```

The code is a little strange, in that the name of the database, although it is a character string, must *not* be in quotes. The logical name of the file *can* be in quotes, and the name of the physical file *must* be in quotes. And you do have to supply the complete path, including the disk drive, for the physical name.

MANAGING DATABASE GROWTH

In the database example, we put in some upper limits for the size of the files, rather than letting them fill up the disk. Most databases tend to grow, and some just seem to take on a life of their own and keep growing endlessly. It would be quite unusual for a database to shrink over time, and if you see that happening in your company, it may be time to update your résumé. There are situations where a database will shrink, such as when you decide to drop customers who have not placed an order in the last two years. Or perhaps you bought a mailing list that contained vast numbers of duplicate and incorrect addresses, and you have removed the inaccuracies. You might occasionally clean up your database, or you might even have a scheduled monthly task to drop records or archive data that you don't need online any more. But usually, growth happens continuously as a function of doing business, and shrinkage happens less often under the control of the administrator. Archiving or deleting data is usually done to free up space for new incoming data.

As we mentioned earlier, SQL Server 7.0 introduced a whole new model for data storage and added the ability for the RDBMS to grow databases automatically. This is a neat feature and can save a lot of trouble if, for example, someone is loading in a large volume of data and runs out of space part way through the load procedure. Should you use this feature to handle the growth of your database? Should you start with a 2MB database and allow it to grow as needed? We suggest not. Do the numbers and size your database, accounting for future growth. Use the automatic growth feature as a safety mechanism only. Otherwise, you may find that your database has grown to occupy all of the available disk space, and it will do so at the most inopportune time.

When you create a database, you set the parameters for growth. You can specify no growth, and then expand the database manually when required. Or you can allow the database to grow by a percentage, or by a fixed increment in megabytes or kilobytes (megabytes or gigabytes would be more useful these days). If you go with the percentage option, keep in mind that it is a percentage of the current size, so the bigger the database gets, the more space it grabs with each growth step. If you set the database to grow, use a generous increment, for two reasons. First, it takes time to add space to the database. SQL Server has to find the free disk space, claim it, update its information about disk space, and allocate the space to the database tables. Meanwhile the user is kept waiting. So you don't want to repeat this process frequently. Second, if you use small increments, your database will end up scattered in multiple fragments across the hard disk, and this can adversely effect query performance.

Although the database can grow a file, it cannot extend the file onto another disk. So when you run out of disk space, the automatic growth option is not going to help. You can also set an upper limit on the database growth so it does not unexpectedly take over a disk—if, for example, someone ran a query that selected data into a table and got far more rows returned than planned. If you want the database to stay the same size, you can set the growth options to zero or you could set the maximum size equal to the original size to prevent automatic file growth. The defaults are to allow the database to grow by 10 percent each time, with no upper limit until it fills the disk.

If your database plans call for growth, it's not a bad idea to build the database initially at a size that allows room for data growth. As far as we know, there's no penalty for making a database larger than it needs to be, other than the cost of the hardware and data storage. There are some performance issues, both pro and con, if you choose to spread your data out across this space to make inserting new records easier, but we'll talk about that in our upcoming discussion of indexes.

If you wanted to manually increase the size of the Strawberry database, say to 200MB, you would use the ALTER DATABASE command, which looks like this:

```
ALTER DATABASE Strawberry
MODIFY FILE (NAME = Strawberry_data, SIZE = 200Mb)
GO
```

That's all there is to it. You don't need to give the physical filename, as SQL Server knows what physical file is associated with the logical filename Strawberry_data. The change happens immediately.

SHRINKING DATABASES

As we said, a shrinking database may not be a good sign, but there are times when you need to clean out old data, or perhaps you've just found that your initial estimates were too generous and you want to reclaim the disk space for another application. Perhaps the database grew automatically because of a runaway query or someone rebuilding indexes with far too much free space, and now you want to shrink the database back again. Shrinking a database can be done manually by typing a command in the Query Analyzer, or from Enterprise Manager by simply adjusting the numbers. Although shrinking a database would normally be handled by the DBA, one question might come up that requires some input from the designer. If the database was created with too much space, it's not obvious that you can shrink it below the initial size. In fact, Books Online will confirm that you cannot shrink an entire database below its original size. The key word here is *entire*. You can shrink individual files below the size they were when first created, but not the entire database. Unless your database is in only one data file, the DBA might want to work with the designer to plan those files that can be shrunk and those files that should be left alone. Not only can you compact the data within the files and shrink each file, but if you originally spread the database over three files, for example, you can shrink the data back to one or two files and delete the third file.

The command to shrink a database looks like this (from SQL Books Online):

```
DBCC SHRINKDATABASE
  ( database_name [ , target_percent ]
    [ , { NOTRUNCATE | TRUNCATEONLY } ]   )
```

where *database_name* is the name of the database, and *target_percent* is the percent of free space left in the database file after the database has been shrunk.

NOTRUNCATE causes the freed file space to be retained in the database files (if not specified, the freed file space is released to the operating system).

TRUNCATEONLY causes any unused space in the data files to be released to the operating system and shrinks the file to the last allocated extent, reducing the file size without moving any data. No attempt is made to relocate rows to unallocated pages. *Target_percent* is ignored when TRUNCATEONLY is used.

To truncate Strawberry so that it has 10 percent free space, and release the extra space to the operating system, run this code:

```
DBCC SHRINKDATABASE (Strawberry, 10)
```

To shrink a database from Enterprise Manager, select the database to shrink in the database hierarchy, right-click, point to All Tasks, and then click Shrink Database.

Removing Databases

Removing or dropping a database in SQL Server is very easy—perhaps too easy. All you have to do from Enterprise Manager is right-click on the database, select the Delete option, and confirm that yes, you really do want to delete the database. (This is where DBAs start to understand the significance of the unit of time known as the "ohnosecond"—that brief instant between clicking Yes and realizing you've selected the wrong database.) Like everything else in SQL Server, there's a SQL command to drop databases, either one at a time or several together. From SQL Books Online:

```
DROP DATABASE database_name [ ,...n ]
```

It's common practice when creating a database to include a statement in the SQL script to check for the existence of the database and drop it if it already exists. Note that you will *not* see an error message if the database exists, nor will you be asked for confirmation—the point of the existence check and the drop statement is to avoid getting an error message if the database *is* already there. Unlike pre-7.0 versions of SQL Server, when you delete a database, it's gone. You don't have to delete any NT data files in addition to the SQL drop command.

Attaching and Detaching Databases

New to version 7.0 is the ability to "detach" a database. When you detach a database, using the sp_detach_db stored procedure, all references within SQL Server to that database are dropped and the database is now just a series of files on the hard disks. You can also detach a database from Enterprise Manager. Just right-click on the database, select All Tasks, Detach Database. These files can be reattached at any time, either to the same server or to a different server, using the sp_detach_db stored procedure. Or from Enterprise Manager, right-click on Databases, select All Tasks, Attach Database. The ability to detach and reattach databases is a great tool for moving databases from one server to another. Suppose you have built several databases on one server and it becomes overloaded. You could detach one or two of these databases, move the files to another server, either across the network or on some removable media, and then reattach the databases to a new server. Or perhaps you have just bought a fancy new server that can handle the load previously spread over two or three older computers. This two-step procedure is a quick way to consolidate all your databases on the new server. You will have to change some of your client connections (of course) to point to the new server when you move databases from one computer to another. You could even copy the files to the target computer, and then reattach the database to its original location. So now you would have two copies of the database running. You can probably think of situations where this might be useful, including making test copies of databases, trying out new hardware, testing new client software, and so on. The code for these commands is very simple:

```
sp_detach_db 'strawberry'
```

and

```
sp_attachdb 'Strawberry', 'd:\mssql\data\Strawberry.mdf',
d:\mssql\data\Strawberry.ldf'
```

If the database is a single file, as in the case of our example database, you can use sp_attach_single_file_db and not even worry about the log file—SQL Server will build a new one for you. If you plan to copy the database to a read-only device, such as a CD-ROM, you have the option to run the UPDATE STATISTICS procedure before detaching. When you run UPDATE STATISTICS on a database, you're making sure that the tables and indexed views in the database you'll be distributing on CD all have the most current information about index key distributions. You want to do this to ensure that you'll have good query performance. We'll talk a lot more about this procedure when we get to Chapter 16.

DATABASE CONFIGURATION OPTIONS

SQL Server supports multiple databases, and each database has a set of configuration parameters that should be set for each specific database. These options can be viewed and modified through Enterprise Manager by right-clicking on the database name and selecting Properties from the pop-up dialog box. This action brings up a tabbed dialog box. Select the Options tab, shown in Figure 5-3. You can also see the properties listed and change their settings from the Query Analyzer using the sp_dboption stored procedure. Let's take a look at these options with a view to how they should be set for test databases and production databases.

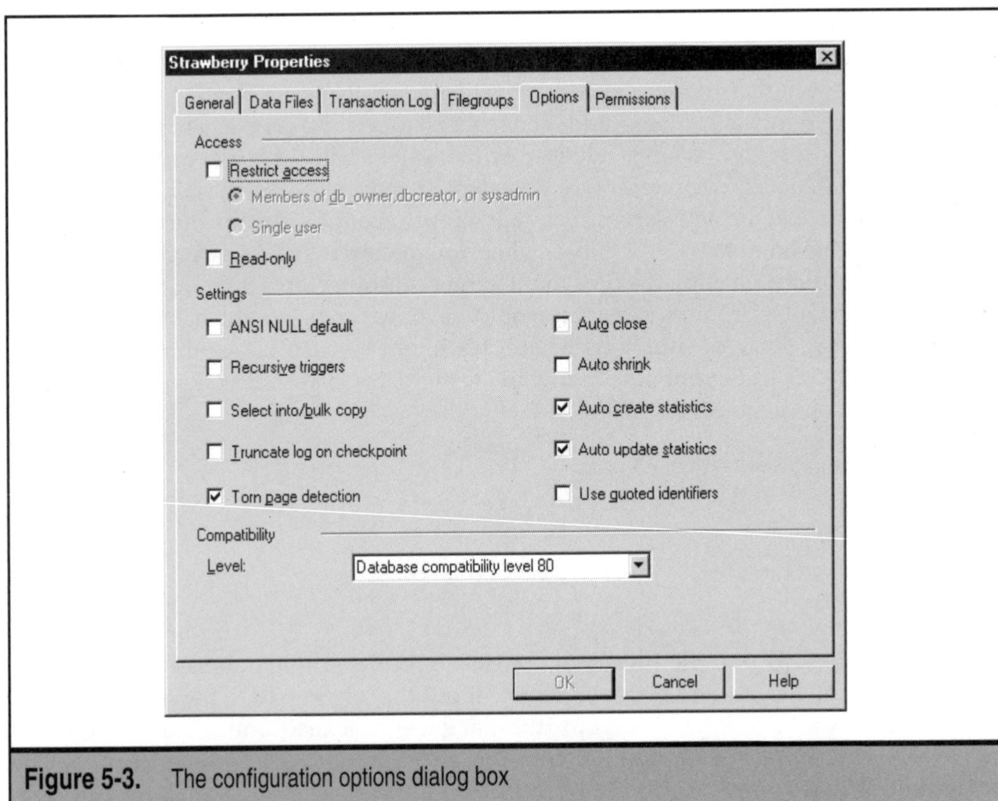

Figure 5-3. The configuration options dialog box

Security Access

When you are developing a database, you may want to keep the data users out of the database. Normally you can do this by simply not giving them user access to the database and not adding a guest account. If you want to be a little more secure, you have two options: either restrict access to the database or make the database read-only. If you opt to restrict access, you can further limit access only to members of the database_owner, dbcreator, or sysadmin roles, or you can simply make the database single user. If you decide to make the database read-only, no user can make any user data changes. SQL Server will still be able to perform its internal functions, such as reading and writing pages.

If you decide to go ahead and restrict access to the database, you'll have to remember to make your database programmers members of one of the db_owner, dbcreator, or sysadmin database roles, rather than just db_ddladmins. We would suggest leaving these settings for the DBA to use when creating or restoring databases.

Read-Only

This option looks obvious, but let's look a little more closely. If you have a truly read-only database—for example, a database containing archived data that by definition should not be changed—the read-only setting might be very handy. By default, whenever a query selects data from an updateable database, it has to lock the data so that nobody can change it while the data is being read. Even if locking is happening at the page level, it takes time to lock the page, read the rows, and unlock the page. But if the database is read-only, SQL Server knows that nobody can change the data, so it does not bother to lock the data as it is being read. The result is a significant increase in the query performance. There are other ways to achieve similar results with locking mechanisms and transaction isolation levels, which we'll talk about later, but for now, think about this option for your archive databases. The only downside is that when the DBA refreshes or loads in new data, she will have to disable the read-only property for the load operation. Then the DBA can reset it when the load is done. This is easily achieved with a script.

ANSI NULL Default

Of all the database options, this is the one with the most potential for confusion. SQL Books Online gives the deceptively simple explanation, "specifies whether database columns are defined as NULL or NOT NULL by default." But there's more to it than that, and you need to be aware of other settings, too. Every column in a table can either allow NULL values if the column is created with the NULL property, or the column can require a value be supplied if it has the NOT NULL property set for that column. The ANSI standard is that if you do not specify NULL or NOT NULL, the column will allow NULLs.

When you look at this database options list, notice that this box is not checked by default. This implies that the ANSI standard is not being enforced. But if you create a table in Enterprise Manager and check the columns, you will find that they allow NULLs. Remember, this is not the only way you can create a table, and even an application can modify the ANSI NULL setting. The ANSI standard option can be set in several different places: for the server, for the database, or for the connection. When you use Enterprise Manager, for example, the ANSI standard is enforced (NULL by default). If you run a script in the Query Analyzer to create a table and don't specify NULL or NOT NULL, nullability will be determined by the setting in this properties window (see Figure 5-3). If you create a table from an application like MS Access that uses an ODBC or OLE-DB connection to the SQL Server, (generally) the default will be NULL or the ANSI standard.

Really, there's only one approach that works all the time, and that is to specify for every column you create whether it should be NULL or NOT NULL. This ensures that you will get the NULL behavior you're expecting even if you generate a script from an existing database and re-create it on another database, another server, or even on a different RDBMS.

Recursive Triggers

Once again, the entry in SQL Books Online gives little indication of the potential for trouble contained in this option. We'll be talking about triggers in much more detail later on, but briefly, a *trigger* is code that is activated when a table is modified. An example might be that you add a column to a table that records the username of the person who last updated the row. Rather than expecting the user to remember to update this column, you write a trigger, so whenever the user updates any column, SQL Server grabs the username and inserts it into the LastModifiedBy column. But the trigger is itself modifying the table, which could cause the trigger to fire again, which would insert the username, which would then fire the trigger, and so on. This would be an infinite loop if not for the 32-level limit on triggers activating triggers imposed by SQL Server. By default, SQL Server prevents this kind of runaway trigger action by not allowing a trigger to activate the triggers again on the *same* table. It can still modify another table, activating a trigger that modifies a third table. There are a few cases, such as Gantt charts, where recursive triggers might be useful, and we'll go into more detail when we get to triggers later in the book. The big gotcha here is that the recursive trigger option is a database option—if you turn it on, all your triggers will be recursive, and if you leave it turned off, you cannot use a recursive trigger for just a single situation. Ideally, you want to be able to specify, for any given trigger, whether it should be recursive or not. Check future releases of SQL Server to see whether this feature is ever implemented.

Select Into/Bulk Copy

This option would usually be set by the DBA before performing a bulk import of data, so it might be useful when you are building databases. It allows nonlogged operations (inserts), meaning that SQL Server does not write an entry to the transaction log for every row inserted. Obviously that is a big time and space saver compared to a logged insert, especially when importing many hundreds of thousands of rows. However, it is not possible to perform a nonlogged insert on a table that has indexes, because the index values have to be updated as each row is inserted. The same limitation applies where there is a primary key or unique constraint on the table, because they are built on an index. Some DBAs, when they have large amounts of data to import, like to drop the indexes and constraints, import the data, and then reapply the constraints and rebuild the indexes. As the designer, you may be called upon to assist in setting up the scripts to make sure that the constraints and indexes are rebuilt correctly. Later, if you modify the indexes or constraints, you may want to coordinate with the DBA to make sure she is aware of the changes you've made.

Truncate Log on Checkpoint

It is quite common to see this option set on test databases and very unusual to see it on a production database. When a checkpoint occurs (and we'll be talking about checkpoints more when we discuss transactions later in the book), the changes that have been made to data in memory are written out to the physical database. This option, when activated, instructs SQL Server to remove the entries from the transaction log that have been written to the database on disk. The intent is to free up space in the log and make sure the log does not overflow or auto-grow so that it fills up the disk. The danger with this scheme is that if there is a problem with the data disk, you could lose data. With Truncate Log On Checkpoint checked, you've thrown away your transaction log so you cannot restore the most recent changes to the database. The best you can do is to restore the most current backup. Any changes that have been made to the database since you made this backup are lost. That's why it is not a good idea to use this option on production databases. You might use it on an archive database, where you can reload the most recent data should the database crash, but you would not use it on a production database. The test databases that come with SQL Server—Pubs and Northwind—have this option checked because normally you wouldn't bother to back them up or care if any changes you make are preserved or not.

By the way, in the Install directory of your SQL Server installation, on the hard disk, are two script files: instnwnd.sql and instpubs.sql. They can be run from the Query Analyzer to rebuild Northwind and Pubs, respectively, so you don't need to worry about messing up these two databases in your testing.

Torn Page Detection

You would need this option only if you were having hardware problems. Suppose you have some data on a page and you delete the record, freeing up the space. You begin to write another record over the top of the old one, but part of the way through writing, an error occurs. Now you have part of the new record and part of the old record, which is obviously going to cause problems when you try to read the record. It is exactly like looking at a torn page in a book, where you can see part of the page and part of the page below it. (Don't try that experiment on this book, please.) While selecting this option may give you an extra level of error checking, it does add some overhead, as SQL Server checks the pages on both read and write operations. This option was not selected by default in previous versions of SQL Server, but it is now selected by default in SQL Server 2000. For a performance enhancement, turn it off.

Auto Close

This option closes databases that have no current user connections. It will also free up any resources—such as memory—being used by that database. If you are so low on resources that this option looks worth implementing, you need to think about moving one or more databases to another server or adding more resources to your current database server.

Auto Shrink

If this option is turned on, the database will automatically shrink itself. Periodically, SQL Server will check to see whether there is enough free space in the database to justify shrinking itself and reclaiming the free space.

Auto Create Statistics

There's really no reason to turn off this option. As you will see when we discuss indexes, the Query Optimizer uses the statistical information about the indexes to determine the optimal way to run the query. It can even calculate statistics for columns that are not indexed if it thinks that information will be of value in optimizing a query.

Auto Update Statistics

This option partners with the previous option, and again, we see no reason to turn it off. Actually, if you create statistics but don't update them, performance could really suffer over the long run because the Query Optimizer would be basing its decisions on out-of-date statistical information, and that might be worse than not having any statistical information at all.

Use Quoted Identifiers

One of the features introduced in SQL Server 7.0 is a feature that users of databases such as Microsoft Access have had for years: the ability to use spaces in object names, like the Order Details table in Northwind. We're still not convinced that allowing spaces in table names is a good idea, but there's no going back now. Even if SQL Server can handle spaces in names, you may find that you have to interact with other database management systems that do not support this feature.

If you do use spaces, you'll have to decide how you will tell SQL Server that there is a space in the name. Otherwise SQL Server will get confused. For example, it might try to parse "Order Details" as the Order table and not know what to do with the word "Details." You can use square brackets, as in [Order Details], which always works. In fact, if you ask SQL Server to generate scripts for you, you will see that it puts square brackets around every object name. That way it does not have to decide whether there's a space in the name or not.

The alternative is to turn on Quoted Identifiers. Normally SQL Server is very flexible about whether you can use single or double quotes for text strings and such. If you turn on this option, double quotes are used to designate an object name, such as "client name." Then you *must* use single quotes for text strings, as in 'Hamilton.' It's a personal preference, but we prefer to stay with no spaces in object names (use an underscore for readability), use the square brackets if totally necessary, and retain the full flexibility of single or double quotes in queries.

Database Compatibility Level

It is possible to make SQL Server 2000 behave like earlier versions of SQL Server, at least versions 6.0, 6.5, and 7.0. The compatibility level is really restricted to certain SQL statements, so your scripts, triggers, and stored procedures that may have been created under a previous version of SQL Server will run the same way they used to. But SQL Server still uses the new performance enhancements, storage mechanisms, query optimization, and so on from the latest version. If you are just getting started with SQL Server, and you're on the 2000 release, you should leave this compatibility setting alone, at the default of version 8.0 (default level 80). SQL Server 2000 is its "public" name, but it really is SQL Server V 8.0.

If you upgraded your databases from an earlier version, SQL Server will set this compatibility level to the correct value for the version under which the databases were running. In other words, if you upgraded a SQL Server 7.0 database, the database compatibility level should be automatically set to level 70. You can check your code to make sure it runs correctly—and as expected—under version 8.0, at which point you can change the database compatibility level setting to 8.0.

CHAPTER 6

Building Tables

In this chapter, we will start building the tables for our example application and discuss how you can translate the models you built previously into a set of tables with the appropriate columns, containing the correct type of data. We will look at how data is stored in SQL Server and how that impacts your table design strategy. And we will examine how the automatic numbering schemes work in SQL Server. First, though, we need to discuss datatypes, how they are used, and the pros and cons of user-defined datatypes.

DATATYPES IN SQL SERVER 2000

A datatype in SQL Server is a property of a column. It specifies the type of data and the format of the data that can be entered into the column. Examples of datatypes include numeric, alphanumeric or character, date/time, money, and so on. Every column must have a datatype defined when it is created. Some datatypes, such as integer, occupy a fixed number of bytes. Other datatypes, such as character, require that you specify the size or width of the column. Whenever data is entered into a column it must be presented in the correct format for the datatype, and in many cases it must fit within an allowed range of values for that datatype. Once you create the column it is possible to go back and change the datatype, from either the table design interface in Enterprise Manager or by using T-SQL. However, you should be very careful about doing this, because of the risk of data truncation or loss.

SQL Server makes a set of system-supplied datatypes available. At first glance it might appear that you can extend this with user-defined datatypes, but the user-defined datatypes are really just variants of the system-supplied datatypes.

System-Supplied Datatypes

Knowing the various available datatypes and their behavior will allow you to make the best choice for each column, keeping in mind the storage requirements of each datatype and the range of values each can handle. You should also keep in mind that you may have to remain compatible with other database management systems, so you might not be able to use every T-SQL datatype. Each database management system has its own variation on the standard set of datatypes, so if you plan on cross-platform replication of data or updating multiple heterogeneous databases, stay with the most basic of the datatypes.

As an example, the following SQL statement will create the Person table in your Strawberry database:

```
CREATE TABLE tblPerson (
      PersonID INT IDENTITY NOT NULL,
      LastName VARCHAR(20) NOT NULL,
      FirstName VARCHAR(20) NOT NULL,
      MailingAddr VARCHAR(40) NULL,
      City VARCHAR(20) NULL,
      State CHAR(2) NULL,
      Zip CHAR(10) NULL,
      PersonType CHAR(1) NULL)
ON PRIMARY
```

The CHAR and VARCHAR columns contain alphanumeric (text) data. Assuming that you're using the United States format, the state and zip codes are always the same length, so they will use the fixed-length character (CHAR) datatype. But the names, street address, and city can vary in length, so you will use the VARCHAR or variable-length character datatype. The only noncharacter datatype in this table is PersonID, which is an integer (INT) datatype with the identity property, which is the automatic number-generator for values of PersonID, without any intervention on the part of the user.

Let's take a look at each of the system-supplied datatypes and see how you might use them in your database design.

Character Datatypes

Two of the SQL Server 2000 character datatypes, CHAR and VARCHAR, can be as long as 8000 bytes. Version 7.0 raised the limit on character data from 255 bytes to 8000. While this change has made the character datatype more flexible, you might encounter some problems when your client interface, such as MS Access, doesn't have the capability to handle such long strings of data. Until the client tools catch up with this database functionality, you'll have to limit the maximum length of your user interface character data fields to match the capability of the tool you're using.

As you saw in the example above, some character fields can be a fixed length, and some can be variable length. Use the CHAR datatype for columns whose value set will always (or nearly always) contain the same number of bytes. For instance, the State column is a CHAR(2) datatype. U.S. state codes are always 2 bytes long. U.S. zip codes are always either 5 or 10 bytes long (zip + 4), thus you should make the Zip column a CHAR(10) and store the formatting.

You use the VARCHAR datatype for these columns whose contents will vary in length, but you specify the maximum length permitted for the column. The VARCHAR datatype is great for columns such as first and last names, street addresses, city names, and so on, which are typically between 6 and 15 characters, but could be up to 30 or 40 characters in length. Obviously the intent here is to store less data by storing only the data string rather than the data string plus spaces. Later in this chapter, when we discuss data storage, we'll look at the trade-offs between more compact storage and the extra CPU cycles required to handle variable-length data. The question you need to ask when designing the table is whether you'll really be saving significant amounts of space. In other words, if you have a column like LastName that may occasionally require up to 20 characters but is typically around 6 to 10, it may be worthwhile using a variable-length datatype. But if you are looking at a column where the values set is normally nearly as long as the datatype length, it may not be worth the added overhead to make this a variable character datatype. You would not, for example, use a variable-length datatype for a product code, where 98 percent of your products have a five-character code and only 2 percent have an older three-character code.

SQL Server 7.0 introduced Unicode datatypes, where 2 bytes are used instead of 1 to represent a character. The two newest character datatypes are NCHAR and NVARCHAR, for fixed or variable-length data, respectively. The benefit of using Unicode datatypes is the ability to handle foreign languages, including Pacific Rim graphical-based character sets like Chinese and Japanese. The downside is that your storage requirements (hard disk and RAM) will double, and it will take longer to read and write the data. Sometimes you have to use Unicode datatypes. Case in point: Your Pacific Rim affiliate has sent data in their native language, and you have to import it into your database. When you installed SQL Server you chose a character set that wouldn't support Chinese characters. SQL Server 2000 gets around many of the problems of previous versions by allowing you to control the collation order at the table level. Collation determines how your result sets will be ordered. It's similar to sort order and is applied across multiple languages rather than just to one character set. So you are no longer limited by a fixed sort order and character set for the entire server. This gives you the flexibility to store data in multiple languages. If you need to find out what character set and sort order was chosen during installation, run the stored procedure SP_HELPSORT and it will show you the settings for your current database.

Numeric Datatypes

There are so many numeric datatypes in SQL Server that it's tricky to keep track of them. Another numeric datatype, BIGINT, was added with SQL Server 2000. The integer datatypes are often used not only for entering data values, but also as a row number or identifier. We'll talk later about the identity property, which SQL Server uses to automatically increment numbers, such as an invoice number or customer number, without any interaction on the part of the end-user. The four integer datatypes are INT, SMALLINT, TINYINT, and BIGINT. They vary in the number of bytes of storage that they occupy and therefore in the size of the number they can represent. The INTEGER datatype is 4 bytes long and can handle numbers between -2,147,483,648 and 2,147,483,647. You might think that this value of over 2 billion would be enough to allow for unique record identifiers for any application, but some users wanted larger numbers, hence the introduction of BIGINT, which uses 8 bytes to handle values from -2^{63} to $(2^{63} - 1)$, or -9,223,372,036,854,775,808 through 9,223,372,036,854,775,807. BIGINT should be good for almost anything except astronomical applications and the national debt.

At the other end of the scale, you have the option of using SMALLINT, which is quite economical at only 2 bytes, on the understanding that you can use only values between -32,768 and 32,767. Perhaps this would work for the set of employee numbers in a small company or product numbers if your company manufactures only a few dozen products. It might work for an employee identifier in the Strawberry database, as it's unlikely that you'll be tracking more than 32,000 employees. But it might be risky using SMALLINT for product numbers in Northwind, as the day may come when you are importing more than 32,000 products (a large supermarket may have 40,000 products in stock or available for order).

If you are feeling parsimonious about your disk space, consider TINYINT, which at 1 byte is positively frugal. However, it can accommodate only values from 0 to 255, with no negative numbers. You might use this to number your branch offices if you do not plan to add more offices than the datatype allows, or it might be suitable for allocating bin numbers in your private wine cellar (you wish!).

Decimal Values

Integers are relatively simple to work with—just determine the range of values to be stored and pick the appropriate datatype. Things get a little more complex once you start dealing with decimal points. To pick the right datatype for a column, you need to know what type of decimal values you are storing and how you want the values returned. If this seems confusing, remember that the computer is not storing decimal values, it is storing ones and zeros. Some decimal values, such as the decimal equivalent of one tenth, or 0.1, can be represented accurately. Other values, such as one third, or pi, cannot, because they never end. So you have two types of decimal values—those that can be stored as an exact equivalent and those that cannot and must be stored as an approximation. For exact numeric values, you want to use the DECIMAL or NUMERIC datatype. This datatype stores and returns exactly what you type in, to the degree of accuracy you define. You must specify the total number of digits to be stored, which is referred to as the *precision*. You also have to say how many digits will appear to the right of the decimal point, in an area known as the *scale*. So decimal (12.5) will have a total of 12 digits, up to 7 to the left of the decimal point and 5 to the right. You don't count the decimal point (that warning is for anyone who used to program in Fortran or COBOL, where you do count the decimal point).

On the other hand, in some situations you may be storing scientific measurements, for example, where the last decimal place is within the margin of error. In this case, the FLOAT or REAL datatypes may be a better choice. These datatypes store a very close approximation of the data entered, so sometimes there may be a tiny difference between what was entered and what was returned. You shouldn't use them with comparisons where you are looking for exact matches, such as the equal or not equal operator. It's okay to perform comparisons looking for all values greater than or less than some limit—just avoid the exact comparisons.

Money as a Datatype

Two datatypes are used specifically for money values, called MONEY and SMALLMONEY. Again the difference is in how many bytes they occupy in storage. MONEY takes 8 bytes, and SMALLMONEY takes 4 bytes. MONEY can store values of plus or minus 922 trillion, and SMALLMONEY, the financial datatype for the rest of us, stores plus or minus 214,748. (A student in one of our classes, who must have been depressed at the time, asked if there was a TINYMONEY datatype. There is not, nor is there a BIGMONEY for all the dot-com entrepreneurs out there.) Both MONEY and SMALLMONEY store the data to five decimal places of accuracy but display four. This brings up an interesting point: many brokerage companies use the DECIMAL datatype instead of the MONEY, because they deal in 1/32 parts of shares that require five decimal places. Another factor in your decision about money datatypes is the currency in which you will be entering data. There are quite a few countries where the SMALLMONEY limit of 214,748 in local currency will just buy you a cup of coffee. In these cases, you could use the MONEY datatype or you could make the column an integer, because in currencies where it costs 50,000 lira to buy a snack, nobody uses decimal points.

Dates and Times

Date and time handling and storage in SQL Server 2000 still leave something to be desired. The problem is an old one: Date and time are stored as a combined field. There's no way to separate them at the table level. Figure 6-1 is an example of the combined DATETIME datatype. The first query extracts a start date and an end date from the Event table. Notice that, while the dates are displayed in an acceptable format, the times, by default, are set to midnight. This is more than annoying: it is misleading. If you don't have or don't want to store a time in a column, and all you have available is a DATETIME datatype, then at the very least the time component of the DATETIME datatype should be set to NULL, not to midnight.

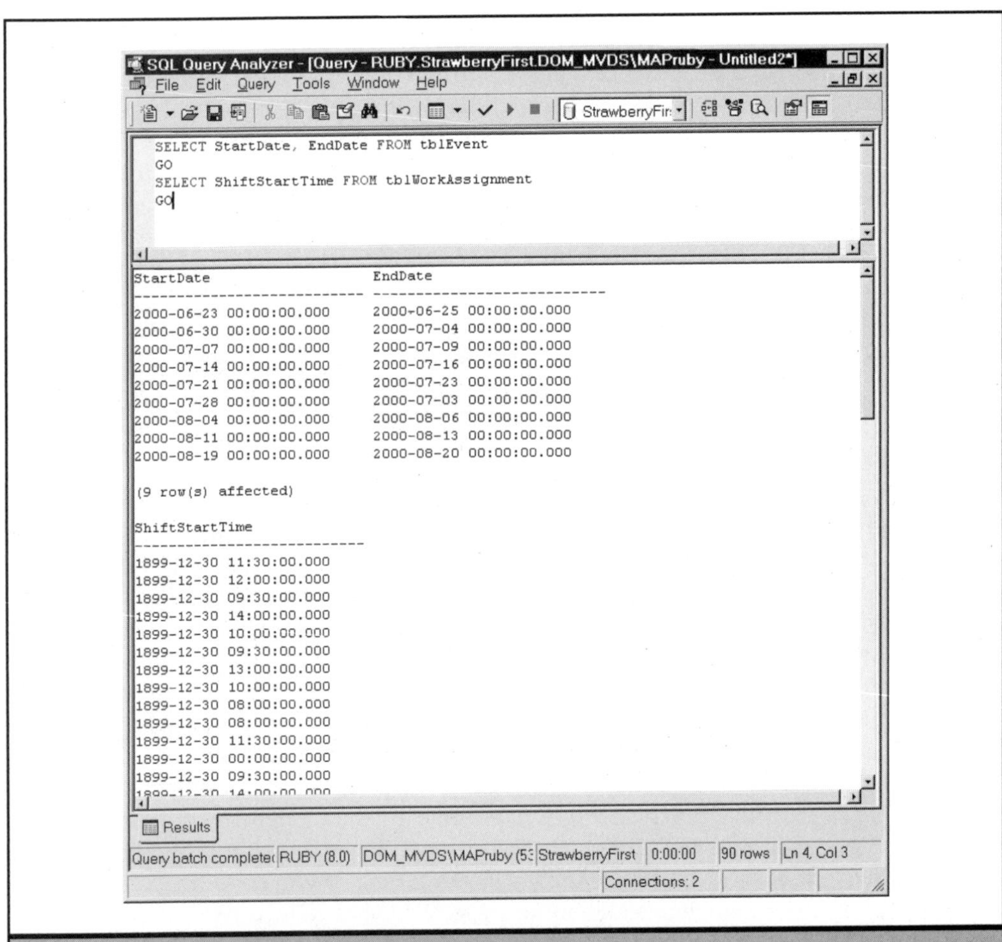

Figure 6-1. The T-SQL DATETIME datatype, in which both date and time are combined

Similarly, the second query extracts time data from the WorkAssignment table. Notice that, while the times are displayed in an acceptable format (if you like the 24-hour clock), the dates are set to the 30th of December 1899! Once again, if you don't want to store date data in a column, the date component of the DATETIME datatype should be set to NULL. By plugging in a default value that is a real date when you actually mean "nothing" or "unknown," you're compromising the integrity of the data in your database. At some point, Microsoft will wake up and introduce separate date and time datatypes. The functions for manipulating times and performing date/time calculations are also rather awkward to use. There are two date/time datatypes, DATETIME and SMALLDATETIME. The DATETIME datatype is stored as a pair of 4-byte integers. The first 4 bytes store the number of days before or after January 1, 1900, the base date or system reference date. The second 4 bytes store the time of day in milliseconds since midnight. The SMALLDATETYPE datatype is less precise; it's stored as a pair of 2-byte integers, the first of which stores the days after January 1, 1900, the second of which counts time in minutes since midnight.

The question to ask with these datatypes is whether you really need the extra precision of the DATETIME datatype, and in many cases the answer is no. The SMALLDATETIME can represent dates between 1 January 1900 and 6 June 2079. It's accurate to the minute, so it would work fine for fields such as when a database record was last changed or when an order was placed. Even if you are planning ahead, it's quite likely that by 2079 we will be using SQL Server Version 48, which (we hope) will support a different set of date and time datatypes. Use the DATETIME datatype only if you need to store dates beyond the range that SMALLDATETIME can handle or if you need more up-to-the-millisecond accuracy. The DATETIME datatype stores data to the millisecond, although it's accurate only to 1/300 of a second, or 3.33 milliseconds. It also can represent years between 1753 and 9999. The upper limit is fairly obvious: We don't want to return a five-digit year to a client application that isn't ready to handle it. (Can you see the beginning of a Y10K problem here?) But why is 1753 the DATETIME lower limit? Is it a technical limit based on the storage capability of the 4-byte datatype? (No.) We'll discuss this question later. For now, regard it as today's brainteaser.

Binary Datatype

If you need to store binary data—streams of bits—you have the same choice as for character data: either fixed-length columns or variable length with a maximum specified. These datatypes are known as *binary* and *varbinary*. Capacity for each (maximum length) is 8000 bytes. SQL Server Books Online suggests that you "use binary data when storing hexadecimal values such as a security identification number (SID), a GUID (using the uniqueidentifier datatype), or a complex number that can be stored using hexadecimal shorthand."

TEXT, NTEXT, and IMAGE Datatypes

SQL Server treats TEXT and IMAGE datatypes different from other system-supplied datatypes. TEXT is the term used for variable-length, non-Unicode character data that is too large to fit into the 8000-byte limit of a CHAR or VARCHAR column. It has a maximum capacity of 2,147,483,647 characters or bytes (2 gigabytes). You could store an employee's résumé, a production description, or a legal document in a TEXT column. The NTEXT datatype is variable-length, Unicode character data with half the capacity of the TEXT datatype (1,073,741,823 characters). If you recall, Unicode datatypes use 2 bytes to store a single character, unlike non-Unicode datatypes that store a character in a single byte.

Image data—sometimes referred to as BLOBs (binary large objects), such as digital or scanned images, word processor files, and scanned documents—can easily exceed the 8000-byte limit imposed by the CHAR and VARCHAR datatypes. They need a little special treatment. SQL Server has the IMAGE datatype, with a storage capacity of 2 GB. Only a pointer to the image data is stored in the table; the image itself is stored in a set of pages elsewhere in the database. SQL Server uses different storage strategies depending on the size of the BLOB being stored, but all work on the same basic principle of a pointer in the row that points to the start page of the set of pages that contain the image data.

SQL Server 2000 introduced an exception to storing the image outside the table with the "text in row" feature of the SP_TABLEOPTION system stored procedure. You can set a limit in bytes, up to 7000, and force SQL Server to store TEXT or IMAGE data smaller than this value directly in the table. When the TEXT/IMAGE data exceeds this length, SQL Server reverts to setting a pointer in the row and placing the TEXT/IMAGE outside the table, as a set of separate pages. For example, the syntax to set the storage cut-off point at 2400 bytes would be this:

```
EXEC SP_TABLEOPTION 'tblPerson', 'text in row', 2400
```

While being able to store TEXT or IMAGE data in the database sounds very useful, you may want to think carefully before designating columns as TEXT, NTEXT, or IMAGE datatypes. Columns of these datatypes are trickier to work with than most other datatypes. Inserts, updates, and even data retrieval is different from other datatypes. Changes made to these columns are usually not logged; this complicates recovery in case of a system failure. One reason why TEXT, NTEXT, and IMAGE data is not logged is because the transaction log would fill up very rapidly—imagine keeping the "before" and "after" images of an NTEXT file—potentially causing the SQL Server to come to a screeching halt as the transaction log fills the entire hard disk. Then you have to consider how your client interface software is going to handle this type of data. Because of the complexity introduced by TEXT, NTEXT, and IMAGE data, some developers choose to handle data storage manually. They don't list this data as a column in a table. Instead they store the data in external NT system files, and in the database, they store a path to these files, as a UNC or a URL. Either approach is complex!

The TEXT datatype should be used for plain text data. If you want to store Microsoft Word documents or Excel spreadsheets in their native formats, you'll have to use the IMAGE datatype. This seems a little odd, but it may help to think of TEXT as the extended datatype for character data, and IMAGE as the extended datatype for binary data. Thus you would use the IMAGE datatype to store documents as binary representations of themselves. SQL Server can perform full-text indexing on Word, Excel, PowerPoint, and HTML files, in addition to being able to index text and character data. Full-text indexing allows you to do fuzzy-logic searches for words and phrases in a document. If you implement full-text search capability, you'll have to plan for an extra column in the table to store the file extensions for each of your image columns. This gives SQL Server a hint about what type of data is stored in the IMAGE column. Also, keep in mind that while you can use the full-text indexing feature on TEXT, NTEXT, or IMAGE datatypes, you cannot build a regular index on columns of this type.

We suggest that if you really need to track a lot of Word or Excel data you might consider a third-party software package such as PC Docs, which is itself built on SQL Server and is already optimized for document management.

Special Datatypes

There are some datatypes that do not belong to any of the categories we've discussed so far, and that are used for specific purposes. They are known as special datatypes. One of these is the BIT datatype, which is an integer with a value of 0 or 1. It's used for true/false or yes/no values. For example, in the Pubs database, the Authors table includes a BIT datatype to designate whether or not the author has a contract. If you have several of these flags in the table, it can be a very economical datatype because it can store up to eight values in one byte. However, you have to make sure that the complete set of valid values for this column with a BIT datatype will be yes, no, or NULL. As soon as you need to add a fourth value, you'll need to modify the datatype to at least a CHAR(1).

TIMESTAMP is a datatype that causes some confusion because of its name. It really is not a date or time value. Rather, it is a binary value assigned by a SQL Server to track the relative sequence in which events take place. It has a number of uses, including being an important part of the recovery process when the SQL Server restarts after a shutdown. It also is used when updating records through a client application such as Microsoft Access. The record is handed off to the client application with a timestamp. When the client submits the change, SQL Server checks to make sure that the timestamp on the record being submitted matches the timestamp of the record on the SQL Server. If there is a match, the update can proceed. If not, someone has modified the record on the server while the client was in the process of making changes, and the client update is rejected. This avoids having records locked by clients such as Access, which may download large numbers of records but only update one or two. In fact, if you use the Upsizing Tools to convert your database from Access to SQL Server, you will find that the upsizing process adds TIMESTAMP columns to your tables. Because the TIMESTAMP column is internally generated within the SQL Server, timestamps from one server mean nothing to another server, and hence TIMESTAMP columns cannot be replicated to another database as timestamps. If you try, you will find they get converted to binary values. There is no way to convert a timestamp to a time and date, so if you need to track when a record was last modified, you can add a column with the DATETIME or SMALLDATETIME datatype and update that column with a trigger when the data changes.

Also new in SQL Server 2000 is the SQL_VARIANT datatype, which offers the interesting option of storing different data values of different datatypes all in one column. The flexibility comes at a price, because SQL Server has to store for every record the data plus some metadata about that data value—including the datatype, its maximum size, the scale and precision, and the collation used. You can see that the overhead for this datatype can be significant.

The last datatype we'll look at is also new in SQL Server 2000, the TABLE datatype. It has a very specific use, which is to define a local variable of datatype TABLE, to store the result set from some processing routine to feed it to a subsequent process. Think of it as temporary storage for a set of rows returned from a query. Obviously this is not a datatype that you need to consider when designing your user tables.

User-Defined Datatypes

User-defined datatypes (UDTs) in SQL Server are datatypes that you can define for your own use in your own environment. They are constructed using system- supplied datatype building blocks. There can be some real benefits to defining your own datatypes, but there can also be some significant potential problems. As so often in the computer world, you have to consider the trade-offs, so before you start defining and implementing user-defined datatypes, carefully consider if they will be helpful in your environment or if they will be more trouble to maintain than they're worth.

One reason to use UDTs is to enforce consistency throughout your company or organization. Let's suppose that you define a ZIPCODE datatype of CHAR(10). (For non-U.S. readers, the zip or postal code in the U.S. has the format 12345-7890. But often only the first five digits are used or supplied, because the Post Office initially designed a five-digit postal code.) This new ZIPCODE datatype would avoid potential problems where one programmer uses a 10-character field, another decides that 5 characters is enough, and a third decides to store the full zip code but leave out the dash, so she uses 9 characters. A fourth programmer, who should have given the problem more thought, makes Zip Code a numeric field. He must have been raised on the West Coast, or he would realize that there are zip codes in the east which look like 000nn, but if stored as numeric data, would show as nn, dropping the leading zeros. Faced with this confusion, you decide to enforce a standard by making all the programmers use the ZIPCODE datatype anywhere a zip code is stored—for customers, suppliers, employees, and any other entity that uses a zip code.

User-defined datatypes, such as ZIPCODE, are specific to the database in which they were created. But you can take your standardization a step further if you wish, by defining this new datatype in the Model database. The datatype will then appear, and can be used, in any new database you create from that point on. You now have a corporate standard—or at least a standard for all databases on this SQL Server. For a true corporate standard, you would have to put the datatype into the model database on every server. As we suggested in a previous chapter, rather than go to all of this trouble, you might just have a script with all your standards defined and mandate that the programmers run the script immediately after creating a database to populate it with all of your standard objects.

One real benefit to UDTs is that they can also have defaults and rules associated with them. We'll talk in more detail about rules and defaults and how they work in Chapter 15. So, for example, you might define a datatype called STATECODE, making it a CHAR(2). Then you could add a rule to restrict the allowed values to the list of the 50 U.S. states, D.C., and the Canadian province codes. You might also add a default state code for the state where your company is located. From this point on, whenever you use the STATECODE datatype, the rule and the default come with it and are automatically applied. This sounds like a way to reduce the programming workload, but defaults and rules are not ANSI standard. So your code might not be portable to another database management system.

A real drawback to UDTs shows up when you try to port the application to a different database management system, even a relational one. While Oracle and Informix know how to handle character, number, and datetime data, they have no idea what to do with a STATECODE datatype or a ZIPCODE datatype. You'll see this problem not only if you port the application across database platforms, but you'll also see it if you start to replicate data between servers, even between SQL Servers, unless you've made sure when you set up replication that both servers have the same datatypes defined.

Another reason for not choosing to employ UDTs is their very limited scope, being only variations on system-supplied datatypes, albeit with the length, nullability, rules, and defaults all defined. Unlike a truly object-oriented database management system, in SQL Server you cannot create a whole new datatype with its own rules and behaviors. This is where UTDs could be really useful. For example, if you were building a GIS (Geographic Information Systems) application, it would be nice to be able to define datatypes for latitude and longitude, along with rules about how these datatypes should be handled in calculations. Unfortunately that is not yet possible with SQL Server 2000, although it is on our wish list. But SQL Server 2000 has made a step in the right direction with the introduction of user-defined functions, so if we could store the data in a convenient format, we could indeed write functions to handle the calculations (if we understood spherical trigonometry, that is).

Creating a User-Defined Datatype

You can create UDTs from within Enterprise Manager. If you expand a database listed in the hierarchy, you will see a symbol for User-Defined Data Types. Right-click on the symbol or in the right pane of the MMC window, and open a window for defining a datatype, as shown in Figure 6-2. Notice in this dialog box that there is a drop-down list labeled Data Type; this allows you to choose the system-supplied datatype on which to base this UDT. You will also see that you can bind a rule or a default to a UDT here, so that whenever the datatype is used, the rule and the default are invoked along with it. There is also a button (grayed out in this figure) that will show where the datatype is used once you have associated it with a column or columns.

The T-SQL syntax for setting up a UDT is

```
EXEC SP_ADDTYPE  name, datatype, nullability, owner
```

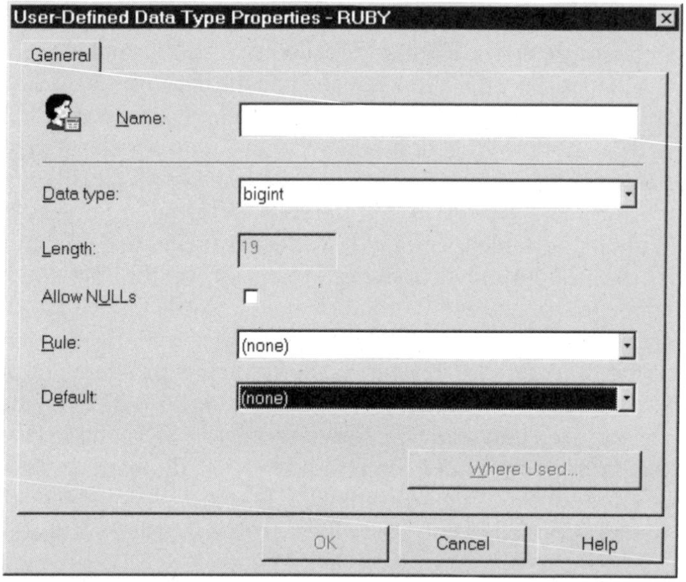

Figure 6-2. Creating a user-defined datatype is as easy as filling out a form.

This command has changed a little from SQL 7. The fourth argument, owner, is new in SQL Server 2000. It is meant to specifically designate the owner or creator of the new datatype being created. When not specified, it defaults to the current owner. So, to create a ZIPCODE datatype:

```
EXEC SP_ADDTYPE zipcode, 'char(10)', 'NOT NULL', 'dbo'
```

Notice that the foundation system datatype, the 'char(10)', has to be in quotes because it contains punctuation (the parentheses). Also, the 'NULL' or 'NOT NULL' and the owner name, if given, *must* be in quotes.

About that DATETIME Question

We promised that we would explain why 1753 is the earliest date you can enter in a DATETIME column. It all goes back to the time when the change was made from the Julian calendar to the Gregorian calendar. On the Julian calendar, by the early eighteenth century, the dates were out of synch with the seasons by almost two weeks. Pope Gregory XIII introduced the calendar we use today, which included a system of leap years—the one that caused all the confusion about whether the year 2000 was supposed to be a leap year or not. But it took a while before all countries adopted the new calendar, in part because the Protestant countries thought that it was a Catholic plot to cheat them of several weeks of their lives. Finally, by 1753 all countries that had been on the Julian calendar were converted to the new system, including Great Britain, where there had been riots when people were "robbed" of 14 days when the calendar was moved forward. (And we thought Y2K was a big deal.)

But during the 30 or so years of the transition, depending on which country you were visiting, you could cross a border and step from the 1st of May to the 14th of May. Literally, from one country to another there was a fortnight's difference in the date. Sybase made the decision early on to sidestep this problem altogether by not allowing dates before 1753, and Microsoft has not changed that. In addition to the fortnight differential in date, there was an additional problem, in that the calendar year used to begin in March. September, from the Latin word *septum* for seven, is our ninth month, and December, derived from the Latin *decem* for ten (decimal), is our twelfth month. This naming convention makes sense only if the year begins in March, which it used to. So if you want to know what day of the week was Groundhog Day in 1620 (assuming they had Groundhog Day back then), you would have to know if you were talking about the second month of 1620 or the eleventh. Confusing, to say the least. But unless you are a historian, you probably don't have a whole lot of contacts or customers or events in your database to track before 1753.

If you do need to store dates prior to 1753, there are a couple of schemes you could institute. If you don't need to worry about proper date formatting (February 2, 1620, for instance), you could store date detail in a character field, defining it as CHAR(8) and then populating it with date values in the format of YYYYMMDD (for example, 16200202).

CREATING TABLES

Once any UDTs are set up, it's time to start creating tables. In this chapter we are not generating the tables directly out of a CASE tool. We will look at how we would create tables using the Enterprise Manager tools or by writing our own Transact-SQL scripts.

Understanding Data Storage Allocation

When you start to build tables, it helps to keep in mind how SQL Server stores data and design your tables to work within these limits. The fundamental unit of storage in SQL Server 7/2000 is the page, which is 8KB (8192 bytes) in size. This is a big increase over version 6.5 and before, where the page size was 2KB. Because a row cannot span pages, the upper limit for any row is 8060 bytes—there's some overhead that accounts for the 132-byte difference between the total page size and the useable page size. If you add up all of the column sizes in a table, the total has to be less than 8060 bytes. So what happens with variable-length columns? The rule is that the data contained in the columns cannot exceed 8060 bytes. You can get away with building a table where the sum of the maximum column sizes in bytes is greater than 8060. When you create this table you will get a warning from SQL Server, because you are gambling that you will never "hit the jackpot" and try to max out each of the variable-length columns (fill them to capacity). If you ever do encounter a situation

SQL Server Row Size

In some books or articles, you might see the upper limit on row size given as 8092 rather than 8060. The reason stems from this peculiarity: Whenever you modify a row, the row information is written to the transaction log, along with a 32-byte description of the operation being performed. The difference between 8092 and 8060 is the size of the entry in the transaction log describing the modification operation. So the practical limit for your data is 8060 bytes.

where you need to use the maximum length of the variable-length columns, and you exceed the limit of 8060 bytes, you're out of luck. SQL Server will refuse to insert that row. It won't truncate the data; it'll just reject the entire row.

In SQL Server, the page is the smallest unit input or output (I/O). For random access processing, SQL Server will read a single page at a time. This means that whenever a query requests a row for processing, SQL Server reads the entire page. When a change is made to a single field of a single row, the entire page is written back to the hard disk. Pages are allocated to tables or indexes in 64KB blocks called *extents*. Each extent contains eight contiguous 8KB pages. At the start of the database file is a Global Allocation Map (GAM), containing a list of the allocated extents, which tables and indexes they are allocated to, and a list of the available free extents. So it's a quick task for SQL Server to allocate more extents as the tables and indexes grow. However, as the extents are allocated to the tables and indexes, the database file quickly becomes fragmented as the various table and index pages get interleaved. When we discuss indexes, we'll look at how index fragmentation can be minimized. But with the GAM, user table page fragmentation is not that big of a problem—SQL Server can quickly locate all the extents for a given table. The extent is also the unit of sequential I/O in SQL Server. When you back up your databases or when you launch a sequential process, SQL Server will read the data off the disk in extents, eight pages at a time.

Storing Variable-Length Columns

When we talked about variable-length columns earlier in this chapter, we pointed out how they can be space savers for most character data. However, variable-length columns do require a little more administration; SQL Server has to keep track of how many bytes occupy each column. The actual length of data in storage is the length of the character string plus 1 byte, so for example the name "Mary" will occupy 5 bytes—4 for the character string and 1 for the length byte. To optimize the storage and retrieval of data, SQL Server stores all the fixed-length columns first. This way it knows exactly where each column begins and how long it should be. If it interleaved fixed and variable-length columns, it would have to continuously calculate where each column began. Then it stores all the variable-length columns, and at the end of the row, it stores the data that lists the lengths of the variable columns and also stores flags to show whether the columns that allow nulls actually contain NULL. Organizing the different datatypes like this speeds up the retrieval process.

Fixed vs. Variable-Length Columns

This discussion swings back and forth with each release of SQL Server. The question is, are variable-length columns worth the space savings over fixed length, even though they do require that one extra length byte? Fixed-length columns always take the same amount of space, regardless of the length of the various character strings populating the column. But with fixed length there's no need to figure out how long the column is, and there's no need to break up the row data bytes into the correct variable-length columns. Obviously there's some CPU overhead involved in processing variable-length data. But there's also a benefit to reading and writing less data, which is what's happening with variable-length data. So you're trading CPU cycles for disk I/O. Which is better? It may depend on the speed of your processor(s), the speed of your disk arrays, the number of users accessing the system, and the way in which they are working with the system. This is definitely a case where you need to test both approaches, modeling after the way your clients will be using your system.

Two more points to keep in mind: variable-length columns don't make good candidates for indexing because of the increased overhead associated with handling of variable-length data, and there are update issues with variable-length columns. If a row is updated, and the data in a variable-length column is not going to fit back in the place on the page where it came from (an "update in place"), it has to write the row with the modified data to a new location and delete the original row. So, unless the update is an "update in place," you're looking at an insert followed by a delete operation.

Nulls and Storage

You might think that a column of worth NULL would not take up any space, but that's actually not always true. With SQL Server 7/2000, Microsoft changed the way it handles NULL. Now, if a column is a fixed length, it is *always* the set number of bytes as defined in the CREATE DATABASE statement. If it is NULL, it still occupies the same amount of space and the flag is set to indicate that this column is indeed considered NULL. If the column is variable length, when it is NULL its length is set to zero and the NULL indicator flag is set to TRUE. This differs from previous versions of SQL Server, where any fixed-length column that allowed NULLs automatically was treated as though it were a variable-length column. A fixed-length column could have a defined length if the instance had a value, or else be zero length if the instance were NULL. Programmers thought they were using fixed-length columns, but in fact they incurred the overhead of a variable-length column. From SQL 7 onward, you do indeed have a fixed-length column regardless of whether or not the instance is NULL, at the expense of a few bytes of storage. So a fixed-length column allowing NULL might not be a good choice for a second line of a street address, as chances are it will more often than not be NULL.

Creating a Table from the GUI

The SQL Server graphical user interface keeps getting better, and for creating tables, it's almost as good as the GUI in Microsoft Access. In fact, it looks very much like the interface from Access. To start designing a table from Enterprise Manager, expand the hierarchy and select the Database symbol. Expand the Database symbol so that the Tables symbol is visible. You should see the system tables, even in a brand new database. If you don't, back up and right-click on the Server name, select Edit SQL Server Registration Properties, and in the pop-up dialog box check the Show System Databases And System Objects check box. If you prefer not to clutter the interface with the system tables, uncheck that box, but if you do that, the Master and MSDB databases will not be visible.

Okay, back to the database. Right-click on Tables, or right-click in the right pane, and select New Table. You will see a window that looks like the one in Figure 6-3. For each column, the four critical values are shown in the grid. These are Column Name, Data Type, Length, and Allow Nulls. In SQL Server 2000, the other attributes of the column, including its description, default value, and precision/scale, have been moved to a lower window. The datatype offers a drop-down list, with the system datatypes listed first followed by the user-defined datatypes. It is possible to change the datatype or length of an existing

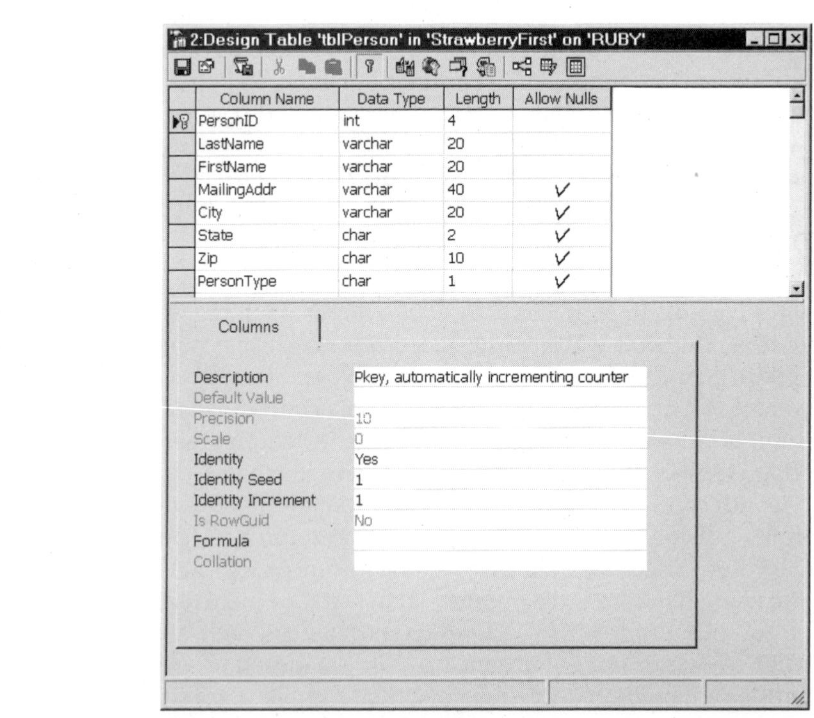

Figure 6-3. The graphical design-table interface gives you the opportunity to manage table architectures with ease.

column. Be very careful if you do that after you have loaded data, as you could truncate or totally lose data.

You can even change the name of the column. That's all right at the early stages of data modeling, but once you start creating relationships between tables, you should avoid changing object names. If you simply must change an object name once you've got relationships established and data loaded, seriously consider a third-party software package such as Speed Ferret, which will let you track down every place where the object is referenced and make the change. You can also change the Allow Nulls property of a column, but again, this raises potential problems—what if you need to change a column from NULL to NOT NULL even though the table contains some instances where this column is NULL? You're going to have to remedy the NULL conditions before you can make this change. It's better to take a little more time at the beginning to get the design right, rather than try to make changes later, once the database is in production!

There is one feature of the GUI that we find useful and cannot duplicate using T-SQL. When you use T-SQL to add a column, it is added to the end of the record and thus the column list when you retrieve the data in no special order, as in a "SELECT *" expression. SQL Server doesn't care about the column order, and most of the time you will not either. However, if this lack of order bugs you, you can use the GUI to rearrange the order of the columns. In the GUI, highlight the table name and right-click; then select Design Table. You can right-click on any column and select Insert Column to add the new column anywhere you want. If you simply want to reposition columns, you can click in the left margin of the column you want to move, wait until the cursor changes to an arrowhead, hold down the left mouse button, and drag the column to the new position. You can use this feature to keep associated columns close to each other—for example, when you add a second line for the street address and want to position it right after the first line and before the city name. (Another piece of trivia: In Great Britain, to be a city, you have to have a cathedral; otherwise, it's a town. In the United States, it appears that to qualify as a city, you need a post office or a saloon.)

Creating a Table with T-SQL

Let's take another look at that T-SQL script we used to start the chapter:

```
CREATE TABLE tblPerson (
      PersonID INT IDENTITY NOT NULL,
      LastName VARCHAR(20) NOT NULL,
      FirstName VARCHAR(20) NOT NULL,
      MailingAddr VARCHAR(40) NULL,
      City VARCHAR(20) NULL,
      State CHAR(2) NULL,
      Zip CHAR(10) NULL,
      PersonType CHAR(1) NULL)
ON PRIMARY
```

There are other options we can add here, including constraints, but we'll leave those for a later chapter and concentrate on the basic syntax. Note that every column has either NULL or NOT NULL specified. This is to avoid confusion regarding the default NULL behavior. ON PRIMARY instructs SQL Server to place the table on the primary filegroup. If you wanted to place the table on a different filegroup, as we discussed in Chapter 5, assumedly for performance reasons, you would simply give the filegroup name here. If you are not concerned about filegroups, you can leave out that one line because you would have left the primary filegroup as your default filegroup.

The Identity Property

The SQL Server identity property is an automatically incrementing number. There are many situations where an automatically incrementing number is very useful, such as for invoice numbers, employee numbers, purchase order numbers. Although this is not a datatype—it can be used with any one of several datatypes, including all the integer datatypes—it seems appropriate to mention it here. The automatically incrementing feature is actually a column property, allowing it to be used with various number datatypes. You can specify the starting value or "seed" and the increment, and either of those can be negative if you wish. The Northwind sample database makes extensive use of the identity property for values such as EmployeeID and OrderID. Most of the tables of the Strawberry database have identity properties, as we saw in Chapter 4. These incrementing values make good candidates for primary and foreign keys. They are typically small—the INT datatype is only 4 bytes—so they make for efficient indexing, and a single simple column is a lot easier to manage than combining multiple columns to come up with a unique identifier for each record.

We recommend building primary keys out of identity columns rather than trying to design what some refer to as a derived or "intelligent" primary key. An intelligent primary key contains values that are derived from some attributes of the data, such as the first four letters of a person's last name plus the last two digits of the year they were born. This string contains meaning. Programmatically it's neat to be able to extract information by parsing the primary key value. This scheme might work initially, but sooner or later the meaning will change or will become outdated. An employee changes her last name; the date of birth was originally entered incorrectly, thus rendering that part of the primary key value incorrect; someone joins the company who has the same last name and year of birth as someone else who already works here. You cannot live with duplicate primary keys, so you have to assign the new employee an EmpID that is a variation on the theme, thereby voiding the point of the "intelligent" primary key.

Only one column in a table can have the identity property. So you could not assign the identity property to both a sequential employee number and a sequentially numbered key to the health club, assuming that both columns are part of the same table. You can achieve the desired result with triggers, of course.

The Global Unique Identifier

One of the ongoing challenges facing managers of data warehouses is how to identify data from disparate sources as it is consolidated in their data store. Often different data sources have used different numbering schemes, and it is common to assign a new sequence number (an identity) to each incoming record to ensure that there is at least one guaranteed unique, reliable identifier per table. Another approach, new with SQL Server 7, is the *global unique identifier*. This is a datatype, and the concept is that it will generate a unique value, which will not be duplicated on any other SQL Server. It's generated using an algorithm that combines the MAC address of the network card in the SQL Server computer with the system clock time. This is a good solution for companies with offices in different locations, each of which may want to have an automatically incrementing sequencer without the risk of overlapping numbers. The payoff comes when you have to merge the data from the different branches into a data warehouse. You know that there will be no overlapping or duplicate values in this column.

Unlike the identity property, the global unique identifier (GUID) is implemented as a datatype, so you define a column with this datatype in your table. You then have to populate the column for every row you insert by calling the NEWID function, which then generates a value.

To create a Customer table with a GUID column, use the Enterprise Manager GUI, or from the SQL Query Analyzer window, run the following T-SQL:

```
CREATE TABLE tblCustomer
(CustomerID UNIQUEIDENTIFIER NOT NULL DEFAULT NEWID(),
 GivenName  Varchar(30) NOT NULL,
 FamilyName Varchar(30) NOT NULL,
 Address    Varchar(30) NOT NULL,
 City       Varchar(30) NOT NULL,
 StateCode  Char(2)    NOT NULL,
 ZipCode    Char(10)    NOT NULL )
```

In Chapter 10, when we look at how to modify data, we will examine how to insert values into a table when one of its columns is a GUID.

TABLE MAINTENANCE

It would be nice if, after you created the tables, you never had to change them. However, we've said it before and we'll surely say it again, change happens. Corporate direction and purpose change over time, companies buy up other companies and assimilate their databases. Your database will have to change to support what the company does. It's good to know that SQL Server has a set of commands that make table maintenance and modification easy.

However, just because operationally it's easy to drop or add a column, a table, or a stored procedure doesn't mean you should do so without regard for the consequences. In a production database, you *must* consider what repercussions your proposed action might have. If you rename a stored procedure, are there programs that reference it that will no longer run? If you want to drop a column that's been published as part of an article, and there are subscribers to this article, you won't be able to make this change. (We'll talk more about replication in Chapter 19.) If you want to add a column or a table, what kind of impact will that have on the normal form of the database? You need to go back to the data models, incorporate your proposed change, evaluate the impact, modify the new columns and tables as needed, and then add them to the database.

Adding and Dropping Columns

As we mentioned earlier, you can add a column or drop a column, even after you have started loading data into the database. You need to keep a couple of things in mind when you do this. First, when you drop a column, the data goes away—that sounds pretty obvious, but the point is that it really is gone. You cannot execute a ROLLBACK and recover the column and the data. The second thing is that when you add a column, you have to either allow NULL or supply a default value. This makes sense, because the column is added to existing rows in the table, and each instance of the newly added column must either be NULL or it must contain the default value you provided. For example, if your company is going international, you could add a country code column to all of the tables that contain address information, make it NOT NULL, and give it a default of USA. The data you currently have in your database is all from the United States; therefore the default value of USA is correct. Subsequent records added to the table will need a country code, because you indicated that records added to the table must be NOT NULL.

Adding a column from the Enterprise Manager GUI is as simple as opening a table in design mode, selecting a column name if you want to insert or clicking after the last column name if you want to append, right-clicking, and choosing Insert Column. Deleting a column is just as easy: open the table in design mode, select the column from the list, and then right-click, select Delete Column, and it's gone. At least, it's that easy if the column is not part of a relationship, as SQL Server will not make changes that would adversely impact referential integrity. To delete a column that is involved in a relationship you would first have to remove the relationship. SQL Server will actually offer to do this for you. It also requires that you remove any check constraints on the column, although it does not offer to do this for you—it just gives you a warning and then refuses to save the changes. And again, if the column is being replicated, you won't be able to drop the column.

If you want to use T-SQL to add or delete a column, the syntax is as follows:

```
ALTER TABLE tblCustomer
ADD Country VARCHAR(30) NOT NULL
DEFAULT  'USA'
```

Because the column is defined as not allowing NULL, and you have supplied a default, SQL Server will fill in all the existing rows with the default value. But what about adding a column that does allow NULL? In that case, you have a choice as to whether you leave the new column NULL or fill it in with a default value. If you supply a default value, that's what will be used for new records from this point forward. If you want to go back and fill in the old records with the default, use WITH VALUES to tell SQL Server to put the default value in all existing rows as well:

```
ALTER TABLE tblCustomer
ADD Country VARCHAR(30) NULL
DEFAULT  'USA' WITH VALUES
```

The T-SQL command to drop a column is

```
ALTER TABLE tblCustomer
DROP COLUMN Country
```

This looks simple enough, but there are a couple of gotchas you should know about. First, notice that you have to say that you are dropping a column, even though you did not need the keyword COLUMN in the ALTER TABLE...ADD statement. Second, there's a little problem with dropping a column if you've defined a default for the column. Microsoft has changed the way defaults are treated. In previous versions of SQL Server, this default would have been considered a "default constraint." However, in SQL 2000, supposedly a default such as this is not considered a constraint anymore. In fact, if you use Enterprise Manager Design Table to check the default constraints, you won't find defaults listed in the grid, as they were in SQL 7. Instead, defaults have been moved down into the properties box for each column. The defaults aren't even listed under the Defaults entry in the Database Hierarchy of Enterprise Manager. So a default looks like it's a column property. Okay so far, until you try to drop the column. Then you get a message that looks something like this:

```
Server: Msg 5074, Level 16, State 1, Line 1
The object 'DF__tblCustom__Count__09946309' is dependent on column
'Country'.
Server: Msg 4922, Level 16, State 1, Line 1
ALTER TABLE DROP COLUMN Country failed because one or more objects access
this column.
```

And of course, 'DF__tblCustom__Count__09946309' is a constraint name. SQL Server supplies names like this for constraints if you don't supply one. To really see defaults you have to run the following code:

```
SELECT * FROM sysobjects WHERE type = 'd'
```

So this default is in fact a constraint, and to get rid of it you will have to run this:

```
ALTER TABLE  tblCustomer
DROP CONSTRAINT  DF__tblCustom__Count__09946309
```

Then you can drop the column.

Removing Data from a Table

Occasionally you'll have a need to remove data wholesale from a table. This is typically a task reserved for test or development databases, where you need to "refresh" the data set. The fastest way to do this is to remove all the data from a table by truncating the table and then reload the table using the BCP utility.

Neither the TRUNCATE command nor the BCP utility are logged, so they both have minimum impact on the database server. Here's how to truncate or remove all of the data from a table:

```
TRUNCATE TABLE tblCustomer
```

As this operation is not logged, there's no changing your mind and rolling back the operation. The data is gone. You'll not be able to truncate a table if it has been published for replication or if it is involved in a relationship and is the parent table of the two. If it's the child table, you can truncate the data. If it's the parent table, you have to truncate the child table first before you can truncate the parent, or you have to drop the foreign key constraint between the two tables before you can truncate the parent table.

Removing a Table from the Database

Again, in a test or development environment, and once in a great while in a production environment, you'll need to remove a table from the database. Like the TRUNCATE command, the DROP TABLE command is not logged. The difference between these two commands is that while the TRUNCATE command removes just the data, the DROP TABLE command removes data plus structure. To remove a table from the database:

```
DROP TABLE tblCustomer
```

You will not be able to drop a table if it has been published for replication or if it is involved in a relationship and is the parent table of the two. If it's the child table, you can drop the table. If it's the parent table, you have to drop the child table first before you can drop the parent, or you have to remove the foreign key constraint between the two tables before you can drop the parent table.

Temporary Tables

Temporary tables are used in interim steps when you're processing large data sets or when your processing routines are lengthy or complex and you need to store partially processed data until the next step of your processing routine is ready for the input. Temporary tables are stored in the tempdb database, and all activity against these temporary tables is, in fact, logged. The logging is so that transactions can be rolled back; tempdb is not used to recover a SQL Server on system restart. There are two types of traditional temporary tables: local and global. To create a local temporary table, here's the syntax:

```
CREATE TABLE #MyLocalTempTable
(ID    INT           PRIMARY KEY,
 ColA                Varchar(30) NULL,
 ColB                Varchar(30) NULL,
 ColC                Varchar(30) NULL )
```

The pound or number sign (#) that precedes the table name indicates to SQL Server that this is a local temporary table. It's visible only to the session that created it. SQL Server will drop a local temporary table automatically at the end of the session that created it. If a local temporary table is created by a stored procedure, the table is dropped when the stored procedure completes. In this case, if a process (A) calls a stored procedure (B) that then creates the temporary table #MyLocalTempTable, only the stored procedure (B) can access the table. Process (A) cannot see or write to #MyLocalTempTable.

In the case where the stored procedure (B) is called by many processes (A, A1, A2), it's possible that there would be multiple copies of #MyLocalTempTable instantiated at the same time. SQL Server 2000 has a contingency plan: it appends to the temporary table name a system-generated numeric suffix to ensure uniqueness among multiple copies of #MyLocalTempTable. Because of this suffix, the limit on local temporary table names is 116 characters.

The second kind of temporary table, the global temporary table, is created very similarly to the local temporary table:

```
CREATE TABLE ##MyGlobalTempTable
(ID    INT           PRIMARY KEY,
 ColA                Varchar(30) NULL,
 ColB                Varchar(30) NULL,
 ColC                Varchar(30) NULL )
```

Two pound or number signs (##) are used to precede the table name. Global temporary tables are visible and useable by all active sessions, not only by the session that created it. SQL Server drops global temporary tables when the session that created them is terminated *and* when all other tasks (T-SQL queries) are no longer referencing the global temporary tables. To continue our example, if a process (A) creates the global temporary table ##MyGlobalTempTable, processes (A1) and (A2) can also access the data in ##MyGlobalTempTable. ##MyGlobalTempTable isn't removed until all tasks from processes (A), (A1), and (A2) have finished accessing the table. Also, if process (A) calls the stored procedure (B) that then creates ##MyGlobalTempTable2, all the processes, the stored procedure (B), the calling process (A), and the other processes (A1) and (A2), can access the table.

There's a third type of "temporary table," and that's a table you would create in tempdb to use for the same reasons that you would create a traditional temporary table. The tempdb database is rebuilt every time the SQL Server restarts, so any tables created on tempdb would indeed be temporary! These so-called "temporary tables" would be available even after the creating process terminated. They would be available until the next SQL Server system restart, specifically. Another added benefit: You can directly assign permissions to these "temporary tables." That's different from both local and global temporary tables. You can't assign permissions on local temporary tables, and you can't restrict anyone from seeing the contents of a global temporary table. We would suggest two things if you decide to use this type of "temporary table." First, develop a naming convention that is self-identifying, such as this:

```
CREATE TABLE tempdb.dbo.MyTempTabl …
```

Second, arrange to cycle your SQL Server at least once a day, so you don't overload or stress tempdb.

OBJECT OWNERSHIP

We cannot leave a chapter on building tables without discussing object ownership. Every database and every object has an owner, usually the person who created that object. You may wish to include in your design plans some discussion of who is going to own which objects in the database, but the bottom line is quite simple. In a production database, the database owner (dbo) owns all objects within a database. In a development database, all objects that are to become part of the final product are owned by the user dbo, perhaps with the exception of test objects and copies of data tables for testing, which might be owned by an individual developer. For this to work, everyone who is creating objects needs to get into the habit of creating objects with the dbo as owner. So the syntax of a CREATE TABLE statement should be

```
CREATE TABLE dbo.tblPerson …
```

If you do not follow these rules about object ownership, different people on the development team will own different objects. This is a security nightmare and vastly complicates assigning permissions. You may also find that two people might have used the same object name. It would be quite possible for Pubs to have tables called dbo.authors, michael.authors, michelle.authors, becky.authors, and so on, leading to confusion as each developer tried to place his or her table into production. An additional problem is that if Joshua owned an object in the database and left the company to become a dot-com entrepreneur, you could not delete his login because he still owns objects in the database. SQL Server won't delete the login and leave orphan objects floating around in the database. Fortunately, there is a stored procedure that you can use to change the ownership of an object:

```
Exec sp_changeobjectowner joshua.table1, dbo
```

This code will make the dbo the new owner of Joshua's table, table1.

A particular concern is when you run scripts that were originally built in SQL Server 6.5 and earlier databases. These scripts will probably not have any owner specified for the objects, so whoever runs the script will end up owning the objects. You need to modify these script to ensure that a dbo actually is given the ownership. This situation exists because, back in the good old days of SQL Server 6.5, the usual security model was to map all the developer logins to the dbo user account in the development database. Then any objects they created were by default owned by the dbo user account. This did result in a lack of accountability, because everyone showed up in the database as dbo. And very often the developers would require system administration privileges, which gave them almost unlimited powers over that database and any other databases on the server. The new security model from SQL Server 7 onward is to place all of your developers in the db_ddladmin role within a database. This gives them the right to create objects and to write data definition language (DDL) like CREATE TABLE and CREATE VIEW statements, but they still keep their individual SQL Server login and user names, and their Windows NT logins are also readily tracked. So now you know who is doing what in the database. Just remember, all developers now have to remember to add "dbo" in front of the object name when creating database objects.

PART III

Information Retrieval

CHAPTER 7

Data Retrieval

One of our deeply held beliefs is that the prime function of a database is *not* for storing data, it is for making information easily accessible. Studies have shown that more than 90 percent of all the pieces of paper filed in file cabinets are never looked at again. Hopefully, the data entered into your database will not suffer the same fate, even if it is used only to generate summary reports and analyze trends. If an individual record is needed, it should be easily and quickly retrieved. In this chapter, we will look at some SELECT statements, and focus on using the SQL 2000 Query Analyzer to optimize your queries.

SQL Server is the server side of a client/server software solution; it does not have a dedicated data reader/data writer interface for non-administrative users. You would not expect the typical end-user to query the database using the SQL Query Analyzer. Query Analyzer is a development tool we will use throughout the rest of this book. An end-user, a data reader or data writer, will most likely have a GUI interface to access the data, created from software such as Microsoft Access, Visual Basic, or PowerBuilder, and connected to the SQL Server databases. So why would you need or want to build and run queries on the SQL Server side, if you have an Access interface that will run queries? The answer is that by running queries on the server you're leveraging the client/server technology, which is an integral part of SQL Server. A client application (Access) can call a query (a stored procedure, usually) on the server, and will get in return only those rows that it specifically asked for. If the client application issued a request for a single row out of a 100,000-row customer table, the SQL Server would process this query and return to the client a single row of data. This is very quick, and places very little stress on the network. The other scenario is to locate all of your queries in the client program, which imposes a large load on the desktop computer (that is, the client) and on the network. If SQL Server is acting merely as a data store and the client computer is controlling the data processing, all queries are executed on the client and the entire set of tables involved in a query has to be transferred across the network, from the server to the client. Once at the client, the row restrictions and summarizing and processing of data take place. Data not in the result set is discarded. Contrast this to queries executing on the server, and it's obvious how inefficient this latter scheme truly is.

Quite often, when companies use the Microsoft upsizing tools to move an Access application to SQL Server, they find that the initial performance is not what they had hoped for. But really all that happened during the upsizing is that the data that was once stored in the Access database is now stored in a SQL Server database. None of the program code was optimized or modified to take advantage of the new client/server environment. In fact, if the Access application had, prior to upsizing, been used by only one person (it was contained entirely on his or her desktop computer), you may actually see a decrease in performance. The solution is to start rewriting code, and then move the processing off the client computers and onto the server.

The key to fast performance is to write queries and then compile them as stored procedures on the server. The client applications can call these stored procedures whenever they need to retrieve or modify data. The stored procedures are run on the SQL Server, which in most cases resides on a more powerful computer. The only network traffic is the result set from the query, plus some interaction between the client and the server computers. The stored procedures have to be written in T-SQL, of course, which for an Access programmer may mean learning a new programming language. But looking on the bright side, the stored procedures are written once in T-SQL and can then be called from any client application, whether it be written in Access, Visual Basic, PowerBuilder, or any other development environment. So it is possible to design and optimize the procedures once, on the SQL Server, and make them available for all the client applications to use.

In Chapter 17 we take a look at stored procedures, but in this chapter, the focus will be on the T-SQL component of these stored procedures, and also on the ad hoc queries that may be run by system administrators and a few power users or developers. As we discuss in Chapter 17, the capability to cache even ad hoc queries in memory for re-use, introduced in SQL Server 7, means you can see really good results with pass-through queries from the client. A pass-through query is one where the query code is sent directly from the client application to the server and run on the server, instead of the client sending a request to run a compiled stored procedure on the server.

AN INTRODUCTION TO THE QUERY ANALYZER WINDOW

As usual with SQL Server, when you have a choice of two ways to do a task, you'll be choosing between running your queries in a graphical environment (the Query Analyzer) or using the text-based option (the command-line O-SQL). O-SQL replaces the older I-SQL from versions 6.5 and earlier. If you don't already know how to use O-SQL, don't bother to learn now. O-SQL has an interface that looks like the old DOS editor Edlin. It is present only for backward compatibility, as there are some die-hard database administrators who have database administration scripts that they run by piping them into an O-SQL or I-SQL session. As far as we know, Microsoft plans to continue support for a command-line interface, so if you're one of these folks, rest easy. The Query Analyzer window is the place for everyone else. It is an excellent interface for running queries, and it gains more neat new features with every release of the software.

The newest features of the Query Analyzer window, introduced in SQL Server 2000, make writing T-SQL statements really easy. You don't have to switch back and forth between windows to check what columns are in the tables, because the Object Browser window, new in SQL Server 2000 and shown in Figure 7-1, contains all of this information. You can copy or drag and drop column objects from the list on the left into the Query window (upper right), and then run the query. You can right-click an object (the table object tblEvent in Figure 7-2) and have SQL Server script the DDL, in this case, into the window for you. You can even use the supplied templates (choose the Template tab, as shown in Figure 7-3) for many common queries and database tasks, and literally just fill in the blanks—or rather, substitute the right object names to finish the Create Table Specifying Filegroups script.

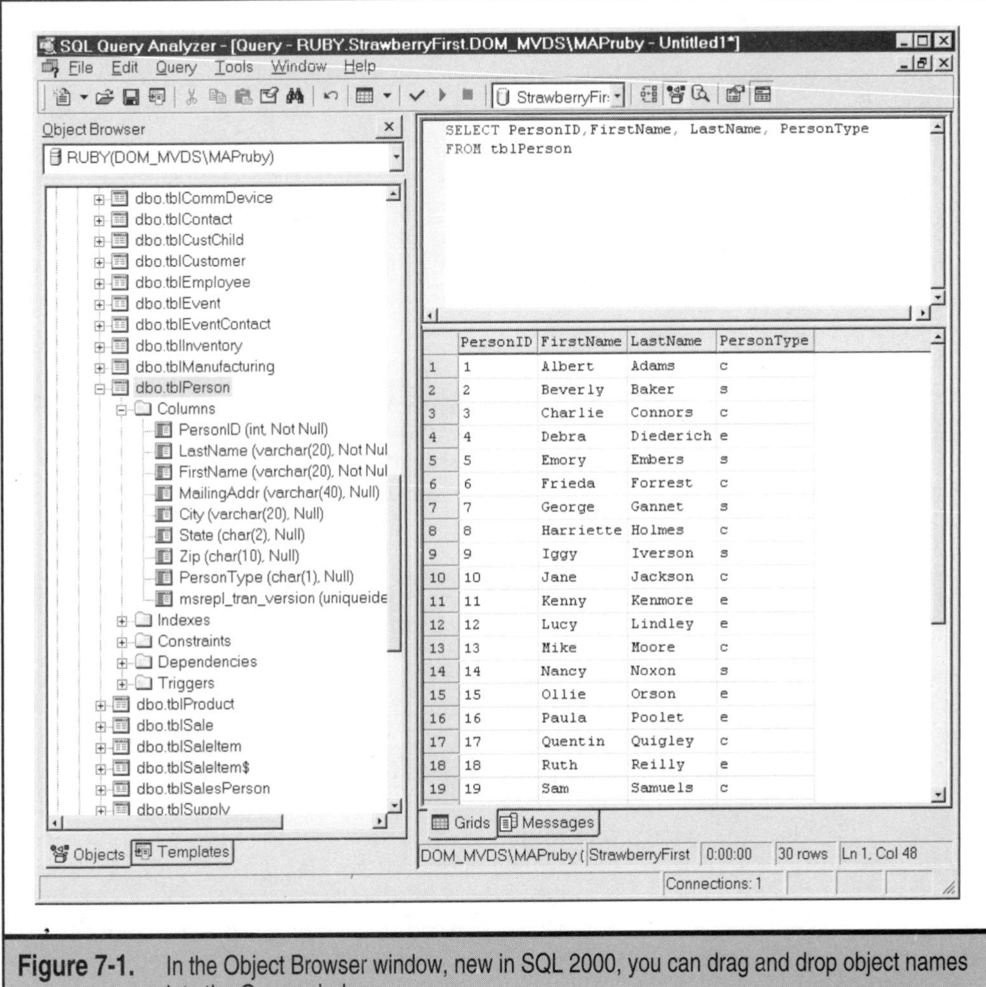

Figure 7-1. In the Object Browser window, new in SQL 2000, you can drag and drop object names into the Query window.

You can have multiple windows open in the Query Analyzer, which is handy if you need to run a quick check on some object or table while you are writing a query on a different database. Keep in mind that every time you open a new window, you have opened another connection to the database. In a development environment, you're probably not worried about the number of open user connections, unless you happen to be working with the Desktop or Personal editions of SQL Server. These are limited by a concurrent workload governor that slows down all of the T-SQL batches when more than five batches are running. Also, you might notice a problem when you have multiple windows open, all of which are retrieving large amounts of data at the same time. It's possible that you could block your own processes if two or more of your windows are retrieving the same or overlapping data sets.

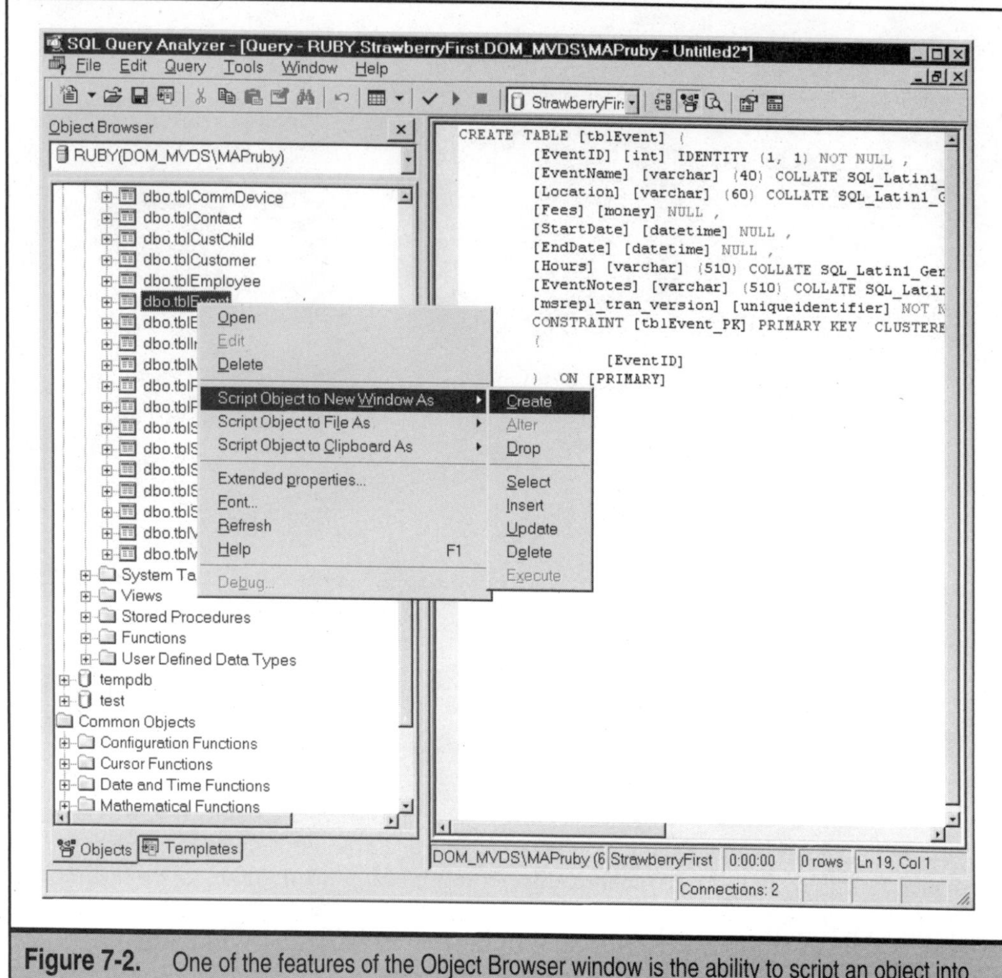

Figure 7-2. One of the features of the Object Browser window is the ability to script an object into the Query window as DDL or DML.

One of the most powerful features of this Query window is the capability to show the execution plan for a query in graphical form. This feature was introduced in SQL Server 7. The display, shown in Figure 7-4, shows you how SQL Server plans to optimize the query, taking into account the way the query is phrased, the amount of data to be returned, and the statistical information about the data. Even though you might write two different queries that return the same result set, don't be surprised if the execution plans look the same for these two queries. SQL Server 2000 reinterprets your T-SQL code and constructs the optimal execution plan, so it may come up with the same plan for two different queries.

One other feature of the Query Analyzer window you need to know about is Undo. Sometimes when you're writing code you might delete a line that you didn't mean to, and

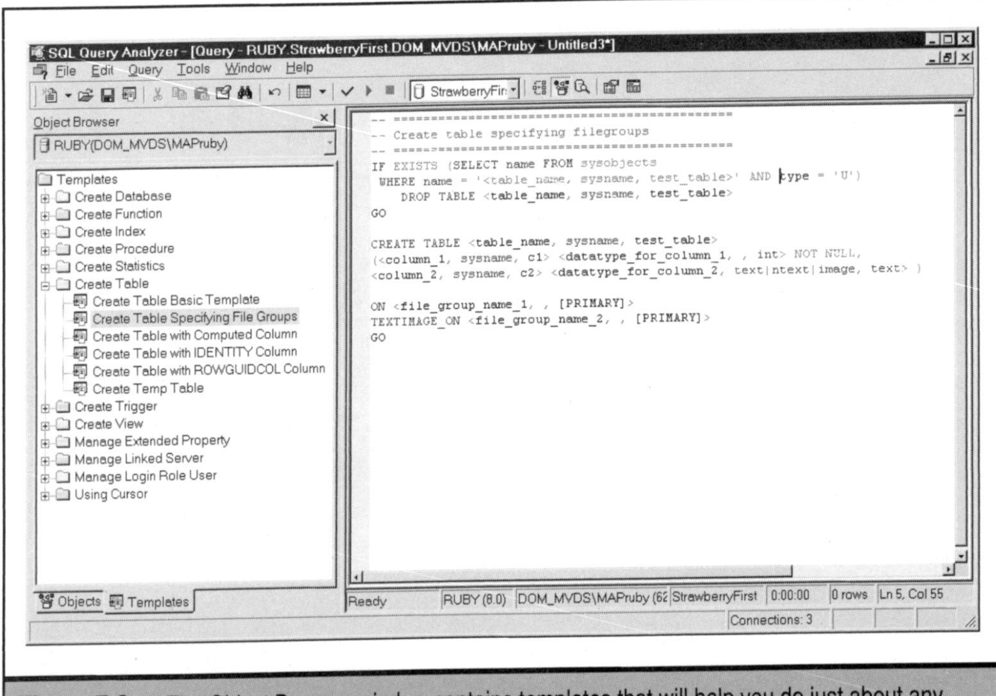

Figure 7-3. The Object Browser window contains templates that will help you do just about any T-SQL task.

it's nice to be able to quickly undo this change. CRTL-Z undoes the change, and will actually undo the last 20 changes by default. You can reduce this setting if you want by selecting Tools | Options from the Query Analyzer top menu, and then select the Editor tab from the pop-up dialog box, as shown in Figure 7-5.

SQL Server 7 introduced color-coding to the Query Analyzer window, making the code easier to read, and providing a visual confirmation that you are typing in the object names correctly. You can change the default colors if you or someone on your staff has a problem with the color combinations. Go to Tools | Options on the Query Analyzer window top menu, and select the Fonts tab, as shown in Figure 7-6. Under Category, make sure that Editor is selected. Under Colors, you will see the various items that can appear in the Query Analyzer window, and below that the foreground and background color. By default, system table names appear in green. If you do try to change color selections, you'll find that what is offered in the drop-down lists is a strange palette, but you can always choose custom colors.

The Object Browser Window

In previous versions of SQL Server, while you were writing code, the only way to keep track of the table names, column names, and so on, was to run a query to list the objects, like so:

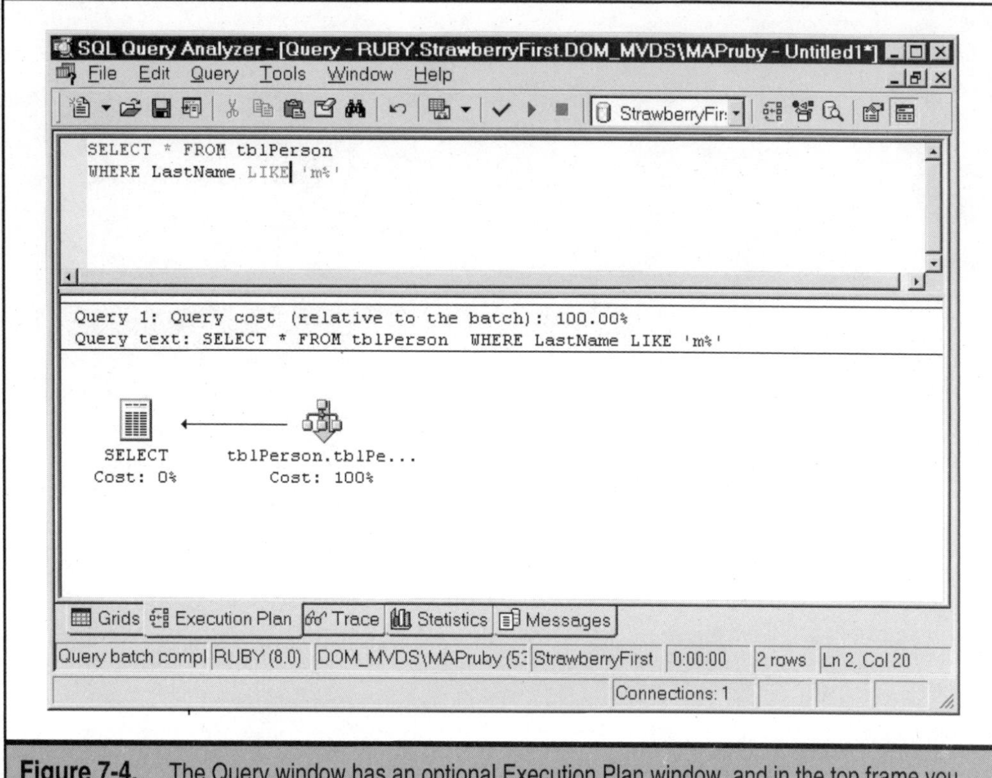

Figure 7-4. The Query window has an optional Execution Plan window, and in the top frame you can see the execution plan that SQL Server proposes to use to resolve the query.

```
SELECT * FROM sysobjects Where type  = 'u'       --  lists the tables
SP_HELP tblPerson  -- lists columns and properties for the Person table
```

So you usually had one Query Analyzer window open with the result of these listings, and then a second window open in which you would write the query, often cutting and pasting the table and column names. In SQL Server 2000, you now have the Object Browser window, which we introduced earlier in this chapter. If the Object Browser window is not visible when you open the Query Analyzer, as shown earlier in Figure 7-1, click Tools | Object Browser from the top menu, or press F8 and it will open. To close the Object Browser, click the "x" in the upper-right corner of the window, or choose Tools | Object Browser again from the top menu, or press F8. Not only can you see the object names in the browser pane, you don't even need to cut and paste them, because you can simply drag and drop table names or column names from the Object Browser into the Query window. And, as we showed in Figure 7-2, when you right-click an object, a menu pops up that allows you to script the object into a new window, to a file, or to the clipboard. So if you have an object in one database, and want a copy of the

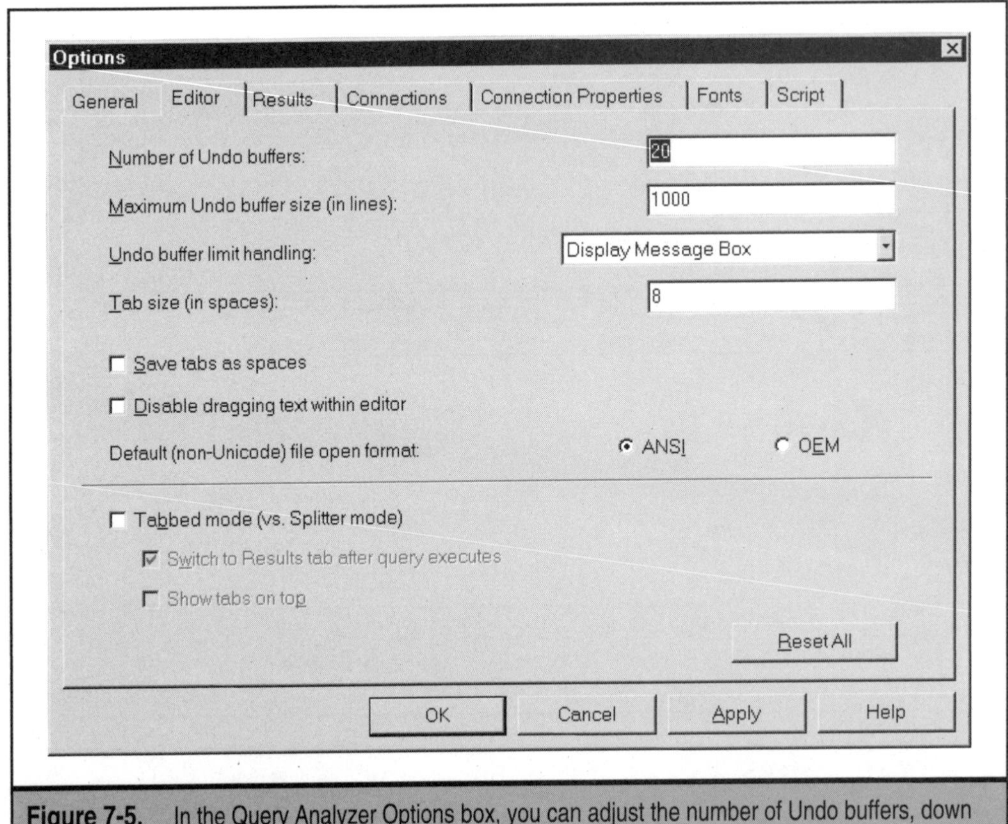

Figure 7-5. In the Query Analyzer Options box, you can adjust the number of Undo buffers, down from the default of 20.

same table in another database, you can generate the script to the clipboard, paste it into the new database, and run it. You aren't limited to creating the object, either, as there are options for selecting columns, inserting data, or updating records.

This is really powerful stuff, and makes writing T-SQL code much easier than it was in earlier versions, and less subject to small typing errors in object names that can be so frustrating to track down. Combine the ability to keep track of your objects with the power to script functions right into the query window, and you really can build some complex code in record time. You still have to know what to ask for and how to construct the code, of course, because although this is an impressive and powerful tool, it will still do what you said, not what you meant.

If you prefer to use some of the more traditional SQL Server tools to examine objects in the database, the SP_HELP stored procedure will give you information about the current database, if you run it with no arguments. If you supply the name of a table, SP_HELP will show the metadata for the columns in that table. And if you instead supply the name of a

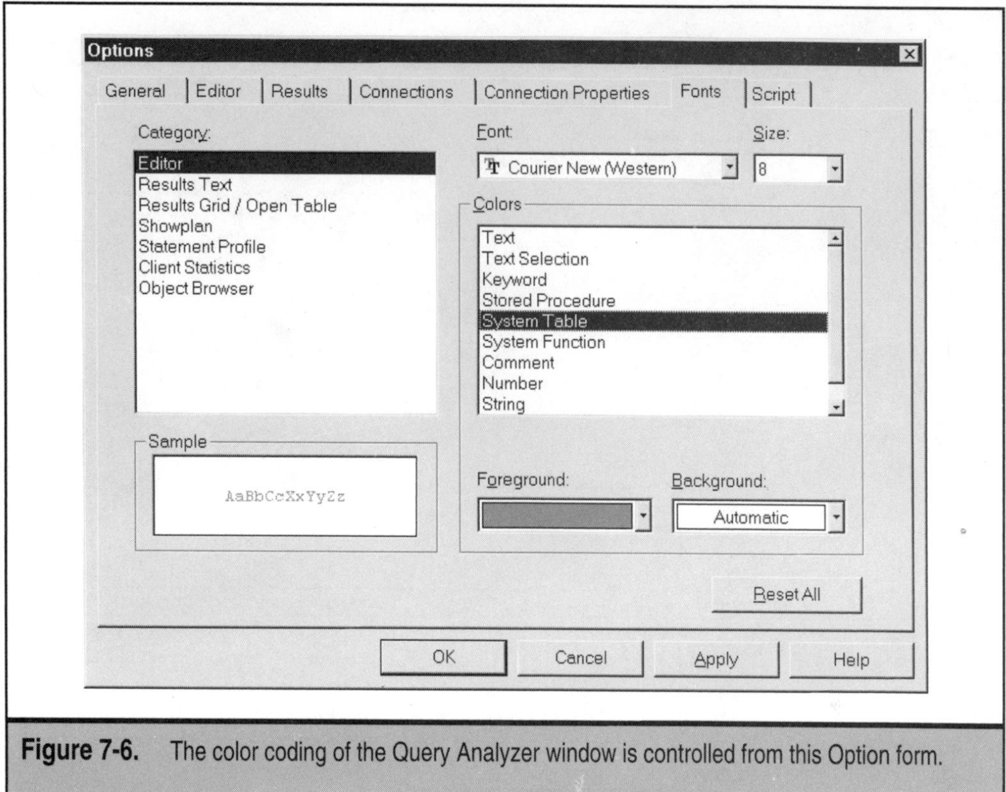

Figure 7-6. The color coding of the Query Analyzer window is controlled from this Option form.

datatype, it will tell you about that datatype. You don't even need to run SP_HELP—just highlight the name of the datatype and press ALT-F1. This feature used to be in SQL Server 6.*x*; it vanished in version 7, and now it's back.

The Object Search Window

The list of new features in SQL Server 2000 continues on, and there's another one hiding out in the Query Analyzer window. It's the Object Search window. You activate it by clicking Tools | Object Search from the top menu, or by pressing the F4 key. This window will let you track down all the columns, views, user tables, stored procedures, triggers, and other objects and constraints in your database, as shown in Figure 7-7. However, this feature looks like it still needs a little work. The results are shown ordered only by object name. It would be nice to be able to order the output by any of the column names in the grid. This functionality has not yet been implemented. Close the Object Search window by clicking the little "x" in the upper-right corner of the window, once for each time that you activated a search operation.

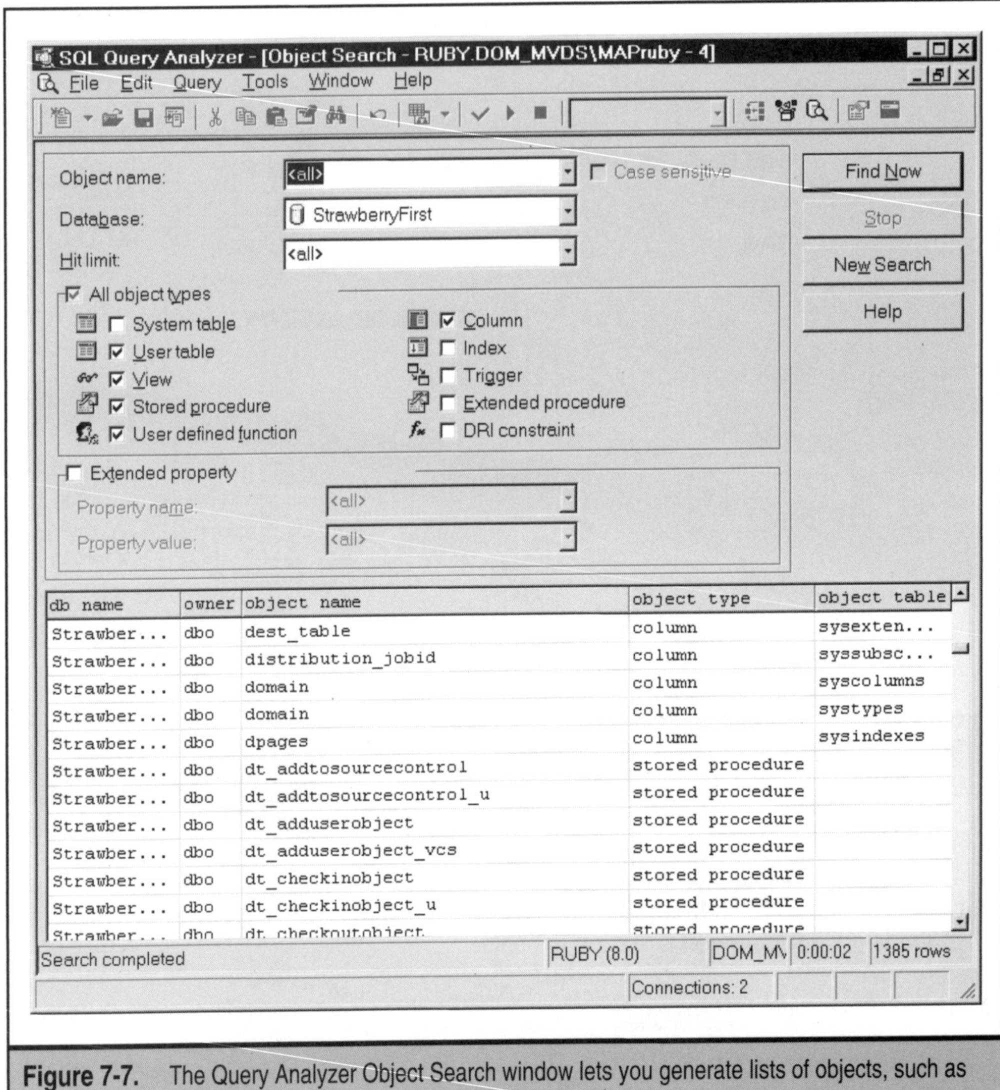

Figure 7-7. The Query Analyzer Object Search window lets you generate lists of objects, such as tables, views, columns, and stored procedures.

How to Run Queries

We're going to make an assumption that you are not going to use the O-SQL command-line interface. Rather, we'll assume that you'll use the Query Analyzer window for your T-SQL coding. You can open the Query Analyzer from the SQL Server program group. You can also open it from within Enterprise Manager, by clicking on Tools | SQL Server Query Analyzer from the top menu. The Query Analyzer window has a full menu bar and a full toolbar, with a lot of capability. There are a few very important command buttons you'll want to know about, however. First, to execute a query, you can click the little green right-pointing arrow from the toolbar, or you can press CTRL-E or F5 from the keyboard, or you can choose Query | Execute from the top menu. To stop a query in progress, you can click the little box next to the green arrow on the toolbar (it turns red when the query is running), or you can press ALT-BREAK from the keyboard, or you can choose Query | Cancel Executing Query from the top menu.

You can write many lines of code in the Query window and execute all or part of them, simply by using the cursor to highlight the code that you want to execute and then clicking the green button (or press CTRL-E or F5 or choose Query | Execute from the top menu). Only the highlighted portion of the code will execute. We find this feature hugely useful and use it extensively when we're building T-SQL scripts. We can then test each step in a script, one at a time, to ensure that it's working as expected, before we commit the script to production runs.

Another very useful feature of the Query Analyzer window is that you can jump directly to the associated help page in SQL Server Books Online just by highlighting any command (use the cursor to do this) and pressing SHIFT-F1. This saves all those intermediate steps of having to bring up the Books Online application, type the command in the search window (or cut and paste the command into the window), and wade through the options offered by the Books Online search engine. SQL Server Books Online isn't an Internet application, even though the interface is browser-based. SQL Server Books Online is the set of help files for SQL Server that comes on the installation CD-ROM. It's usually installed on any computer from which you're going to administer SQL Server. The word "Online" is used here in its traditional and proper sense of "available on the computer" and not in the more recent sense of "we couldn't be bothered to build a proper help system—so we threw a few HTML pages up on our Web site, and if you have a really fast Internet connection, you might be able to find what you need there." We usually keep SQL Server Books Online open when we are coding.

SIMPLE SELECT STATEMENTS

You probably already know how to write basic SELECT statements, so let's try writing some while using the new Object Browser. If you don't have the Query Analyzer window open, do so now, and also open the Object Browser (Tools | Object Browser). Highlight the Strawberry database and expand it so that you can see the User Tables | dbo.tblPerson entry. Right-click the table name, and then choose the option for Script Object To New Window As Select. The SELECT statement will appear in the Query Analyzer window, as shown by Figure 7-8. It's all written out on one line, so you may want to insert a couple of line breaks for readability, as we've done. Notice that all the object names are in square brackets. This is just in case you've done the naughty and used spaces in your object names. In this instance there are no spaces, but SQL Server doesn't bother to check—it just plays safe and puts the brackets in there anyway. It also puts the database name and owner along with the table name in the FROM clause. And it doesn't create a WHERE clause. Actually, neither the SELECT nor the INSERT queries are scripted with a WHERE clause, but the UPDATE and the DELETE both are. The consequences of running an UPDATE or a DELETE statement without a WHERE clause could be disastrous!

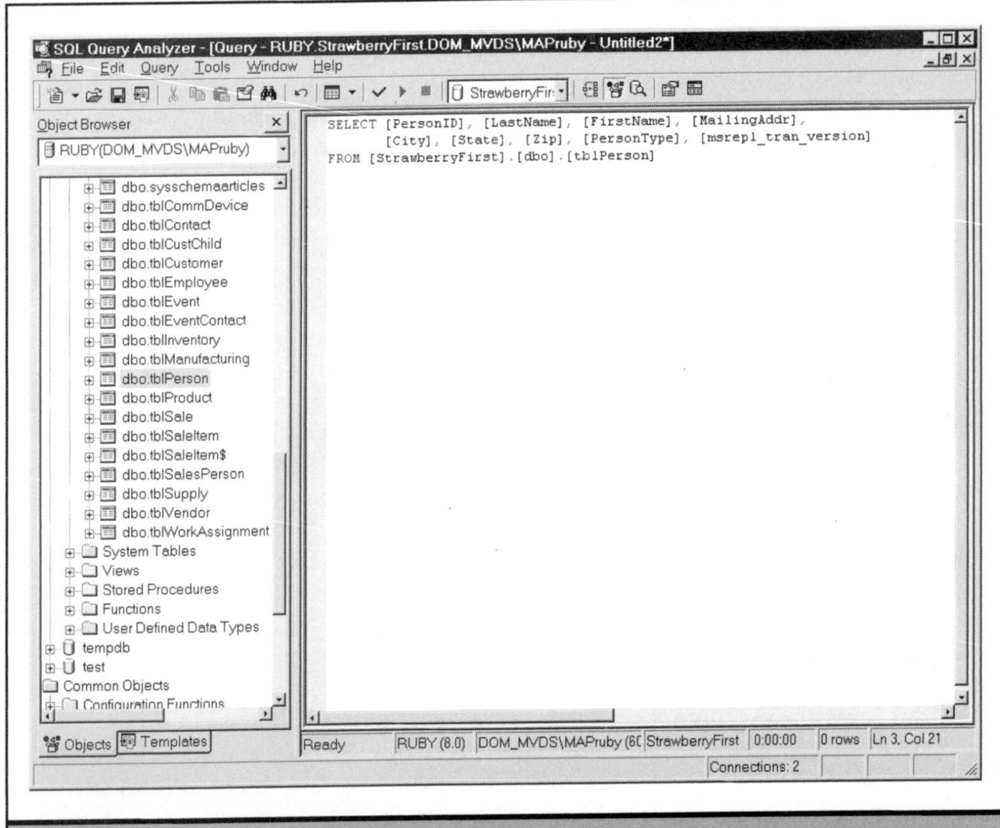

Figure 7-8. With the Object Browser feature, you can generate scripts to select, insert, update, or delete from a table object.

Suppose you want to test the query code, just to see if it will work and see what the output column headings would be, but you don't want to execute the query just yet. Here's a trick, which at first looks strange:

```
SELECT * FROM tblPerson
WHERE  0 = 1
```

Of course, 0 will never equal 1, so the condition in the WHERE clause always evaluates to false. But the query will execute and will return an empty result set, and if you have the column headings turned on, you will see them also. If for some reason you don't want to see the column headings in your output, you can turn them off by selecting Tools | Options from the top menu and then choosing the Results tab. Select Default Results Target As Results To Text, and uncheck Print Column Headers(*), as shown in Figure 7-9. Then, if you rerun the above query, you won't see any column headers at all. This option is especially useful if you're preparing data for export as a tab-delimited output file.

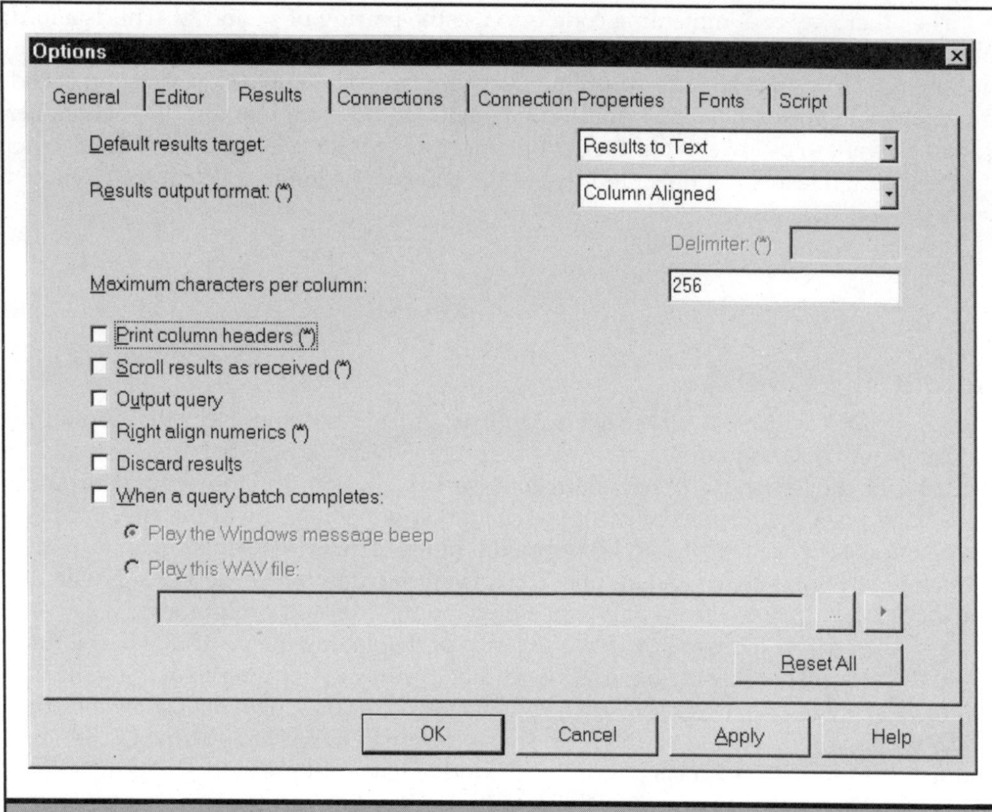

Figure 7-9. To modify the default appearance of your query results, simply use the Options dialog box to remove printed column headings from your result set.

Commenting the Code

In our opinion, real programmers *do* comment their code. In fact, we sometimes write the comments before the code. This is an old programming design technique called pseudo-coding. It helps to firm up the specifics of the design and breaks the code into manageable chunks. It also makes sure that the code is commented! It's way too easy to write the code with every good intention of commenting it later and never finding the time to go back and finish the job. Then, six months later, as you try to figure out what you did, you're wondering why you didn't annotate the code. What a waste of time!

In T-SQL syntax, there are two ways to comment code. The inline technique uses a double dash; this indicates that anything to the right of the double dash is a comment and should be ignored by the query processor, as in this example:

```
SELECT * FROM tblPerson      -- this is a comment
```

The other way of commenting code is to use the pairing of /* and */. This is a fairly universal scheme; anything between these symbols is treated as a comment, including line breaks. Now you can write multiline comments. If you want to skip a section of code during testing, this is how you would do it—you would comment out the section. Perhaps you want to put in some extra debugging code in your regular code stream. When you're through testing, you needn't delete the code; just comment it out, so it's there if you ever need it again.

```
/* This is a comment line
     and so is this      */
```

Formatting the Output

After you work with SQL Server for just a little while, it becomes clear that formatting output is not its strong point. This is not surprising, because SQL Server was really intended to be the server component of a client/server solution, and formatting the output has always been the responsibility of the client component. Many of the client applications such as Microsoft Access and Excel have a range of tools for formatting data, both as printed reports or as charts and graphs. The formatting tools in SQL Server are basic, and you would normally use them only while developing tests and prototypes.

As of SQL Server 7, you now have a choice of displaying query results in the traditional text window or displaying in a grid format. If you run two queries at the same time and request the results in a grid format, you will get the grids shown one below the other, all on one page, as shown in Figure 7-10. This is new in SQL Server 2000. In SQL Server 7, you would get one page for each result grid, kind of like multiple worksheets in an Excel workbook. You can change the way the default results are presented by selecting Tools | Options from the top menu, and then choosing the Results tab on the ensueing dialog box and altering the display settings. But if you just want to switch between text and grid displays, it may be easier to use the toolbar icon that looks like a little spreadsheet, or you can use the hotkeys CTRL-T for the text display and CTRL-D for the grid display.

Controlling the Column Order

In Chapter 6, we talked about how SQL Server stores data. If you recall, for each row, SQL Server stores all the fixed-length columns first and then it stores all the variable-length columns; and at the end of the row, it stores the data that lists the lengths of the variable columns, and the flags to show whether the columns that allow nulls actually contain NULL. You might think that if you don't request columns in any order, using the asterisk to retrieve all the columns, SQL Server would return the columns in storage order—but that's not the case. SQL Server returns the columns in the order in which they were created. If you want the columns in a different order, just ask for the columns in the order you want. Here's an example:

```
SELECT FirstName, LastName, Zip, PersonType  FROM tblPerson
will return a differently arranged result set than
SELECT PersonType, Zip, LastName, FirstName  FROM tblPerson
```

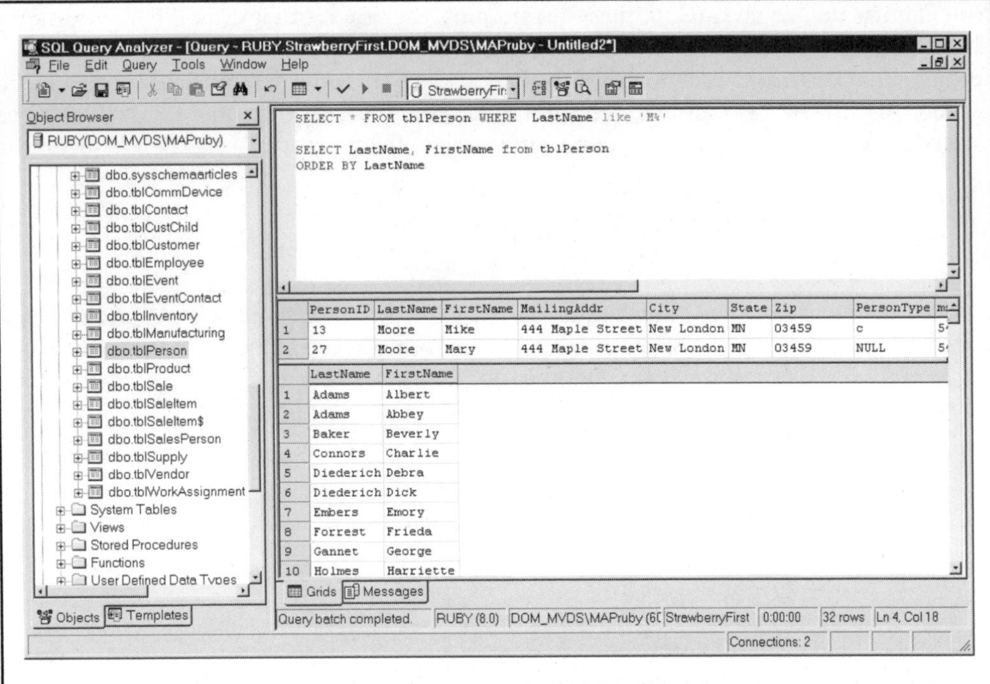

Figure 7-10. SQL Server 2000 can present the results of multiple queries on a single page, even when the display is formatted as a grid.

Labeling the Columns (Column Aliases)

If you don't specify anything different, the column headers in the result set will be the names of the columns, as they were created. If you want to label the column headings with something different (a column alias), you can do that in one of several ways.

You can declare the column alias like this:

```
SELECT 'Person First Name' = FirstName,
       'Person Last Name'  = LastName
FROM tblPerson
```

Or you can use the alternative technique:

```
SELECT FirstName AS 'Person First Name',
       LastName AS 'Person Last Name'
FROM tblPerson
```

You can even leave out the AS in the second option:

```
SELECT FirstName 'Person First Name',
       LastName  'Person Last Name'
FROM tblPerson
```

You can use any or all three of these techniques, as shown in Figure 7-11. We think it's easier to use the AS variation, because it makes very clear to the next person who looks at the code that this query is using column aliases. Here are some examples of confusing situations. If you use a single-word column alias, you don't need to quote it. For instance, you could rewrite one of the preceding queries like this:

```
SELECT PersonFirstName = FirstName,
       PersonLastName  = LastName
FROM tblPerson
```

It's not abundantly clear in this example which term is the column name and which is the column alias. While this query would not compromise data integrity or skew the meaning of a report, a programmer would have to do some investigating to find out which term is which. That's only lost time. But here's an example that might be a little more worrying:

```
SELECT city state FROM tblPerson
```

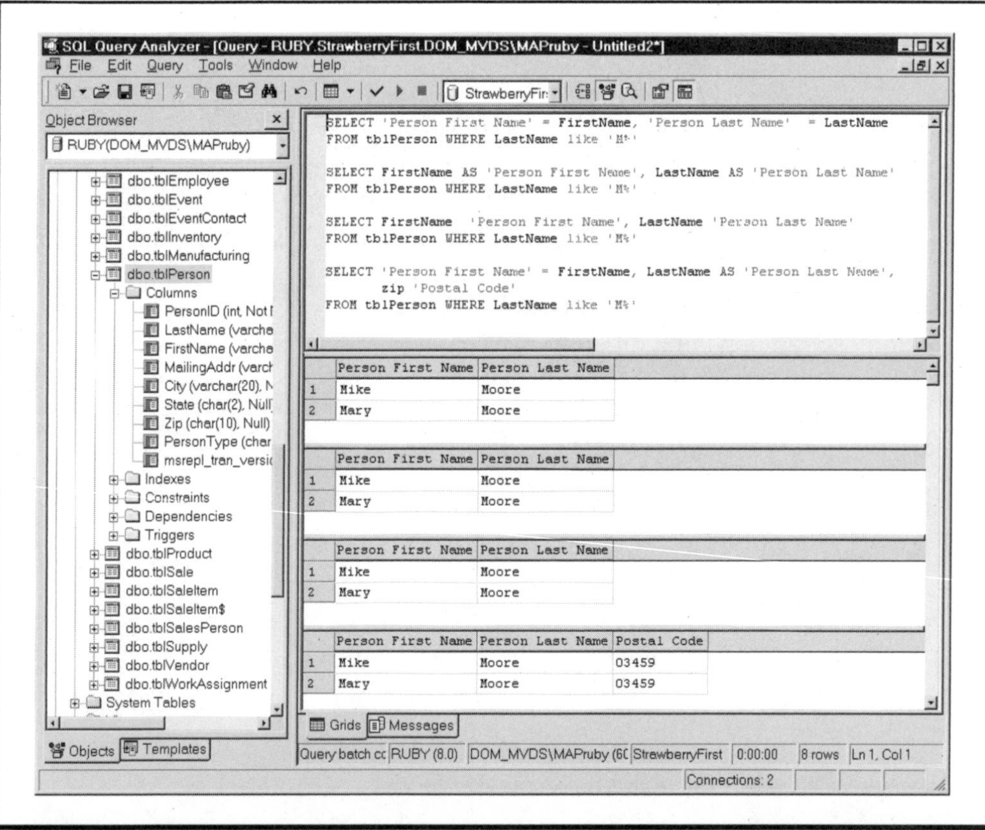

Figure 7-11. Column aliases enhance the readability and meaning of result sets, and you can use any or all of the techniques shown here to create these temporary labels.

At first glance, this query looks okay, except that the result set would contain a listings of cities with a column label "state." Unusual? What actually happened was that the programmer meant to write a query that extracted city plus state; but he left out the comma between city and state, so the state column name was treated as if it were a column alias. This is not only lost time, but inaccurate results. So if you ever find a column missing from your output, and the column labels don't look quite right, check to make sure you have all your commas in the right places.

A column alias is not a persistent object. You declare it in the query where you want to use it, it appears in the result set, and then it's gone. If you want to use the same column alias in a second query, you have to declare it in the second query. Either the column name or the column alias can be used in an ORDER BY clause, as in the following example:

```
SELECT 'Person First Name' = FirstName,
       LastName AS 'Person Last Name',
       Zip 'Postal Code'
FROM tblPerson
ORDER BY 'Person First Name'
```

The ORDER BY clause sorts the result set, by default, in ascending order. Neither the ORDER BY nor the column aliases modify the data in storage. The ORDER BY only reorganizes the data in the result set; the column alias only re-labels the columns in the result set.

Concatenating Columns and Literals

In a normalized database, it's quite likely that some fields (such as a person's name) will have been parsed into its component pieces (first, middle, and last names) and these pieces will have been stored separately. Of course, users want to see these pieces reunited on their reports. In the Person table, for example, you have split the person's name into two fields, FirstName and LastName. You have separated the address into four parts, MailingAddr (the street number, name, and extension, as in 123 Water Street), City, State, and Zip. When you select this data, either the parts are displayed in different cells of the grid display, or—if you opt for a text display—the parts are separated by large gaps. You can combine the various parts into one or two output fields. You would do this for more than just readability in the Query Analyzer window. You might have to send the result set to a client application that has only one text field for the person's name and one long text field for the person's address. So you concatenate the pieces using the plus (+) symbol. For readability, add some other character data, such as spaces, or a comma and a space, between the parts, as in the following code:

```
SELECT FirstName + ' ' + LastName AS 'Person Name',
       MailingAddr + ', ' + City + ', ' + State + ' ' + Zip
        AS 'Person Address'
FROM tblPerson
ORDER BY LastName
```

Because you are creating a column in the result set that doesn't exist in the user table, you should give it a label, like the column aliases in Figure 7-12. That's especially true when you're going to feed the results of this query into another table, like a temporary table, for further processing. In this case, if you didn't use a column alias for the computed column, you would not be able to select it directly. You'd only be able to issue a SELECT * command to retrieve the data.

To retrieve a set of data into a temporary table for further processing, use the SELECT… INTO command, as shown next.

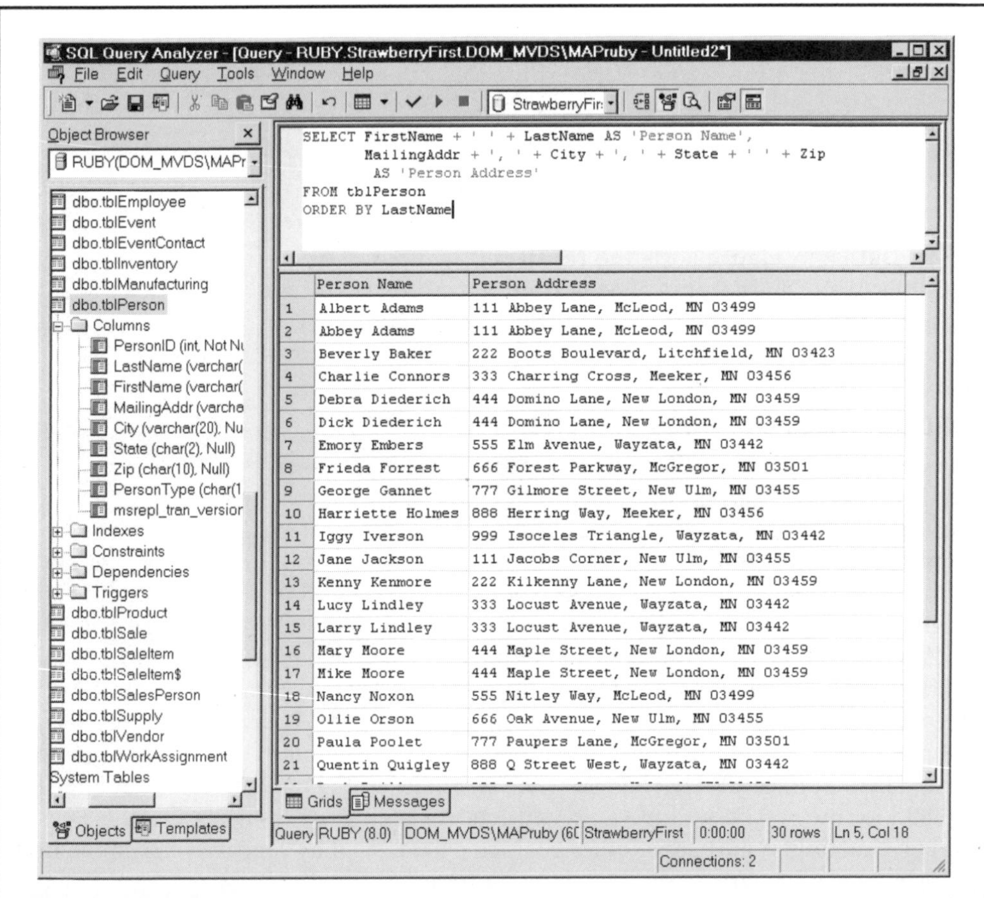

Figure 7-12. When you concatenate two or more columns to produce one output string in the result set, use a column alias to identify the new computed column.

```
 SELECT FirstName + ' ' + LastName AS 'Person Name',
        MailingAddr + ', ' + City + ', ' + State + ' ' + Zip
        AS 'Person Address'
INTO #tempPerson
FROM tblPerson
```

Figure 7-13 shows the results of this operation. The first query (labeled Query 1) creates the temporary table #tempPerson and populates it with data from tblPerson based on the conditions in the WHERE clause. The second query (labeled Query 2) in the figure

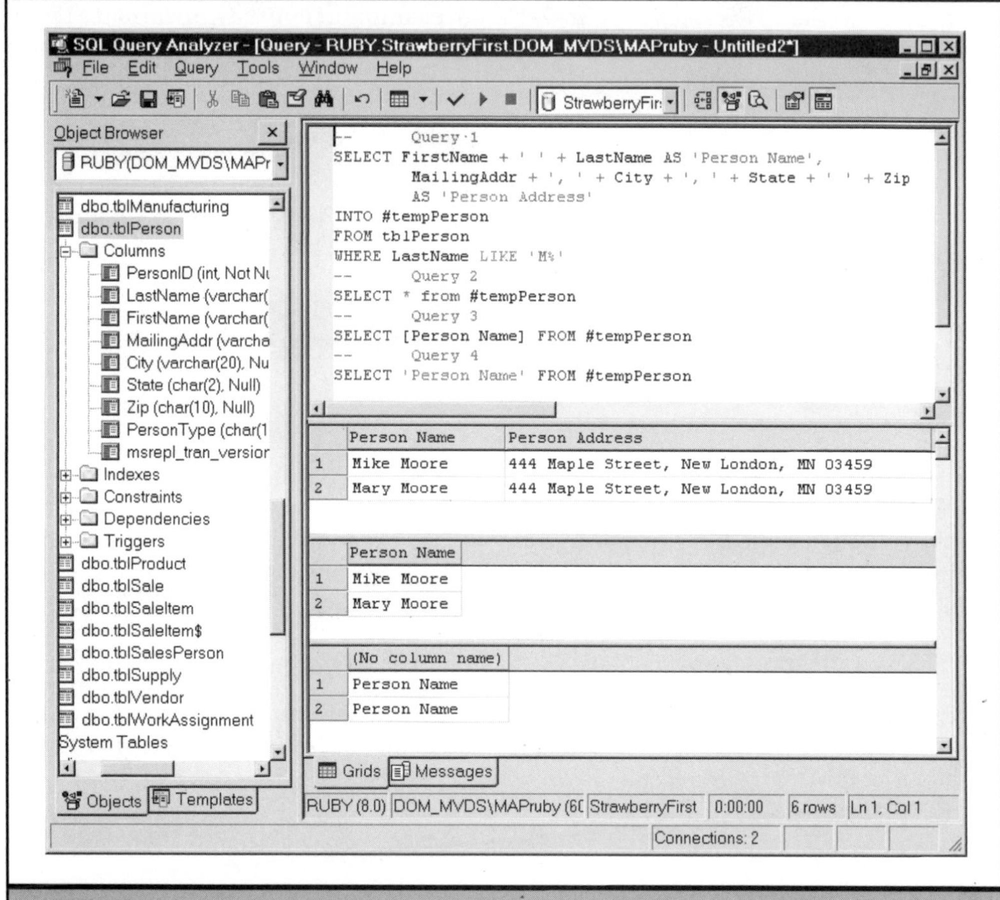

Figure 7-13. The SELECT ... INTO command allows you to dynamically create a temporary table and populate it in the same step.

displays the contents of the temporary table, #tempPerson. Both of the columns in #tempPerson have column labels, which are the column aliases declared in Query 1. If you wanted to return only the first column of #tempPerson, you would be able to do so with the following query, Query 3 in the figure:

```
SELECT [Person Name] FROM #tempPerson
```

Remember that you have to enclose an object name that has embedded spaces with brackets before you can use it in a query. In the SELECT clause, you can't quote (') a column with embedded spaces, because the SQL Server query processor thinks that this is a string literal and will print it *verbatim* in the result set, as shown by Query 4 in the figure.

String literals are simply alphanumeric text strings that are included in the result set and are used to clarity the report. Figure 7-14 is an example of two ways to format a report with string literals. Query 1 extracts from #tempPerson and is using only concatenated spaces to format the output:

```
SELECT [Person Name] + ' lives at ' + [Person Address]
FROM #tempPerson
```

Query 2 extracts data from the Person table, and uses both spaces and the SPACE() function to format the output:

```
SELECT  'The person'  +  SPACE(1) + FirstName + SPACE(1)
        + LastName  + SPACE(2) + 'lives in' + SPACE(2)
        + City + ',  ' + State + SPACE(2) + Zip
FROM tblPerson
```

Character Data Functions

SQL Server provides a range of string functions that allow you to manipulate character data. If you open the Query Analyzer window and expand the Object Browser, under Common Objects you will see an entry for String Functions, as shown in Figure 7-15. These include the usual SUBSTRING function:

```
SUBSTRING (column_name, start, length)
```

This allows you to return just a portion of a character string. For example, if you wanted to retrieve the last name, a comma, and then the first initial of the first name, you would write this:

```
SELECT LastName + ', ' + SUBSTRING(FirstName,1,1) + '.' AS 'Person List'
FROM tblPerson
ORDER BY LastName
```

Because there is no LEFT function, use the SUBSTRING function, starting at character 1 and continuing to the right as many bytes as you want. Use the RIGHT function if you want to list characters from the right side of a column:

```
RIGHT (column_name, length)
```

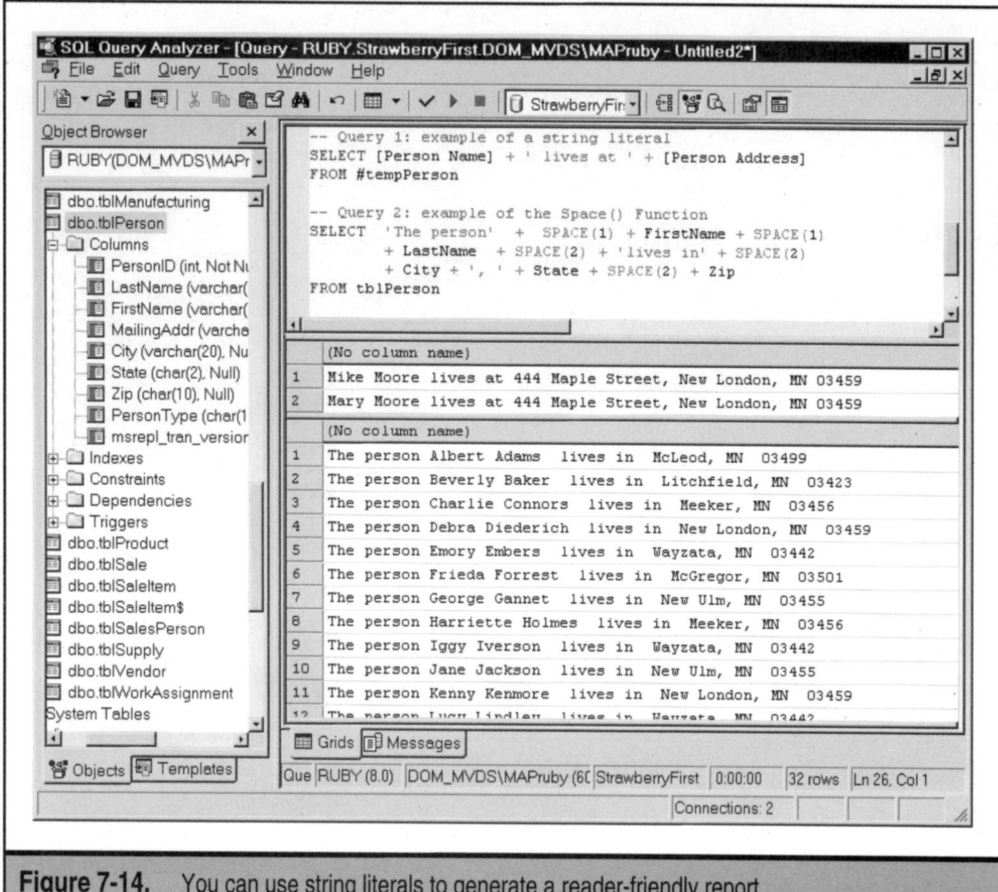

Figure 7-14. You can use string literals to generate a reader-friendly report.

For example, here's how you can display the last four digits of a Social Security number:

```
SELECT PersonID, RIGHT(SSN, 4)as 'Last Part of SSN'
FROM tblEmployee
ORDER BY PersonID
```

The usual functions such as removing leading and trailing blanks (LTRIM, RTRIM) and converting to upper or lower case (UPPER, LOWER) are also available. One function we have found useful is the STUFF function:

```
STUFF (column_name, start, length, replacement_character_expression)
```

It replaces any part of a character string with another string, which you define.

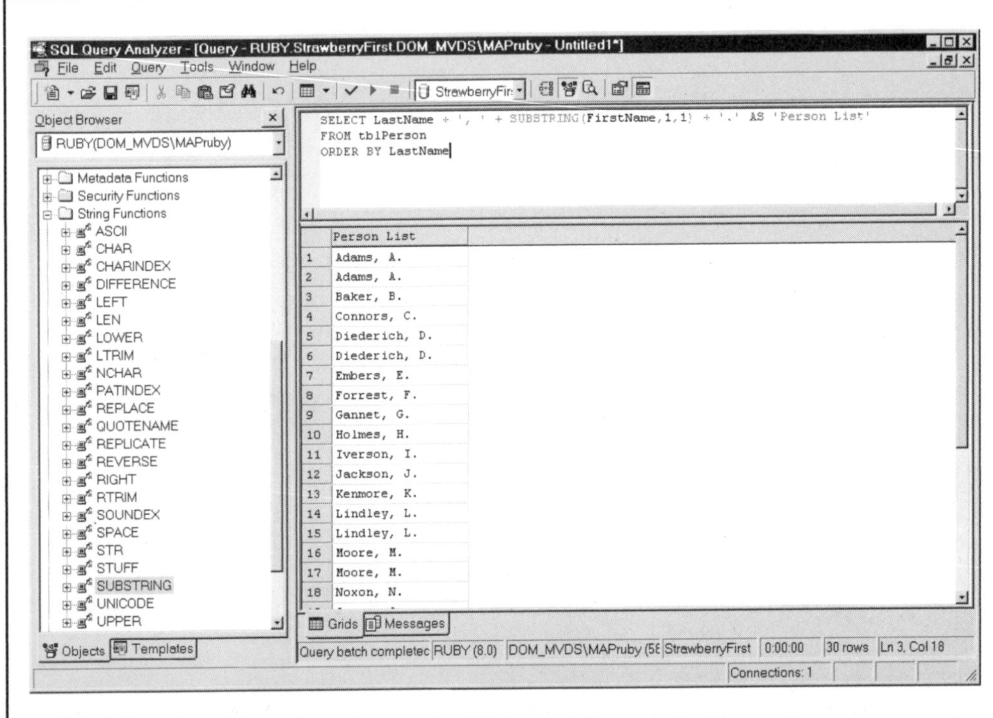

Figure 7-15. The SUBSTRING() function allows you to extract the first letter of the first name.

Suppose you want the company receptionist to be able to verify each employee's identity when they call in, but you don't want to make the complete SSN available to her. Write the following code:

```
SELECT Lastname,  Firstname,  STUFF(SSN, 1,6,'XXX-XX') AS 'Employee ID'
FROM tblEmployee JOIN tblPerson
    ON tblEmployee.PersonID = tblPerson.PersonID
```

The output looks like the result set shown in Figure 7-16.

Converting Data

SQL Server provides two functions for converting data, CAST and CONVERT. The CONVERT function has been with SQL Server from the beginning, but the CAST function is new in version 7. The syntax of the two functions is somewhat different, but the idea is the same—that is, to convert from one datatype to another. The most common use is to convert diverse datatypes in a result set to character data, often for export to another program.

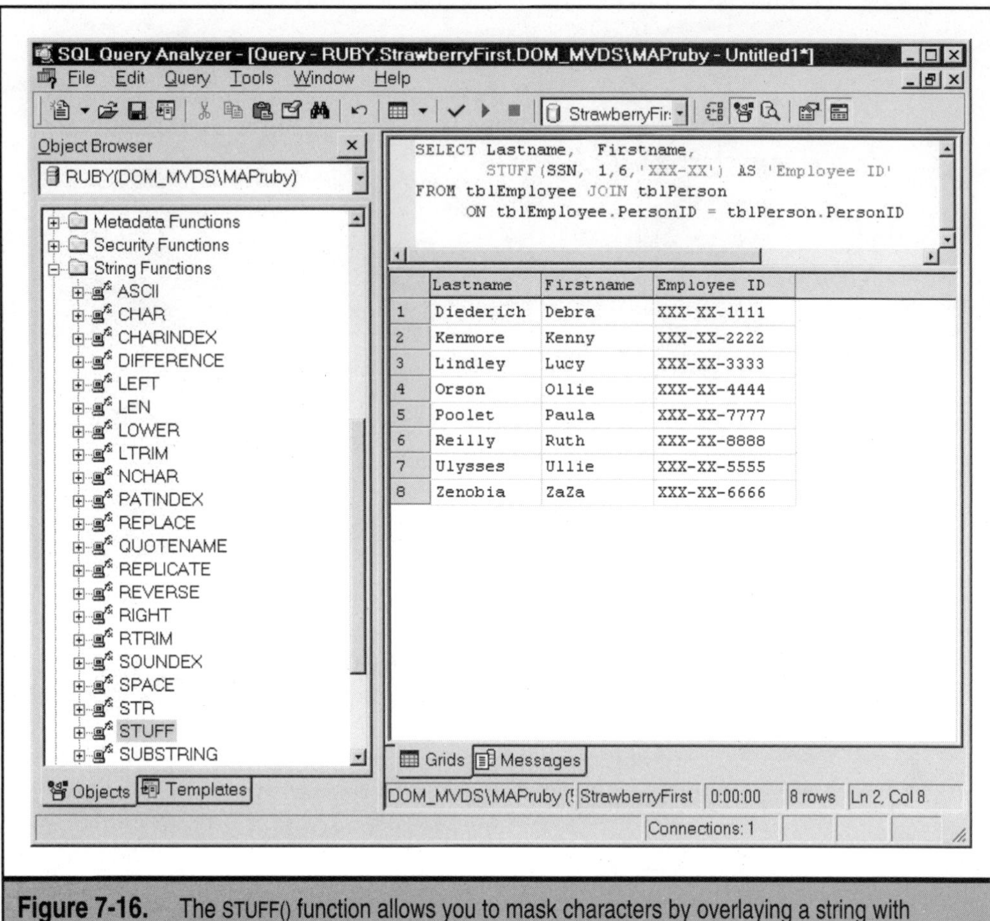

Figure 7-16. The STUFF() function allows you to mask characters by overlaying a string with a string.

The CONVERT program is frequently used to format datetime data. Many companies do business overseas, with their own branch offices or with other companies. As you cross international boundaries, you find that there are different standards for how dates are shown and interpreted. In the United States, you will use 12-31-2000 to indicate the 31st of December; but in Europe, it would be 31-12-2000. Europeans often use the 24-hour clock, with 4:00 P.M. written as 16:00. If you run the code SELECT GETDATE(), what you will see by default is the ANSI-preferred date format, as shown in Figure 7-17. It is a composite string that contains the year, month, day, hour, minute, second, and milliseconds in descending order from left to right. This is known as the canonical date. While this format is logical, as Mr. Spock would say, nobody but a computer person would express a date like that. On the other hand, adopting this format offends nobody, as it does not give preference to any one nation's date and time format. This may be the way SQL Server likes to

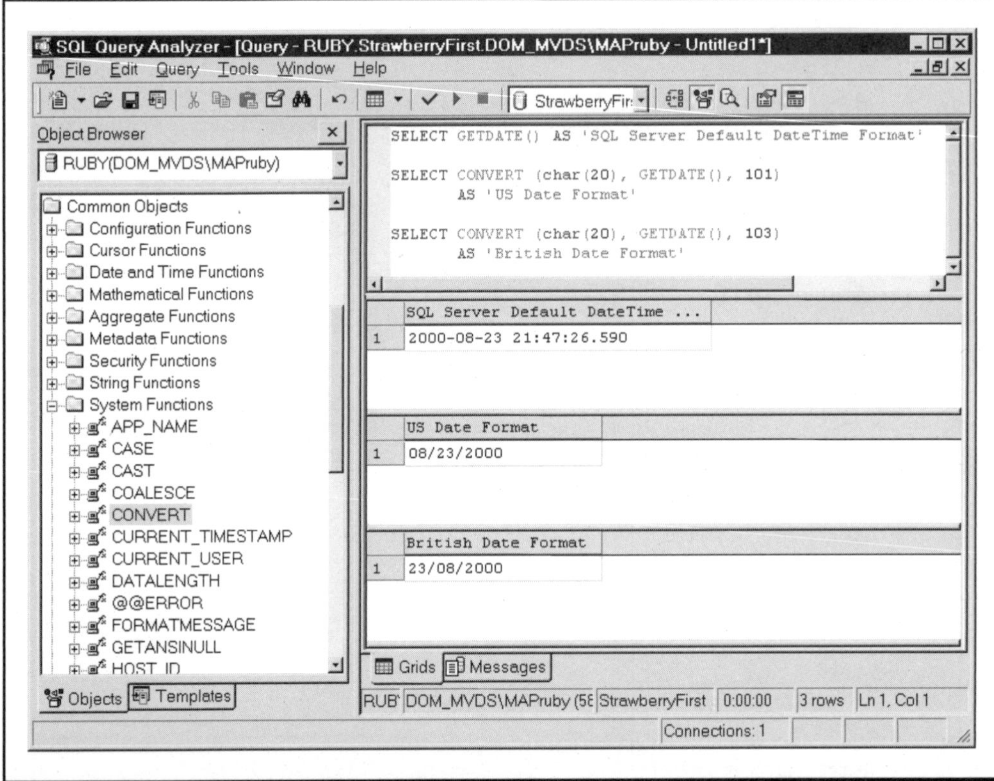

Figure 7-17. The GETDATE() and the CONVERT() functions allow you to retrieve the system date and convert it to reader-friendly formats, respectively.

report dates, but what should you do to format your reports to be reader-friendly? SQL Server has many different style formats you can use to present the date and time data. For example, the following queries return the date in U.S. and British formats:

```
SELECT CONVERT (char(20), GETDATE(), 101)AS 'US Date Format'
SELECT CONVERT (char(20), GETDATE(), 103)AS 'British Date Format'
```

The results are shown in the second and third result sets of Figure 7-17. A frequent source of confusion is the SET DATEFORMAT command:

```
SET DATEFORMAT format
```

This command, which takes the argument in the form *mdy*, *dmy*, *ymd*, *ydm*, *myd*, and *dym*, is used to specify how SQL Server will interpret an incoming date string. It has nothing whatsoever to do with how the datetime column is stored or how dates and times are displayed.

DATA MANIPULATION

In Chapter 3 we discussed data normalization. At that time we said that it's not a good idea to store calculated data in the user tables. Instead, we suggested that you compute it dynamically, on request. This will eliminate the possibility of errors creeping in if you were to modify the base data but forgot to update the calculated data. Even if you elect to keep calculated data and update it with a trigger, the trigger code for the calculations will be similar to computing the results on the fly. We said similar but not identical, as the trigger will most likely be applying incremental changes rather than accumulating totals for a range of dates or values. A good example would be paychecks. When the print-paycheck program runs, it has to print year-to-date deductions and year-to-date salary for each paycheck recipient. You can store these as calculated columns in the database, and each time the print-paycheck program runs, it initiates trigger code that adds the new values to the accumulated totals. Alternatively, you can have the print-paycheck program call for on-the-fly calculations for year-to-date deductions and year-to-date salary for each paycheck it prints. In order to do this, the equations to actually do the calculations must be stored within the print-paycheck program, and the historical paycheck data must be available to the program at runtime.

Regardless of which approach you choose for your applications, you'll find that there are various arithmetical, mathematical, and custom operations available in T-SQL.

Arithmetic Calculations

The basic arithmetic functions—add, subtract, multiply, and divide—are handled much the same way that you would handle numbers on a calculator. The operators and operations look like this:

```
SELECT fees, fees + 10 as '$10 increase in fees' FROM tblEvent
SELECT fees, fees - 10 as '$10 decrease in fees' FROM tblEvent
SELECT fees, fees*2 as 'Double fee structure' FROM tblEvent
SELECT fees, fees/2 as 'Halve the fee structure' FROM tblEvent
```

and you can see the result sets in Figure 7-18. These arithmetic functions are not listed in the Object Browser. (Don't be misled by the "System Statistical Functions"—that object is used to query the system for values such as total reads and writes.) You need to remember a few rules when you use these arithmetic operators:

- Calculations are performed left to right.
- If you have a string of calculations without parentheses, multiplications and divisions are done first, and then additions and subtractions are performed.
- If you want to control the order of calculations, use parentheses. Calculations within parentheses are performed first, and those without are performed last.

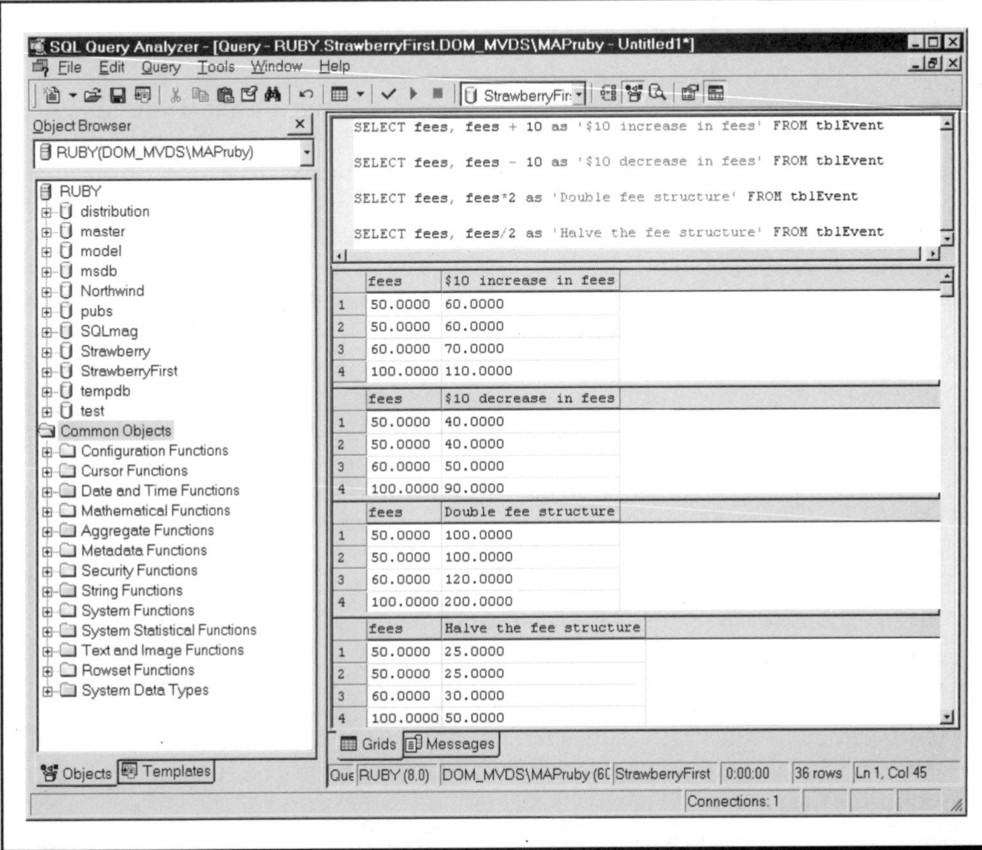

Figure 7-18. The four arithmetic operators—add, subtract, multiply, and divide—and the respective result sets

Just remember this:

```
100 - 3 * (2 + 4)    does not equal  100 - 3  * 2 + 4
```

These arithmetic operators work with integer and number datatypes, including the money datatype, but they won't work with character and datetime datatypes. Datetime datatypes have their own operators, or more correctly stated, they have functions that you can use to manipulate datetime data. There are also some statistical functions such as variance and standard deviation, and we will leave the explanation of how these work to those who understand such things.

Mathematical Functions

You will find the mathematical functions in the Object Browser, under Common Objects. Most of them will be familiar from your high school or college math classes, such as the trigonometry functions (SIN, COS, TAN), square and square root, log functions, and so on. The two functions you might not have encountered yet are FLOOR and CEILING, which are T-SQL extensions, not ANSI standard functions. From SQL Books Online, the *Transact SQL Reference*, the FLOOR function returns "the largest integer less than or equal to a given numeric expression." In other words, take the expression and move in the direction of decreasing values. The FLOOR value of a positive value would move toward zero, but the FLOOR value of a negative value would be more negative, as shown in Figure 7-19. The FLOOR function takes an argument of a single number, so it won't calculate the FLOOR value of a series.

The CEILING function returns the "smallest integer greater than or equal to the given numeric expression." So, in this case, the function searches in a positive direction for the next integer value, as shown in Figure 7-20.

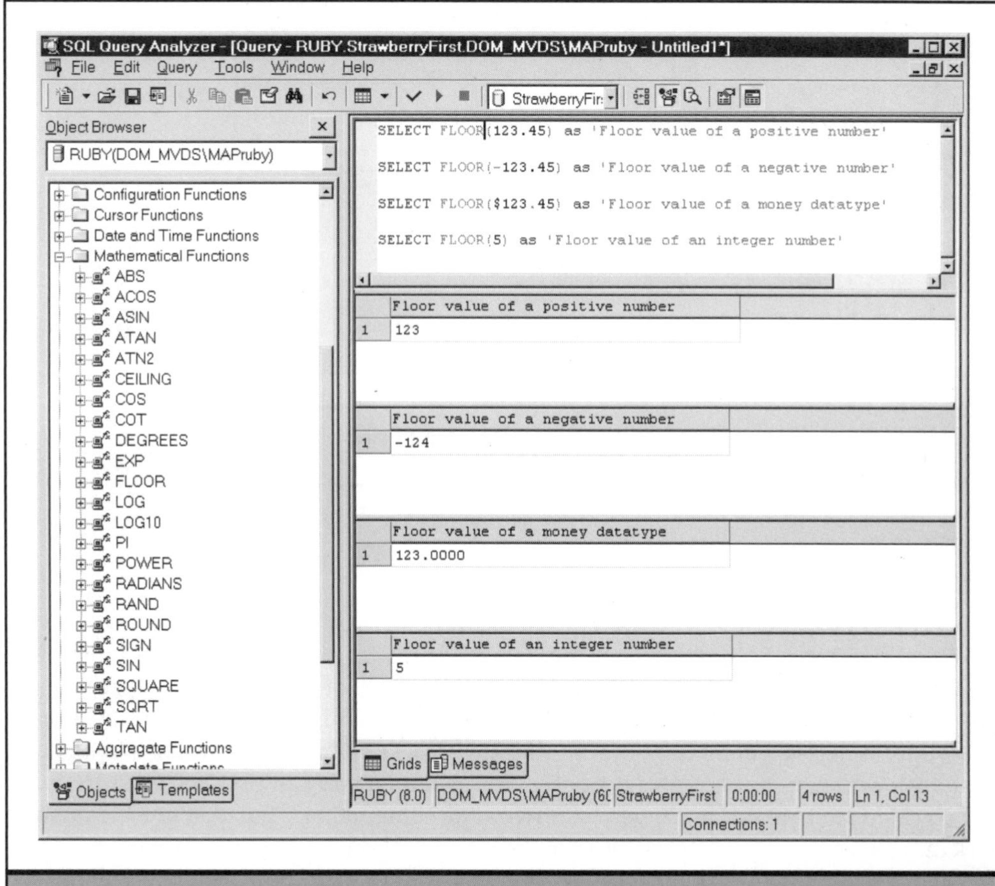

Figure 7-19. The FLOOR function returns an integer value that is less than or equal to the function argument.

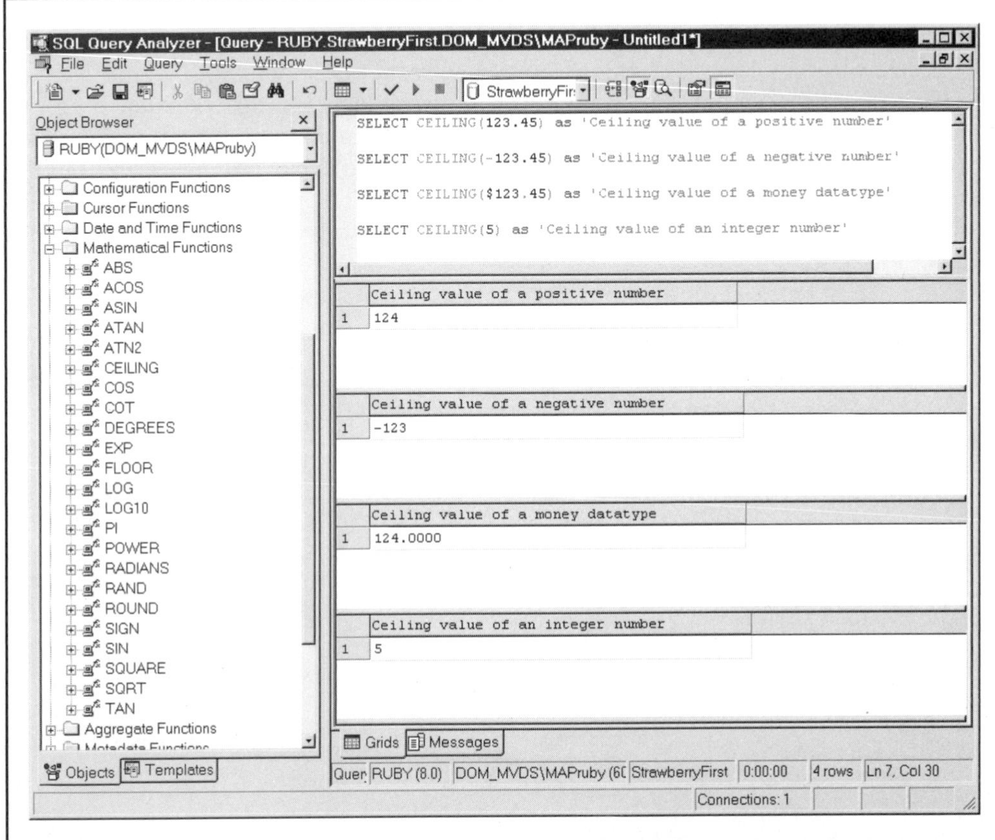

Figure 7-20. The CEILING function returns an integer value that is greater than or equal to the function argument.

Date-Time Calculations

As we mentioned earlier, you cannot use arithmetic or mathematical functions with datetime datatypes. You have to use the date and time functions, which you can find in the Common Objects | Date and Time Functions section of the Query Analyzer Object Browser. The way SQL Server handles date and time values is less than elegant. Unfortunately, this reflects on database programmers, who get a bad rap because it looks like you don't know how to format dates properly. For example, you can use the DATEDIFF function to calculate the difference between two date/time values. But you get the answer back in whichever units you specify—weeks *or* days *or* hours *or* minutes, but not a combination of units. You might get an answer of 3.75 weeks or 26.25 days, but you will not see a useful answer like 3 weeks, 5 days, 6 hours, 10 minutes. Figure 7-21 is an example of the limitations of the DATEDIFF function.

The query

```
SELECT EventName, DATEDIFF(dd, StartDate, EndDate) as
  'Number of Days for Each Event'
FROM tblEvent
```

says "show me the event name and the number of days each event runs." The result set looks reasonable. The second query asks for the same information, only in hours, not in days:

```
SELECT EventName, DATEDIFF(hh, StartDate, EndDate) as
  'Number of Hours for Each Event'
FROM tblEvent
```

The result set strains credibility. It's highly unlikely that even the Meeker County Agricultural Festival will run for 96 hours straight! Part of the problem is the table design. If you want to query at the hour and minute level, you have to store data at the hour and minute level. As you can see in Figure 7-21, that's not happening. The columns StartDate and EndDate are just that—starting and ending dates. The time component of these two columns is set to all zeros—you're not using them. You've put the hours of operation into

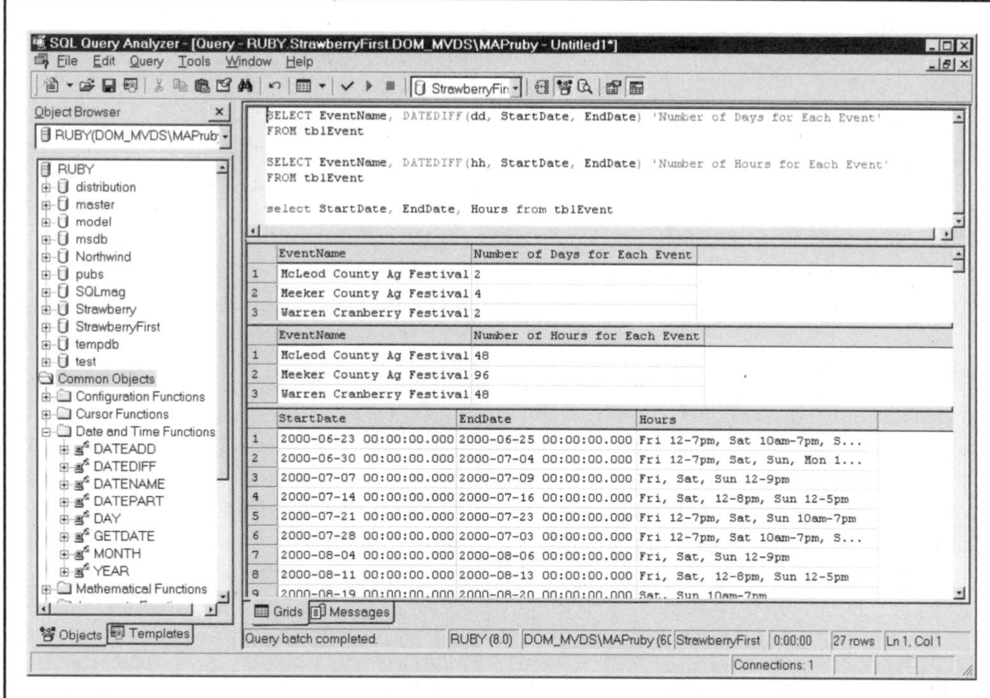

Figure 7-21. The DATEDIFF function gives correct information on days but not on hours with your event data.

a character column that is very easy to publish on a print report or Web page, but is impossible to use with a datetime calculating function. In conclusion, you cannot use the DATEDIFF function to get the total hours of operation with this table architecture.

The situation worsens if you want to add 5 days, 2 hours, and 27 minutes to a datetime value. You'd start with the DATEADD function, and you'll need to run it three times. The first time you add five days; the second time you add two hours; the third time you add 27 minutes. This is probably the easier approach, because the alternative is to preprocess the data—divide the hours by 24 to get a decimal equivalent of 2/24 of a day; divide the minutes by 1,440 to get the decimal equivalent of 27/1440 of a day; and then add the fractions together and append to the five days. Then you can run the DATEADD function. Either technique is not what you'd call a slick operation.

Because the datetime datatype always refers to a point in time, not a duration of time, you cannot store a value like four hours. If you try it, you'll see that the data you inserted looks like 4:00 A.M. This makes it tough to store durations for tasks, for example, such as a time-tracking system that doesn't require start time and end time for a task. To do this, you'd have to use decimal or integer datatypes and write your own code to calculate the total hours on a project.

These functions work really well when you use largest granularity (days versus hours/minutes) or for the simple case. As an example, if you wanted to add two weeks to the present date and time, you'd use GETDATE() to determine the current date and time, and just add two weeks to it:

```
SELECT DATEADD (ww,2, Getdate()) as 'Two weeks from today'
```

SEARCH CRITERIA IN QUERIES

Sometimes you do want to include the entire table in a result set, but more often you want just one record or a subset of the records. That's especially true when you are updating or deleting data, to ensure that you apply the change only to the relevant rows and not to the whole table. In a query, the WHERE clause limits the number of rows affected by the query.

Restrict Operations

The WHERE clause of the query can direct the query processor to search for all rows in which a column, or a calculated column, is compared with a fixed value, with a corresponding value in another table, or with a declared variable. The comparison operators include equal (=), not equal (<> or !=), greater than (>), less than (<), and combinations of these. You can select everyone who lives in a particular city by restricting on the city name:

```
SELECT * FROM tblPerson WHERE  city = 'McLeod'
```

or you can ask for every row in which the zip code is greater than 03500:

```
SELECT * FROM tblPerson WHERE zip > '03500'
```

In this second case, you have to know your data. Zip code is a character datatype, so the "greater than" comparison is evaluated on the ASCII character value, not the numeric value.

Booleans AND, OR, NOT

You can use the comparison operators in combination with AND, OR, and NOT operators, but you need to make sure that you are coding what was requested. When you sit down with the client or your users, you'll most likely have to interpret what they say so that they get what they want. Suppose, for example, the marketing VP says she wants "a report of our customers who bought from us more than three times last year and have incomes of over $80,000." Does she mean that she wants information on all the customers who made more than three purchases last year, narrowing the results by imposing the further restriction of income level? If yes, the query would require an AND to bind the two conditions into a single search condition. Or is the VP thinking of two groups of customers—the frequent repeat buyers (more than three purchases last year) and the group with disposable income? In that case, you would have to use the OR operator to look for people who belong in either result set. For those customers who fall into both groups, the query processor will return their data only one time. It's confusing for a non-tech to be told that she needs to ask for "A *or* B" when she actually wants both group A *and* group B! What she really was saying was "our customers who bought from us more than three times last year and (our customers who) have incomes of over $80,000." T-SQL can handle both of these requests; but as there are two ways of interpreting the original request, and Murphy's Laws often apply in situations like this, it's better to clarify a request in the requirements phase than to have to go back and fix it after the fact—and be thought the worse for it!

Let's delve into the technology behind the query for a moment. The Query Optimizer treats an AND operation differently than it treats an OR operation. You can use both AND and OR in the same WHERE clause, but AND binds tighter than OR. This means the Query Analyzer will parse through your query expression, building *search arguments*, called SARGs. A search argument, or SARG, is composed of one or more conditions expressed in the WHERE clause; it limits the amount of time the query processor will spend scanning the data. A SARG will specify an exact match, a range of values, or multiple conditions that have been AND-ed together in the WHERE clause. Conditions that can be used as SARGs are optimizable—they can use indexes for fast data retrieval.

To backtrack just a moment, SQL Server can retrieve data in two ways: by using indexes or by doing a table scan. We talked about indexes in Chapter 4 and saw how they can enhance data retrieval. A table scan is just what it sounds like—each page of the table is scanned, its contents compared to some condition in the WHERE clause of a query. If a table is small or if it has few pages, it's often more efficient for the query processor to do a table scan than to go to the trouble of reading in the index pages, finding the match, and then reading in the data pages. If a table is large or the query has multiple conditions that require retrieving data that lies at the intersection of these conditions, it's more efficient for the query processor to use the indexes to find the match, and read in only those data pages that contain data for the result set. Either way, it's the Query Optimizer and Query Analyzer that will create the execution plan, and the execution plan will contain instructions for an index search or for a table scan, as deemed appropriate.

If two conditions in the WHERE clause have been OR-ed together, there's no way the Query Optimizer can combine these into a single SARG. Instead, the Optimizer will create two SARGs and use both of these to build the result set. In the preceding example for those customers who fall into both groups, the query processor executes each SARG in turn. It then combines the two intermediate result sets; and when it finds duplicate rows, it will filter out only a single instance of that row. If the data sets being evaluated are very large, and the SQL Server has multiple processors, the Query Optimizer will evaluate the potential for parallel query execution. If the potential is high, and the query processor decides to execute the plan in parallel, each SARG will be processed by a different processor, and the independent results recombined at the end of the query operation.

Back to the query level, when you're AND-ing and OR-ing conditions in the WHERE clause, you should be careful. It's possible that you'll get what you asked for, but not what you want! Figure 7-22 is an example of what we're talking about. The first query is asking for data from the Sale table that meet either of the two conditions shown next.

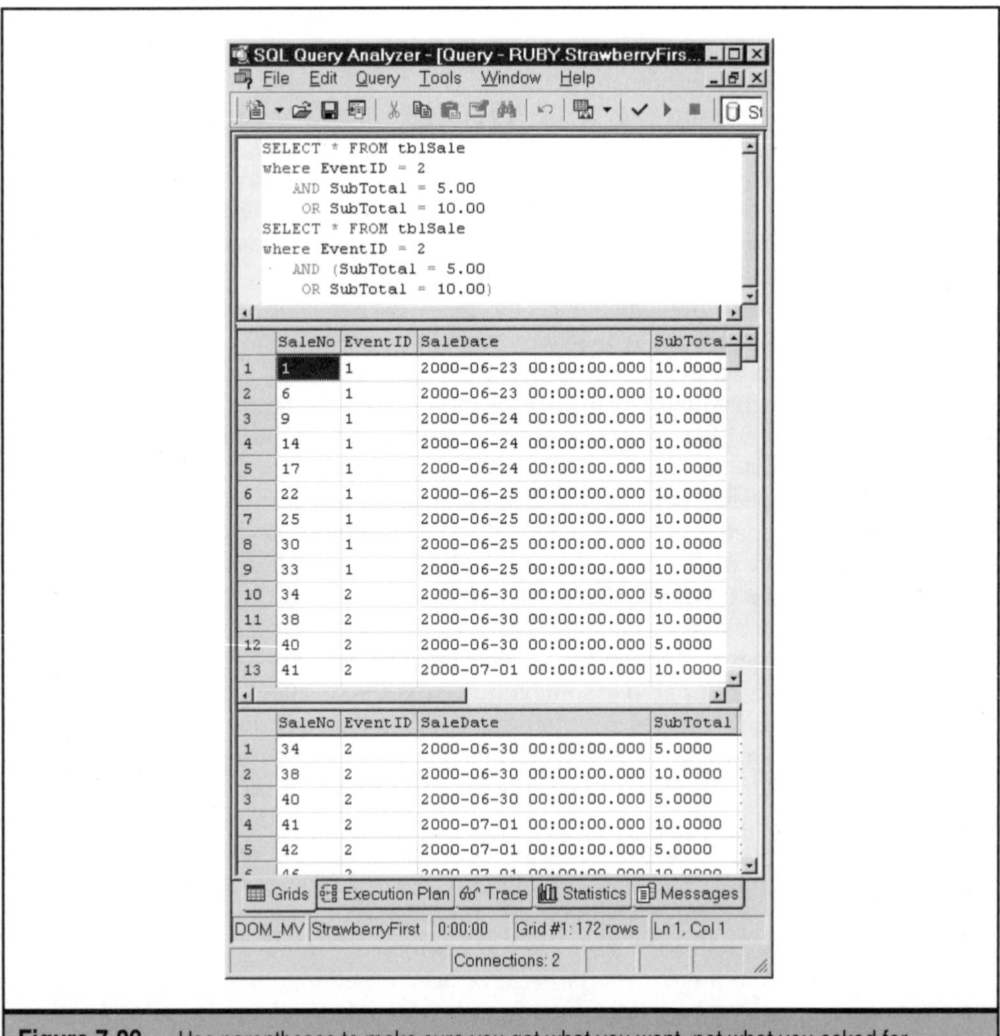

Figure 7-22. Use parentheses to make sure you get what you want, not what you asked for.

- ▼ All rows in which the subtotal equals $10.00
- ▲ Rows from EventID 2 whose subtotal is $5.00

The second query has parentheses bounding the subtotal conditions. It is asking for rows from EventID 2 whose subtotal is either $5.00 or $10.00. There is a big difference between these two result sets. Use parentheses in the WHERE clause to ensure that you've explicitly declared which conditions are to be AND-ed together and which are to be OR-ed, to make sure you get back what you want.

Not every condition specified in the WHERE clause is optimizable. If a condition contains a NOT, for instance, the execution plan generally will not be able to use an index, and instead revert to a full table scan to determine the result set. The NOT operator can be used with any of the comparison operators; it inverts the query, so you could ask for all of your customers who do not live in New York, for example. Usually, there's a way to rewrite a query as a positive statement, rather than resort to using the negative NOT. If this is impossible, use the Execution Plan window of the Query Analyzer to evaluate the proposed execution and then to monitor how the query is running. Watch for performance hits if you must use a NOT operator.

Restricted IN Operator

If you need to cite a lot of conditions in a query, such as retrieve all your customers who live in Utah, Tennessee, Oregon, Kansas, and Maryland, you can do this in two different ways. You can OR together these five conditions, so your query looks like this:

```
SELECT au_lname, au_fname, state, zip
FROM pubs..authors
WHERE state = 'UT'
   OR state = 'TN'
   OR state = 'OR'
   OR state = 'KS'
   OR state = 'MD'
```

or you can write the query using a restricted IN operator. The restricted IN operator allows you to list the variables that make up the arguments of the conditions. The previous query can be rewritten like this:

```
SELECT au_lname, au_fname, state, zip
FROM pubs..authors
WHERE state IN ('UT', 'TN', 'OR', 'KS', 'MD')
```

Range of Values

If you need to retrieve all data that falls in a range, say between a starting date and an ending date, you can easily do this in one of two ways (is this beginning to sound repetitive?).

For instance, if you wanted to retrieve all data from the EventContact table, but only for the first half of the month of May, you could write it this way:

```
SELECT PersonID, DateOfContact, EventID, ContactNotes
FROM tblEventContact
WHERE DateOfContact > = '05/01/2000'
  AND DateOfContact < = '05/15/2000'
```

You can rewrite this query to use the BETWEEN operator. The BETWEEN operator produces the same result as the previous query:

```
SELECT PersonID, DateOfContact, EventID, ContactNotes
FROM tblEventContact
WHERE DateOfContact BETWEEN '05/01/2000' AND '05/15/2000'
```

The BETWEEN operator is inclusive, as you can see from Figure 7-23. The limits of the date range are 5/01/2000 and 5/15/2000, and both these dates appear in the result set. However, like the first query above, if the data set were missing either of these limiting date values, the query would run anyway. The result set would include all rows whose date value falls between the limiting values.

You can combine multiple BETWEEN conditions in the same query, as in the following query, where you want to see all event contact records from the month of May, but only for events of EventID value 1, 2, or 3:

```
SELECT PersonID, DateOfContact, EventID, ContactNotes
FROM tblEventContact
WHERE DateOfContact BETWEEN '05/01/2000' AND '05/31/2000'
  AND EventID BETWEEN 1 AND 3
```

These examples raise an interesting issue with datetime fields; it's a trap many people have fallen into, and we'd like to discuss it here. Let's suppose you know for a fact that you spoke to someone on May 31, but the person does not show up in the result set after you queried for this record. So you run a query that shows all this person's contact records, and sure enough, there's the contact record dated May 31. There is a simple explanation for this apparent anomaly. The DateOfContact column was programmed to automatically fill in the current system date, using the GETDATE function. This function fills in not only the date, but also the time. This record you were looking for may have looked like 2000-05-31 11:44:23. Remember that it's a datetime field, and both the date component and the time component are filled in by the GETDATE function. When you queried using "05/31/2000" as the date, the query processor interpreted that as 2000-05-31 00:00:00. This is not a match, so you wouldn't see any records from the last day of May.

Imagine what this anomaly could do to your monthly summary data. All your monthly sales totals could be low by the number of sales on the last day of the month! It's very possible that sales figures for any month could be off by as much as 3 percent. The solution to this situation is manyfold. You can use 2000-05-31 11:59 P.M. as the upper limit

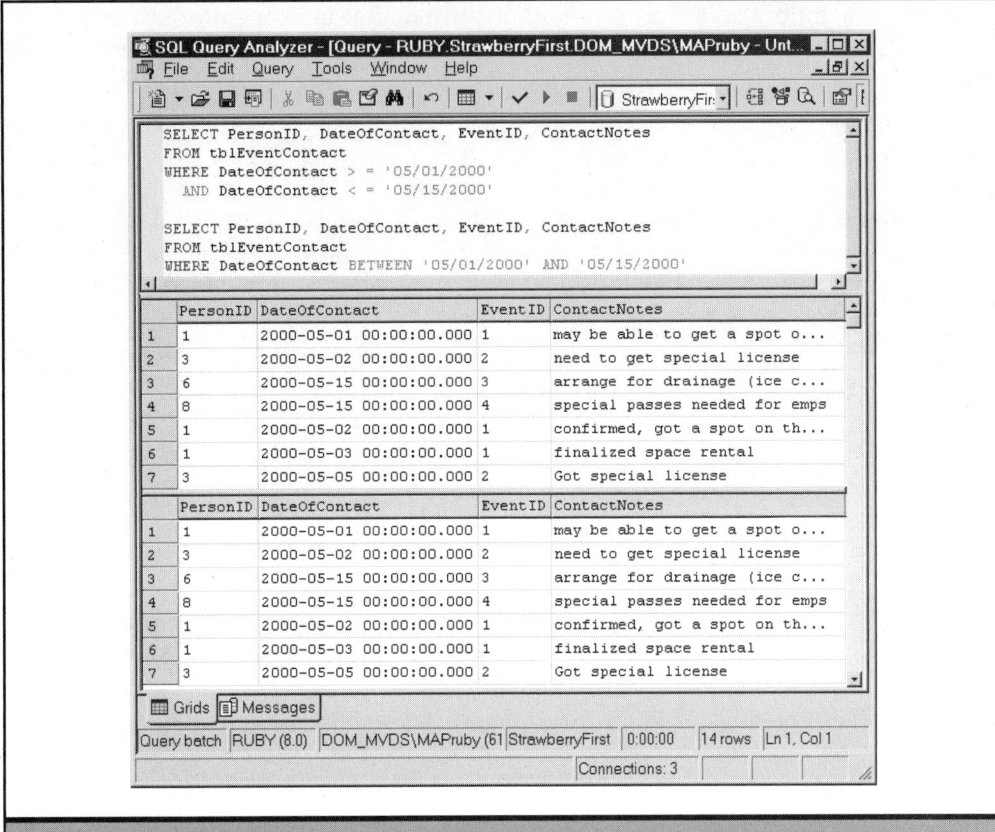

Figure 7-23. The BETWEEN operator returns rows that include the date limits expressed in the query.

of the monthly date range. You can set 06/01/2000 as the upper limit of the range, assuming that you will not have any sales recorded on the stroke of midnight on the first day of the month. Or, if you know you will be having sales posted around the clock, you can modify the query format to read

```
WHERE DateOfContact > = '05/01/2000'
  AND DateOfContact <  '06/01/2000'
```

Searching for Character Data

There are many ways that you can search for character data with T-SQL. You can search using an equal (=) operator, as in

```
SELECT * FROM tblPerson WHERE LastName = 'Thompson'
```

Another operator that's more or less equivalent to the equal operator in T-SQL is the LIKE operator. The LIKE operator works similarly to the equal operator and is often used in place of the equal operator with character data (remember, for number data you must use the equal operator):

```
SELECT * FROM tblPerson WHERE LastName LIKE 'Thompson'
```

The LIKE operator has a special property, and that's the capability to search for data by using *pattern matches*. A pattern match is a template you set up with wildcard characters in the WHERE clause. It can then be used to search through string values; and where it finds a match, you get that row in your result set.

For instance, suppose you want to find all entries in the Person table whose last name begins with a specific letter. A query like this uses the wildcard % symbol, meaning "substitute any number or type of characters from this point forward." The following query will return any string that begins with the letter T:

```
SELECT * FROM tblPerson WHERE LastName LIKE 'T%'
```

The T-SQL version of the LIKE operator is not quite ANSI standard. According to the ANSI standard, the LIKE operator is meant to be used only with pattern-matching wildcards, to find a substring of the LastName value in the preceding example, for instance.

The T-SQL dialect of ANSI-standard SQL has taken liberties with the LIKE operator, so for at least the time being, you can use it interchangeably with the equal operator. However, if you're working in a heterogeneous database environment, you'll want to stick to the ANSI standard intent, which is to use the equal operator when you're searching for a full string value and use the LIKE operator when you're going to use a wildcard character and pattern matching.

If you wanted to list all the entries whose last names begin with A through M, you would specify this range as

```
SELECT LastName, FirstName FROM tblPerson
WHERE LastName LIKE '[A-M]%'
```

Don't forget to include the dash between the letter A and the letter M; otherwise, the pattern LIKE '[AM]%' will return rows in which the last name begins with *either* A or M. If you forget the square brackets, the query will look for last names that begin with the three-character string A-M. (Just a note: If you write a search query using LIKE '%-%', you will be able to return hyphenated names such as Forbes-Hamilton. In Britain this is known as a double-barreled name.)

To track down your Celtic contacts (or ancestors if you're into genealogy) and find all the contacts whose names begin with the letters Mc, you would modify the preceding query to read like so:

```
SELECT * FROM tblPerson WHERE LastName LIKE 'Mc%'
```

On the other hand, if you really wanted to leave out all authors whose last name begins with an Mc, you would use the construct LIKE 'M[^c]%'. The caret symbol tells SQL Server to exclude that character when scanning and comparing the data, and in this example you're saying that you want names that begin with M but do *not* have a c as the second character. Be very careful with the syntax here. The square brackets must go around the character being excluded. So, LIKE '[M^c]%' returns names that begin with M or C, and the exclusion request (^c) is ignored.

Searching for names that begin with a given character or a range of characters is an operation that can take advantage of an existing index, in this case on the LastName column. The index is sorted alphabetically, so it can be used in the search for a name that begins with a certain letter or a range of letters. This is not the case if you begin your pattern with a wildcard character, such as this:

```
SELECT * FROM tblPerson WHERE LastName LIKE '%son'
```

SQL Server will most likely have to scan through the entire Person table, looking for matches to the pattern '%son'. We know that an index search would be faster than a table scan when looking for a limited range of values; but in this case, there's no way to avoid the table scan.

Handling Apostrophes, Quotes, and Special Characters

If you have programmed in MS Access or Visual Basic for Applications, you know that you have to be really careful when you include apostrophes in character data. Trying to get the right number of quotes in all the right places can be quite frustrating. SQL Server offers a couple of options regarding handling apostrophes. The simplest technique may be to just repeat the single quote. When SQL Server sees two single quotes together, it assumes that you mean the first one as a text delimiter and the second one as an apostrophe. For example, suppose you want to find your Irish contacts whose names begin with O':

```
SELECT * FROM tblPerson WHERE LastName LIKE   'O''%'
```

Whether you use single or double quotes as text string delimiters depends on whether or not you've turned on the database option Use Quoted Identifiers. If Use Quoted Identifiers is on, double quotes denote an object name, as in the Northwind table Order Details. Then single quotes *must* be used for text strings. If you have not turned on the Quoted Identifiers, and are instead using square brackets for object names that have embedded spaces, you can use either single or double quotes, although it's not good style to mix the two. You could write the preceding query like this:

```
SELECT * FROM tblPerson WHERE LastName LIKE "O'%"
```

so that the double quotes are the text string delimiters and the single quote is the apostrophe. Quote handling in SQL Server can be confusing and downright awkward at times, so you should establish a standard for quotes and apostrophes and stick with it.

CHAPTER 8

Joins: Combining Data from Multiple Tables

Back in the first few chapters, when you were designing your database, you normalized the tables so that your data was logically grouped into many small tables. In most cases, retrieving useful information will require combining data from two or more of these tables. In this chapter, we will look at the different ways of joining data from multiple tables. We will also see how the Execution Plan window in the Query Analyzer can be used to see exactly what type of join SQL Server will propose for each query.

There are two slightly different ways of writing joins in SQL Server. There's the older convention, which we will call the T-SQL method, as it has been part of T-SQL since SQL Server 1.0. There is also the ANSI standard method, and Microsoft is encouraging its use. In fact, their documentation really makes little or no mention of the older, T-SQL syntax. If you were going to be only involved with new applications, we wouldn't mention it either. But it is quite possible that you will at some point have to maintain or update older code written using the T-SQL syntax, so you should be aware of how it works. We do suggest using the ANSI syntax for any new code, partly because there are a few cases in which the old syntax doesn't work (we'll give an example shortly). Also, we don't know what Microsoft's plans are, and the old syntax may go away in some future version of SQL Server. In fact, SQL Server Books Online specifically states that the older outer join syntax "will not be supported in a future version of SQL Server." For now, both versions will compile and run.

To clarify the nomenclature and be totally accurate, both the "T-SQL" method and the "ANSI standard" method of programming SQL code are ANSI standards. The American National Standards Institute has released multiple standards for programming SQL code over the last two decades. The "T-SQL" method is the original, or ANSI-1, standard, which was developed circa 1986–1989. Typical of first releases, it didn't have all the features wanted or needed by vendors of SQL databases, such as the outer join. The Microsoft "ANSI standard" method is a revision and extension of ANSI-1. Most of the ANSI standard code we'll present here is ANSI-2, which was released in 1992, and some of the code is ANSI-3, which is still under development. Let's take a look at the different types of joins, consider how they might be used, and look at their proposed execution plans.

INNER JOINS

An INNER JOIN is used if you want to return all rows in which there is a match between the two tables. A match means that the value in a column (or combination of columns) in table A matches the value in a corresponding column in table B. You need to specify the columns on which to match, and they will most likely be either a primary key/foreign key combination or a unique column/foreign key combination.

Suppose you want to write a query to combine the Person table and the CommDevice table, so you can get a listing of people and ways to contact them (phone numbers, email addresses, and so on). In the older style T-SQL, you would write this as shown next:

```
SELECT LastName, FirstName, CommType, CommValue
FROM tblPerson, tblCommDevice
WHERE tblPerson.PersonID  = tblCommDevice.PersonID
```

Table A (tblPerson) is joined to table B (tblCommDevice) based on matches found by the SQL query processor in the values of table A's join column (PersonID) compared to the values of table B's join column (PersonID).

The SELECT clause specifies which columns you want in the result set, the FROM clause lists the tables, and the WHERE clause tells SQL Server the columns to use for joining the tables. You would also use the WHERE clause to restrict the rows returned, if you wished to do so. In this case, the person identifier, represented by the PersonID column, is the common link between the Person table and the CommDevice table. Now here's the same query in the ANSI syntax:

```
SELECT LastName, FirstName, CommType, CommValue
FROM tblPerson INNER JOIN tblCommDevice
  ON tblPerson.PersonID  = tblCommDevice.PersonID
```

Notice that you now type the word JOIN in the query, in between the names of the tables taking part in the join. The word INNER is optional, because it is the default type of join. Also notice that, in this example, there is no WHERE clause. In the ANSI syntax, you use the ON keyword to specify on which columns to base the join operation. You still use the WHERE clause when you want to restrict the rows returned in the result set. Keeping the JOIN expression and the row restriction expressions separate might make it easier to figure out what the query is meant to do when you review the code months later.

In either syntax, the order in which you list the tables is not critical, because SQL Server is going to optimize the order in which the tables are read. So,

```
SELECT LastName, FirstName, CommType, CommValue
FROM tblPerson INNER JOIN tblCommDevice
  ON tblPerson.PersonID  = tblCommDevice.PersonID
```

gives you the same result as

```
SELECT LastName, FirstName, CommType, CommValue
FROM tblCommDevice INNER JOIN tblPerson
  ON tblCommDevice.PersonID  = tblPerson.PersonID
```

where the order of the tables in the FROM clause is reversed. Our preference is to list the columns in the SELECT clause in the order desired for the output data, and then list the tables in the FROM clause—beginning with the master table and then adding the detail table. Remember, a JOIN combines data from two tables that have a 1:M relationship, thus the need to join the two on the primary key/foreign key combination.

Using Table Aliases

Operationally, it gets tedious, keying in all those long table names when you're writing join queries all day long. To the rescue: the table alias. A table alias is a substitute for a table name in a join query. In the previous query, you can define an alias for tblCommDevice and a second alias for tblPerson, as follows:

```
SELECT p.LastName, p.FirstName, c.CommType, c.CommValue
FROM tblCommDevice c INNER JOIN tblPerson p
  ON c.PersonID  = p.PersonID
```

Using the T-SQL syntax:

```
SELECT p.LastName, p.FirstName, c.CommType, c.CommValue
FROM tblCommDevice c, tblPerson p
WHERE c.PersonID  = p.PersonID
```

You define the table alias in the FROM clause. Once you have defined an alias, you cannot use the table name anywhere in the query. If you tried, for instance, to write the preceding query with both table names and table aliases modifying the column names, as in

```
SELECT p.LastName, p.FirstName, c.CommType, c.CommValue
FROM tblCommDevice c INNER JOIN tblPerson p
  ON c.PersonID  = tblPerson.PersonID
```

you would see the following error message:

```
Server: Msg 107, Level 16, State 3, Line 1
The column prefix 'tblPerson' does not match with a table name or alias
name used in the query.
```

The table alias literally assumes the identity of the table it's referencing for the duration of this query, but no longer. The alias is a local variable (not shared with other queries) that exists only for the duration of the query that it is a part of. It's dynamically defined when the query is parsed, used in lieu of the table name while the query is resolved, and then released as soon as the result set is returned to the user. As far as the SQL Server query processor is concerned, the table names in the preceding query are "c" and "p."

The table alias is typically one to three characters in length, any combination of letters and numbers. One purpose is to save you having to key in the long table names you see in the queries thus far. The second purpose is to allow you to join a table to itself, something we will talk about later in this chapter. Technically, it's not necessary to modify a column name with a table name or alias, unless you have two column names the same in one query. When this happens, you *must* modify each of the duplicate column names with the appropriate table name or alias, so the SQL Server query optimizer and query processor will know which of the two columns to use in the query. We suggest that you might want to get into the habit of modifying all columns in a query with the appropriate table alias, as a form of documenting your code. In the above query, LastName and FirstName came from the Person table, while CommType and CommValue came from the CommDevice table. From this point on, we'll use table aliases wherever appropriate.

Generating the Execution Plan

If you want to see what happens when the tables are processed in different orders, you can do so with the SET FORCEPLAN ON option. The SET FORCEPLAN ON option says to SQL Server "access the tables in the order I've specified them in the query." Generally, you won't want to use this option, because the SQL Server query optimizer can probably choose a more cost-effective scheme to access the data than you can. From the top menu, choose Query | Show Execution Plan. Type **SET FORCEPLAN ON**; then run both queries, as shown in Figure 8-1. After the query executes, you'll see a third tab labeled Execution Plan, which is where the Query Analyzer shows the plan that SQL Server will use to execute the query. Most of the time, if you run tests, reversing the order of table access in your queries, you'll see a marked difference in the execution plans.

In Figure 8-1, the Query Analyzer window is divided into two panes. The upper pane contains the batch of queries, with FORCEPLAN on. The lower pane is divided into two parts; each part shows the execution plan for one of the queries. Above each execution plan is a statement of query cost relative to the batch. 100% is the total cost to run the entire batch, both queries. The query optimizer evaluates how "expensive" each query is and calculates a ratio of the query cost to the total. Query 1, tblPerson INNER JOIN tblCommDevice, takes 63.66% of the total cost; while query 2, tblCommDevice INNER JOIN tblPerson, only takes 36.34% of the total cost. In other words, query 2 "costs" about half as much to run as query 1 does. If you had left off FORCEPLAN, the SQL Server query optimizer would have chosen execution plan 2. To prove this to yourself, run this test. Set FORCEPLAN off. Highlight the first query, and run it. Check the execution plan. The query cost, relative to the batch, is now 100%, but that's because this one query is the entire batch. The actual execution plan that was used to run this query is the less expensive one, the second plan from Figure 8-1.

If you want to see the execution plan for one query, you can use CTRL-L (instead of the normal CTRL-E) key combination to show the *estimated* plan, without running the query. Or, if you prefer using the top menu, choose Query | Display Estimated Execution Plan. If you want to see the execution plan for the query as it's running, use the CTRL-K key combination; or, from the top menu, select Query | Show Execution Plan, and then run the query. There's also an item on the toolbar that looks like a little spreadsheet or grid; this controls the Execute mode, so you can turn the Execution Plan on and off from here, too. When you run the query, you will have to click the Execution Plan tab at the bottom of the window in order to see the plan, as the Query Analyzer default behavior is to show the query results.

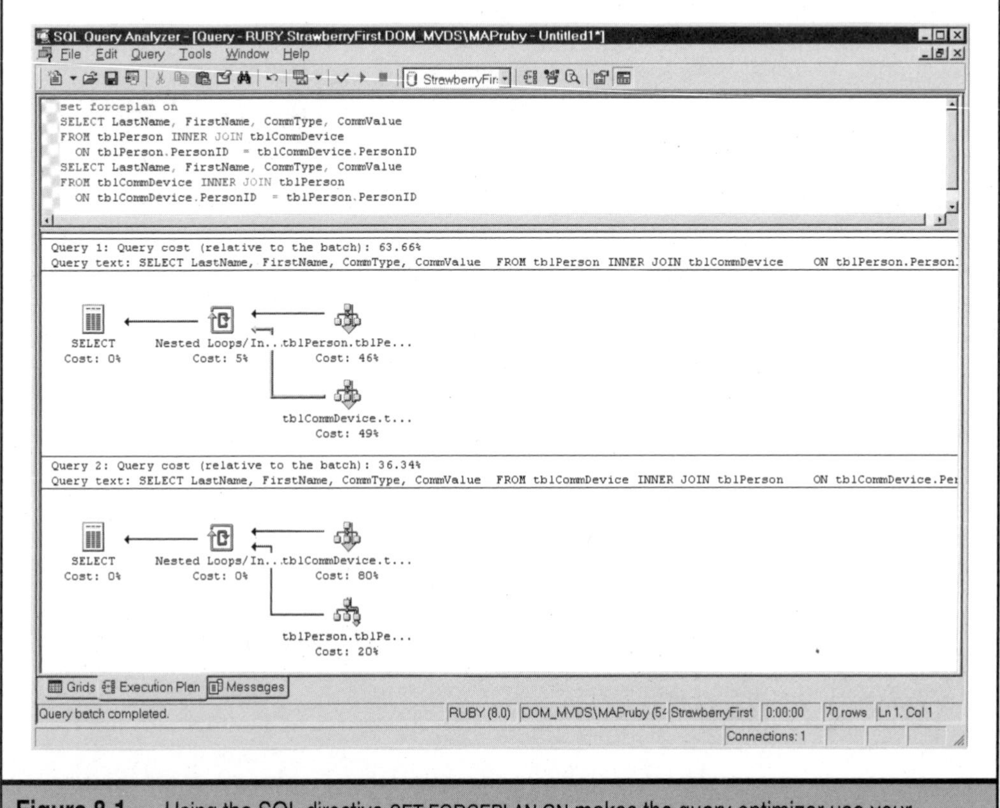

Figure 8-1. Using the SQL directive SET FORCEPLAN ON makes the query optimizer use your execution plan rather than its own.

Figure 8-1 shows the plan for the query listed earlier. If you place the cursor over any of the elements in this picture, you will see an overlay, as shown in Figure 8-2. The overlay will provide information about the operation, including the type of join, whether an index is being used, which index is being used, and the estimated I/O and CPU cost for that step. You can also see the percentage of the total cost contributed by each step. In Figure 8-2, step 1 (read from right to left) is a clustered index scan on the Person table. We'll talk later about clustered indexes, but briefly, in a clustered index, the data is physically sorted in the order determined by the index. The scan of the index is fed into the nested loop/inner join (step 2, to the left of step 1), which then scans the second table, CommDevice, for matching records.

So why does SQL Server always run the query the same way, even when you swap the order of the tables? SQL Server has a very powerful cost-based query optimizer, so it

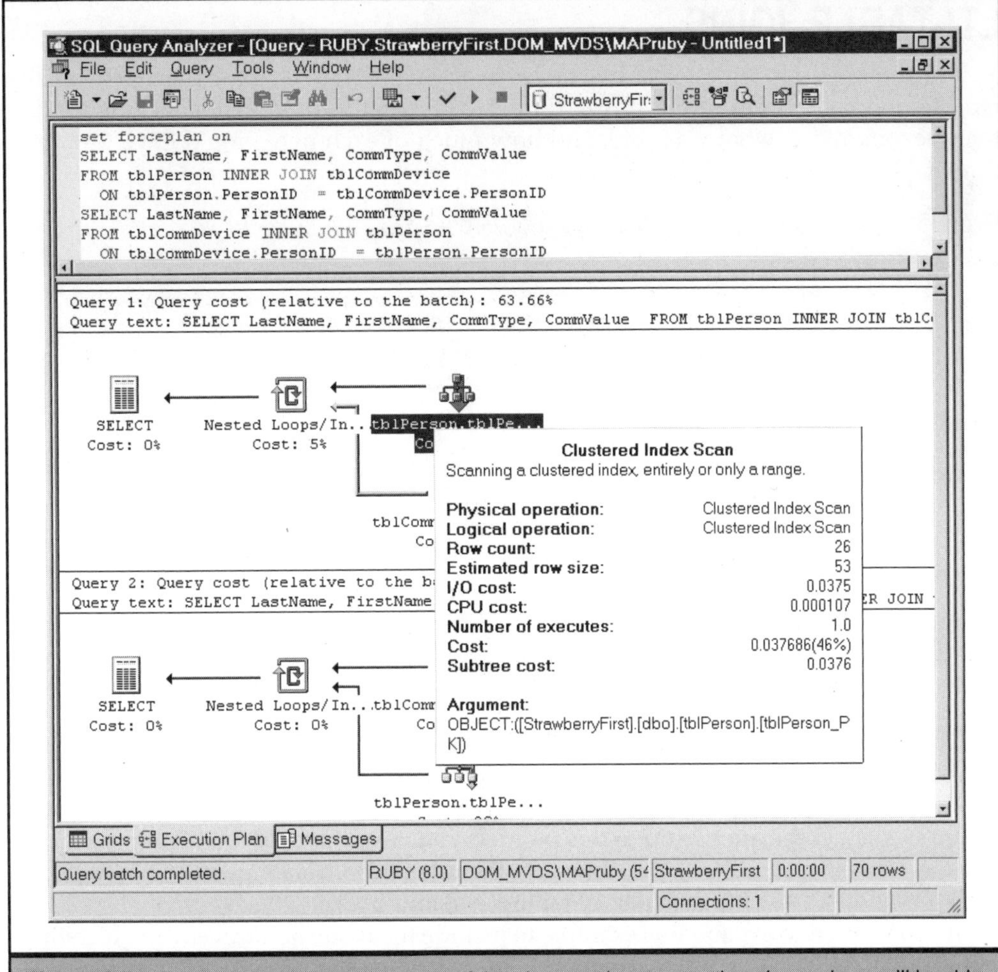

Figure 8-2. Position your cursor over any of the elements in an execution plan and you will be able to see a full explanation of the steps involved in this part of the plan.

makes sense to let it figure out the best way to run the query. Most of the costs involved in a query are physical and logical I/O, and very little is CPU time. So the optimizer typically looks for the plan that will reduce the number of page reads to a minimum.

When you've finished experimenting, remember to run SET FORCEPLAN OFF or else the query optimizer will be constrained to do just exactly what you tell it to do for the rest of this session.

MULTI-TABLE JOINS

You're not limited to joining just two tables in any relational database management system environment. For example, if you wanted to get a listing of sales that include the date the sale took place, what was sold, and how much of each item, you'd have to write a three-table join query, as follows:

```
SELECT s.SaleDate, s.SaleNo, p.ProductDscr, i.QuantitySold,
       i.UnitPrice, i.ItemCost
FROM tblSale s    INNER JOIN tblSaleItem i
                        ON s.SaleNo = i.SaleNo
                  INNER JOIN tblProduct p
                        ON i.ProductCode = p.ProductCode
ORDER BY s.SaleDate, s.SaleNo
```

Using the T-SQL syntax:

```
SELECT s.SaleDate, s.SaleNo, p.ProductDscr, i.QuantitySold,
       i.UnitPrice, i.ItemCost
FROM tblSale s, tblSaleItem i, tblProduct p
WHERE s.SaleNo = i.SaleNo
  AND i.ProductCode = p.ProductCode
ORDER BY s.SaleDate, s.SaleNo
```

The result set looks like Figure 8-3. The rule for writing multi-table join queries is that for each *pair* of tables, you'll need to write one join statement. If you have two tables (table A and table B) in your join query, you'll need a single join statement (table A JOIN table B), as you've seen in the queries up to this point. If you have three tables in your join query (table A, table B, and table C), you'll need to include two join statements (table A JOIN table B JOIN table C, one for each pair of tables (A-B and B-C).

If you wanted to expand this example to include the name of the event at which these sales took place, you'd need to expand the query to a four-table join query, as follows:

```
SELECT e.EventName, s.SaleDate, s.SaleNo, p.ProductDscr,
       i.QuantitySold, i.UnitPrice, i.ItemCost
FROM tblEvent e   INNER JOIN  tblSale s
                        ON e.EventID = s.EventID
                  INNER JOIN tblSaleItem i
                        ON s.SaleNo = i.SaleNo
                  INNER JOIN tblProduct p
                        ON i.ProductCode = p.ProductCode
ORDER BY s.SaleDate, e.EventName, s.SaleNo
```

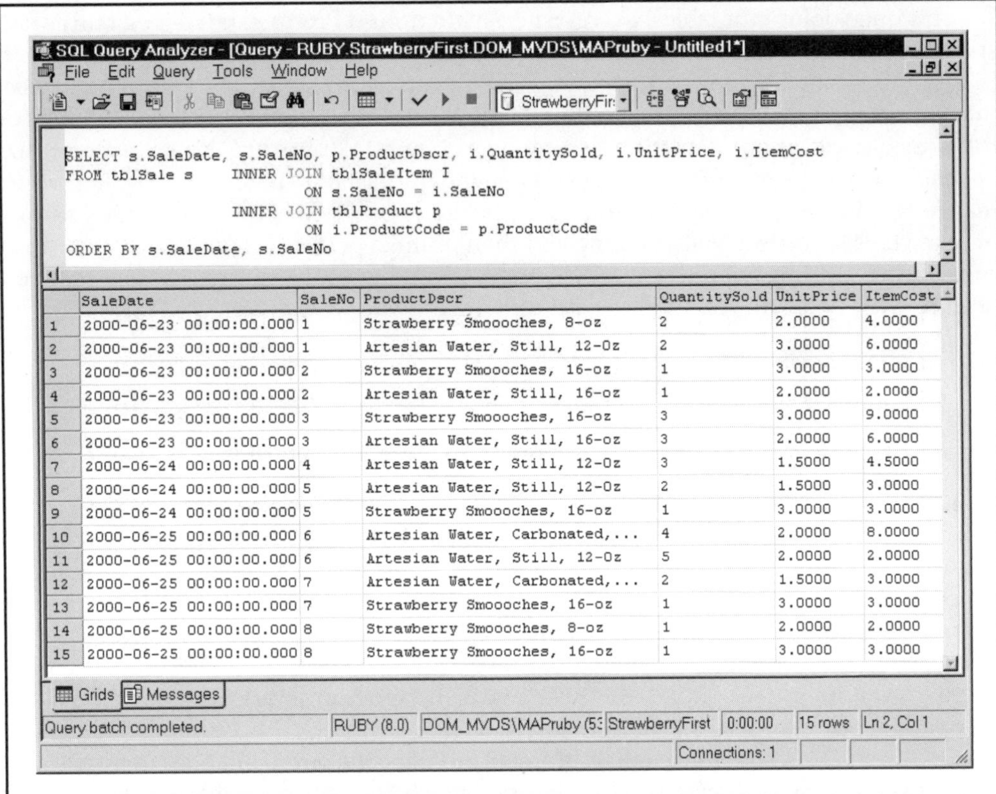

Figure 8-3. A three-table join requires two joining statements, the first that joins tblSale to tblSaleItem, the second that joins tblSaleItem to tblProduct.

Using the T-SQL syntax:

```
SELECT e.EventName, s.SaleDate, s.SaleNo, p.ProductDscr,
       i.QuantitySold, i.UnitPrice, i.ItemCost
FROM tblEvent e, tblSale s, tblSaleItem i, tblProduct p
WHERE e.EventID = s.EventID
  AND s.SaleNo = i.SaleNo
  AND i.ProductCode = p.ProductCode
ORDER BY s.SaleDate, e.EventName, s.SaleNo
```

This query joins four tables: Event, Sale, SaleItem, and Product. It will need three join statements for the three *pairs* of tables: Event-Sale, Sale-SaleItem, and SaleItem-Product. In the SQL Server 2000 environment, you can join up to 255 tables, in theory. In practice, the more tables you join, the longer it will take for the query optimizer to evaluate all of the possible execution plans; thus, the longer it will take to run. At some point, the optimizer will have to quit analyzing and go with the best plan it has found so far, which may not be the most optimal solution. As a practical limit, once you start to get beyond six or seven tables, you might start seeing less-than-optimal performance; so it may be worth considering splitting the query into two parts. If you have a 10-table join query that you need to write and run, you might want to create the following batch job:

1. Join five tables in each of two queries.
2. Output the results to temporary tables.
3. Run a third query that joins the two temporary tables for the final output.

If you create true temporary tables by prefixing the table name with the # sign, you will be using up some of the space in the tempdb database, and possibly you'll be competing with other users for this resource. To be considerate, you could delete the temporary tables immediately after the third join query is run by including a DROP TABLE command in the batch. The other possibility would be to create "work" tables in your own database, and again delete them when you have finished. Or, if you'll be doing this operation frequently, you can use the TRUNCATE TABLE command to remove just the data and reclaim the space, while retaining the table structure itself.

One thing to keep in mind with multiple table joins: the outer join does not work correctly if you join more than two tables. It is possible to have a three-table outer query run and produce results, with no warnings, but they're not the correct results. In each of our tests, the query processor reinterpreted all join statements in the query as inner joins. The query executes and returns a result set, but rows from the outer table that do not have a match are not included as part of the result. It seems odd that the Microsoft SQL Server development team does not pick up this problem and do something about it. In fact, sometimes it will give you a message saying that what you are asking is not permitted. Thus, you have a situation that is not only inconsistent, but sometimes it actually returns misinformation.

EQUI-JOINS AND NATURAL JOINS

Database theoreticians have defined two special types of inner join. Although you may never use these terms yourself, knowing what they are will help you if someone starts dropping these terms at the next SQL Server Users Group meeting. The two types of inner joins are the equi-join and the natural join. If you request both the join column from table A and the join column from table B, you've written an equi-join. This illustrates the point that, when a column name occurs in both tables, you have to declare which one of the two same-name columns you want by adding the table name in front of the column name.

```
SELECT p.PersonID, p.FirstName, c.PersonID, c.CommValue
FROM tblPerson p INNER JOIN tblCommDevice c
  ON p.PersonID  = c.PersonID
WHERE c.CommType = 'home'
```

If you were to write the above query like so:

```
SELECT *
FROM tblPerson p INNER JOIN tblCommDevice c
                 ON p.PersonID  = c.PersonID
WHERE c.CommType = 'home'
```

the result set returned would be an equi-join—that is, you'd see two columns, each of which was labeled PersonID. The default behavior of SQL Server under these query circumstances (SELECT *) is to do an equi-join.

A natural join, on the other hand, displays just one copy of the join columns, which is actually a more realistic way of presenting data. Does it matter which of the matching columns you display, seeing that they are identical? No, it doesn't matter. Just pick the column you prefer.

```
SELECT p.PersonID, p.FirstName, p.LastName, c.CommValue
FROM tblPerson p INNER JOIN tblCommDevice c
  ON p.PersonID  = c.PersonID
WHERE c.CommType = 'home'
```

Using the T-SQL syntax:

```
SELECT p.PersonID, p.FirstName, p.LastName, c.CommValue
FROM tblPerson p, tblCommDevice c
WHERE p.PersonID  = c.PersonID
  AND c.CommType = 'home'
```

OUTER JOINS

Data that is missing from the database can be as important as data that is present in the database. Suppose you want to see a list of all vendors and which inventory items each vendor is supplying. That's no problem: you can write an inner join query to relate the Vendor table to the Inventory table, using the primary key/foreign key combinations, and you'll have your report. However, you'll notice that some vendors found in the Vendor table are missing from this report. That's because you haven't purchased from some vendors recently, so there will not be an entry in the inventory table for these vendors. An inner join does not return a row for that product. For cases like this, you will need to use an outer join.

The Left Outer Join

A left outer join returns all rows from table A, whether or not there is a match in table B. For those rows from table A that have no match in table B, the row will be padded with NULL, as shown in Figure 8-4. In the ANSI syntax, a left outer join looks like this:

```
SELECT v.VendorName, i.InventoryDscr
FROM tblVendor v LEFT OUTER JOIN tblInventory i
              ON v.VendorID = i.VendorID
ORDER BY v.VendorName
```

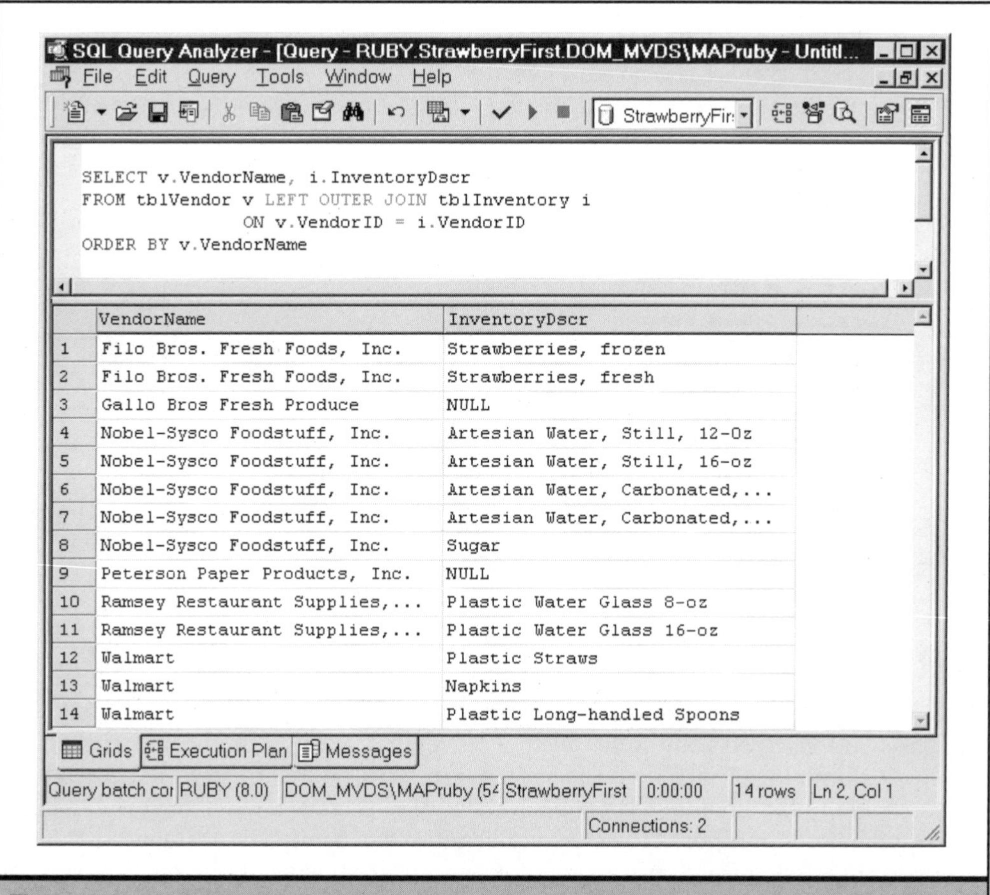

	VendorName	InventoryDscr
1	Filo Bros. Fresh Foods, Inc.	Strawberries, frozen
2	Filo Bros. Fresh Foods, Inc.	Strawberries, fresh
3	Gallo Bros Fresh Produce	NULL
4	Nobel-Sysco Foodstuff, Inc.	Artesian Water, Still, 12-Oz
5	Nobel-Sysco Foodstuff, Inc.	Artesian Water, Still, 16-oz
6	Nobel-Sysco Foodstuff, Inc.	Artesian Water, Carbonated,...
7	Nobel-Sysco Foodstuff, Inc.	Artesian Water, Carbonated,...
8	Nobel-Sysco Foodstuff, Inc.	Sugar
9	Peterson Paper Products, Inc.	NULL
10	Ramsey Restaurant Supplies,...	Plastic Water Glass 8-oz
11	Ramsey Restaurant Supplies,...	Plastic Water Glass 16-oz
12	Walmart	Plastic Straws
13	Walmart	Napkins
14	Walmart	Plastic Long-handled Spoons

Figure 8-4. This left outer join returns all rows from tblVendor whether or not the vendor has supplied anything for the company inventory table.

This is a left outer join because you're returning all the data from the table on the left (table A)—that is, all of the vendors, plus the corresponding data, if any—from the table on the right (table B) of the join. The word "outer" is optional because a left join can only be an outer join, but it's customary to use the phrase "left outer join."

The Right Outer Join

A right outer join is the opposite of a left outer join—it returns all rows from table B, whether or not there's a match in table A. Once again, if there is no matching row in table A, the result set row is padded out with NULL. You can write the above left outer join query as a right outer join query by swapping the order of the tables, with the same result set as that shown in Figure 8-4:

```
SELECT v.VendorName, i.InventoryDscr
FROM tblInventory i RIGHT OUTER JOIN tblVendor v
               ON i.VendorID = v.VendorID
ORDER BY v.VendorName
```

Internally, SQL Server doesn't bother to evaluate a right outer join; it just flips the order of the tables and treats it as a left outer join, as you can see in Figure 8-5. In both cases, the Vendor table is first sorted into VendorName order, ascending. Then, for each row in the outer table (tblVendor), it scans the inner table (tblInventory) and outputs matching rows.

If you are maintaining some older code, you might see an outer join written in the T-SQL syntax. Whereas in the ANSI syntax the word LEFT or RIGHT is fairly obvious, the T-SQL syntax is harder to spot:

```
SELECT v.VendorName, i.InventoryDscr
FROM tblVendor v,  tblInventory I
WHERE v.VendorID *= i.VendorID
ORDER BY v.VendorName
```

The only indication that this is an outer join is in the WHERE clause. There is an asterisk before the equal sign. You know that in a SELECT clause the asterisk means "get everything." The *= means "get everything from the table on the left of the equal sign (table A) and any matching data from the table on the right side (table B)." This code listing produces the same result set as the ANSI standard code listing for the left outer join, above. To write a right outer join, use the designation =*.

Does it matter which of the join columns you display (if you choose to display that column at all) when you're writing an outer join? Yes, it does. You should display the join column from the outer table, so that each row in the result set will have a non-NULL value in the join column. If you were to choose the join column from the inner table, you might have NULL in some of the result set rows for which there is no match in the inner table.

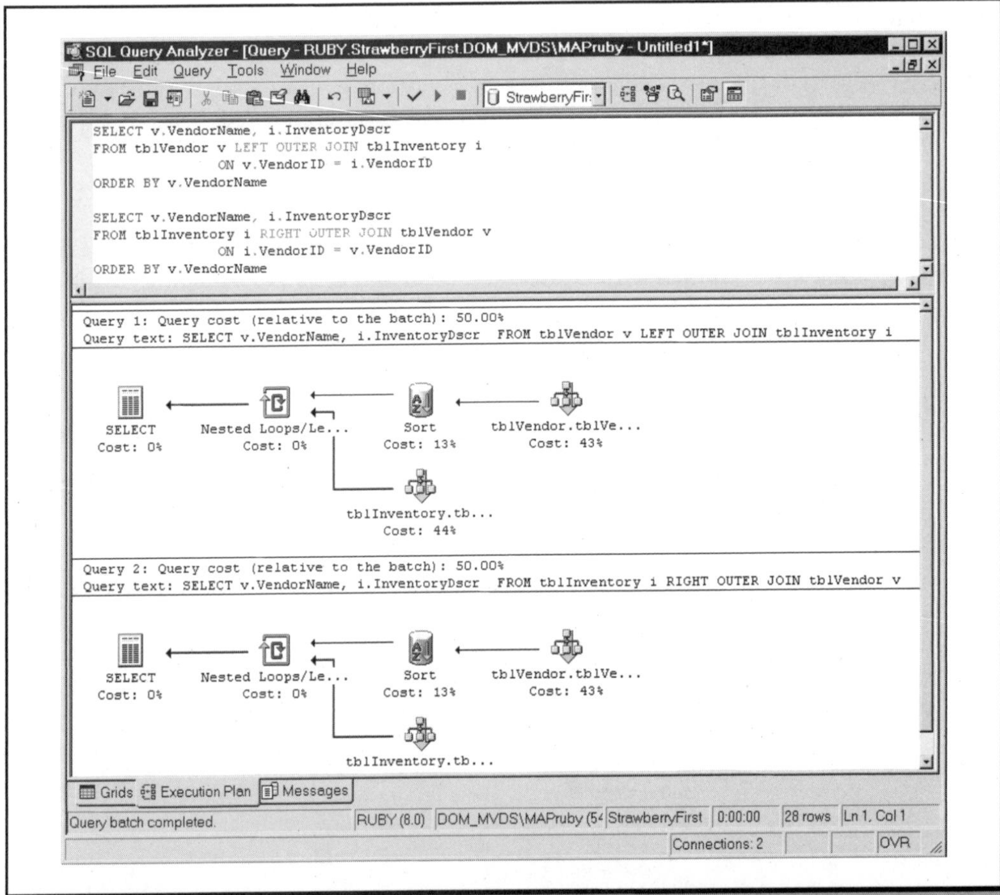

Figure 8-5. SQL Server, if left to its own devices, will treat a left outer join and a right outer join the same way.

The Full Outer Join

The full outer join is a new feature introduced in SQL Server 6.5. The full outer join combines the left and the right outer joins; and it gives you all the data from both table A and table B, matching rows when appropriate and filling in NULLs when there is no match. You have to write the full outer join in ANSI syntax, as there is no *=* notation for the T-SQL syntax.

The full outer join syntax looks like this:

```
SELECT v.VendorName, i.InventoryDscr
FROM tblInventory i FULL OUTER JOIN tblVendor v
              ON i.VendorID = v.VendorID
ORDER BY v.VendorName
```

And the result set, as you can see in Figure 8-6, contains rows padded with NULL on both the right and the left ends. The left outer joins you wrote earlier in this chapter didn't pick up the inventory items that aren't associated with a vendor, such as water for Smoooches and ice cubes. Even the right outer join didn't list these items, because we swapped the positions of the vendor and inventory tables to show that you can generate

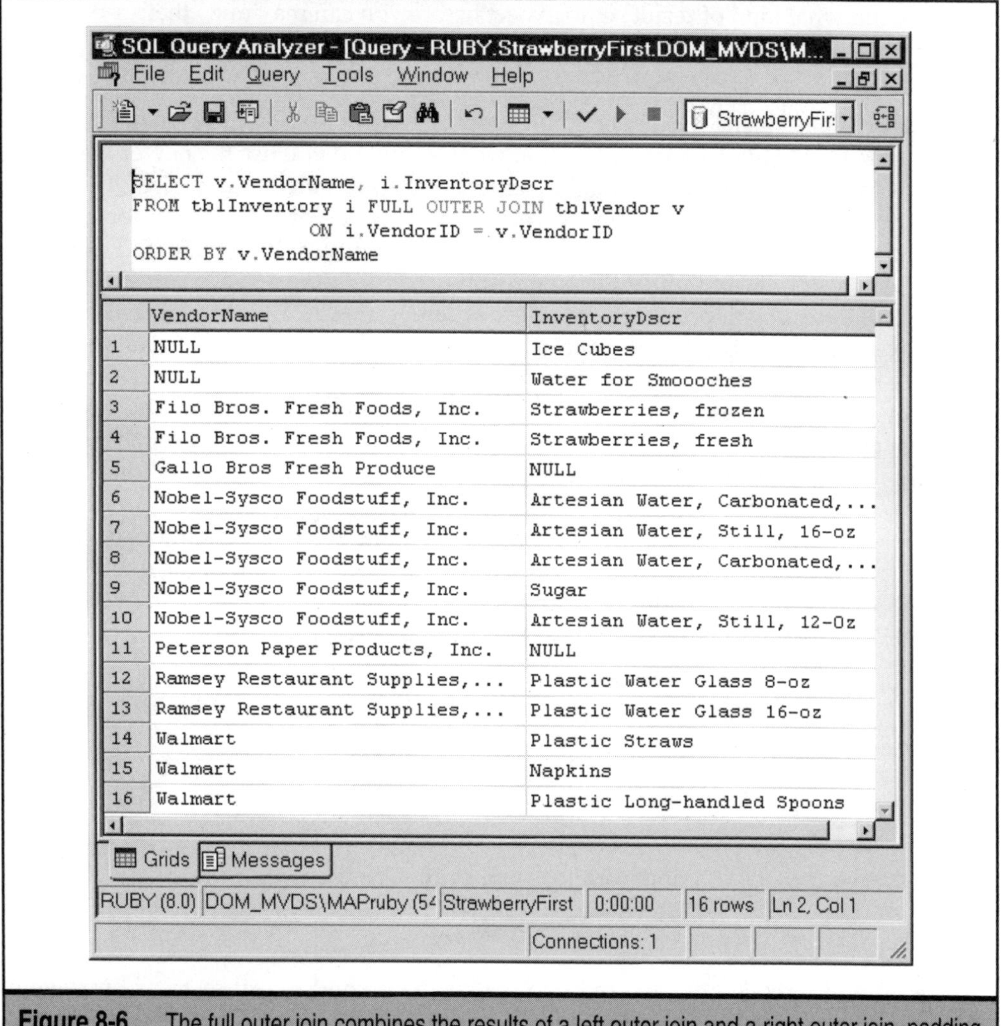


```
SELECT v.VendorName, i.InventoryDscr
FROM tblInventory i FULL OUTER JOIN tblVendor v
            ON i.VendorID = v.VendorID
ORDER BY v.VendorName
```

	VendorName	InventoryDscr
1	NULL	Ice Cubes
2	NULL	Water for Smoooches
3	Filo Bros. Fresh Foods, Inc.	Strawberries, frozen
4	Filo Bros. Fresh Foods, Inc.	Strawberries, fresh
5	Gallo Bros Fresh Produce	NULL
6	Nobel-Sysco Foodstuff, Inc.	Artesian Water, Carbonated,...
7	Nobel-Sysco Foodstuff, Inc.	Artesian Water, Still, 16-oz
8	Nobel-Sysco Foodstuff, Inc.	Artesian Water, Carbonated,...
9	Nobel-Sysco Foodstuff, Inc.	Sugar
10	Nobel-Sysco Foodstuff, Inc.	Artesian Water, Still, 12-Oz
11	Peterson Paper Products, Inc.	NULL
12	Ramsey Restaurant Supplies,...	Plastic Water Glass 8-oz
13	Ramsey Restaurant Supplies,...	Plastic Water Glass 16-oz
14	Walmart	Plastic Straws
15	Walmart	Napkins
16	Walmart	Plastic Long-handled Spoons

Figure 8-6. The full outer join combines the results of a left outer join and a right outer join, padding incomplete rows with NULL.

the same result set from a left outer or a right outer join. Had we left the tables in their original positions, as in

```
SELECT v.VendorName, i.InventoryDscr
FROM tblVendor v RIGHT OUTER JOIN tblInventory i
               ON v.VendorID = i.VendorID
ORDER BY v.VendorName
```

then you would have seen the two items in inventory that have no associated vendors. The outer joins—left, right, and full—are extremely powerful; but you have to know what each one does and what kind of result set to expect before you can maximize their use.

Nulls in a Join

We've talked about using the newer ANSI syntax and the older T-SQL syntax for writing joins, and now we'd like to state clearly that we recommend you use the newer ANSI syntax, in all cases, for two reasons. First, Microsoft has clearly stated that the T-SQL join syntax will be dropped from some future version of SQL Server (when, we don't know). Secondly, and more importantly, there are some conditions under which the T-SQL syntax will return strange and unpredictable results.

As you've seen from previous examples, when you write an outer join, some of the rows may be NULL, representing no data matches with the inner table. This raises a question: does this NULL really exist in a row in the inner table, or was it created as a result of the join query? You have no way of knowing without searching the inner table to confirm the presence or absence of a specific foreign key value. In our Strawberry database, the tables are small and the search would be relatively painless. In a real production system, it might take hours to find the answer to this question.

There's a further complication: when you try to limit the above-mentioned query by restricting the rows to those WHERE xxx IS NULL, the T-SQL version of the query returns some very odd results. Consider these two queries that follow and the result sets shown in Figure 8-7:

```
SELECT v.VendorID, v.VendorName, i.InventoryDscr, i.QuantityOnHand
FROM tblVendor v,  tblInventory i
WHERE v.VendorID *= i.VendorID
```

and

```
SELECT v.VendorID, v.VendorName, i.InventoryDscr, i.QuantityOnHand
FROM tblVendor v,  tblInventory i
WHERE v.VendorID *= i.VendorID
  AND i.QuantityOnHand is NULL
```

The only difference between the two is that the second query restricts on rows in which the QuantityOnHand value is missing (is NULL). The first query result set is correct—there are three rows with no QuantityOnHand value: Peterson Paper Products, Gallo Bros. Fresh Produce, and Walmart Plastic Straws. The second query result set is completely inaccurate. Yet, if you were dealing with large data sets and were not cogni-

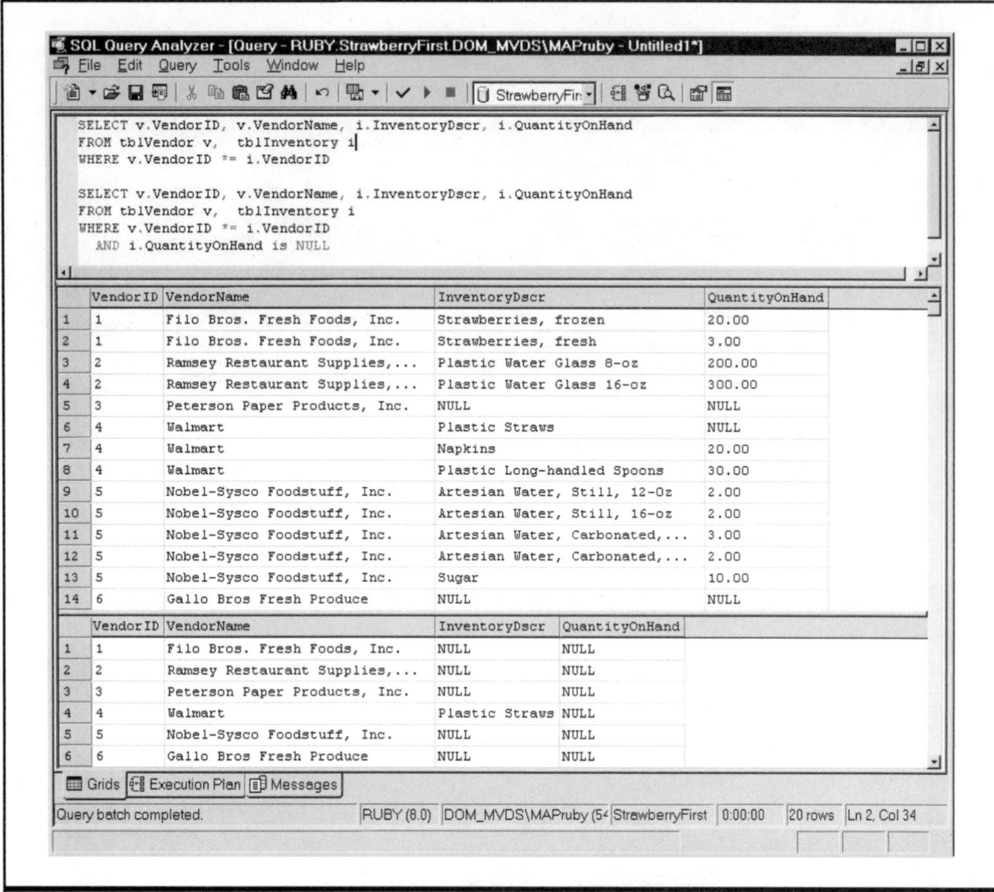

Figure 8-7. The T-SQL syntax of the left outer join can fail to return correct results if there's a row restriction (where QuantityOnHand is NULL) on the inner table.

zant of this limitation of the T-SQL left outer join construct, you might never realize that this query has returned misinformation. Even more interesting is the fact that *the execution plans of these two queries are almost exactly the same,* as you can see from Figure 8-8, so whatever's happening to mess up the second result set is happening internally.

These two queries highlight the fundamental problem with the T-SQL syntax. In the T-SQL query, the WHERE clause is used for both the join criteria and the restrict conditions. The restrict expression "i.QuantityOnHand is NULL" is somehow getting mixed in with the join, producing what are obviously incorrect results.

In the ANSI syntax, as shown in Figure 8-9, the join operation is handled in the JOIN clause and row restrictions are handled by the WHERE clause. There is apparently no confusion between the two, and the result set is correct. The execution plan for this query, shown in Figure 8-10, is quite different from the execution plans of the preceding two queries (Figure 8-8). Although you can't see it, in the bottom execution plan shown in

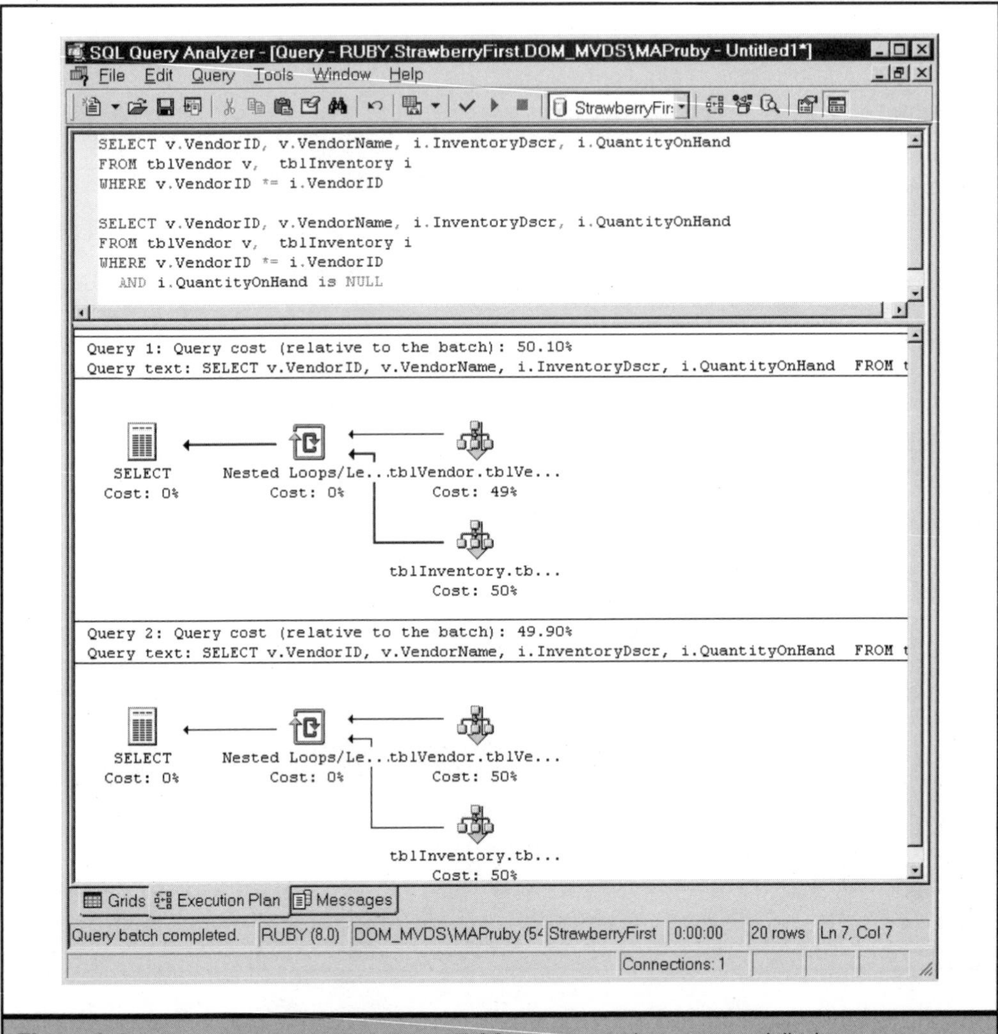

Figure 8-8. The execution plans of the two T-SQL syntax queries are essentially the same, even though one query returns correct results and the second returns incorrect results.

Figure 8-8, the filtering of rows containing NULL QuantityOnHand is done in the first (far right) step, which makes sense. For efficiency of resources when doing a join, you would first restrict the row sets being joined to the smallest they can be and still be joinable. Thus, if there are three rows in the Inventory table that have NULL QuantityOnHand, these are the only three rows that need to be processed in the join operation—right? So, theoretically, this execution plan should have worked, and should have returned the correct result set. However, the T-SQL outer join syntax simply doesn't work right when there's a NULL record set from the inner table.

The execution plan shown in Figure 8-10, from the ANSI syntax version of this query, uses all rows from both tables for the join operation; then it filters just prior to returning the

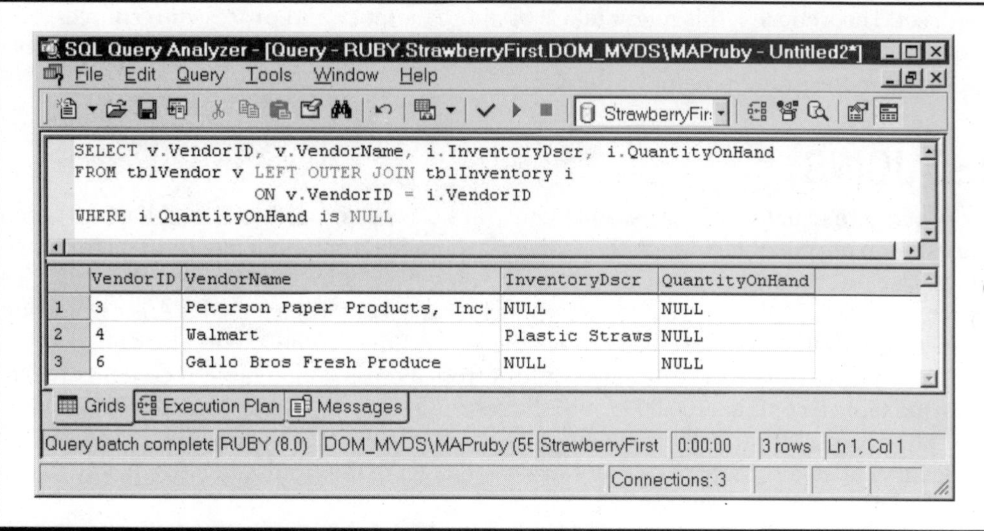

Figure 8-9. The ANSI syntax version of this query returns correct results, despite the presence of a NULL row restriction on the inner table.

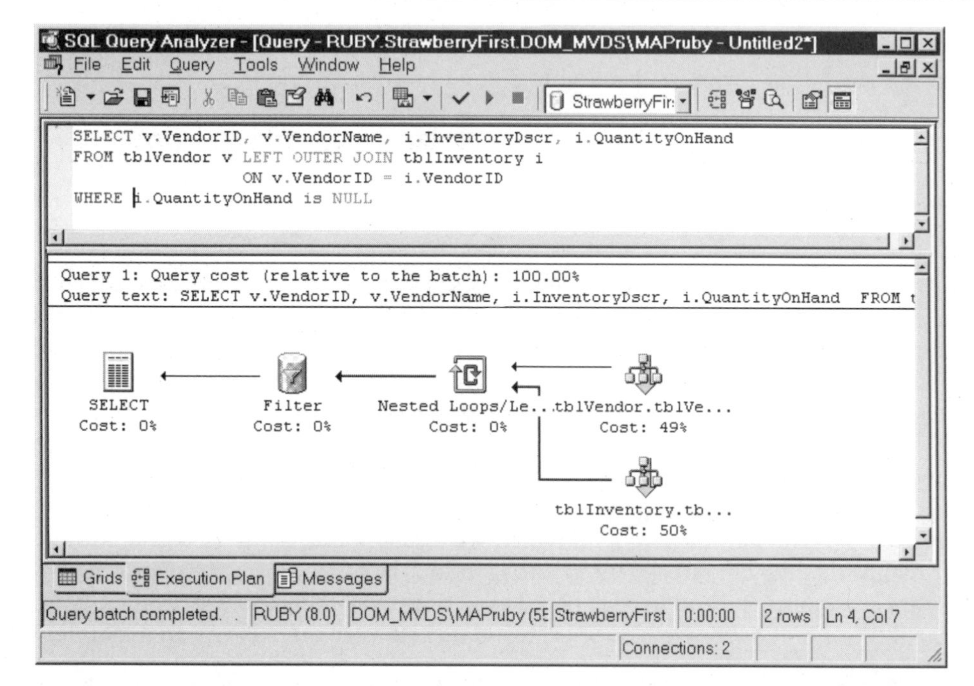

Figure 8-10. The execution plan for the ANSI syntax version of this query is very different from the T-SQL syntax execution plan.

result set. Theoretically, this might take a bit more memory and processor resources; but, apparently, it gets the correct data set returned to the user—and that's really what's most important in the grand scheme of things.

CROSS JOINS

Cross joins are usually bad news. Also known as Cartesian products, they happen when you ask—on purpose or accidentally—for every possible combination of the data from two tables. Usually, the results make no sense—if you get a chance to see the result set, that is! The characteristic style of a cross join resembles a runaway job; so if the DBA is monitoring processing activity, he's most likely to kill the job and then come looking for you.

It's easy to calculate the estimated output from a cross join. If table A contains 10,000 rows and table B contains 100,000 rows, the result set from the table A cross join table B is one billion rows. Multiply the number of rows in table A times the number of rows in table B, and that's how many rows you can expect to get in the result set. Now do you know why the DBA is looking for you?

If you want to try this for yourself, here's a code example you can key into the Query Analyzer:

```
SELECT VendorName, InventoryDscr
FROM tblVendor CROSS JOIN tblInventory
```

The Vendor table contains 6 rows. The Inventory table has 14 rows. Six times 14 equals 84 rows that contain all possible combinations of vendor name and inventory item, as shown in Figure 8-11.

The T-SQL syntax for the cross join is simply the lack of any join statement:

```
SELECT VendorName, InventoryDscr
FROM tblVendor, tblInventory
```

and you get the same result as if you used the ANSI syntax. This is another reason why the ANSI syntax is the preferred syntax. When you use the ANSI syntax, you must intentionally type the word **cross** in order to execute a cross join query. This is hard to do accidentally. In the T-SQL syntax, all you have to do is forget the join statement in the WHERE clause that specifies how the tables are to be joined. If you're writing a multi-table join, this could easily happen. If you're joining six tables in a single query and you write only four join statements, not five as you should have, your result set will contain a partial Cartesian product. In a large result set, you may not detect that this has happened; and certainly, if you're producing a summary report (which we'll talk about in the next chapter), you'll never realize that the data that went into the summarized values was incorrect.

So are cross joins evil and to be avoided at all times? No. You can use the data-generating capabilities of the cross join to build test data sets very quickly. As an example, let's

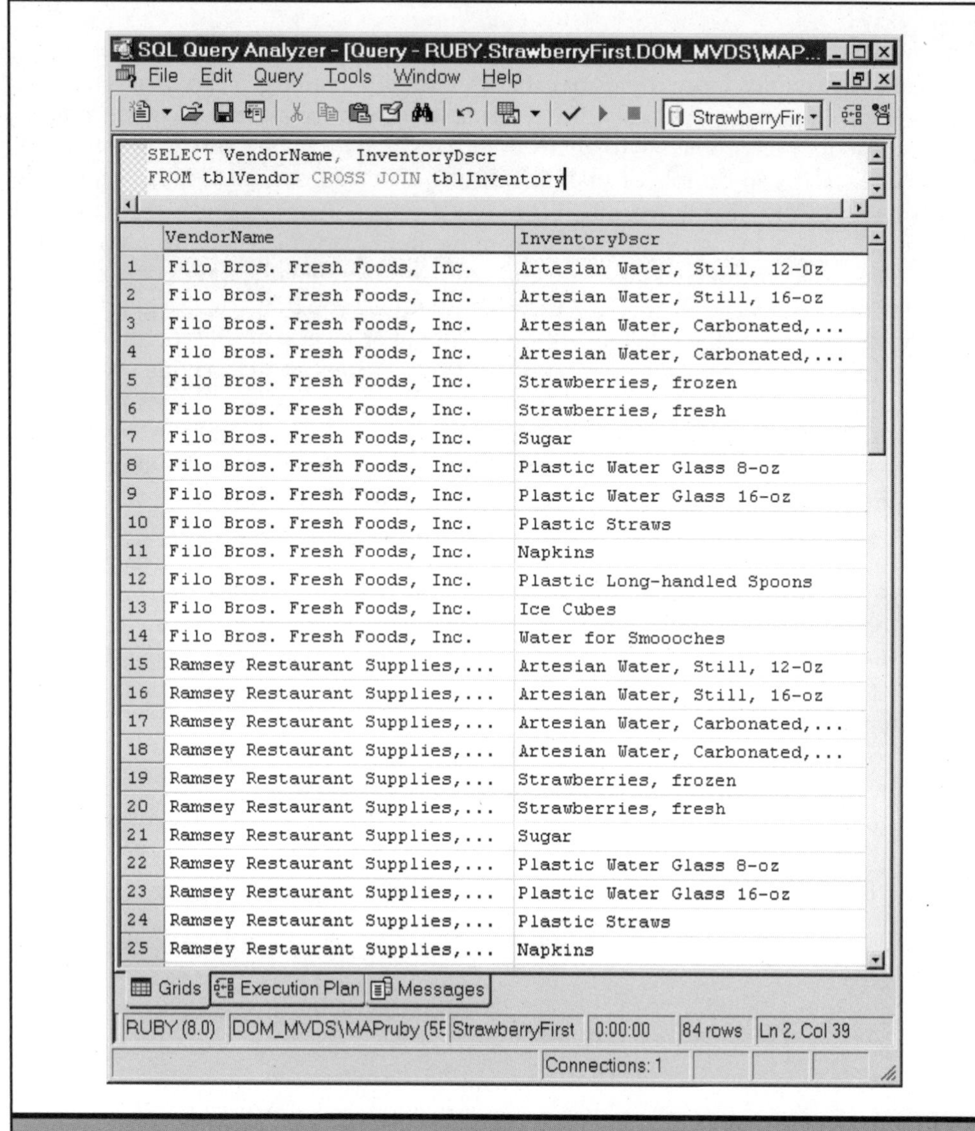

	VendorName	InventoryDscr
1	Filo Bros. Fresh Foods, Inc.	Artesian Water, Still, 12-Oz
2	Filo Bros. Fresh Foods, Inc.	Artesian Water, Still, 16-oz
3	Filo Bros. Fresh Foods, Inc.	Artesian Water, Carbonated,...
4	Filo Bros. Fresh Foods, Inc.	Artesian Water, Carbonated,...
5	Filo Bros. Fresh Foods, Inc.	Strawberries, frozen
6	Filo Bros. Fresh Foods, Inc.	Strawberries, fresh
7	Filo Bros. Fresh Foods, Inc.	Sugar
8	Filo Bros. Fresh Foods, Inc.	Plastic Water Glass 8-oz
9	Filo Bros. Fresh Foods, Inc.	Plastic Water Glass 16-oz
10	Filo Bros. Fresh Foods, Inc.	Plastic Straws
11	Filo Bros. Fresh Foods, Inc.	Napkins
12	Filo Bros. Fresh Foods, Inc.	Plastic Long-handled Spoons
13	Filo Bros. Fresh Foods, Inc.	Ice Cubes
14	Filo Bros. Fresh Foods, Inc.	Water for Smoooches
15	Ramsey Restaurant Supplies,...	Artesian Water, Still, 12-Oz
16	Ramsey Restaurant Supplies,...	Artesian Water, Still, 16-oz
17	Ramsey Restaurant Supplies,...	Artesian Water, Carbonated,...
18	Ramsey Restaurant Supplies,...	Artesian Water, Carbonated,...
19	Ramsey Restaurant Supplies,...	Strawberries, frozen
20	Ramsey Restaurant Supplies,...	Strawberries, fresh
21	Ramsey Restaurant Supplies,...	Sugar
22	Ramsey Restaurant Supplies,...	Plastic Water Glass 8-oz
23	Ramsey Restaurant Supplies,...	Plastic Water Glass 16-oz
24	Ramsey Restaurant Supplies,...	Plastic Straws
25	Ramsey Restaurant Supplies,...	Napkins

Figure 8-11. A cross join produces a Cartesian product of the contents of the two tables in the join.

suppose that you build a table and populate it with 50 first names. Then you build a second table of 50 last names. When you SELECT INTO a third table of first and last names, cross joining the first two tables, voilà! You have 2,500 customer names with almost no effort at all.

SELF JOINS

Do you ever get two or more copies of catalogs and bulk mailings? The names and addresses are *almost* identical, but not quite. You are in the vendor's database twice, at least. This is a very common problem with many databases, and it can be a very expensive situation, especially if you do lots of mailings. It also annoys your customers, who quite rightly think they are paying too much for your products to cover the costs of mailing three or four catalogs to each household. Retaining more than one record for each of your customers is also inefficient, taking more disk storage space. Finally, it reduces your ability to really market effectively to your customers, because you don't have a good picture of their buying habits, as the statistics are spread out over several profiles per individual. Here's a likely scenario: A customer is supposed to get a discount after having spent more than a set amount, say $10,000, with your company—but the customer is not seeing this discount applied to the orders. On further investigation—probably initiated by an irate customer—you see the customer had purchases listed under three different customer names in the database, for amounts of $6,000, $5,500, and $4,200.

This is the classic "dirty data syndrome," and you've got to do something about it. If you have the budget, you could invest in a product like dfPower Series 3.3, a data-quality management product offered by DataFlux/SAS (http://www.dataflux.com/). Products like this tend to be expensive, so you might have to resort to creating your own filters. In order to eliminate these duplicates, you'll have to use some form of self join in which a table is joined to itself, and pattern match searches are made for matching data. The trick is that you don't want to see the match of each record with itself, you only want to check for the match of each record with every other record. Also, you will need some way of restricting the result set to ensure that you only see the duplicates.

You don't have very dirty data in the Strawberry database, but you can do a simulation. The following code will join the Person table to itself, so you can find people who have the same last name:

```
SELECT a.FirstName, b.FirstName, a.LastName
FROM tblPerson a INNER JOIN tblPerson b
                 ON a.LastName = b.LastName
WHERE a.personid > b.personid
ORDER by a.LastName, a.FirstName
```

Using the T-SQL syntax:

```
SELECT a.FirstName, b.FirstName, a.LastName
FROM tblPerson a, tblPerson b
WHERE a.LastName = b.LastName
  AND a.personid > b.personid
ORDER by a.LastName, a.FirstName
```

You can see the result set in Figure 8-12. The two copies of the Person table are joined on last name; so the LastName column in each row of table Person-A is compared to all the rows of table Person-B, and any matches are added to the result set. The inequality operator (>) on the last line ensures that matches that are a row matched to itself are not included in the result set. We chose to use PersonID for this inequality match because numbers compare faster than characters. We could have used FirstName and gotten the same results. The "less than" inequality was used instead of "not equal" because the "not equal" would return the inverse matches as well—that is, (Person-A match Person-B) and (Person-B match Person-A).

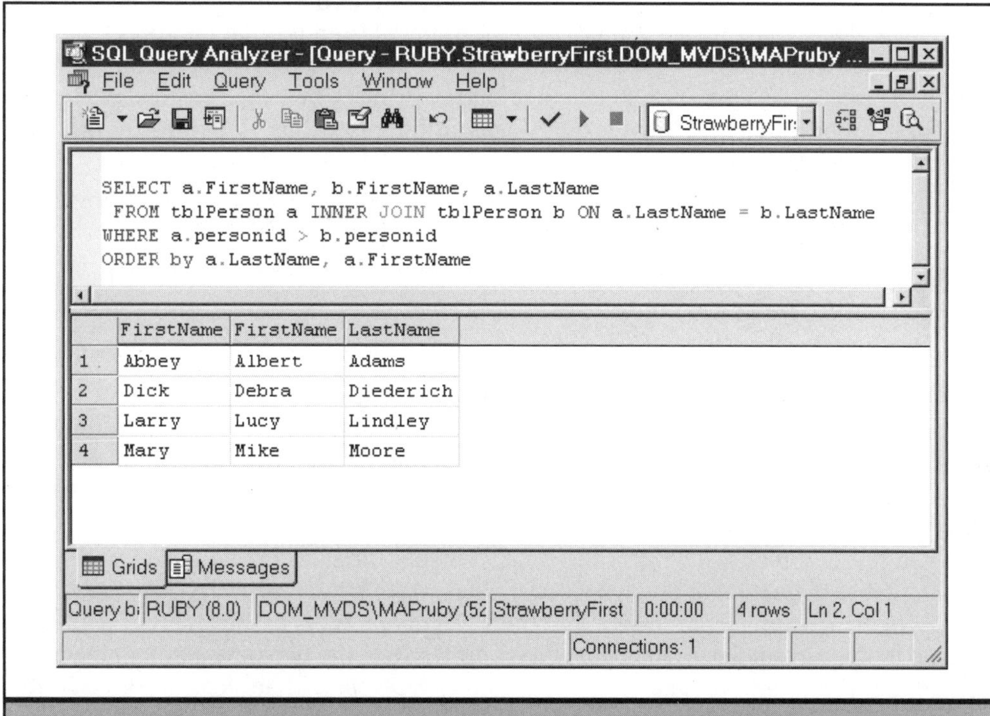

Figure 8-12. A table joined to itself will allow you to search for certain criteria, such as people with the same last name.

UNION OPERATORS

The union operator is the command you use when you need to append one data set to another and present the two data sets as a single output. The most typical situation in which you would do this is with data archiving. You've decided to archive the Strawberry sales data for previous years to a different set of tables. This will speed up modifications to the Sales table, which now has fewer rows in it. You've also placed the archive Sales table on a different filegroup on another disk, so now there's more room on the primary filegroup for new sales data. This also simplifies your backup strategy. Now you can back up all the archive sales data much less frequently than the current sales data by using a filegroup backup strategy.

All was going going well until the VP of Marketing wanted a report that included sales figures for the past 24 months. It wasn't a problem to query the current data for the information for this report. But the data for the previous year is off in a set of separate tables. The archive sales tables contain more or less the same columns as the current sales table (the archive tables always have an additional column, ArchiveDatetime, that indicates when the row has been archived). You don't want to write a join to match rows in the old tables to rows in the new table—they don't have that kind of primary key–to–foreign key relationship. The solution is to write the same query against the current Sales table and the other archive tables, and combine the output with the UNION operator, as follows:

```
SELECT SaleNo, SaleDate, EventID, SubTotal, SalesTotal
FROM tblSale
UNION
SELECT SaleNo, SaleDate, EventID, SubTotal, SalesTotal
FROM tblSale_Archive
ORDER BY SaleDate, SalesTotal
```

The T-SQL syntax for a UNION query is the same as the ANSI syntax. Although you can't see it here, the column names in the ORDER BY clause are always columns from the first SELECT clause in the UNION query. As with a JOIN query, you can UNION as many as 255 tables together.

When you archived last year's sales data, you kept the sales for December in the current sales table, even though you removed the data from January through November, because of open accounts. That means that the December data is in the archive Sales table and also in the current Sales table. So, when you UNION the two data sets together, you would think you'd see duplicate rows. Fortunately, SQL Server handles this for you automatically and filters out the duplicate rows. If, for some reason, you decided that you wanted to see those duplicate rows, you could write the following query:

```
SELECT SaleNo, SaleDate, EventID, SubTotal, SalesTotal
FROM tblSale
UNION ALL
```

```
SELECT SaleNo, SaleDate, EventID, SubTotal, SalesTotal
FROM tblSale_Archive
ORDER BY SaleDate, SalesTotal
```

There's an extra performance benefit from writing the UNION ALL operator. If you know for a fact that there are no duplicate rows (because of the way you archived, all the data in a table is from one year and only from that one year, with no overlap), you can tell the UNION operator not to worry about eliminating duplicate rows. This saves a little work and speeds up the query.

SEMI JOINS

As you're viewing the execution plans, you will sometimes see that SQL Server has used a semi join. This might be a left or right semi join, or even a left anti–semi join. So what is a semi join, and why is SQL Server using one when you wrote something quite different? What's even stranger, when you try to code a left semi join, SQL Server says that the syntax is wrong. You cannot code a semi join. The query optimizer has the option of using it, but you cannot directly call a semi join. A semi join behaves sort of like an inner join, where there is a match between two tables. The difference is that the result set requested contains data from only one table. For example, you might ask for a list of people who are also employees. You only want to see first names and last names, but you have to reference the Employee table to separate the employee-Person from the other entries in the Person table. We haven't talked yet about subqueries, which are the types of query you would write to invoke a semi join; but for now, we'll demonstrate what we're talking about with this subquery:

```
SELECT * FROM tblPerson
WHERE PersonID IN (select PersonID from tblEmployee)
```

The outer query says "display first names and last names from the Person table where the ID values are found by a reference operation in the Employee table." The T-SQL syntax is the same as the ANSI syntax.

MERGE JOINS

The most basic join in SQL Server is a simple nested loop, in which SQL Server takes a row from the first table and uses the value to scan the inner table, searching for a match. But sometimes you will see in the execution plan that SQL Server used a merge join. A merge join is not something you can directly call in your SQL code. It is one of the approaches used by SQL Server to optimize joins, and it was introduced in version 7.0. It is possible that the Query Optimizer will use a merge join in conjunction with an inner or outer join query, a semi join operator, or a union query. When the required conditions are met and SQL Server can use a merge join, there is a real performance benefit due to the reduced I/O required. In a merge join, both inputs have to be sorted on the merge columns, the columns that are in the equality clause of the join (the ON clause). The ON clause join predicate must be an equal, not some other operator, for the merge join to be used. The Merge Join operator takes a row from each input and compares them to see if there is a match. In the case of Inner Join, for example, both rows would be returned if there is a match. If there is not a match, and the rows are not equal, the row with the lowest value is discarded; and the next row is read from that input, and the comparison repeated. This continues until all the rows have been processed.

The requirement that both inputs be sorted implies that when existing indexes are available, this merge join approach can be used; indeed it is very fast on large data sets that have the necessary indexes. Even without a suitable index, the optimizer may use a merge join when there is an ORDER BY, GROUP BY, or CUBE in the query, because a sort has to be performed anyway—so the merge join can take advantage of the sort operation. Occasionally, the optimizer itself may decide that it can place a sort operator in the query plan and still come out ahead, although that is not something you will see very often.

HASH JOINS

Another type of join that shows up on execution plans is the hash join. Like the merge join, this join was new in version 7.0. The Query Optimizer will use a hash join when it decides that it would be more efficient than using a nested loop join or a merge join. That would usually be when there is no index that can be used to resolve the query. Hashing is a technique for allocating data into sets of a manageable size, based on some characteristic of the data. As an analogy, suppose that you have a closet full of shirts or blouses. You might sort them by type, such as formal, dress shirts, casual, polo, t-shirts, and so on. Or you might group them by color. So when you want a blue casual shirt, you can zero in on it quickly, rather than having to sort through the entire closet. The hash join also tries to rapidly narrow the search and look at just a few rows, rather than scanning whole tables looking for a match.

An algorithm known as a hash function is applied to the data, usually to the columns being employed in the join. The output of the algorithm is a hash value. The tables you are joining are assigned as the probe input and build input. The build input will be the join column from the table that has the smaller number of rows. SQL Server creates a hash table in memory to store the column values from the build input. The data from the hash table is divided into hash buckets based on the hash values. Each row from the build input is run through the hash algorithm to compute a hash value, and then the row is assigned to the hash bucket with the same hash value. Because more than one input can produce the same hash value, the row data is stored in the hash bucket in a linked list format. Next, the rows in the probe input are hashed and a hash value computed. Identical inputs to the hash function will produce identical outputs, so if there are matching rows, they will fall in the same hash bucket with the same hash value. The hash value is used to identify the one hash bucket that might contain a match to this row. So the process has eliminated most of the rows from consideration, and now all that remains is to compare the row from the probe input with the few rows from the build input that are stored in the linked list in the hash bucket. If there is a match, the row becomes part of the result set. Then the process moves on to the next row in the probe table. If, as it runs the query, SQL Server determines that it would be better to reverse the assignments of probe and build tables, it will do so dynamically.

The hash process has the aim of narrowing the search as quickly as possible, so the key comes up with a hash function that produces an optimal number of hash buckets, with an optimal number of rows in each bucket. Choosing the attribute on which to base the hash is also important. These choices will vary depending on datatype, the number of rows, size of the columns, and many other factors. Fortunately, SQL Server handles all this internally, if it decides that a hash join is what it wants to use.

Although it looks like an efficient algorithm, especially when compared with a nested loop on tables with no indexes, the hash join relies for its performance on being able to keep the hash table in memory; so it does require a significant amount of available memory. This memory may not continue to be available if you have a large number of users querying against the same server, or if you are running the join on a desktop system with just barely enough memory to accommodate the operating system and SQL Server. If the memory is not available, SQL Server may decide to use this algorithm anyway, but it will have to split the hash table into partitions that are written out to disk and read back in as needed. Obviously, this increases the amount of I/O required and drives up the cost of this query. SQL Server is able to use a technique by which some of the partitions are written out to disk as necessary and some are retained in memory, in an attempt to reduce the I/O.

CHAPTER 9

Summarizing Data and Reporting

The reporting tools available within SQL Server are fairly basic—you might even say primitive. Generally, if you build a SQL Server–based application, you'll use some other software such as Access, Visual Basic custom applications, Excel (Microsoft Query), or any of a host of software tools to create the reports that are part of the client interface. But it's useful to know about the SQL Server tools for prototyping and testing purposes and for client interface support purposes. These tools can be used to produce views, stored procedures, and triggers that support the client interfaces directly by causing the data processing to be done on the SQL Server instead of at the client computer, where the interface is located. These tools also can be used to create summary and aggregate data that can then be moved into a data warehouse, where storing calculated data is a very common thing to do.

In this chapter, we will look at how to write this aggregate and summary code. Then we will look at some of the ways in which you can use these aggregate and summary functions. We will use the execution plan display to see what is going on behind the scenes.

AGGREGATE FUNCTIONS

Aggregate functions are functions that aggregate, or combine, values in a data set so that you end up with a single number solution. Typical aggregate functions are COUNT(), SUM(), AVG(), MAX(), and MIN(). You can find these functions in the Query Analyzer Object Browser (Tools | Object Browser), classified under Common Objects, Aggregate Functions.

Aggregate functions are used to create summary reports. Up to this point, you've been writing queries that produce detail reports—row after row of itemized detail data. Now you'll write queries that summarize whole sets of values.

COUNT()

The COUNT() function is a useful one when you are developing a query, because it will tell you how many rows will be returned without actually bringing back any data. For example, if you want to know how many rows are in the Event table, you could use this:

```
USE Strawberry
SELECT COUNT (*) FROM tblEvent
```

COUNT(*) simply returns the total number of rows in the table. It counts every row, including any that contain NULL values. If you want to know how many events were scheduled in July, you can modify this query to read

```
SELECT COUNT (*) FROM tblEvent
WHERE StartDate BETWEEN '07-01-00' AND '07-31-00'
```

The result set contains the number of rows that meet the criteria. You can use the COUNT() function to count any kind of data, number, character, or date. You'll always get a number value returned. Another question you might ask is how many different values are in a column, something called *variance*. Variance is not the total number of rows in the table, nor is it the total number of instances of a column in a table (total number of rows less NULL instances). Variance is the number of distinct values in a column. For instance, if you had a column in the Person table called "gender," you would expect to find three distinct values in the set of data that comprises this column: male, female, and NULL. In another example, you can find out how many different types of communications devices you have in the CommDevice table by using the DISTINCT clause in this query:

```
SELECT COUNT(DISTINCT CommType)
FROM tblCommDevice
```

The result set indicates that four different types of device (home phone, cell, fax, and so on) are in use at present. The DISTINCT keyword tells SQL Server to ignore duplicate values of CommType. The execution plan for this query, as shown in Figure 9-1, shows (reading right to left) first a scan of the data or the relevant index, and then a Sort/Distinct operation that orders the data by the values of CommDevice. Then there's a stream aggregate, where the values in each distinct group are summarized. Finally, there's a scalar computation where the sum is divided by the number of records to get the average, and the presentation of the result set.

New in SQL Server 2000 is the COUNT_BIG() function, the only difference being that COUNT_BIG returns a value as a bigint datatype, while the COUNT function returns an integer value. So if you need to count value sets in a multi-terabyte database, you might need to use the COUNT_BIG() function instead of COUNT().

SUM(), AVG()

The SUM() and AVG() aggregate functions can be used only with numeric datatypes, including the various integer and numeric/decimal datatypes, and the result set is also a number. The SUM() function sums up the values in a column. The AVG() function takes the sum of the values and divides by the count—in other words, it gets an average value of the set of data you've specified. For example, suppose you wanted to know the amount of the next payroll. Summing the payroll amounts for all your employees can be done simply:

```
SELECT SUM (PayAmount) AS 'Payroll' FROM tblEmployee
```

If you want to know the average paycheck for the group, add an AVG() function to the query:

```
SELECT SUM (PayAmount) AS 'Payroll', AVG (PayAmount) AS 'Average'
FROM tblEmployee
```

The execution plan for this query, as displayed in Figure 9-2, shows that SQL Server computes only one stream aggregate, in which it calculates the sum and also keeps count of the number of records. You haven't included a distinct or sorting operation in this query, so the Sort/Distinct step shown as Figure 9-1 is not present. The next step is a

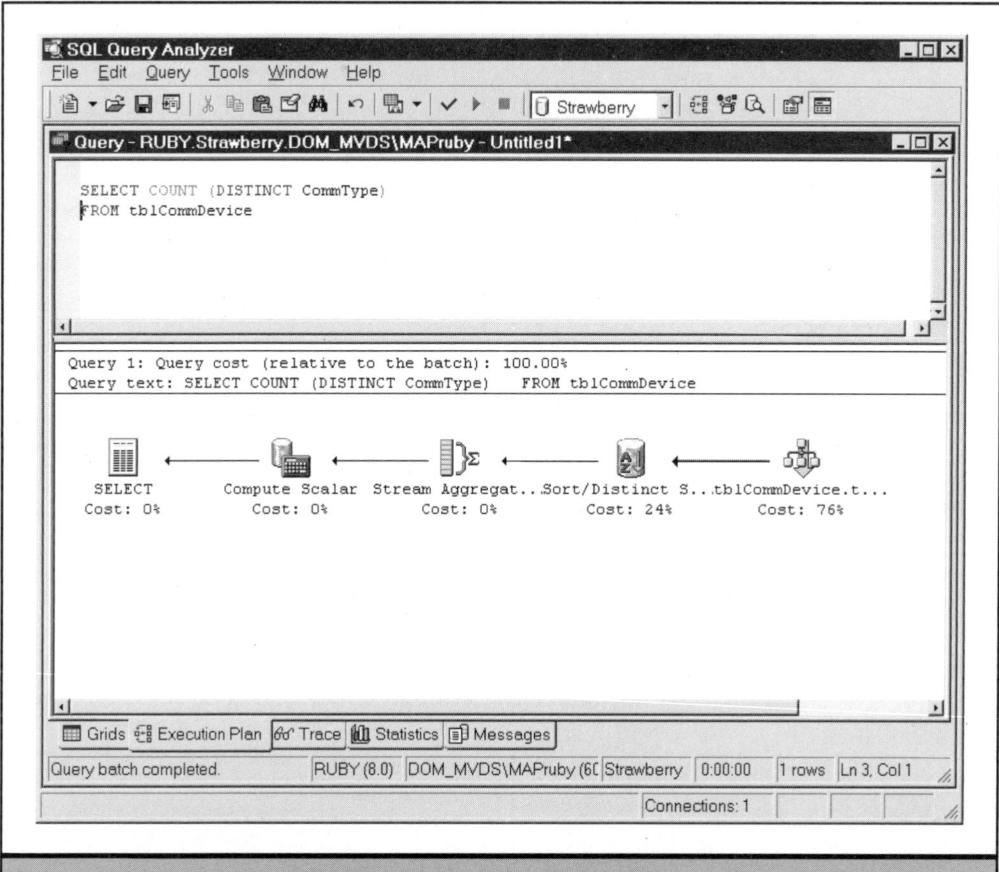

Figure 9-1. The execution plan of a COUNT (DISTINCT) has five steps.

Compute Scalar, where it takes the sum and divides by the number of records to get the average. Interestingly, the row count is kept in the stream aggregate. This is so that if there were no rows that met your row search criteria, had you applied one with a WHERE clause, the result returned would be NULL, not zero. Remember, NULL and zero are not the same. For example, suppose that in the previous query you had included a WHERE clause requesting the payroll only for employees whose job title is Subcontractor. A return of zero would imply that you had successfully selected a group of subcontractors, but their paychecks would be zero this week. NULL would suggest that there were no subcontractors on your payroll.

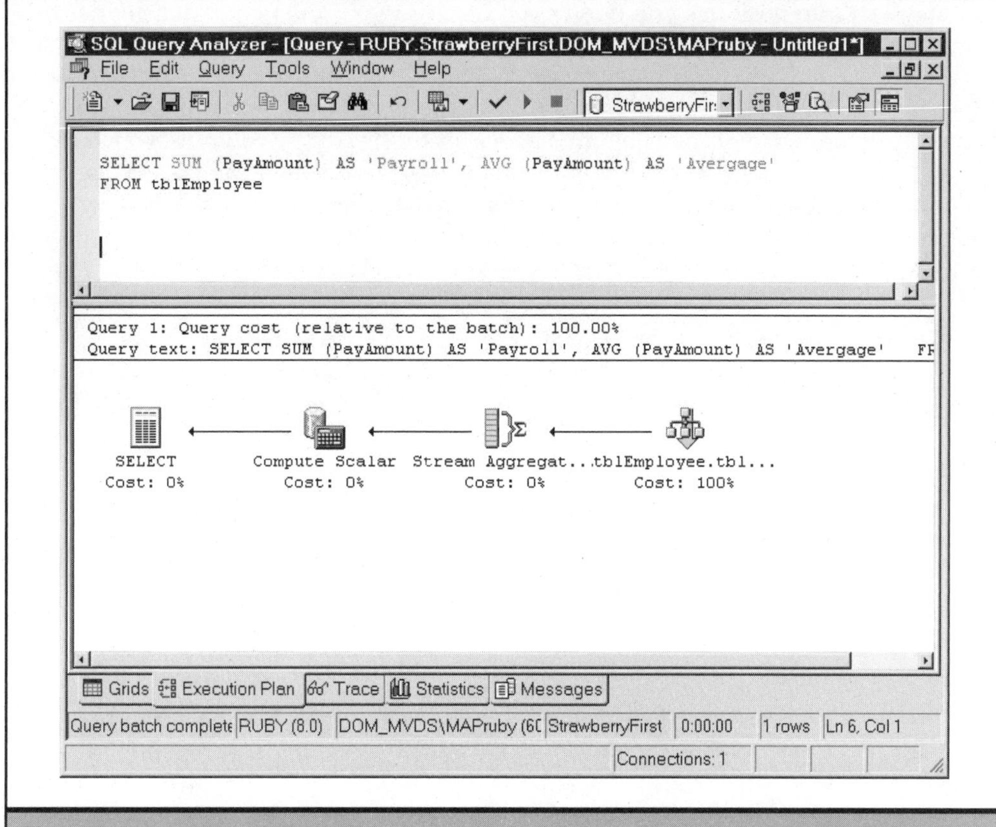

Figure 9-2. The execution plan for an unsorted, indistinct SUM() plus AVG() query will use only a single stream aggregate.

MIN(), MAX()

The MIN() and MAX() functions return what you would expect, the minimum or the maximum values, respectively, of a set of numbers. MIN() and MAX() can be used with any datatype, and the result set will return the same datatype. For instance, if you ask for the MIN() of the set of numbers {1, 2, 3}, the result would be {1}. If you ask for the MIN() of the set of character strings {apple, orange, pear}, the result, all other things being equal, would be {apple}. You do have to be careful what you ask for. As you can see, numeric datatypes are predictable: the MIN() is the smallest number in the set, and the MAX() is the largest. Sometimes, however, the order of alphanumeric data can vary depending on the sort order and character set used in the database, and that will influence the MAX() and MIN() values returned. Certain foreign alphabets, for example, have additional characters that may sort into positions you don't expect, so test your data and your queries thoroughly before putting any code into production!

When you're working with aggregate functions, you should give column aliases to the aggregate column output. If you don't use column aliases, the result set shows up with "(No column name)" as a column header for the aggregate columns, which can really make for confusing output. If you plan to use the results of an aggregate query in a temporary table for additional processing, it's even more important to provide names for these computed columns. Otherwise, you'll have no way other than using the ubiquitous "SELECT * FROM #temp_table" to access the computed columns in the temporary table.

```
SELECT MIN(LASTNAME) AS 'Start', MAX(LASTNAME) AS 'End' FROM tblPerson
```

If you're just generating a printed report rather than sending the result set to another table, you could also use string literals to make the output very readable, as shown in Figure 9-3.

```
SELECT 'The names in tblPerson range
       from '+ MIN(LASTNAME) + ' to ' + MAX(LASTNAME)
       AS 'The Person Table Report'
FROM tblPerson
```

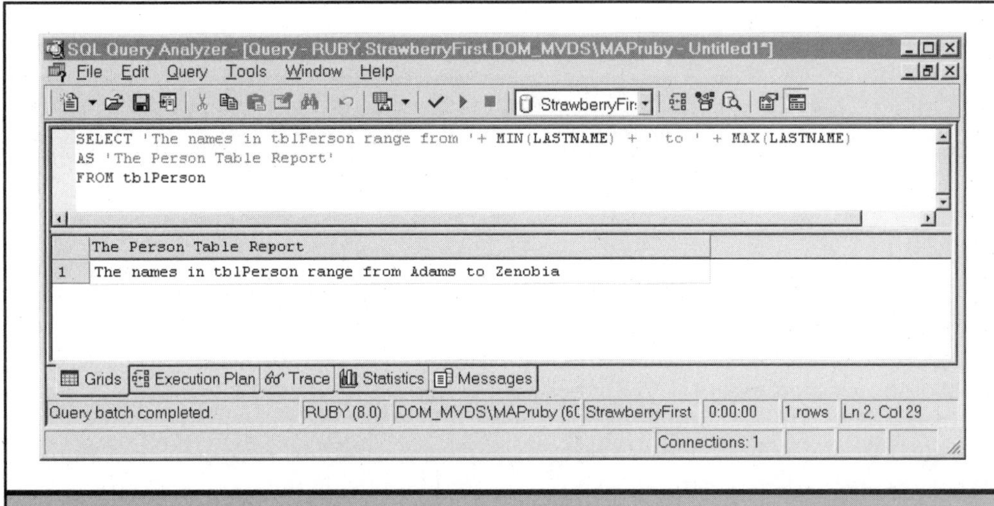

Figure 9-3. You can use string literals to produce a person-friendly, readable, and informative report of the Person table.

GROUP BY SUMMARY FUNCTIONS

The GROUP BY function is used when you want to see data aggregated by subsets or groups, rather than running an aggregate function on the entire set of data. For example, you might want to see next week's payroll, broken down by job title. When you add a GROUP BY to one of your previous queries, you can break out or group the results by job title, as shown in Figure 9-4. The rule for a GROUP BY function is that each column in the SELECT list must be either a computed value or in the GROUP BY list. Those columns in the GROUP BY list are called *partitioning* or *grouping* columns.

```
SELECT JobTitle, SUM (PayAmount) AS 'Payroll'
FROM tblEmployee
GROUP BY JobTitle
```

Conceptually, SQL Server has to gather all the information for the employee-owners, do the same for the employees, and then do it again for any other category of employee you might have stored in the table. Once the information for each group is gathered, it can compute the total payroll *for each group*. The execution plan, Figure 9-5, shows the steps as shown on the following page.

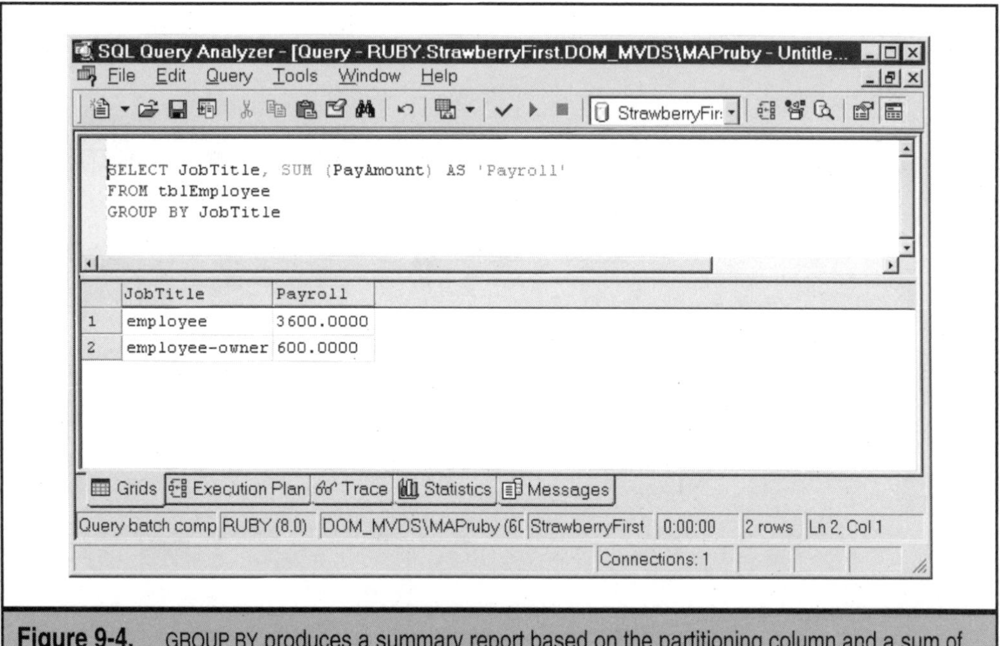

Figure 9-4. GROUP BY produces a summary report based on the partitioning column and a sum of the aggregate column.

1. Scan the table using the clustered index of the Employee table, 8 rows output.
2. Order by JobTitle, 8 rows output.
3. The stream aggregate, computing summary values for groups of rows, 2 rows output.
4. Compute scalar value, 2 rows output.
5. Present result set.

As a result of this execution plan, the result set is returned in alphabetic order. That seems reasonable, given that the execution plan sorts the data early on in the operation.

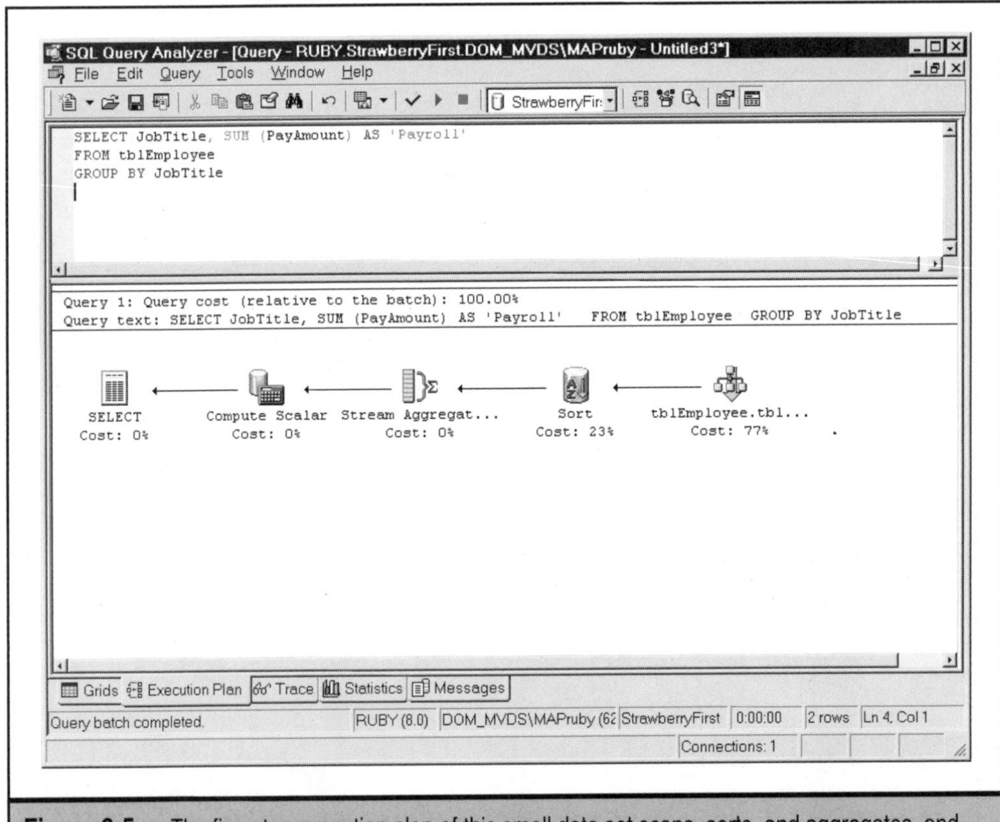

Figure 9-5. The five-step execution plan of this small data set scans, sorts, and aggregates, and then it computes a scalar value and presents the results.

But what happens when you group a larger data set? Let's look at the SaleItem table, which has substantially more records than the Employee table. You want to know how many of each product you sold over the course of the summer season:

```
SELECT ProductCode, SUM (QuantitySold) AS "Total Units Sold"
FROM tblSaleItem
GROUP BY ProductCode
```

If you run this query, as shown in Figure 9-6, you would expect it to be sorted by ProductCode, in ascending order, as in Figure 9-4. But it is not. The data seems to be in reverse order by ProductCode. This query, although it looks similar to the ones in Figures 9-4 and 9-5, uses quite a different execution strategy. This query does the following:

1. Scan the table using the clustered index of the SaleItem table, 1,280 rows output.
2. Run a hash match and aggregate, inserting rows into groups, 6 rows output.
3. Compute scalar value, 6 rows output.
4. Present result set.

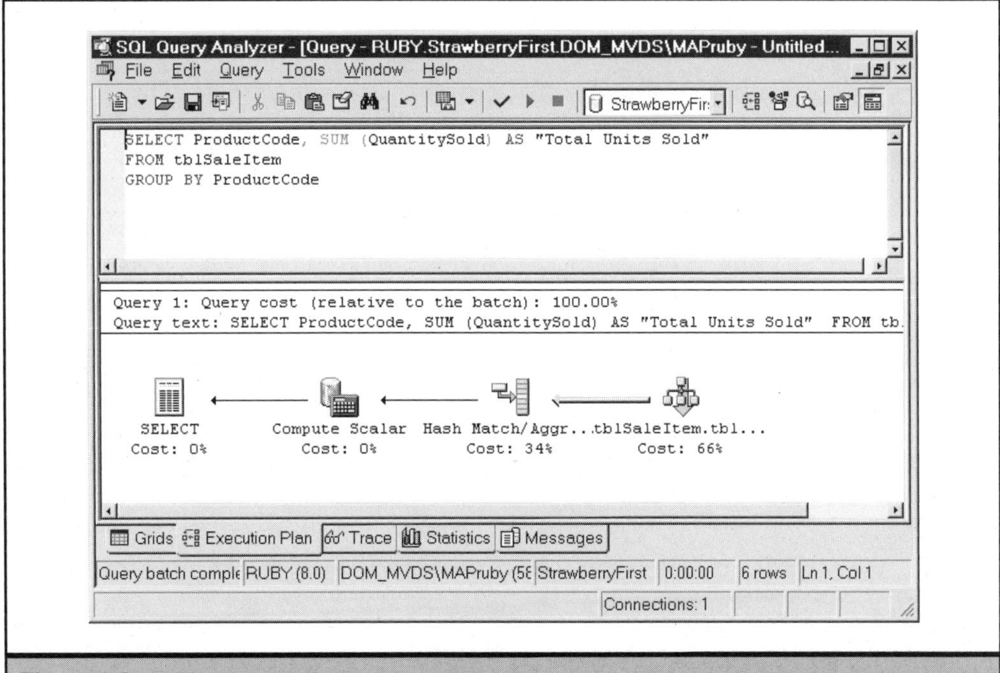

Figure 9-6. This execution plan uses an efficient four-step process to get the summary report.

This execution plan has one less step than the previous plan. Step 2, the hash match and aggregate function, is much more efficient than steps 2 and 3 from the previous execution plan, for large data sets. Rather than sort 1,280 rows and then sum the quantities, SQL Server built hash buckets and then summed the data in each hash bucket in the same step. You could think of this in programming terms as setting up six registers, one for each product code, and then incrementing the appropriate register value based on the quantity sold in each input row. With this technique, there's no need to sort the data. The decision to use the hash depends on many factors, including the number of rows input, so you cannot tell whether or not the Query Pptimizer will use a hash.

Here's a test: run the following two queries using the SaleItem table and look at the execution plans for the queries. They are shown in Figure 9-7.

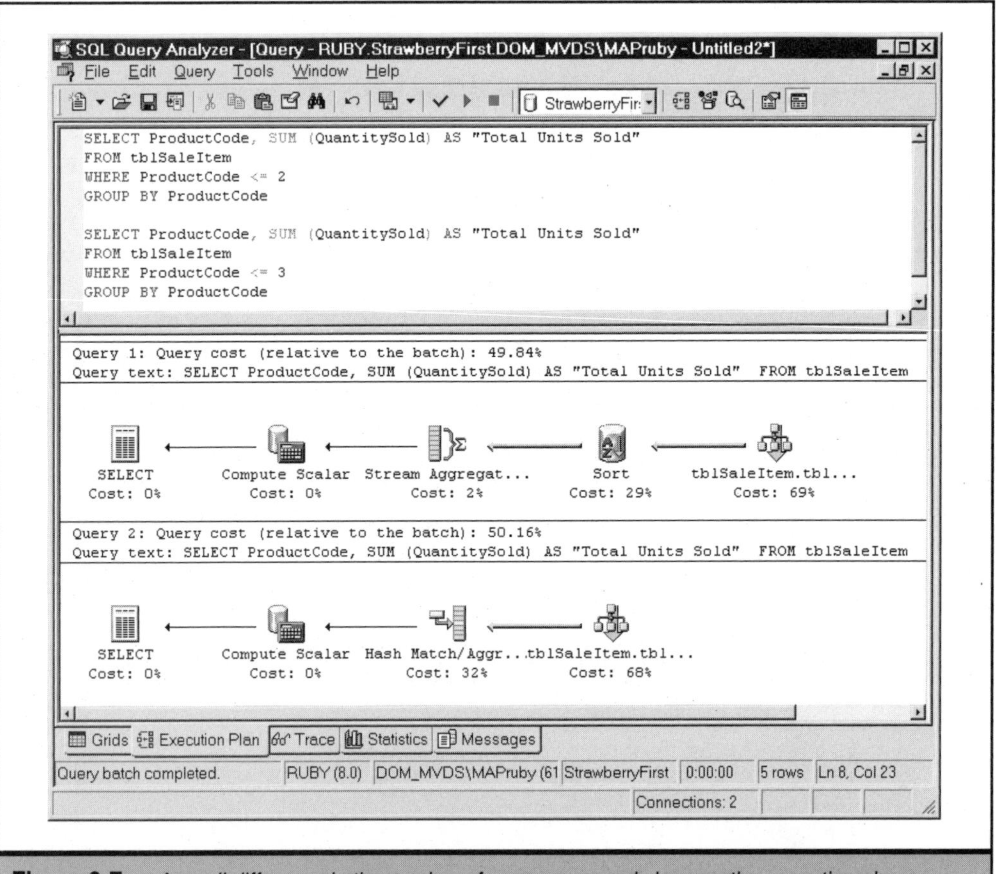

Figure 9-7. A small difference in the number of rows processed changes the execution plan for the query.

```
SELECT ProductCode, SUM (QuantitySold) AS "Total Units Sold"
FROM tblSaleItem
WHERE ProductCode <= 2
GROUP BY ProductCode
GO

SELECT ProductCode, SUM (QuantitySold) AS "Total Units Sold"
FROM tblSaleItem
WHERE ProductCode <= 3
GROUP BY ProductCode
GO
```

The only difference between the two queries is that the cutoff for the ProductCode changes from 2 to 3. For small data sets, it is more efficient to sort the data, discarding rows that are not required, and then sum the values. For larger data sets, it's more efficient to use the hash match/aggregate step.

There's nothing magical about the numbers 2 and 3—they just happen to be what works for this data set. Each data set will have a different switch-over point, and we found the switch-over point simply by trying different values. It's not easy to predict exactly what solution the Query Optimizer will use in any given situation. The bottom line is that if you want the data returned in a specific order, say so by including an ORDER BY clause in your query. Despite the fact that the GROUP BY seems to imply some ordering to the data, these new methods of data handling can't be trusted to return data in the order you think it ought to be in.

Try running the query shown in Figure 9-6 with an ORDER BY clause, as shown in Figure 9-8, and see what happens. The execution plans are similar, except for near the end, just before the presentation step in Figure 9-8. There's an additional step, the Sort step, in which the output from the hash match/aggregate is sorted into ascending order. The sort involves only six rows, but even so, it's extra effort. As we said, a lot of variables can influence the decisions made by the Query Optimizer.

GROUP BY ALL

GROUP BY has an optional parameter, ALL, which can be used in combination with the WHERE clause to make sure that all rows in the table are represented. Suppose that you want to see how you did for the first half-dozen sales at the beginning of the season, so you put in a WHERE clause to limit the Sale Numbers to 1–6. It might have been possible that some products did not sell at all in this sampling, and ordinarily they would not show up in the result set. If you use a GROUP BY ALL, all Product Codes will be listed, and

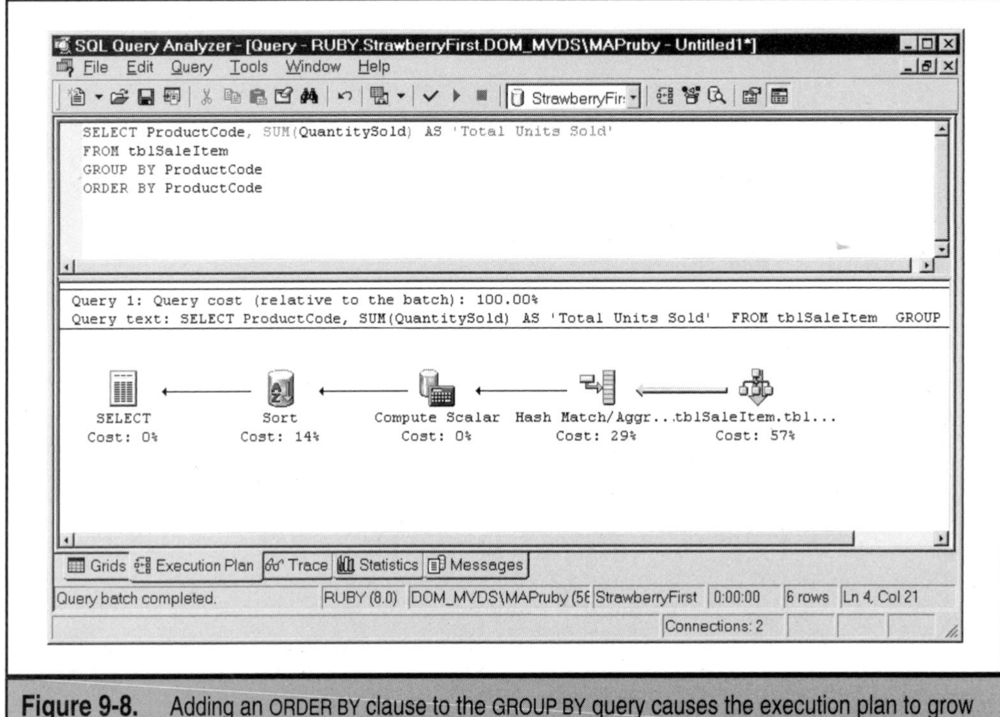

Figure 9-8. Adding an ORDER BY clause to the GROUP BY query causes the execution plan to grow by the addition of a Sort operation.

any product that did not sell would show a NULL for the Quantity Sold. Figure 9-9 shows this example from the SaleItem table. The result set from the upper query has five rows, each of which has a value for Qty Sold. The lower result set has six rows returned, the previous five values for Qty Sold and one NULL, which indicates that ProductCode 3 did not sell during this period.

```
SELECT ProductCode, SUM(QuantitySold)AS 'Qty Sold'
FROM tblSaleItem
WHERE SaleNo <=6
GROUP BY ProductCode
GO
SELECT ProductCode, SUM(QuantitySold)AS 'Qty Sold'
FROM tblSaleItem
WHERE SaleNo <=6
GROUP BY ALL ProductCode
GO
```

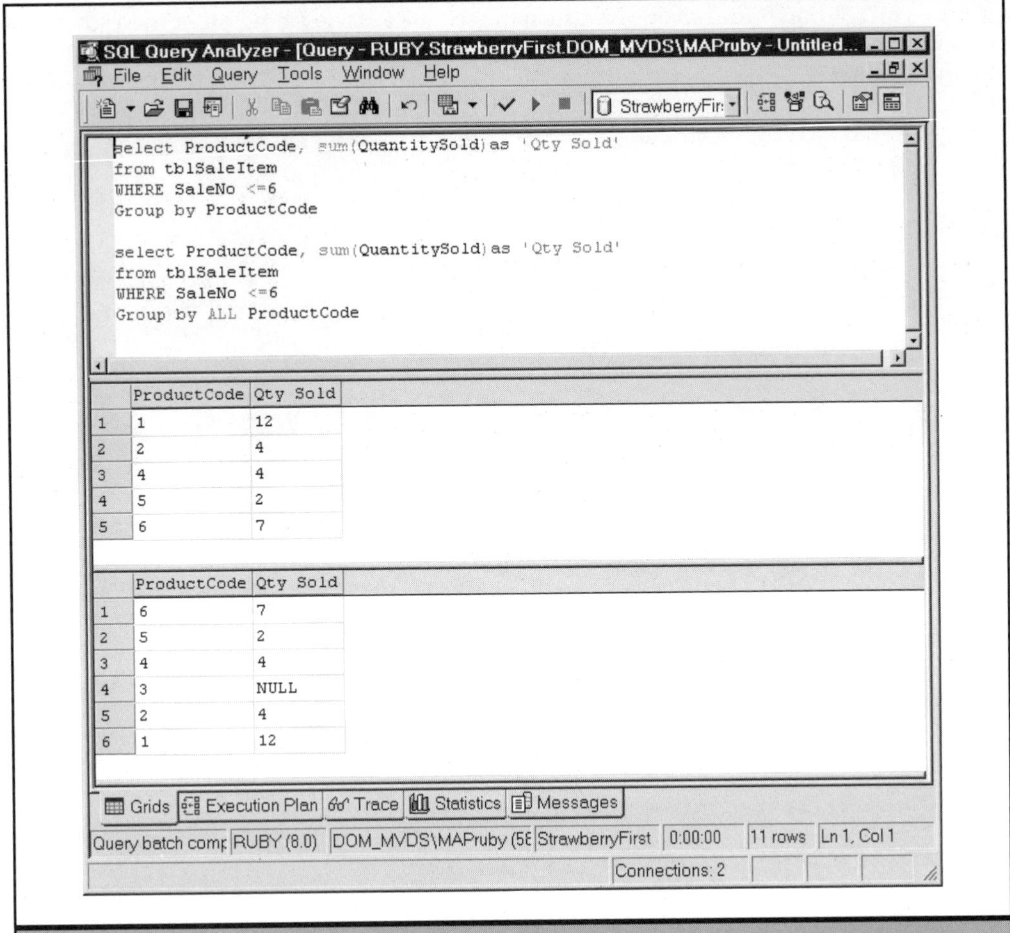

Figure 9-9. The GROUP BY ALL function includes rows that would not otherwise appear in the result set, rows that have no aggregate value to report.

GROUP BY with Multiple Columns

SQL Server 2000 displays a rather strange behavior when the GROUP BY has two partitioning columns, two columns to GROUP BY. We've already demonstrated that the Query Optimizer may use different strategies with a GROUP BY query based on factors such as number of rows in the source data set. There is no guarantee of the data being returned in the order you want unless you include an ORDER BY clause after the GROUP BY. We've found an even stranger behavior in the GROUP BY with two partitioning columns. With any GROUP BY, but especially when you have a multi-column GROUP BY query, there really is an expectation that the data will be grouped by column A, and then within column A grouped on column B, and so on. To return the result set in anything other than sorted order based on the requested groupings is a waste of time and resources. Figure 9-10, with the following code, illustrates this point.

```
SELECT CAST(SaleDate AS char(12)) AS "Sale Date", ProductCode,
      SUM(ItemCost) AS "Total $$"
FROM tblSale s INNER JOIN tblSaleItem i ON s.SaleNo = i.SaleNo
GROUP BY SaleDate, ProductCode
SELECT SaleDate, ProductCode, SUM(ItemCost) AS "Total $$"
FROM tblSale s INNER JOIN tblSaleItem i ON s.SaleNo = i.SaleNo
GROUP BY SaleDate, ProductCode
```

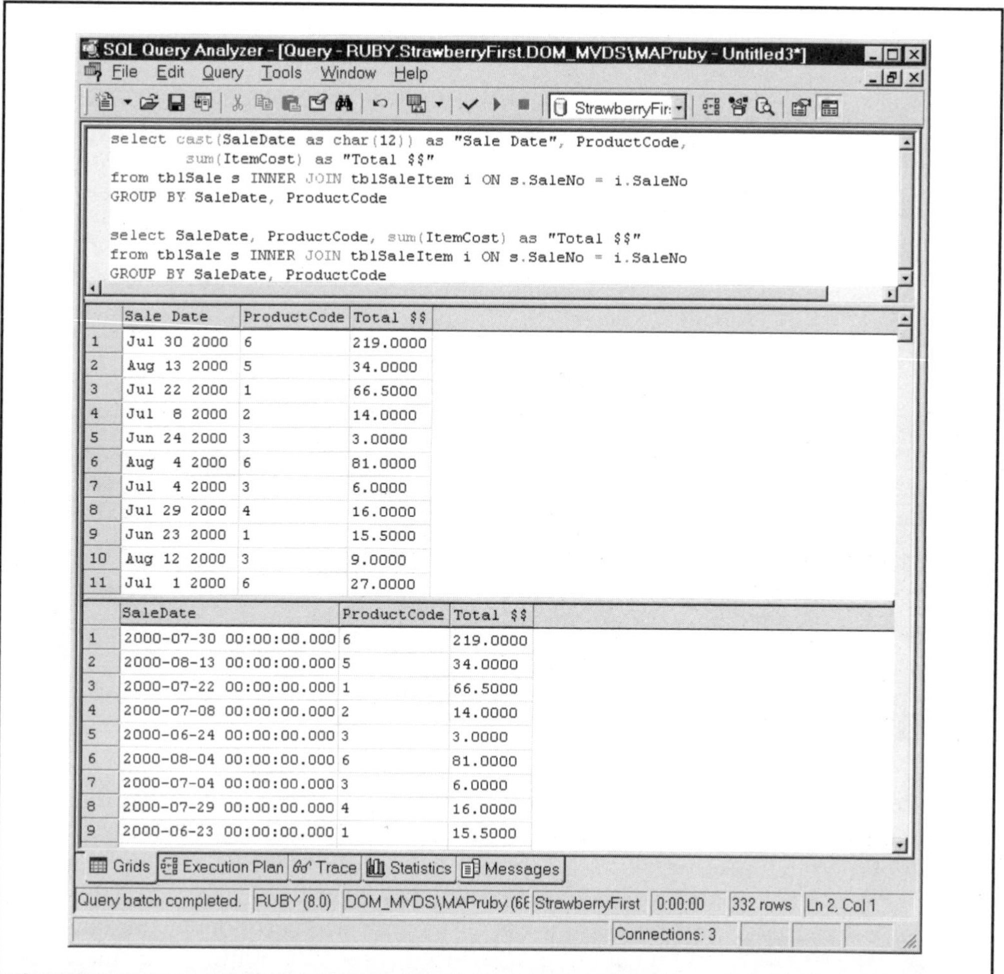

Figure 9-10. A GROUP BY that has two partitioning or grouping columns will return the results in apparent random order, thus defeating the purpose of the grouping request.

In this example, the first query is using the CAST() function to convert the dates into data that presents well and is informative. The second query is the check query—you can see that the column SaleDate has not been converted to a character string, and that it is also hard to read. If you look carefully, you'll see that the portions of the two result sets returned contain the same data, but it's been formatted differently. You've asked for the data to be grouped first by SaleDate and then by ProductCode. In SQL Server 6.5, you would get back all of the earliest date records (6/23/2000); and then within each date grouping you'd have the ProductCodes arrayed 1 through 6; and, last, the "Total $$" for each row. In SQL Server 2000, the results can best be described as random. If you look at Figure 9-11, the execution plan for these queries, you'll see why. The CAST() function doesn't substantially alter the execution plan or the query results. It simply adds another Compute Scalar operation at the end, just before the presentation of the results. This second Compute Scalar converts the standard datetime display format shown in the second query into the display format shown in the first query. The random appearance of the result set is due to the Hash Match/Aggregate operation, present in both execution plans. If you recall from Figure 9-6, the Hash Match/Aggregate operation uses hash buckets to store same-value rows (the groups), and then sums the data in each hash bucket in the same step. There is no sorting of the groups involved in a Hash Match/Aggregate operation. The Hash Match/Aggregate is used when SQL Server has a lot of records to process. Would you see the same result if you limited your record set to two days' worth of sales?

Figure 9-12 is a composite that shows the GROUP BY query limited to two days, the result set, and the execution plan. Despite the fact that the query asked for data grouped by SaleDate and then ProductCode, the result set seems to indicate that the data is first grouped by ProductCode and then by SaleDate. A look at the execution plan gives you a clue what has happened. The Hash Match/Inner Join is used only to resolve the join of tblSale to tblSaleItem. The next step (moving left) is a Sort. On the interactive Query Analyzer screen, you can see that the Sort instruction is ORDER BY [i].[ProductCode] ASC, [s].[SaleDate] ASC—the reverse of what you requested in your GROUP BY query! It appears that if the grouped data sets are few, and a Sort is used in the execution plan, the result set will be ordered backward from the way you asked for it to be presented. If the grouped data sets are many, the execution plan will use a Hash Match/Aggregate operation, and the result set will be in apparent random order. Neither situation is very pleasant, nor is this what you would expect as output. We consider this situation of random display or a transposed sort from the GROUP BY to be a bug in SQL Server 7 (where it first appeared) and 2000.

If you increase the number of partitioning or grouping columns in the GROUP BY to three, and if the execution plan includes a Sort, the results are returned in exactly the order you expected, and the execution plan shows that the sort order is the order you specified in the GROUP BY clause. You can run the following code and test for yourself:

```
SELECT EventID, CAST(SaleDate AS char(12)) AS "Sale Date", ProductCode,
      SUM(ItemCost) AS "Total $$"
FROM tblSale s INNER JOIN tblSaleItem i ON s.SaleNo = i.SaleNo
WHERE CAST(SaleDate as char(12)) BETWEEN 'Aug  4 2000' AND 'Aug 20 2000'
GROUP BY EventID, SaleDate, ProductCode
```

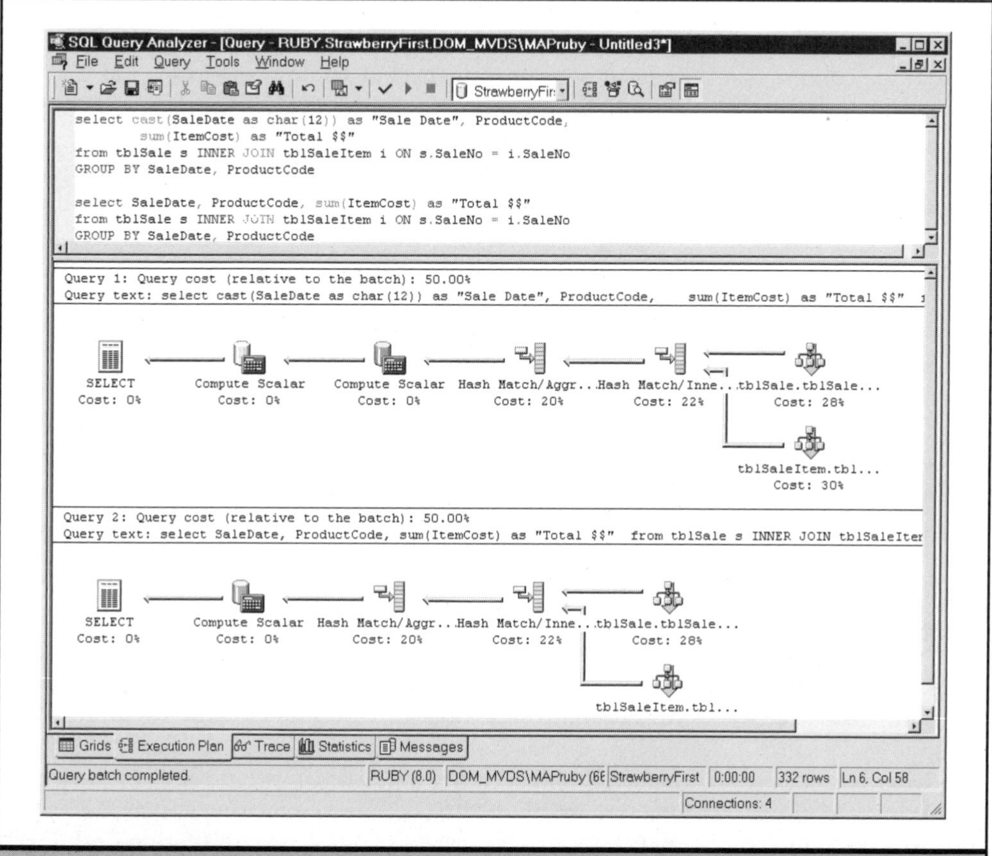

Figure 9-11. The apparent randomness of the result set in this example is because the Query Analyzer selected the Hash Match/Aggregate to do most of the work.

Interestingly, even larger data sets with many groupings seem to return to normal behavior when the number of grouping columns in the GROUP BY is increased to three. The composite Figure 9-13 shows your original large data set, but now it's grouped first by EventID, then by SaleDate, and last by ProductCode; so you're seeing a result set that shows total dollars earned for each product, on each day, during each event. The superimposed execution plan shows a different strategy than Figure 9-11, when only two grouping columns are involved. Figure 9-13 shows an execution plan that reads Hash Match/Inner Join to join the two tables, a Sort with the argument ORDER BY [s].[EventID] ASC, [s].[SaleDate] ASC, [I].[ProductCode] ASC, and then a stream aggregate for computing

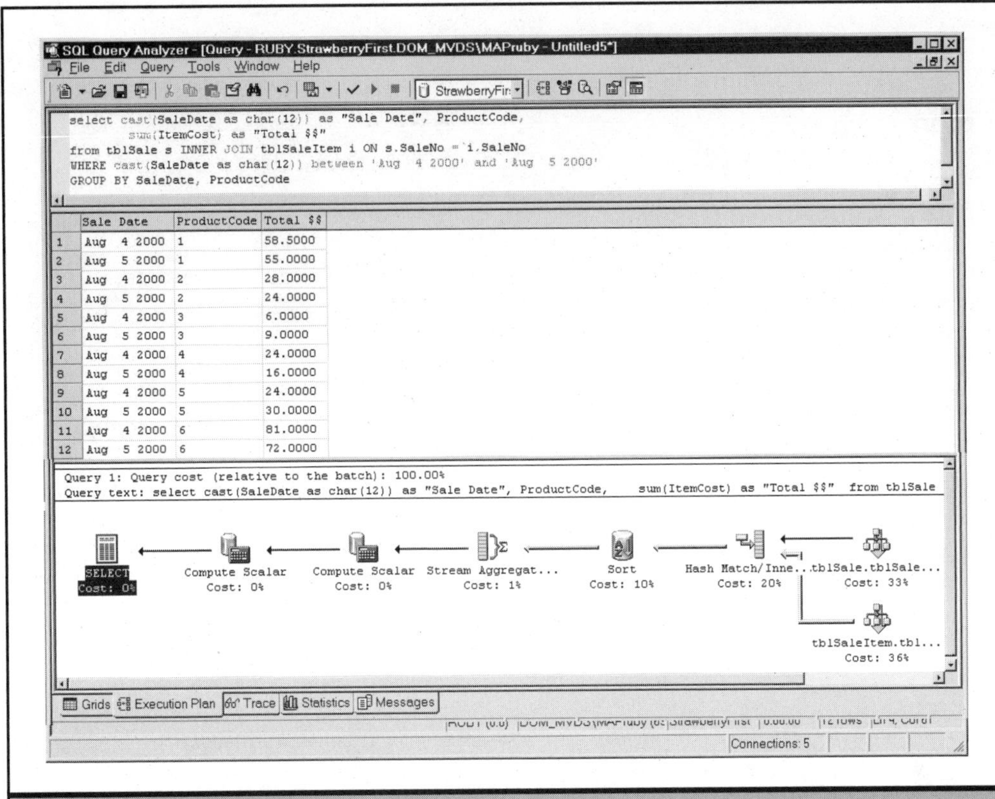

Figure 9-12. A composite view of a GROUP BY query that asks for data grouped by SaleDate and then by ProductCode; the result set is reversed.

summary values. Apparently, with three grouping columns, the Query Optimizer has abandoned the Hash Match/Aggregate operation and the resulting random result set output.

This inconsistent behavior in the GROUP BY query is something you want to take precautions against, and you do that by always including an ORDER BY clause in the query. We feel that this inconsistent behavior diminishes the veracity of SQL Server 7 and 2000, as there's not much point in grouping data unless you also present it grouped as specified in the query. Simply because this is a new version of SQL Server, it shouldn't be necessary for you to have to remember to include an ORDER BY clause in your GROUP BY queries; but for now, you have to do this.

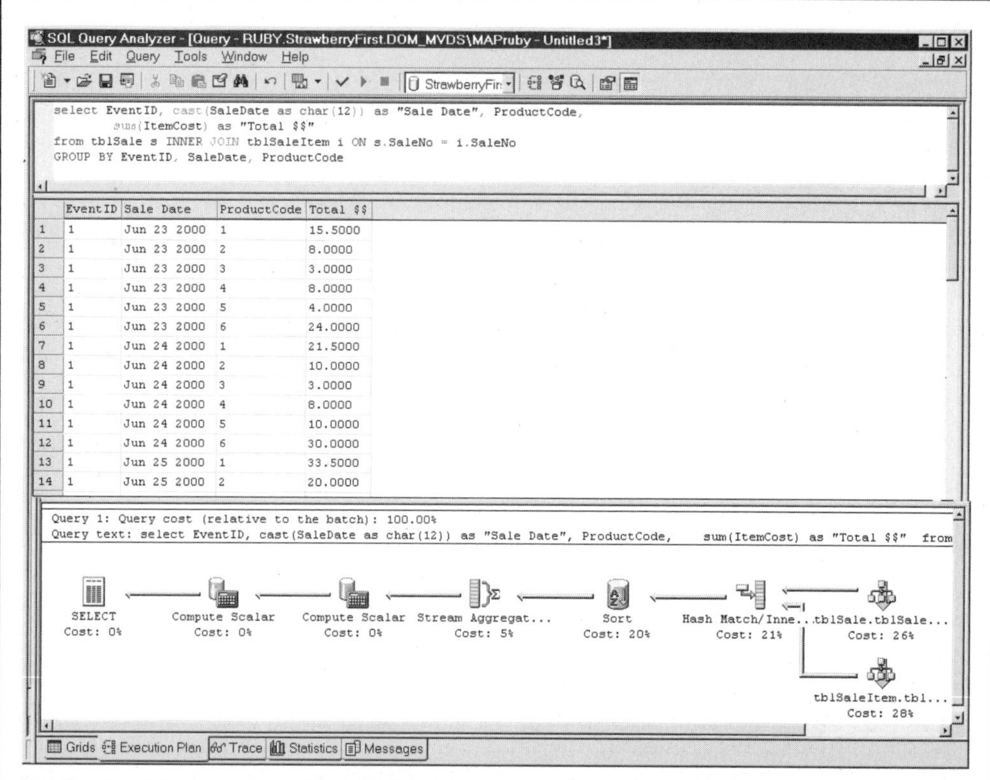

Figure 9-13. A GROUP BY that uses three grouping columns returns results that are grouped in the order in which the query specifies.

GROUP BY...HAVING

You know that the WHERE clause in a query will restrict the rows returned in the result set. If you say you want to see sales figures for all customers whose name begins with the letter M, you know that SQL Server will discard all the rows that do not meet this criteria and will return just what you asked for. But what if you ask a question like, "Show me all the customers who have purchased more than $10,000 worth of products in the last year"? This question is not simple because the restriction is placed on aggregated data, not on the raw data rows as it is when you use a WHERE clause. A customer may have many records in the sales table, none of which exceeds $10,000, but if this customer's records were summed, this customer would meet your requirement. In other words, you need to first compute the aggregate and then apply the restriction. You do this not with the WHERE clause but with the HAVING clause of the GROUP BY function. A HAVING clause looks very similar to a WHERE clause, but it is applied *after* the grouping and the aggregation. This means that you have to compute all of the aggregates first, and then discard many of them according to the specifications in the HAVING clause, which is a lot of extra work for SQL Server. In your customer example, you would have to sum the orders for all your customers, grouping by CustomerID, and then go through and discard those CustomerIDs where the total is less than $10,000. There's no way to shortcut this process. Consider this example from your Strawberry database, illustrated in the composite Figure 9-14. You're looking for your very best product-selling days.

```
SELECT EventID, CAST(SaleDate AS char(12)) AS "Sale Date", ProductCode,
      SUM(ItemCost) AS "Total $$"
FROM tblSale s INNER JOIN tblSaleItem i ON s.SaleNo = i.SaleNo
GROUP BY EventID, SaleDate, ProductCode
HAVING SUM(ItemCost) > 100
```

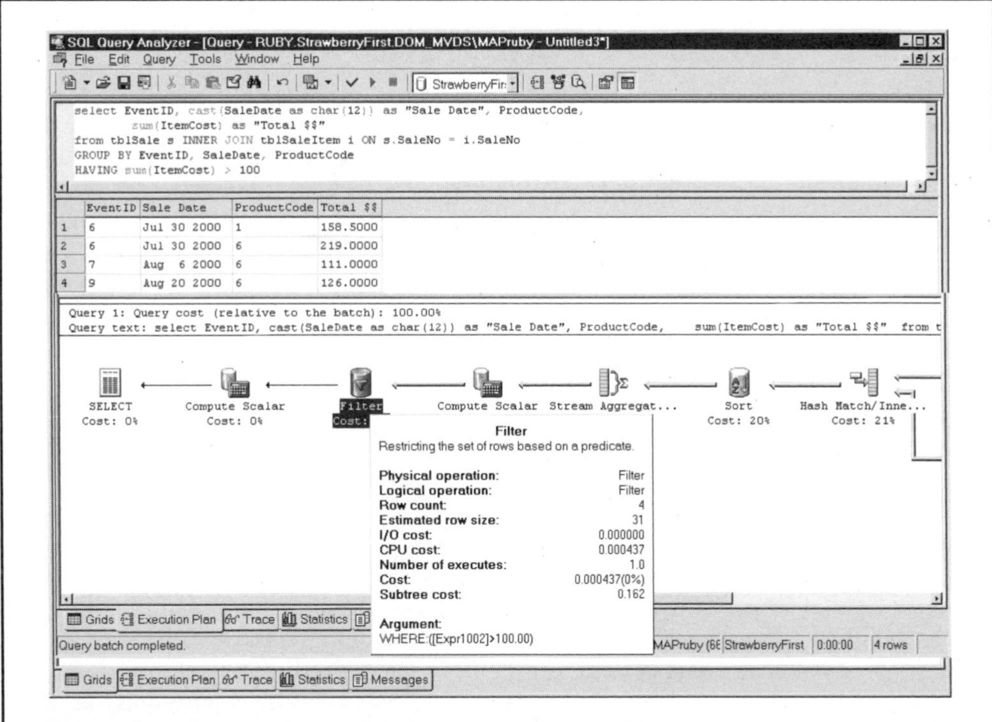

Figure 9-14. The execution plan shows the HAVING clause implemented as a filter after the aggregate function has been computed.

The execution plan uses a final filter with the argument WHERE [Expr1002]>100.00, which is caused by the HAVING clause of this GROUP BY function. The filter's apparent contribution to the total cost of the query is zero, so it appears that the HAVING clause won't have an adverse impact on query performance. The same query without a HAVING clause returns 166 rows, while the addition of the HAVING clause gives back only 4 rows. That means that the HAVING version of the query discarded 162 rows after calculating the sum of ItemCost. It's in this discard that the hidden costs lie. On a per-row-returned basis, the GROUP BY...HAVING queries take a lot longer to run than if you had just been able to ask for the data of these four rows; but until you compute the sums, you don't know which rows you need. There's no way around this problem. A query with a HAVING clause is just going to take longer to run than you might expect based on the number of rows returned.

You might expect that, once you had aliased the SUM(ItemCost) AS "Total $$", you should be able to use that alias in the HAVING clause. In other database management system environments you might be able to do this, but not in the SQL Server world. You have to specify the aggregate function a second time. Fortunately, you can see from the execution plan that SQL Server does not need to compute the aggregate function twice!

COMPUTE BY SUMMARY FUNCTIONS

One of the limitations of GROUP BY is that the result set contains only summary data, not the original detail records. What happens if you have a request for a report with the original detail records, subtotals, and grand totals, all together? You can do this with a third-party report writer, such as Microsoft Access or Crystal Reports, but the learning curve on these products might be a little too long to allow you to make your deadlines. One way to do this within SQL Server is to use the COMPUTE BY function. Keep in mind that this function is not ANSI standard, and therefore there is no guarantee that it will be supported in future releases. The output from this function is non-relational, because some rows have data in every column and other rows contain nothing but the subtotals and totals, with no primary key data or any other unique identifier in the subtotal and total rows. This makes it difficult to pass the results of a COMPUTE BY into a temporary table, for example, for further processing. Realistically, you would use the COMPUTE BY just to generate a quick prototype to confirm results, and then use some other tool to generate the production report. T-SQL doesn't really have extensive formatting capabilities like some other database management systems, so you really don't have what you need if you are going to generate production reports for management. Better to use tools like Access, Excel, or Crystal Reports, which have better formatting and can generate charts and graphs to enhance the presentations. Having said that, let's go ahead and take a look at COMPUTE BY so you can use it in your test applications to produce prototypes.

When you use COMPUTE BY, you're asking to see the individual records and the subtotals, so you must take charge of sorting the data in the correct order. For instance, if you wanted to get a report of each of the events, the work assignments, and the hours worked, you'd use the following code:

```
SELECT e.EventName, w.WorkAssignmentDscr, w.HoursWorked
FROM tblEvent e INNER JOIN tblWorkAssignment w ON e.EventID = w.EventID
ORDER BY e.EventName, w.WorkAssignmentDscr
COMPUTE SUM(HoursWorked)
```

Figure 9-15 shows part of the result set. There are 81 rows in the detail portion of the report, one for each work assignment. At the end is a summary figure, a total of all the hours worked at all the events. Unfortunately, there's no way to add a more informative column alias to the summary portion of the report.

Now you want a more detailed report—one that breaks out each event and subtotals the hours worked by event, and then totals the hours worked for all events. You also want to see who (by PersonID) worked each event. You can ask for multiple levels of subtotal. The rule is that whatever columns you have in the ORDER BY clause you can use in a

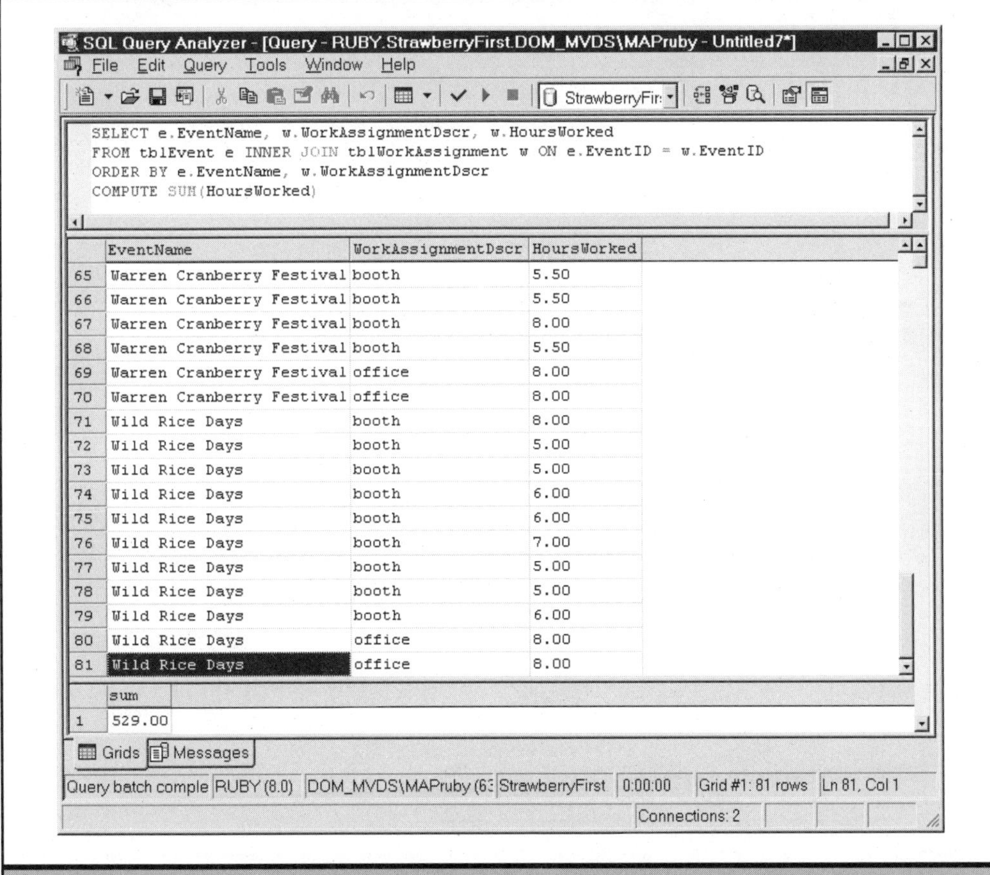

Figure 9-15. The COMPUTE BY result set is non-relational; it includes both detail rows and rows that contain just summary data.

COMPUTE BY clause. For instance, if you order by columns (A, B, and C), you can COMPUTE BY (A), or by (A and B), or by (A, B, and C). You cannot write a COMPUTE BY (B and C) or (C and A), or by any other combination that's not in the ORDER BY clause.

```
SELECT e.EventName, w.WorkAssignmentDscr, w.PersonID, w.HoursWorked
FROM tblEvent e INNER JOIN tblWorkAssignment w ON e.EventID = w.EventID
ORDER BY EventName, WorkAssignmentDscr, PersonID
COMPUTE SUM(HoursWorked) BY EventName
COMPUTE SUM (HoursWorked)
```

Figure 9-16 shows part of the result set. Each of the seven events listed (you can only see the last two in this figure) have a subtotal of hours worked, and the detail records in-

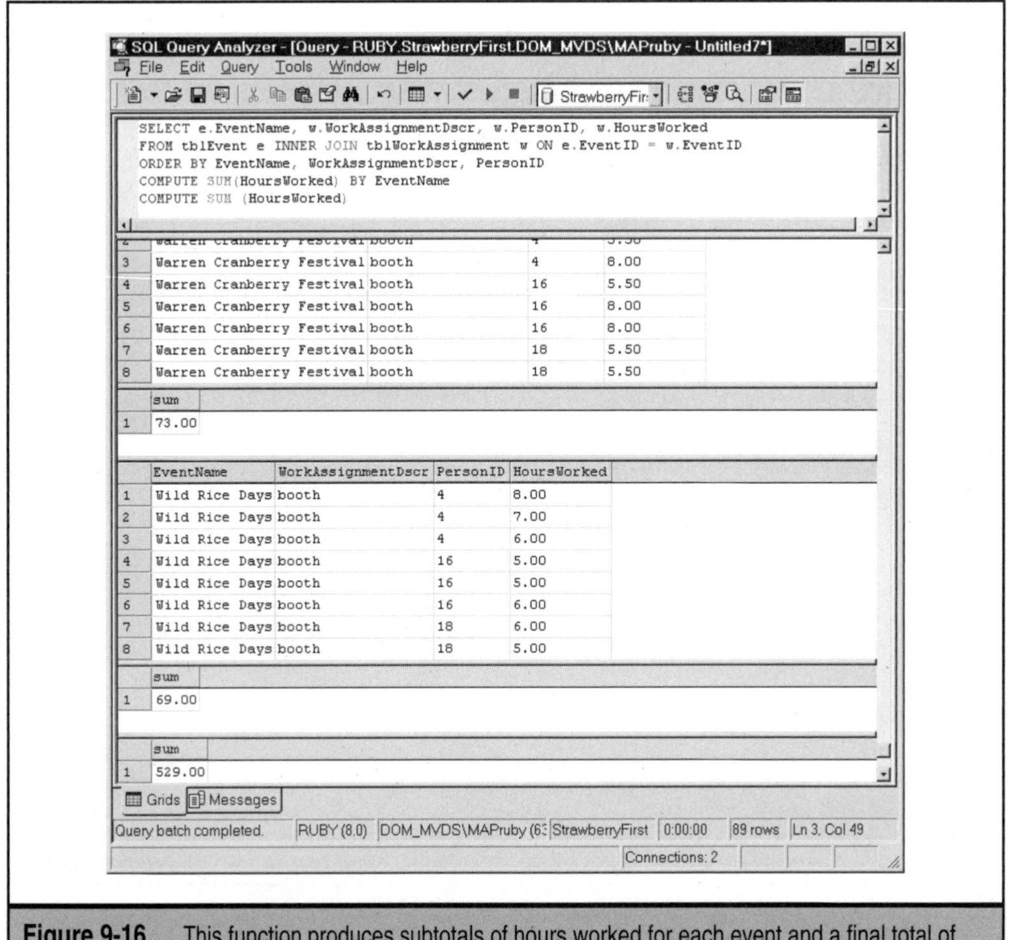

Figure 9-16. This function produces subtotals of hours worked for each event and a final total of hours for all events.

clude who (by PersonID) was working. Then, at the end of the report, is a grand total of 529 hours, which includes all hours worked at all events.

As you can see from these examples, the output is not formatted in a very readable manner. You may want to look at using the text output rather than the grid output, as it's a little more readable. However, neither output is anything we would care to show to a client or to management.

ROLLUP AND CUBE FUNCTIONS

There are a couple more ways to generate aggregate data in SQL Server, and while these options do produce relational output, they are difficult to interpret. The ROLLUP operator does just that—it takes an aggregate and rolls it up to progressively higher levels. The CUBE operator takes the aggregate and turns the question around, looking at the aggregate from different points of view. This is something akin to an Excel pivot table. Once again, we would suggest using these functions for prototype development and for making sure that your concepts are correct and that you have the information you need in the database to generate the required output reports. In that light, let's first look at a GROUP BY function of the Events and WorkAssignments from previous figures:

```
SELECT e.EventName, w.WorkAssignmentDscr,
       SUM(HoursWorked) as "Hours Worked"
FROM tblEvent e INNER JOIN tblWorkAssignment w ON e.EventID = w.EventID
GROUP BY e.EventName, w.WorkAssignmentDscr
ORDER BY EventName, WorkAssignmentDscr
```

This code produces the output shown in Figure 9-17. Looking at the first two rows, you can see that you spent a total of 55.5 hours in the booth at the Greater Wayzata Festival and 16 hours in the office.

Now you want to determine how many hours total you spent at each event. You can use the ROLLUP operator to do this, while still retaining the information you've just generated from this last query:

```
SELECT e.EventName, w.WorkAssignmentDscr, SUM(HoursWorked) as "Hours Worked"
FROM tblEvent e INNER JOIN tblWorkAssignment w ON e.EventID = w.EventID
GROUP BY e.EventName, w.WorkAssignmentDscr
WITH ROLLUP
```

Figure 9-18 shows what the result set looks like with a ROLLUP function. The results of the ROLLUP appear as additional rows in the output, one for each event, with the WorkAssignmentDscr listed as NULL. The HoursWorked entry for these rows is a subtotal for each event; so for the Greater Wayzata Festival, you worked a total of 71.5 hours—55.5 in the booth and 16 in the office. The last row of the result set has a NULL EventName and a NULL WorkAssignmentDscr, and a total number of hours worked for all events.

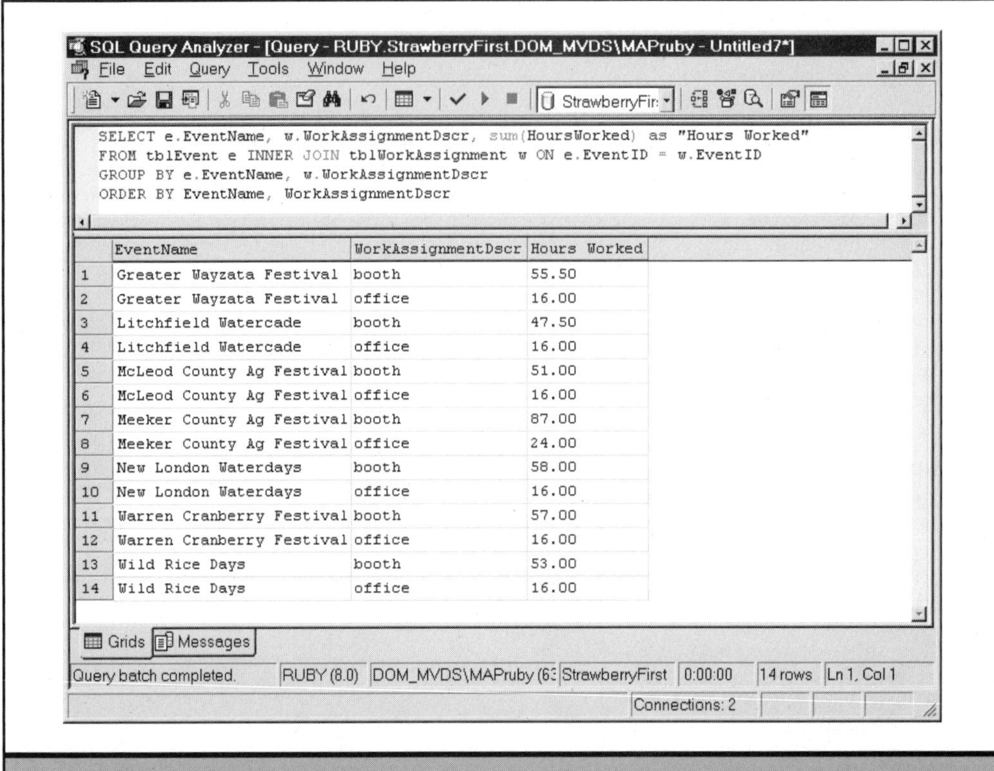

	EventName	WorkAssignmentDscr	Hours Worked
1	Greater Wayzata Festival	booth	55.50
2	Greater Wayzata Festival	office	16.00
3	Litchfield Watercade	booth	47.50
4	Litchfield Watercade	office	16.00
5	McLeod County Ag Festival	booth	51.00
6	McLeod County Ag Festival	office	16.00
7	Meeker County Ag Festival	booth	87.00
8	Meeker County Ag Festival	office	24.00
9	New London Waterdays	booth	58.00
10	New London Waterdays	office	16.00
11	Warren Cranberry Festival	booth	57.00
12	Warren Cranberry Festival	office	16.00
13	Wild Rice Days	booth	53.00
14	Wild Rice Days	office	16.00

Figure 9-17. This GROUP BY function shows how many hours you spent at each event doing different jobs.

This is what is meant by the term "rollup," as the operator moves from one level to another, rolling up first each subtotal and then the grand total.

One thing you will have to watch for is the condition where a column value is NULL. Are these NULLs created by the ROLLUP operator or are they actually data?

You can use the ROLLUP operator to show both the detail row data and the summary data, but in a row-and-column relational format, which may work better than the output from the COMPUTE function. The ROLLUP function can be extremely useful, as in the following query, in which you see both a sum and an average of hours worked:

```
SELECT e.EventName, w.WorkAssignmentDscr, w.PersonID,
       AVG(HoursWorked) AS "Avg Hours Worked",
       SUM(HoursWorked) AS "Total Hours Worked"
FROM tblEvent e INNER JOIN tblWorkAssignment w ON e.EventID = w.EventID
GROUP BY e.EventName, w.WorkAssignmentDscr, w.PersonID
WITH ROLLUP
```

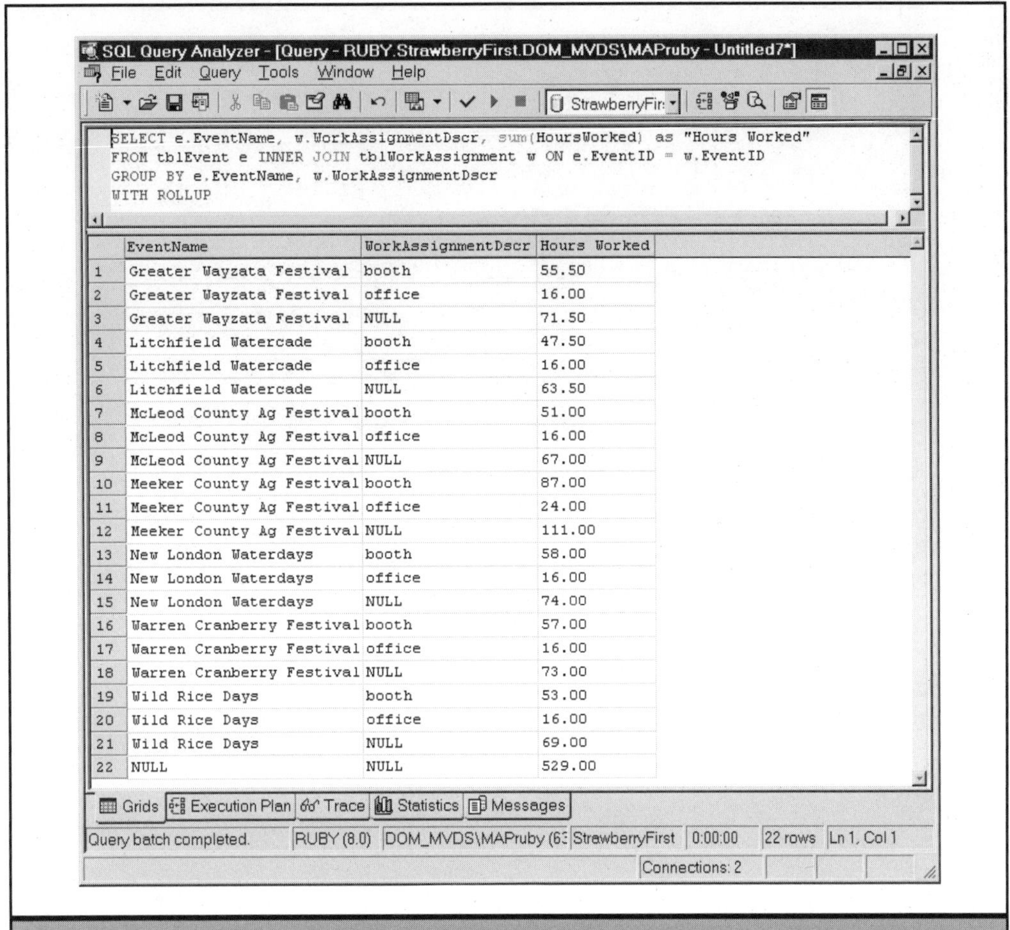


```
SELECT e.EventName, w.WorkAssignmentDscr, sum(HoursWorked) as "Hours Worked"
FROM tblEvent e INNER JOIN tblWorkAssignment w ON e.EventID = w.EventID
GROUP BY e.EventName, w.WorkAssignmentDscr
WITH ROLLUP
```

	EventName	WorkAssignmentDscr	Hours Worked
1	Greater Wayzata Festival	booth	55.50
2	Greater Wayzata Festival	office	16.00
3	Greater Wayzata Festival	NULL	71.50
4	Litchfield Watercade	booth	47.50
5	Litchfield Watercade	office	16.00
6	Litchfield Watercade	NULL	63.50
7	McLeod County Ag Festival	booth	51.00
8	McLeod County Ag Festival	office	16.00
9	McLeod County Ag Festival	NULL	67.00
10	Meeker County Ag Festival	booth	87.00
11	Meeker County Ag Festival	office	24.00
12	Meeker County Ag Festival	NULL	111.00
13	New London Waterdays	booth	58.00
14	New London Waterdays	office	16.00
15	New London Waterdays	NULL	74.00
16	Warren Cranberry Festival	booth	57.00
17	Warren Cranberry Festival	office	16.00
18	Warren Cranberry Festival	NULL	73.00
19	Wild Rice Days	booth	53.00
20	Wild Rice Days	office	16.00
21	Wild Rice Days	NULL	69.00
22	NULL	NULL	529.00

Figure 9-18. The ROLLUP function adds rows for the subtotal of hours worked per event and a grand total at the end for all events.

At first glance, this looks like an odd way to query the data, until you realize what you are trying to show. In Figure 9-19, you can see part of the result set. The GROUP BY is grouping on EventName, WorkAssignmentDscr, and PersonID, so now you can see who was working which events and what they were doing. Furthermore, you can see the average length of a shift and the total hours worked on a shift by all people. Then the ROLLUP adds to the information set. The last row of each event is a rollup of the numbers to show you what the average length of a shift is, regardless of what the work assignment was, and the total number of hours worked by all people at this event (don't count the summaries by WorkAssignmentDscr!). Finally, the last row of the result set is the grand total, the

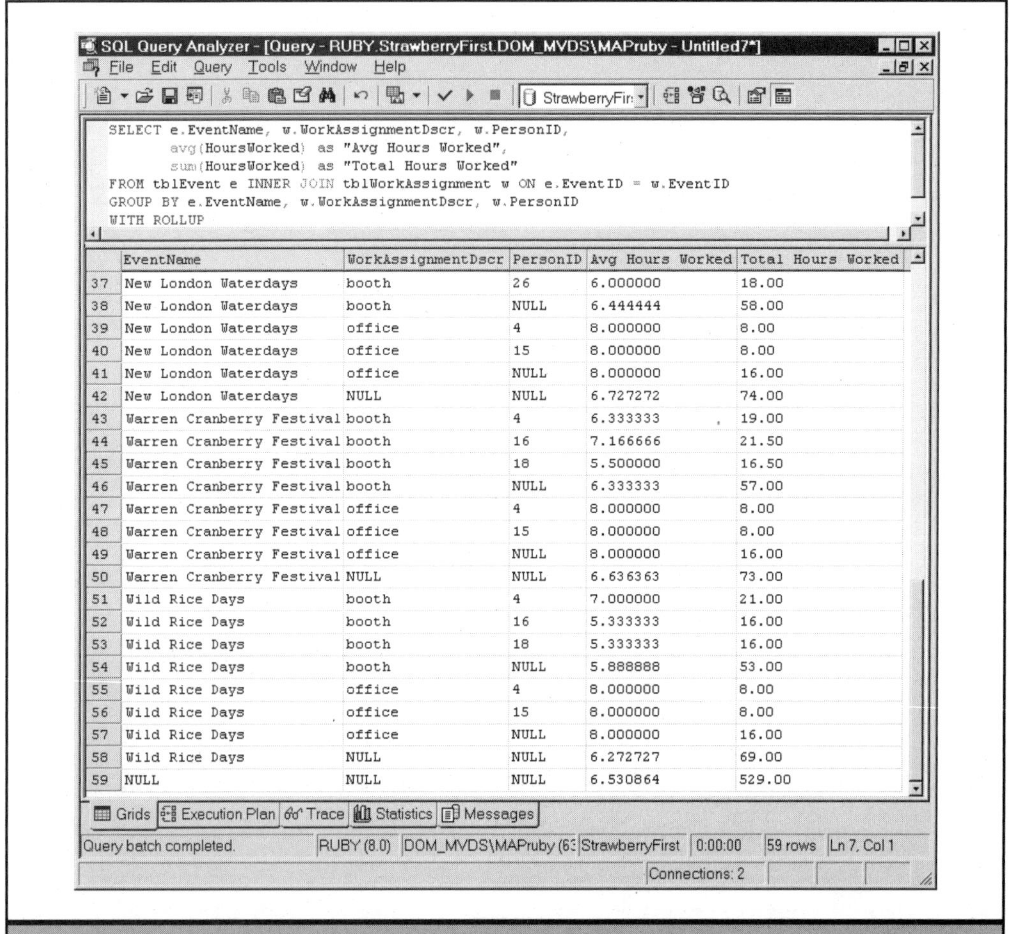


```
SELECT e.EventName, w.WorkAssignmentDscr, w.PersonID,
       avg(HoursWorked) as "Avg Hours Worked",
       sum(HoursWorked) as "Total Hours Worked"
FROM tblEvent e INNER JOIN tblWorkAssignment w ON e.EventID = w.EventID
GROUP BY e.EventName, w.WorkAssignmentDscr, w.PersonID
WITH ROLLUP
```

	EventName	WorkAssignmentDscr	PersonID	Avg Hours Worked	Total Hours Worked
37	New London Waterdays	booth	26	6.000000	18.00
38	New London Waterdays	booth	NULL	6.444444	58.00
39	New London Waterdays	office	4	8.000000	8.00
40	New London Waterdays	office	15	8.000000	8.00
41	New London Waterdays	office	NULL	8.000000	16.00
42	New London Waterdays	NULL	NULL	6.727272	74.00
43	Warren Cranberry Festival	booth	4	6.333333	19.00
44	Warren Cranberry Festival	booth	16	7.166666	21.50
45	Warren Cranberry Festival	booth	18	5.500000	16.50
46	Warren Cranberry Festival	booth	NULL	6.333333	57.00
47	Warren Cranberry Festival	office	4	8.000000	8.00
48	Warren Cranberry Festival	office	15	8.000000	8.00
49	Warren Cranberry Festival	office	NULL	8.000000	16.00
50	Warren Cranberry Festival	NULL	NULL	6.636363	73.00
51	Wild Rice Days	booth	4	7.000000	21.00
52	Wild Rice Days	booth	16	5.333333	16.00
53	Wild Rice Days	booth	18	5.333333	16.00
54	Wild Rice Days	booth	NULL	5.888888	53.00
55	Wild Rice Days	office	4	8.000000	8.00
56	Wild Rice Days	office	15	8.000000	8.00
57	Wild Rice Days	office	NULL	8.000000	16.00
58	Wild Rice Days	NULL	NULL	6.272727	69.00
59	NULL	NULL	NULL	6.530864	529.00

Figure 9-19. The ROLLUP with a GROUP BY will produce an extensive report with averages, total hours worked per person, subtotals, and totals.

average length of a shift worked by anyone, at any event, plus all hours worked by everyone, everywhere.

The CUBE function is similar to the ROLLUP, and expands the ROLLUP by adding some rows to the result set. In addition to the subtotals for each event and the grand total for all events, the CUBE function adds two rows, one for each WorkAssignmentDscr value. These rows contain, for each job description, the average shift length for all events and the total number of hours worked. Figure 9-20 shows the query and the result set.

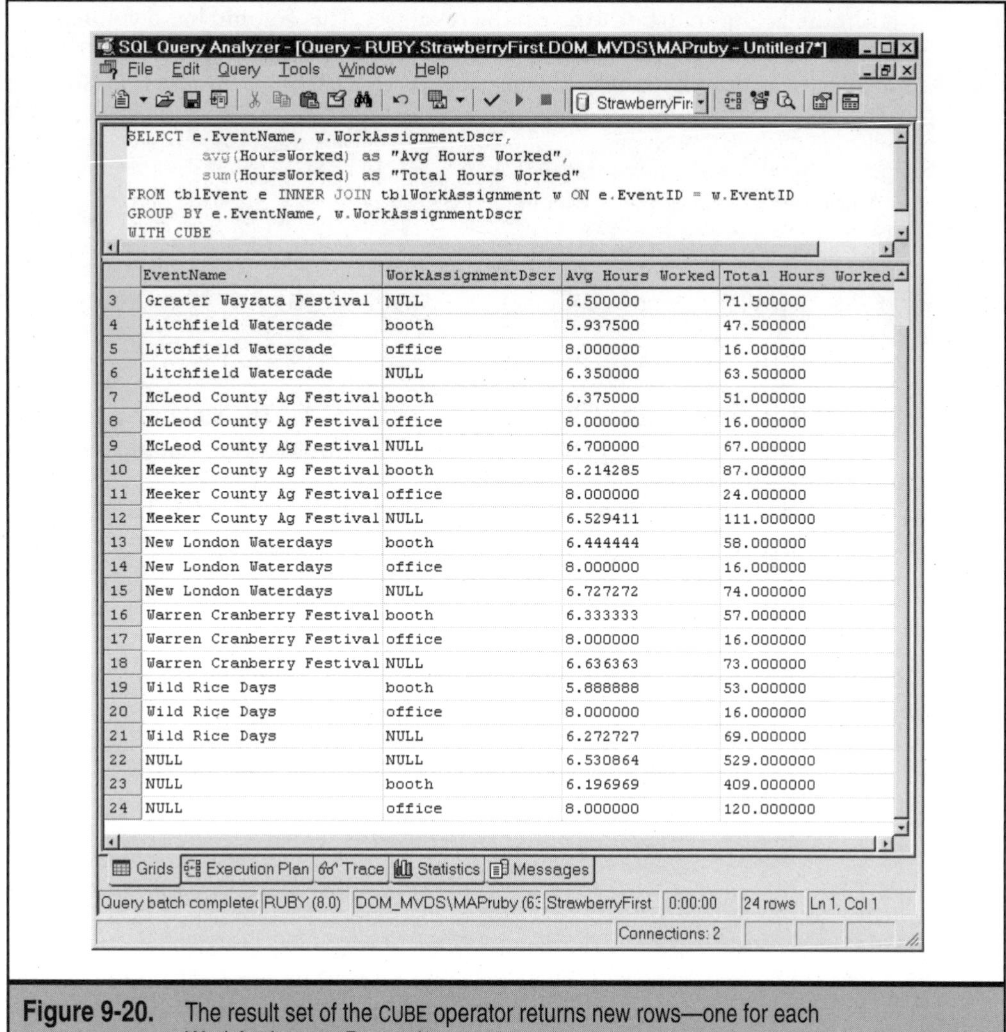


```
SELECT e.EventName, w.WorkAssignmentDscr,
       avg(HoursWorked) as "Avg Hours Worked",
       sum(HoursWorked) as "Total Hours Worked"
FROM tblEvent e INNER JOIN tblWorkAssignment w ON e.EventID = w.EventID
GROUP BY e.EventName, w.WorkAssignmentDscr
WITH CUBE
```

	EventName	WorkAssignmentDscr	Avg Hours Worked	Total Hours Worked
3	Greater Wayzata Festival	NULL	6.500000	71.500000
4	Litchfield Watercade	booth	5.937500	47.500000
5	Litchfield Watercade	office	8.000000	16.000000
6	Litchfield Watercade	NULL	6.350000	63.500000
7	McLeod County Ag Festival	booth	6.375000	51.000000
8	McLeod County Ag Festival	office	8.000000	16.000000
9	McLeod County Ag Festival	NULL	6.700000	67.000000
10	Meeker County Ag Festival	booth	6.214285	87.000000
11	Meeker County Ag Festival	office	8.000000	24.000000
12	Meeker County Ag Festival	NULL	6.529411	111.000000
13	New London Waterdays	booth	6.444444	58.000000
14	New London Waterdays	office	8.000000	16.000000
15	New London Waterdays	NULL	6.727272	74.000000
16	Warren Cranberry Festival	booth	6.333333	57.000000
17	Warren Cranberry Festival	office	8.000000	16.000000
18	Warren Cranberry Festival	NULL	6.636363	73.000000
19	Wild Rice Days	booth	5.888888	53.000000
20	Wild Rice Days	office	8.000000	16.000000
21	Wild Rice Days	NULL	6.272727	69.000000
22	NULL	NULL	6.530864	529.000000
23	NULL	booth	6.196969	409.000000
24	NULL	office	8.000000	120.000000

Figure 9-20. The result set of the CUBE operator returns new rows—one for each WorkAssignmentDscr value.

The more partitioning or grouping columns you add to the mix, the more complex the result set will be. You can imagine how quickly the cube could get out of control, returning combinations of results that most likely would not be useful.

To get around the problem of not knowing whether the NULL values are really data or were introduced by the ROLLUP or CUBE functions, Microsoft has given us the GROUPING aggregate, which is declared in the SELECT clause. The GROUPING aggregate function causes an additional column to be output in the result set. This column has a value of 1 if the row has been added by either the CUBE or the ROLLUP operator, and a value of 0 if not. You need to specify a column name as the argument for the GROUPING function, such as GROUPING(PersonID), as shown in the following code:

```
SELECT e.EventName, w.WorkAssignmentDscr, w.PersonID,
       AVG(HoursWorked) AS "Avg Hours Worked",
       SUM(HoursWorked) AS "Total Hours Worked",
       GROUPING(PersonID)
FROM tblEvent e INNER JOIN tblWorkAssignment w ON e.EventID = w.EventID
GROUP BY e.EventName, w.WorkAssignmentDscr, w.PersonID
WITH ROLLUP
```

The result set, shown in Figure 9-21, shows what happens. The rightmost column, with a column labeled (No column name), is the result of the GROUPING aggregate function. The rows with value 1 are generated by the ROLLUP function. Those with value 0 are truly data rows from the joined tables. This column is essentially a flag field that indicates the origins of the output data.

TOP *n* VALUE QUERIES

Once again Microsoft has redefined reality, and in this case, redefined the English language. The TOP function does not return the top anything; it returns the first *n* set of rows in the result set. Suppose that you want a report that shows you the five largest quantities for any product sold on a single order, along with the sale number. You would write this as

```
SELECT TOP 5 s.SaleNo, p.ProductDscr, s.QuantitySold
FROM tblSaleItem s INNER JOIN tblProduct p ON s.ProductCode = p.ProductCode
ORDER BY s.QuantitySold DESC
```

Figure 9-22 shows the result set. The TOP 5 portion of the query is restricting the result set to only the first five rows returned. The TOP keyword must immediately follow the SELECT; but the columns can be written in the order you want—because the TOP does not apply to what is in the select list, but rather to the entire result set. In Figure 9-22, it's not looking for the TOP 5 SaleNo values, or for the TOP 5 product descriptions or quantities sold. It's not looking for the TOP anything. It's looking for the first five rows returned as a result of the sorting initiated by the ORDER BY clause. The ORDER BY clause determines the order in which the data is returned, and in this example, you have asked for the data sorted by quantity. And, to ensure that you get the rows with the TOP 5 quantity values, you have to remember to include DESC (descending) in the ORDER BY to make sure that the results go from largest to smallest. If you forget to include the DESC in a SELECT TOP query, you could end up giving achievement awards to your five worst performing salespeople. In the absence of an ORDER BY clause, the SELECT TOP 5 will give you the first five rows returned by the query in the order they are presented in the result set, no matter what kind of data they contain.

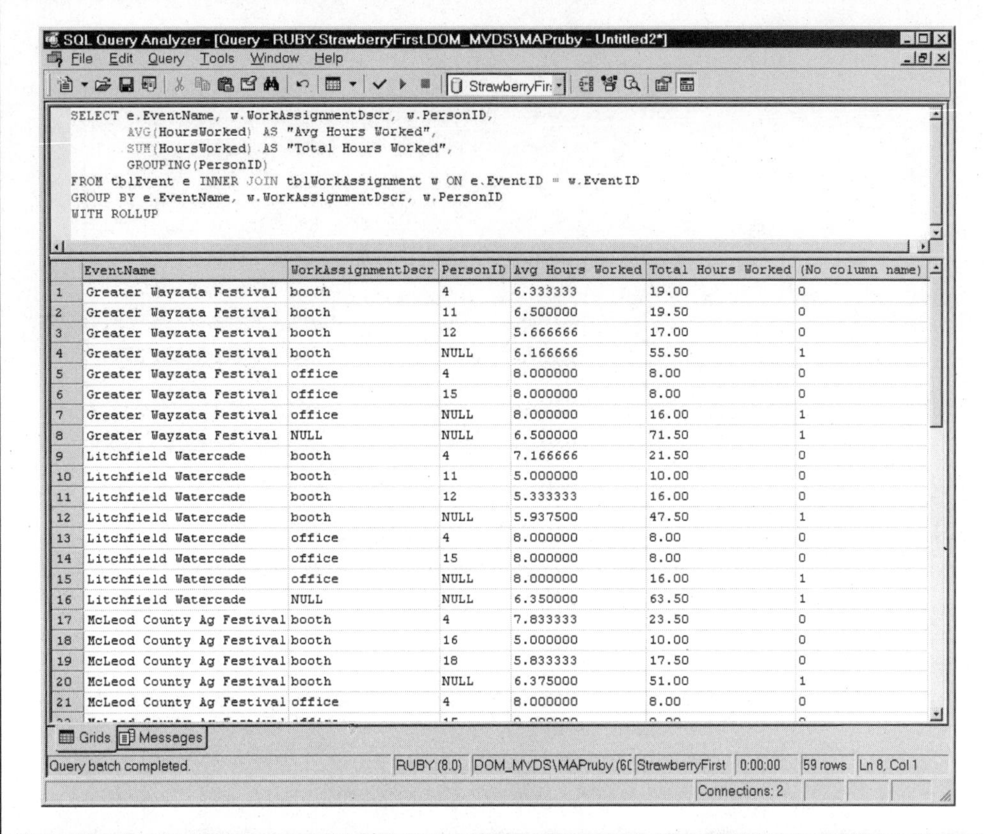


```
SELECT e.EventName, w.WorkAssignmentDscr, w.PersonID,
       AVG(HoursWorked) AS "Avg Hours Worked",
       SUM(HoursWorked) AS "Total Hours Worked",
       GROUPING(PersonID)
FROM tblEvent e INNER JOIN tblWorkAssignment w ON e.EventID = w.EventID
GROUP BY e.EventName, w.WorkAssignmentDscr, w.PersonID
WITH ROLLUP
```

	EventName	WorkAssignmentDscr	PersonID	Avg Hours Worked	Total Hours Worked	(No column name)
1	Greater Wayzata Festival	booth	4	6.333333	19.00	0
2	Greater Wayzata Festival	booth	11	6.500000	19.50	0
3	Greater Wayzata Festival	booth	12	5.666666	17.00	0
4	Greater Wayzata Festival	booth	NULL	6.166666	55.50	1
5	Greater Wayzata Festival	office	4	8.000000	8.00	0
6	Greater Wayzata Festival	office	15	8.000000	8.00	0
7	Greater Wayzata Festival	office	NULL	8.000000	16.00	1
8	Greater Wayzata Festival	NULL	NULL	6.500000	71.50	1
9	Litchfield Watercade	booth	4	7.166666	21.50	0
10	Litchfield Watercade	booth	11	5.000000	10.00	0
11	Litchfield Watercade	booth	12	5.333333	16.00	0
12	Litchfield Watercade	booth	NULL	5.937500	47.50	1
13	Litchfield Watercade	office	4	8.000000	8.00	0
14	Litchfield Watercade	office	15	8.000000	8.00	0
15	Litchfield Watercade	office	NULL	8.000000	16.00	1
16	Litchfield Watercade	NULL	NULL	6.350000	63.50	1
17	McLeod County Ag Festival	booth	4	7.833333	23.50	0
18	McLeod County Ag Festival	booth	16	5.000000	10.00	0
19	McLeod County Ag Festival	booth	18	5.833333	17.50	0
20	McLeod County Ag Festival	booth	NULL	6.375000	51.00	1
21	McLeod County Ag Festival	office	4	8.000000	8.00	0

Figure 9-21. The GROUPING() aggregate indicates the origin of data: 1 for data from the CUBE or ROLLUP, and 0 for data from a joined table.

In this example, you may notice that the results show a value of 5 for the first five rows. That might lead you to wonder whether there are more rows with quantity 120 that were omitted by the cutoff of only five rows. The solution to this question is to include WITH TIES in the TOP query. Any additional rows with the same value will also be returned, as you can see in Figure 9-23.

```
USE Northwind
SELECT TOP 5 WITH TIES orderid, productname, quantity
FROM [order details] JOIN products
   ON [order details].productid = products.productid
ORDER BY quantity DESC
```

In addition to the TOP *n* rows, you can also ask for the TOP *n* percent, which again will return the first *n* percent of your rows, based on whatever order you have specified.

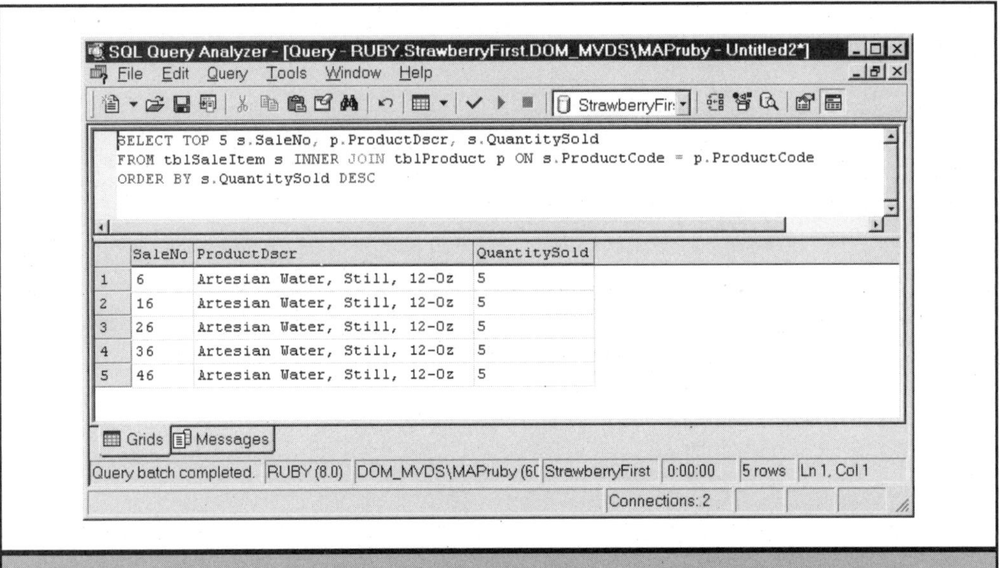

Figure 9-22. The TOP function limits the output to the first *n* rows in the result set.

SQL Query Analyzer - [Query - RUBY.StrawberryFirst.DOM_MVDS\MAPruby - Untitled1*]

File Edit Query Tools Window Help

```
SELECT TOP 5 WITH TIES s.SaleNo, p.ProductDscr, s.QuantitySold
FROM tblSaleItem s INNER JOIN tblProduct p ON s.ProductCode = p.ProductCode
ORDER BY s.QuantitySold DESC
```

	SaleNo	ProductDscr	QuantitySold
50	496	Artesian Water, Still, 12-Oz	5
51	506	Artesian Water, Still, 12-Oz	5
52	516	Artesian Water, Still, 12-Oz	5
53	526	Artesian Water, Still, 12-Oz	5
54	536	Artesian Water, Still, 12-Oz	5
55	546	Artesian Water, Still, 12-Oz	5
56	556	Artesian Water, Still, 12-Oz	5
57	566	Artesian Water, Still, 12-Oz	5
58	576	Artesian Water, Still, 12-Oz	5
59	586	Artesian Water, Still, 12-Oz	5
60	596	Artesian Water, Still, 12-Oz	5
61	606	Artesian Water, Still, 12-Oz	5
62	616	Artesian Water, Still, 12-Oz	5
63	626	Artesian Water, Still, 12-Oz	5
64	636	Artesian Water, Still, 12-Oz	5

Grids Messages

Query batch complete(RUBY (8.0) DOM_MVDS\MAPruby (61 StrawberryFirst 0:00:00 64 rows Ln 4, Col 1

Connections: 1

Figure 9-23. The WITH TIES option shows additional rows beyond the TOP 5 that have the same values as the TOP 5.

CHAPTER 10

Data Modification

Although we said that databases are for retrieving information, not storing data, we do realize that you have to get the data into the tables somehow, and you have to keep that data current for the extracted information to have some business value. There are many ways to get data into SQL Server tables, including the bulk copy program (BCP), Data Transformation Services (DTS), replication, and entering data through a client interface such as Excel or Access. In this chapter, we will look at how you enter and modify data using SQL Server's own T-SQL commands. You may have to enter data directly into SQL Server when you are developing test databases and need to populate them. Or you may have to use these commands to clean up a database that has become corrupted or one that includes contradictory data. You may also want to code these T-SQL commands into stored procedures, so that instead of an application updating the database directly, it calls a stored procedure and passes the data values as parameters to that stored procedure. SQL Server performs an actual update, and a confirmation of success or notification of failure can be passed back to the client application.

Only a few commands for modifying data are available in SQL, but they are sufficient to get the job done and powerful enough to inflict severe damage on the database if used carelessly. Let's take a look at these commands. We'll also talk a little about triggers, which we'll cover in much more detail in Chapter 18.

THE INSERT COMMAND

When you insert a new row into a table, you may choose to supply a value for every column, or you might input values for just a few of the columns. If you supply a value for every column, you do not need to list the columns in the INSERT statement. If you supply values for just some of the columns, you'll need to list which columns you are providing input values for. The columns for which you do not supply values must either have a default value defined or must allow NULLs. For some columns, the default may be a system function, rather than a fixed value. For example, functions can be very useful if you want to insert the name of the person making the change to the database, and the date and time when the row was inserted. We'll look at examples of each of these conditions in a moment.

The one column for which you never supply a value is the identity column, because SQL Server will fill in the value for you. In fact, you write the INSERT statement as if the identity column did not even exist. You might think that a timestamp column would be handled the same way, as SQL Server will generate the value, but that is not the case. You have to specify either NULL or DEFAULT for the timestamp column.

Inserting by Position

If you want to supply a list of values for the INSERT statement, you will have to specify the values for each column in the exact order in which it appears in the table or in the SP_HELP *tablename* command. If you want the default value to be filled in, just type in the word **DEFAULT**. If you want a NULL, type in **NULL**. Neither NULL nor DEFAULT should be quoted.

Unlike some other database software (Access comes to mind), you cannot skip a value. The input values are separated by commas, and a double comma is interpreted as a syntax error. If the data value being input is a character or date datatype, it must be quoted (single quotes); number datatypes do not have to be quoted. An example of an INSERT statement for the Person table that supplies values for every column would look like this:

```
INSERT INTO StrawberryFirst.dbo.tblPerson
VALUES ('Anderson', 'Arne', '1212 Arcadia Avenue',
       'Akershus', 'MN', '03555', 'e')
```

This code and the results are shown in Figure 10-1. We could have left out the name of the database in this statement, and we probably would do that if we were just writing a quick INSERT statement to get some data into a test database. But it does no harm to have it in there, and it may be needed, especially in a stored procedure that you might call from another database.

CAUTION: If you have replication turned on in your SQL Server database, you need to provide a DEFAULT at the end of the value list. Replication adds a column to the table msrepl_tran_version. This is a unique identifier, and you shouldn't provide a value for it. Instead, you simply provide the value DEFAULT, as in the following code:

```
INSERT INTO StrawberryFirst.dbo.tblPerson
VALUES ('Anderson', 'Abram', '1212 Arcadia Avenue',
        'Akershus', 'MN', '03555', 'e', DEFAULT)
```

Inserting with Column Names

As an alternative to inserting in column position, you can list the columns, or just a subset of the columns, and then specify the input values in the same order as the columns are listed. In this case, the column list does *not* have to be in the same order as the columns were created. Again, any columns not listed, other than the identity column, must have a default value, be an identity column, or allow NULLs. As an example, suppose you have a name to enter into the Person table, but you don't have an address yet. You could enter this record using the following INSERT statement:

```
INSERT INTO StrawberryFirst.dbo.tblPerson
        (PersonType, FirstName, LastName)
VALUES  ('c', 'Billy Bob', 'Boudreau')
```

The query and results are shown in Figure 10-2. Notice that the PersonType column appears first instead of last, and the order of the first and last name columns have been swapped. All that matters here, though, is that the VALUES in the value list correspond to the columns in the column list.

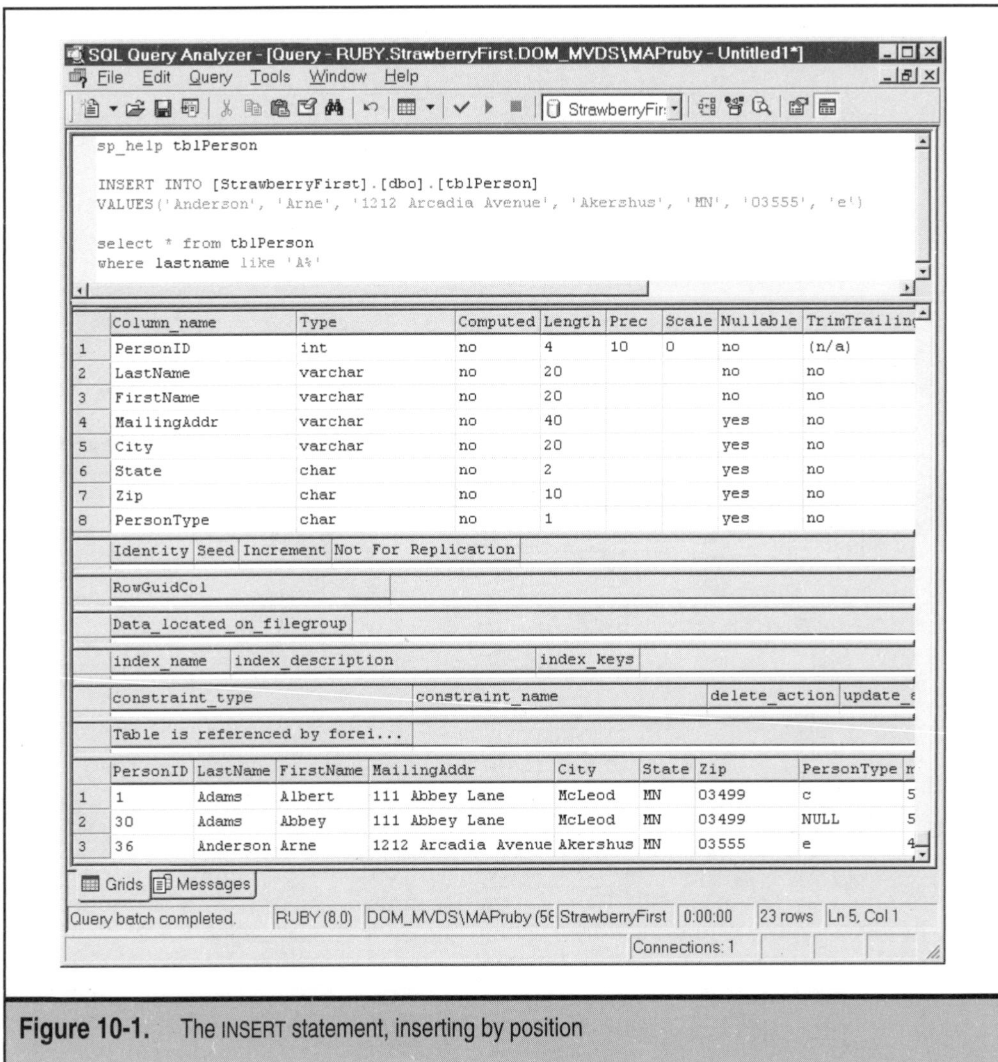

Figure 10-1. The INSERT statement, inserting by position

Inserting Data from Other Tables

You can select data from one or more tables and insert it into a different table in two ways. You can use a regular INSERT statement, but instead of listing the values, you use a SELECT statement. The same rules apply as for any other INSERT statement. If you do not list columns, the SELECT will have to return from the source table exactly the comparable number and type of values to insert into the rows of the target table. The returned values must be compatible datatypes. If your SELECT returns only some of the insert values, you will have to specify which columns these values go into by using a column list. Then the remaining columns have to be accounted for, by specifying either DEFAULT or NULL.

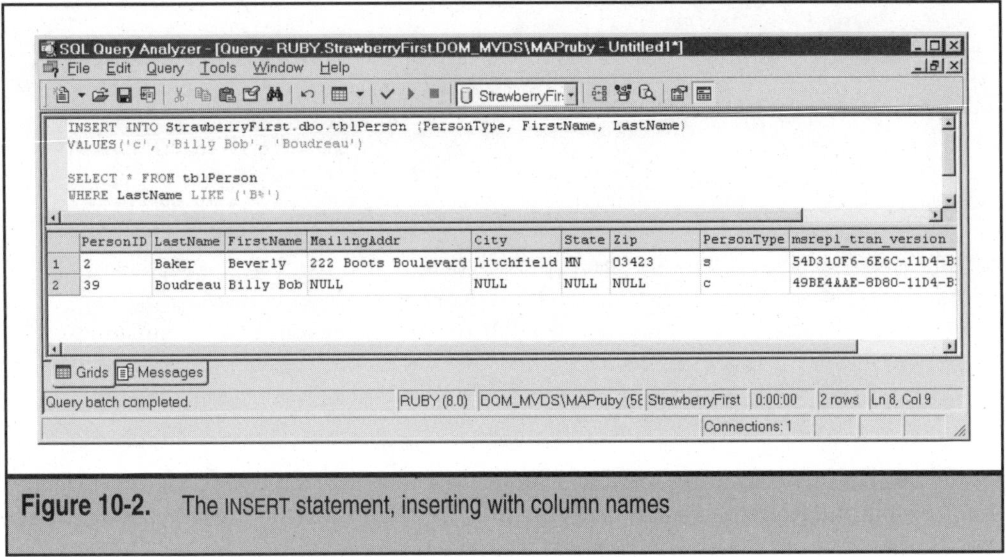

Figure 10-2. The INSERT statement, inserting with column names

It is quite possible that your SELECT statement will return data from more than one table. It can even retrieve data from another database. For example, before you run the payroll this week, you could run a SELECT query on the Personnel Department database to see whether any new employees have been hired; if so, you would insert their records into the Payroll table. It's very possible that your SELECT query will return more than one row—in this case, more than one new employee. SQL Server can easily handle multiple row inserts from a single INSERT query, although you may want to consider this carefully. When we discuss transactions in Chapter 13, we'll talk about how a transaction can be rolled back or undone. If you insert many rows all at once, as part of a single operation, and there is an error near the end of the operation, it is possible that SQL Server will have to roll back all the rows that were inserted as part of this operation. You might prefer to set up a loop in your code that processes the inserts one at a time. Even though this would take longer, there is less risk of having to roll back a large volume of transactions.

The syntax for an INSERT statement using a SELECT clause is shown next. You have created a table called SalesStaff for this example, and you will drop the table when you are through with it. Note that when you do the insert, you list the columns. This is not strictly necessary, because you are providing values for every column, and the columns are in the correct sequence for loading:

```
CREATE TABLE SalesStaff
( PersonID        INT             NOT NULL PRIMARY KEY,
  VendorName      varchar (40) NOT NULL ,
  LastName        varchar (20) NOT NULL ,
  FirstName       varchar (20) NOT NULL ,
  MailingAddr     varchar (40) NULL ,
```

```
  City           varchar (20) NULL ,
  State          char (2)     NULL ,
  Zip            char (10)    NULL ,
  OfficeLocation varchar (60) NULL )
GO

INSERT INTO SalesStaff (PersonID, VendorName, LastName, FirstName,
                        MailingAddr, City, State, Zip, OfficeLocation)
SELECT s.PersonID, v.Vendorname, p.LastName, p.FirstName, p.MailingAddr,
       p.City, p.State, p.Zip, s.OfficeLocation
FROM tblSalesPerson s   JOIN tblPerson p  ON s.PersonID = p.PersonID
                        JOIN tblVendor v  ON s.VendorID = v.VendorID

SELECT * FROM SalesStaff
```

Figure 10-3 shows the code and the result set. The SalesStaff table contains data from the Vendor table and from the Person table, but only those people who are salespeople. Don't drop the SalesStaff table yet; you'll need it for more code examples in the next section.

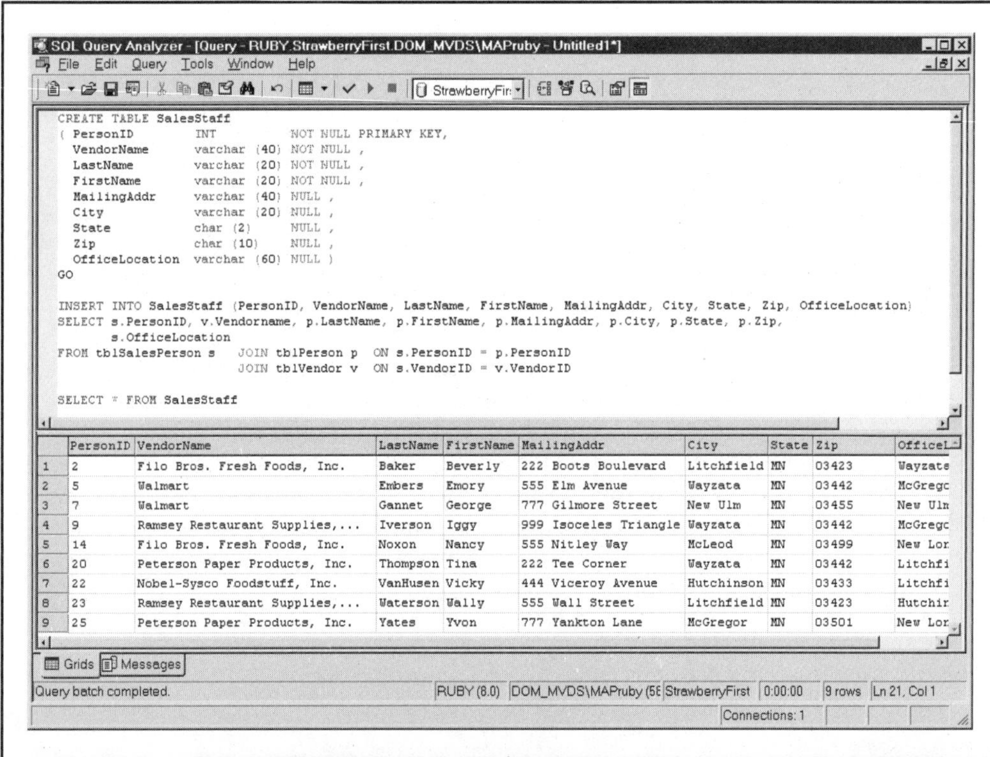

Figure 10-3. Inserting data into the SalesStaff table by issuing a SELECT against a join of the Salesperson, Person, and Vendor tables.

Inserting Data from a Stored Procedure

The previous example shows the results of a SELECT query being inserted into a table. You can also query using a stored procedure and return those results into a table, using an INSERT statement. To illustrate this, you will take the SELECT query from the previous section and convert it to a stored procedure (which we will cover in more detail in Chapter 17):

```
CREATE PROCEDURE SalesStaffLoad
AS
SELECT tblSalesPerson.PersonID, Vendorname, LastName, FirstName,
MailingAddr, City, State, Zip, OfficeLocation
FROM tblSalesPerson JOIN tblPerson
     ON tblSalesPerson.PersonID = tblPerson.PersonID
JOIN tblVendor
     ON tblSalesPerson.VendorID = tblVendor.VendorID
GO
```

Next, you remove the data that you loaded with the previous result set with a TRUNCATE TABLE command, which we'll explain in more detail in the section "DELETE" later in this chapter.

```
TRUNCATE TABLE SalesStaff
```

Now you'll execute the INSERT statement with the stored procedure instead of all the code shown in Figure 10-3:

```
INSERT INTO SalesStaff
( PersonID,  VendorName,  LastName,  FirstName,
  MailingAddr, City, State, Zip, OfficeLocation)
EXEC SalesStaffLoad
GO
SELECT * FROM SalesStaff
GO
```

Figure 10-4 shows the query and the result set from this INSERT using a stored procedure. The SalesStaff table once again contains data about Vendors and Salespeople. Now it's time to drop the SalesStaff table, using the following code:

```
DROP TABLE SalesStaff
DROP PROCEDURE SalesStaffLoad
```

Building a Table with SELECT INTO

You can use a variant of SELECT to insert data into a table: the SELECT INTO command. This is not an ANSI-standard SQL command, although you will find this same command in other RDBMS languages. SELECT INTO differs from an INSERT statement with a SELECT

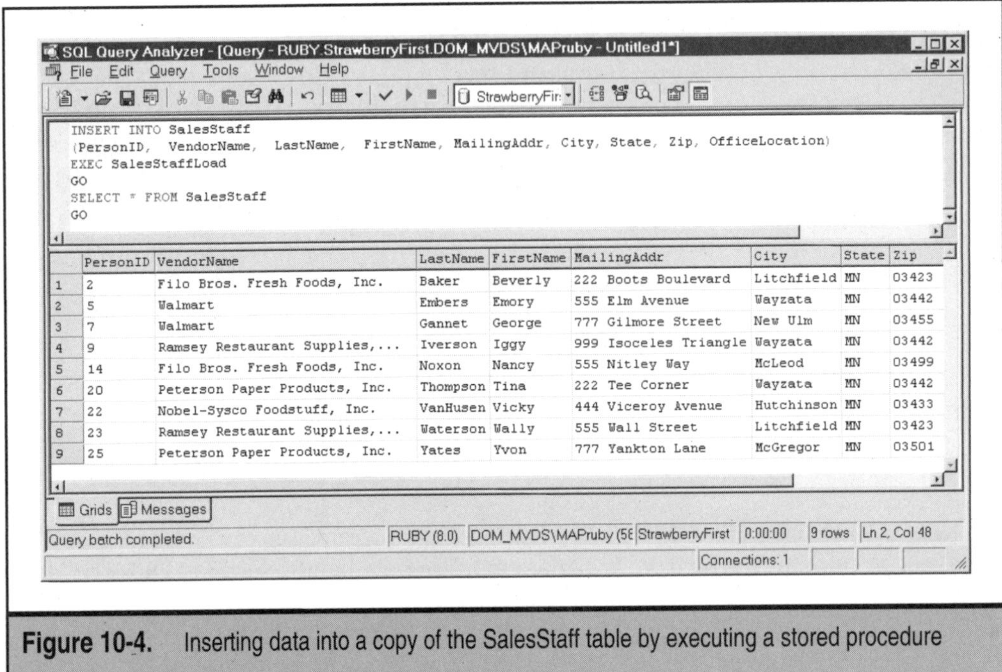

Figure 10-4. Inserting data into a copy of the SalesStaff table by executing a stored procedure

clause in several significant ways. First, the SELECT INTO dynamically creates a new table and then inserts the data, all in the same operation. The INSERT statement, on the other hand, needs to have an existing table into which it can insert the row. Also, the SELECT INTO is a non-logged operation—there are no copies of the inserted records retained in the transaction log. For the SELECT INTO to run, you must turn on the Select Into/Bulk Copy option on the database properties page, or you can add a line of code before the SELECT INTO that activates this option. The implication of a "non-logged" operation is that recovery in the event of a system failure might be difficult or impossible, forcing you to take manual recovery action. Typically, if you were able to determine that the SELECT INTO operation was halted partway through, you would delete the target table from the database and restart the SELECT INTO.

SQL Server 2000 offers some new backup options, including Full Recovery and Bulk-Logged Recovery, which do allow you to recover from a failure, even though you've used non-logged operations such as SELECT INTO. Full Recovery actually does log everything and allows you to restore the database to the point just before the system failure. As you can imagine, the overhead of this level of transaction logging is very high. Bulk-Logged Recovery allows you to recover to the point of failure if, and only if, you have the data files available. If they are damaged or unavailable, the best you can do is to recover up to the end of the last transaction log backup. Everything that happened afterward will be lost. The name Bulk-Logged is a little confusing at first, because it is not logging the bulk operations row by row. Think of it as "logging in bulk," in the same way that the warehouse clerk might note the arrival of a truckload of computer paper, rather than logging in 400 boxes, one at a time.

You can rewrite the previous example so that you do not create the table first. Instead, you can have the SELECT INTO create the table for you. To add a little variety, and to review column aliases, you have also combined two columns into one—the last and first names—so you need to supply a column name for your new column in the new table. The syntax for SELECT INTO looks like this:

```
SELECT s.PersonID, v.Vendorname,
       p.LastName + ', ' + p.FirstName AS "Full Name",
       p.MailingAddr, p.City, p.State, p.Zip, s.OfficeLocation
INTO SalesStaff
FROM tblSalesPerson s JOIN tblPerson p ON s.PersonID = p.PersonID
                      JOIN tblVendor v ON s.VendorID = v.VendorID
GO
SELECT * FROM SalesStaff
GO
DROP TABLE SalesStaff
```

As you can see in Figure 10-5, the execution plan shows the three-table join, first Sales-Person to Vendor, and then that result to the Person table. Next, the scalar computation is creating one computed column from the directive:

```
p.LastName + ', ' + p.FirstName AS "Full Name"
```

The TOP operation is selecting the first *n* rows based on a sort order, most likely to get the dimensions for the new table that will be created, because the very next step, the table insert, actually inserts the rows from the join operation into the target table.

When you've finished reviewing the results and the execution plan, run the DROP TABLE command to remove the SalesStaff table and its contents from your database.

DELETE

Deleting data is really easy in any relational database management system, including SQL Server. In fact, it's too easy, so you should use this command with care. If you forget to put in a WHERE clause to restrict the rows for the DELETE operation, you'll find that all the rows will disappear from the table. For example,

```
DELETE FROM tblEmployee
```

will wipe out all the entries in the Employee table. This particular example will fail, because there's a foreign key relationship from Employee to another table that prevents the removal of rows from the Employee table. We'll talk about foreign key relationships in Chapter 15.

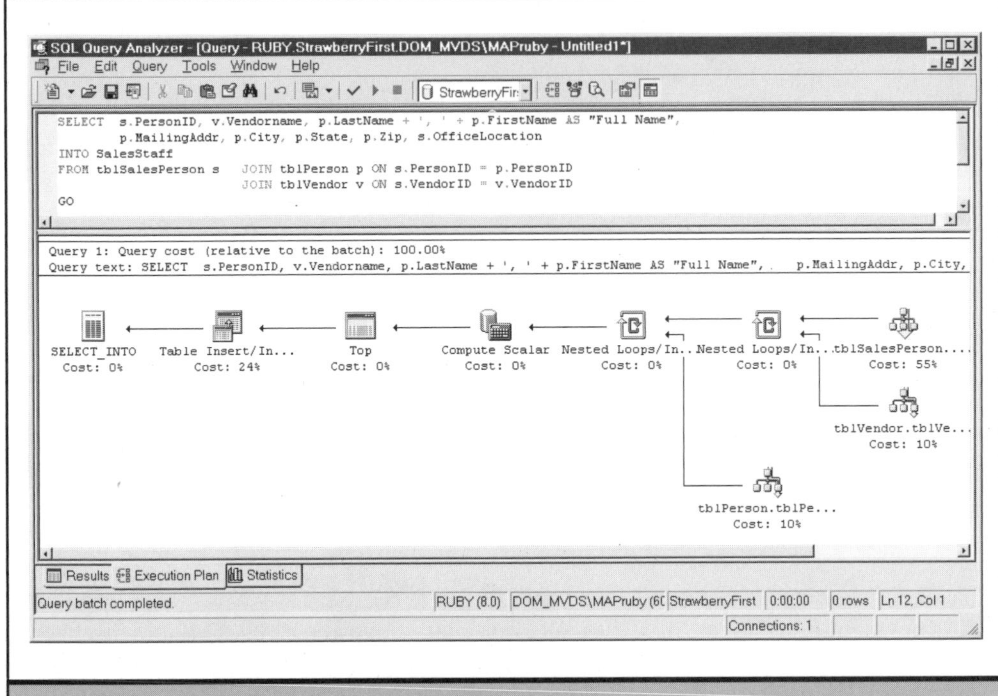

Figure 10-5. Using the SELECT INTO statement to create and populate a copy of the SalesStaff table in one operation.

A more reasonable example of the DELETE might be to remove Arne, Abram, and Billy Bob, and return the Person table to the way it was before you inserted these rows:

```
DELETE FROM tblPerson
WHERE PersonID IN (36, 37, 39)
```

As you've probably surmised, Arne, Abram, and Billy Bob have PersonID values of 36, 37, and 39, respectively. If you recall, the PersonID is an identity datatype that automatically increments with each row inserted into the table. If you're following along with the examples, you may have to adjust the preceding code to work with your database.

Figure 10-6 is the execution plan for the preceding DELETE statement. Notice how many tables are scanned (shown on the right side of the window). Each of these tables has an enforced relationship with the Person table, and SQL Server must first determine whether there are any referenced rows in these tables before it will allow a row from the Person table to be deleted.

As we've mentioned before, we will be covering the topic of transactions in Chapter 13; but for now, we should mention that the DELETE statement shown above is a complete transaction in SQL Server. If you hadn't changed the default behavior, SQL Server would initiate a transaction, run the command, and commit the transaction. This behavior is different from Oracle, for instance, in that Oracle initiates the transaction, runs the command,

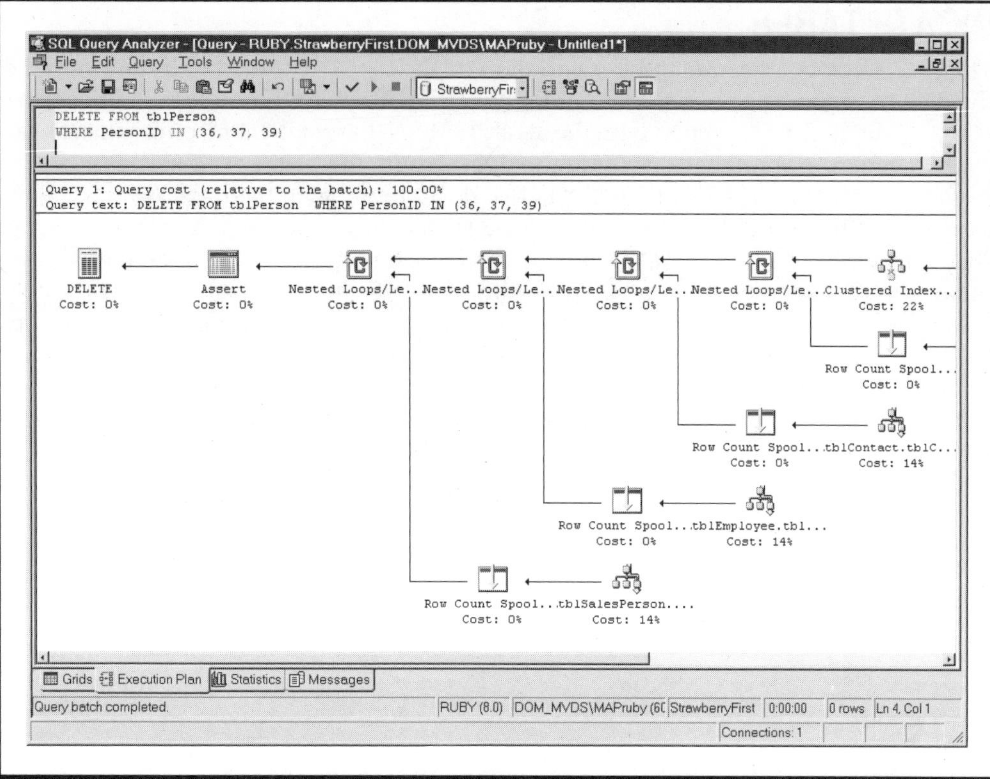

Figure 10-6. The execution plan for a DELETE statement includes scanning related tables for associated records.

and leaves the transaction pending until you commit it or roll it back. We mention this because some people with a background in Oracle might believe that you could recover from deleting the entire table or the wrong set of rows by issuing a ROLLBACK command. In SQL Server default behavior, the ROLLBACK command will not work unless you have specifically started a transaction with a corresponding BEGIN TRANSACTION command. If you just type in a DELETE command on its own, the data is gone.

The DELETE command is logged, so if you delete an entire table or the wrong set of rows, and you cannot roll back the operation, you may be able to recover by restoring from the transaction log or from a recent backup of the table.

It is possible to use a SELECT query in the WHERE clause and query another table to determine which rows to delete. For example, you might delete all the rows from your Customer table in which the date of the last order is more than two years past. The WHERE clause would contain a SELECT that would scan a second table to determine the date of last order, and the result set would then determine which rows to delete from the Customer table. You can write this type of sub-SELECT statement, as it's called, as either a join or a subquery. We'll expand on subqueries in Chapter 11.

TRUNCATE TABLE

The TRUNCATE TABLE command is a variation on the DELETE command. It removes all of the data from the table, but it does not log the deletes on a row-by-row basis. So even if you had initiated a transaction with the BEGIN TRANSACTION statement, once you truncate a table, you cannot roll back or undo the damage. On the positive side, the TRUNCATE TABLE is quick; it is far faster than a DELETE (which does log all the rows as it is deleting them). Both the DELETE and the TRUNCATE TABLE delete just the data; they leave the table structure intact. The TRUNCATE TABLE command is sometimes used with test databases to remove the exhausted test data before reloading a fresh set. Another use for TRUNCATE TABLE would be in archiving production tables. At the end of each month, you could copy all the data from one table into another table, an archive copy of the first table, using a SELECT INTO command. You would then truncate the production table with the TRUNCATE TABLE command, so it's ready for the next month's data entry. This technique prevents your production table from growing too large and unwieldy.

The TRUNCATE TABLE command looks like this:

```
TRUNCATE TABLE tblEmployee
```

There is no WHERE clause to indicate which rows are affected. This command operates on the entire table.

UPDATE

As with the DELETE command, when you update an existing row, it is important to make sure that you've used a WHERE clause to restrict the rows to which the UPDATE is applied. If you forget the WHERE restriction, SQL Server will do a global update—it will update all of the rows. When you update a row, you have to indicate which row you want to change, which column(s) you are changing, and what the new value should be. You can change more than one column at a time, as this example from Strawberry shows. You are changing the employee-owner from a weekly paycheck to bi-monthly and therefore changing the amount paid per pay period:

```
UPDATE tblEmployee
SET PayAmount=1250, PayPeriod= 'bi-monthly'
WHERE JobTitle = 'Employee-Owner'
```

As we've shown in Figure 10-7, it's always a good idea when you're writing an interactive T-SQL UPDATE statement to first check the data with a SELECT, to make sure that you know what your UPDATE statement will be doing. Typically, I write a SELECT statement to get the result set I need, and then I copy the WHERE clause from the SELECT and use it in the UPDATE statement.

The execution plan in Figure 10-7 is pretty straightforward. It starts on the right with a clustered index scan to find the row that meets the criteria in the WHERE clause, and that

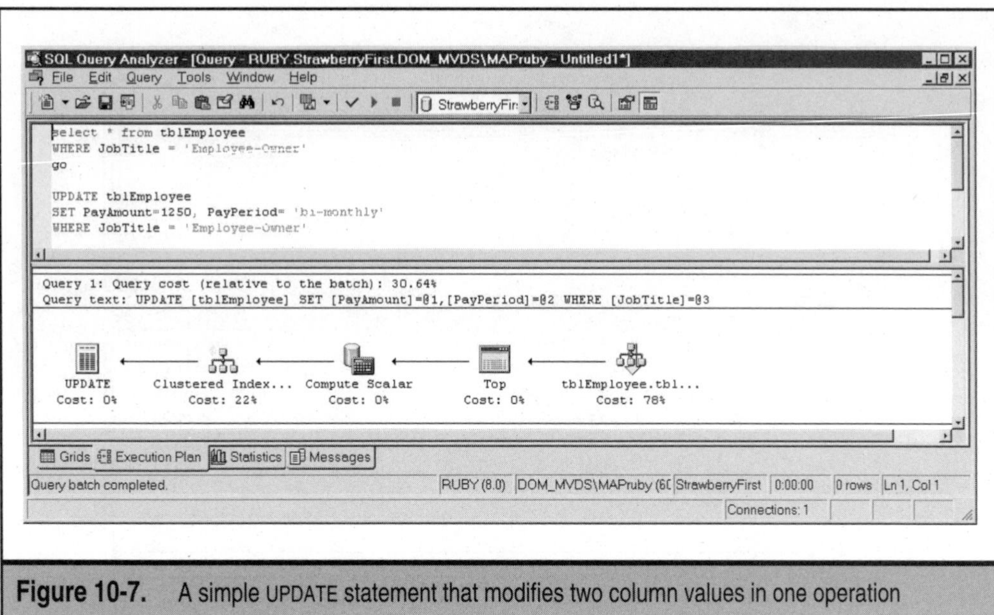

Figure 10-7. A simple UPDATE statement that modifies two column values in one operation

takes up most of the time (78 percent). Then there is a TOP operation and a Compute Scalar operation, both of which have to do with figuring out whether SQL Server can update in place (the new values will replace the old values and the row will not physically move on the hard disk) or if it will have to rewrite the row somewhere else in the file. From the subsequent Clustered Index Update, it looks like the latter operation was needed, which required nearly all of the rest of the cost for resources (22 percent). Finally, the single row was updated, a new physical record was written to disk, and the old version of the record was marked for deletion.

You can also update data by modifying existing values, using the arithmetic and mathematical functions. Suppose that profits are up and you want to give the employees a 10-percent pay increase. You'd use the multiplication operator that we covered in Chapter 7:

```
UPDATE tblEmployee
SET PayAmount= PayAmount*1.1
WHERE JobTitle = 'Employee'
```

As you can see from Figure 10-8, the rows in the Employee table have been updated. The execution plan, which we're not showing, is similar to that for Figure 10-7, which indicates that SQL Server could not do an update in place; instead, it had to rewrite the rows to a different place on the hard disk.

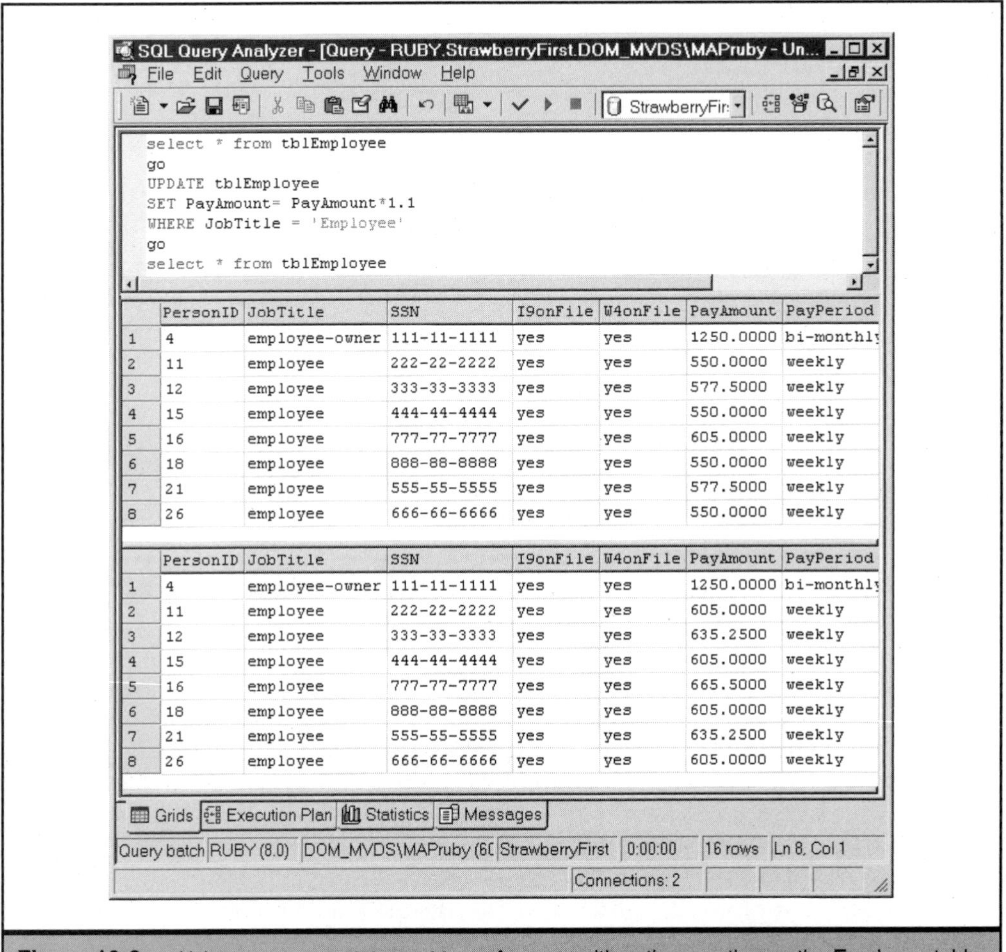

Figure 10-8. Using an UPDATE statement to perform an arithmetic operation on the Employee table

As with the INSERT statement, the UPDATE can reference data from other tables to base its decision on which row to update. You have to be careful about how you phrase the SELECT statement that accesses the other tables, because an UPDATE statement can only update a row based on a single value returned for that row. For instance, suppose that you want to increase an employee's paycheck to account for special pay allocated during the past week. You would use a query with the date range for the past week to find out which events had taken place that week. The WorkAssignment table will provide the special pay value for the employee. But it could be possible that this employee had worked two events during this time period. This means that two entries will appear in the WorkAssignment table, each of which may have a value for special pay. Because of the update-once rule, you can't add them both to the PayAmount in the Employee table. The solution to this problem is to ask for the SUM of the SpecialPay column, which produces a single output row for each EventID. Once you have the summed value, the UPDATE operation will work fine.

To see how this works, you'll need to do a bit of setup. First, add a row to the WorkAssignment table, giving person 15 additional special pay for event 1:

```
INSERT INTO tblWorkAssignment
VALUES ('backup', 1, 15, 'Saturday', '8:00', '12:00', 4, 15.00, default)
GO
```

Now add some special pay values to the WorkAssignment table:

```
UPDATE tblWorkAssignment
SET SpecialPay = 20.00
WHERE workid IN (3,7,11)
GO
```

Run a detail report confirming that the payroll figures for the pay period are accurate. The ISNULL function will convert any SpecialPay value that is NULL to zero, so that the Total Pay value doesn't come out NULL. This is a default behavior of SQL Server 2000, that NULLs propagate—a NULL multiplied by a number yields NULL.

```
SELECT e.SSN, p.LastName, p.FirstName, e.PayPeriod,
       v.EventName, v.StartDate, v.EndDate,
       e.PayAmount AS "Regular Pay", w.SpecialPay,
       e.PayAmount + ISNULL(w.SpecialPay, 0) AS "Total Pay"
FROM tblPerson p INNER JOIN tblEmployee e       ON p.PersonID = e.PersonID
                 INNER JOIN tblWorkAssignment w ON e.PersonID = w.PersonID
                 INNER JOIN tblEvent v          ON w.EventID = v.EventID
WHERE v.StartDate = '2000-06-23'
ORDER BY SSN
GO
```

Now create a separate payroll table for Event 1 and display the results:

```
SELECT * INTO PAYROLL_Event1
FROM tblEmployee
WHERE PersonID IN (SELECT PersonID FROM tblWorkAssignment
                   WHERE EventID = 1)
GO
select * from PAYROLL_Event1
GO
```

Add three simple columns. The first (Special Pay) will hold data from the Work Assignment table. The other two will hold first name and last name from the Person table:

```
ALTER TABLE PAYROLL_Event1
ADD SpecialPay money NULL,
    LastName varchar(20) NULL,
    FirstName varchar(20) NULL
GO
```

Add a computed column to hold the calculated total pay:

```
ALTER TABLE PAYROLL_Event1
ADD TotalPay AS PayAmount + ISNULL(SpecialPay, 0)
GO
```

Finally, update the new payroll table with names and special pay values, and let the computed column calculate the total pay and display the results:

```
UPDATE PAYROLL_Event1
SET LastName = (SELECT LastName FROM tblPerson
                WHERE PersonID = PAYROLL_Event1.PersonID),
    FirstName = (SELECT FirstName FROM tblPerson
                 WHERE PersonID = PAYROLL_Event1.PersonID),
    SpecialPay = (SELECT SUM(SpecialPay) FROM tblWorkAssignment
                  WHERE PersonID = PAYROLL_Event1.PersonID)
GO

SELECT * FROM PAYROLL_Event1
GO
```

Figure 10-9 shows the INSERT statement and the final result, the payroll report. The LastName and FirstName are retrieved from the Person table, where there was a match on PersonID. Values for the SpecialPay column were retrieved from the WorkAssignment table, but because of the very real possibility of more than one row for a PersonID, the SpecialPay values in the WorkAssignment table were added up for each PersonID. This ensured that only one value per PersonID would be returned to the PAYROLL_Event1 table.

Autoincrementing Column Values

A frequently used feature of T-SQL is the capability to generate automatically incrementing numbers for a column. There are many uses for this feature, such as invoice numbers, purchase order numbers, and customer numbers. You can use this autonumbering feature to generate primary key values, rather than trying to come up with some complex combination of columns to define each row uniquely. There are two ways to generate a value: the Identity property and the global universal identifier (GUID), which was introduced in SQL Server 7. Let's first look at the Identity property, which has been part of SQL Server since at least version *6.x*, and which you will find in many existing databases.

The Identity Property

As we mentioned in our discussion of datatypes in Chapter 6, the Identity property is just that—an additional property attached to a column. The column itself can be an integer datatype, or a smallint or a tinyint if the range of available values meets your needs. If you have huge numbers of rows, you can use the bigint datatype, which will allow you to count up to 2^{32}–1. You can even use the decimal or numeric datatypes, but you have to specify no values to the right of the decimal point if you're using these as an identity column.

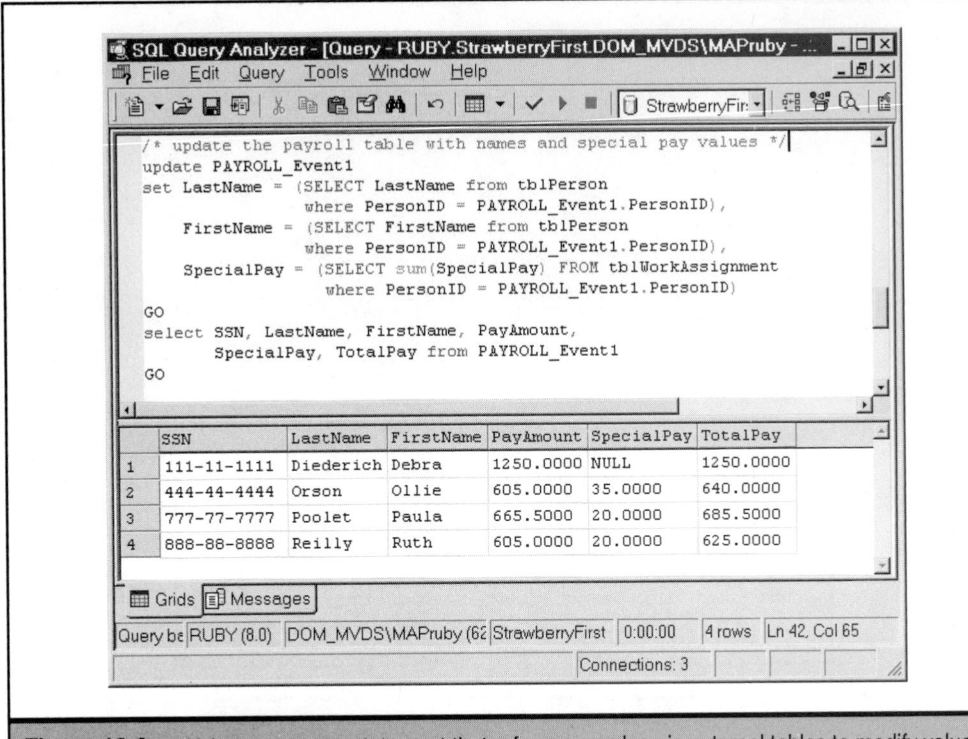

Figure 10-9. Using an UPDATE statement that references values in external tables to modify values in the PAYROLL_Event1 table.

Typically, you would designate a column as having the Identity property when you create the table, as shown in Figure 10-10. You cannot go back and make a column an identity column once it has been created, because it may contain values that are out of sequence and would therefore disrupt the autonumbering. If you want to add a primary key to your table and no suitable column meets the criteria for a primary key, you can add an identity column to the table and have SQL Server populate it with values. An identity column cannot allow NULLs. You can have only one identity column per table.

Keep in mind that just because a column has the Identity property set, it is not an absolute that will contain unique values. As long as nobody overrides the autonumber feature, the automatic incrementing will ensure no duplicate values. But it is possible to manually override the numbering scheme and insert rows with duplicate values in this column. To prevent this, you can designate the identity column as a primary key, or you can create a unique index on the identity column, which will prevent duplicate values.

When you designate a column as an identity column, you can specify a *seed*, or starting value, and an increment. You don't have to increment by 1; you can use whatever increment value you want. You can even use negative values for the seed and increment, if the datatype supports negative values (which tinyint does not).

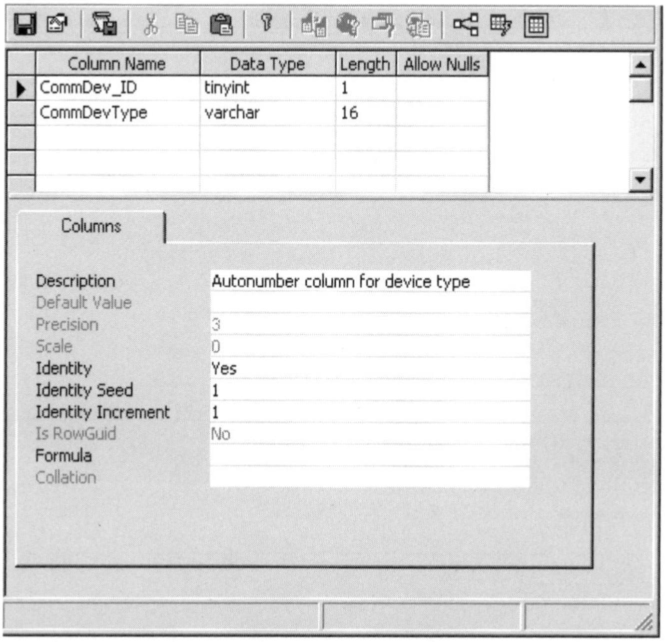

Column Name	Data Type	Length	Allow Nulls
CommDev_ID	tinyint	1	
CommDevType	varchar	16	

Columns

Description	Autonumber column for device type
Default Value	
Precision	3
Scale	0
Identity	Yes
Identity Seed	1
Identity Increment	1
Is RowGuid	No
Formula	
Collation	

Figure 10-10. Assigning an Identity property to the CommDev_ID column at table creation time

To illustrate this, let's add a table to the Strawberry database—a small reference table that lists the valid types of communications devices or links. A table like this can be used to verify that the entries in the CommDevice table, CommType column are valid. This table has only two columns: an autoincrementing number that is the primary key of the table and a device type, which has a unique constraint on it.

```
CREATE TABLE tblCommDevType
      (CommDev_ID      INT IDENTITY(1,1) PRIMARY KEY,
       CommDevtype     VARCHAR(16) NOT NULL UNIQUE)
```

When you add rows to this table, you act as if the identity column does not exist. Then you display the results:

```
INSERT tblCommDevType VALUES ('Office')
INSERT tblCommDevType VALUES ('Home')
INSERT tblCommDevType VALUES ('Fax')
INSERT tblCommDevType VALUES ('Cell')
SELECT * FROM tblCommDevType
```

Figure 10-11 shows the results of the previous code. For column CommDev_ID, the seed value was 1 and the increment was 1, so these four rows will have values of 1, 2, 3, and 4.

Determining the Autonumber Value

When automatic numbering is used in a high-volume environment, such as a Web and telephone-based catalog order entry shop, many people will be inserting rows at a fast and furious rate. The numbers in the identity column of the order table will be incrementing at a high rate of speed. As an order entry operator, you might have to do subsequent processing on the order you last took. You might need to execute more processes, say, for the invoice and the picking-and-packing slip. In so doing, you will need to know the order number you were just assigned. Simply asking for the highest order number in the table will not work, because many other orders have come in and been assigned order numbers between the time this order was initiated and the time it was printed and sent to the shipping department.

This is where the global variable @@IDENTITY comes in. The global variable is not really a variable, in that you cannot assign values to it, and it is anything but global. When you request the value for @@IDENTITY, you'll see the value of the identity column for the

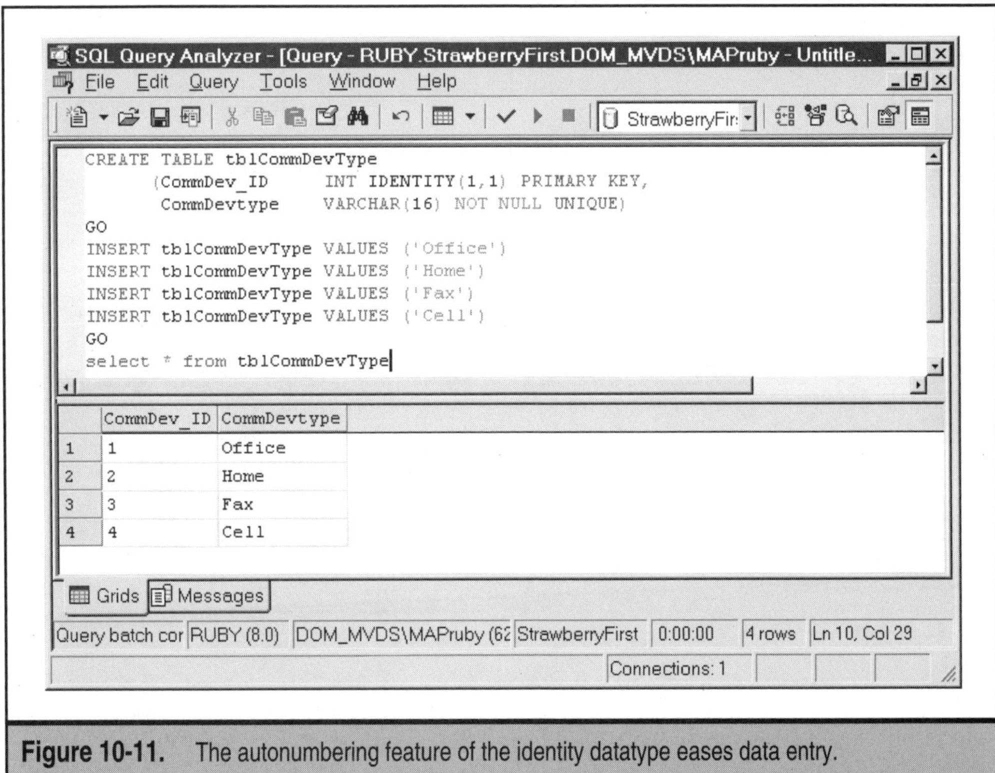

Figure 10-11. The autonumbering feature of the identity datatype eases data entry.

row that you just inserted; and when someone else in the order entry department makes the same request, he will see the value for the row that he just inserted. Far from being global, the @@IDENTITY is local to your connection.

Let's illustrate this with an example. You need to keep in mind that we're talking about two different things when we talk about the identity value (@@IDENTITY) and the maximum number in the identity column in a table. @@IDENTITY is a system counter; its value indicates the last value that was assigned to a table within a user session. The maximum number in the identity for the table, as determined by looking at MAX (IDENTITYCOL), may be higher if other users are also adding records.

```
Select @@identity
```

As you can see in Figure 10-12, the SELECT returns the last identity value generated (@@IDENTITY) for this user's session.

This next query gives the current maximum value for the identity column, but not necessarily the maximum value that has ever been used. In this example, someone else

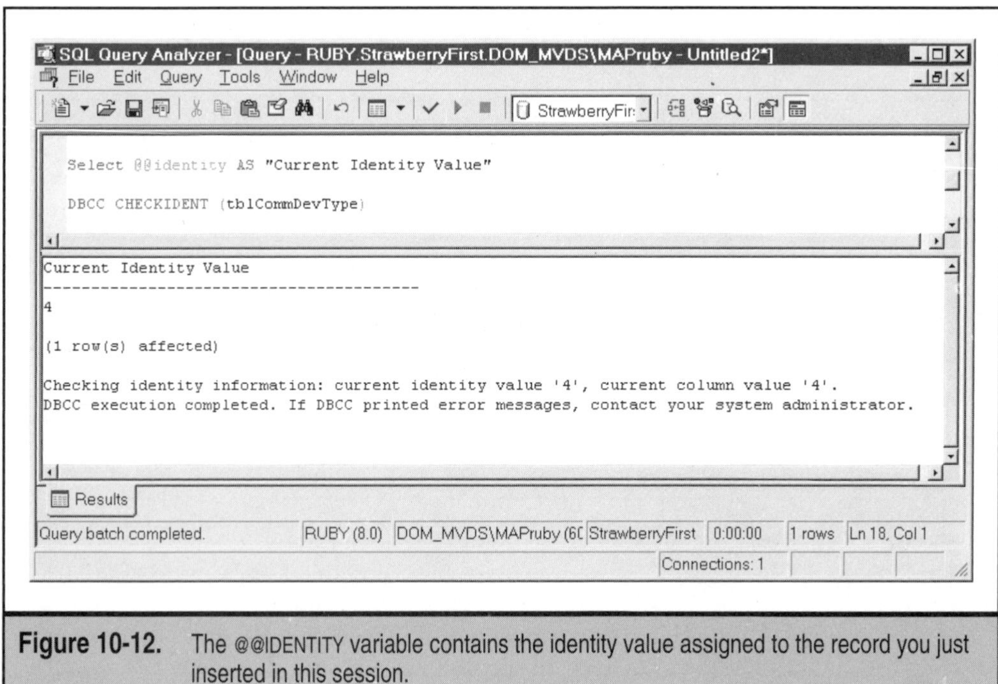

Figure 10-12. The @@IDENTITY variable contains the identity value assigned to the record you just inserted in this session.

added a row, and that row was assigned a CommDev_ID value of 5. Row 5 was then deleted a minute after it was added. When that happens, the next insert will have a CommDev_ID value of 6, and there will be a gap in the sequence:

```
SELECT MAX (IDENTITYCOL)AS "Maximum Identity Value"
FROM tblCommDevType            -- currently is 4

INSERT tblCommDevType VALUES ('Car')                         -- Insert value
DELETE FROM tblCommDevType WHERE CommDevtype = 'Car'    -- Delete value
INSERT tblCommDevType VALUES ('Mobile')                      -- Insert value

SELECT MAX (IDENTITYCOL) AS "Maximum Identity Value"
FROM tblCommDevType            --  now is 6
```

To demonstrate how @@IDENTITY is specific to a user session, you can open another Query Analyzer window and run this query in a different session:

```
INSERT tblCommDevType VALUES ('ISDN')
GO
SELECT @@IDENTITY AS "Maximum Identity Value"
```

As you can see in Figure 10-13, the @@IDENTITY value in the second window is 7. If you then return to the first window and check the value of @@IDENTITY, you will find that it is still 6. What happens in one session has no impact on the @@IDENTITY of the second session. The value of the @@IDENTITY will be unchanged for a given session, until you execute your next INSERT query.

Autonumbering and Triggers

In Chapter 18, we will discuss triggers. For now, we'll just point out that because a trigger can update another table that may also contain an identity column—a table other than the one to which the trigger is attached—you will have to be a little more careful about what the @@IDENTITY value is telling you. SQL Server provides three different functions to give you additional information: @@IDENTITY, SCOPE_IDENTITY, and IDENT_CURRENT.

@@IDENTITY does return the maximum identity value assigned within a session, but it does so across all *scopes*, meaning that all identity values from all tables that are involved in a procedure are included. *Scope* in this sense is a query that you've run, or it could be a trigger or stored procedure activated by your query, so several scopes could be involved when you update a record that fires a trigger that calls a procedure, and so on. @@IDENTITY will return the maximum value from all scopes involved in a procedure.

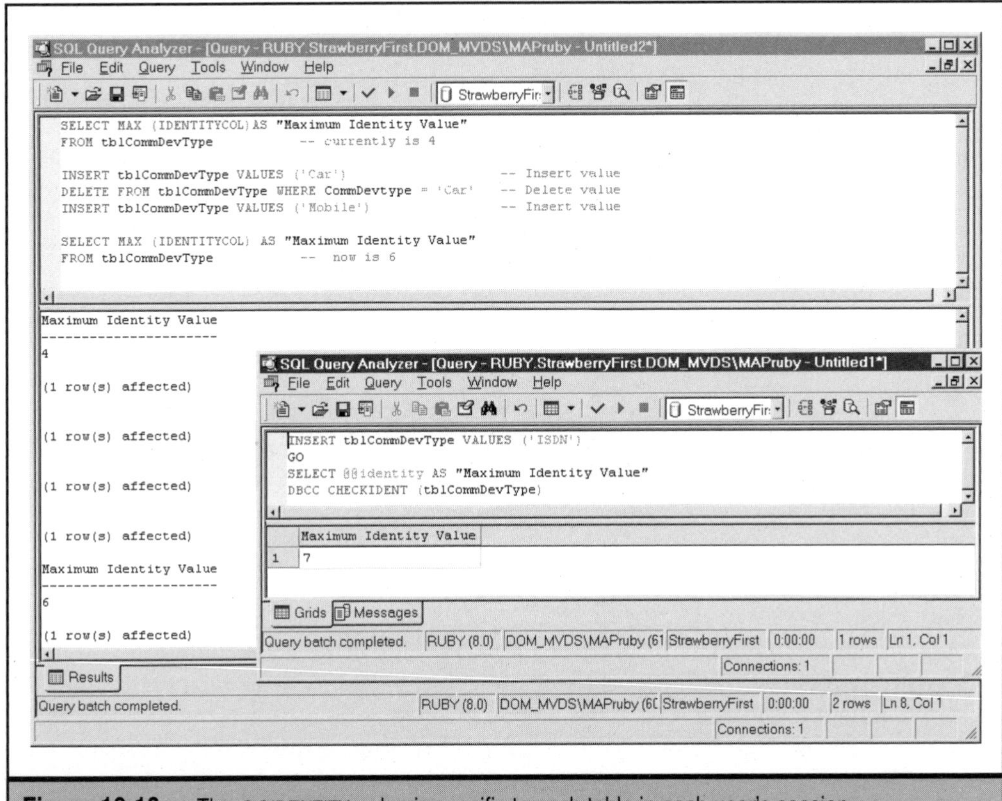

Figure 10-13. The @@IDENTITY value is specific to each table in each user's session.

SCOPE_IDENTITY returns the most recently generated identity value for the current scope and session—in this case, the table you updated.

IDENT_CURRENT returns the last identity value generated for a specific table, but across all sessions and scopes, so it could be the value generated by someone else in his or her session. The one option that seems to be missing is to get the latest value for a specified table within the current scope. That would really be useful, as you could retrieve the identity value assigned by any of the triggers or procedures activated by your initial T-SQL statement. It's on our wish list.

Here's the syntax for these different options:

```
SELECT @@IDENTITY AS "@@identity value"
SELECT SCOPE_IDENTITY() AS "scope_identity"
SELECT IDENT_CURRENT ('tblCommDevType') AS "ident_current"
```

Overriding the Autonumbering

In the example mentioned previously is a gap in the sequence of identity numbers, because the entry for CommDev_ID = 5 was deleted. This is usually not an issue when numbers are skipped, but in this case, let's see how to go back and reuse that value for the identity column. First you need to turn off the autonumbering for your session, so that the identity column behaves just like any other column. Then you insert a row. This time, because autonumbering is turned off, you have to specify the value you want in the ComDevID column:

```
SET IDENTITY_INSERT tblCommDevType ON
INSERT tblCommDevType (CommDev_ID, CommDevType)
              Values (5, 'Car')

SET IDENTITY_INSERT tblCommDevType OFF

select * from tblCommDevType
```

Figure 10-14 shows the result of this operation. CommDev_ID value 5 is back in the table. SQL Server has a few tricks up its sleeve with this Identity property. If the highest value in the table is 7, and someone manually inserts a row using the technique above, but uses a value of 20 instead of 8, the next autoincremented value assigned to the table will be 21. SQL Server will not add in values between 8 and 19. It knows that if it did so it would encounter an error at 20. It doesn't yet have the capability to fill in missing numbers by itself, but it does keep track of the maximum value that has been used in any table. SQL Server tries to make sure that the autonumbering stays error free.

Resetting the Identity Column Values

New to SQL Server 2000 is the DBCC CHECKIDENT, which gives administrators some control over the autonumbering. It shows the identity counter value and will also allow you to reset the seed value and the increment. This ability could be quite handy, for example, if someone has manually updated the table and mistakenly managed to set the seed number to a huge value. An example is shown in Figure 10-12. The DBCC, short for database consistency check, command will check to see what the maximum identity counter value is and how it compares to the current column value. The current identity value—this determines the number assigned to the next row inserted—should not be any lower than the maximum column value currently in the table. If it is, you're about to try to insert duplicate values into the table. To remedy this situation, the DBCC CHECKIDENT can reset the identity value if you have specified the RESEED option. Actually, the RESEED option is the default, so by default the current identity value will be corrected. There's an alternative parameter, NORESEED, which will report a problem but will not try to fix it. With the RESEED parameter, you can specify a new seed value, but be careful when using this, as you are responsible for making sure that the new starting value is larger than the maximum value currently in the table. The trick here is to run the DBCC CHECKIDENT again with no parameters, and if you got it wrong, the CHECKIDENT RESEED will detect the conflict and reset the seed value.

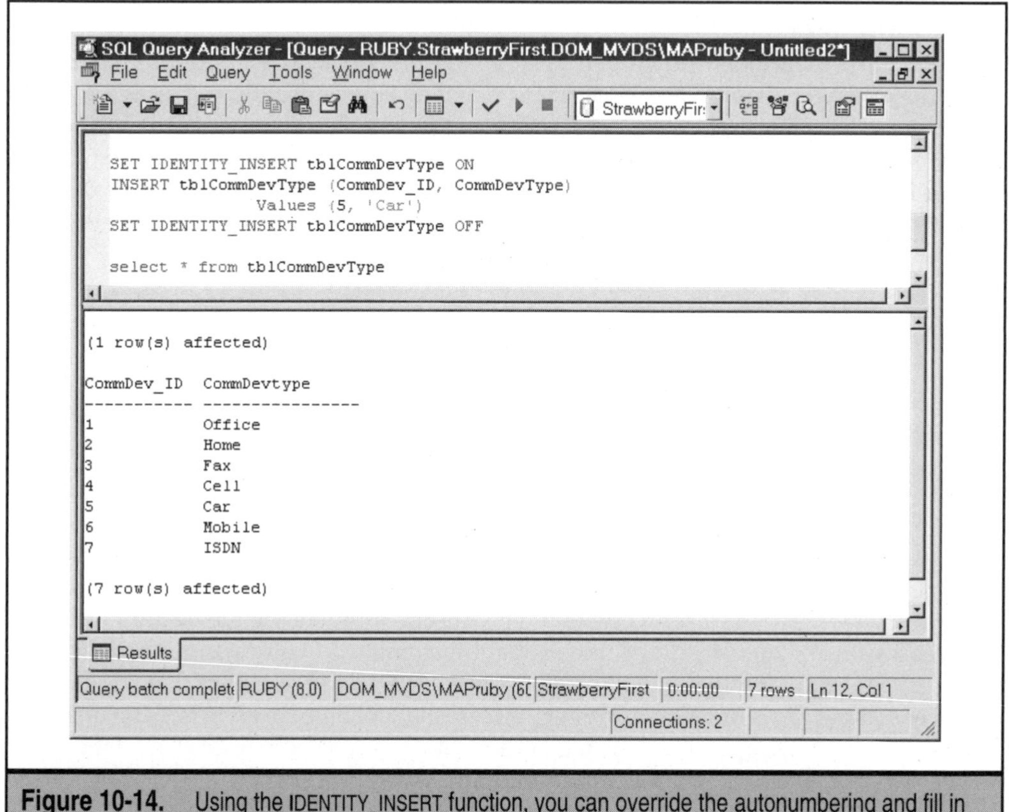

Figure 10-14. Using the IDENTITY_INSERT function, you can override the autonumbering and fill in missing CommDev_ID numbers.

CHECKIDENT is one approach you can use if someone has manually entered and then deleted a very large value, so that the identity value is far higher than the maximum column value in the table, and there's the potential for a very large gap in numbers. Just set the seed value to something low (like 1) and then run the CHECKIDENT to let it pick the right value. Alternatively, run CHECKIDENT to find the current identity value and the current column value, and then use the RESEED option to set the identity value equal to the column value. It's not difficult to fix problems with this new CHECKIDENT tool.

To keep things neat, if you have been following the code in this book on your own server, drop the CommDevType table that you just created:

```
DROP TABLE tblCommDevType
```

Inserting Rows with GUIDs

The global unique identifier (GUID) was introduced to SQL Server in version 7. It is a 16-byte binary value, and Microsoft has assured us that no other computer in the world will generate a duplicate of a GUID value. The datatype that supports the GUID is called the uniqueidentifier datatype, and it was developed primarily to provide unique identifiers to data that is scattered among networked and non-networked computers.

Oddly enough, by default, a GUID column does not automatically generate values like the Identity property does. You have to activate this behavior by designating the uniqueidentifier as having the NEWID() property. Once you do this, one of the side benefits of the GUID is that it will also help keep track of where the data originated. In a data warehouse environment, it is important to know where the data came from, and the GUID will help you with tracking the data source. Part of the GUID is based on the MAC address of the computer's network card, and those addresses are unique, having been generated during the manufacturing process of the cards themselves. The other part of the GUID is based on the CPU clock in the computer. The NEWID function, which is a property of the uniqueidentifier datatype, returns a GUID whose value is composed of the MAC address of the network card combined with a unique number from the CPU clock on the server. The API functions and methods generate a GUID based on the network card plus CPU clock of the client computer—you really can tell where the data was generated! At least, you can if you know the MAC addresses of your client computers, which is probably not something you'd pay much attention to, unless you've carefully inventoried not only your computer equipment but all of the component parts. While this scheme probably will guarantee a globally unique identifier for each row of data, it does raise some questions about what happens if you change the network cards or move the database to a different server. Unfortunately, Books Online does not address these issues, but it's pretty obvious that you'll have to keep a correlation list of network card addresses and computers/users if you want to take full advantage of this scheme.

Although the GUID itself may be a unique value, there's nothing to stop the same GUID from being manually copied to more than one row in the database. The uniqueidentifier datatype does not in itself enforce uniqueness. If you want to ensure uniqueness, you have to apply a primary key constraint or a unique index constraint to the GUID column. You don't always want to do this, which may sound odd if you're thinking of the GUID as a unique identifier. But if you're more interested in the GUID as a method of tracking the source of the data, you really don't care whether or not the values are unique. There's also the one-to-many relationship situation, in which the GUID in the master table must be unique, but in the detail table the same value may appear many times.

It is possible to have more than one GUID column per table, unlike the identity column, which has a limit of one per table. If you know that you'll need to reference the value of a GUID column in your applications, you can designate one GUID column per table as having the ROWGUIDCOL property. Then you can reference the GUID value by using the ROWGUIDCOL keyword in a query.

As we mentioned earlier, the uniqueidentifier datatype is not an autogenerator of values, like the identity column is. Instead, you have to instruct it to generate values with the NEWID() function. One way to do this is to call the NEWID() function in the INSERT statement. An alternative method would be to assign a default to this column (we'll look at default constraints in Chapter 15) and make the default the NEWID() function.

Let's look at an example of this by rebuilding your table for communications device types, but this time you'll use GUID. First you create the table, specifying a uniqueidentifier datatype for the primary key column CommDev_GUID, and give it the capability to autogenerate values:

```
CREATE TABLE tblCommDevTypeGUID
(CommDev_GUID  UNIQUEIDENTIFIER PRIMARY KEY DEFAULT NEWID(),
 CommDevtype   VARCHAR(16) )
GO
```

Now populate the table, using three different techniques to insert the data:

```
Insert tblCommDevTypeGUID values (DEFAULT, 'Office')
Insert tblCommDevTypeGUID values (NEWID(),'Home')
Insert tblCommDevTypeGUID (CommDevType) values ('Fax')
```

Figure 10-15 shows the commands and the result of the SELECT query. In practice, you would not use a uniqueidentifier datatype in a table like this, because this lookup table is so small that the primary key should be a tinyint datatype, rather than a 128-bit (16-byte) hexadecimal value. Plus, you're a little limited in the type of operations that you can perform on a GUID. You can do comparison operations (=, <>, <, <=, >=, or >), you can check for a NULL condition, and you can ORDER BY—but that's all.

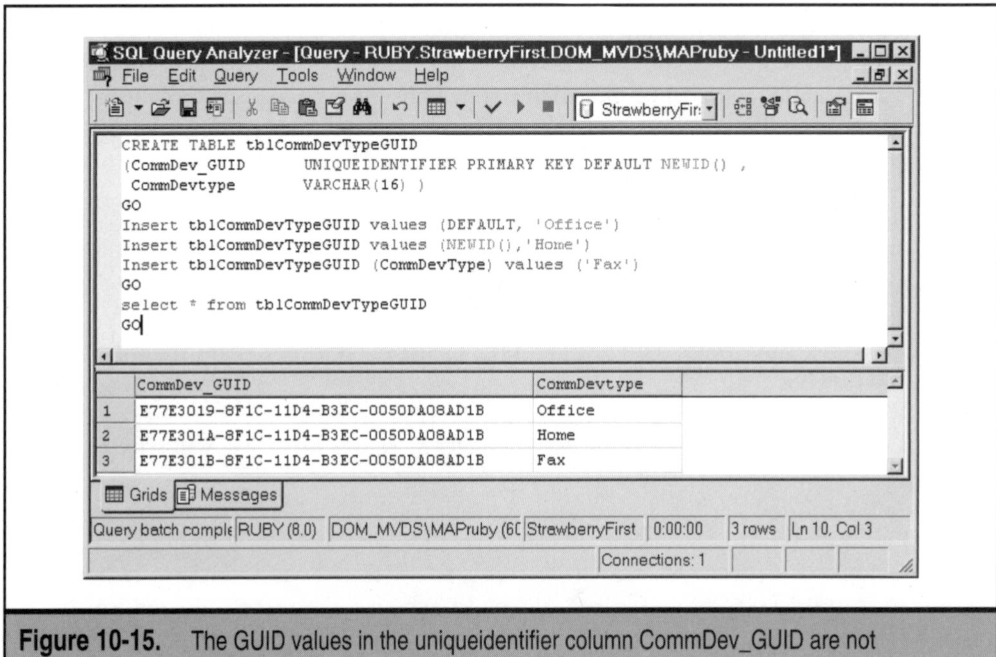

Figure 10-15. The GUID values in the uniqueidentifier column CommDev_GUID are not particularly user friendly.

In addition to the storage issues and the operational constraints, who on earth would remember that E77E3019-8F1C-11D4-B3EC-0050DA08AD1B means "office phone"? So there is a usability issue in addition to the other limitations of the GUID. These are the major drawbacks to using GUIDs. They are great to use when you need a primary key value that maintains uniqueness across and beyond the network but that no one will ever see. They are, as Books Online says with an amazing degree of understatement, "long and obscure. This makes them difficult for users to type correctly, and more difficult for users to remember." They don't have any recognizable pattern (except for the last section of the number, which is the IEEE 802 identifier for the NIC), and they don't really have any order, especially when you remember that multiple client computers will be generating values based on their own network card address and CPU clock. The uniqueidentifier is not the best choice when you need a sequence of incrementing numbers such as invoice numbers. You're much better off using a plain integer or bigint datatype with the Identity property. Indexing on a 16-byte column will result in longer comparisons and searches than the integer (4 bytes) or the bigint (8 bytes) datatypes. Use the uniqueidentifier datatype carefully; don't just use it as an across-the-board substitute for the autonumbering integer with an Identity property.

CASCADE UPDATE/DELETE

For many years Microsoft endured a lot of criticism because SQL Server lacked the ability to cascade updates and deletes to key columns. When you modify the value of a primary or candidate key that is part of an enforced one-to-many relationship, you want that change to cascade down to all foreign key instances in the database. Similarly, when you delete a row in the master table of this enforced relationship, you want the delete operation to cascade down and automatically delete all related detail records in the database as well.

Some of the discontent on the part of SQL Server developers was spurred by the presence of cascade update and cascade delete functionality in Microsoft's desktop database management system, Microsoft Access. From the very beginning, Access has had this functionality. And, of course, Oracle has had cascade update and cascade delete functionality for a long time. Add to this set of reasons, the SQL-3 Standard now lists CASCADE as one of the supported rules of data manipulation for referential integrity. It's a given that SQL Server 2000 would support cascade update and cascade delete.

Like most powerful features, cascade update and cascade delete can be good or bad depending on how you use them. Cascading updates can be very useful in propagating changes through a database. For example, suppose you work for a publishing house, and you had based the production database on the Pubs sample database that comes with SQL Server. Because the Microsoft database designers had carelessly implied that the Social Security number would be the unique identifier (au_id) in the Authors table, you simply followed suit. Now you're finding that many authors are incorporating, so that royalties have to be paid to the author's company, not directly to the author. The author is using a federal tax ID number instead of an SSN. So now what do you do? Do you treat the author using the federal tax ID as a different person from the same author who used to use an SSN? Probably not, as this action would cause total confusion and unrestrained redundancy in your database. In addition, you've been getting uncomfortable about using SSN as a unique identifier (you read some of the books on privacy and security listed in our bibliography). So, to clear up the confusion and put your mind at ease, you decide to add an extra column to the Authors table that will hold either SSN or tax ID; however, the author wants to be paid. Now you have to assign a different set of values to the au_id column. But wait, these au_id values are used to connect the authors to the books they wrote through the TitleAuthor table. So you need to change the corresponding values in the TitleAuthor table. If you don't, you know from our discussion of foreign key constraints that you won't be able to change the au_id column values in the Author table. Referential constraints will not allow a value of au_id to exist in the TitleAuthor table that doesn't already exist in the Author table. Actually, without the cascade update function, making a modification like this is a tricky task. The cascade update will do all the changes in the AuthorTitle table for you, after you make the update to the values in the Author table. The cascade update feature is an enormous time saver.

Cascading deletes, on the other hand, can have a serious and unintended impact on your data. For example, in your active customer table you have records of customers who have not ordered in the last year. Typically, you archive these records—delete them from the active customer table and insert them into the archive customer table. When you delete these customer records from the active customer table, do you really want to delete all the orders, invoices, and other data that you've accumulated on these customers? Your statistician is looking at trends and needs several years' worth of data to do her analysis. If you start deleting orders and invoices when you delete the associated customer records, you'll be skewing the results. You could even bury a trend. If your western sales force is not being effective, so that current customers are not placing orders, your statistician might be able to spot this trend before the competition corners that market. However, if you start deleting old sales records from the database, it's going to look like you had bad sales in the past. It may even appear that this year's sales are up in comparison to those of two years ago, instead of way down!

Ideally, you should archive old data rather than delete it. But your company may want to reduce its exposure on privacy issues, and thus will want to remove customer data for people who no longer place orders. If you do not cascade the deletes, your foreign key relationships will prevent you from deleting the customer records when there are related sales records. If you cascade the delete, you lose valuable information on sales volumes and products. If you don't cascade the delete, you risk exposure on privacy issues, plus you're carrying more data on disk than you need to. If you eliminate the foreign key constraints between Customer and Sales, it's possible that you could have a sale that belongs to a nonexistent customer. What a quandary!

In this case, we suggest a compromise. Set the sensitive data in the Customer table—such as name, address, phone number, and credit card number—to some substitute value, like all Xs. Make sure that your mailing-label queries drop these rows, of course. Now the statistician will have the demographic information from the Customer table, such as city, state, and zip, and will know that a certain number of orders were placed from a given state and zip code; but she'll have no way of knowing too much about an individual. Be very careful of cascade deletes, some of which can ripple a long way through your data before you have evaluated their impact on the database and on the organization.

We'll discuss the syntax and use of cascade update and cascade delete in Chapter 15, when we deal with constraints.

CHAPTER 11

Subqueries

In Chapter 7, we looked at some basic queries, and in Chapter 8, we discussed joins. In this chapter, we want to go another level deeper into the subject of retrieving data by introducing subqueries. A *subquery* is a query within a query. Subqueries come in two types: simple and complex. We'll explore the simple subquery first. We will also look at modifying data based on the results of a query, as we promised in Chapter 10.

SIMPLE SUBQUERIES

As an example of a subquery, suppose that someone asks you a question such as "Which products cost more than the average?" or "Which of our salespeople contributed more than 10 percent of sales last month?" The first step in answering such a question is to find out what the average cost of a product is or to look at the total sales and take 10 percent of that figure. Then you can substitute the number you calculated into the first part of the question ("Which products…" or "Which of our salespeople…") and find the answer. This is exactly what a simple subquery does. The general format of a subquery looks like this:

```
SELECT outer_column_list
FROM outer_table_name
WHERE outer_table_field_name subquery_operator
         (SELECT inner_column_list
            FROM inner_table_name
            WHERE subquery_predicate_or_restriction_on_rows)
ORDER BY outer_column
    [example subquery operators: IN, NOT IN, =, <=, =>, <>, etc.]
```

The outer query retrieves data based on the reference created by the inner query. You can only display data from the table in the outer query; the table from the inner query contains the data that is being used for reference. Typically, in this simple subquery statement, the inner SELECT is solved first. The answer is then passed back to the outer SELECT as the value for the WHERE clause, and the outer SELECT is then solved and the answer displayed to the user.

There are many subquery operators. In the simple subquery, you can use any of the comparison operators (=, <>, >, >=, <, <=) or you can use the IN operator. You can also use NOT with any of these operators, so that you can find rows from the outer table that do not have a reference in the inner table. The ANY operator and the SOME operator both produce the same results. And there's an ALL operator. The EXISTS operator actually works better with the correlated subqueries, which we will talk about in the next section.

Let's work through these operators with examples. To explain the comparison operators—the equal (=) operator specifically—suppose that you want to find out who the contact person is for the last event that you entered into the Event table. For simplicity, let's break this query into two parts.

In part 1, the outer query uses only the EventContact table to return a PersonID. The subquery (the second SELECT, which is in parentheses) will find the most recent entry

(MAX(EventID))in the Events table. The MAX(EventID) value is then returned to the outer query, which uses this value as an argument in its WHERE clause. Then the row (or rows) that meet the WHERE criteria are returned from the EventContact table:

```
SELECT  PersonID FROM  tblEventContact
WHERE EventID = (SELECT MAX(EventID) FROM tblEvent)
```

Notice that between the outer query and the inner query, a comparison is made between the outer table and the inner table on a single column, EventID. This is the way all the subquery operators work, with the exception of the EXISTS operator.

Part 2 adds a join to the Person table in the outer query that converts the PersonID to a first and last name, which is the kind of output that you'd expect to see:

```
SELECT  p.PersonID, p.FirstName, p.LastName
FROM  tblPerson p JOIN tblEventContact e ON p.PersonID = e.PersonID
WHERE e.EventID = (SELECT MAX(EventID) FROM tblEvent)
```

Figure 11-1 is a display of the query results in the Query Analyzer. You can see that the part 1 query returns the value 24 for the PersonID, while the part 2 query returns the name data for PersonID 24.

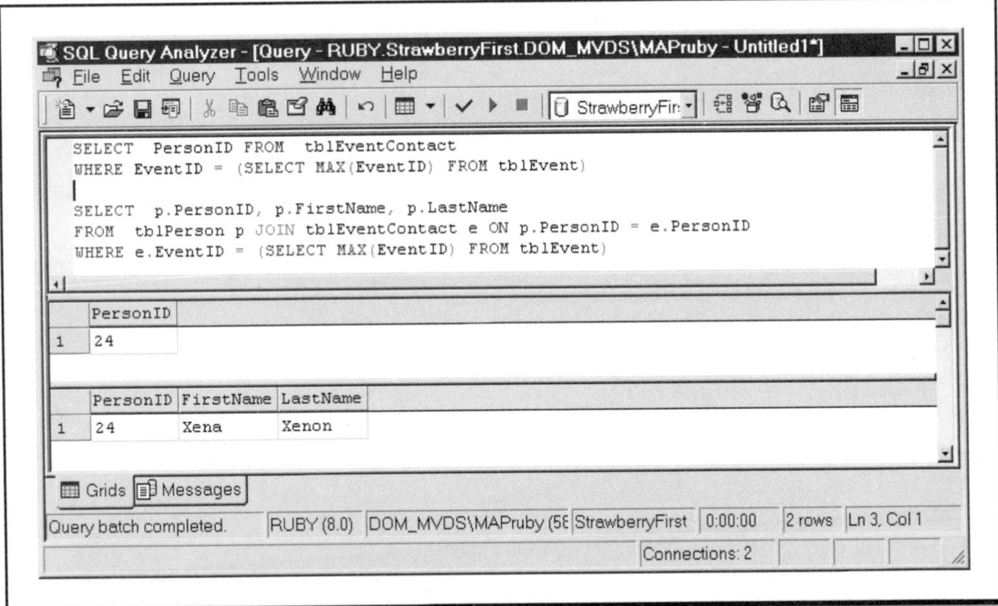

Figure 11-1. The result sets of these two simple subqueries show the structure of the subquery expression.

Figure 11-2 is the execution plan for the same set of queries. In both cases, the inner query (the SELECT on table Event) was executed first, and the results were returned to the outer query. In the part 1 query, the Event table is sorted in reverse order based on its clustered index, which is the EventID index. Then the TOP function takes the first few values returned, which includes the largest EventID, the last one entered into the table. The stream aggregate places this first row value into the MAX function, so now the query knows the value of the maximum EventID. Then the nested loop uses that value to scan through the EventContact table and find the PersonID that corresponds to the Event with the largest EventID.

The part 2 query starts out like the part 1 query, but it's complicated a little by the addition of an inner join to the Person table after the nested loop. This join requires a second nested loop to find the first and last names for the PersonID that has been returned by the inner query.

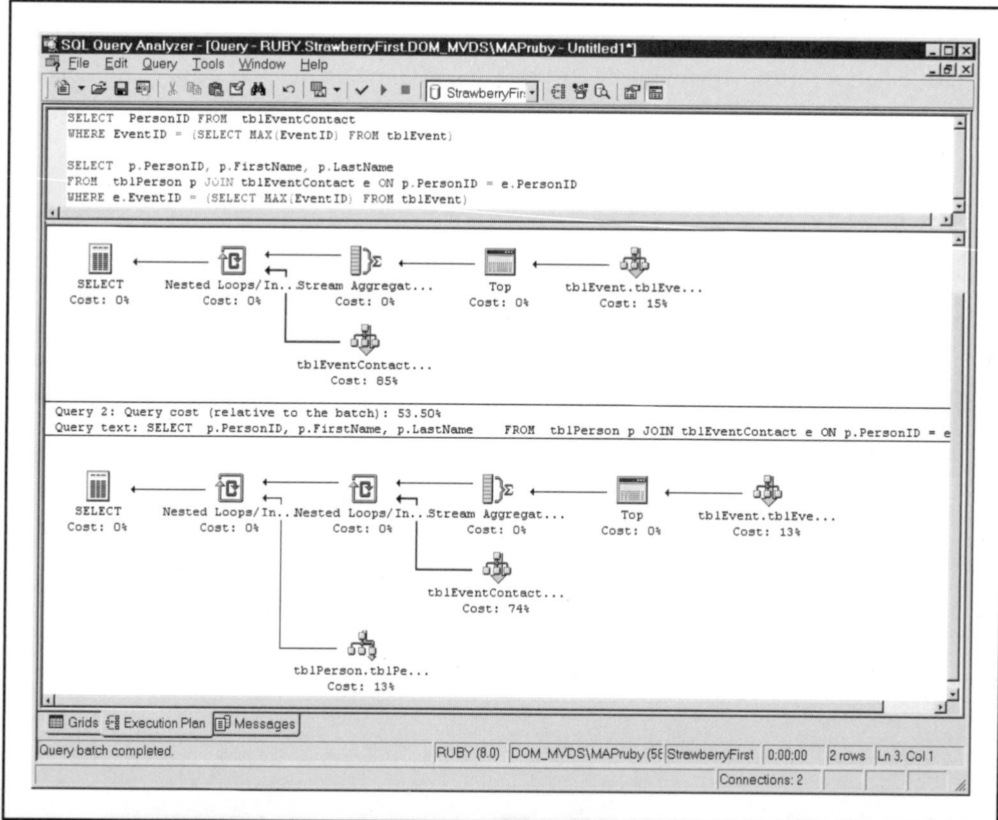

Figure 11-2. The execution plans for these simple subqueries show how the inner query is evaluated first.

You can test a subquery expression to determine whether it is a simple subquery or a complex subquery—it's a simple test. Will the inner query run on its own? If the inner query is a valid query in its own right, and you can highlight it in the Query Analyzer window and run it successfully (as you could the inner query in Figures 11-1 and 11-2), you've got a simple subquery. You must enclose each inner query in parentheses, so that SQL Server knows where it starts and ends. You can have more than one inner query in the subquery expression, and you can nest queries within queries. There's no system limit to how deep you can nest the queries—it's more a question of how many levels deep you can go and still keep track of what you are doing. Of course, the more complex your subquery expression, the longer it is going to take to parse, optimize, and run, and the more system resources you'll need. If the subquery expression gets too complex, you might consider taking part of the subquery expression logic and running it as a standalone query. Then you can place the result from this standalone query into a variable, which you can feed into in the main query expression, or you can put the results into a temporary table and reference that table from the main query expression.

A subquery expression doesn't necessarily have to return just a single row. It can return multiple rows, as in the following query from the Pubs database that uses the IN operator. The business question here is, "Which authors live in the same cities as the publishers in the database?" First, you retrieve a list of cities in which the publishers live. Then you match it to the authors table, looking for authors who live in the same cities as the publishers. Note that this query doesn't mean to imply that the authors write for the publishers who live in the same city—they just happen to be located in the same city. Don't read more into the reports than what is intended, and protect against this by using meaningful column aliases to accurately identify the data:

```
USE pubs
SELECT au_id as "AuthorID",
       au_lname + ', ' + au_fname as "Names of authors who live in the
                                       same cities as our publishers",
       City as "City"
       FROM Authors WHERE City IN
                (SELECT City FROM Publishers)
```

Most simple subquery expressions can also be written as joins. The following code, which produces the same result set as the previous, may look a little more familiar to you:

```
SELECT a.au_id as "AuthorID",
       a.au_lname + ', ' + a.au_fname as "Names of authors who live
                                   in the same cities as our publishers",
       a.city as "City"
FROM Authors a JOIN Publishers p ON a.City = p.City
```

Figure 11-3 shows the result set from this pair of queries—both return exactly the same data. However, looking at the execution plans for these two queries, shown in Figure 11-4,

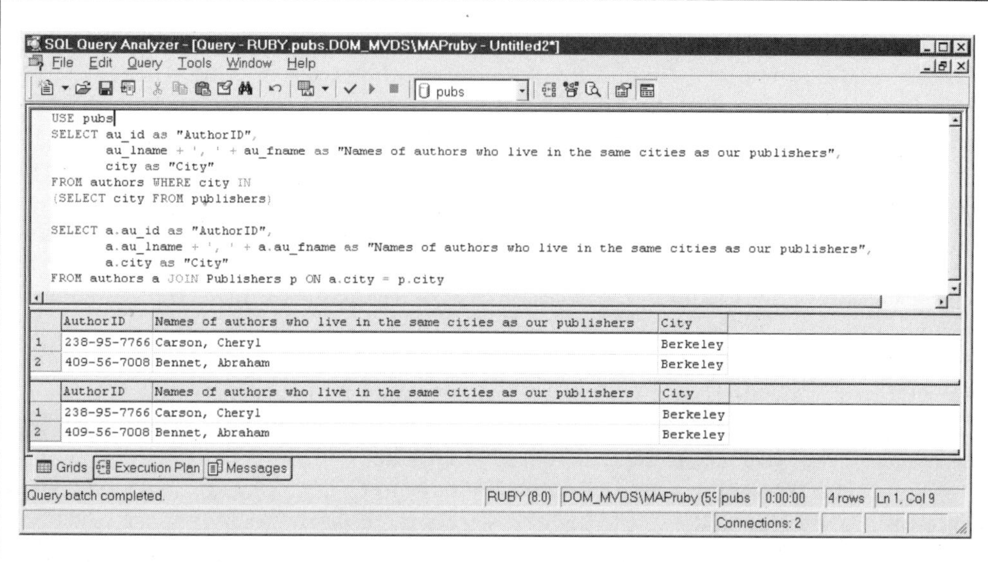

Figure 11-3. The result sets of these two queries—the first a subquery expression, and the second a join—are identical.

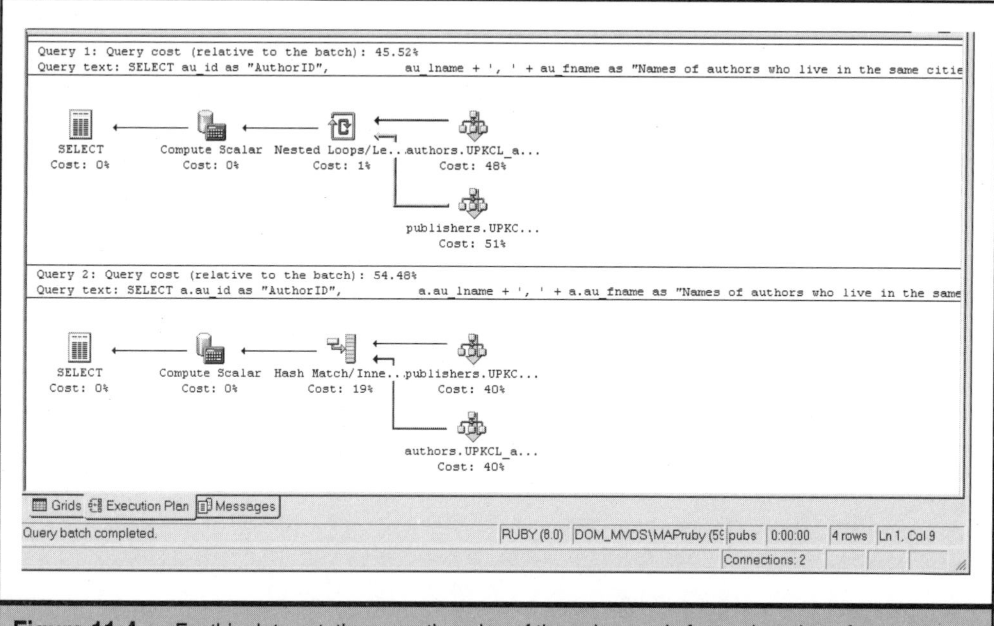

Figure 11-4. For this data set, the execution plan of the subquery is faster than that of an equivalent join operation.

you can see that in this case the subquery expression (the uppermost of the two) runs more efficiently than the join, even though the join uses a hash match, which is an extremely efficient operation. With other tables, different indexes, and larger data sets, the join might be faster, but there are so many variables to consider that it's hard to generalize and say that one is always more efficient or always faster than the other. So rather than try to come up with a rule to decide which to use—a join or a subquery expression—do some testing on your own data sets.

How would you quickly find the most expensive item in a list? You could display the entire product listing and order by price, which would be fine for your little Strawberry database, but could be very tedious if you were looking at a 1,000,000-row Product table. Alternatively, you could use the ALL operator, as in the following code:

```
SELECT * FROM tblProduct ORDER BY ProductCost DESC
GO
SELECT ProductCode, ProductDscr, ProductCost
FROM tblProduct WHERE ProductCost >=ALL
                (SELECT ProductCost FROM tblProduct)
GO
```

Figure 11-5 shows the output result set of this code. The first query is a listing of products from the Strawberry Products table, sorted in reverse order so that the most expensive item in your inventory is displayed as the first row. The second query returns a single row, the most expensive item in the Product inventory. The second query reads "Show me the product whose product cost is equal to or greater than all the products in the Product table." The execution plan for the second query, shown in Figure 11-6, shows that two instances of the Product table are scanned and then joined in the following manner: "For each row in the top (outer) input, scan the bottom (inner) input, and output matching rows." Interpreted, each row in the Product table is compared against all other rows in the Product table, and if there is a row in the table that has a higher product cost, the operative row is discarded. The only row that will be returned is the one with the highest ProductCost. In the case of a tie, both rows will be returned.

The ANY and SOME operators have equivalent meaning and produce identical results. The question this time is, "Which products cost more than the minimum cost of all the products in the Product table?" The code to do this is shown here:

```
SELECT ProductCode, ProductDscr,ProductCost FROM tblProduct
GO
SELECT MIN(ProductCost) FROM tblProduct
GO
SELECT ProductCode, ProductDscr,ProductCost
       FROM tblProduct WHERE ProductCost >ANY
            (SELECT ProductCost FROM tblProduct)
```

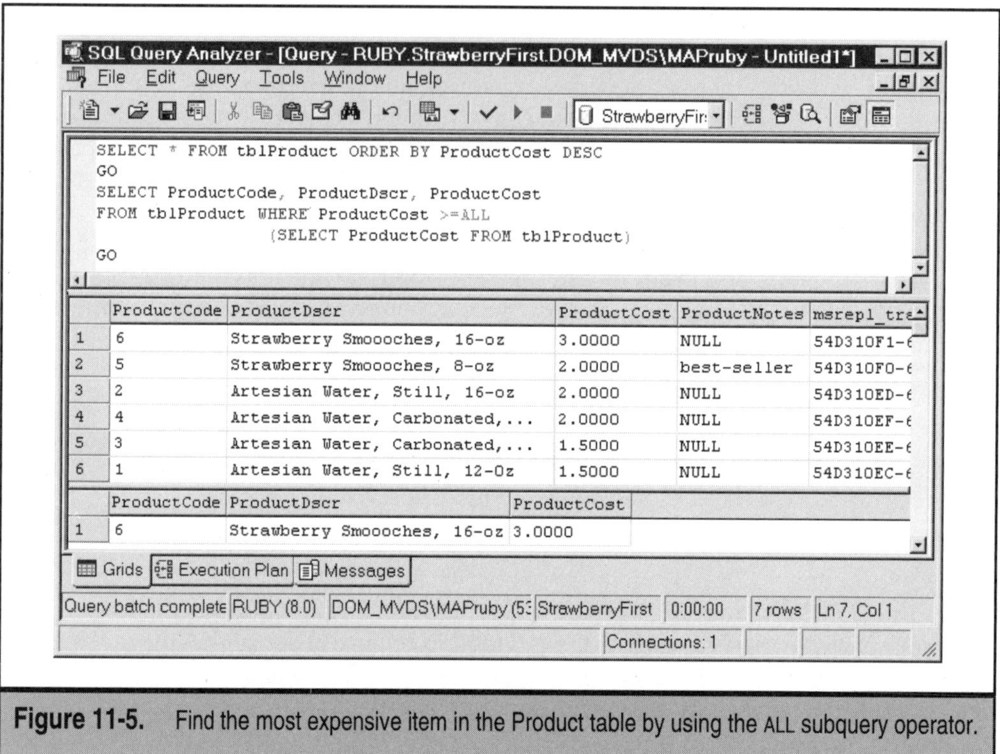

Figure 11-5. Find the most expensive item in the Product table by using the ALL subquery operator.

As shown in Figure 11-7, the first query is a control that shows the product costs in the Product table. The second query is another control that shows the average product cost in the table. The third query is the subquery expression that uses the ANY operator. It reads "Show me the products where the product cost is greater than the lowest cost of all the products in the table." The lowest priced product is $1.50. All the products are more expensive than this except for the 12-ounce carbonated artesian water. Figure 11-8 shows that, indeed, the ANY and the SOME operators are identical, even to the steps of the execution plan. Both start with scanning the Product table to find the minimum cost of a product. Then the two instances of the Product table are joined; and for each row in the outer table, the inner table is scanned and rows that meet the criteria are output. In this example, SQL Server actually decided that using the MIN() function was more efficient.

CORRELATED SUBQUERIES

A *correlated subquery* is much more complex than a simple subquery. The type of question you might ask that would need a correlated subquery is, "What are the total sales from each event, listed by event name, in descending order from the most profitable to the least?" In this query, to get the total sales for each event, the correlated subquery operation must first read each row in the outer query and get the identifier—in this case, the

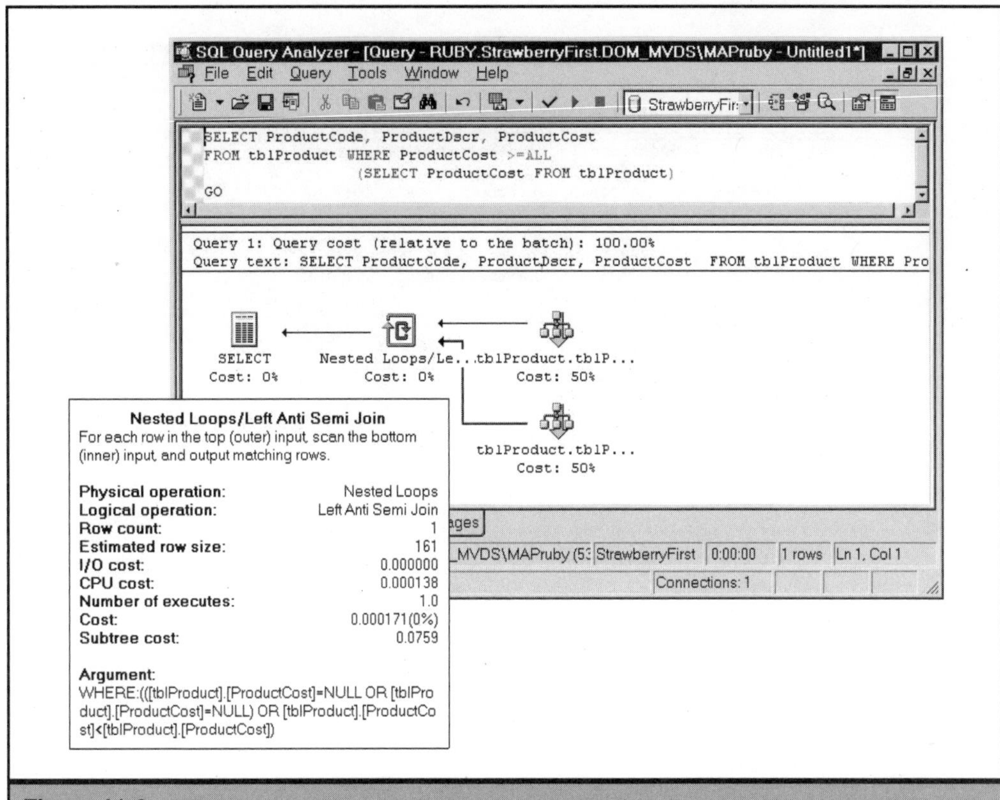

Figure 11-6. The ALL subquery operator causes each row of the Product table to be scanned against all other rows of the Product table.

EventID from the Event table. Then, taking the first EventID value, the operation sums the SaleTotal values for the Sale table in the inner query, by joining the EventID from the outer query with the EventIDs from the inner query. The result is a sum of sales for just this EventID. Then it goes back to the outer query, gets the second EventID, and repeats the summing of rows in the inner table, this time joining with the second EventID. It repeats this operation with each of the EventIDs from the outer query, until all the EventIDs in the outer query have been processed. In this example, you have nine events, so the join in the inner query has to be executed nine times.

The example we've been talking about looks like this:

```
SELECT EventName, CONVERT(CHAR(10),StartDate,1) AS "Start Date",
   CONVERT(CHAR(10),EndDate,1) AS "End Date",
   "Total Sales" = (SELECT SUM(SaleTotal) FROM tblSale
FROM tblEvent
  WHERE tblSale.EventID = tblEvent.EventID)
  ORDER BY "Total Sales" DESC
```

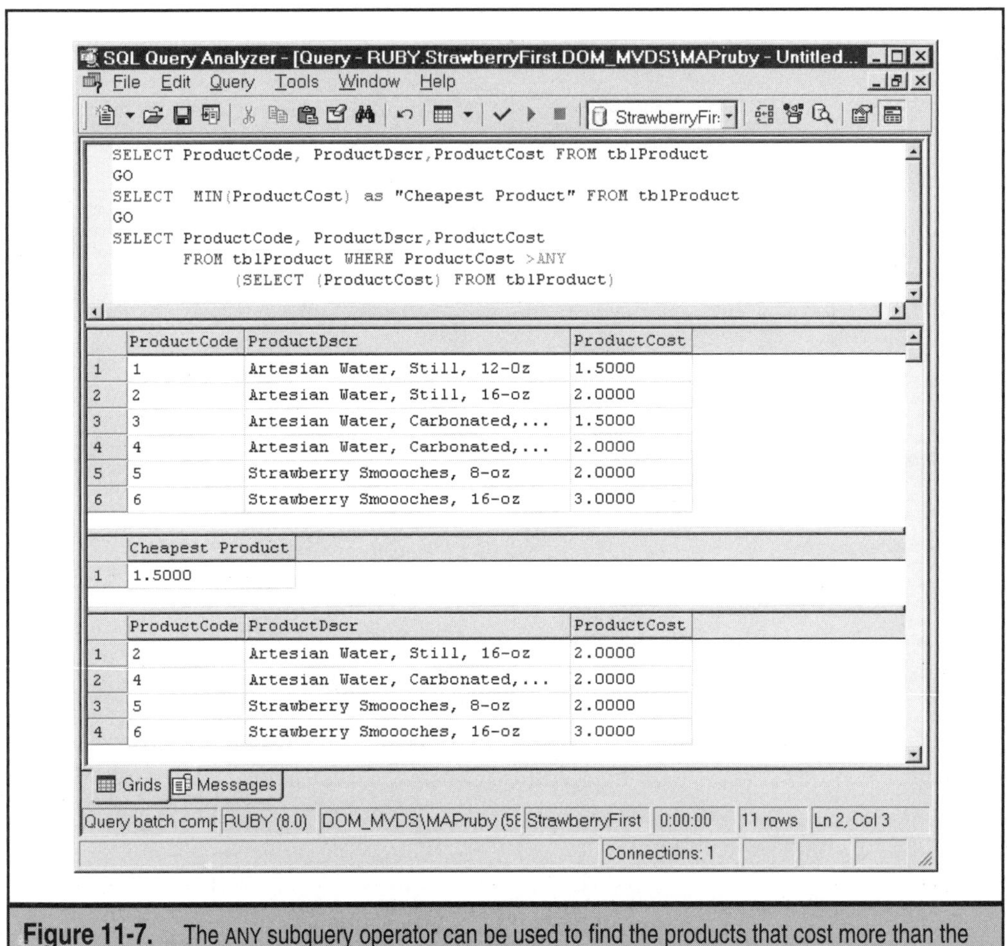

Figure 11-7. The ANY subquery operator can be used to find the products that cost more than the lowest cost of all products.

The outer query (from the Event table) retrieves data based on the reference created by the inner query (from the Sale table). As with the simple subquery, you can only display data from the outer query table. The table from the inner query contains the data that is being referenced. As you can see in Figure 11-9, all the columns in the result set are from the Event table, except the calculated column Total Sales. To get Total Sales for each event, you would use a correlated subquery expression that sums the individual SaleTotal rows from the Sale table by comparing the EventID from the Sale table (the inner query) to the EventID from the Event table (the outer query). The EventID from the Event table is the outer reference.

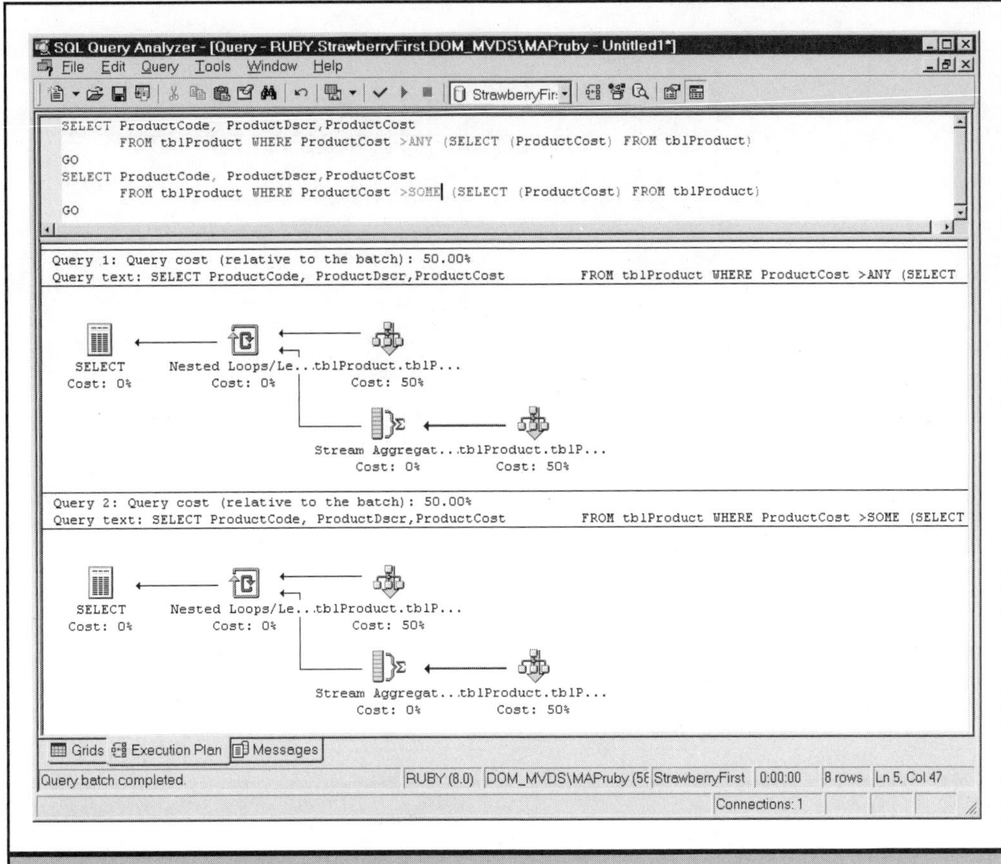

Figure 11-8. The execution plans of the ANY and the SOME subquery operators are exactly the same.

Despite the idea that, conceptually, for each row retrieved from the outer query there's a join operation performed with the inner query, the SQL Server Query Optimizer can sometimes make this a less-cumbersome operation. For example, in Figure 11-10, the execution plan from the example code shows that SQL Server first reads the Sale table and then sorts it by EventID; then it groups and sums by EventID (the Stream Aggregate) in preparation for the joining with the Event table, which has also been sorted by EventID. The impact of the join operation has been mitigated by matching rows from two sources that have been presorted on the joining columns.

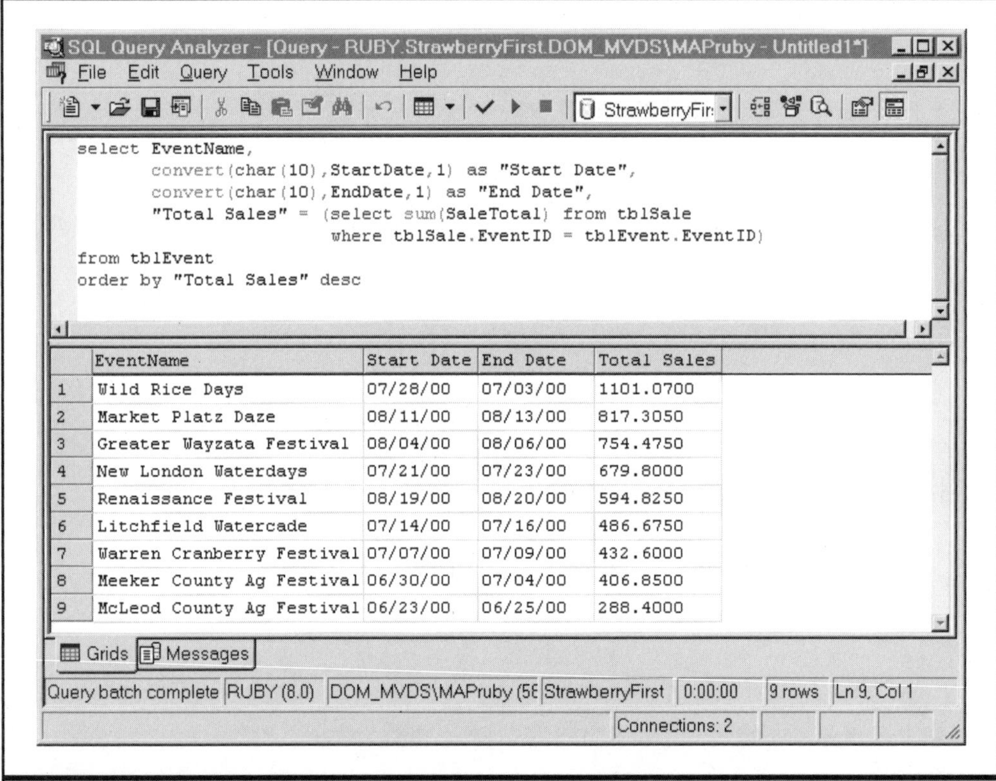

Figure 11-9. The correlated subquery expression contains a join in the inner query that references values from the table in the outer query.

It's easy to tell a correlated subquery just by looking at it—it has a join in the inner query. Unlike a simple subquery expression, the correlated subquery expression will *not* run on its own. If you were to try it, you'd get an error message because the query has a reference to a table that is not defined within itself—the outer reference.

The subquery operators for the correlated subquery expression are the same as those for the simple subquery: the comparison operators (=, <>, >, >=, <, <=), NOT, ANY, ALL, and EXISTS.

You should be careful with correlated subqueries, or you'll most likely get some strange results. For example, consider these two queries run on the Titles and Sales tables of the Pubs database. They each compute the total sales for each book, and they look deceptively similar:

```
SELECT title, type, price,
'SalesTotal' = (SELECT SUM(qty) FROM sales
WHERE sales.title_id = titles.title_id
```

```
  AND ord_date BETWEEN '01/01/92' AND '01/01/95')
FROM titles
GO
SELECT title, type, price,
'SalesTotal' = (SELECT SUM (qty) FROM sales, titles
 WHERE sales.title_id = titles.title_id
 AND ord_date BETWEEN '01/01/92' AND '01/01/95')
FROM titles
GO
```

The first query result set contains the correct answers, as you can see in Figure 11-11. The second query shows that every book has a total sales quantity of 493 units. Not only would this be a highly unusual coincidence, but it's just not plausible given the individual sales records that went into the calculations in the query! The difference between the two queries is that the first is a true correlated subquery expression. The inner query evaluates once for each row in the outer query, and the correct summed value for sales of each title is calculated. The second query is not a correlated subquery expression at all. Both the Sales table and the Titles table are included in the FROM clause of the inner query, so it is totally self-contained. It doesn't have an outer reference, and it doesn't need to refer back to the outer query for an individual book title.

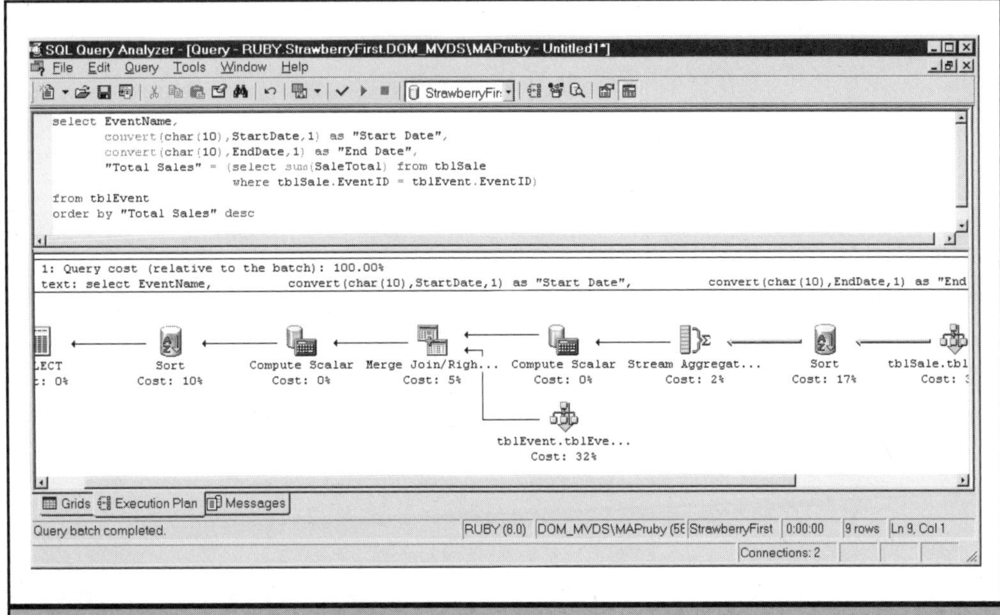

Figure 11-10. In a correlated subquery, both data sets are presorted on the joining columns to minimize the workload.

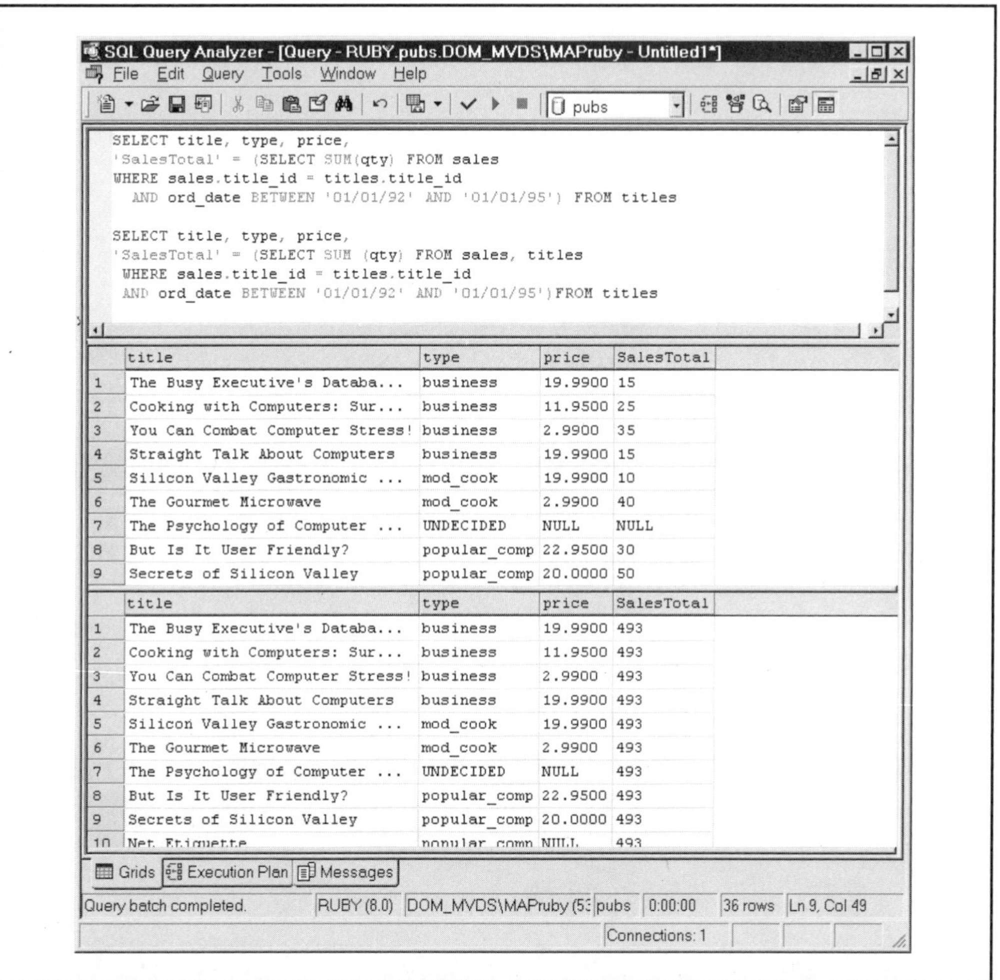

Figure 11-11. Two queries, extremely similar, give vastly different results; only the first is the true correlated subquery.

THE EXISTS CONDITION

Subquery expressions that use the EXISTS condition should be treated as a special case. Testing for existence of a row via a subquery is different from retrieving results to be used by an outer query. When SQL Server is testing for the EXISTS condition, you will find that the execution plan shows what looks like a join, and in fact that's really what the EXISTS does—it returns data from table A where there is a matching row in table B. The EXISTS is not typical, because once one matching row has been found, the condition is true—and the search can be terminated without looking at more rows. The NOT EXISTS operator is similar; like the left anti semi join, it returns all rows in table A where there is no match in table B. In this case, depending on how the Query Optimizer decides to execute the query, once a matching row has been found, the NOT EXISTS evaluates to false and it is not necessary to continue to search for matching rows.

To demonstrate how the EXISTS operator performs an existence check on data, let's answer the question, "Which people are employees?" You could easily resolve that question with a simple subquery:

```
SELECT LastName, FirstName, PersonType FROM tblPerson
WHERE PersonID IN (SELECT PersonID FROM tblEmployee)
```

But you also can write a correlated subquery and get the same exact results, as shown in Figure 11-12.

```
SELECT LastName, FirstName, PersonType FROM tblPerson
WHERE EXISTS (SELECT * FROM tblEmployee
           WHERE PersonID = tblPerson.PersonID)
```

So what's the deal? Why would you want to write a correlated subquery expression when a simple subquery will do? For one thing, the EXISTS operator alleviates the need to know the column names and which columns are the joining columns—something all other subquery operators require. And what's more, the SQL Server Query Optimizer treats these two pieces of code exactly the same, as shown in Figure 11-13. So the EXISTS operator, used in a correlated subquery expression, can be as efficient as the simple subquery expression IN operator. The choice of which to use is yours.

The EXISTS operator can be written as a simple subquery, as in the following:

```
SELECT LastName, FirstName, PersonType FROM tblPerson
WHERE EXISTS (SELECT * FROM tblEmployee)
```

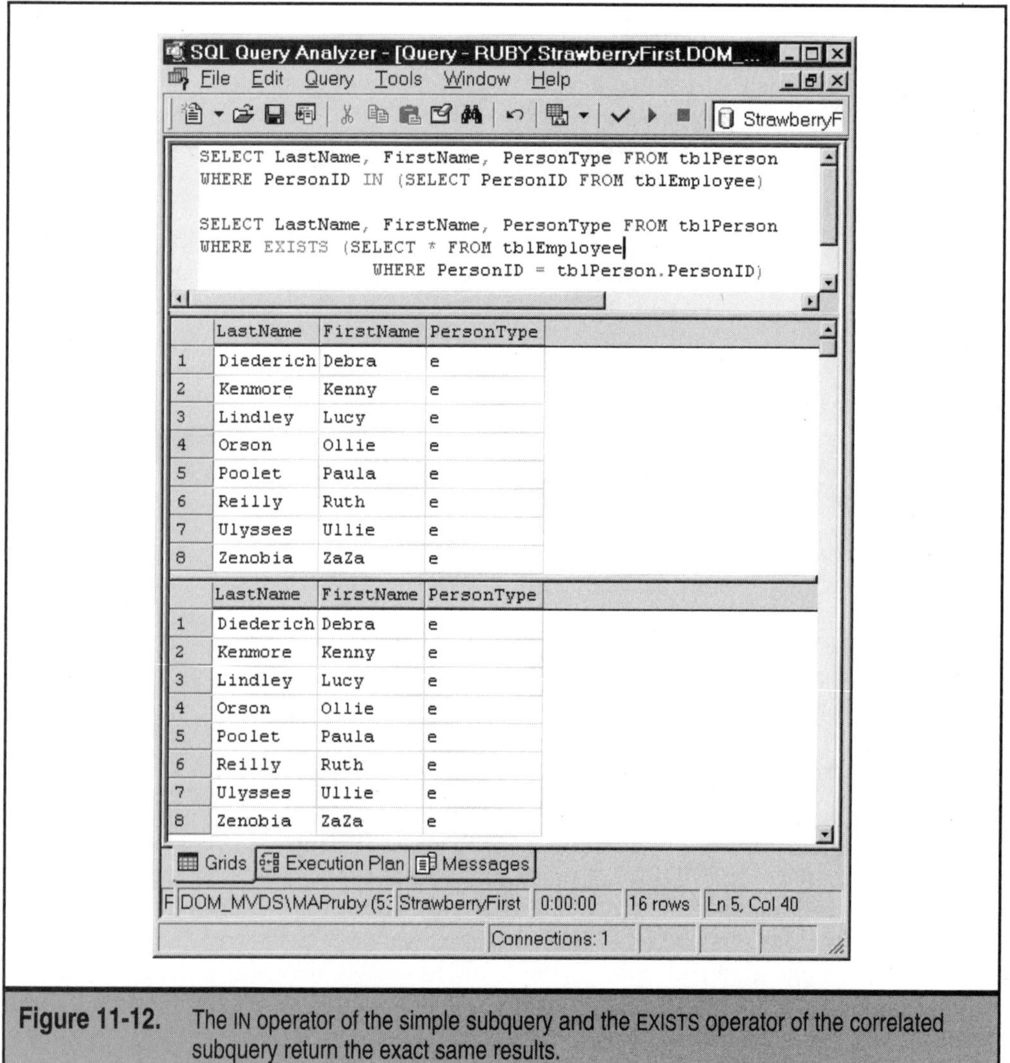

Figure 11-12. The IN operator of the simple subquery and the EXISTS operator of the correlated subquery return the exact same results.

However, there is a flaw in the logic here. As you can see from the result set in Figure 11-14, all rows are returned, which is not what we wanted to see. If the EXISTS operator is used like this and if a single row of the inner query evaluates to true, all conditions in the outer query are assumed to be also true, and the entire data set defined by the outer query will be displayed. For specific situations, the EXISTS operator can be very useful.

Note that between the WHERE EXISTS phrase and the inner query you can't add any arguments except the negative, NOT. The EXISTS operator may be one of the simplest of the correlated subquery operators to use and one of the most understandable.

In the next example, you'll use the Pubs test database. You're looking for information about authors who have published books. You don't want any information about books,

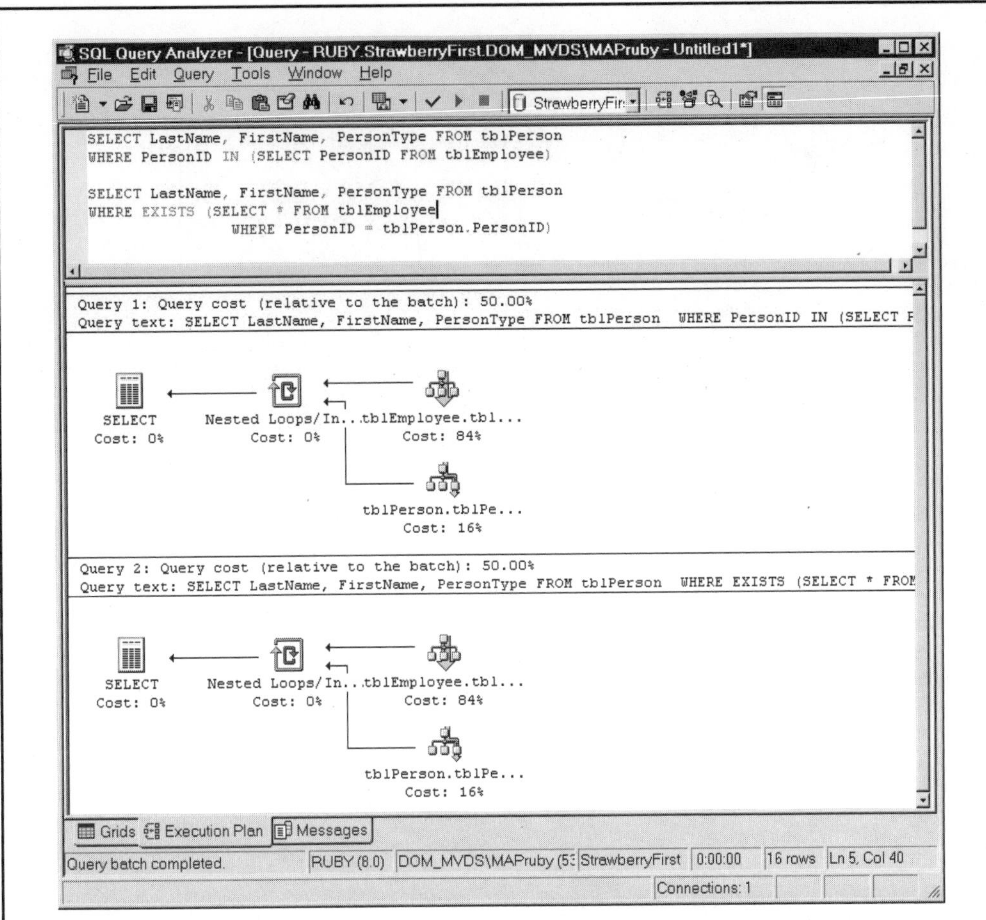

Figure 11-13. The execution plan of the simple subquery operation and the correlated subquery expression that uses EXISTS are the same.

just about the published authors. The query passes the au_id value, the author ID, into the subquery and checks for a match between the au_id in the Authors table and the au_id in the TitleAuthor table. If a match is found, the subquery returns a positive response, so the row for that author is included in the output data set. The convention is to write the subquery with a SELECT *, rather than name a column, because the EXISTS does not return data—it just returns a response of yes or no on the existence check:

```
SELECT au_id, au_lname, au_fname
FROM authors WHERE EXISTS
 (SELECT * FROM TitleAuthor WHERE TitleAuthor.au_id  = Authors.au_id)
```

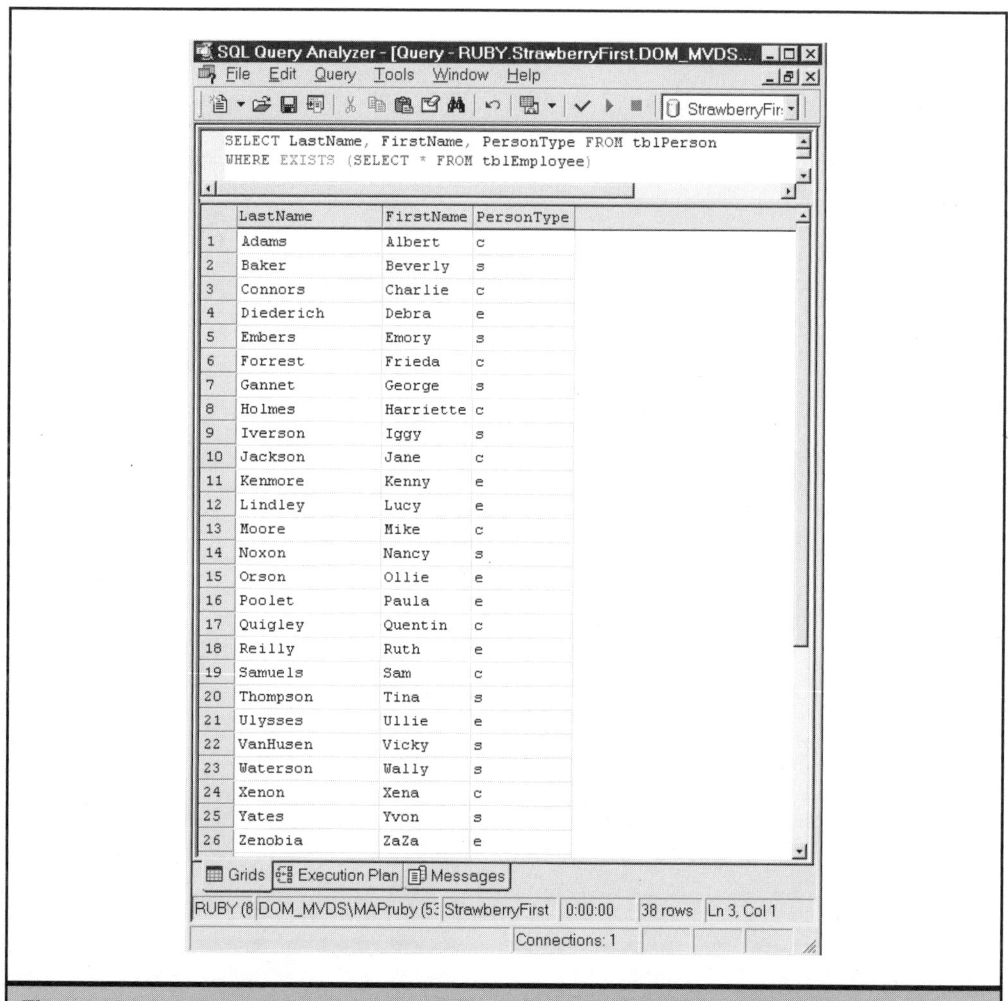

	LastName	FirstName	PersonType
1	Adams	Albert	c
2	Baker	Beverly	s
3	Connors	Charlie	c
4	Diederich	Debra	e
5	Embers	Emory	s
6	Forrest	Frieda	c
7	Gannet	George	s
8	Holmes	Harriette	c
9	Iverson	Iggy	s
10	Jackson	Jane	c
11	Kenmore	Kenny	e
12	Lindley	Lucy	e
13	Moore	Mike	c
14	Noxon	Nancy	s
15	Orson	Ollie	e
16	Poolet	Paula	e
17	Quigley	Quentin	c
18	Reilly	Ruth	e
19	Samuels	Sam	c
20	Thompson	Tina	s
21	Ulysses	Ullie	e
22	VanHusen	Vicky	s
23	Waterson	Wally	s
24	Xenon	Xena	c
25	Yates	Yvon	s
26	Zenobia	ZaZa	e

Figure 11-14. If the EXISTS operator is used in a simple subquery sense, it acts like a truth test.

In the execution plan, shown in Figure 11-15, you can see that the EXISTS query uses a stream aggregate—in other words, a group by—on the Author ID column in the TitleAuthor table. The SQL Server Query Optimizer is interpreting the request as wanting to know whether the author exists in the TitleAuthor table; the Optimizer doesn't care how many times the same author appears in the table. By inserting the stream aggregate, the Query Optimizer has reduced the number of rows that will be joined. Although that action may not make much difference on a small data set like this, it could have some serious performance implications (and benefits) on a large data set. The benefits could be significant if the one-to-many ratio was large, rather than the one-to-one or one-to-two ratio we see here with authors and titles.

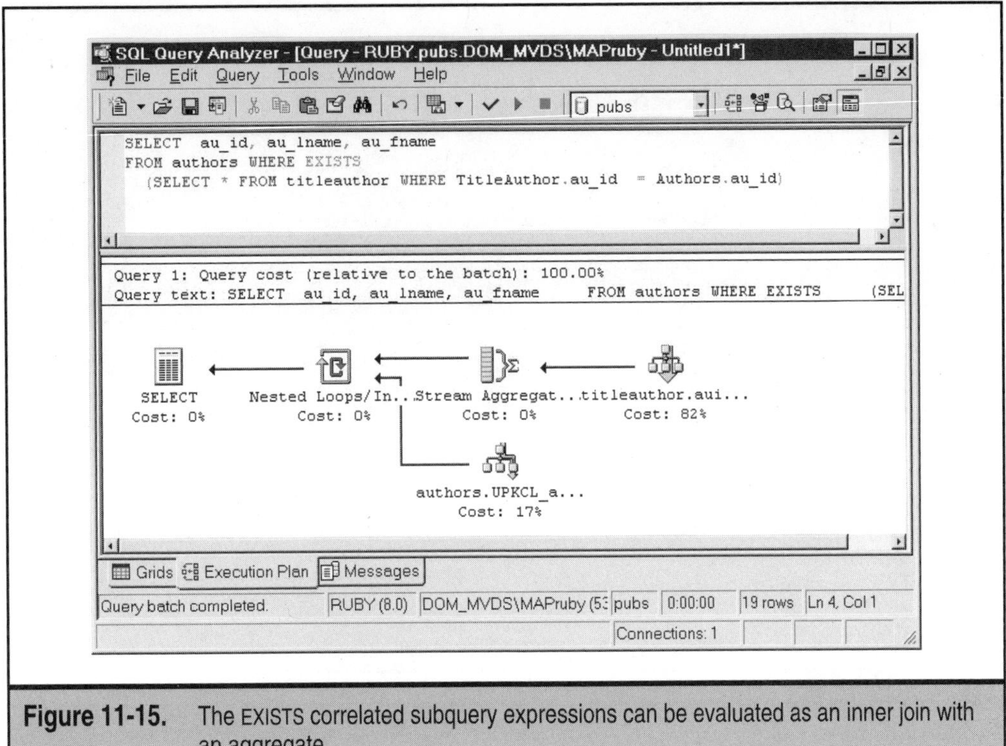

Figure 11-15. The EXISTS correlated subquery expressions can be evaluated as an inner join with an aggregate.

If you were to use the FORCEPLAN option on this query, as shown in Figure 11-16, the execution plan looks a little different, even though the result set remains the same. The stream aggregate is gone, and instead of an inner join there is now a left semi join. You will recall that in Chapter 7 we said that a left semi join is just like an inner join, except that the result set output contains columns from only one of the tables in the join. In this example, we have data output only from the Authors table. Running the two queries together and looking at the execution plans shows that the semi join takes slightly more than 50 percent of the total batch cost, and the stream aggregate/inner join takes a fraction less than 50 percent. Notice that the Authors table now becomes the outer table in the join—it's now at the top of the execution plan display. This might be because the Authors table has fewer rows than the TitleAuthor table, or it might be because it has a more appropriate index that the Query Optimizer can use. Or it may just be that SQL Server doesn't do right semi joins; it flips them around to become left semi joins, so it makes the Authors table the outer table in the left semi join. Sometimes you just have to accept what the Query Optimizer does, because Microsoft is a little reluctant to discuss all the tricks and strategies that it has programmed into the Query Optimizer—and for good reason.

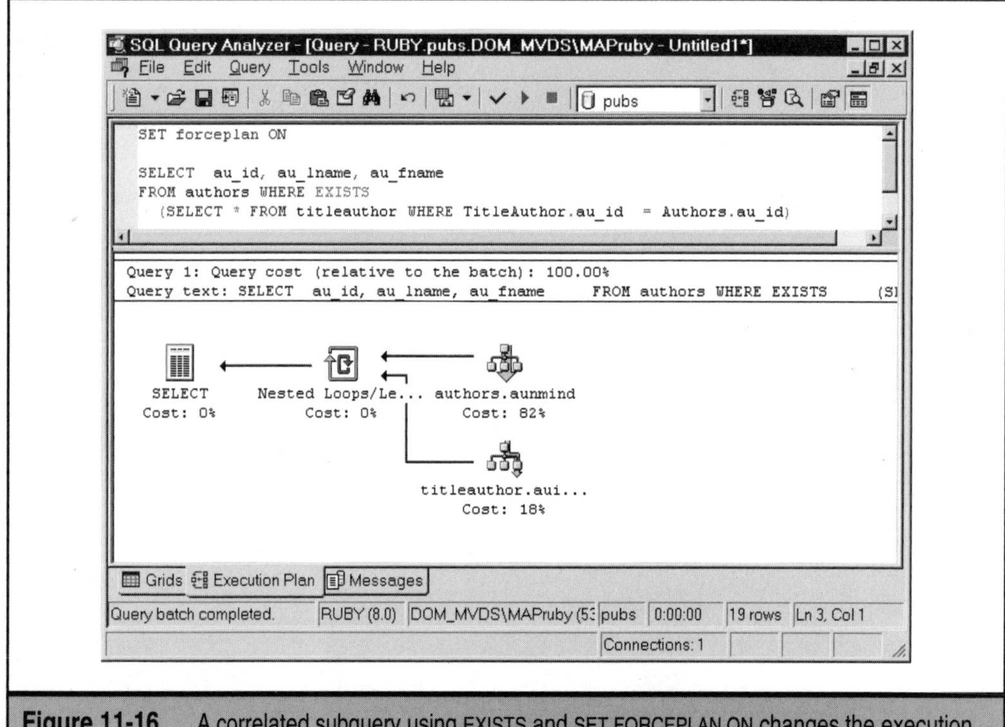

Figure 11-16. A correlated subquery using EXISTS and SET FORCEPLAN ON changes the execution plan from a stream aggregate to a left semi join.

It is often possible to write a correlated subquery expression as a join expression, and in this case, the equivalent statement would be this:

```
SELECT distinct authors.au_id, au_lname, au_fname
FROM authors INNER JOIN TitleAuthor
ON authors.au_id  = titleauthor.au_id
```

Notice in Figure 11-17 that to get the same results with only one row per author in the output data set, you have to include a DISTINCT qualifier in the join query. The EXISTS query did that for us automatically. The inner join will by default give all matching rows, and as some authors have written more than one book, their names will show up more than once in the match list. Hence the need for the DISTINCT.

Running this query with the OPTION (FORCE ORDER), which acts like the SET FORCEPLAN ON, shows that left to itself, the Query Optimizer will pick the left semi join solution. The code to do this is shown here:

```
SELECT DISTINCT authors.au_id, au_lname, au_fname
FROM authors INNER JOIN TitleAuthor
ON authors.au_id  = titleauthor.au_id  OPTION (FORCE ORDER)
```

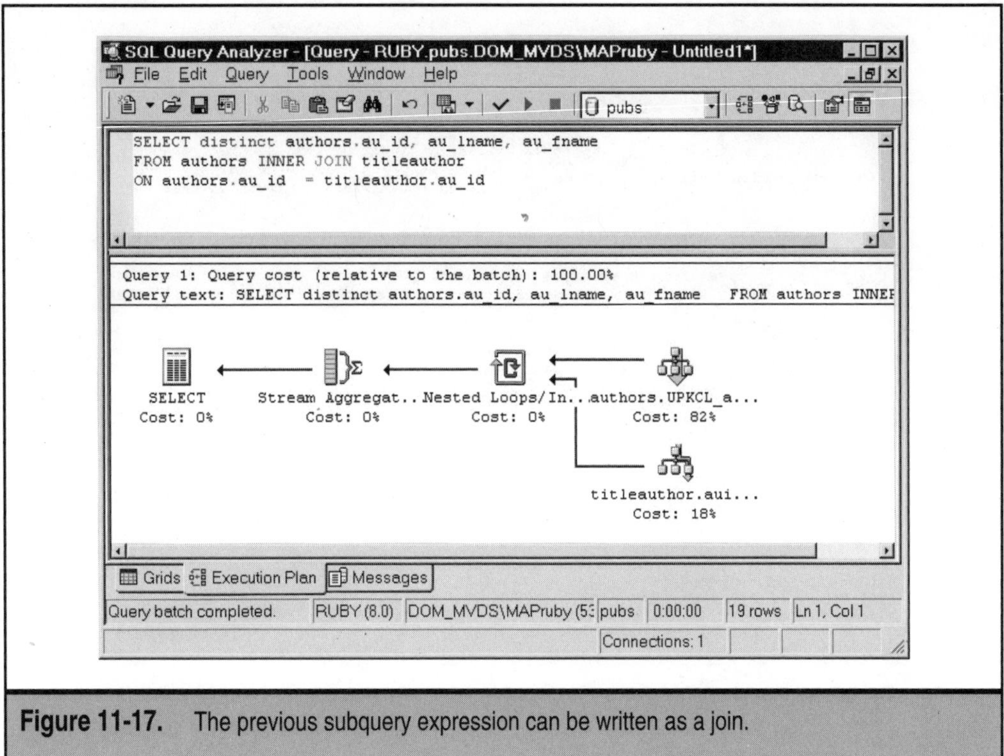

Figure 11-17. The previous subquery expression can be written as a join.

If you make the Optimizer process the query in the order you stated in the query, it does an inner join *followed by* a stream aggregate to get only one row per author, as you can see in Figure 11-18. The stream aggregate is now being done on output from the join operation. This differs from the EXISTS correlated query expression. With FORCE ORDER turned on, you are joining more rows than without, and then you're discarding some of those rows with the stream aggregate. This is less efficient than the left semi join operation; so left to its own devices, the Query Optimizer will pick the left semi join.

We mentioned when we talked about joins in Chapter 8 that it's easy to find all the matches between two tables using an inner join. What is less easy is finding the rows that do not match. One approach is to use a NOT EXISTS subquery operator. An example from Pubs would answer the question "Which authors do not have book titles listed with us?" These authors will not have an entry in the TitleAuthor table, which cross-correlates Authors and Titles:

```
SELECT au_id, au_lname, au_fname  FROM authors
WHERE NOT EXISTS (SELECT * FROM TitleAuthor
                  WHERE titleauthor.au_id  = authors.au_id)
```

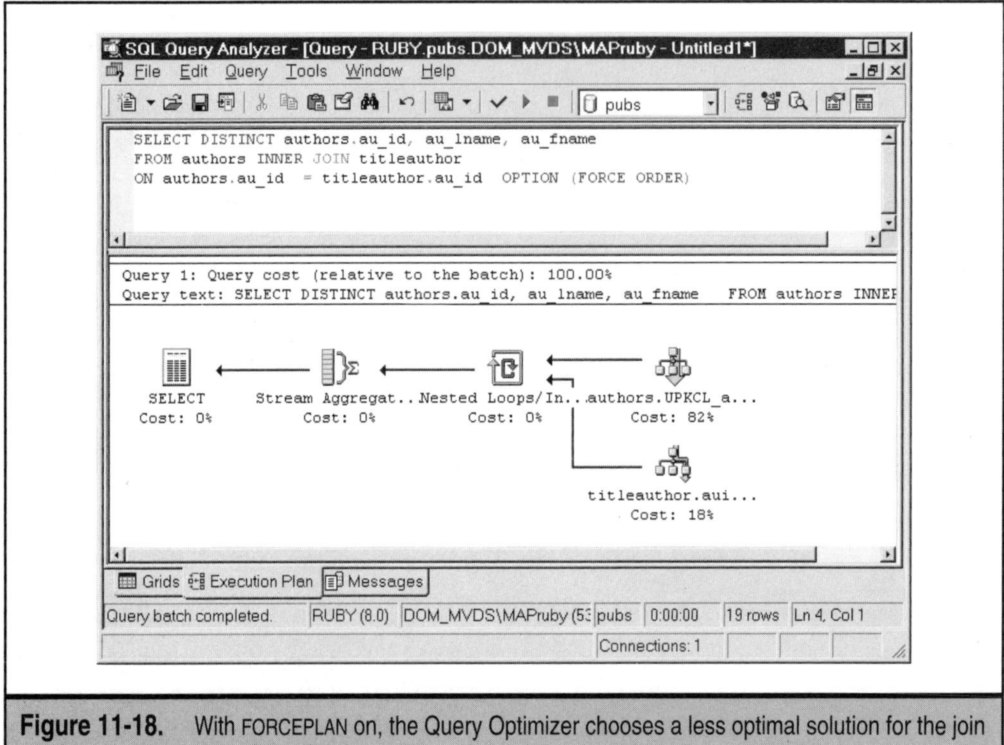

Figure 11-18. With FORCEPLAN on, the Query Optimizer chooses a less optimal solution for the join operation.

This query returns a list of the four authors who have not yet written books. You can also write this as a join, although the syntax is a little more complex:

```
SELECT a.au_id, au_lname, au_fname, t.au_id
FROM authors a LEFT OUTER JOIN TitleAuthor t ON a.au_id  = t.au_id
WHERE t.au_id IS NULL
```

In this case, we do not need a DISTINCT in the join operation, because we know that each author can appear in the Authors table only once and we are looking for a row in which the author from the Authors table and a NULL in the TitleAuthor table appear. Given the way the left outer join works, only one row per author can contain a NULL for the titleauthor.au_id.

Figure 11-19 shows the identical result sets from both queries. The corresponding execution plans are shown in Figure 11-20, and from these plans you can see that there is a very slight benefit to using the NOT EXISTS subquery expression rather than the join operation.

Normally when you see a NOT query, you should be wary of using it, because often it makes for a highly inefficient query. The Query Optimizer usually cannot make use of any available indexes with negative criteria, and it is forced to do a table scan. At least, that was the case in earlier versions of SQL Server. Now the Optimizer is getting smarter.

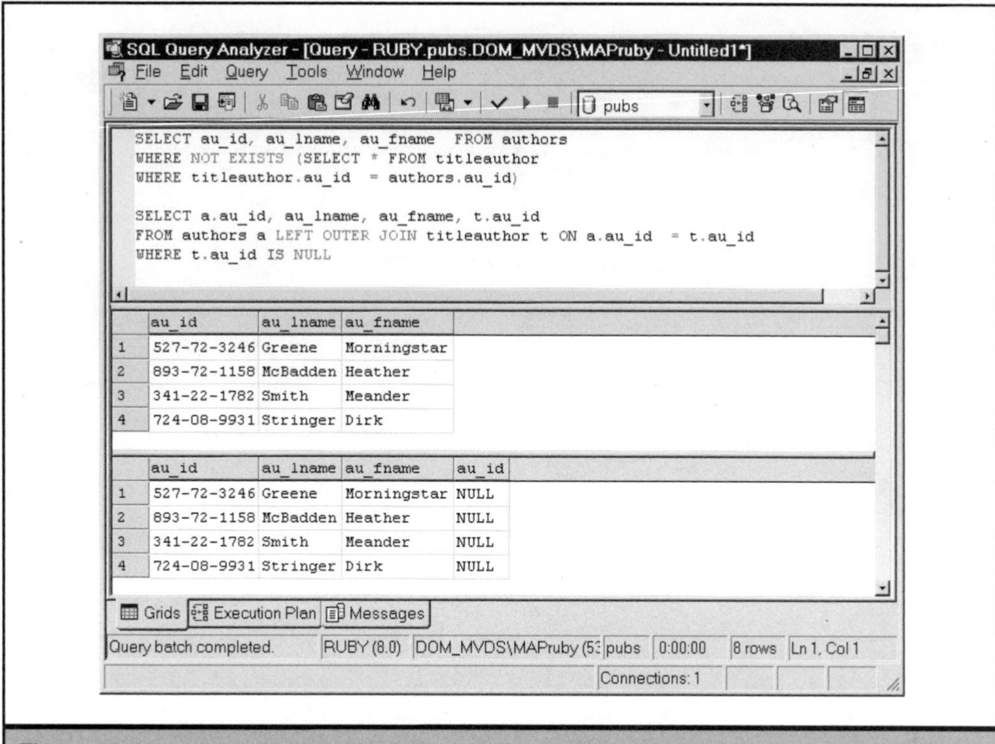

Figure 11-19. You can use a NOT EXISTS or a left outer join to show authors who don't have books in our title listing.

For example, if you run the following query on the Person table in your Strawberry database, SQL Server will use the clustered index on PersonID to scan the data:

```
SELECT * FROM tblPerson WHERE LastName BETWEEN 'Holmes' AND 'Moore'
```

When you change the query to read

```
SELECT * FROM tblPerson WHERE LastName NOT BETWEEN 'Holmes' and 'Moore'
```

it will still use the same clustered index, and furthermore, it rewrites the query to read this way:

```
SELECT * FROM tblPerson WHERE LastName <  'Holmes' OR LastName >  'Moore'
```

That's pretty impressive, but don't rely on the Query Optimizer to bail you out and rewrite your code for you all the time. Try to express your queries as positive statements rather than negative ones. The exception, as we hope we have made clear in this chapter, is the NOT EXISTS subquery expression, which is a special case of an operator can be very efficient in some instances.

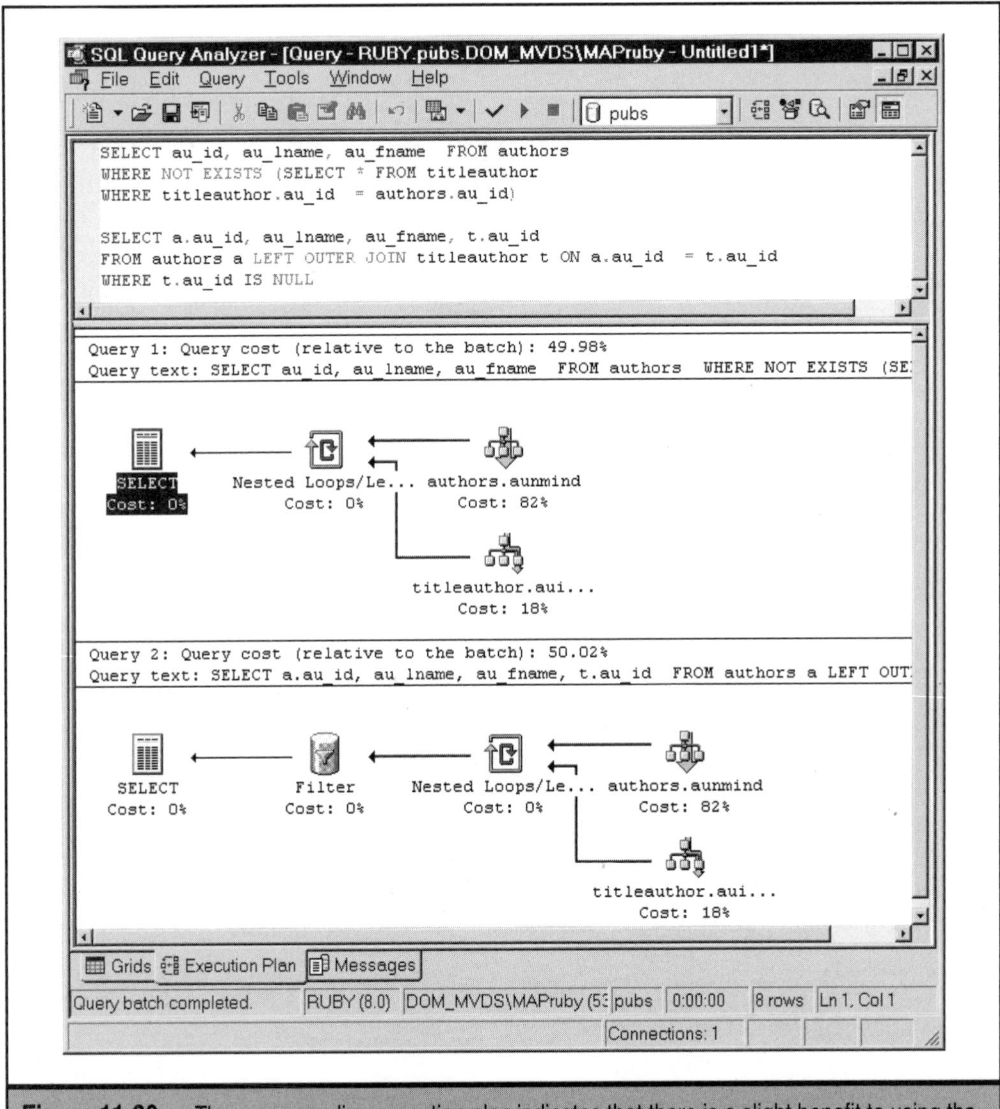

Figure 11-20. The corresponding execution plan indicates that there is a slight benefit to using the NOT EXISTS subquery expression.

MODIFYING DATA BASED ON THE RESULTS OF A QUERY

One of the more powerful features of the subquery is its ability to make changes in a table by referencing data in another table. This is a lot easier than it sounds, and a lot less complex. You can insert rows into a table by selecting them from another table, delete rows from a table based on their presence or absence in another table, and update rows in a table based on values of data in another table.

Inserts

In the previous chapter, we showed that you could create a table, called SalesStaff, and then, with an INSERT statement, use a SELECT statement to bring data into the table. In this case, the SELECT statement was a subquery and the outer query just happened to be an INSERT statement instead of another SELECT. To refresh your memory, let's re-create the SalesStaff table:

```
CREATE TABLE SalesStaff
(PersonID           INT           NOT NULL,
VendorName          varchar(40)   NOT NULL ,
LastName            varchar(20)   NOT NULL ,
FirstName           varchar(20)   NOT NULL ,
MailingAddr         varchar(40)   NULL ,
City                varchar(20)   NULL ,
State               char(2)       NULL ,
Zip                 char (10)     NULL ,
OfficeLocation      varchar (60)  NULL )
GO
```

Now let's reload the table, using an INSERT statement with an inner SELECT clause:

```
INSERT INTO SalesStaff (PersonID,  VendorName,  LastName,  FirstName,
                        MailingAddr, City, State, Zip, OfficeLocation)
SELECT s.PersonID, v.Vendorname, p.LastName, p.FirstName,
       p.MailingAddr, p.City, p.State, p.Zip, s.OfficeLocation
FROM tblSalesPerson s JOIN tblPerson p ON s.PersonID = p.PersonID
                      JOIN tblVendor v ON s.VendorID = v.VendorID
GO
SELECT * FROM SalesStaff
```

Deletes

It's time to clean up the Vendor table. You'll do it all with subqueries. Suppose a couple of vendors are not currently supplying anything to your company. First, so you don't mess up the Strawberry database, make a temporary copy of the Vendor table:

```
SELECT * INTO ##Vendor FROM tblVendor
GO
SELECT * FROM ##Vendor
```

Before you delete from a table, make sure you know what it is you're deleting! Show the vendors who are not currently providing anything to Strawberry:

```
SELECT * FROM ##Vendor
WHERE VendorID NOT IN(SELECT VendorID FROM tblSupply)
```

The result set contains records for Filo Bros. Company and the Gallo Bros. Company. Let's go ahead and get rid of these two rows:

```
DELETE FROM ##Vendor
WHERE VendorID NOT IN(SELECT VendorID FROM tblSupply)
```

Or you can use the NOT EXISTS subquery operator:

```
DELETE FROM ##Vendor
WHERE NOT EXISTS(SELECT * FROM tblSupply
                 WHERE VendorID = ##Vendor.VendorID))
```

Now show the remaining vendors:

```
SELECT * FROM ##Vendor
```

If you somehow mess up a table, you can rebuild it quickly and easily. If the table is part of the Pubs or Northwind database and you decide that it is messed up too badly to repair, open a Query Analyzer window and go to File | Open. In the \MSSQL\INSTALL directory, you will find files called INSTPUBS.SQL and INSTNWND.SQL. Open the appropriate file, run it, and it will rebuild Pubs or Northwind.

Updates

The UPDATE command can use a subquery instead of a value list to modify data in the table by referring to data in another table. In this example from the Strawberry database, you're first going to increase the price of each item in the SaleItem table by 50 cents. Then you'll update the SubTotal values in the Sale table by executing a subquery that will go out to the SaleItem table and calculate a value that is the sum of the ItemCost for each sale. After that, you'd better redo your SalesTax and SaleTotal columns in the Sale table. Once again, you'll create temporary work tables to do this exercise.

First, create the temporary work tables ##Sale and ##SaleItem:

```
SELECT * INTO ##Sale FROM tblSale
GO
SELECT * FROM ##Sale
GO
SELECT * INTO ##SaleItem FROM tblSaleItem
GO
SELECT * FROM ##SaleItem
GO
```

Now add 50 cents to each item in the ##SaleItem table:

```
UPDATE ##SaleItem
SET ItemCost = ItemCost + .50
GO
```

Ready to recompute the SaleTotal in the ##Sale table:

```
UPDATE ##Sale
SET  SubTotal=(SELECT SUM(ItemCost) FROM ##SaleItem
               WHERE ##Sale.SaleNo = ##SaleItem.SaleNo )
GO
```

Now calculate the SalesTax (3 percent) and the SaleTotal in the ##Sale table:

```
UPDATE ##SALE
SET SalesTax = SubTotal * .03,
    SaleTotal = SubTotal + (SubTotal * .03)
GO
```

Take a look at the end result:

```
SELECT * FROM ##SALE
```

All the data in the ##Sale table is successfully updated. Notice that the UPDATE statement that calculates the value of SalesTax and SaleTotal is using the formula (SubTotal * .03) two times. The first time it's used to update the column SalesTax. The second time it's used to help calculate the SaleTotal. You have to set up the calculation this way, because you're updating two columns in the same statement, one of which is dependent on the value of the other. If you didn't, the value of SaleTotal would be short by the SalesTax amount.

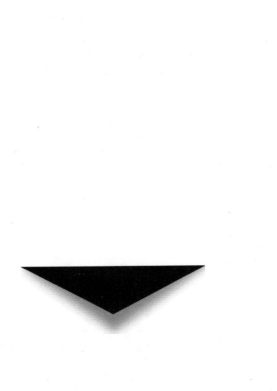

CHAPTER 12

Views

Views are a neat feature of SQL Server that offers a lot of benefit without much in the way of trade-off or drawback. The introduction of indexed views in SQL Server 2000 adds even more reason to consider building your user interfaces on views, rather than directly on the underlying tables. In this chapter, we will look at how to build views and how to modify existing views. We will consider the issues involved with updating data through a view. We'll look at some of the ways in which views can be used, and then we'll discuss the new features added in SQL Server 2000.

WHAT IS A VIEW?

A view is a way of looking at the data. Typically, it's a restricted perspective of the data in the database, which may involve looking at data from more than one table at the same time. A view can include calculated data, data that isn't stored in the database but is dynamically computed when you use a view to look at the data. A view can restrict data to a subset of the rows and columns in one table, or it can combine data from two or more tables to show you a more informational perspective of the data than what is available from the raw table data. A traditional view is a definition based on real tables, and the data you see associated with a view is "borrowed" from the tables that the view is created from. We're going to leave aside discussions of materialized or indexed views for the moment; we'll talk about them later in the chapter. A view takes up very little space in the database, because only the definition is stored in the database catalog.

You use a view in a SQL query as you would a table. When a view is used, the Query Optimizer fetches the definition of the view to determine which tables the view was created from, and then retrieves the data from these tables. What you are seeing is the data in the table itself, so the view is like a window into the data. Views can be thought of as virtual tables. They don't really exist until you use them, like the monsters under your bed; and just like those monsters, they vanish when you stop thinking about them (when the SQL query has finished executing).

Views can also be thought of as stored queries. It might be more accurate to think of them as prefabricated query modules, which can be merged with other modules to build a query. When you SELECT from a view, SQL Server does not run the view, build the result set, and then extract the data from that result set based on the additional WHERE clause conditions in the SELECT statement. Instead, it takes the view definition; merges it with the SELECT conditions; and then parses, optimizes, and compiles the entire query. The same is true when you join a view and a table, or when you join two views. SQL Server takes all the view definitions and all the other SELECT conditions, and integrates them into one query; then it parses, optimizes, and compiles from there. You can demonstrate this for yourself by running a SELECT on a view (Titleview in the Pubs database is a good choice for this), then running the SELECT statement you used to build the view (highlight Titleview in Enterprise Manager, right-click, choose Properties), and comparing execution plans. The execution plans are identical—there's no extra SELECT statement in the first query. Merging the definitions of the views and the conditions placed on the tables allows the Query Optimizer to determine the best overall plan for execution of the query, rather than trying to optimize for the view and then again for the query containing the view.

WHY USE VIEWS?

When you normalize a database, you end up with data that is broken out into many small tables. To retrieve useful information, you have to join these tables together. It may not be easy for end-users (including non-SQL programmers) to write those joins, as doing so requires knowledge of the internal structure of the database and knowledge of the SQL language. Even if your users always connect to and interact with the database through a customized application built in VB or Access, they're still going to want information. They're not going to want to have to navigate through the database, table by table, trying to make sense of the data they find. This is especially a concern when you have some power users, such as data analysts and statisticians, who need to connect to SQL Server data using an interface such as Excel or MS Query, or those who want to build their own Access applications. Instead of expecting them to write these table joins, you can build views that present the information from the joined tables.

A view is a database object and is treated much like a table by MS Access or by Excel, so these applications can connect directly to a view instead of a table. In fact, you really should have a naming convention that distinguishes between tables and views, because from Access or Excel you cannot tell whether you are looking at a view or a table. You use the prefix *tbl* for tables, but views are prefixed with an underscore. The underscore ensures that all the views sort at the head of the list—so that when your power users connect to the database with Excel, they'll see these views listed first. We have found the combination of Excel and views easy to use and very powerful in the hands of users who have some background in PC applications.

Views are a great tool for establishing initial security. Step 1, make sure that no users have any right to access the database tables directly. Step 2, construct views for each business application or function, and give the users permissions on the new views. This approach is especially useful when you want to restrict access to certain columns in a table. Setting column-level permissions can be tedious, and it's easy to overlook something in the process. Checking column-level permissions can be tedious for the SQL Server, too, and can consume a lot of system resources—now that you can have 1,024 columns in a table. The ability to set column-level permissions through the Enterprise Manager was omitted in SQL Server 7; we thought it was gone for good, but it showed up again in SQL Server 2000. Actually, SQL 7 users aren't missing much because trying to set column-level permissions in a graphical environment involves too much clicking and mousing around. Typically, you write security scripts that are easily tracked, easily modified, and, more important, easily perused to determine who can do what. But, really, a better approach is not to use column-level permissions at all. Instead, create views in which the column list includes only the columns you want the user to see. Then give the user permission to select from the view.

About the only time that column-level permissions could be useful is on a table with really sensitive data, such as payroll information, Social Security numbers, or passwords. Here you want to make sure that access is denied to most users. A good data modeler would tell you that if one or two columns in a table are really that sensitive, perhaps they need to be moved to a separate table, with special security permission levied against the table to protect the contents from most users.

Views are also useful for delivering a subset of the data to specific members of your user community. Not only can you define which columns they see, but you can also add a WHERE clause to the view and define a subset of the rows. For example, you could set up a view for your San Diego office to see only customers from California, and a second view for the Charlotte, North Carolina, office showing only customers from North and South Carolina.

With Data Transformation Services (DTS), introduced with SQL Server 7, there is less call for BCP (bulk copy program) for data export. But if you are still using BCP, you prob ably know that there are no BCP switches that will allow you to restrict the columns and rows being exported, other than by a count of rows processed. This is of limited use with rows and no help at all with restricting the export of columns. To export a subset of a table, you need to use a view, and you can specify the columns and rows in the SELECT and WHERE clauses of the view. If you have converted to DTS for your import and export, you can export from a query or a view in a DTS package. Certainly DTS gives you a lot more control over what gets exported; but if you already have a view set up for the exact data set you want, why not use it?

HOW TO DEFINE A VIEW

Defining a view involves nothing more than writing a SELECT statement, making sure it works, and then defining the view as that statement. There are a couple of options to think about, but views are not complicated to create. As usual when creating new database objects, you have to be the database owner, a member of the db_ddladmin role, or a system administrator to create a view. As it creates the view, SQL Server puts an entry in the sysobjects table for the view name, and the code for the view definition is written in the syscomments table. The syntax for a view is

```
CREATE VIEW view_name [(column [,...n])]
[WITH ENCRYPTION]
AS
select_statement
[WITH CHECK OPTION]
```

As an example from the Strawberry database, let's create a view that shows a list of employees by name and their job titles:

```
CREATE VIEW dbo._EmployeeList
AS
SELECT p.PersonID, p.LastName, p.FirstName, e.JobTitle
FROM tblPerson p JOIN tblEmployee e ON p.PersonID = e.PersonID
GO
SELECT * FROM _EmployeeList
```

You would expect to have to name the view, just as you would any new object; but notice that, optionally, you can name the columns as well. If each column in the view corresponds to one column in the underlying table, you don't need to specify column names. As you can see in Figure 12-1, the view columns inherit their names from the table on which they're built.

If you are computing values for a view column, you should specify the column names. If you do not, these columns will be without a name. The users of the view won't have a way to specify the unnamed column; they'll either have to SELECT just named col-

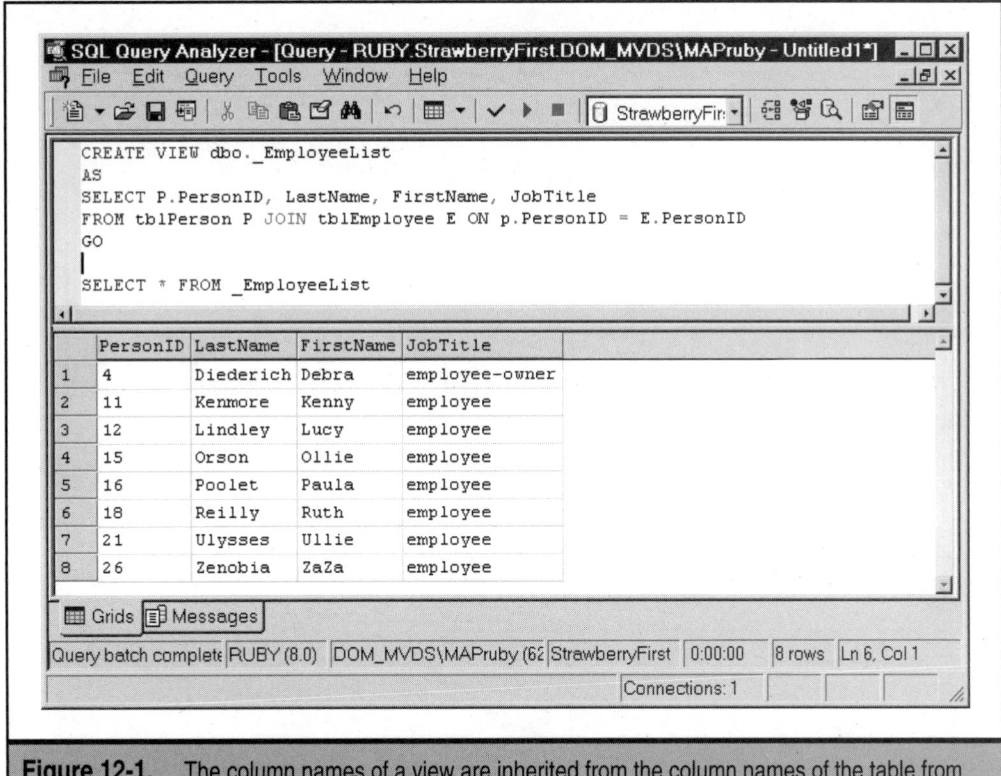

Figure 12-1. The column names of a view are inherited from the column names of the table from which the view is built.

umns, or they'll have to SELECT * (select all columns). Of course, you can also specify new column names if you want to rename the columns in the view, perhaps substituting more user-friendly names than those used in the tables. The following example and the result set shown in Figure 12-2 illustrate how you can name the computed column in the view definition.

```
CREATE VIEW dbo._EmployeeList1 (PersonID, Name, JobTitle)
AS
SELECT p.PersonID, p.LastName + ', ' + p.FirstName, e.JobTitle
FROM  tblPerson p JOIN tblEmployee e  ON p.PersonID = e.PersonID
GO
SELECT * FROM _EmployeeList1
```

In an alternative approach, you can name the columns when you create them in the SELECT statement of the view expressions, as shown in Figure 12-3. This avoids having to list out all the columns in the view, when most of them will retain their original names, and only one or two columns are computed.

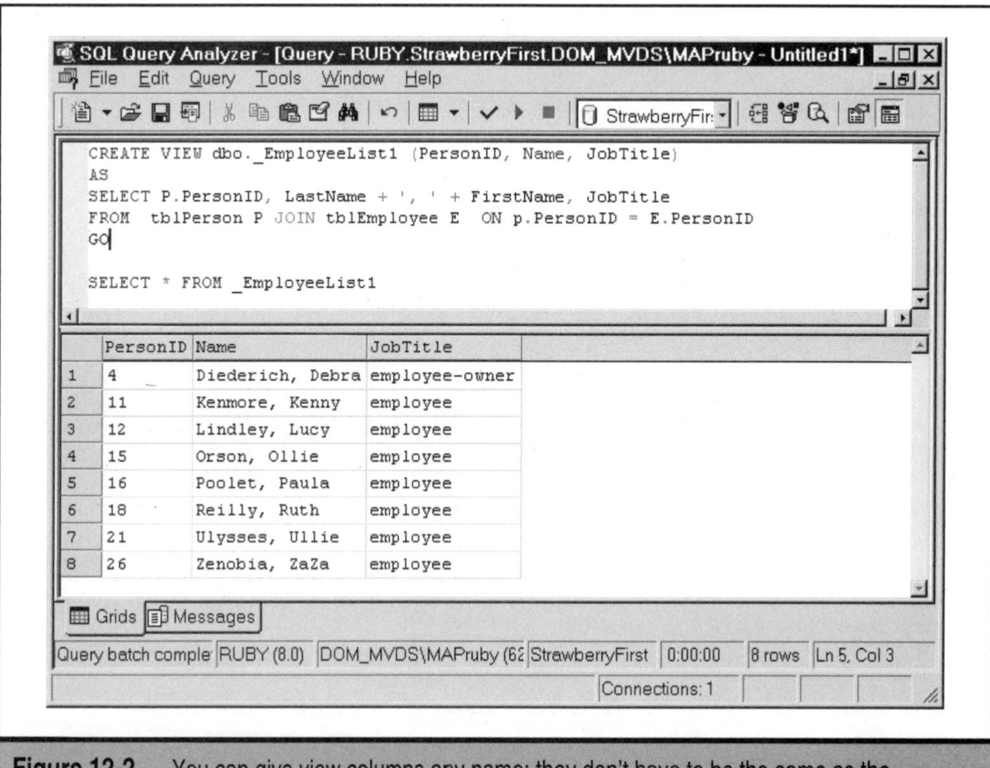

Figure 12-2. You can give view columns any name; they don't have to be the same as the underlying table columns.

```
CREATE VIEW dbo._EmployeeList2
AS
SELECT p.PersonID, p.LastName + ', ' + p.FirstName AS 'Name', e.JobTitle
FROM  tblPerson p JOIN tblEmployee e  ON p.PersonID = e.PersonID
GO
SELECT * FROM _EmployeeList2
```

As with stored procedures and triggers, the code for the view can be encrypted in storage. There is probably less need to encrypt a view than there is to encrypt the algorithms in stored procedures, but perhaps when you compute columns you might wish to hide the details of the calculation. Otherwise, anyone with access to the syscomments table in the database can look at the code. Encryption is one way of preventing people from accessing the code, but this means that you cannot ask SQL Server to return the unencrypted code. There's no way to supply a key or password and have SQL Server reverse the encryption. SQL Server can rebuild the view definition, for example, when you upgrade from one version to the next, but ordinary mortals (and database

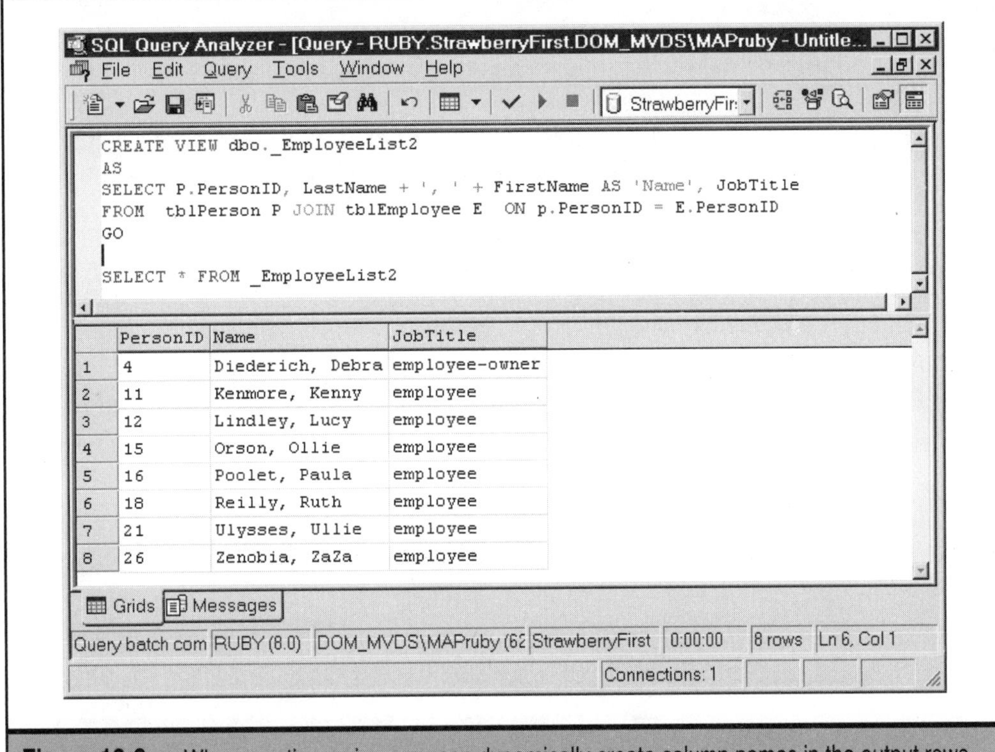

Figure 12-3. When creating a view, you can dynamically create column names in the output rows.

administrators) cannot decrypt the code. So, as with any software, make sure that you have a copy of the code stored somewhere safe.

Normally, SQL Server will not allow "orphan" objects, because it enforces referential integrity within the system tables. One exception to this rule is that you can drop a table without first deleting the views built on it. These views do not go away, nor will you see an error or even a warning message when you drop the parent table. The SQL Server architects assume that you might want to drop a table and then re-create it, and it would be inconvenient if you had to drop and rebuild all the views that were associated with that table. (Pre-SQL 7 versions did not support the ALTER TABLE command, so dropping and rebuilding a table was the only way to remove a column, rename a column, or modify the datatype of a column.) Taken in this context, the decision to allow orphan objects makes sense, except it does mean that if you drop a table permanently, the next person who tries to use the view will get an error message, "invalid object name." SQL Server has a stored procedure, SP_DEPENDS 'PARENT_object_name', that shows what objects (including triggers and stored procedures) are dependent upon a parent object, so that you can see what the implications are before you drop an object. You can view this dependency information in graphical form in Enterprise Manager, as shown in Figure 12-4, if you right-click the table name and then select All Tasks | Display Dependencies.

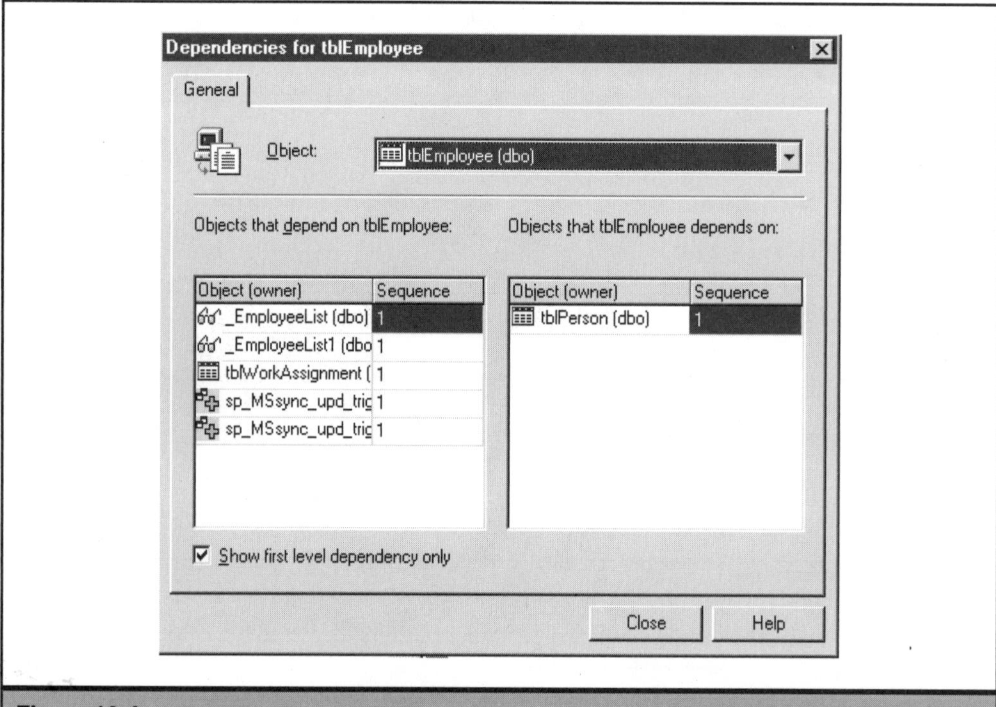

Figure 12-4. You can view dependencies for any table by using this feature of Enterprise Manager.

ALTERING AND DROPPING VIEWS

To change a view prior to SQL Server 7, you had to drop the view and re-create it. Because the view did not contain any stored data, this was a quick process. The only problem was that when the view was dropped, all the permissions that had been granted on that view also vanished. So after you rebuilt the view, you had to reapply all the permissions. (We always made sure that we kept backup SQL scripts that included the permissions statements on the file server or used the Generate SQL feature to script all permissions before dropping objects.) SQL Server 7 introduced the ALTER VIEW command, which rebuilds the view with the modifications but does not drop it first, so you don't lose and have to re-create the permissions. This is a really neat feature and a time-saver, but it is not ANSI standard, so don't expect it to work in other RDBMSs. In this example, you change the order of the output columns for the view _EmployeeList2:

```
ALTER VIEW dbo._EmployeeList2
AS
SELECT e.JobTitle , p.PersonID, p.LastName + ', ' + p.FirstName AS 'Name'
FROM  tblPerson p JOIN tblEmployee e  ON p.PersonID = e.PersonID
GO
SELECT * FROM _EmployeeList2
```

As you can see in Figure 12-5, the first SELECT retrieves the data from the view as it was originally created, with the columns in the order PersonID, Name, and JobTitle. The ALTER VIEW command switches the order of the columns, so the second SELECT retrieves the data with the columns in the order JobTitle, PersonID, Name.

Dropping views is as simple as executing a DROP VIEW statement and naming the view to be dropped, as in the following code:

```
DROP VIEW _EmployeeList, _EmployeeList1, _EmployeeList2
```

Views of a View

Views can be built to reference other views or to reference a combination of other views and tables. Effectively, you are building views on top of other views. We call these *second-level views*. There is no theoretical limit to how deep you can stack views; the limit is more of a practical one. If you have two views that each join four tables, and then you build another view that joins the first two views, you have an eight-table join, and performance is likely to suffer as you add more and more tables into the join. Remember, SQL Server does not run each of the first two views and then build the third view by

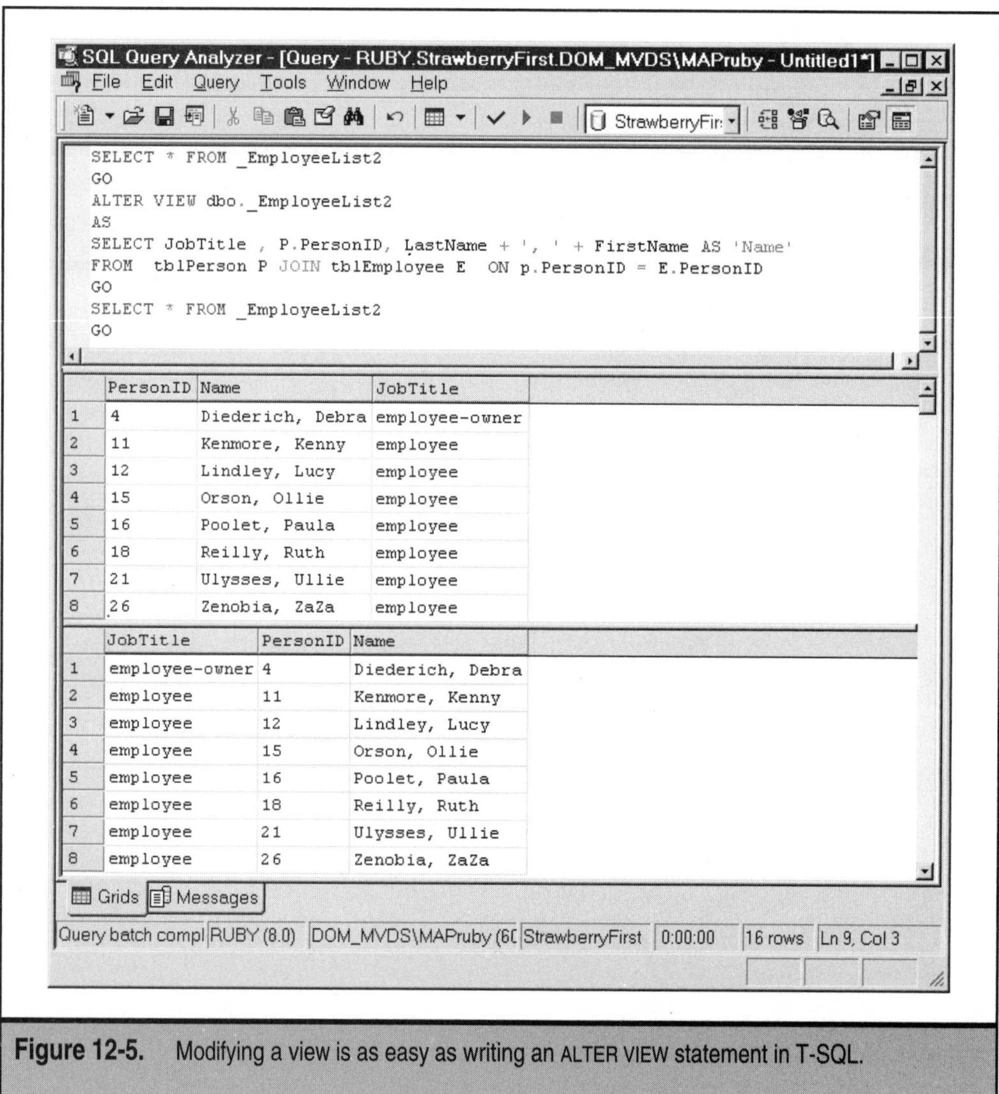

Figure 12-5. Modifying a view is as easy as writing an ALTER VIEW statement in T-SQL.

merging the result sets. It merges the definitions and runs the complete query as one, as the following example will demonstrate:

```
/* create the _EmployeeList view by joining two tables*/
CREATE VIEW dbo._EmployeeList (EmpID, Name, Title)
AS SELECT p.PersonID, p.FirstName + ' ' + p.LastName,  e.JobTitle
```

```
FROM  tblPerson p JOIN tblEmployee e  ON p.PersonID = e.PersonID
GO
/* create the _EventSales view by joining two tables*/
CREATE VIEW dbo._EventSales
          (Event_ID, Event_Name, Start_Date, Event_Fee, Total_Sales)
AS SELECT e.EventID, e.EventName, CAST(e.StartDate AS char(12)),
         e.Fees, SUM(s.SaleTotal)
FROM tblEvent e JOIN tblSale s ON e.EventID = s.EventID
GROUP BY e.EventID, e.EventName, e.StartDate, e.Fees
GO
 /* create the _EventWorkers view by joining two views and a table*/
CREATE VIEW dbo._EventWorkers
AS SELECT DISTINCT e.EmpID, e.Name, s.Event_Name, s.Total_Sales
FROM _EmployeeList e JOIN TblWorkAssignment w ON e.EmpID = w.PersonID
                     JOIN _EventSales s ON w.EventID = s.Event_ID
GO
/* display the contents of the _EventWorkers second-level view */
SELECT Event_Name, Name, Total_Sales from _EventWorkers
ORDER BY Event_Name, Name
```

Figure 12-6 shows the execution plan from the SELECT statement that displays the contents of the second-level view called _EventWorkers. Even though the input to the view _EventWorkers is two views that are in themselves created from a total of five tables, the result set from _EventWorkers is created from a four-table join: tblPerson, tblWorkAssignment, tblEvent, and tblSale. The SQL Server Query Optimizer is quick enough to figure out that adding tblEmployee into this mix would gain nothing, as it's determining the _EventWorkers result set without referring to the previously created view definitions. This four-table join is executed in response to the SELECT ... FROM _EventWorkers, each time the SELECT is issued.

If you were to drop one of the first-level views (such as _EmployeeList), just like the behavior we talked about earlier with parent tables, the second-level view _EventWorkers would not be impacted. However, the next time you try to access data by using _EventWorkers, you'll get an error message at runtime: "invalid object name." Again, this is a backward compatibility issue, to allow you to drop a "parent" view and re-create it with a different definition before the ALTER VIEW command was added.

MODIFYING DATA THROUGH A VIEW

You can update, insert, and delete records through views, but you must follow a few rules and realize some limitations on what you can do. Obviously you cannot change any value in a parent table that you cannot see in the view. Taking that one step further, to be

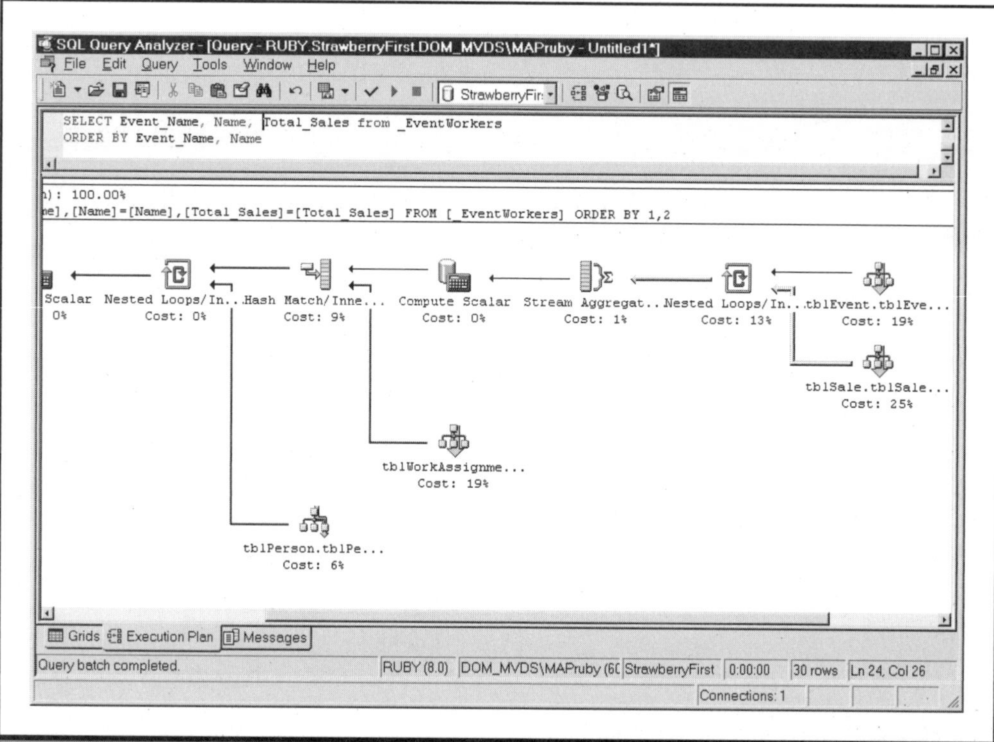

Figure 12-6. You can create a view from a view, but the execution plan for the second-level view still involves a four-table join.

selective with the updates and deletes, you should always specify a WHERE clause that indicates which rows to change or delete. The column or columns referenced in the WHERE clause must appear in the view. You cannot specify which rows to update or delete based on a column that might be in the table but is not in the view.

On a view built upon a single table, updating and deleting rows is rarely a problem, although for data accuracy reasons you'll want to be able to see and use the primary key values of these rows. Updates are possible only in the columns visible in the view. For columns that have been hidden from you (not included in the view), you have no way of supplying values.

Inserting rows may pose a greater challenge to you, however. You can insert a row if 1) columns are automatically populated on the INSERT command via the autonumbering feature of the identity property or by default values; 2) columns allow NULLs; or 3) you provide date values in the INSERT statement. You cannot insert a row if it has one or more

NOT NULL columns that have not been included in the view, and if SQL Server is not set up to supply values for these columns, either by using defaults or the identity property.

When the view is based on more than one table, modifications become much more complex. SQL Server will not update more than one table at a time with a single update statement, as shown in the following example:

```
/* change the job titles of employees 12 and 15 */
UPDATE _EmployeeList
SET Title = 'Employee-Senior'
WHERE EmpID in (12, 15)
GO
```

In this example and in Figure 12-7, the UPDATE query is modifying only one table. As long as SQL Server can determine which table the updated columns belong to, it can handle an update to a multi-table view. If you need to update more than one table, you can code the update as a multi-step transaction, changing one table at a time. If the view is the basis for a data entry form in VB or Access, for example, you can have the client application call a stored procedure to perform the update at the server, and write the code for that procedure to update the tables in the correct order, one at a time.

It is possible to use the BCP utility to bulk copy data into a view, but the same rules apply to views as about working with multiple tables. BCP will insert into a view only when all the columns involved in the BCP operation are from the same table. Also, when data is bulk copied into a view, NULLs are inserted for undefined columns, even if you have a default value specified for that column.

Non-Updateable Views

There are some operations that you *cannot* do with a view that you *can* do with a table. Some columns you simply cannot update in a view, because the columns are computed from other data and do not exist beyond the view. For example, suppose that you have a payroll system and you want to generate a view that lists employees' year-to-date salary. Year-to-date salary is not stored anywhere in the payroll system, so you know that this column has to be computed by summing all the paychecks so far this year, each time the view is used. If there is an error in one of the rows in the YTD-salary column, it cannot be fixed by updating the view. To fix it, you have to go back to the source table and update the data in the parent column. In the future, it might be possible to conceive of computed columns where you can define logic that will deduce which input value to the computation has changed and roll that back to the source data, but that involves an artificial intelligence component, and you're not quite there yet.

In general, a view will not be updateable if any of the following criteria are met:

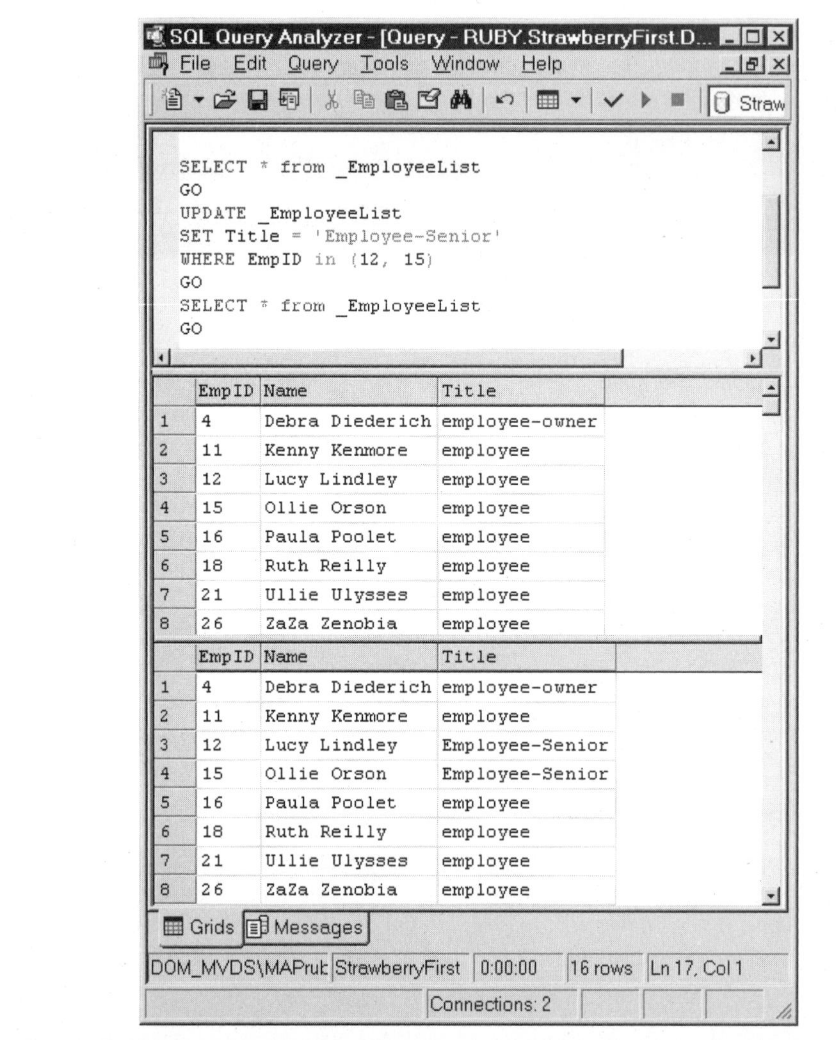

Figure 12-7. You can modify using a view instead of the underlying table, as long as the SQL statement refers to only one table.

- The view was created with a SELECT DISTINCT operator.
- The view was created with a UNION operator.
- The INSERT does not contain all NOT NULL columns of the parent table, or some other mechanism (such as the default or the autonumbering identity property) is not available to populate these columns.

- The UPDATE references multiple tables (assuming the view was created with a join).
- The DELETE references multiple tables (assuming the view was created with a join).

In addition, a column in a view will not be updateable if the column is a computed column.

The WITH CHECK Option

Users can see only data that conforms to the row and column restrictions in the view. So what happens when they enter data, deliberately or accidentally, that does not meet those requirements? The new row could be quite valid as far as the database is concerned, and if so, the INSERT is accepted by the database. But the data entry operator might not have permission to view the new record! For example, say you have an insurance company with offices in both Colorado and California. Someone in the Oakland, California, office, who can see only data where the state is "CA," accidentally types "CO." CO is a valid state code (Colorado), so the row is entered. But the person in Oakland will not see it, because it does not fit within the limits of her view. You know what happens next. She assumes that the computer lost the record and retypes the data. Now you have one customer with the same name, same street address, same city and zip, and two different state codes in the database.

One possible solution to this quandary is to use the WITH CHECK option when you first create the view. This option prevents anyone from entering data that does not meet the requirements of the view. In the preceding example, any attempt to enter data with the wrong state code would be automatically caught and the data entry operator would be prompted to correct the error before the record would be accepted by the database.

But you cannot assume that using the WITH CHECK option will always keep you from storing inaccurate data. Suppose that some records were entered with incorrect data before you instituted these views that segregate user views in different states. A clerk in the Fort Collins office of the insurance company, who can see the Colorado data, spots a record with the state set to Colorado but a California zip code, and attempts to fix the problem. But she cannot, because she is not allowed to enter "CA" for the state code (the WITH CHECK option is turned on). While she is trying to figure out whether to call the California office (which would be a total waste of time anyway, because her counterpart in the California office wouldn't be able to see the record to change it), a customer calls. The customer is moving from Colorado to California and would like his records transferred. Can you begin to see the depth of this problem? The Colorado agent cannot change the address to California. The customer hangs up, thinking he will call the California office after the move. He does so, but the California office cannot see the Colorado record to change it. Frustrated, the customer decides to buy insurance from a competitor. The WITH CHECK option has its uses, but you need to consider carefully your "need to know" policy and how it will impact issues like customer service. You need to allow some employees, perhaps those at the supervisory level, to be able to access the data through a less-restrictive view.

NEW IN SQL 2000: INDEXED VIEWS

Standard views are activated on demand, used, and then discarded. Because data is not stored as part of the standard view, you always get the most current data from the parent tables at the time you run the view. However, when you have the same view being used over and over by multiple users and programs, this is not a very efficient approach. The view may be computing aggregate values or concatenating strings (as in your view _EmployeeList in the previous section) in addition to displaying table data. The aggregate values are being computed every time the view is used. Wouldn't it be nice to be able to keep the view in memory or on disk, and be able to reuse it, and maybe even make a single instance of the view available to more than one user? Of course, SQL Server would need some way of keeping the view current—a live link from the parent table(s) to the view—so, as the table data changes, the view changes as well.

SQL Server 2000 has added the ability to retain views as data sets and build indexes on them so that they can be accessed quickly and efficiently just like any other indexed table. It can even build indexes on computed columns that don't exist in the original tables. You are making a trade-off between additional storage space (which is cheap) and people-time (which is expensive). There's also an additional cost in maintaining these views, the live links. Any change to the parent data is reflected in the view and its indexes.

These permanent views are called "indexed" views. That's because the way you make the view persistent is to build a unique clustered index on the view. We will discuss indexes in more detail in Chapter 16, but as we have mentioned before, a clustered index is one in which the data is physically sorted and stored in the order dictated by the clustering column. The structure has to be a clustered index, and the clustering column has to be unique, because this is the most efficient way for changes to be applied to the correct rows in the view. Once the clustered index is built, you can define other indexes on this view. Not only do these indexes speed up queries on the view, the Query Optimizer can also consider them to see if they would help resolve other queries. In other words, the Query Optimizer adds the indexes built on indexed views as part of its set of tools for resolving queries.

There is a performance benefit when retrieving data with indexed views; but conversely, there is a performance penalty when doing inserts, updates, and deletes. That's because the views need to be kept synchronized with the table data. This requires that each time a change is made to the table, all associated views will need to be updated the same way. In a query-intensive environment, such as a decision-support database or a data warehouse, this penalty may be acceptable. In an online transaction environment, it is going to take stress testing to determine whether the benefits of indexed views will outweigh the performance hit, because there will be a hit.

There are some restrictions on creating an indexed view. These include the following:

- The ANSI NULLS and QUOTED IDENTIFIER options must be on when the view is created, and the ANSI NULLS option must have been on when all base tables were created.
- The view may not reference another view; it must be built directly on the base tables.

- All the tables have to be in the same database and have the same owner.
- The view must be created with the SCHEMABINDING option specified. This option ties the views to the underlying tables, thereby avoiding the problem of the table being dropped and the view left in place. That strategy works for traditional views; but, obviously, it is not going to be possible to drop a table yet keep an indexed view that depends on that table.

The syntax to create an indexed view is as follows:

```
CREATE VIEW _EmployeeList  WITH SCHEMABINDING
AS SELECT p.PersonID, p.LastName, p.FirstName, e.JobTitle
FROM dbo.tblPerson p JOIN dbo.tblEmployee e ON p.PersonID = e.PersonID
GO
CREATE UNIQUE CLUSTERED INDEX IV1 ON _EmployeeList (personID)
GO
```

Notice that the table names must be specified as two-part names—the owner name and the table name—separated by a dot. You create the indexed view with the SCHEMABINDING option, and then you create the index itself in a separate step.

In the final beta version of SQL Server 2000, indexed views were supported only in the Enterprise edition of the product; they were absent from the Standard addition and presumably from all other, more minor editions. SQL Books Online indicates that indexed views were meant to be supported only in the Enterprise edition, even in the released product version of Books Online. However, perhaps because of beta participation feedback and customer pressure, it seems that indexed views are, in fact, now supported in the released-to-market SQL Server 2000 Standard edition! Whatever the reasoning, we applaud Microsoft's decision, because this is a tremendously powerful feature. You can now build indexed views in the Standard edition. Run the preceding code to create the indexed view _EmployeeList, and then look for the view and the index in the Query Analyzer Object Browser.

PARTITIONED VIEWS

SQL Server 7 laid the foundation for distributed databases, and the combination of SQL Server 2000 and Windows 2000 built upon this foundation. It is now possible to have not only a database but even a table spread across two or more servers. The benefits are easy to see: having multiple CPUs crunching the data, and having faster response time on individual queries if the splits are done correctly. As usual, there is a cost, and it comes when you need to query across multiple servers to retrieve a large result set. Your design has to take into account the best way to distribute the data to minimize the overall cost.

When we say that you can partition a table, we're talking about horizontally partitioning a set of records. Several database servers are configured with databases that contain identical table structures, having the same column definitions. Then the data records are spread across the different servers, using some criteria to determine which records belong on each server. Each table has the same column architecture but contains a different set of data. To create identical table structures, you can run the same SQL script to create the tables on each server, or you can copy over the table definitions using Data Transformation Services (DTS). If you had to store the customer list for a major corporation's clients or for contributors to a national-level charity, for example, you might decide to split the list among more than one server.

There's a reason why we decided to introduce the topic of partitioned data here in this chapter on views. Views greatly simplify the handling of partitioned data, at least from the end-user's viewpoint. If views were not available as a programming tool, the client applications would need to have logic added to them to figure out where the requested data resides, and then they would need to have queries specially written to access the data on the appropriate server or servers. In other words, whatever logic you used to partition the data would have to be built into the applications also, allowing them to reverse the effects of the partitioning and collect the data together when all data needs to be retrieved. Worse yet, when you change the partitioning logic, perhaps by distributing the data across four servers instead of three, all your client applications would have to be modified.

With views, you can add a level of abstraction between the client application and the location of the data. Suppose that you had a huge customer table, which we'll call tblPerson. You split it across three servers; and to keep things a little more clear, you renamed the tables as tblPerson1, tblPerson2, and tblPerson3. To join the tables together, you would create a view, using the UNION operator to combine the results. Each server contains a database called Mail_List. You would define a view on Server1, and the code looks like this:

```
CREATE VIEW _Person AS
SELECT * from tblPerson1
UNION ALL
SELECT * from Server2.mail_list.dbo.tblPerson2
UNION ALL
SELECT * from Server3.mail_list. dbo.tblPerson3
```

As mentioned earlier, we start view names with an underscore for sorting purposes. Notice that the code above uses a UNION ALL and not just a UNION operator. The UNION ALL query runs faster than the UNION query because it doesn't have to filter out any duplicate records. UNION ALL instructs SQL Server not to worry about duplicate records when it joins the result sets, because there should be no records that occur more than once. One record shouldn't be in more than one table. If you do encounter this condition, you'd better rethink your partitioning scheme and your applications logic! When you build the partitioned tables, the range of values stored in each table is limited by a CHECK constraint, which we will talk about in Chapter 15. There should be no overlap in record ranges. Your client applications can now treat the view _Person as if it were a single table. If a client sitting on Server1 requests data that is on Server3, Server 1 behind the scenes generates a distributed query that grabs the data from Server3 and returns it to the user on Server1. The same reasoning applies if a client on Server3 requests data from Server1, although they will, of course, have a slightly different version of the view definition, with Server3 as the local server and Servers 1 and 2 as the remote servers.

Using a view, the client applications do not need to know where the data is located or what logic was used to partition it. If you decide to repartition the data—for example, partitioning by geographic region instead of by the client number—the front-end applications will not know the difference if you modify the view. If you change from three servers to four and reallocate the data, the client applications again cannot tell the difference once the view has been adjusted to compensate for the change. And if the view is an updateable view, the client applications cannot tell that _Person is a view, not a table. (Of course, your naming convention might be a giveaway.)

Although SQL Server will handle these distributed queries efficiently, your design should try to minimize the number of distributed queries and maximize the number of queries that can be handled locally. For example, if you have several branch offices around the country, you might choose to split the customer data based on geographic location. If each office handles its own customers from its own region, with little or no overlap, this distribution makes sense. It would not make sense to split this data based on an autonumber customer ID; this would cause each region's customers to be scattered among all the servers. If you have deliberately set up the customer ID to depend on the region in which the customers live, what happens when a customer moves—do you change their identifier value, or do you allow customer ID anomalies? If you allow anomalies, you can't partition by customer ID, and you have to partition by region… and so it goes. We never promised it would be simple. Then there's an issue, no matter which way you partition, of assigning customer identity numbers to the identity column property. Should you allocate different ranges of numbers for each region, or should you go with the GUID, the global universal identifier?

So you decide to partition the _Person table by region. What about other tables? Is the same strategy applicable to all tables in your distributed database? Product inventory might be a good candidate for horizontal partitioning, if you have regional distribution centers. Each region can then query the other regions if they need to cover an out-of-stock situation. On the other hand, the vendor table does not look like a good candidate for partitioning, because each region orders from the same vendors. But if a table is not partitioned, where should it be located? At the head office? On one of their servers? Keep in mind that the list of vendor companies is a table that changes slowly and is probably a lot smaller than your customer or sales tables. The vendor table can be placed on each of the servers. The original version is maintained at the head office, and it is then replicated to each of the other servers. Then, no matter which server a user is connected to, the products table will always be local.

Updateable Partitioned Views

We mentioned that if the partitioned view is updateable, it looks and acts just like a table. SQL Server 7 supports partitioned views; but because it did not have the ability to update partitioned views, they were effectively read-only. SQL Server 2000 added the ability to update partitioned views. SQL Server 2000 also added features to the Query Optimizer, so that it can minimize the amount of data that has to be transferred as the result of distributed queries. In addition, SQL Server 2000 scales to much larger queries than previous versions could handle. Each of the servers holding part of the partitioned table is known as a *member* server. A group of member servers acting together to respond to a query constitutes what Microsoft calls a *federated database*. No one server is in charge, but all the servers cooperate to provide each other with the requested data, so the client application believes there is a complete copy of all the data on one server, in one table.

PART IV

Programming for Performance

CHAPTER 13

Introduction to Transactions

In an ideal world, you could make changes to your database as needed without worrying about possible conflicts with other users, system failures, disk crashes, power outages, accidental or deliberate data corruption, and all the other dangers that exist in the real world. But because you are in the real world, you have to be able to recover from situations that might damage the data, corrupt the data values, or even lose the data entirely. The concept of transactions, which is common to all data processing and RDBMSs, allows you to maintain the integrity of your data. When you write scripts, stored procedures, or triggers, you need to keep in mind how best to use transactions to protect your own data but at the same time minimize the impact on other users of the SQL Server.

With a shared data resource, such as a database, many people may be trying to make changes to the same record at the same time. Controlling this potentially chaotic (and dangerous!) situation is one of the many tasks that SQL Server handles. In the next chapter, we'll talk about how the SQL Server operationally handles these concurrency conflicts. However, for the SQL Server to apply its decision-making routines in these conflict situations, it has to know which transactions it is dealing with.

In this chapter, we will look at transactions and how you can control them in your applications. We will look at the transaction log and discuss how the code you write can impact the log. And we will introduce the idea of distributed transactions, which are data updates across multiple servers. Later, in Chapter 19, we'll look at some other approaches to managing distributed data.

WHAT IS A TRANSACTION?

A *transaction* is a logical unit of work and a logical unit of recovery. A transaction is one or more SQL modification statements that must either complete as a unit or not at all. If a transaction is partly complete when a system or processing failure occurs, it is better to remove all traces of the transaction than to leave some of the data changed and some of the data not changed. A transaction has to pass the ACID test. A transaction must be

- **Atomic** All transaction operations must be executed to completion or not at all. It is the responsibility of the database management system to ensure atomicity as described by the program code.
- **Consistent** Each transaction must preserve business data integrity. It is the responsibility of the database programmer to define correctly what constitutes a business transaction. Once defined, the database management system will enforce the definition.
- **Isolated** One transaction cannot interfere with another. This is the responsibility of the database management system, which usually enforces isolation through the use of locks and/or timestamps.
- **Durable** Each transaction must result in a permanent modification to the database. This is the responsibility of both the programmer and the database management system. If the programmer writes the code correctly, the database management system will enforce the code.

The classic example of a transaction is a bank balance transfer: The bank takes $1,000 from your checking account and transfers it to your savings account. Two separate update actions are required for this transaction. The first update debits $1,000 from your checking account. The second update credits $1,000 to your savings account. If the system failed for any reason immediately following the first step, $1,000 would be missing from your checking account, with no corresponding credit to your savings account. To prevent this from happening, the two steps (debit plus credit) are designated as one transaction. So when both steps complete successfully, there are no inconsistencies in the data and the books balance. If something were to happen to the server during the transaction, such as a power failure, so that only part of the transaction was executed, SQL Server would be able to undo that portion of the transaction as it started itself up again.

Whenever the SQL Server service starts, it always goes through a process called *automatic recovery*. It looks through the transaction log to identify any complete transactions that need to be written to disk, and it checks for incomplete transactions that have to be rolled back or undone. There is no way to turn off this automatic recovery process.

Begin Tran, Commit, and Rollback

When you need to link several modification statements into a single transaction, the first thing you have to do is open a transaction with the BEGIN TRANSACTION or BEGIN TRAN command. By default, T-SQL requires that you explicitly state that you are beginning a transaction, and all queries and statements that follow, up to and including the COMMIT statement, are part of that transaction. You can, if you wish, give the transaction a name (for example, BEGIN TRAN UPDATE_EMPS), but the name is really no more than a label to help you keep track of the transaction boundaries in your code. If you supply the same name with the COMMIT statement at the end of the transaction (for example, COMMIT TRAN UPDATE_EMPS), you can quickly pair up the start and end statements for this transaction, making the code self-documenting and a little easier to read.

NOTE: If you *do* label the transaction in the COMMIT statement, you then have to use the longer variation BEGIN TRAN *transaction _name*/COMMIT TRAN *transaction_name*. You can't use just a simple COMMIT.

You'll note that at the beginning of the previous paragraph we said several modification statements are linked together into a single transaction. If at all possible, keep non-modification statements, such as the SELECT statement, outside the boundaries of the transaction. This has everything to do with locking and shared resource availability, which we'll discuss in the next section.

In T-SQL it is possible to nest transactions, so your transaction naming convention will help you track these transactions within a transaction. A BEGIN TRAN statement opens the transaction, but nothing is actually written to the transaction log until the transaction performs an action such as an INSERT, an UPDATE, or a DELETE. After the BEGIN TRAN, you list the T-SQL statements that are the component parts of the transaction. Each level of a nested transaction needs to have its own COMMIT statement. So, in pseudocode, a nested transaction will look like this:

```
BEGIN TRAN OUTER_TRANSACTION
  SQL STATEMENT 1
  SQL STATEMENT 2
      BEGIN TRAN INNER_TRANSACTION
        SQL STATEMENT A
        SQL STATEMENT B
      COMMIT TRAN INNER_TRANSACTION
  SQL STATEMENT 3
  SQL STATEMENT 4
COMMIT TRAN OUTER_TRANSACTION
```

You might want to take note that nested transactions are unique to T-SQL, in its two major dialects: Microsoft SQL Server and Sybase System *x*. And they are not supported by any of the ANSI SQL standards. If you're writing code that is meant to run cross-database platform, you'll want to shy away from nested transactions altogether.

When SQL Server reaches the last step in a transaction, it needs to COMMIT the transaction. Remember that SQL Server first makes all changes to the copy of data in memory, not to the data that's stored on the hard disk. If a record is not available in memory, the appropriate page is read from the hard disk into memory and the changes made to the page in memory. The page is then marked for update, and it's considered a *dirty page*. The SQL statements COMMIT, COMMIT TRAN, and COMMIT TRANSACTION mean that the transaction is written out to the transaction log file. This ensures that the changes to the data in memory are recorded in the transaction log file.

Note that other processes, such as the CHECKPOINT process and the "lazy writer," write changed (dirty) pages in memory to the transaction log file and to the database on disk. Because so many processes are running simultaneously on the server, it is quite possible that some parts of a transaction will have been written to disk before the COMMIT statement is executed. The COMMIT isn't written to the transaction log file until all the modification statements that are part of the transaction have been written to the transaction log file. We will discuss some of these other processes later in this chapter.

For a multi-step transaction (two or more modification statements that make up a transaction), you specify the BEGIN TRAN and COMMIT statements in your code. For a single-step transaction (one modification statement), SQL Server can automatically commit the data modifications. This is SQL Server's default behavior, which can be altered. We will discuss the Implicit Transactions setting, which is the controlling setting for this behavior, shortly. Once the COMMIT statement has been written to the transaction log file, you can rest assured that your data changes are secure. These changes will either be written to the database on disk during the current session, or else, in the event of a system crash, the changes will be written to the database on disk when the SQL Server restarts. The one point of failure that could compromise this operation is if you were to lose the database file(s) *and* the log file because of a major computer failure, flood, fire, earthquake, theft of the computer, meteor strike, or other major disaster. To mitigate some of this potential for disaster, *always* allocate file space for the transaction log file on a physical disk separate from the database files.

When the SQL Server restarts after an unexpected shutdown, any incomplete transactions are rolled back. *Incomplete* in this context means that they were not committed—the COMMIT statement was not recorded on the transaction log file. Parts of the transaction might have been written to the transaction log file and/or to the database on disk; but if this has happened and the corresponding COMMIT is not recorded on the transaction log file, the changes must be undone. You also have another option during any transaction, to undo the changes by coding in a ROLLBACK command, as long as you have not yet committed the transaction. You might have to do this if there is a problem with the transaction, and for some reason a step does not complete, as in the following pseudocode:

```
BEGIN TRAN OUTER_TRANSACTION
  SQL STATEMENT 1
  SQL STATEMENT 2
      BEGIN TRAN INNER_TRANSACTION
        SQL STATEMENT A
        SQL STATEMENT B
        IF SOME_CRITICAL_CONDITION_NOT_MET
        ROLLBACK ELSE
      COMMIT TRAN INNER_TRANSACTION
  SQL STATEMENT 3
  SQL STATEMENT 4
  IF SOME_CRITICAL_CONDITION_NOT_MET
  ROLLBACK TRAN OUTER_TRANSACTION ELSE
COMMIT TRAN OUTER_TRANSACTION
```

Perhaps, in your bank balance transfer example, moving $1,000 out of the checking account works, but the $1,000 cannot be placed into the corresponding savings account because it would take that account over the $100,000 limit for FDIC insurance. The second update is rejected, so the first one must also be rolled back and the $1,000 reinserted into the checking account. On encountering the error in the second update, your transaction would issue a ROLLBACK command, which would undo the first step and terminate the transaction.

As an example from the Strawberry database, let's add a new employee. This means you need to make an entry in the Person table and in the Employee table at the same time. We'll demonstrate how to use nested transactions; how to label transactions; how to declare, assign value to, and use variables; and how to test for a successful operation and, based on the success or failure, either commit or roll back the transactions.

```
BEGIN TRAN A1
-- 1. open the outer transaction and insert a row into the Person
-- table, allowing PersonID value to be assigned automatically
INSERT INTO tblPerson
  (LastName, FirstName, MailingAddr, City, State, Zip, PersonType)
```

```
VALUES
  ('Carter', 'Cecily', '345 Cherry Creek', 'Denver', 'CO', '80001', 'e')
GO
  -- 2. open the nested transaction
  BEGIN TRAN A2
  -- 3. declare variable to hold PersonID value
  DECLARE @pers_id int
  -- 4. initialize @pers_id with the identity value assigned to tblPerson
  SELECT @pers_id = @@identity
  -- 5. execute the insert statement into the Employee table
  INSERT INTO tblEmployee
    (PersonID, JobTitle, SSN, I9onFile, W4onFile, PayAmount, PayPeriod)

VALUES
     (@pers_id, 'employee', '987-65-4321', 'yes', 'yes', 550, 'weekly')
-- 6. test error code, commit or roll back entire transaction
  IF @@ERROR <> 0 ROLLBACK ELSE COMMIT TRAN A2
-- 7. display the results to the screen (remove for production runs)
SELECT * FROM tblPerson WHERE PersonID = @pers_id
SELECT * FROM tblEmployee WHERE PersonID = @pers_id
-- 8. commit outer transaction
COMMIT TRAN A1
```

This example is a little more complex than previous examples, so we'll take it step by step. Step 1, "open the outer transaction and insert a row into the Person table, allowing PersonID value to be assigned automatically," does just what the comment says. As you're using labels, you have to open this transaction with the statement BEGIN TRAN A1. The Person table primary key, PersonID, is an identity datatype that is automatically assigned each time a new row is inserted. This is what happens in this transaction.

Step 2 is "open the nested transaction." We decided to write this as a nested transaction to show you how such a transaction can be set up. In addition, as the Person table has a parent/child relationship with the Employee table, using a nested transaction seems appropriate. Again, because you're using labels, you have to begin the transaction with the longer command BEGIN TRAN A2.

Step 3 is "declare variable to hold PersonID value." We haven't talked about variables yet, but we need to because you really can't write any but the most simple of T-SQL code without using and passing variables. A variable in T-SQL is the same as a variable in any other programming language; it's a dynamically initialized named memory buffer that holds a value or values that are used in processing. The T-SQL naming convention for user-defined variables is an @ sign with a name that is meaningful to you, the programmer. In this case, we've defined a variable, @PERS_ID. When you define a variable, you also need to assign it a datatype, indicating what kind of data can occupy the memory buffer. @PERS_ID is an integer datatype; therefore, only whole numbers (not characters, dates, or fractions) can be stored in this variable memory buffer.

Step 4 is "initialize @PERS_ID with the identity value assigned to tblPerson." To capture the identity value that was assigned to the row you just inserted into the Person table in the outer transaction, you're going to use the system-defined variable @@IDENTITY. This variable contains the last identity value assigned for a user session. So, if, in the outer transaction, you had inserted a row into the Person table and immediately inserted a row into a second table that also had an identity datatype, @@IDENTITY would contain the identity value inserted into the second table. Each user session (you log on, I log on, that's two user sessions) has its own @@IDENTITY that tracks inserted identity values. Be careful when you use @@IDENTITY. In this case, you did only the one insert into the Person table, so you know that @@IDENTITY contains the value you want to use to populate the PersonID in the Employee table, and you set the value of your user variable @PERS_ID to that of @@IDENTITY.

Step 5, "execute the INSERT statement into the Employee table," does just what it says; it inserts the row into the Employee table, using the variable @PERS_ID in lieu of a scalar value for PersonID. You know that @PERS_ID contains the value that was just inserted into the Person table, so you have synchronized the PersonID values between the Person table and the Employee table.

Step 6 is "test error code, commit or roll back entire transaction." SQL Server returns codes after each operation indicating success, warning, or failure. A zero is a successful completion of the operation; a nonzero value indicates a problem. You should test for nonzero conditions and take appropriate action. You do this by sampling the system-defined variable @@ERROR. Like @@IDENTITY, each user session has its own @@ERROR variable. If the value of @ERRCODE is not equal to (<>) zero, you roll back the entire INSERT operation and end the procedure, or else you COMMIT the INSERT into the Employee table.

Step 7 is "display the results to the screen (remove for production runs)." This is a test and development step only, so that you, the programmer, can confirm that the inserts you've just done are, in fact, correct. Remove or comment out the SELECT statements for production.

Step 8 is "commit outer transaction." If the operation makes it past the check of @@ERROR in the nested query, you COMMIT the INSERT into the Person table.

INTRODUCTION TO LOCKING

There's an entire chapter coming up on locking (Chapter 14), but we need to say a bit about this topic because locking and transactions are so intimately connected. SQL Server's default locking behavior prevents users from changing records that are being updated—in other words, records that are involved in a transaction.

In the bank balance transfer example, checking account records are modified first, and then the saving account records are modified. Until you have finished all the steps in the transaction, both checking and savings account records are locked against updates by a user other than the initiator of the transaction (you). More than one person should not be updating the same record at the same time, or you risk one person overwriting the changes made by another person.

Modification operations need to be serialized, or single-threaded, to ensure that data integrity is maintained. The longer and more complex your transaction, the more records will be locked and for a longer period of time, so the impact on other users will be more noticeable. They may see reduced response times or even have their queries and updates time out if your transaction is too long-running. So when you're writing transaction code, be cognizant of how much work you define in a transaction.

Try to keep SELECT statements outside the boundaries of a transaction, because even a SELECT requires a form of lock on the records selected that could easily interfere with other retrieval and modification operations. Consider how you would structure an operation that needed to update each row in a table. Writing a transaction that updates and commits one row at a time might make your program run longer, but it will minimize the impact on the other users of the system. Writing a program that updates all the rows of a table within a single transaction might get the job done faster if you are the only user on the database. This job will request a lock on the entire table, and, once it gets the lock, it will hold it until it has finished with the updates and has committed the changes. If something were to go wrong near the end of this process, SQL Server might have to roll back all the changes it made! That would keep the table locked for an even longer period of time and greatly diminish the capability to share the data involved in the transaction.

In the next chapter, we will return to the topic of locking and look at some of the locking strategies available to the T-SQL programmer. In the meantime, remember the rules: keep your transactions as limited as possible without compromising the business data integrity, and try to keep SELECT statements outside the transaction code.

THE TRANSACTION LOG

A transaction log is a file that is an integral part of any relational database. All transactions are written to the transaction log before they are written to the database file. In the SQL Server environment, every change to both system and user tables is written to the log. By reading through the log, the SQL Server can re-create the sequence of changes to its environment if it needs to. Along with the change instructions, data is also written to the log. For an update operation, the entry contains images of the before and after versions of the data record. For an insert operation, the entry is only the new record—the after-image; there is no before-image. For a delete operation, the entry is the record deleted—the before-image only, because there is no after-image. Because the log contains these images of changed records, it enables the SQL Server to roll back or undo changes in the event of a system crash. It also allows the administrator to restore the data, including all the recent changes, if there is a disk failure and the database records are lost or damaged.

There are some exceptions to the statement that every change is written to the log, because SQL Server supports several non-logged operations, such as the BCP program, the TRUNCATE command, and the SELECT INTO command. But even these non-logged operations may end up being logged, depending on the level of restore capability you elect. If you select the full-recovery option, all operations on the database are fully logged, even those just mentioned that normally are not. You will be able to recover any loss to the database *as long as the log file is undamaged*. This option imposes an extra load on the SQL Server, both in writing to the log and in the storage required for the log.

The bulk-logged recovery option is not as resource intensive for the SQL Server, as it performs a minimal amount of logging. Instead of storing the entire content of an inserted row, it stores only a reference to the row and a description of what the operation was. Then when you back up the log to disk or tape, it grabs the row out of the database and backs it up along with the instructions stored in the log. Should the system fail, you can then reapply this log entry that contains the data and the instructions and recover the data as it was before the crash. SQL Server includes other useful backup options, including the differential backup scheme introduced in SQL Server 7.0. For a complete discussion of the flexible backup and restore options for SQL Server 2000, you'll want to consult a book on the administration of SQL Server.

The transaction log is always stored in a separate file or files that have the extension .ldf, and the log is in its own file group. When you first create a database, it will have at least one .ldf log file. As we said when talking about creating databases, the log files should be on a separate physical disk or disks, for both safety and performance reasons. Ideally, whatever disks the log files are located on should also be mirrored. SQL Server mirroring was discontinued with version 7, so to mirror the .ldf files you'll have to use Windows NT mirroring, RAID, or some other external scheme.

In SQL Server 6.5 and earlier, the log was a table in the database, and you could select from it like any other table. It didn't help to be able to do so, as the entries were not in a format that was easily interpreted. Now that the log is in a separate file, it is not possible to look at it using a query. Because it's no longer a table in the database, the log has its own optimized internal format, so it is not readable with conventional tools. The log has its own cache that is handled separately from the data cache, again allowing for optimal handling of the log file pages.

Checkpoints

Most of the time, a checkpoint is something that happens automatically behind the scenes in SQL Server. But it is possible to call for a checkpoint in your program, if you have an administrative login, so it helps to know what a checkpoint does and what the implications are of calling a checkpoint in a script or procedure.

A checkpoint is a way of synchronizing all the disparate pieces that constitute a database. We mentioned, when talking about the COMMIT, that a COMMIT means changed data pages are written to the transaction log file. That takes care of the log, but the changes also have to be written to the database. As part of a checkpoint operation, all of the changed data pages are written out, first to the transaction log file and then to the database. Note that *all the changed pages*, not just those that are part of committed transactions, are written out. A checkpoint synchronizes the pages in memory with the pages on the hard disks. So it is quite possible that changes for current transactions will be written out to the disk at a checkpoint, especially those that belong to long-running transactions, even though those transactions have not yet been committed. If something happens to make these transactions roll back, the changed pages have to be backed out of the database. This means extra work for the SQL Server.

From a programming point of view, once the transaction is committed—that is, written to the transaction log file—it will be written to the database. As long as the database administrator is taking care of regular backups, and the logs are on different disks from the user data files, there should be no problem with data loss. Checkpoints happen frequently enough that changes to data will be written to the database shortly after they occur. The busier the SQL Server is, the more often it makes sure that the changed pages are written out to the database. If it is not very busy, it is possible that a changed page could wait for minutes or even hours before being written out to disk.

By default, the checkpoint process wakes up every minute and looks to see how much work it has to do. If there are lots of changes, it issues a checkpoint command. If there's not much to be done, it decides that it can put off doing anything until the next time and goes back to sleep (sounds like some people we know). It decides whether to get to work or hit the snooze button based on the recovery interval. The recovery interval is the time it takes per database for the server to recover from a sudden failure, assuming the hardware is undamaged and still operational. The default recovery interval is one minute per database. If you allow a longer recovery interval, SQL Server can afford to build up a bigger backlog of changes that have not yet been written to the database. In that case, it checkpoints less often. If the administrator sets a shorter recovery interval, SQL Server knows it needs to minimize the number of changes not yet written out to the database, so it does more frequent checkpoints.

The impact of a checkpoint on the users is minimal. If the checkpoints are frequent, the amount of data written each time is not large, so the number of pages locked are few. If the checkpoints are infrequent, it is because the server is not busy, so again the impact is minimal, even though the number of locked pages increase. With a longer recovery interval, the number of log and data pages written each time there is a checkpoint will increase, but the impact to the user community should still be slight. A checkpoint typically takes about a second to complete.

A question for the program developer is, "have you made some changes that are critical enough to warrant a checkpoint in the code?" Usually there is no need for a checkpoint, no matter what kind of data changes you've made. However, when you make system changes, such as structural changes to the tables, you might want to consider adding a checkpoint to your code. Permission to execute a checkpoint belongs to the sysadmin, db_owner, and db_backupoperator roles and is not transferable. That is, permission to execute a checkpoint cannot be granted to any other user role.

SQL Server issues checkpoints automatically, following certain operations such as SP_DBOPTION and server shutdown. Also, SQL Server will automatically checkpoint if the Truncate Log On Checkpoint option is set to True and an alter database statement is executed, or if some non-logged operation such as BCP, TRUNCATE TABLE, or SELECT INTO is run.

Even in moderately busy production databases, including a checkpoint as a normal part of your scripts or stored procedures may not only be overkill, it may have a negative impact on the server. The checkpoint in a script applies to the entire database, not just to those changes that happen as a result of the script. If everyone included checkpoints in their code, it is quite possible that the database may be checkpointing more often than necessary and wasting time by doing so. However, if you do feel that you have performed some critical operation that alters the database structure and you want to checkpoint it, then after the transactions are done, add the command CHECKPOINT to your code.

The Lazy Writer and Worker Threads

We mentioned that other processes might write out changed pages to the disk, even before a commit has been reached in a transaction or a checkpoint issued. Windows NT and Windows 2000 have active *worker threads*, which scan the data cache and look for dirty pages (that is, changed pages) and write them out to disk. The idea is to keep the data cache available for incoming data, so by clearing out all the dirty pages, use of the data cache can be optimized. The worker threads can perform this task in the interval between when they schedule an asynchronous read and when that task completes, so they are using what would normally be idle time to do some housekeeping tasks (we could use a few worker threads around here, we can assure you…). One of the benefits is that checkpoints can be done less frequently because fewer changed pages still need to be written to the disk, so it's less work for the checkpoint process to do.

The *lazy writer* is a thread that wakes up at intervals and looks at the data cache. In particular, it looks at the number of free buffers in the data cache that can be used for incoming data. Not only does SQL Server read data into the cache as it is needed, it also tries to anticipate or predict what will be needed next (a form of pre-fetch or read-ahead processing), so the lazy writer keeps moving changed pages out of cache whenever the amount of free space falls below a certain level. If SQL Server is installed on Windows 95/98, neither of which does asynchronous writes with worker threads, the lazy writer does most of the work of freeing up cache space and writing dirty pages.

Although all these processes are responsible for writing data to the disk files, there's a difference in their purposes. The worker threads and the lazy writer make sure that free space is available in the data cache. The checkpoint operation is there to synchronize the database environment and ensure that changes do get written to the disk at some point.

Savepoints

It is possible to designate a point in your transaction code as a *savepoint*. A savepoint is an interim point—a milestone, if you will—in a transaction. It is also a way to enforce partial rollbacks. A savepoint can be defined with a name so that, later in the transaction, you can roll back to the savepoint. The transaction, which has been interrupted only temporarily, can then continue on from the savepoint. This introduces an extra level of complexity into the transaction. Obviously, you wouldn't normally put something in your code and then deliberately undo it. For savepoint logic, you would typically check with an IF condition to decide whether to let the changes stand or roll them back. If the changes are valid, the transaction is processed all the way through from start to finish. If, for any reason, the changes are canceled, none of the instructions between the savepoint and the rollback are applied to the data. This does undermine the concept of a transaction being an all-or-nothing operation, so it is totally up to the database programmer to properly define the transaction boundaries so that the integrity of the data is retained.

One situation in which Microsoft suggests that the savepoint might be useful is when you have a slow connection between the client application and the SQL Server, and the rollback to the savepoint happens infrequently. The idea is that, instead of running a check first to make sure that your transaction will run successfully, you just run the transaction and then test for the returned error code. If errors occur, roll back the transaction.

The following example uses pseudocode to illustrate what happens with a savepoint in the code:

```
BEGIN TRAN A1
     SQL STATEMENT 1
     SQL STATEMENT 2
         SAVE TRAN SAVE1
     SQL STATEMENT 3
     SQL STATEMENT 4
         IF (test condition fails) THEN ROLLBACK SAVE1
     SQL STATEMENT 5
     SQL STATEMENT 6
COMMIT TRAN A1
```

In this scenario, SQL statements 1, 2, 3, and 4 are executed. Then if the test condition fails, the rollback removes the changes made by SQL statements 3 and 4. It then continues on with SQL statements 5 and 6 and COMMITs the changes. So in some cases the affected records will have SQL statements 1 through 6 applied, and in some cases only statements 1, 2, 5, and 6.

Another possible scenario is that you check for SQL statements 3 and 4 running correctly, and if they do not, then and only then would you run statements 5 and 6:

```
BEGIN TRAN
     SQL STATEMENT 1
     SQL STATEMENT 2
         SAVE TRAN SAVE1
     SQL STATEMENT 3
     SQL STATEMENT 4
  IF (test condition fails) THEN
      BEGIN
        ROLLBACK TRAN SAVE1
        RETURN
      END
  ELSE
     SQL STATEMENT 5
     SQL STATEMENT 6
COMMIT
```

In this example, SQL statements 1 and 2 might insert information about a new customer. Statements 3 and 4 are placing an entry in the orders table and updating inventory. But if the inventory update fails because the item is out of stock, the IF condition, checking for errors, evaluates to true. The order is rolled back, but the customer information is retained. If the item ordered is in stock, the rollback does not take place and statements 5 and 6 generate invoice and shipping information. The ELSE is really not needed, but it makes the pseudocode a lot easier to read.

The following is code you can use to demonstrate to yourself how the savepoint works:

```
/**** #1 ******/
-- connect to the Pubs database
USE Pubs
GO
-- begin a transaction
BEGIN TRAN
  -- make changes to two rows in the AUTHORS table
  UPDATE authors   SET AU_LNAME = 'BLACK' WHERE AU_LNAME = 'WHITE'
  UPDATE authors   SET AU_LNAME = 'BLUE' WHERE AU_LNAME = 'GREEN'
-- now view the changes to confirm that they were made correctly
SELECT * FROM AUTHORS
/***** #2 *****/
    -- establish a savepoint (SAVE1)
    SAVE TRAN SAVE1
  -- modify two more rows from the AUTHORS table
  UPDATE authors   SET AU_LNAME = 'BENT' WHERE AU_LNAME = 'STRAIGHT'
  UPDATE authors   SET AU_LNAME = 'BORING' WHERE AU_LNAME = 'DULL'
-- and view the changes to confirm that they were made correctly
SELECT * FROM AUTHORS
/***** #3 *****/
    -- now roll back the changes made after savepoint SAVE1
    ROLLBACK TRAN SAVE1
-- and view the table to confirm that the changes were undone
SELECT * FROM AUTHORS
/***** #4 *****/
  -- change two more rows
  UPDATE authors   SET AU_LNAME = 'HOOD' WHERE AU_LNAME = 'LOCKSLEY'
  UPDATE authors   SET AU_LNAME = 'HASHIMOTO' WHERE AU_LNAME = 'YOKOMOTO'
-- now commit the changes
COMMIT
-- and view the table to see which of the changes were saved
SELECT * FROM AUTHORS
/***** #5 *****/
--Reset the changed rows back to the original values
```

```
BEGIN TRAN
  UPDATE authors   SET AU_LNAME = 'White' WHERE AU_LNAME = 'BLACK'
  UPDATE authors   SET AU_LNAME = 'Green' WHERE AU_LNAME = 'BLUE'
  UPDATE authors   SET AU_LNAME = 'Locksley' WHERE AU_LNAME = 'HOOD'
  UPDATE authors   SET AU_LNAME = 'Yokomoto' WHERE AU_LNAME = 'HASHIMOTO'
COMMIT
SELECT * FROM AUTHORS
```

For best viewing, you should run the code in sections, each section being indicated by a /***** *#n* *****/ line, rather than all at once. Section 1 connects to the Pubs database, which you should have available on your SQL Server. This database is built as part of the installation process and is typically used for testing programs and program behavior. In Section 1 you make the first changes, and you UPDATE a pair of rows from the Authors table and view the changes, without having committed these changes. The SELECT statement is, obviously, not something you would include in a production transaction because of the additional overhead of locking and unlocking records. We're using it in this code as a means of quality control, to ensure that our modification statements did what we thought they should do. You would do something like this while you're developing and testing your code. Then, before releasing the code to production, you'll want to remove or comment out the SELECT statements that are used for quality control.

At the beginning of Section 2, you establish a savepoint with the SAVE TRAN command, and then you update a second pair of rows and view them to make sure the changes are correct. In Section 3, the fun begins—you roll back the changes you've just made in Section 2, all the way to the savepoint you've just established. Then you view the results to confirm that the second pair of rows that were modified in Section 2 have, indeed, had those changes undone.

Now, in Section 4, you're changing a third pair of rows, but this time you're going to COMMIT the changes. When you view the table, which pair of row changes do you expect to see? That's right, the first pair and the third pair. The second pair of row changes was rolled back.

NESTING TRANSACTIONS

You can nest transactions within other transactions, as you saw earlier in this chapter. The caveat: Nested transactions are indigenous to T-SQL. They're not supported by other RDBMS platforms, so don't use these if you're writing cross-platform or transportable code.

SQL Server has a function, @@TRANCOUNT, that shows you how deep you are in the nesting scheme. Each BEGIN TRAN statement increments the @@TRANCOUNT counter by one, and each COMMIT decrements it by one. However, nesting transactions is really only useful for organizing your code into manageable steps for programming. Once you have begun a transaction, nothing is actually committed until the final COMMIT is executed, which is another way of saying that nothing is committed until @@TRANCOUNT reaches zero. Furthermore, you cannot COMMIT the entire transaction from within a nested transaction. Even if you specify the outer transaction name in the inner COMMIT statement, it's just ignored. A COMMIT in an inner transaction really does nothing more than decrease @@TRANCOUNT by one.

A rollback, in the absence of a savepoint, cannot take a name other than the name of the outermost transaction. If a rollback with no transaction name occurs anywhere, regardless of the level of nesting, it rolls back the entire transaction all the way to the top. The same is true of a rollback that names the outermost transaction. You cannot begin a nested transaction, get several levels deep into the nesting, and then roll back a single level of nesting. The only exception is if you had named a savepoint; then you can roll back to the savepoint.

IMPLICIT TRANSACTIONS

We mentioned that SQL Server will automatically commit a single-step instruction, and that is actually the server's default behavior. When you run an UPDATE statement, for example, there is an implied BEGIN TRAN in front of the UPDATE command and an implied COMMIT TRAN after it. You cannot roll back this UPDATE.

This behavior differs from some other RDBMSs, such as Oracle, which allows you to issue an UPDATE command that can be followed by a ROLLBACK. The reason you can do this is that these RDBMSs open a transaction with the first SQL statement issued following a COMMIT or ROLLBACK, and keep it open until the next COMMIT or ROLLBACK. They do not automatically add a COMMIT to the command; you have to do it in your code. Should you forget to COMMIT your changes, the default behavior is to COMMIT for you when you close your SQL session or end the program. However, if your session or program is abruptly terminated (disconnected), or the system crashes before you finish, your changes will vanish, because these are uncommitted changes and they will be automatically rolled back. This is the ANSI standard behavior. Once the ANSI-compliant database management software has opened a transaction, it keeps adding subsequent commands to the same transaction until you issue a COMMIT or ROLLBACK. It does not keep opening new transactions for every command, as does the implicit transaction we described at the beginning of this section. As an analogy, think of SQL Server default behavior as a fast-food burger shack where you pay for your meal as you get it. If you go back for extra fries, a second drink, or a dessert, you pay for each of these when you get them. The ANSI behavior is more like a sit-down restaurant. You order the soup, and they start a bill for your table. As you order more courses, they are added to the bill, and finally you pay at the end of the meal.

You can change the behavior of SQL Server so that it follows the ANSI standard. Be careful about the syntax here because Microsoft has once again redefined reality and coined a confusing naming convention for the commands. First, the default behavior where every command stands alone and is committed as soon as it completes (normally termed *implicit transactions* in the non-Microsoft world) is now referred to as *auto-commit mode*. If you want to switch to the ANSI standard behavior, you run this command:

```
set implicit transactions on
```

This can be really confusing, because most people think that the default behavior, with SQL Server handling the BEGIN TRAN and COMMITs automatically, would mean that each command was implicitly a transaction. Microsoft says that this is not so, that setting this IMPLICIT TRANSACTIONS option on causes a transaction to be opened and kept open, and that is an implicit transaction. And (are you ready for this?), when you open a Microsoft "implicit" transaction, it has to be closed *explicitly* with a COMMIT or ROLLBACK. When this IMPLICIT TRANSACTIONS option is set to the ANSI standard, Books Online states that "If the connection is already in an open transaction, the statements do not start a new transaction." That is not quite correct. When SQL Server executes the first command after IMPLICIT TRANSACTIONS is turned on, it implicitly opens a transaction and sets the @@TRANCOUNT value to 1. Then SQL Server executes the first UPDATE statement, increases the @@TRANCOUNT value to 2, executes the instructions, and follows up with an implicit COMMIT. This COMMIT has no real effect on saving data, because it's a nested transaction. However, it does set @@TRANCOUNT back to 1. The main transaction is still open, and nothing will be committed until it closes. Each subsequent modification command does the same thing—initiates a nested query, bumping @@TRANCOUNT to 2 in the process, auto-committing, and dropping @@TRANCOUNT back to 1.

If you had a way of capturing @@TRANCOUNT during each command, you would see this happening. It so happens that we did just that. We built a little table with an identity column and a second, integer column. Then we started inserting the current value of @@TRANCOUNT into the integer column, so we could see what the value is right in the middle of a transaction. Understand that this is not something you would normally do, but to satisfy our unbounded curiosity, we *had* to do this. (If you had just spent months locked away in a small room, working on a SQL Server book, you might think this was interesting, too.)

In the following code, we set up some nested transactions using the auto-commit default behavior and tracking the value of @@TRANCOUNT. Then we turn IMPLICIT TRANSACTIONS ON and repeat the transaction set, again tracking the value of @@TRANCOUNT. Then, at the end, we switch back to the default behavior, because we really don't like the ANSI standard behavior at all. This code is best viewed by running each section (indicated by /***** #*n* *****/) separately:

```
/***** #1 *****/
-- Make sure that implicit transactions are turned off
-- build the test table
-- run the first test and observe (use the SELECT) the trancount
SET IMPLICIT_TRANSACTIONS OFF
GO
IF EXISTS (SELECT * FROM dbo.sysobjects WHERE id = object_id('nesttran') )
DROP TABLE nesttran
GO
CREATE TABLE nesttran (id Int IDENTITY(1,1) NOT NULL , transcount INT )
GO
-- begin the transaction tests, "auto-commit" mode
INSERT nesttran          -- implicit open transaction, trancnt=1
```

```
VALUES (@@trancount)      -- inserted values are 1,1 in SS7, 1,2 in SS2000
                          -- auto-commit closes transaction, trancnt=0
GO
SELECT * FROM nesttran WHERE id = 1      -- display results from test#1
SELECT @@trancount                       -- display @@trancount value

/***** #2 *****/
-- begin second test, transaction explicitly declared
-- using BEGIN TRAN and COMMIT
BEGIN TRAN              -- set transcount=1
INSERT nesttran         -- insert opens nested transaction, trancnt= 2
VALUES (@@trancount)    -- inserted values are 2,2
                        -- auto-commit closes transaction, trancnt=1
COMMIT                  -- commit closes transaction, trancnt=0
GO
SELECT * FROM nesttran WHERE id = 2  -- display test #2
SELECT @@trancount                   -- display @@trancount value

/***** #3 *****/
-- begin third test, nested transaction explicitly committed
BEGIN TRAN                -- begin tran sets trancnt=1
 BEGIN TRAN               -- begin tran sets trancnt=2
  INSERT nesttran         -- insert opens transaction, trancnt=3
  VALUES (@@trancount)    -- inserted values are 3, 3
                          -- auto-commit closes transaction, trancnt=2
  SELECT @@trancount
 COMMIT                   -- close inner transaction, trancnt=1
SELECT @@trancount
COMMIT                    -- closes outer transaction, trancnt=0
GO
SELECT * FROM nesttran WHERE id = 3   -- display test#3
SELECT @@trancount                    -- display value of @@trancount

/***** #4 *****/
-- set ANSI implicit transactions on, begin test #4 (a repeat of #1)
SET IMPLICIT_TRANSACTIONS ON
GO
                        -- first operation opens a transaction, trancnt=1
INSERT nesttran         -- insert opens nested transaction, trancnt=2
VALUES (@@trancount)    --    inserted values are 4, 2
                        -- auto-commit closes nested transaction, trancnt=1
COMMIT                  -- commit closes transaction, trancnt=0
GO
SELECT @@trancount
SELECT * FROM nesttran  -- any operation opens a transaction, trancnt=1
WHERE id = 4
SELECT @@trancount
COMMIT                  --  commit closes transaction, trancnt=0
SELECT @@trancount
```

```
GO

/***** #5 *****/
-- begin test #5 (a variant of #2 and #3)
INSERT nesttran      --  any operation opens a transaction, trancnt=1
VALUES (@@trancount) --  insert begins nested transaction, trancnt=2
                     --     inserted values are 5,2
                     --  auto-commit closes transaction, trancnt=1
BEGIN TRAN            --  begin transaction, set trancnt=2
 INSERT nesttran      --  insert opens new transaction, trancnt=3
 VALUES (@@trancount) --     inserted values are 6,3
                      --  auto-commit closes transaction, trancnt=2
 COMMIT               --  commit closes transaction, trancnt=1
COMMIT                --  commit closes transaction, trancnt=0
GO
SELECT @@trancount    -- display latest @@trancount value
SELECT * FROM nesttran  -- SELECT opens transaction, trancnt=1
 WHERE id = 5 or id = 6
SELECT @@trancount
COMMIT                  --  commit closes transaction, trancnt=0
SELECT @@trancount      -- display latest @@trancount value
/***** #7 *****/
--  reset the server to its default behavior
SET IMPLICIT_TRANSACTIONS OFF
DROP TABLE nesttran
GO
```

DISTRIBUTED TRANSACTIONS

As your SQL Server database grows larger and larger, you may have to split it across more than one server. In another scenario, you may find that you're trying to integrate multiple databases, created for various reasons by different departments, while bringing some measure of consistency to them. In either scenario, you'll find that you need to write transactions that update tables located on more than one server. For example, you might have a new employee who has to be added to the personnel department database and also to the payroll database in the accounting department. These two records should be inserted together, as they constitute a business transaction; otherwise, you might have an employee who is not being paid, or someone who is taking home a paycheck but is not officially an employee. Obviously, the two updates should be treated as a single SQL transaction, so that if either modification fails, the other is rolled back.

A transaction on one server, even across two different databases, is not that complex, because one SQL Server instance is controlling the reads, writes, and record-locking. But when you have a transaction that updates across two instances of SQL Server, the two SQL Servers have to work together to make sure that the transaction proceeds smoothly and completely. The two instances can reside on the same computer, or they can be on separate computers. The instances have to be coordinated, and that task is handled by the Distributed Transaction Coordinator (DTC). The practical definition of a *distributed* transaction is that the transaction affects more than one instance of SQL Server. Actually, technically speaking, a transaction across two or more databases on the same server is a distributed transaction; but the single instance of SQL Server handles it internally without making the user aware of what is happening. It looks to the user like a local transaction. (A local transaction is defined as a transaction against the single database that the user is logged in to.)

The DTC is a service that is installed along with SQL Server and can be automatically started when the server starts, just like SQL Server and the SQL Server Agent. The service can be started and stopped from the Service Manager or from the Support Services section of the Enterprise Manager. DTC needs to be running on only one of the servers involved in a multi-server transaction. Each of the SQL Servers participating in the transaction is referred to as a *resource manager*. The DTC has the role of *transaction manager*. Although it may seem redundant to define these terms, other database management systems can participate in the distributed transaction as either resource or transaction managers. In the personnel/payroll example mentioned, it's quite possible that payroll is actually part of an Oracle Financials installation. Interoperability between RDBMSs is getting better and will continue to do so to the point at which distributed transactions across different products from different vendors will be considered the norm.

When coding a distributed transaction, you designate it with a BEGIN DISTRIBUTED TRAN command, and you end it with a COMMIT, as usual. You cannot nest distributed transactions (as we mentioned earlier in this chapter, only SQL Server and Sybase support nested transactions), but you can nest BEGIN TRAN...COMMIT pairs inside the distributed transaction. You can use one BEGIN TRAN...COMMIT pair for the instructions for each of the servers involved, making the code easier to read. In a distributed transaction, savepoints are not supported, as all RDBMSs do not support savepoints the same way the SQL Server does. The entire transaction must commit or else all changes are rolled back.

When the distributed transaction starts, the DTC keeps track of the various resource managers involved. When the commit point for the entire transaction is reached, the transaction manager has to ensure that all of the resource managers commit, or they all roll back. It does this through a process known as a *two-phase commit*. First, it sends a "prepare to commit" command to each of the resource managers involved in the transaction. At this point, the resource managers have each processed its own portion of the transaction, and upon receiving the "prepare to commit" command, it does whatever is needed to make the transaction durable or permanent—short of committing it. All the memory buffers containing the log images for the transactions are written to the disk. Once each resource manager is ready to commit, it sends a success notification to the transaction manager. If there's a problem with the transaction, the resource manager sends a failure notification to the transaction manager.

Once the transaction manager has received success notifications from each of the resource managers, it sends a COMMIT command to each resource manager. The resource managers complete the COMMIT operations and report back again to the transaction manager. If they all report back as successfully committing their changes, the transaction manager returns a success status notification back to the calling application that initiated this distributed application. However, if any resource manager reports a problem with the "prepare to commit," or fails to report back (implying that it's offline), the transaction manager will instruct every resource manager to roll back its changes. The riskiest part of the process is while everyone is reporting in but before the final commit order is issued, because a network failure at that time would leave some resource managers wondering which way the vote went. They do not know whether they are supposed to commit or roll back. All records affected by the distributed transaction are going to stay locked until the network communications are re-established.

Distributed transactions tend to be expensive, and not just because of the back-and-forth communication among the systems. If any of the servers is down or the network is not available, none of the participants in the transaction can commit any changes. The records remain locked or the changes are rejected, and in the meantime the users cannot get on with their work. In a distributed environment, the computers must be running on uninterruptible power supplies (servers should always be on a UPS, anyway) and backup generators. The network has to be very reliable and highly redundant, with backup strategies to ensure that data can still get through even if part of the network is down. Your client applications have to be written to accommodate the possibility that the transaction might not complete and compensate for such conditions.

You might want to rethink some of the applications that at first glance appear to be good candidates for distribution. For example, when the personnel department adds a new employee, is it really necessary for that employee to be entered into the payroll database at exactly the same time? And will the people in the personnel department put up with not being able to add a new employee to their database just because the network is having problems? You need to examine several alternative strategies when considering distributed applications.

One alternative approach to the question of adding new employee records to two databases would be to have the payroll database send a query to the personnel database, requesting a list of all the new employees added to the personnel database since the previous time this query was run. You might run this query once a day or once a week, perhaps just before running the payroll for that week. This is still a distributed transaction, although now the payroll server would be the transaction manager and it would send the query over to the personnel server. Of course, if the network is down and you cannot update the payroll tables (and subsequently print the paychecks), you might have a few upset employees. Another possible solution is to implement a replication strategy. With replication from the personnel database to the payroll database, new or modified employee records would be copied from the personnel database to the payroll database on a scheduled basis. The scheduled copy operation can be set to happen every few minutes, or the timing can be modified to run once a day—it depends on the level of replication required. Then, if the network is down for a while, the people in the personnel office can keep making changes that will be sent to payroll as soon as the network comes back up.

Long-Running Transactions

When coding transactions, you should try to make the transaction as efficient as possible. This includes not just the resources used by the transaction, but you also need to consider the impact on other users of the database and data resources. A long-running transaction can lock records or tables and prevent other users from doing their jobs. Another effect of a long-running transaction is that it may cause the transaction log to fill up. The transaction log file cannot be truncated as long as there is an open transaction. When the administrator runs a backup of the transaction log to disk or tape, the log would normally be truncated, and inactive transactions—those that have been written to the database and to the transaction log backup file—would be discarded. This frees up the space in the log for the next round of transactions. The truncate process, though, can truncate only up to the first entry for the oldest active transaction. It cannot remove entries for any transaction that might commit or might roll back—active transactions. Nor can it sort through the transaction log, discarding entries for inactive transactions and retaining entries for active transactions.

As an analogy, think about what happens when you write a check. Writing a check is like opening a transaction. When the check is deposited, the transaction is committed. Even though the changes have not shown up in your bank account yet, it is only a question of when, not if, the changes will be made. A checkpoint is like balancing your checkbook. You enter all the checks you have written recently, including some that have been deposited by the recipient and some that have not. Now let's suppose that each month, you archive the transactions from the previous month. It doesn't matter whether this archiving is on paper or in electronic form—the idea is the same. You want to reconcile your checkbook, perhaps retire the current paper register, and move on. But there's an outstanding check from six months ago! You cannot archive the checks since that time, as you don't know what is happening with this outstanding check. This is especially true of electronic checking systems in which the software does not understand a command to "archive everything older than 60 days except for this one check." So you have to make a choice: not archive the account, or decide that the check is not coming back and cancel it.

The same logic applies to a long-running transaction. At some point, it may cause the transaction log file to fill up. Even if the database has the Truncate Log On Checkpoint option turned on, to avoid the log filling up, SQL Server still cannot truncate past the start of the oldest active transaction—just as you couldn't archive the transactions because of one outstanding check. So, in fact, even with the Truncate Log On Checkpoint option set to True, a SQL Server transaction log can fill up. If this happens, the database administrator may have to dump the log file. This will kill the long-running transaction, forcing a loss of all the changes made thus far. And, to further inconvenience users, when the database administrator dumps the log file under these circumstances, the recommended procedure to follow is to do a full offline backup of the database.

Guidelines for Transactions

There are a few steps you can take to avoid the problems associated with long-running transactions. All these suggestions will minimize record locking and avoid possible violations of data integrity.

You should never include any user interaction inside a transaction, such as returning values to the calling application and waiting for the user to make a choice. While this is tricky to do with T-SQL alone, you can imagine a transaction being passed from a Visual Basic application interacting with a user in this way. You'll find that you have to write code to handle violations of data integrity and possible incomplete transactions when the client session is interrupted, like when the user steps away from the computer to go to lunch.

Try to do as much error checking on the parameters for the transaction on the front end as possible. We'll be looking at stored procedures in Chapter 17, but for now, let's just say that within a stored procedure, you should first check to make sure that all the parameters passed to the procedure are valid and consistent before you send them to the server for processing. This approach will minimize the number of transactions that will have to be rolled back.

A frequent cause of long-running transactions is when someone does a major modification to all the rows in a table. Suppose that you are running an import/export business, similar to the Northwind Traders sample database. Every night you update all of your prices for every item based on the foreign currency exchange rate for the country of origin for that item. If you open a transaction and then start the update operations, the entire table will be locked until you are through. If there is a problem with the update process, all of the changes will have to be rolled back. Murphy's Law being what it is, if a problem arises, it will be with an item from Zimbabwe, not from Antigua. So to minimize the impact on your co-workers, you might break down this large update into a series of smaller transactions.

If you're designing a database for a client, you may want to ask them about the difference in these two approaches. It may be that the client prefers to update the table all at once when the users are not busy on the system. In this case, a table lock is a better choice for this method than individual record locking, as the total time the records will spend being locked is far less than the individual record method. So you'll want to consider setting up this job to run during off–prime-time hours.

Updating the entire table at one time, or individual records one at a time, also raises the question of consistency. If the update process starts and it takes five minutes to complete, and a customer places an order two minutes into the job, do they get the old price or do they get the new one? If your process applies a table lock, you know that the customer (when they finally get a response from the system) will be quoted the new price. If you are updating record by record, you'll have a hard time telling which price the customer was quoted until the order invoice is generated.

Moving the data into a data warehouse, you might be faced with the same problem as the transaction update, if you assume that an order placed on a certain date was billed at a certain rate for that date. There are pros and cons about a transaction that does a full table lock versus one that initiates row locking; as usual, you need to understand the business requirements in order to make the right choice. You may be able to craft a compromise. If you start a transaction that locks the table, that will prevent inconsistencies. Then you can perform the updates using small groups of records for each nested transaction, establishing savepoints to avoid a full rollback in the case of a system problem. We'll look at locking strategies in the next chapter.

CHAPTER 14

Locking

One of the reasons you're implementing a SQL Server solution is because you want to make data readily available to the people who need it. You also want to make sure that all users see the same version of the data. Both objectives can be met by storing one copy of the data where all users can access it.

The benefits of keeping one centralized copy of data are well understood, but the database management system must take some precautions to avoid conflicts when two or more people try to update the same data at the same time. SQL Server uses locks to avoid this type of problem, and it helps in your design and implementation strategy to know when to let SQL Server handle the contention between users and when to give it an assist. It also helps to look at how users are accessing the database and to understand what the optimum strategy for preventing them from interfering with each other's updates might be, while maximizing throughput for everyone.

Some sort of conflict management is done by nearly every RDBMS. Conflict management, also called *concurrency control,* is implemented by one of two general types of concurrency protocols (ways of handling the conflict situation): by locking records or by time stamping records. Some RDBMSs even use a combination of these two schemes, and SQL Server, when front-ended by ODBC or OLE DB applications, does just that. In this chapter, we're going to look at SQL Server locking techniques. We'll also discuss how to make SQL Server behave more like an Oracle database, for those readers who are more comfortable with the approach taken by Oracle.

Databases have to balance concurrency (record availability) with the potential for user conflicts and rollbacks. To optimize for one means to sacrifice the other. Along these lines, databases can apply locks either *pessimistically* or *optimistically*. Pessimistic locking means that the database management system will lock resources with the first operation—even a SELECT statement—that accesses data. The assumption here is that the possibility of user contention and associated rollbacks is high, so to avoid this SQL Server sacrifices some concurrency. Optimistic locking works in the opposite vein, on the assumption that user contention is low and the possibility of rollbacks is correspondingly low, so it won't lock a record until the instant of the actual change operation. In an optimistic locking environment, concurrency is high, but the database will have the occasional rollback to deal with.

POTENTIAL PROBLEMS ADDRESSED BY LOCKING

If each database had only one user, you wouldn't have this problem of concurrency control. Unfortunately, because a database is a shared resource, concurrency control protocols come with the package! It might help you understand concurrency to look at some of the classic conflict situations that can arise in the absence of concurrency controls. These scenarios are known as the *lost update*, the *uncommitted dependency*, and the *inconsistent analysis*.

The Lost Update (Overwriting Updates)

If two users modify the same record at the same time, and each of them commits the modification and writes the record to the database, in the absence of concurrency control the second update will overwrite the first. Although the first user believes that her transaction finished because the application returned a successful completion message, when she looks at the record it will show the updates made by the second user. The second user updated just after the first user, so the most current update wins. To prevent this happening, the RDBMS must lock the record so that only one person at a time can update a record.

The Uncommitted Dependency (Dirty Reads)

Under normal circumstances, when a user is updating records in a table, the records will be locked so nobody else can update them. What happens if someone is just interested in *reading* the data? As the update queries are being executed, the pages in memory are simultaneously being changed. Could someone else read those pages and see the records before the changes are committed? The default SQL Server behavior doesn't allow this, although there is a way to change that. The assumption is that because it may be possible for the first user's updates to be rolled back, the second user will not want to see inaccurate data. The ability for the second user to view data that is in the process of change, which may or may not be saved to the database, is called a *dirty read*.

For example, suppose that ten cases of widgets are in stock, and a customer is placing an order for eight of them with one of your sales associates. While the sales associate is entering this order, you get a call from a second customer for six cases of the same widgets. When you check the quantity on hand, you see that the supply of widgets is now down to two cases. The reorder point is five, so you order another ten cases from the manufacturer. You sell two cases to your customer and register a backorder for another four cases to be shipped to your customer when they arrive. But hold on—now the sales associate finds that her customer's credit is shaky, so the sale is deferred and the first order for eight cases is rolled back. Now what have you got? There are still ten cases of widgets in the warehouse and another ten coming in from the manufacturer. You have a very irate warehouse manager who has to find room for all these widgets. You have a boss who wants to know why you are ordering more of an item that is already in stock, spending the company's money on items that don't need to be resupplied. And you have to explain why you only shipped two cases of widgets to your customer and have four cases on backorder, despite a warehouse full of the things! You got yourself into trouble because you made a decision based on uncommitted data. This is exactly the sort of situation that SQL Server is set up to avoid by default. Its locking mechanism prevents you from seeing records until they have been committed. If you recall, *committed* means that the changes have been written to the transaction log file, but not necessarily to the database. However, once the changes are committed, you can read the updated pages in memory.

The Inconsistent Analysis (Unrepeatable Reads and Phantom Records)

The inconsistent analysis is going to be a problem if you have to query the data twice within a single transaction, and you cannot have any changed or missing records between the first select and the second select. If this is a high-activity data set, with you and many others making changes to the data, you would expect to find differences between the same record sets when they're read and reread, even if the two reads happened in rapid succession. You have an unrepeatable read situation on your hands.

An unrepeatable read situation can be described succinctly (paraphrasing from the ANSI SQL-92 Standard): Transaction 1 reads a record. Transaction 2 reads the same record and modifies or deletes it before Transaction 1 can COMMIT. If Transaction 1 were to reread the record, it would get different data. The read cannot be repeated, in that the result set returned the second time is different from the first result set. In the case of the record DELETE by Transaction 2, Transaction 1 might even get no rows returned when it rereads!

A phantom read is a little different. Transaction 1 reads a group of records that meet some criteria in the WHERE clause. The criteria doesn't have to be a range of values; it can designate a set of discrete values. Transaction 2 does an INSERT or an UPDATE, which adds rows to this group of records. Now, the same query reissued by Transaction 1 will return more records than the first time it was run. These additional records returned are called phantom records.

The only way to ensure identical sets of data records is to lock the data at the very beginning of the process, so that when the select is run a second time, the results will be the same. This does not necessarily mean locking the table, but it does mean locking the rows that meet the requirements of the SELECT query or, in the case of avoiding phantom reads, locking the entire extent of records so that none can be inserted into the range of records involved in this operation. If the query affects a large number of rows, the impact on the other users will be significant. For example, if you ran a query with a WHERE clause that restricts data based on STATE = 'TX', none of the Texas records can be changed until you have read the data for the second time. This may adversely impact concurrency in the database and frustrate your user community.

Here's another example of an unrepeatable read that leads to an inconsistent analysis: You need to compute the percentage of your customers in each zip code in the United States. You start with 100,000 customers. In zip code 00012 are 270 customers, or 0.27 percent. By the time the calculation reaches zip code 99998, with 140 customers, someone has modified the customer table so that now it shows 275 customers in zip code 00012, plus the total number of customers in the database has risen to 100,020. Now, should you divide the 140 by 100,000 or by 100,020? Should you return to zip code 00012 and recalculate the percentage? If you divide each zip code by the total number of rows, the total number of rows is changing, so the results are not internally consistent. If you asked for a count of the number of rows at the beginning of this process and used it as a fixed variable for each calculation, the results for the higher zip codes will be slightly off. This is an inconsistent analysis of the highest order.

One possible approach to making the numbers right is to lock the entire customer table while performing the calculations, so that no changes can be made and the results are guaranteed consistent. But that approach would have a negative impact on the sales staff who are trying to add new customers. In this case, locking the table would not be the practical solution. Requiring that a read be repeatable is a serious restriction in a multiuser database.

If a repeatable read is what you need, you as the database administrator are caught in the classic conflict between data entry people, who want fast response time on data modifications, and data analysts, who need to run large queries that sometimes involve entire tables in the database. The best way to resolve this conflict is to eliminate it altogether by giving the data analysts their own copy of the data to work with. You can implement this concept simply by making copies of the tables and putting them where your data analysts can access them. You could replicate the database so that it is relatively up to date (snapshot replications every hour) and always available to the analysts. You could replicate to another database on the same server or a different server—and if you are thinking "replicate to a server on a different planet," you must have seen this type of conflict before. We'll look at replication in more detail in Chapter 19, but for now, we will mention that the replicated database can contain the same data as the source or a subset of the data, but it can have completely different indexes, locking, and security settings.

SQL SERVER LOCKS

SQL Server uses an elegant locking scheme traditionally known as *multiple granularity concurrency protocol*. It can lock user data at four different levels: the table, the extent (eight pages of 8K each), the page, and the record, and it can lock both individual index keys and ranges of keys. SQL Server 7.0 onward has had the ability to lock at the row level, the page level, or the table level. This is a significant improvement over version 6.5 and earlier in which row-level locking was not an option, and the page was locked even if only one row on that page was being modified. Understand that row-level locking is not always an improvement over page-level locking. The advantage is in the capability of SQL Server to dynamically adjust locking to the optimum level for any given situation. This is a giant step forward for SQL Server.

A little history here: Prior to SQL Server 7, Microsoft used to endure a lot of criticism for not having row-level locking. Much of the criticism was based simply on the fact that Oracle had row-level locking and had had it for years. Now let's review a situation: You've written a procedure that will update a large number of rows in a table. What is more efficient, locking 100,000 rows or locking 5,000 pages? Locks have to be managed (by the Lock Manager, no less!). Each lock is an entry in the lock table in the Master database. These locks have to be added and then removed when no longer needed. It'll take fewer resources (less work) to lock 5,000 pages than to manage 100,000 rows, obviously, but it is also more likely that, under this scenario, there will be more conflicts with other users of the data. In the past, SQL Server was optimized "out of the factory" to minimize lock management, with the idea that if the locks were applied and released quickly, and programmers wrote transactions that requested locks on just a few records at a time, that would in itself minimize concurrency contention.

That was a good idea for its time, but it limited SQL Server in its ability to scale. Now we're in a new era, and the good news is that SQL Server can do more than elect to lock at the row level or the page level. It can actually adjust the locks while a transaction is in progress, depending on the demands made by other processes on the data.

SQL Server can also lock index pages. This makes sense, because index pages are read and modified just the same as data pages, and the same considerations apply to index pages about not changing values when they are being modified by someone else. However, while you might think it's a good or necessary idea to be able to influence the locking strategy on tables or pages, locking on indexes is something you're going to have to leave to the SQL Server. Still, it's worth keeping in mind that indexes can and will be locked as the data entry staff adds and modifies records, and that locking might account for delays in queries run by the analysts. It's yet one more reason why, for online transaction processing (OLTP), you should have as few indexes as possible on the data.

SQL Server has several types of locks—or lock modes, as they are called in Books Online. These are share, update, exclusive, intent, and schema. These locks are applied at different levels, as we'll discuss in a moment. The various locks interact with each other so that, for example, two different users can each have share locks on the same record at the same time, but only one user can have an exclusive lock on a record at any time. Also, an exclusive lock cannot be obtained if the record already has a share lock on it—no surprises there.

Table 14-1 is a lock decision table. A picture is worth a thousand words, and with one look you can determine which locks peaceably coexist and which ones will be in a state of contention. You read the lock table from the viewpoint of a transaction. For instance, if Transaction 1 has a share lock on a resource (row/page/table), can Transaction 2 obtain a share lock? Yes. Can Transaction 2 obtain an update lock? No. Can Transaction 2 obtain an intent lock? Yes. An exclusive lock? No. And so on.

Now let's take a closer look at each of these lock modes.

Share Locks

By default, SQL Server places share locks on resources (rows/pages/tables) that are SELECTed. The share lock is acquired when a transaction is reading the data (SELECT) but not updating it. As the name implies, share locks can coexist with other locks, especially other share locks. Multiple transactions can each request a share lock on the same resource, as indicated by Table 14-1. A share lock won't interfere with another share lock, so there's no problem with other transactions reading the same records. However, a share lock can block other locks. As long as one transaction has a share lock on a record, no other transaction (unless it happens to be the one that already has the share lock) can get an exclusive lock on the same record. Because a transaction needs an exclusive lock on a record to change the record, the data will remain unchanged until the last transaction that has a share lock on the record has completed, and the share lock is released.

Locks are held as short a time as necessary. A share lock is held only long enough to read the row or page. For example, if SQL Server is scanning a table, it drops the share lock on that page just after it has acquired a share lock on the subsequent page, so as to impact concurrency as little as possible.

Trans 2

Trans 1	Share Lock	Update Lock	Exclusive Lock	Intent Share	Intent Exclusive Lock	Share with Intent Exclusive Lock	Schema Stability Lock	Schema Modification Lock	Bulk Update Lock
Share Lock	Yes	Yes	No	Yes	No	No	Yes	No	No
Update Lock	Yes	No	No	Yes	No	No	Yes	No	No
Exclusive Lock	No	No	No	No	No	No	Yes	No	No
Intent Share	Yes	Yes	No	Yes	Yes	Yes	Yes	No	No
Intent Exclusive Lock	No	No	No	Yes	Yes	No	Yes	No	No
Shared with Intent Exclusive Lock	No	No	No	Yes	No	No	Yes	No	No
Schema Stability Lock	Yes	Yes	Yes	Yes	Yes	Yes	Yes	No	Yes
Schema Modification Lock	No	No	No	No	No	No	No	No	No
Bulk Update Lock	No	No	No	No	No	No	On	On	Yes

Table 14-1. The Lock Mode Decision Table Helps You Determine Which Locks Are Compatible with Which Other Locks

Exclusive Locks

Exclusive locks ensure that only one transaction at a time can update a record, and by default, nobody else can read that record while it is being updated. Other transactions cannot see the changes until they have been committed. Table 14-1 indicates that an exclusive lock is inconsistent with any other lock mode (except the schema stability lock, which we'll explain in a moment). An exclusive lock is held until the end of the transaction, by which time the changes will have been committed. In other words, it is not possible to "read through" an exclusive lock in SQL Server as it is in some other RDBMSs. However, you can change the behavior of SQL Server for a connection, as we will explain a little later.

Update Locks

Update locks are also called *intent locks*. You can think of an update lock as a "read-with-intent-to-update" lock. It's the kind of lock that SQL Server acquires when there is a data modification operation that first needs to search through a table to find the record or records that will be modified. By itself, an update lock isn't enough to allow data changes. Once the record to be modified has been located, the update lock is escalated to an exclusive lock, the change is made, and the exclusive lock is released. As you can see in Table 14-1, only one transaction can hold an update lock on a resource. The update lock blocks other requests for update or exclusive locks on the same resource, although other transactions can acquire share locks on the same resource.

Intent Locks

SQL Server uses intent locks to handle multiple incoming requests for locks and to speed the process of making locking decisions. An intent lock makes a statement that a transaction needs to place a comparable lock at a lower level in the locking hierarchy. For example, an intent exclusive lock at a table level says that a transaction needs to place exclusive locks on certain pages within the table. This would prevent a second transaction from coming in and trying to place an exclusive lock on the entire table. Intent locks help with performance, because the second transaction simply has to look for the presence of the intent exclusive lock on the table, rather than looking to see if all the pages are free of exclusive locks, before it tries to place its exclusive lock on the table.

A problem you may have detected when we were talking about multiple share locks and the conflict with update and exclusive locks is lock *starvation*. For example, if Transaction 1 has a share lock on a record and Transaction 2 needs to update that same record—and, therefore, Transaction 2 needs to place an exclusive lock on that record—Transaction 2 will have to wait until Transaction 1 finishes its read operation and releases the share lock. Transaction 2 acquires an update lock on the record in the meantime. While Transaction 2 is waiting, Transaction 3 also places a share lock on the same record. By the time Transaction 1 has released its share lock, Transaction 4 has requested and is granted a share lock on the aforementioned record, so Transaction 2 still cannot update it. At this rate, you might think that Transaction 2 may never get to update the record in question! It's being "starved."

In versions of SQL Server prior to 7.0, Transaction 2 would have to wait in the queue a little while before it was granted permission to upgrade to an exclusive lock, because share locks took precedence over exclusive locks. The Lock Manager could issue as many as four share locks while Transaction 2 was waiting for its exclusive lock to be granted. Then, to avoid lock starvation, the Lock Manager would block any more requests for share locks on the record in question. Transaction 2's update lock would be escalated to an exclusive lock, the update process could execute, the exclusive lock would then be released, and the blocked share lock requests in a WAIT state would be granted.

The SQL Server 7 and 2000, Lock Managers have changed a little. The precedence of share locks over exclusive locks has diminished. Today, Transaction 2 has to wait only while a single share lock request jumps the queue before it (Transaction 2) gets the go-ahead to upgrade to an exclusive lock.

Schema Locks

SQL Server applies these locks automatically. The Sch-M (schema modification) lock makes sure that no queries or updates are allowed to execute while the table is being modified, such as what would happen if you were adding a column to the table. The Sch-S (schema stability) lock does the opposite: these are applied while compiling queries, so that a table definition cannot be modified while a query is being run. The Sch-S lock is the only lock mode that is compatible with an exclusive lock.

Deadlocks

A deadlock is not a type of lock. It's a condition that arises when two users or processes are updating the same set of records. Each process needs to update a row the other has locked. If neither one will release its lock, potentially both updates could wait indefinitely for the resources to become free. SQL Server detects this problem, selects one of the transactions as a victim, and kills it. The user application must then handle the returned error code 1205 and resubmit its transaction. Actually, the victimized transaction (the one that was killed) needs to reevaluate itself to see whether it is still relevant, because the successful transaction has changed the data and the changes proposed by the killed transaction may no longer be appropriate.

As an example, suppose two travel agents are booking flights. Agent A books seat 12A on the Monday outbound flight, and then wants to book seat 27F on the Friday return flight. However, travel agent B has 27F on Friday locked and wants to book 12A on the Monday flight. If neither one of them is willing to give up the seat they are holding, neither transaction can complete. SQL Server recognizes this within a second or two and will roll back one of the transactions. It'll pick the transaction that takes the least amount of work to roll back, but there's really no way to predict for sure which transaction will get the ax, as there are many factors that influence this decision. In a deadlock resolution situation, the killed transaction will get an error code 1205 and a message stating that the transaction was deadlocked and was chosen as the victim. It doesn't allow the winning transaction to complete and then automatically reapply the killed transaction. Rather, it forces the user of the killed transaction to do a reread of the data to avoid any possible data anomalies. In our travel agent example, after the deadlock resolution in which the second agent's program got the 1205 error code, travel agent A is now holding seats 12A and 27F; these seats are no longer available to travel agent B. Agent B has to do another search for available seats and resubmit the booking request.

One way to avoid this situation would be to impose a rule that says that all updates must be done through stored procedures, and these stored procedures always update tables in a certain order. In the preceding example, you could make a rule that all bookings must be done by seats in chronological order. The travel agent A would book seats 12A and 27F; travel agent B would find these seats already taken and would continue searching for alternative seats. With this rule in place, a deadlock, with its associated costs of killing and rolling back transactions, is much less likely to happen.

In the real world, you may face opposition to implementing such rules, and the arguments against doing so may be valid. Back to the two travel agents, agent A and agent B. Suppose that agent B is dealing with a customer who wants to leave on Sunday and return on Thursday. Agent B books a Sunday departure, but there's nothing available on the return flight on Thursday. So agent B books a return flight on Friday, in seat 27F. Now the customer decides that if she has to return Friday, she's going to shift the outbound flight from Sunday to Monday. So agent B tries to book 12A on the Monday flight, while holding 27F on the Friday flight, and promptly deadlocks with agent A, who had just locked seat 12A-Monday. Because the user application needs maximum flexibility, you sometimes have to live with these situations.

Another design issue that will affect the likelihood of deadlock is the length of your transactions—that is, how long they run. The longer you keep resources locked, the higher the probability that someone else will try to access and lock those same resources. For example, it might not be a good idea to keep the airline seats locked while the travel agent searches for a rental car and hotel rooms. Good application design would mandate that you commit the transaction on the airline seats rather than hold the locks on the data until acceptable hotel rooms are found. If it turns out that no hotel is available, you can release the airline seats. In this case, you have to balance the reduction in lock contention against the possibility that occasionally a customer may be told that no seats are available, yet a minute or two later, seats do become available. That's a business decision you'll have to make, rather than a technical decision.

HOW TO DETECT LOCKING PROBLEMS

Severe locking problems will make themselves apparent with poor response time, timeouts to client applications, and unhappy users. Unfortunately, there's more than one way to create these situations, so you need to be able to pinpoint the cause. If many deadlocks occur, you'll find that users are getting a 1205 error code and that they have to resubmit their transactions.

One of the first places to start looking for deadlocks is in Performance Monitor. When you install SQL Server, it adds new objects to the Windows NT/2000 Performance Monitor that are specific to SQL Server operations, as you can see in Figure 14-1. Each SQL service that's installed or initiated, such as replication, adds even more counters to Performance Monitor.

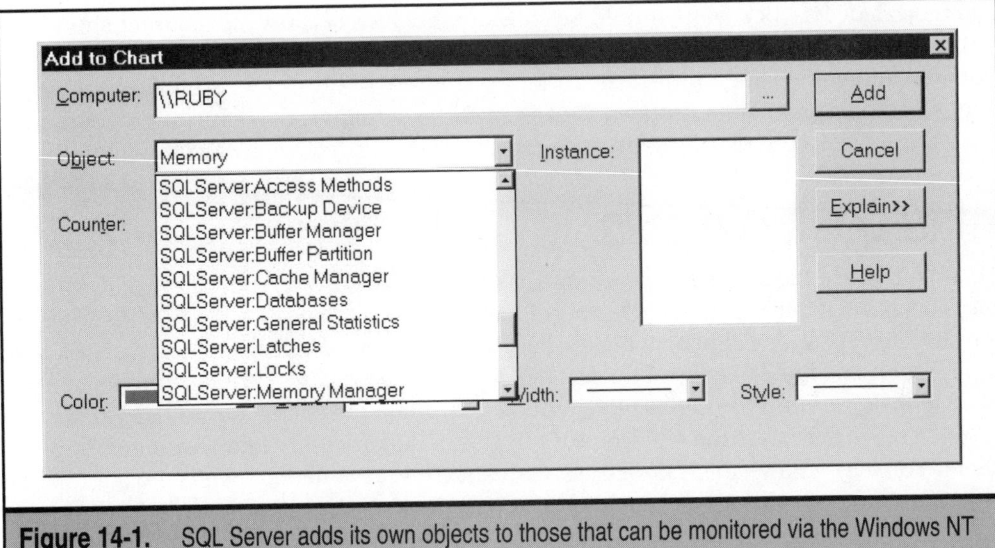

Figure 14-1. SQL Server adds its own objects to those that can be monitored via the Windows NT Performance Monitor.

The counters for SQL Server locks (shown in Figure 14-2) include Lock Requests/sec, Lock Waits/sec, and Number of Deadlocks/sec, among others. In a busy data entry environment, you would expect to see a substantial number of lock requests as data is entered

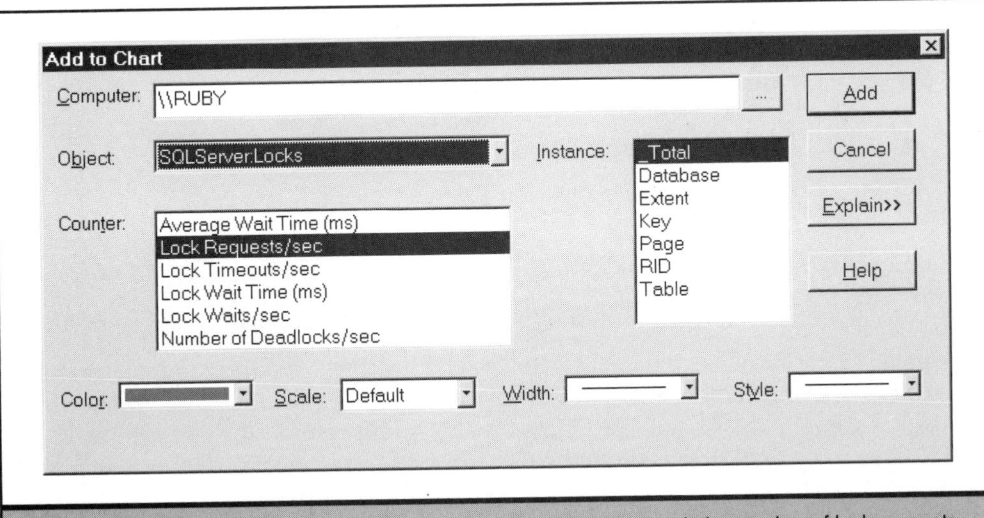

Figure 14-2. The SQL Server lock object counters allow you to track the number of lock requests and the wait times to satisfy these requests.

and modified. The lock waits should be considerably less, because this counter shows the number of lock requests that could not be satisfied immediately, forcing the calling application to wait before being granted the lock. The number of deadlocks occurring should be very small or none at all. If this isn't the case, you need to investigate further to determine what is causing the deadlocking situation, and you need to determine how to alleviate it.

SETTING LOCK OPTIONS

You can modify the SQL Server lock options when you execute your SQL code. Most of the time, it's a better idea to let SQL Server handle the locks, because it can adjust its locking strategy dynamically to provide the best response to multiple users. But there may be times when you need to control the locking for a single process. Perhaps you decide you need to lock the entire Products table while you update the prices. Or perhaps you want to allow users to browse data in a table while it is in the process of being changed by other users. You can achieve these objectives with a technique called *lock hints*. Lock hints are stronger than just hints; they override the normal locking decisions made by SQL Server. Lock hints are supplied with a SELECT or an UPDATE statement.

Suppose that you want to find out what percentage of unit sales is represented by each product. For this query, you don't want users making changes to the sales data while you are doing the calculations, as that would alter the numbers. (Note: Please don't try this on your production server or without the consent of your senior database administrator, as this code can adversely affect SQL Server concurrency!)

```
USE Strawberry
GO
BEGIN TRAN
SELECT  ProductCode, SUM(QuantitySold)AS 'Quantity of product',
    (SELECT SUM(QuantitySold) FROM tblSaleitem) AS 'Total units',
     CONVERT (Decimal (8,3), SUM(QuantitySold)* 100.0) /
          (SELECT SUM(QuantitySold) FROM tblSaleitem) AS 'Percent'
FROM tblSaleItem  WITH (HOLDLOCK)
GROUP BY ProductCode
ORDER BY ProductCode
```

Before you commit this transaction, switch to the Enterprise Manager and expand the hierarchy for the server, and then choose Management | Current Activity. Expand the Locks/Object hierarchy, and you will see hundreds of "key" locks (1,292, to be exact, in our version of the Strawberry database) for the entry Strawberry.dbo.SaleItem, as shown in Figure 14-3. SQL Server is using row-level locking on the SaleItem table of the Strawberry database. ALT-TAB back to the Query Analyzer and commit the transaction.

To see how you can drastically reduce the lock management overhead, change WITH (HOLDLOCK) to WITH (PAGLOCK, HOLDLOCK). WITH (PAGLOCK, HOLDLOCK) instructs the SQL Server to place page-level locks on the data instead of row-level locks. Again, run the transaction but do not commit it. ALT-TAB back to the Enterprise Manager and refresh the

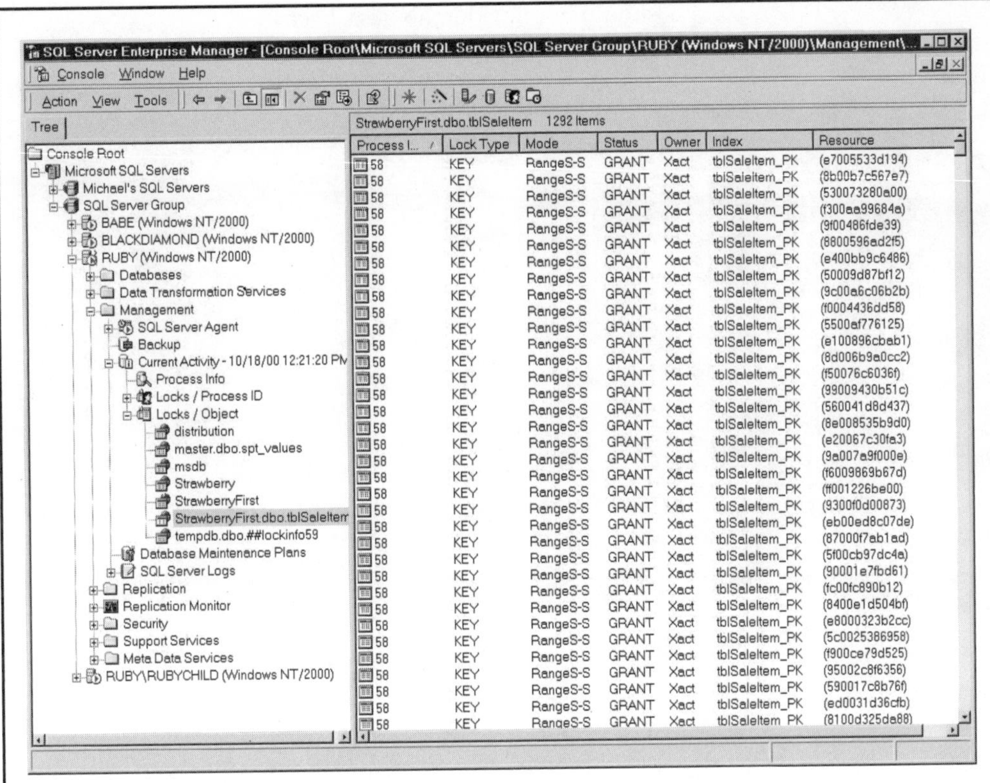

Figure 14-3. The SQL Server Lock Manager window displays the status granted to a process during a transaction.

Current Activity item (highlight Current Activity, right-click, and choose Refresh). You'll have to reopen the hierarchy. (Ironically, even though it is called Current Activity, the display does not automatically refresh itself.) Click to open Locks/Object and highlight Strawberry. Notice far fewer locks for the entry Strawberry.dbo.SaleItem—11 page locks (as you can see in Figure 14-4) as opposed to 1,292 row locks—because you forced page-level locking with the WITH (PAGLOCK, HOLDLOCK) lock hint. ALT-TAB back to the Query Analyzer and commit the transaction.

To reduce the number of locks even further, change WITH (PAGLOCK, HOLDLOCK) to WITH (TABLOCK, HOLDLOCK). Run the transaction a third time. ALT-TAB to Enterprise Manager, refresh Current Activity, and now you'll see only a single table-level lock for the entry Strawberry.dbo.SaleItem, as shown in Figure 14-5. You've minimized the Lock Manager overhead, but you've also managed to minimize the concurrency on the SaleItem table. Go ahead and commit the transaction.

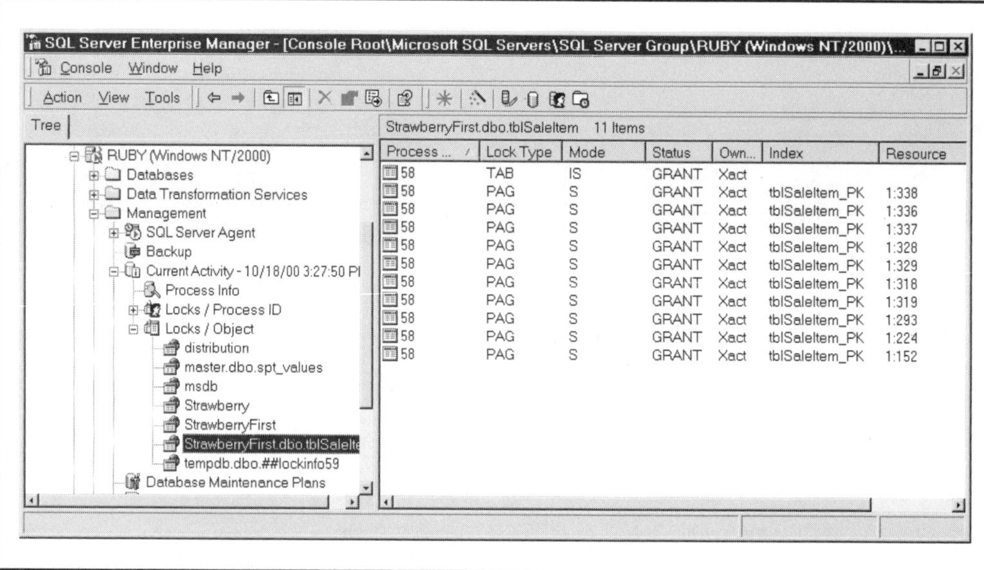

Figure 14-4. You can manually reduce the total number of locks granted per transaction by using the lock hint PAGLOCK.

If you decide that you need to lock a table while performing calculations or making updates, a table-level lock by itself is a lot more efficient than the (TABLOCK, HOLDLOCK) combination. Placing a HOLDLOCK on data instructs the SQL Server to maintain the lock until the COMMIT is executed—a much longer time than is normally needed. You can

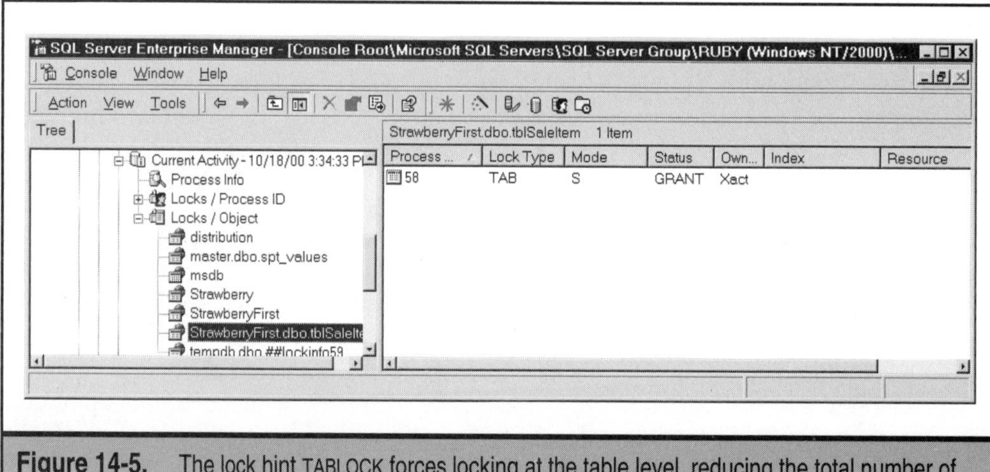

Figure 14-5. The lock hint TABLOCK forces locking at the table level, reducing the total number of locks granted to one, but also reducing concurrency in the database.

negatively impact database concurrency and productivity if you use these lock hints incorrectly or too often; so if you must supply lock hints, make sure that you choose the appropriate one for the job, and try not to use HOLDLOCK at all.

The NOLOCK Option

One lock option we have found very useful is NOLOCK. In our code example, change WITH (TABLOCK, HOLDLOCK) to WITH (NOLOCK). As you can see from Figure 14-6, there isn't even an entry for locks on Strawberry.dbo.SalesItem—no locks, just as you instructed. The single lock you are seeing in Figure 14-6 is the share lock on your StrawberryFirst database. (StrawberryFirst is the master copy of all the Strawberry databases you have scattered around on your network of servers.)

If someone needs to browse the data, with no intent to update, and doesn't really need totally accurate and up-to-date values, this option is one you want to utilize. The NOLOCK option can improve response time for the browsing user because the SQL Server doesn't have to spend any time adding and removing locks, so the query runs faster. It also means that the NOLOCK query will have less impact on other users of the system, because the data readers will not be blocking access to records they might be trying to modify.

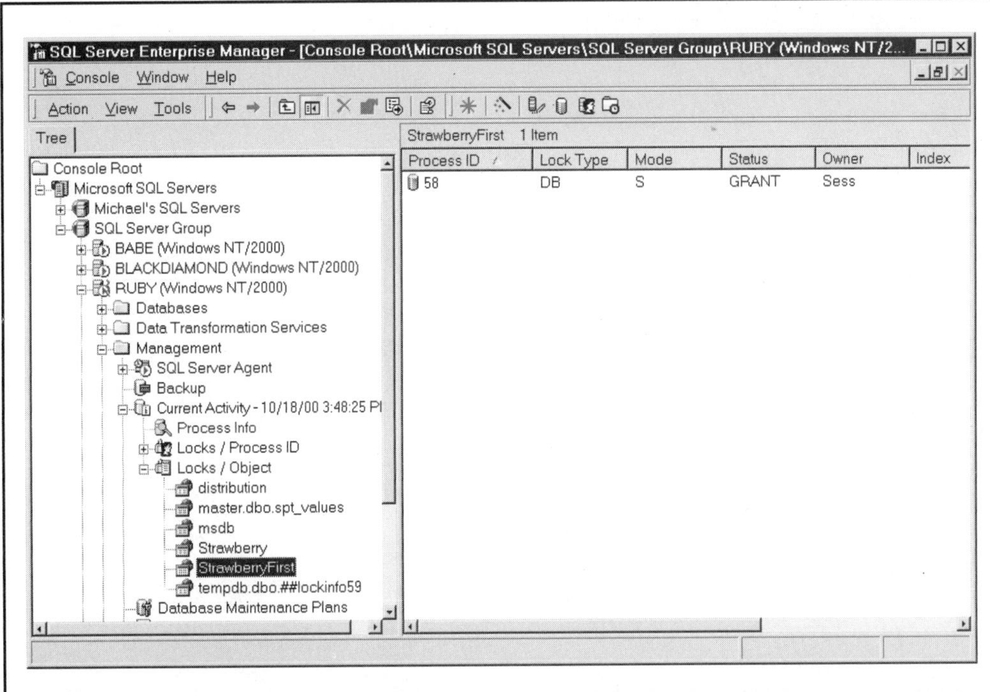

Figure 14-6. The NOLOCK lock hint obviates record, page, and table locks, thus enhancing concurrency within the database.

Transaction Isolation Levels and What to Do About Them

The transaction isolation levels determine how one transaction will be affected by other concurrent transactions from other SQL sessions that are accessing the same data, so that the transactions do not interact or influence each other. The setting of the transaction isolation level determines the locking decisions made by the SQL Server.

By default, SQL Server uses a conservative approach to data sharing. This is sometimes referred to as a pessimistic locking approach because it assumes a worst-case scenario, as we described at the beginning of this chapter. Other relational database management systems, including Oracle, default to optimistic locking. The presumption in an optimistic locking scheme is that most transactions will complete successfully and you will rarely have to roll back a transaction. It is possible to make SQL Server use optimistic locking for individual connections, and we'll look at how that is done in just a moment.

One factor that seems to have a direct influence on whether you should implement pessimistic or optimistic locking is the size of the data set being accessed and the number of users who are actively accessing it. You can categorize use-case scenarios from A to Z, A being a very small data set with lots of data readers and data writers, and Z being a very large data set with few data readers and even fewer data writers. Scenario A will tend to incur lots of conflicts, as many data readers and writers contend over very few records. The probability of rollbacks in this situation is high; therefore, you'd most likely want to use pessimistic locking to mitigate the probability and cost of undoing updates. Scenario Z is a sparsely hit large data set. The few data writers who are making modifications to this data set will most likely never contend with each other; therefore, a rollback is an unlikely event. You can safely use optimistic locking in this kind of environment.

Arguably, the typical Oracle database contains larger data sets than the typical SQL Server database (although with the advent of SQL 7 and SQL 2000, this stereotype is breaking down fast), while the population of data readers and data writers in the two camps are about the same. Proportionately, the ratio of data to user in the Oracle environment is greater than the proportion of data to user in the SQL Server environment. You might be able to draw the conclusion that the optimistic philosophy of locking works for Oracle users, because there is less chance of you bumping into another user while you're working with a data set.

In the SQL Server environment, the decision to implement optimistic or pessimistic locking depends on at least three factors: the potential liability of exposing incorrect, inaccurate, or phantom data to your user community; the probability of a transaction ROLLBACK instead of a COMMIT; and the length of the transactions themselves. The longer a transaction takes to run, the more likely that some other user may need to read the data involved in this transaction. You need to consider who your users are, what type of understanding they have about the data as it is presented, and what they're using the data for. You might want to stay with pessimistic locking for the operator who places the resupply orders to avoid inaccurate inventory counts. But you might go with optimistic locking for a manager who is just browsing through the data looking for trends. As long as the manager understands that the numbers shown are not to be taken as exact values, there's no problem with allowing optimistic locking—also known as "dirty reads" because the pages are marked for update. In fact, there is a benefit to this, because this manager's queries will run faster if they do not have to wait on changed data to be committed. In a volatile and high-transaction environment, using the optimistic locking scheme may be the best way to get quick response for the user.

You can manipulate the locking scheme from pessimistic to optimistic for a user session by using the transaction isolation levels. The transaction isolation–level setting determines the locking decisions made by the SQL Server. The ANSI SQL-92 Standard defines four isolation levels, all of which are supported by SQL Server 2000:

- Read committed (default behavior)
- Read uncommitted
- Repeatable read
- Serializable read

Let's look at each of these transaction isolation levels in detail.

Read Committed (Default)

Read committed is the default behavior for SQL Server, and it translates to pessimistic locking. In this mode, it is not possible to read data that is part of a transaction until the data has been committed. Nonrepeatable reads and phantom reads can still happen, because record inserts, updates, and deletes can be committed by other processes between the first and second read operations.

Read Uncommitted (Dirty Read)

Read uncommitted translates to optimistic locking. It is considered the lowest transaction isolation level of the four, in that the read uncommitted transaction isn't isolated at all from data change operations, even when these operations involve the records being read. Phantom reads and nonrepeatable reads are probable, because this mode essentially acquires no locks.

Repeatable Read

A repeatable read is typically an operation bounded by two SELECT statements, and the two SELECT operations must return the same data set each time. However, while the existing data that satisfies the query cannot change, phantom reads can occur as records are added into the data set between the first and second reads.

Serializable Read

The serializable read is the highest transaction isolation level, which means that it's the most restrictive of the four levels. Transactions are totally isolated from each other. A transaction will lock not only the records it needs to operate on, but also any records that happen to fall within the record range. No new records can be inserted into the range, and no records within the range can be updated or deleted by some other operation.

The transaction isolation level for the SQL Server is read committed. This cannot be changed at the server level, so you cannot make the overall behavior of SQL Server imitate some other RDBMS. You can control the transaction isolation level for a session only. You can do this in scripts, inside a stored procedure, or in your VB code when connecting from Visual Basic or Access applications. Once the level is set for a session, it remains that way until the session is terminated or until you set the transaction isolation level to something different.

To test the effects of the transaction isolation levels, let's make a change to a table and see what happens when another user tries to read the data. First, open a Query Analyzer window and run this code to change the Employee table. The transaction isolation level is read committed—that's the server default. Don't commit the transaction yet; just leave it in limbo. And again, please don't try this on your production system!

```
BEGIN TRAN
UPDATE tblEmployee
SET W4OnFile = 'No'
WHERE PersonID = 11
```

SQL Server's default behavior causes the Employee record to be granted an exclusive lock, as you can see in Figure 14-7. The record with key value 11 is X-locked, exclusively locked. The page that contains the record is IX-locked, intent exclusive, and the table is also IX-locked.

Now open a second window and run a query against the Employee table:

```
SET TRANSACTION ISOLATION LEVEL READ UNCOMMITTED
GO
SELECT * FROM tblEmployee
WHERE PersonID  = 11
```

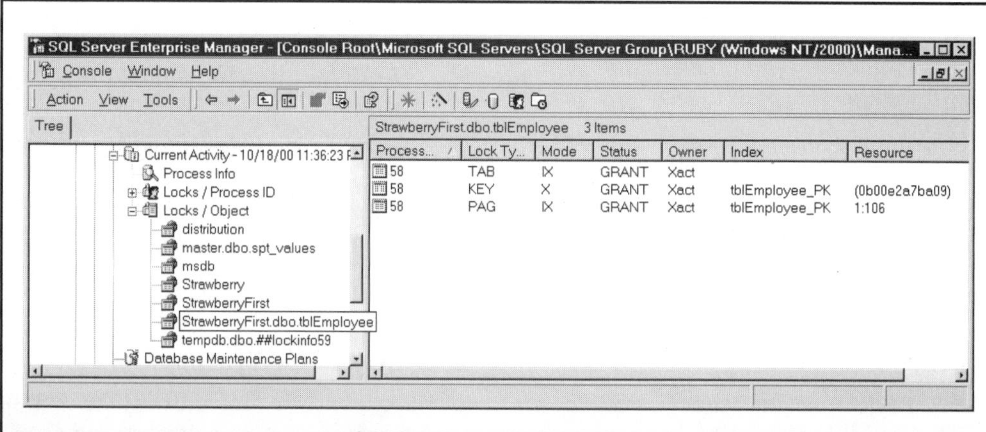

Figure 14-7. The record being modified is immediately granted an X-lock, while the page and table that contain the record are granted IX-locks.

This query will execute because you have set the transaction isolation level to read uncommitted. Figure 14-8 shows the result set, and lo and behold, there is the W4onFile value that the first transaction had changed to "No." You're reading dirty data, because this change has not yet been committed.

If you were to take a look at the lock table after this second query had executed, it would look exactly like Figure 14-7. Remember that a read uncommitted acquires no locks.

Let's try this again. Reset the transaction isolation level to read committed and rerun the second query:

```
SET TRANSACTION ISOLATION LEVEL READ COMMITTED
GO
SELECT * FROM tblEmployee
WHERE PersonID  = 11
```

Did you get a result set? You shouldn't have. The first query is blocking this second query. A blocked query is different from a deadlock, because as soon as you COMMIT or ROLLBACK the first query (the one that changed the value of W4onFile), this query will run. But before you do that, let's look at the lock table.

Figure 14-9 shows what is going on. Process 58 is the update process you saw previously in Figure 14-7. Added to the Lock Manager is Process 62, this last read operation. Notice that the key is waiting to acquire an S-lock, share lock, while the page and the table now also have been granted IS-locks, intent-share locks. This is a typical blocked process.

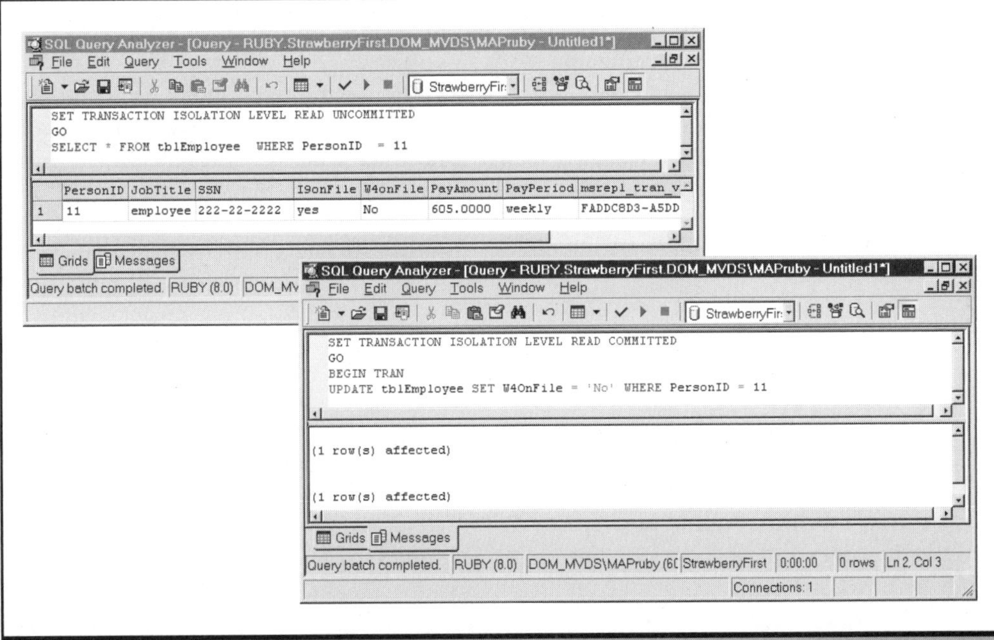

Figure 14-8. Transaction isolation–level read uncommitted allows one process to read data that is being modified.

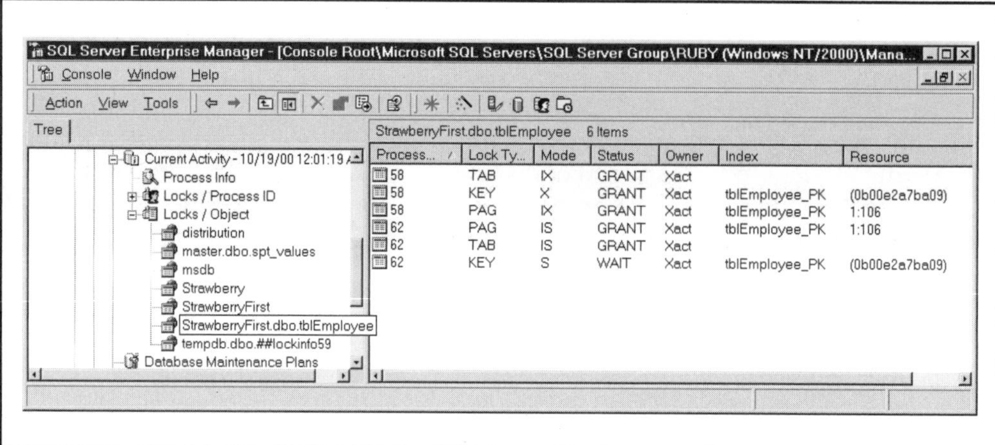

Figure 14-9. Transaction isolation–level read committed will cause a process (62) to wait before it can read data that is being modified.

Okay; you've hung the system long enough. Tile the Query Analyzer windows so you can see the action when you release the bottleneck. In the first Query Analyzer window, execute a ROLLBACK to undo the change, and then watch the action in the second window. Additionally, ALT-TAB to the Enterprise Manager lock table and refresh. All locks for Strawberry.dbo.tblEmployee are gone.

Let's try an exercise that tests concurrency constraints on the system when you use the repeatable read and the serializable read, so you can see how they differ. We'll start with a simple example, and once again you'll need to use the two Query Analyzer windows you should still have open. This following bit of code sets the transaction isolation level to a repeatable read. Then it selects from the Employee table, makes modifications to a range of values in the table, and then rereads the Employee table:

```
SET TRANSACTION ISOLATION LEVEL REPEATABLE READ
GO
BEGIN TRAN
SELECT * FROM tblEmployee
UPDATE tblEmployee
   SET W4onFIle = 'no' WHERE PersonID BETWEEN 15 and 21
SELECT * FROM tblEmployee
```

Run this code in the first Query Analyzer window, as shown in Figure 14-10, but don't commit the transaction. Now, ALT-TAB to the second Query Analyzer window and run this following bit of code, but again, don't commit it:

```
SET TRANSACTION ISOLATION LEVEL READ COMMITTED
GO
BEGIN TRAN
INSERT INTO tblEmployee
```

```
    (PersonID, JobTitle, SSN, I9onFile, W4onFile, PayAmount, PayPeriod)
VALUES (19, 'employee', '000-00-0000', 'yes', 'yes', 650.00, 'weekly')
SELECT * FROM tblEmployee
      WHERE PersonID = 19
```

As you can see in Figure 14-10, this second modification statement works! But, you ask, don't I have the entire range of PersonID values between 15 and 21 locked for update? After all, the UPDATE statement says "SET w4onfile = 'no' WHERE personid BETWEEN 15 AND 21."

When you use the repeatable read transaction isolation level, you do not, in fact, have the range of values locked; you have the individual records that are being updated locked. Figure 14-11 shows the lock table; and sure enough, four keys (records) are X-locked (PersonIDs 15, 16, 18, and 21), while all the rest of the records are S-locked—or share locked. The page and table are both IX-locked, intent exclusive, but neither the share lock nor the intent exclusive lock will block an INSERT. Execute a ROLLBACK in each of the two Query Analyzer windows.

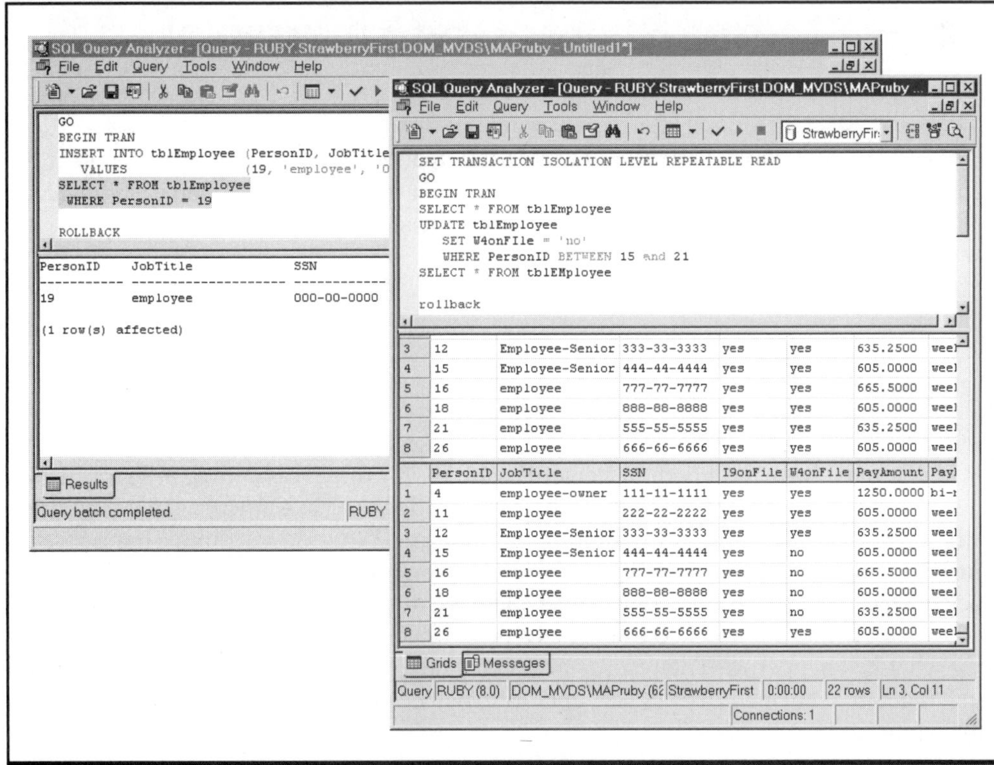

Figure 14-10. Transaction isolation–level repeatable read allows insert concurrency; a process can insert a record into a set, but it cannot change existing records.

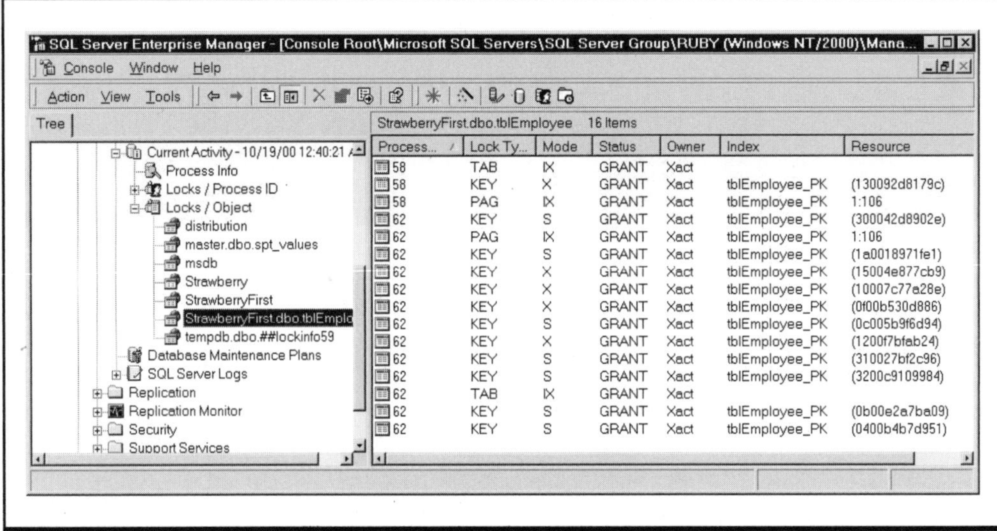

Figure 14-11. The repeatable read isolation level X-locks only the discrete records that are involved in a transaction.

Now let's try this exercise again, but this time you're going to attempt to prevent the second process from inserting record 19. You'll use a serializable transaction isolation level.

In the first Query Analyzer window, change the statement

```
SET TRANSACTION ISOLATION LEVEL REPEATABLE READ
```

to

```
SET TRANSACTION ISOLATION LEVEL SERIALIZABLE
```

and run the code, again without committing the transaction. Again, you should see the values of W4onFile were modified for PersonIDs 15, 16, 18, and 21, as shown in Figure 14-12. Now switch over to the second Query Analyzer window and execute the same bit of code as the previous exercise, again without committing it. What do you think happens this time? As you can surmise from Figure 14-12, nothing happens. The INSERT operation is blocked by the UPDATE operation, because you have mandated that the entire range of values between 15 and 21 be locked exclusively. A quick check of Figure 14-13 shows that's exactly what has happened. The records now have range locks, RangeX-X, exclusive locks, and RangeS-S, share locks. The INSERT operation will be blocked until the UPDATE operation either commits or rolls back.

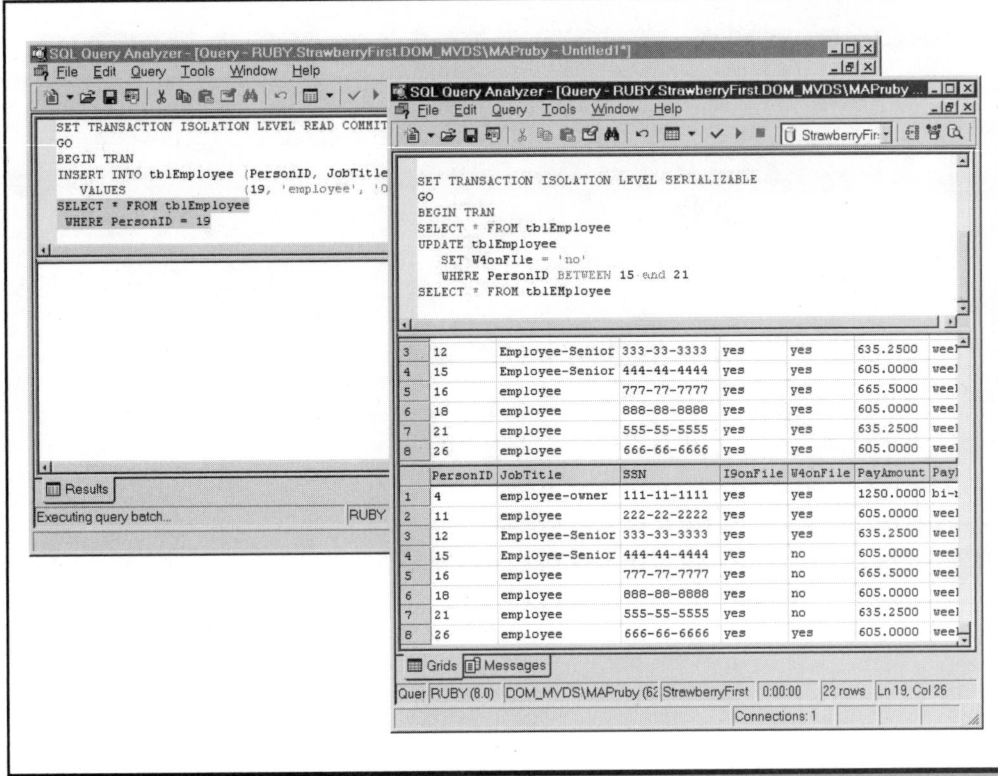

Figure 14-12. Transaction isolation–level serializable blocks an insert attempt; it prevents any process from inserting new records into the range being modified.

As in the previous exercise, arrange the two Query Analyzer windows so you can see what will be happening in both. In the first window (the UPDATE operation), execute a ROLLBACK and watch the action in the second window as the UPDATE operation succeeds. Before you shut down the Query Analyzer windows, execute a ROLLBACK in the second window, to undo the INSERT operation.

SQL Server doesn't provide automated blocked process detection. This is something you'll have to resolve by monitoring the lock table or by writing a stored procedure that periodically reads the lock table and searches for blocked processes.

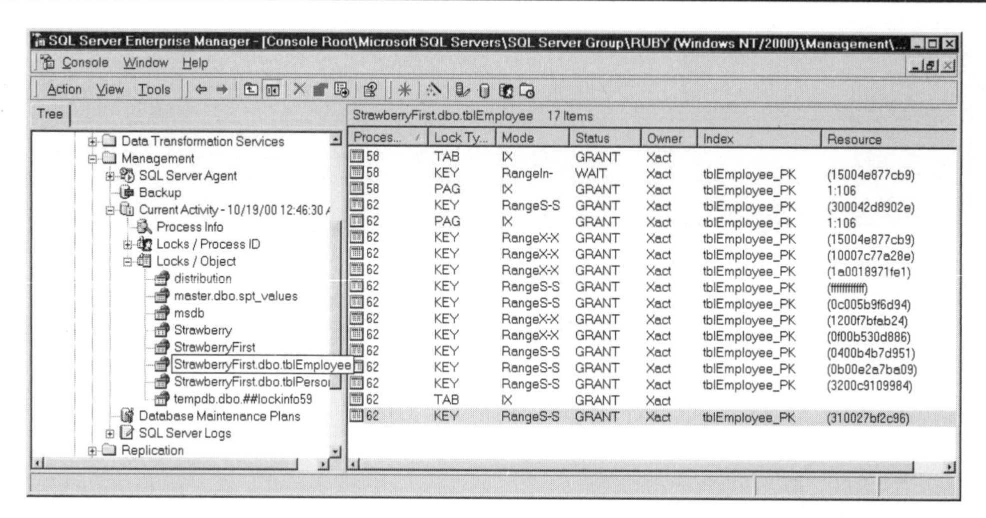

Proces...	Lock Ty...	Mode	Status	Owner	Index	Resource
58	TAB	IX	GRANT	Xact		
58	KEY	RangeIn-	WAIT	Xact	tblEmployee_PK	(15004e877cb9)
58	PAG	IX	GRANT	Xact	tblEmployee_PK	1:106
62	KEY	RangeS-S	GRANT	Xact	tblEmployee_PK	(300042d8902e)
62	PAG	IX	GRANT	Xact	tblEmployee_PK	1:106
62	KEY	RangeX-X	GRANT	Xact	tblEmployee_PK	(15004e877cb9)
62	KEY	RangeX-X	GRANT	Xact	tblEmployee_PK	(10007c77a28e)
62	KEY	RangeX-X	GRANT	Xact	tblEmployee_PK	(1a0018971fe1)
62	KEY	RangeS-S	GRANT	Xact	tblEmployee_PK	(ffffffffffff)
62	KEY	RangeS-S	GRANT	Xact	tblEmployee_PK	(0c005b9f6d94)
62	KEY	RangeX-X	GRANT	Xact	tblEmployee_PK	(1200f7bfab24)
62	KEY	RangeX-X	GRANT	Xact	tblEmployee_PK	(0f00b530d886)
62	KEY	RangeS-S	GRANT	Xact	tblEmployee_PK	(0400b4b7d951)
62	KEY	RangeS-S	GRANT	Xact	tblEmployee_PK	(0b00e2a7ba09)
62	KEY	RangeS-S	GRANT	Xact	tblEmployee_PK	(3200c9109984)
62	TAB	IX	GRANT	Xact		
62	KEY	RangeS-S	GRANT	Xact	tblEmployee_PK	(310027bf2c96)

Figure 14-13. The serializable read isolation level X-locks the entire range of records involved in a transaction.

CHAPTER 15

Data Integrity

In Chapter 14, we talked about how locking prevents data from being corrupted when two users try to update the same record at the same time. In this chapter, we'll look at some techniques for making sure that each user enters data or makes changes using only data values within approved limits—limits that you, as the database administrator, have established. We'll also look at how SQL Server enables you to define primary and foreign key relationship properties quickly, and how it can enforce other rules and restrictions.

Enforcing rules and restrictions can be done in one of three places: at the server, at the client, or midway between, at something called a "rules server." There are pros and cons associated with implementing enforcement at each of these locations. These rules and regulations, also called "application logic," map directly to the business rules you discovered during the requirements gathering that we discussed in Chapter 1.

Enforcing the application logic at the client is something you can do most easily if you tend to develop "fat client" applications, such as those written in Visual Basic or created in MS Access. The code that enforces the business rules is buried in these applications. Every application that accesses the database must have this same code embedded in it. Every time the rules change or a new rule is added, the application code—all of it—must be modified. Many shops have found that this approach is programming maintenance intensive, and they find they have problems keeping the rules synchronized from client application to client application.

Enforcing the application logic in a third-tier rules server is an option that has gained a lot of popularity with the increasing capability of object technology and the Web. Philosophically, this is the most elegant of the three proposed solutions, because it adds an intervening layer between client and server computers. The primary purpose of this layer, often manifested in another server-quality computer, is to administer the business rules and regulations and take some of the processing load off the client-side and server-side computers. An everyday example of this middle tier is the presence of a backup domain controller (BDC) on the Windows NT network. As you log into the network, you are often authenticated by the BDC, not by the primary domain controller (PDC). The BDC is stepping in to take the load off the PDC and is acting as an authentication server.

Enforcing the application logic on the database server is a tried-and-true method, and one that is very easily and quickly implemented. The benefits are obvious: one set of rules, one place to manage them. The rules are applied equally to all applications that access the database, regardless of what route they take to get there—ODBC/OLE DB connections, Web connections, or named pipes. The downside is that the database server now has additional work to do, authenticating and validating as it does the query processing and data retrievals. Nevertheless, it is the approach we prefer, and we're going to look at it in more detail.

For an expanded discussion of client/server architecture as it impacts business and application logic, we'd like to refer you to the *Client/Server Survival Guide, Third Edition*, listed in our bibliography in Appendix F of this book.

DEFAULTS AND RULES

Defaults and rules are older technology inherited from the Sybase days of SQL Server. You may encounter defaults and rules if you are working with an older version of SQL Server or an upgrade of an older version. Note that anything you can do with rules and defaults you can also do with constraints. Each technology has benefits and limitations. By the end of this chapter, we hope that you will be comfortable making a decision to go with one or the other.

A default is just a way of supplying a value for a column when the user does not supply one during an INSERT operation. A rule is a method for defining limits on which values can be written into a column during an INSERT or an UPDATE operation. Rules and defaults are database objects; they are created independently of the tables and columns they modify. Once created, each has to be bound to a column or a datatype. The column or datatype then inherits the properties of the rule or the default. Although defaults and rules are older technology, they actually offer the benefits of reusable code. A rule or a default, once defined in your database, can be used anywhere you need it and as many times as appropriate. One rule or default can be bound to more than one column or datatype.

For example, let's suppose you define a default called df_StateCode and make the default value 'MN' for Minnesota. Now, any time you have a state code column in any table, you can bind this default to it. You might have a state code as a column in tables such as Person, SalesPerson, Employee, Contact, Event, and even Sales. You can bind the same default to each of the StateCode columns in these tables. You can also set up a rule that restricts the value of StateCode to 'MN', 'ND', 'SD', 'WI', and 'IA' and apply this same rule to each state code column in each of the tables. Defaults and rules apply only to the database in which they are created, so create them first in the Model (system) database before you start creating new user databases, or create a T-SQL script that adds and binds these objects, and then run it immediately after creating each new user database.

Creating Defaults and Rules

The syntax for creating a default is fairly simple and straightforward:

```
CREATE DEFAULT default_name
AS  constant_expression
```

For example, to create a default value of MN, you would run the following code:

```
CREATE DEFAULT df_StateCode
AS 'MN'
```

The default value must be a constant, mathematical expression, or built-in function. It cannot refer to other columns or any other database object. Whatever value you supply has to be compatible with the column datatype you intend to bind to, and it has to follow all the rules and constraints applied to that column.

You can also create a default from within Enterprise Manager. Highlight the Strawberry database and expand its hierarchy. Right-click on Defaults. Select New Default, and then supply a name and a value, as shown in Figure 15-1. In the case of the df_StateCode default, you'll have to put 'MN' in single quotes because it's a text string.

It's almost as easy to add a rule, although rules require more code to define the conditions for the rule. The syntax for creating a rule is shown here:

```
CREATE RULE rulename
AS  rule_conditions
```

For example, if you did want to restrict the values allowed in the StateCode column to the five mentioned previously, you would write the rule code like this:

```
CREATE RULE rl_StateCode
AS @scode IN ('MN', 'ND', 'SD', 'WI', 'IA')
```

The @scode is simply a placeholder. Once the rule is bound to a column, the name of the column is substituted for the placeholder. This means you can build the rule before you know the column name or apply the same rule to multiple columns with different column names.

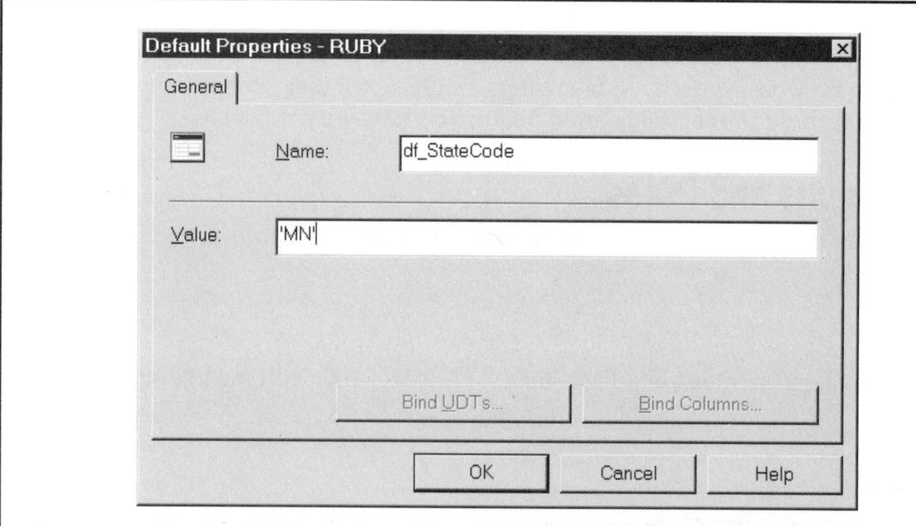

Figure 15-1. Create a SQL Server default object in Enterprise Manager Default Property window.

As with defaults, rules can be created within the Enterprise Manager, again by expanding the database hierarchy, right-clicking Rules, and selecting New Rule. Give the rule a name and then type the code in the text box, as shown in Figure 15-2.

Binding Defaults and Rules

Once you have defined the rules and defaults, the next step is to bind them to the columns you want them to modify. Rules and defaults can also be bound to a user-defined datatype, so any columns created afterward with that datatype automatically inherit the rule or the default, or both. The T-SQL syntax for binding a default to a column or datatype has the following general structure:

```
SP_BINDEFAULT default_name, [table_name.]object_name
```

where the object_name is the name of the column or the datatype. If you're binding to a column, you have to specify the column name in the format table_name.column_name. If you're binding to a datatype, use only a single object name, with no period in the name.

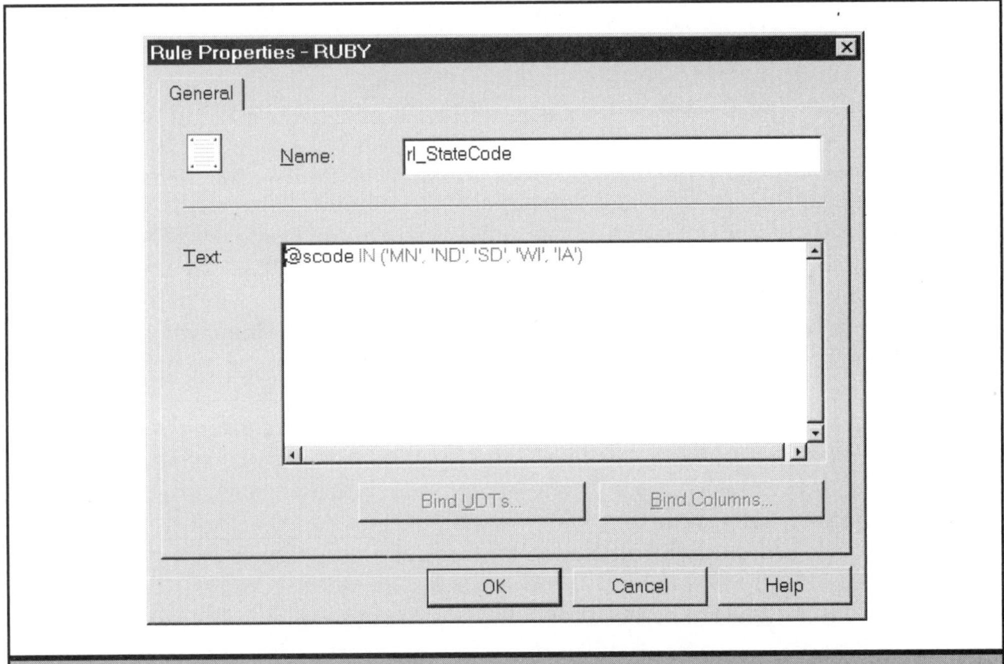

Figure 15-2. A SQL Server rule is an object you can create and manage from the Enterprise Manager Rule Properties window.

For datatypes only, there is an extra parameter called FUTUREONLY. The syntax for the FUTUREONLY option is simply this:

```
SP_BINDEFAULT default_name, object_name, futureonly
```

You might be creating a default for an existing datatype that is already in production, bound to columns, with data already stored in the columns. If you specify FUTUREONLY, you're saying that you want this default value to apply only to columns that you create from this point onward with this datatype. While this seems like it might be quite a handy feature, it has its limitations. For instance, if you drop a table that uses the datatype you've defined with FUTUREONLY and then re-create the table, the column will have a default that it didn't have before. This may not be the kind of behavior you want or expect from this re-created table.

To bind the default df_StateCode to a column, you would write the following T-SQL code:

```
SP_BINDEFAULT df_StateCode, 'tblPerson.State'
```

To bind this default from Enterprise Manager, expand the database hierarchy, select the database, highlight Defaults, and double-click the default df_StateCode. The Default Properties window opens. Now click the Bind Columns button. The Bind Default to Columns window opens. From here you can choose the Person table and then the State column, as shown in Figure 15-3. Apply the bind.

If you want to bind this default to a UDT, from the Default Properties window, click the Bind UDTs button. From the list of UDTs presented, select the one to which you want to bind the default. The FUTUREONLY option is a check box on the UDT row.

A different way to bind rules and defaults is to use the UDT list in the Enterprise Manager hierarchy. From the database hierarchy you can choose User Defined Data Types, highlight the UDT, double-click it, and add the rule and default from the drop-down list boxes in the dialog window that opens, as shown in Figure 15-4.

Still another way to bind defaults to columns is via Enterprise Manager's table design mode. If you open a table in design mode, you will find that you can bind a default object to a column—it's in the column properties at the bottom of the screen, as shown in Figure 15-5. The default objects are shown in a drop-down list and have the format dbo.objectname. Make your choice from this drop-down list. However, there's no place to bind a rule from this screen. This is because Microsoft strongly recommends that you use constraints instead of rules; we'll look at why shortly.

Rules can also be bound to columns or to user-defined datatypes. Everything we've discussed about binding defaults also applies to rules, including comments regarding the FUTUREONLY setting. To bind a rule to a column or a datatype, the syntax is similar to that for the default:

```
SP_BINDRULE rulename, objectname, [future_only]
```

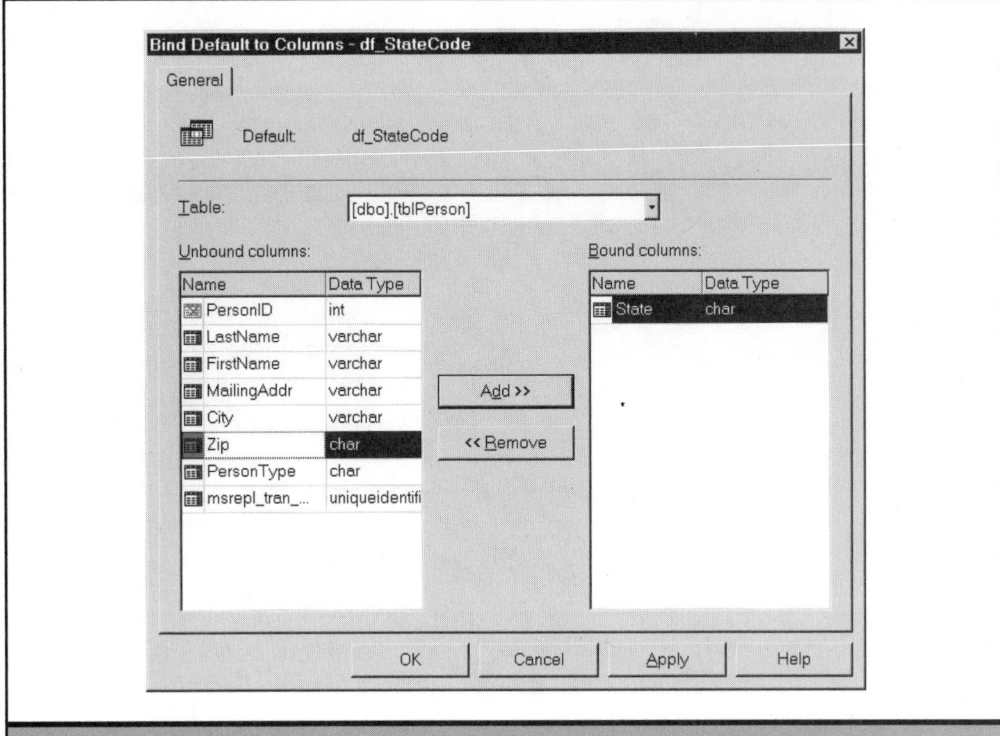

Figure 15-3. A default object can be bound to one or more columns in the database.

For example, you might bind the state code rule using either of the following statements. The first statement binds the rule to the State column of the Person table. The second statement binds the rule to the statecode datatype.

```
SP_BINDRULE rl_StateCode, 'tblPerson.State'
SP_BINDRULE rl_StateCode, 'statecode', FUTUREONLY
```

Binding a new rule to a column never involves checking data that's already stored in the table. The rule always applies to data entered in the table after a column has been bound. Binding a rule to a datatype doesn't retroactively evaluate table contents, either. When you bind a rule to a datatype without FUTUREONLY, you're governed by the rule each time you enter data into a column of that datatype. If you bound the rule to a datatype with FUTUREONLY, you won't be impacted by the rule when entering data into any existing column that uses that datatype, but you will if you create a new column with this datatype.

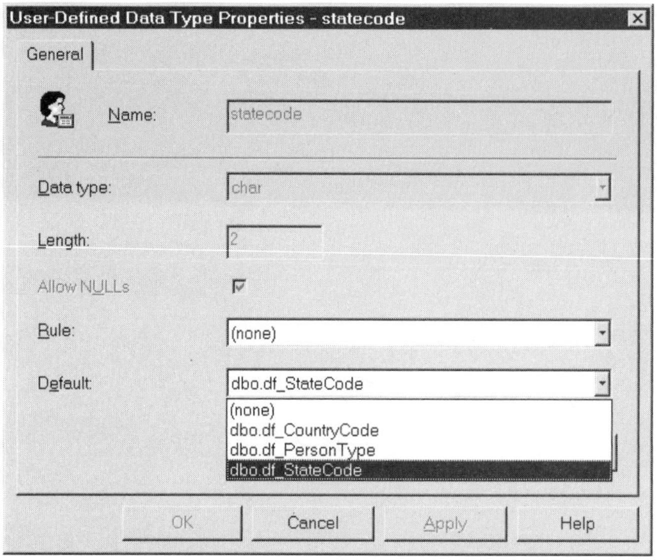

Figure 15-4. You can bind a default object to a user-defined datatype from the UDT Properties window.

Unbinding Rules and Defaults

If you decide that you don't want a rule or a default to be applied any longer, you can run the SP_UNBINDRULE stored procedure. The syntax is very straightforward:

```
SP_UNBINDRULE objectname
SP_UNBINDEFAULT objectname
```

where objectname refers to a column name or a UDT. So to unbind the default on the State column of the Person table, and to unbind the rule on the UDT statecode, you'd write this:

```
SP_UNBINDEFAULT 'tblPerson.State'
SP_UNBINDRULE 'statecode'
```

You do not need to supply the rule name or default name, because only one rule or default can be associated with each column or datatype. Whatever rule or default is bound to the object gets unbound.

In Enterprise Manager, you can highlight the individual rule or default, right-click and choose Properties, and then deselect the column or datatype to unbind the rule or default. You can also go directly to the UDT and remove the rule and/or the default associ-

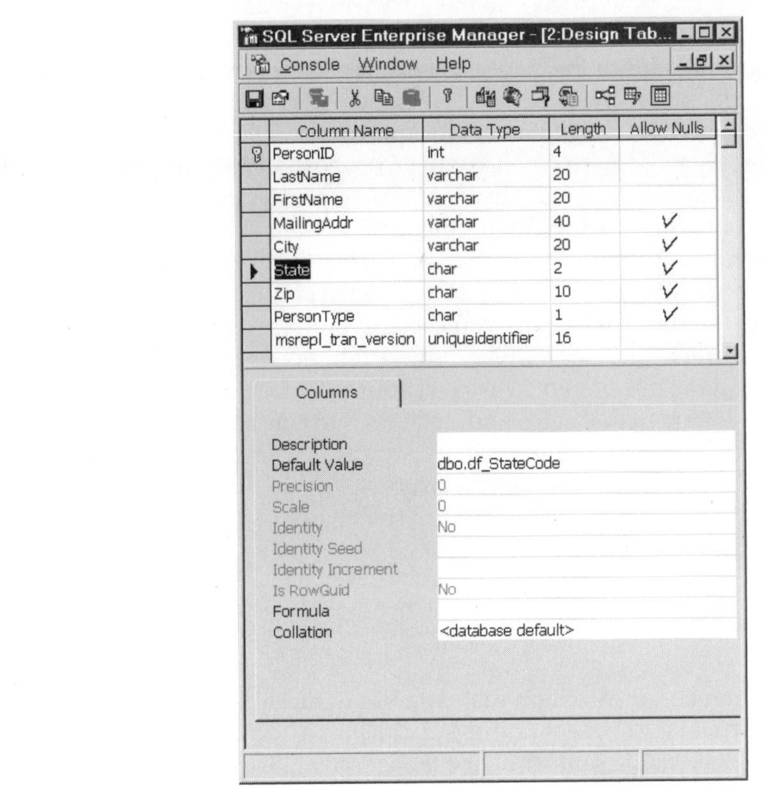

Figure 15-5. You can bind a default object to a column in a table by assigning it as the default value in the Design Table window.

ated with that datatype. You can open a table in design mode and remove a default from a column—but again, there's no way to either add or remove a rule from this interface.

One thing to remember with unbinding rules and defaults: SQL Server has issues about leaving orphan objects, so it will not let you drop a rule or a default if it is in use. In other words, you cannot drop a rule or a default if it is still bound to a column or a datatype.

Reasons for Not Using Defaults and Rules

Defaults and rules seem to be an elegant solution. After all, they are reusable objects, and that fits with an object-oriented approach to program development. But there are two reasons why you might want to migrate away from using rules and defaults and begin to use constraints instead. The first reason is a seemingly minor point. A rule or a default is a separate database object. It is not loaded into memory when an associated column/table is loaded. Instead, it is loaded the first time it is called. There will be a slight delay the first time a row is inserted into a table or the first time a row in a table is modified. If the rule or default is used often, this impact will be minimized because chances are good that the rule or default will remain in cache (memory) for quite a while. If the rule or default is used infrequently, the impact on performance will be proportionately greater, as the rule or default object must be continually read back into cache with each use.

The second argument against using T-SQL rules and defaults is more serious. We said that they are older technology, and in fact the rule and the default object are not part of any of the ANSI standards. They were obviously developed to fill in some of the holes left by the various SQL standards. This means you can count on them not being portable if you need to move the code to another RDBMS, unless it happens to be a Sybase system.

Microsoft is encouraging developers to use constraints that are ANSI compliant. Furthermore, there is no guarantee that rules and defaults will continue to be supported in every future release of SQL Server. While you may argue that constraints are not the perfect solution (as you will see shortly), at least their future seems assured at Microsoft. Following our discussion of constraints, we will return to the discussion of which technique to use—defaults and rules, or constraints.

CONSTRAINTS

A constraint is a requirement or condition that data has to meet before it can be entered into a database. A constraint is not a separate object; it is part of the table it was created on. A constraint can be defined at the same time the table is created, or it can be added later with an ALTER TABLE command. A constraint can be removed from a table without affecting the table structure or the data. There are several different types of constraints, each of which performs a specific function. A table can contain multiple constraints, and even a column can have more than one constraint applied to it. The CREATE TABLE command syntax from Books Online is quite complex, as you can see, because so much of it refers to creating the constraints:

```
CREATE TABLE
    [ database_name.[ owner ] . | owner. ] table_name
    ( { < column_definition >
        | column_name AS computed_column_expression
        | < table_constraint > } [ ,...n ]
    )
[ ON { filegroup | DEFAULT } ]
[ TEXTIMAGE_ON { filegroup | DEFAULT } ]
< column_definition > ::= { column_name data_type }
    [ [ DEFAULT constant_expression ]
      | [ IDENTITY [ ( seed , increment ) [ NOT FOR REPLICATION ] ] ]
    ]
```

```
    [ ROWGUIDCOL ]
    [ COLLATE < collation_name > ]
    [ < column_constraint > ] [ ...n ]
< column_constraint > ::= [ CONSTRAINT constraint_name ]
    { [ NULL | NOT NULL ]
        | [ { PRIMARY KEY | UNIQUE }
            [ CLUSTERED | NONCLUSTERED ]
            [ WITH FILLFACTOR = fillfactor ]
            [ON {filegroup | DEFAULT} ] ]
        ]
        | [ [ FOREIGN KEY ]
            REFERENCES ref_table [ ( ref_column ) ]
            [ ON DELETE { CASCADE | NO ACTION } ]
            [ ON UPDATE { CASCADE | NO ACTION } ]
            [ NOT FOR REPLICATION ]
        ]
        | CHECK [ NOT FOR REPLICATION ]
        ( logical_expression )
    }
< table_constraint > ::= [ CONSTRAINT constraint_name ]
    { [ { PRIMARY KEY | UNIQUE }
        [ CLUSTERED | NONCLUSTERED ]
        { ( column [ ASC | DESC ] [ ,...n ] ) }
        [ WITH FILLFACTOR = fillfactor ]
        [ ON { filegroup | DEFAULT } ]
    ]
    | FOREIGN KEY
        [ ( column [ ,...n ] ) ]
        REFERENCES ref_table [ ( ref_column [ ,...n ] ) ]
        [ ON DELETE { CASCADE | NO ACTION } ]
        [ ON UPDATE { CASCADE | NO ACTION } ]
        [ NOT FOR REPLICATION ]
    | CHECK [ NOT FOR REPLICATION ]
        ( search_conditions )
    }
```

Let's dissect the parts of this command that pertain to constraints. If you take constraints a bit at a time, they will become understandable, and creating them will be less intimidating than it appears in this definition of the CREATE TABLE command!

Column- and Table-Level Constraints

In the preceding code listing from Books Online, and elsewhere, you will see references to "column constraints" and "table constraints," or "column-level" and "table-level" constraints. A column-level constraint is defined on a single column, as part of the column definition as you write the code that creates the table, as in this example code:

```
CREATE TABLE dbo.PersonExample1
(  PersonID        int             IDENTITY(1, 1) NOT NULL ,
   LastName        varchar(20)     NOT NULL ,
   FirstName       varchar(20)     NOT NULL ,    MailingAddr     varchar(40)  NULL ,
   City            varchar(20)     NULL ,
   State           char(2)         NULL DEFAULT('MN'),
   Zip             char(10)        NULL ,
   PersonType      char(1)         NOT NULL
)
```

As you specify the column properties, you add the constraint as though it were also a property (which, in fact, it is), as shown in the column definition for State in the preceding code.

A table-level constraint is defined independently from the column definition. A table-level constraint can be a multi-column constraint. When you need to define a constraint that spans columns of the same table, you have to define the columns first and add a table constraint at the end, as in this example code:

```
CREATE TABLE dbo.PersonExample2
(  PersonID        int             IDENTITY(1, 1) NOT NULL ,
   LastName        varchar(20)     NOT NULL ,
   FirstName       varchar(20)     NOT NULL ,
   MailingAddr     varchar(40)     NULL ,
   City            varchar(20)     NULL ,
   State           char(2)         NULL DEFAULT('MN'),
   Zip             char(10)        NULL ,
   PersonType      char(1)         NOT NULL,
CONSTRAINT pkey_Person2 PRIMARY KEY (LastName, FirstName, PersonType))
```

The table-level constraint in this code example is a primary key constraint. The primary key is a composite of the person's last name, first name, and person type. None of the columns that make up the primary key can be NULL, which is why PersonType has been changed from NULL in the previous code example to NOT NULL in this one.

As we said earlier in this chapter, you can add constraints to a table after the fact with an ALTER TABLE command. When you ask your SQL Server to generate a script of a table, it always generates the CREATE TABLE commands first, without constraints. Then it adds the constraints in an ALTER TABLE command after the table definitions.

Primary Keys

To ensure that your data is in first normal form, and to guarantee that you can update a single row in a table, you must designate a primary key for each table. This key can be a single column, a combination of columns, or an additional column intentionally added to the table for the sole purpose of acting as a primary key (a surrogate key). A primary key is used to enforce data integrity; therefore, the set of primary key values must be unique. Each value must identify one row, and each row must be identified by a single value. A primary key cannot be NULL. Examples of primary keys are employee number, purchase order number, invoice number, check number, and so on.

In the first versions of SQL Server (pre-version 6.0), you could designate a column or combination of columns as the primary key for a table. However, it really was no more than a label on those columns, because a programmer had to write code to enforce the primary key rule. When constraints were introduced in SQL Server version 6.0, life in the DBA lane became considerably easier. Now when you specify a column or combination of columns as the primary key, SQL Server will build a unique index on the column or combination of columns. This is how the uniqueness rule gets enforced. We'll talk about indexes in the next chapter, so for now it's enough that you know that the index is automatically created and that you cannot drop this index manually. The only way to remove this index is to drop the constraint. By default, this primary key index is a clustered index, although you can specify a nonclustered index when you create the primary constraint. Don't assume that a primary key will make the best clustered index.

If you create a primary constraint on a table that already contains data, the data has to meet the limitations of the constraint. Because the primary constraint builds a unique index, and NULLS are not allowed in a primary constraint, if there are duplicate values or NULLS in the data, this will cause the index creation to fail. The primary constraint will not be defined. Obviously, any new rows added to the table must satisfy the conditions imposed by the primary constraint. Changes to data in the primary key column—while not something that you want to do often, if at all—must also meet these conditions.

If someone tries to insert data into a table that violates the conditions imposed by the primary constraint, SQL Server will reject the changes. You don't need to add any code to the database or to your applications to catch potential violations. However, your application, whether a T-SQL stored procedure or an Access or Visual Basic application, will have to include some code to handle subsequent actions after the submitted changes are rejected.

You can have only one primary constraint per table. Some tables will have more than one column suitable for use as a primary key—these are called candidates for the primary key, or *candidate keys*. For example, in an employee table, you might have both an auto-generated employee identifier and a Social Security number. Both of these columns are candidates for the primary key position in the table. For reasons of security and privacy, you choose to use the auto-generated employee identifier as the primary key, and the Social Security number becomes the candidate key.

To create a primary constraint and designate a primary key, you can code it one of two ways. You can indicate it immediately when you write the CREATE TABLE statement, like so:

```
CREATE TABLE dbo.EmployeeExample1
(  EmpID      int IDENTITY(1,1) NOT NULL PRIMARY KEY CLUSTERED,
   SSN        char(10)          NOT NULL,
   LastName   varchar(20)       NOT NULL ,
   FirstName varchar(20)        NOT NULL ,
   Gender     char(1)           NULL,
   JobTitle   varchar(20)       NULL )
```

Or you can create the primary constraint with the ALTER TABLE statement, which should be executed immediately following a plain CREATE TABLE statement:

```
CREATE TABLE dbo.EmployeeExample2
(  EmpID      int IDENTITY(1,1) NOT NULL,
   SSN        char(10)          NOT NULL,
   LastName   varchar(20)       NOT NULL ,
   FirstName varchar(20)        NOT NULL ,
   Gender     char(1)           NULL,
   JobTitle   varchar(20)       NULL )
GO
ALTER TABLE dbo.EmployeeExample2
ADD CONSTRAINT PK_EmplExample2 PRIMARY KEY CLUSTERED (EmpID)
GO
```

If you prefer to use Enterprise Manager, you can easily designate a primary key for a table and invoke the associated primary constraint. Open the database hierarchy, select a table, and open it in design mode. Highlight the column or combination of columns that you want to make the primary key. Either right-click and select the Set Primary Key option or click the key icon on the toolbar, as shown in Figure 15-6. If you're an MS Access programmer or developer, you'll feel right at home with Enterprise Manager's table design mode features.

Unique Constraints

A unique constraint enforces uniqueness in a column or combination of columns. This is how you enforce a candidate key. A Social Security number should be a unique identifier for your employees within your company. If you are working for a trucking company, perhaps the driver's license number is a better candidate key. In this case, you might want to place a unique constraint on the combination of state code plus driver's license number, to allow for the unlikely but theoretically possible situation in which two employees have the same drivers license number issued by two different states.

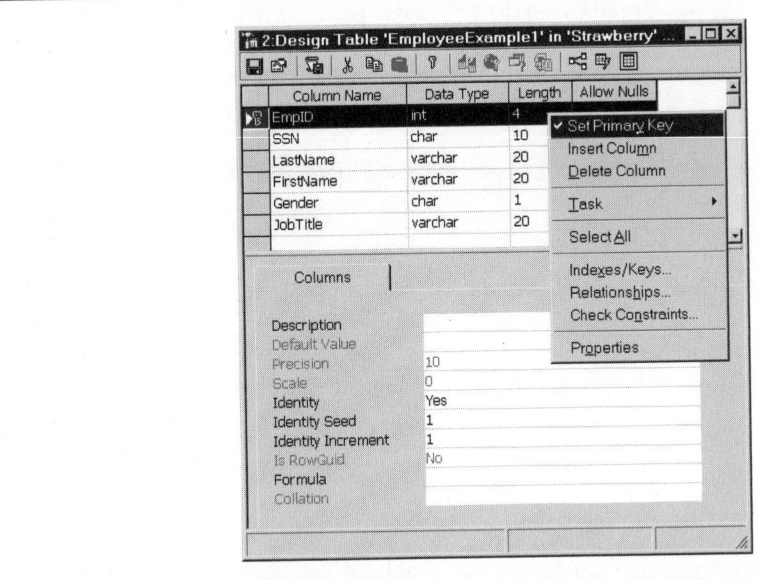

Figure 15-6. Set the primary key for each table from the Design Table window of Enterprise Manager.

The unique constraint is enforced by a unique index, although this unique index defaults to a nonclustered index. A unique index by itself will allow a single instance of NULL, so you have to remember to include a NOT NULL phrase when defining the candidate column. The unique constraint index, just like the index on the primary constraint, cannot be dropped without dropping the unique constraint. If you create a unique constraint on a column or combination of columns that are already populated, the data must conform to the requirements of a unique constraint. Again, when you have defined a unique constraint on a column, SQL Server handles the enforcement of the uniqueness requirement, although your user applications will have to handle any rejected updates or inserts.

To create a unique constraint on a candidate key, you can code it one of two ways. You can indicate it immediately when you write the CREATE TABLE statement, like so:

```
CREATE TABLE dbo.EmployeeExample3
(  EmpID      int IDENTITY(1,1) NOT NULL PRIMARY KEY CLUSTERED,
   SSN        char(10)          NOT NULL UNIQUE NONCLUSTERED,
   LastName   varchar(20)       NOT NULL ,
   FirstName  varchar(20)       NOT NULL ,
   Gender     char(1)           NULL,
   JobTitle   varchar(20)       NULL )
```

Or you can create the unique constraint with the ALTER TABLE statement, which should be executed following a plain CREATE TABLE statement:

```
CREATE TABLE dbo.EmployeeExample4
(  EmpID      int IDENTITY(1,1) NOT NULL,
   SSN        char(10)          NOT NULL,
   LastName   varchar(20)       NOT NULL ,
   FirstName  varchar(20)       NOT NULL ,
   Gender     char(1)           NULL,
   JobTitle   varchar(20)       NULL )
GO
ALTER TABLE dbo.EmployeeExample4
ADD CONSTRAINT PK_EmplExample4 PRIMARY KEY CLUSTERED (EmpID)
GO
ALTER TABLE dbo.EmployeeExample4
ADD CONSTRAINT UK_EmplExample4 UNIQUE NONCLUSTERED (SSN)
GO
```

If you prefer to use Enterprise Manager, you can easily designate a candidate key for a table and invoke the associated unique constraint. Open the database hierarchy, select a table, and open it in design mode. Highlight the column or combination of columns that you want to make the candidate key, and then right-click and select the Indexes/Keys option to open the Properties box. Choose the Indexes/Keys tab and click New. Set the parameters for the unique index, as shown in Figure 15-7. Or you can click the Manage Indexes icon on the Properties window toolbar to bring up the Properties box.

Foreign Key Constraints

The foreign key constraint is how you enforce a one-to-one or one-to-many relationship between two tables. In the Strawberry database, a good example of the one-to-many relationship is the relationship between the Sale table and the SaleItem table. Each Sale record has one or more associated records in the SaleItem table, and each SaleItem record is related back to a single record in the Sale table. The Sale table is considered the master or parent table, and SaleItem is its child table.

When you define a foreign key constraint, SQL Server automatically enforces certain rules on the one-to-many relationship. If you were to define a constraint on the Sale to SaleItem relationship, you could not, for example, insert a record into the SaleItem table for a sale that didn't exist. You would first have to enter the sale record into the Sale table, and then you could enter sale item records. Delete behavior is also restricted. You would not be able to delete an entry from the Sale table without first removing all associated entries from the SaleItem table.

Foreign keys can be single-column or multi-column. Each foreign key in a child table must point to either the primary key or the candidate key of the child's parent. SQL Server has to know exactly which row in the parent table is being referenced by the foreign key in the child table, so the foreign key has to point to a unique value in the parent table.

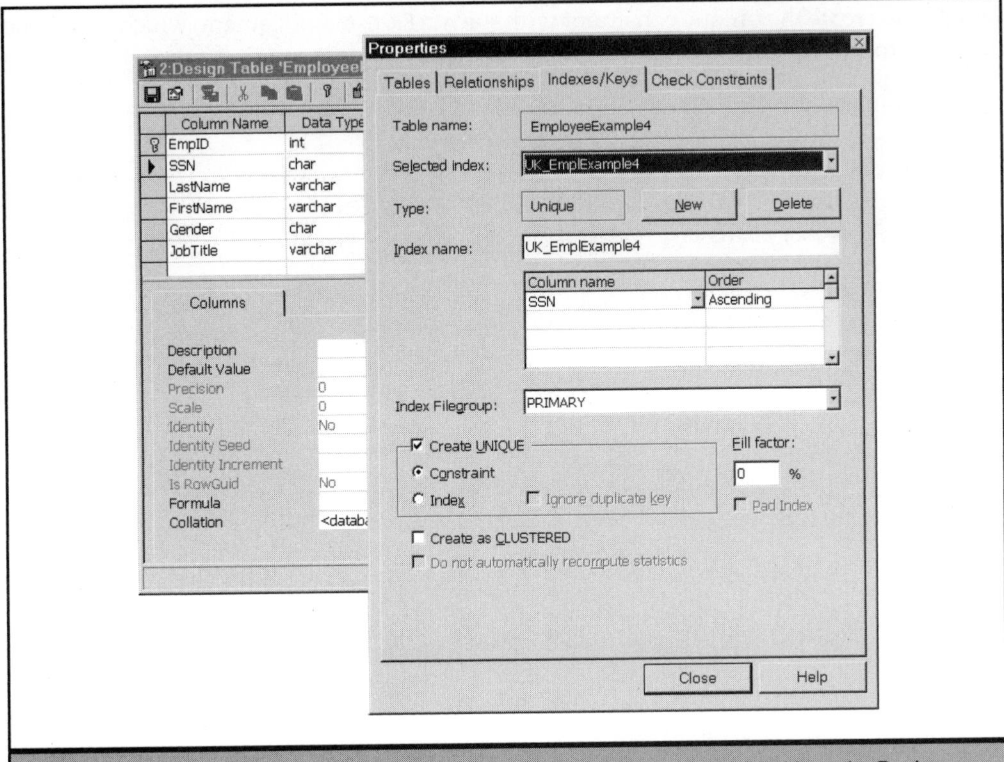

Figure 15-7. Candidate keys, which have a unique constraint, can be defined from the Design Table window Properties box.

Creating a foreign key constraint does not automatically cause an index to be built on the foreign key column. We strongly suggest that you create a non-unique index on each foreign key column or combination of columns, because the foreign key is so often used when joining tables for query retrieval. The index will speed up the join process significantly.

To create a foreign key constraint on a column, you can code it one of two ways. You can indicate it immediately when you write the CREATE TABLE statement, as shown here:

```
CREATE TABLE dbo.SaleItemExample1
(   SaleItemID      int IDENTITY(1,1) NOT NULL PRIMARY KEY NONCLUSTERED,
    SaleNo          int NOT NULL REFERENCES dbo.tblSale(SaleNo)
                             ON UPDATE CASCADE ON DELETE CASCADE,
    ProductCode     int NOT NULL REFERENCES dbo.tblProduct(ProductCode)
                             ON UPDATE CASCADE,
    QuantitySold    int NOT NULL ,
    UnitPrice       money  NOT NULL,
    ItemCost        money  NULL )
```

Or you can create the unique constraint with the ALTER TABLE statement, which should be executed following a plain CREATE TABLE statement:

```
CREATE TABLE dbo.SaleItemExample2
(  SaleItemID      int IDENTITY(1,1) NOT NULL ,
   SaleNo          int NOT NULL ,
   ProductCode     int NOT NULL ,
   QuantitySold    int NOT NULL ,
   UnitPrice       money  NOT NULL,
   ItemCost        money  NULL )
GO
ALTER TABLE dbo.SaleItemExample2
ADD CONSTRAINT PK_SaleItemExample2 PRIMARY KEY
               NONCLUSTERED (SaleItemID)
GO
ALTER TABLE dbo.SaleItemExample2
ADD CONSTRAINT FK_SaleItem2Sale FOREIGN KEY (SaleNo)
    REFERENCES dbo.tblSale(SaleNo) ON UPDATE CASCADE ON DELETE CASCADE
GO
ALTER TABLE dbo.SaleItemExample2
ADD CONSTRAINT FK_SaleItem2Product FOREIGN KEY (ProductCode)
               REFERENCES dbo.tblProduct(ProductCode) ON UPDATE CASCADE
GO
```

If you prefer to use Enterprise Manager, you can easily enforce a foreign key constraint by opening the database hierarchy, selecting a table, and opening it in design mode. Highlight the column or combination of columns that you want to make the foreign key, and then right-click and select the Properties box. Choose the Relationships tab and click New. Set the parameters for the foreign key constraint index, as shown in Figure 15-8. Or you can click the Manage Relationships icon on the Properties window toolbar to bring up the Properties box.

Cascading Changes and Referential Integrity

The Properties box Relationships tab also contains new features that were introduced with SQL Server 2000: the cascade update and cascade delete options. In the preceding examples, we turned on cascade update—changes to the value of a primary key will be automatically "cascaded" to all associated foreign keys—because we wanted to keep the primary key/foreign key values synchronized should a modification of the primary key value be necessary. For the reference to the Sale table only, we have activated the cascade delete also. If a Sale record is deleted, all associated SaleItem records will also be deleted. This is a business decision we decided to enforce in the database. For the reference to the Product table, the cascade delete is not activated. Just because a record might be removed from the Product table, we don't want associated SaleItem records to be removed as well.

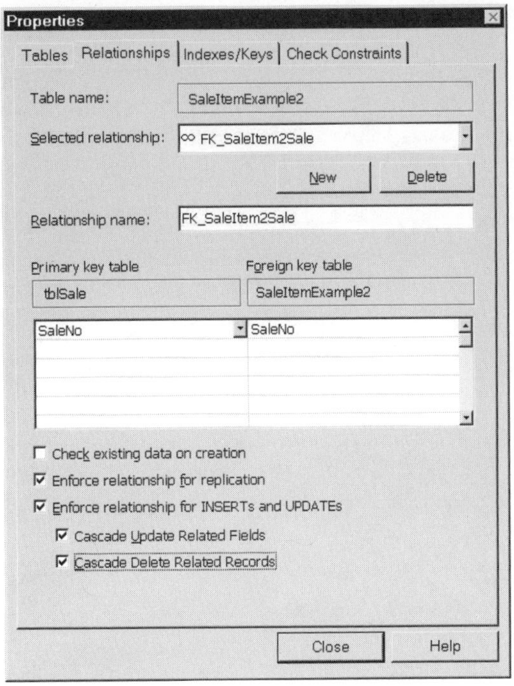

Figure 15-8. Define foreign keys and enforce referential integrity from the Design Table window Properties box.

Recursive Relationships and Referential Integrity

There is a special situation, the case of a recursive relationship, in which the primary key and the foreign key are columns in the same table. A standard example is the Employee table that has both employee identifiers and manager identifiers, so that for each instance of an employee, the employee's manager identifier is also recorded in the same record.

To create a foreign key constraint in this recursive relationship situation, you can code it one of two ways. You can indicate it immediately when you write the CREATE TABLE statement, but you have to treat the reference as though it's a separate table:

```
CREATE TABLE dbo.EmployeeMgrExample1
( EmpID     int IDENTITY(1,1) NOT NULL PRIMARY KEY CLUSTERED,
  SSN       char(10)          NOT NULL UNIQUE NONCLUSTERED,
  LastName  varchar(20)       NOT NULL ,
  FirstName varchar(20)       NOT NULL ,
  Gender    char(1)           NULL,
  JobTitle  varchar(20)       NULL,
```

```
  MgrID      int                NOT NULL
             REFERENCES dbo.EmployeeMgrExample1(EmpID)   )
```

Or you can create the recursive relationship foreign key constraint with the ALTER TABLE statement, and again you have to treat the reference as though it's a separate table. The ALTER TABLE statements always follow a plain CREATE TABLE statement:

```
CREATE TABLE dbo.EmployeeMgrExample2
(  EmpID     int IDENTITY(1,1) NOT NULL,
   SSN       char(10)          NOT NULL,
   LastName  varchar(20)       NOT NULL ,
   FirstName varchar(20)       NOT NULL ,
   Gender    char(1)           NULL,
   JobTitle  varchar(20)       NULL,
   MgrID     int               NOT NULL  )
GO
ALTER TABLE dbo.EmployeeMgrExample2
ADD CONSTRAINT PK_EmployeeMgrExample2 PRIMARY KEY CLUSTERED (EmpID)
GO
ALTER TABLE dbo.EmployeeMgrExample2
ADD CONSTRAINT UK_EmployeeMgrExample2 UNIQUE NONCLUSTERED (SSN)
GO
ALTER TABLE  dbo.EmployeeMgrExample2
ADD CONSTRAINT FK_MgrID2empID FOREIGN KEY (MgrID)
                              REFERENCES dbo.EmployeeMgrExample2(EmpID)
GO
```

Last but not least, when entering data into this table, you'll have to start with the most senior manager in the company, because each employee must have an associated manager identifier already in the table. Additionally, because the MgrID cannot be NULL, the person at the top will have to report to himself/herself.

Default Constraints

A default value is an automatically supplied value for a database object. In this case, we're talking about automatically supplying values for columns during INSERT operations. A default constraint is a rule that enforces the default value. For SQL Server 2000, Microsoft has changed the terminology. What was a "default constraint" in previous versions of the database management system is now referred to as a "default definition." Whatever Microsoft calls it is irrelevant; behind the scenes, the "default definition" still creates a constraint, and you can still name this constraint—albeit for backward-compatibility reasons. To us, they're still default constraints, so we'll continue to refer to them as default constraints.

Default constraints perform the same functions as a standalone default object. Whenever you INSERT a row into a table and you don't supply a value for a column, if that column has a default constraint on it, SQL Server will automatically use the default value to populate this column. Default constraints apply only to INSERT statements, not to UPDATE statements.

You can have only one default value per column, and the default constraint always applies to just a single column. You cannot have both an older version default bound to a column plus a SQL 2000 default "definition" declared on the same column at the same time. Whatever value you specify for the default must be consistent with the column datatype, so you can't declare a default value of "abc" for a column with an integer datatype.

Default values can be constants (string values) or system functions, such as the current date and time or the current user login name. You can use the system functions USER_NAME, CURRENT_USER, or USER_ID to bring back an end-user's identifier. To bring back the current datetime information, you can use CURRENT_TIMESTAMP or the older GETDATE() function. Microsoft claims that SQL Server is moving away from the GETDATE() function, as it's not part of the ANSI-SQL standard, so assume that in some future version the company will drop support altogether for GETDATE(). However, in SQL Server 2000, GETDATE() and CURRENT_TIMESTAMP are functional equivalents, as are USER_NAME and CURRENT_USER.

One downside of these SQL 2000 default "definitions" is that they cannot be created and bound like the default objects we talked about at the beginning of this chapter. And unlike default objects, a default "definition" is defined on one column of one table—it cannot be applied elsewhere. If you want to use the same default for many columns/many tables, you have to define it over and over, for each column/table you want it to apply to. The new-style default has actually become a column property. Fortunately, you can copy and paste the code, and supply the same default definition for each column, in either the SQL scripts or the Enterprise Manager Properties window.

To create a default constraint, you can code it one of two ways. You can indicate it immediately when you write the CREATE TABLE statement, as follows:

```
CREATE TABLE dbo.SaleExample
(SaleNo        INT IDENTITY(10000, 1) NOT NULL PRIMARY KEY CLUSTERED,
 EventID       INT      NOT NULL REFERENCES tblEvent(EventID),
 SalesTaxCode  char(1)  NULL DEFAULT ('T'),
 SaleDate      DATETIME NOT NULL DEFAULT CURRENT_TIMESTAMP,
 SalesTax      MONEY    NULL,
 SaleTotal     MONEY    NULL   )
GO
```

Or you can create a default constraint with the ALTER TABLE statement. The ALTER TABLE statements always follow a plain CREATE TABLE statement:

```
CREATE TABLE dbo.SaleExample2
( SaleNo        INT       IDENTITY(1,1) NOT NULL ,
  EventID       INT       NOT NULL ,
  SalesTaxCode char(1)    NULL ,
```

```
  SaleDate      DATETIME NOT NULL ,
  SalesTax      MONEY    NULL,
  SaleTotal     MONEY    NULL )
GO
ALTER TABLE dbo.SaleExample2
ADD CONSTRAINT PK_SaleExample2 PRIMARY KEY CLUSTERED (SaleNo)
GO
ALTER TABLE  dbo.SaleExample2
ADD CONSTRAINT FK_Sale2Event FOREIGN KEY (EventID)
                             REFERENCES dbo.tblEvent(EventID)
GO
ALTER TABLE dbo.SaleExample2
ADD CONSTRAINT DEF_SalesTaxCode DEFAULT 'T' FOR SalesTaxCode
GO
ALTER TABLE dbo.SaleExample2
ADD CONSTRAINT DEF_SaleDate DEFAULT CURRENT_TIMESTAMP FOR SaleDate
GO
```

Note that in the second example, we supplied a name for each constraint. You could do the same in the first example also, by inserting CONSTRAINT DEF_SALEDATE before the DEFAULT CURRENT_TIMESTAMP and naming the other constraints in the same way. If you don't give the constraint a name, SQL Server will generate one, and it will look something like DF_SaleExamp_SaleD_32616E72. It appends the hexadecimal string onto the end of the name just to ensure that each object name is unique. While this may guarantee uniqueness, it is a real inconvenience for database administrators and database designers to track and manage, especially if you are doing table architecture administration, such as dropping columns out of tables.

If you prefer to use Enterprise Manager to create your default constraints, you know the routine by now. Open the database hierarchy, select a table, and open it in design mode. As we said previously, default values are now treated as column properties, as you can see in Figure 15-9, where the SaleDate default value is listed in the column properties section of the Design Table window. Also notice that, despite the fact that you created the default value for the column SaleDate with a CURRENT_TIMESTAMP, SQL Server converts the CURRENT_TIMESTAMP function to a GETDATE() function.

Check Constraints

A check constraint does what a rule does—it defines the acceptable values for a column. In other words, it is a way of enforcing at least part of a column's domain integrity. With a check constraint, you can enforce a list of discrete values, such as a short list of states or countries. You can enforce a pattern that the data must adhere to (the display layout format in MS Access), like a U.S. telephone number that must consist of a three-digit area code, a space, three more digits, a dash, and four more digits. The check constraint can enforce a range of values, such as a range of zip codes in the Portland, Oregon, area for the

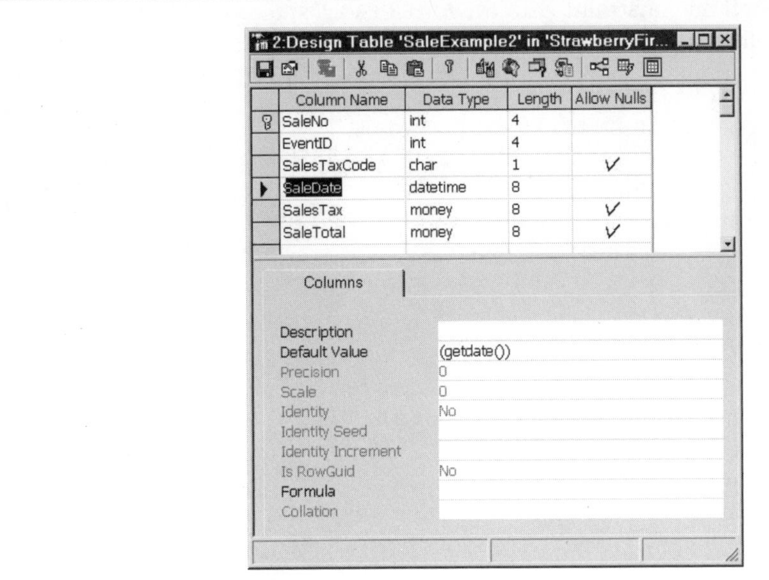

Figure 15-9. Default constraints are created as table properties, in the Design Table window of Enterprise Manager.

data entered from the Portland region, or a date no later than today for the date of a sale. You can put multiple check constraints on a single column, so for example you could ensure that all your telephone numbers follow the pattern just described and also start with area codes from an approved list.

To create a check constraint, you can code it one of two ways. You can indicate it immediately when you write the CREATE TABLE statement, as follows:

```
CREATE TABLE dbo.SaleExample3
( SaleNo       INT      IDENTITY(1,1) NOT NULL PRIMARY KEY CLUSTERED,
  EventID      INT      NOT NULL REFERENCES tblEvent(EventID),
  SalesTaxCode char(1)  NULL DEFAULT ('T'),
  SaleDate     DATETIME NOT NULL DEFAULT CURRENT_TIMESTAMP
                                  CHECK (SaleDate <= CURRENT_TIMESTAMP),
  SalesCounty  varchar(20) NOT NULL CHECK (SalesCounty = 'Jefferson'
                                     OR SalesCounty = 'Arapahoe'
                                     OR SalesCounty = 'Boulder'
                                     OR SalesCounty = 'Douglas'),
  SalesTax     MONEY    NULL,
  SaleTotal    MONEY    NULL   )
GO
```

Or you can create a default constraint with the ALTER TABLE statement. The ALTER TABLE statements always follow a plain CREATE TABLE statement:

```
CREATE TABLE dbo.SaleExample4
( SaleNo        INT         IDENTITY(1,1) NOT NULL ,
  EventID       INT         NOT NULL ,
  SalesTaxCode char(1)     NULL ,
  SaleDate      DATETIME NOT NULL ,
  SalesCounty  varchar(20) NOT NULL ,
  SalesTax      MONEY       NULL,
  SaleTotal     MONEY       NULL )
GO
ALTER TABLE dbo.SaleExample4
ADD CONSTRAINT PK_SaleExample4 PRIMARY KEY CLUSTERED (SaleNo)
GO
ALTER TABLE  dbo.SaleExample4
ADD CONSTRAINT FK_SaleExample4_2Event FOREIGN KEY (EventID)
                                      REFERENCES dbo.tblEvent(EventID)
GO
ALTER TABLE dbo.SaleExample4
ADD CONSTRAINT DEF_SaleEx4SalesTaxCode DEFAULT 'T' FOR SalesTaxCode
GO
ALTER TABLE dbo.SaleExample4
ADD CONSTRAINT DEF_SaleEx4SaleDate DEFAULT CURRENT_TIMESTAMP
                                   FOR SaleDate
GO
ALTER TABLE dbo.SaleExample4
ADD CONSTRAINT CK_SaleEx4SaleDate CHECK (SaleDate <= CURRENT_TIMESTAMP)
GO
ALTER TABLE dbo.SaleExample4
ADD CONSTRAINT CK_SaleExample4SaleCnty CHECK (SalesCounty = 'Jefferson'
                                          OR SalesCounty = 'Arapahoe'
                                          OR SalesCounty = 'Boulder'
                                          OR SalesCounty = 'Douglas')
GO
```

A SQL Server check constraint is sort of like an embedded lookup table. The check constraint is best used when your list or range of values is short and static. If you have long lists of values or rapidly changing values, you'll want to store this data in a lookup table, and then enforce the foreign key reference to the lookup table. For instance, if the short list of counties in the preceding code were to grow into a much longer list of provinces, parishes, and shires (your company went global), you might decide that constantly taking a table offline to modify the check constraint isn't such a good idea. You believe that a much better solution would be to store this long list of rapidly changing values in its own table. Then you and your programmers can use this table of values as a reference or lookup table. However, you won't be able to refer to data in the lookup table with this check constraint—you cannot include a query inside a check constraint definition. So you'll have to drop the check constraint from the SalesCounty column and instead establish a foreign key constraint between table dbo.SaleExample4 and the new lookup table.

If you prefer to use Enterprise Manager to create your check constraints, open the database hierarchy, select a table, and open it in design mode. Highlight the column you want to create a check constraint on, and then right-click and select Check Constraints. Key in the parameters for the check constraint, as shown in Figure 15-10. Or you can click the Manage Constaints [sic] icon on the Properties window toolbar to bring up the Properties box, and choose the Check Constraints tab.

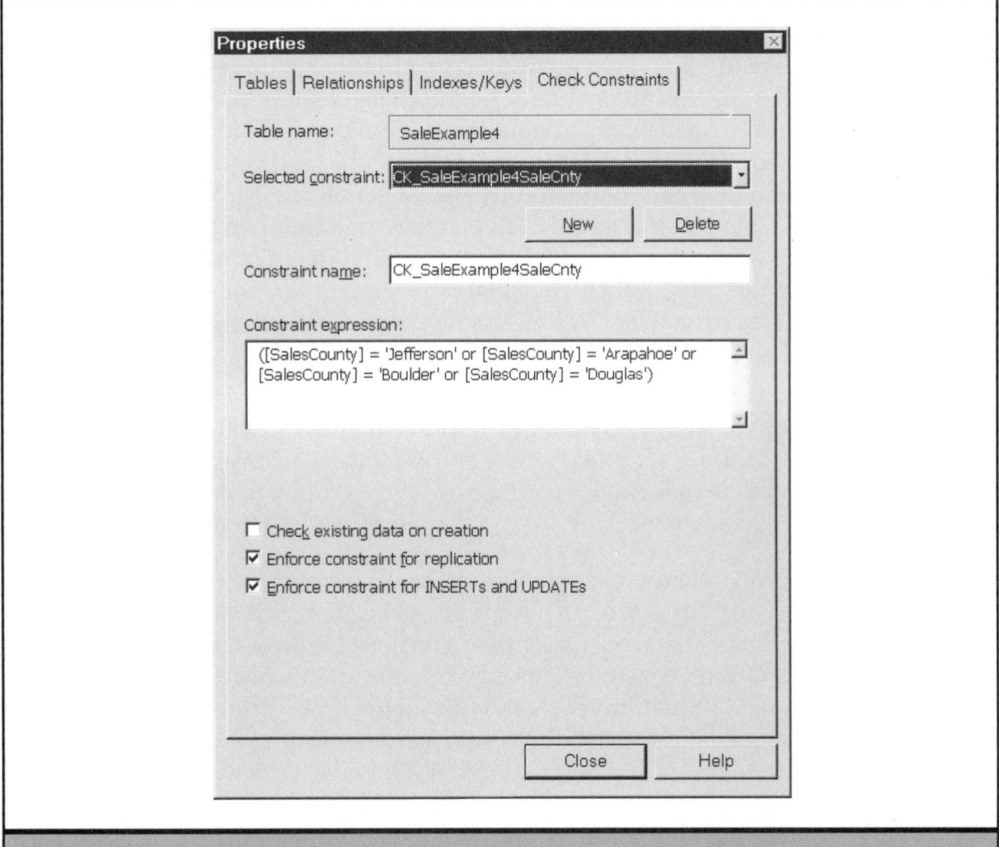

Figure 15-10. Check constraints are created as table properties, from Design Table, Properties window, in Enterprise Manager.

Checking Existing Data

Whenever you create a primary key or a unique constraint, SQL Server will automatically check the data in the table to ensure that it meets the requirements of the constraint. There's no way to turn off this autochecking, because it is part of creating a unique index—which is what SQL Server is doing in the background.

Creating a foreign key constraint does, by default, cause data checking at the time of creation, but unlike the primary key and unique constraints, this checking can be disabled. You might want to turn off checking for two reasons: because the data in the table already meets the conditions of the constraint, or because it does not. This is not as contradictory as it sounds!

- *Reason one:* The data in the table already meets the conditions of the constraint—if you know this is true, why spend the time and cycles to check the data again? In the previous section, you established a check constraint on the column SalesCounty to limit data input to one of four counties. If your business were to grow and you needed to add more counties to the check constraint list, you could opt not to go the route of continually modifying the check constraint. Instead, you could create a new table, CountyList, which would contain a list of counties in which you could sell your product. The initial data you'll put into the CountyList table will come from the check constraint. Then you'll establish a foreign key constraint on the SalesCounty column of the SaleExample table, referencing the SalesCounty column of the new CountyList table. When you create this foreign key constraint, there's no need to check the data, because you know that it is all consistent.
- *Reason two:* The data in the table doesn't meet the conditions of the constraint—if you know this is true, why bother checking the data? You might have put a foreign key constraint on a column to prevent incorrect values from being input in the future, but you know the current data is inconsistent. As time permits, you'll do the cleanup on the current data, but you don't have time right now. You defer checking the old data until some time in the future.

To turn off checking when you add a foreign key constraint, use the WITH NOCHECK option. If you specify WITH CHECK or do not specify any option, SQL Server will check the existing data and will not create the foreign key constraint if there are violations.

When you add a Default constraint, the new constraint does not cause a reevaluation of existing rows of data. It just leaves them with their former values or it leaves them NULL. The only time the default constraint fills in data for existing rows is if you were to add a new column to the table and designate a default value at the same time. The WITH VALUES option instructs SQL Server to use the default to populate the new column; otherwise, it will populate the new columns with NULL. Should the new column not allow NULL, SQL Server will populate it with the default value, whether or not you specified the WITH VALUES option.

A check constraint, like a foreign key constraint, can optionally check or not check the existing data. The default behavior is to check existing data in the table. Again, you might want to turn off checking if you know for sure that all the data meets the check requirements—but only if you are *sure* that the data meets the check requirements. In versions of SQL Server prior to 7.0, turning off checking on existing data you suspect might not be correct is asking for problems later on. This is because of the way that SQL Server pre-7.0 handled check constraints on updates.

The ANSI-SQL standard declares that an update is essentially a delete of an old record followed by an insert of a new record. Any database management system that conforms to this part of the standard will check all columns of a record on an UPDATE statement to see if the contents meets the requirements of the various check constraints. So, in versions of SQL Server prior to version 7.0, even though a value in a column had not changed, it was checked against the constraint anyway—just as if it were being inserted for the first time. This produced some very unpleasant surprises.

This behavior changed with SQL Server 7.0. From this point onward, SQL Server no longer complies with the ANSI-SQL standard. Now, only data that has changed is verified against any existing constraints. The reason behind this is a simple one: performance. Each SQL Server table may have as many as 1,000 columns, each of which may have several constraints. It is not reasonable nor is it efficient to keep checking every column in such a table when only the data in one column has changed.

Enabling and Disabling Constraints

When you have to load a large amount of data into your database, you may want to temporarily disable check and foreign key constraint checking. You would turn off checking of new incoming data for the same reasons you might turn off checking of existing data. For example, you might have a check constraint that makes sure your Dallas branch office enters data only for customers from Texas. At the head office in Toledo, Ohio, the office staff can enter data with a state value of OH only. But when you import the data from Texas, you want to turn off that check constraint.

To disable a check constraint, you would code it as follows:

```
ALTER TABLE dbo.SaleExample4 NOCHECK CONSTRAINT CK_SaleExample4SaleCnty
```

This disables the check constraint you created in the last section. Once it is disabled, if you want to re-enable the constraint, you simply code like so:

```
ALTER TABLE dbo.SaleExample4 CHECK CONSTRAINT CK_SaleExample4SaleCnty
```

You can disable and re-enable check and foreign key constraints on an as-needed basis. To permanently remove a constraint, you drop it, as follows:

```
ALTER TABLE dbo.SaleExample4 DROP CONSTRAINT CK_SaleExample4SaleCnty
```

As you recall, primary key and unique constraints cannot be temporarily disabled, because the associated indexes must still be updated for any INSERT operation. These indexes are charged with enforcing uniqueness.

The NOT FOR REPLICATION Option

If you're using SQL Server replication, some of the same issues that surround checking existing data are relevant to replicated data. In a replication environment, you're copying data from the publishing database to the subscribing databases. If the data has been checked and validated and verified at the publisher, why do it all over again at the subscriber? To disable check constraints on the subscribing databases, use the NOT FOR REPLICATION option. Data added to the table by the replication process is then exempt from the check constraint requirements.

To disable a check constraint from data that is going to be replicated, you would create the constraint on the subscribing database as follows:

```
ALTER TABLE dbo.SaleExample4
ADD CONSTRAINT CK_SaleEx4SaleDate
       CHECK NOT FOR REPLICATION (SaleDate <= CURRENT_TIMESTAMP)
GO
```

This check constraint will apply only to data that is inserted directly into the database by nonreplication users. A replication login, such as sqlrepl, will trigger a suspension of the check constraint. Other constraints, such as the default and foreign key constraints, can also be turned off for replication.

CONSTRAINTS vs. DEFAULTS AND RULES

Constraints have certain advantages over defaults and rules, and they have some disadvantages. Perhaps the biggest factor in deciding which to use is that constraints are ANSI-SQL compliant, and defaults and rules are not. In some future release of SQL Server, support for defaults and rules may not be available. For new databases, you might consider using constraints instead of defaults and rules. There's nothing you can code in a rule or a default that you cannot code with a constraint, so you are not giving up any functionality. Table 15-1 shows some of the features and limitations of the default and rule objects versus the default and check constraints.

CONSTRAINTS vs. TRIGGERS

Should you use constraints or should you use triggers? We'll address triggers in Chapter 18, but a comparison of constraint use and trigger use is appropriate at this point. The answer to the question is easy: If a constraint will do the job, use it rather than a trigger. Otherwise, use a trigger. Constraints (and defaults and rules, for that matter) are more

Defaults and Rules	Constraints
Reusable code: define once, bind to many columns	Separate definitions for each column
Can be bound to user-defined datatypes	Cannot be bound to user-defined datatypes
Ease of maintenance for code changes, change in one place	Code changes require modifications to each object, which is less efficient
Separate object, loads into memory only after associated table is loaded into memory	Part of the table definition, loaded into memory with the table, enhances performance
Not ANSI-SQL standard	ANSI-SQL standard

Table 15-1. Choose Defaults/Rules or Constraints, Depending on Your Requirements

efficient to use than triggers. Constraints, defaults, and rules are all proactive—they stop bad things from happening. A constraint essentially says, "Don't even think about inserting a record unless the state code is CO."

A trigger, on the other hand, is reactive. Most SQL Server triggers fire after the fact—that's why they're called triggers. A condition happens, and it causes a trigger to fire. There is one exception in the SQL Server 2000 INSTEAD OF triggers. These act different, but they are meant for a special use, as we'll discuss in Chapter 18. A trigger would say, "Hey, that record you just inserted has the wrong state code, so I am going to roll back the change." SQL Server has to do more work to enforce trigger code than to enforce constraint code.

So when is it appropriate to use a trigger? Use a trigger when you need to reach beyond the local table, when your code needs to cause actions in another table that are something more than a foreign key constraint. A foreign key constraint can confirm that the records you're entering into the SaleItem table have a valid ProductID, but it cannot tell you if the item is in stock. To do that, your code has to check the data in the Inventory table and return a value, the QuantityOnHand.

Another reason for using a trigger instead of a constraint is that you can code your triggers to include customized error messages and return specific error codes. When a constraint violation occurs, the returned message does indicate which column in which table caused the problem, but it always returns the same error code. If you have a front-end application, such as an Access or a VB application, it probably works with returned error codes rather than trying to parse a long and complex error message. With a trigger, you can define specific error codes with your own customized error messages and have the interface application respond to the various different error codes. You can

even have the error message written to the Windows NT/2000 event log and cause an alert within SQL Server to be fired, notifying someone of a problem.

CAUTION: You can write a trigger on a table that can perform an update or a delete on another table. If the second table has cascade delete or update enabled, though, a cascade chain could be started by the initial trigger. It will ripple through multiple tables.

The bottom line is, triggers are far more powerful than constraints, defaults, and rules, but they are also more complex. They can result in locking contention and performance bottlenecks, as they can access many tables during the performance of the trigger code. They can be written to request and hold more system resources than a comparable constraint or set of constraints. As we said before, if a constraint will get the job done, use it.

CHAPTER 16

Indexes

SQL Server can function without indexes in the same way your car can transport your family without gas—that is, if you don't mind getting out and pushing. You really would not want to run SQL Server without indexes, and "run" would not be the correct word. Planning your indexing strategy should be an integral part of the database design, not an afterthought. The strategy should take into account how the database will be used, and whether it is primarily used for data entry or data analysis. It's also a good idea to plan for maintaining the indexes, to make sure your database continues to perform well.

WHAT IS AN INDEX?

An index is a system-controlled database file—a table—that speeds up data retrieval, allowing SQL Server to directly and rapidly locate a requested record or set of records in a user table. Without an index, SQL Server would have to do table scans for every query, searching through all of the records in a table—thus having a negative impact on data retrieval.

Just like the index at the end of a book helps you find a topic in the book by listing the topic entry and then referencing the page or pages where the topic is discussed, the index on a SQL Server table contains index key values and pointers to the pages or rows where the data can be found. Indexes are also used to enforce database integrity, as we discussed in the previous chapter when talking about primary key and unique constraints. And last but not least, indexes speed up joins and enforce foreign key relationships.

When to Use an Index

An index is most useful for retrieving data. The rule of thumb with creating indexes is that you need an index on columns that will be used for searching, grouping, sorting, or joining. You need to know how your data is going to be used.

When you create a table and specify a column as a primary key or as having a unique constraint, SQL Server automatically creates a unique index on the table created. The unique index enforces the restriction that there will be no duplicates within each set of primary key or unique key values.

As we mentioned in Chapter 15, if you designate a foreign key constraint on a column or set of columns, you will want to create a non-unique index on the foreign key column(s). Your data model may call for one-to-many relationships in the database that are not enforced. You don't create a foreign key constraint on them; but if you'll be using these relationships to join tables, you'll also want to create an index on each unconstrained foreign key.

Columns that are frequently used for searching (in the WHERE clause of a SELECT query or the HAVING clause of a GROUP BY statement), grouping (in the GROUP BY clause), or sorting (in the ORDER BY clause) should also be indexed. "Frequently" is a relative term; you'll need to monitor data usage to confirm which columns need to be indexed and which don't.

When Not to Use an Index

Can you have too much of a good thing? Can you overuse indexes? If indexes are very useful when doing data retrievals, what do they do for data modifications? For every inserted row, each of the indexes that reference that row has to have a comparable row inserted. (Remember, indexes are system maintained; you don't have to write additional code for these index operations.) For each update to an existing row, it's possible that every index that references that row will also have to be updated. What may look like a single-row operation to the programmer is, in fact, a multi-row, cross-table operation. The increased time taken to modify a heavily indexed user table may be the difference between an application that works well and one that users find unacceptably slow.

So the answer is yes, you can overuse indexes. If your database environment is mainly data entry driven, and if your database is a transactional operation (OLTP) that must accept one million inserts/updates a day, then you absolutely can over-index. The trick is to determine, database by database, which indexes help performance and which do not—and which ones may even be slowing things down.

On the other hand, if your database is used primarily for data retrieval, a data mart, or a data warehouse, or if it is a snapshot replicate that contains lots of views for end-user report writing, you can and should index heavily.

What Makes a Good Index?

The point of using an index is to speed up the performance of the database during query retrievals. When you run a query, you want to narrow down the search to a small number of records as quickly as possible. So the more selective the index, the better. Selectivity is a measure of the number of unique values in an *index key*—the column or combination of columns on which the index is built. For example, a search on the State column of your Customer table is not very selective. It has a low selectivity, as you only have 50 different values in the table, and so you will see many rows in the result set. A query on a specific zip code will return a smaller data set than a query based on a state code, as you have thousands of different values in the zip code column—a high selectivity. A query on customer number can be extremely selective, because it can return a single row. The customer number column has as many different values as there are rows in the Customer table. That doesn't mean you shouldn't index on the state or zip code columns. If you frequently query on these columns, you should index them.

The less selective an index, the less likely it will be used. Suppose that instead of a single value of state (or zip code or customer number), you query for a range of 20 values of state code. A query for 20 states is going to return about 40 percent of the rows (low selectivity), so chances are that the Query Optimizer will do a table scan instead of using the state code index. A similar query on a range of 20 zip codes will produce only a small percent of your data (high selectivity), unless your customers are clustered in a few zip codes. The Query Optimizer will most likely use the zip code index in this case. The highest selectivity would come with the query that asked for a range of 20 customer numbers.

This query will return at most 20 records, so the Query Optimizer will most certainly call for the use of the customer number index.

Short columns make better indexes than long columns, because the shorter the index key, the more index records can fit on a page. We'll talk about how indexes are stored in a minute, but for now we'll say that the more index records you can store on a page, the fewer levels in the index. The fewer levels in an index, the fewer I/O operations, so the faster the data retrieval.

Columns with very few unique values are generally not worth indexing. You would not, for example, index the gender column in your Employees table, because at most you'd have three discreet values for gender: M, F, and NULL. This is extremely low selectivity. Any search on "M" or "F" is going to return about half the records, so a table scan would actually return the data faster. A table scan reads the table into memory page after page, in sequence. Data retrieval based on an index will first read the index entries, and then follow the pointers into the data table and retrieve the data pages in index order. The latter technique takes longer than the former, so if the result set is a significant percentage of the whole table size, the Query Optimizer will call for a table scan.

Small tables may not be worth indexing, because they occupy just a page or two, so they may already be in cache if they are frequently used tables such as reference or lookup tables. The overhead involved with referring to the index and then having to retrieve the data from a particular page is just not cost-effective.

Variable-length columns are not good candidates for indexing. The extra overhead involved in handling the variable column lengths works against the purpose of indexing them the first place. However, if you frequently query on these columns, you may have to index them. There's no simple rule to say whether using a variable-length column will hurt or help performance, either for data entry or for data retrieval. If your testing and analysis show that you're not getting the performance gains you would like from a variable-length column, try a test with a comparable fixed-length column.

How to Find Out Which Index Is Being Used

The quickest way to determine which index, if any, is being used for a query or modification statement is to check the Execution Plan window in the Query Analyzer. After executing a query, switch over to the Execution Plan window. Place the cursor over any table object in the execution plan, and you will see a detail overlay window, showing which index was used or whether a table scan was performed. An alternative technique, again from the Query Analyzer, is to choose Query | Current Connection Properties, and check the box for Set Showplan Text. This option shows the various steps in the query plan as text lines, and you can easily spot the index scans, as demonstrated in Figure 16-1. In this figure, a simple SELECT from the Person table is implemented by a scan of the clustered index built on the PersonID column [StrawberryFirst].[dbo].[tblPerson].[tblPerson_PK].

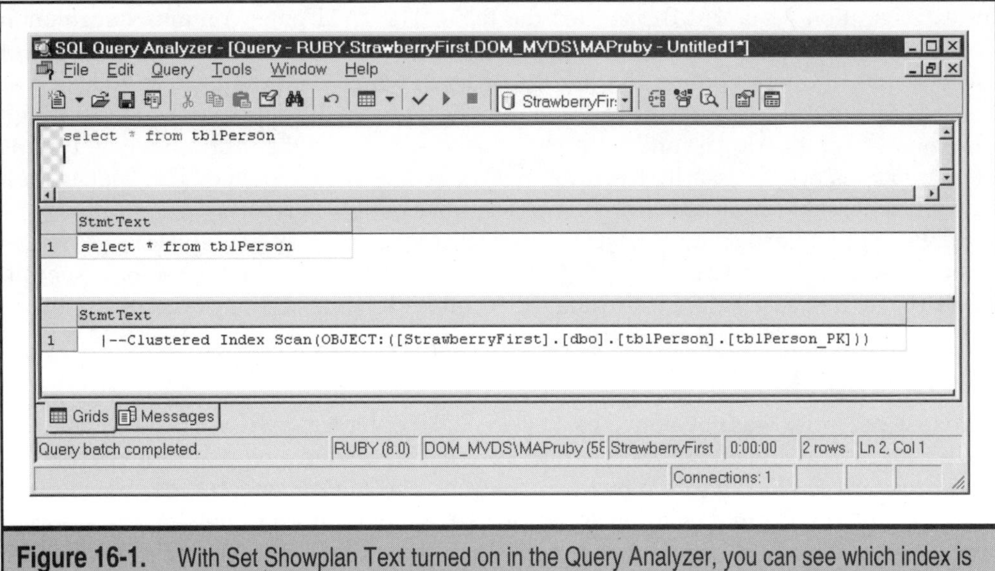

Figure 16-1. With Set Showplan Text turned on in the Query Analyzer, you can see which index is being used to resolve a query.

INDEX FILE STORAGE

Indexes are SQL Server tables, albeit under system control and maintenance, and are stored as such. SQL Server uses the B-tree scheme of file storage and management for both data and index files. The B-tree is tree-shaped, with a root page at the top, one or more intermediate-level pages, and leaf pages at the bottom. The strength of a B-tree file structure is that it is a balanced tree. It can automatically splice or split branches to accommodate file changes, so that the distance (number of levels) between the root and the leaf pages is the same, no matter where you happen to be located in the tree. A search for any data record, using an index B-tree, will always traverse the same number of levels in the tree, thus requiring the same number of page I/O operations.

Depending on which kind of index you're talking about, the leaf pages may contain the actual user data records (the table itself) or they may simply contain pointers to the data records. The pointers in the latter leaf type are row pointers; they point directly at a data page, to where the user record is stored in a table.

Heaps

SQL Server, unless directed otherwise, will not store data in any particular order. Any new records are appended to the end of the existing data file. A query that's searching for data will begin by looking in the sysindexes table and finding the location of the first

Index Allocation Map (IAM) page for the table. The IAM page contains information about the extents that have been allocated to this table. While it now knows the location of these extents, it doesn't bother to track the order in which the extents were allocated or the order in which the rows were inserted into the table. So the data search scans through the extents from first to last and returns the selected rows in the order in which it finds them, which is not necessarily the order in which they were inserted. This makes for a fast, efficient search compared with earlier versions of SQL Server.

If it's imperative that you get data returned in a specific order, you must supply an ORDER BY clause in your queries. Then SQL Server will sort the data in the tempdb (temporary storage) database before returning the result set to your calling program.

Clustered Indexes

The clustered index was developed back when SQL Server was a Sybase product, and it is still a feature of Microsoft SQL Server indexing. It differs from a regular index in that the data pages are physically sorted by the index key—the column or columns on which the index is built. If you build an index on employee number, for example, the data is sorted and stored, generally in ascending employee number order. The clustered index is like a telephone directory or an encyclopedia, in which you look up the key value and the data is right there on the page.

The clustered index can provide some significant performance benefits, especially when you retrieve data based on a range of values in this column. Once SQL Server finds and reads the first record in the range, it just continues reading pages until it reaches the end of the specified range, without needing to refer to the index again. This is a very efficient way to do data retrieval.

There can be only one clustered index per table because there can be only one physical sort order in a table. In some data mart/data warehouse environments, the decision as to which column should be used for the clustered index can result in a strange compromise: Two copies of the table are created and stored, each with a different clustered index. Now the queries will have to access the correct copy of the table, but the performance benefits are worth the extra effort. And, as this is a data retrieval environment we're talking about, there will be no online data entry, so synchronizing the two copies of the file need be done with regular bulk inserts only.

A clustered index key should be as short as possible. Avoid creating clustered indexes on very long columns or combinations of columns, such as first and last name. The clustered index values, or keys, are stored by the nonclustered indexes in their leaf-level pages. The clustered key value is then used to retrieve the record. The nonclustered indexes have to store the clustered index key value, and the longer the clustered index key, the more space it will take up in the nonclustered index page.

One common trap people fall into with clustered indexes is assuming that the primary key has to be the clustered index. By default, when you add a primary key constraint to a table, the index it builds will be a clustered index. But that's only the default behavior, and you can change that. The primary key might make a good clustered index, especially if it's an automatically assigned integer value, 4 bytes long. This makes for a nice short key for all the nonclustered indexes to reference. In a data entry environment, there's less likelihood that you will be running queries to select a large range of data. It's more likely that you will be dealing with one record at a time and inserting, updating, or retrieving. In this environment, you want to choose the clustered index column for its overall efficiency, and a short primary key fills the bill very well. Just keep in mind that you always have the option to make the primary key a nonclustered index.

In case you have to maintain an older application, you might keep in mind that the introduction of row-level locking in SQL Server 7.0 changed the entire mindset on how you assign a clustered index. Previously, especially prior to SQL Server 6.5, if your clustered index was an automatically incrementing column, such as a primary key, you would see a performance hit on row inserts. Each new record added to the table would get the next available incremented value, which meant it was quite likely going to be on the same page as the previous record inserted. With page-level locking, the second insert would have to wait until the first insert completed and released the page lock. To avoid this problem, it was common to deliberately use a column other than the autoincremented primary key for the clustered index. For example, in a catalog order entry system in the Order table, rather than using the autoincremented order number as the clustering index, the programmers might have used the customer number, which is a foreign key in the Order table. As there's no way of knowing which customers will call in to place orders, the effect is a randomizing of pages for row inserts. Each data entry person would be inserting a row at a different point in the Order table, and contention would be significantly reduced.

Keep in mind that a clustered index does not have to be unique (unless it is created by a primary key or unique constraint). If a company regularly sends out mailings to its customers, it may have a customer table in which the clustered index is built on the zip code column, something that certainly is not unique.

In SQL Server 6.5, Microsoft introduced "row-level locking on insert," based on the idea that if two people were both inserting records on the same page, neither of them would be interfering with the other, as they would not even be able to see the other's record until the inserts were complete and committed. Realistically, this "feature" was more about Microsoft being able to claim that SQL Server had row-level locking than about any functional improvement, although it did do much to relieve this known bottleneck. The real resolution to this problem came in SQL Server 7.0, with true row-level locking. Now you can, if you wish, have the order number as the clustered index, and the new orders will not conflict with each other as they are being inserted. If you are working with an older database and wondering why the designer did not use the primary key as the clustered index, this may be why.

A clustered index does not require much storage space on the disk, especially if you use a small, compact key. The root and intermediate levels of the B-tree are index pages.

The leaf pages are composed of the data in the table. The intermediate- and root-level index pages take up some additional space, but typically add only 2–5 percent to the size of the table.

Nonclustered Indexes

A traditional or nonclustered database index is like the index at the back of a book, where the topics are arranged alphabetically, but the pointers to the pages for those topics are not in any particular order. Once you find the index value, you have to turn to a different page in the book to retrieve the data.

A nonclustered index contains the index key values, normally sorted in ascending alphabetic order, along with a pointer to where the data rows are located. If there is a clustered index on the table, the pointers are the clustered key values from the clustered index. If there is no clustered index on the referenced table, the pointers are the row identifiers of the actual rows in the table. Why did Microsoft go to the trouble of having two different ways of accessing the data from within a nonclustered index? It might seem like it's more efficient to be able to jump right to the page and row location of the user data from the leaf level of a nonclustered index, rather than having to traverse through the levels of a clustered index to retrieve the required data. And, in practice, this is true for data retrievals. But retrievals are only part of the picture. Performance on inserts and updates is a major factor to consider, especially in a high-volume data entry environment.

In a clustered index, because the data is sorted in a certain order, any INSERT operation has to insert the data at the right position in the data pages. To do so, it will probably have to relocate some other rows on the page. If there's not enough room on the page, SQL Server will have to move half the existing rows onto a new page, a process known as *page splitting*, and then shuffle the remaining rows on the old page to accommodate the new entry. In each case, as the existing rows are moved, their locations change, and so do the locations of the index entries on the index pages. They all have to be reorganized. When you defragment your table by rebuilding the clustered index, the data is written to a new set of pages, and again all the associated nonclustered indexes would have to be updated. But now that the nonclustered indexes point to the clustered index key instead of the row identifier, they do not know or care where the data is actually stored. Their pointer value is still accurate.

In a data entry environment, there is a definite benefit to building the nonclustered indexes on top of the clustered index for each table. In a data mart/data warehouse situation, the benefits are not as obvious.

Depending on the size of the indexed column or columns and pointer values, a nonclustered index can add a substantial amount to your storage requirements. If a table has many indexes created on it, it could easily double in size.

Which to Use, Clustered or Nonclustered Indexes?

Deciding to use clustered or nonclustered indexes is not really a question of which is better. The real decision is whether to use a clustered index, and, if so, which of the possible candidate columns will make the best clustered index. All other indexes have to be nonclustered. Table 16-1 summarizes the differences between clustered and nonclustered indexes.

TYPES OF INDEXES

If you look at the composition of the index key, there are four different types of indexes: unique indexes, non-unique indexes, composite indexes, and covering indexes.

Unique Indexes

If you need to enforce uniqueness in a column, you need to create a unique index on that column. As we mentioned in the last chapter, the indexes that are automatically built when you designate a column as a primary key or as unique are unique indexes. Once an index has been defined as unique, SQL Server will prevent any attempt to insert a row that has a duplicate value in the indexed column. It will also reject any attempt to make a change to the column values that would result in a duplicate value.

Non-unique Indexes

A non-unique index is just what it sounds like, an index that will allow duplicate values. This is the type of index you would create on foreign key columns, and on columns you often use for searching, sorting, and grouping by. Non-unique indexes can be clustered, but generally they are thought of as being the nonclustered indexes.

Composite Indexes

A composite index is an index that is created by concatenating, or appending, the values of two or more columns. The order of the columns is important. An index on City +

Clustered Index	Nonclustered Index
One clustered index per table	Maximum 249 nonclustered indexes per table
Clustered indexes physically sort the data	Nonclustered indexes have no impact on how the data is stored
The leaf level of a clustered index is the data	The leaf level of a nonclustered index is a pointer to the data

Table 16-1. Differences Between a Clustered and Nonclustered Index

StateCode is quite different from an index built from StateCode + City. Not only are the key values different (GoldenCO versus COGolden, respectively), there is also a difference in the effectiveness of the index. You have 52 different state code values (including DC and Puerto Rico), and you have 10,000 city values. An index on StateCode + City is only moderately selective. It will first narrow the data to approximately 1/50 of the total number of rows, and then it will look for the city matches within this group. Conversely, the index on City + StateCode is highly selective. It will narrow the search down to 1/10,000, and then it will narrow the search even further based on state. The second index is much more selective than the first.

Does high selectivity alone make a better index? Not necessarily, if that's not how you access the data. You have to understand how your data is being accessed to understand what makes a good composite index and what doesn't.

One benefit of a composite index like StateCode + City is that it can also be used for a search just on state values, so there's no need for you to create a separate index on just StateCode alone. When the index StateCode + City is used to retrieve data only on the StateCode component, SQL Server just ignores the second column (City) in the index.

Covering Indexes

A covering index is an index whose key value contains all the data needed to satisfy the query that has called the index. In this case, the index is the end result; there is no need to read the full leaf page (in the case of a clustered index) or follow a pointer to another table (for nonclustered indexes).

Consider this example: Every week you generate an internal company e-newsletter, and email it to every person in the company. The fields you need to email the newsletter are the employee's name and email address, and this information is stored in the Employee table of your database. You know there's already an index on LastName + FirstName. If you could add a column to this index for email address, the index would be a little bit larger than it was before, but when you run the query to generate the email list, it runs faster. What's happening is that once SQL Server gets to the leaf level of the index, it has all the information it needs to resolve the query—the employee name and email address. It doesn't have to search a list of pointers, and it doesn't have to retrieve data from the Employee table. In fact, it doesn't even have to look at the table at all! It has everything it needs, right in the index key values.

When all the information you need is contained in an index, the index is known as a *covering index*. Once it's been changed, other queries that normally use this index will ignore the new column. There might be a small performance hit, because a bigger index means fewer index values on an index page, and therefore SQL Server has to read more pages to scan the same index. Sometimes, though, it is worth a little extra disk storage and perhaps slightly slower performance on some queries to optimize one or more frequently run large queries.

CREATING INDEXES

The syntax of the CREATE INDEX statement is shown here:

```
CREATE [ UNIQUE ] [ CLUSTERED | NONCLUSTERED ] INDEX index_name
    ON { table | view } ( column [ ASC | DESC ] [ ,...n ] )
[ WITH
        [ PAD_INDEX ]
        [ [ , ] FILLFACTOR = fillfactor ]
        [ [ , ] IGNORE_DUP_KEY ]
        [ [ , ] DROP_EXISTING ]
        [ [ , ] STATISTICS_NORECOMPUTE ]
        [ [ , ] SORT_IN_TEMPDB ] ]
[ ON filegroup ]
```

Though the index is not an object that is supported by any of the ANSI-SQL standards to date, it is almost universally used by all relational database management systems to enhance performance. The syntax of the CREATE INDEX statement is simple: create an index—either unique, clustered, or nonclustered—and give it a name. It has to be created on one or more columns of a table or—new to SQL Server 2000—on a view. You can have the index key values sorted in ascending (the default) or descending order. There are parameters to manage its placement, sizing, growth factors, and behavior.

So, for example, to create an ordinary, nonclustered index on the Employee table's JobTitle column, you could code as follows:

```
CREATE NONCLUSTERED INDEX idx_Emp_JobTitle
ON tblEmployee(JobTitle)
WITH FILLFACTOR = 20
```

You can create an index immediately after the table (or view) is created or any time after that. You always want to create the clustered index first, before creating any nonclustered index. If you don't, the nonclustered indexes you create will be built with row pointers. Then, when you create the clustered index, all the nonclustered indexes will have to be rebuilt (this happens automatically, by the way), substituting the clustered index key values for the row pointers. When this happens with a very small table, you will hardly notice it. When it happens with a very large table, the effect on performance can be profound.

When you create a clustered index on a table, the actual data pages from the table are copied over and sorted into index key order, creating the leaf level of the B-tree file. For large tables, this happens section by section—these are called *intermediate sort runs*. The intermediate sort runs are then sort-merged into a full, sorted copy of the user table. Finally, copies of the index key values are used to build the intermediate and root levels of the B-tree index "on top of" the sorted data pages. You will need free space in the user database equivalent to roughly 1.21 times the original table size. This may vary based on the size of the index key you selected and the fill factor. Once the clustered index is built, the pages occupied by the original copy of the table are released. However, during the index build process, the extra space is required.

SQL Server 2000 introduced a new option for the CREATE INDEX statement, SORT_IN_TEMPDB. This instructs the CREATE INDEX process to use the tempdb database to store the intermediate sort runs. If the tempdb database is on a separate disk—a separate spindle, so that the read/write heads for tempdb are a different set from the user database read/write heads—this option will give you some performance gain in two ways. During the reads and writes of the original data pages to the sorted data pages, the writes are happening in tempdb. Having two sets of read/write heads working together—one set to read original data, the second set to write sorted data—will result in more sequential processing, thus streamlining the operation and reducing the amount of time needed to get the read-write operation completed.

The second potential gain is in fragmentation of the index pages, or rather the lack thereof when tempdb is used to help create the index. If SORT_IN_TEMPDB is turned off when an index is created, all reads, writes, and intermediate operations are done in the user database filegroup. The single set of read-write heads now has to do continual back-and-forth, reading from one section of the filegroup and writing to another. The potential for fragmented extents in the index being created is high in this scenario because the write-index-page operations are interleaved with the intermediate sorts and sort-merge runs. The extents used for sorting are pretty much scattered through the filegroup—you can't count on them being contiguous, and you can't request contiguous space for these operations. As the sort work extents are freed, they can be allocated to fill the request for the write-index-page operation. Thus, you can count on the final index pages being noncontiguous.

If SORT_IN_TEMPDB is turned on when an index is created, all reads will be done from the user database filegroup, and all writes and sorts will be done in tempdb. When the final index pages are written back to the user filegroup, the chances of the write-index-page operation securing contiguous pages is much higher in this scenario than in the previous one. Contiguous pages for sequential operations (which is often the case with an index) are much more efficient than noncontiguous pages.

Regardless of whether you use the SORT_IN_TEMPDB option when you're creating an index, you'll still need the 1.21 space factor for the new clustered index in the user database. For additional information on how the SORT_IN_TEMPDB option works, SQL Server Books Online has a coherent, well-written explanation listed under keyword *tempdb and Index Creation*.

Fill Factor and Pad Index

Back in the old days when we had address books made of paper, rather than depending on an assortment of computers, PDAs, electronic organizers, and so on, there always seemed to be a problem with some pages in the address book filling up. One solution was to use a loose-leaf address book, so you could add extra pages as needed. The same thing happens with indexes in a database, because as you add new rows to the user table, any associated index key values have to be inserted into the right spot in the index page. When a page fills up, SQL Server has to find another empty page, transfer half the index values to the new page, rearrange the index records on both pages (these are at the leaf level, remember), and rebuild at least some of the intermediate-level pages in the B-tree. It's unlikely that SQL Server will find a blank page contiguous to the current index page, so it has to use whatever it can find, wherever it happens to be in the database. Although SQL Server has a record of the logical sequence of pages for the index so that it can retrieve in the correct order, physically the pages are now scattered across the disk. This randomizing of page locations hurts performance, especially on data retrievals. Eventually, you will have to restore good performance by a process known as *defragmenting* the index, which we'll talk about later in this chapter.

You can alleviate a lot of index fragmentation if you leave some space on the index pages for additional data to be entered. If there is enough room on a page for 1,000 index values, when you create the index you might designate that only 800 be stored on each page initially. Then up to 25 percent more data in the form of index keys can be added to each page before a page split would be needed. The database administrator should know how much data is being added to each database and so can schedule a periodic rebuild of each index. Rebuilding the indexes restores the free space back to its initial level.

FILLFACTOR is a parameter that indicates the percentage full each leaf page should be when the index is first built. Our example above would have a FILLFACTOR of 80. When you use a FILLFACTOR, you need to allow for more space to create the index—in this case, 25 percent more. If you know you'll be adding this much data anyway, it makes sense to allocate the space ahead of time, rather than have to deal with remedial action after the index performance has diminished.

Page splits and rebuilding index trees take time, so allowing as much free space as you'll need will definitely speed up the data entry process. But as with everything in a computer, you never get something for nothing. The trade-off is more I/O operations to read the entire index as you spread the index over more pages. If the index is heavily used, and the system has enough memory, the entire index may be cached, thus largely eliminating the concern about I/O. Still, it's not a good idea to use a 10-percent fill factor and expect it to suffice for the next two years' worth of additional data. A low fill factor makes sense only if you are planning to do some major bulk data loading in the near future. Typically, if you're bulk data loading large numbers of records, you drop the nonclustered indexes first, load the data, and then rebuild the nonclustered indexes. In the long term, the best plan to avoid index fragmentation is a combination of a reasonable fill factor and a plan to rebuild the index periodically to maintain the fill factor.

FILLFACTOR applies to the leaf level of an index, so in a clustered index, the data pages contain free space to allow for additional record inserts. FILLFACTOR on the clustered index will have a major impact on the size of the table and, if applied to all the tables, could expand the size of the database significantly. You can vary the fill factor by table, and even index by index, so you'll need to work closely with the database administrator on some reasonable values for FILLFACTOR. Tables that change very little, such as reference or lookup tables, might be able to use a FILLFACTOR of 100 percent (totally filled with data records, a single insert will cause a page split) or close to 100 percent. Tables such as the Product table might be set at 90 percent, the Customer table might be set at 85 percent, and the Sale table might be set at 75 percent. The actual percentages will vary depending on how many inserts are anticipated per table and how often the indexes are maintained.

In a data mart/data warehouse environment, where the data is not updated except by bulk loading, a fill factor of 100 percent would make the most efficient use of the data storage available. When data is bulk loaded into the warehouse (presumably on a scheduled basis), it is common practice to drop the indexes and perform a fast bulk load, rather than allow the load operation to update each data row/index row(s) combination. In a data warehouse, especially, you may not have any clustered indexes built on the tables, so the question of dropping and rebuilding clustered indexes is moot, especially if the data being loaded is time sequenced (time of entry determines the sort order). Once the data loading is complete, the indexes are rebuilt, again with the 100-percent fill factor.

FILLFACTOR was introduced in SQL Server 6.0. It was such a success that in version 6.5 the PAD_INDEX option was added. PAD_INDEX applies the same percentage free space to the non-leaf levels of the index tree as specified by the FILLFACTOR value. Finally, regardless of what value of FILLFACTOR you specify, SQL Server always leaves room for a couple of extra rows in each of the upper-level index pages.

Index Statistics

SQL Server uses a cost-based Query Optimizer, and the costs are estimated based on statistical information gathered about the table and its associated indexes. In versions of SQL Server prior to 7.0, gathering index statistics was a big deal. It had to be done manually or at the very least set up as a scheduled task. Statistics gathering is still a big deal, but the statistics maintenance has been automated, meaning that SQL Server is taking care of the statistics behind the scenes.

Each index maintains information about the statistical distribution of the data in the index, showing how the data is spread across the range of values in the index. This distribution shows how selective (or not) this index will be. The distribution shows, for example, whether your clients are clustered in a small range of zip codes or spread evenly across the country. It is this statistical data that the Query Optimizer evaluates to decide which index to use, or even whether or not to use an index. If a query is requesting just a few records returned, and you have built a highly selective index around the selection criteria, the index will be used. But if the query estimate determines that 40 percent to 50 percent of the table records will be retrieved as part of the result set, the Query Optimizer will probably perform a table scan.

If the index statistics get out of date, it is quite possible that the Query Optimizer will make the wrong choice on how to proceed, and this could be a costly error. Using an index when a table scan would work better, or vice versa, could negatively impact your production. In SQL Server versions prior to 7.0, statistical information had to be updated by manually running the DBCC command or the system stored procedure UPDATE STATISTICS. If this were not done, as more and more data was inserted, deleted, and modified in a table, the statistics would get more and more out of date, and performance would suffer. Hopefully, someone would realize that the drop in performance was more than could be explained by simply the volume of changed or added data. That's when the consultants would get called; they'd come in and look busy for a week, running all kinds of tests to determine that there wasn't another problem that was bottlenecking the system. Finally, on Friday afternoon, they would run the UPDATE STATISTICS command on all the tables in the database. And, like a miracle, performance would be restored, the consultants would look like heroes, and the invoice would reflect the time spent on site.

Starting with version 7.0, SQL Server automatically creates and updates the statistics, releasing these consultants to apply themselves to resolve ever more complex questions. In fact, SQL Server 2000 can now create a statistical distribution list for a column *when there is no index on that column*, if it decides that the Query Optimizer might benefit from knowing what the distribution of data is in the column. SQL Server can also independently decide that because a certain number of rows have been added to a table, it is time to update the statistical information for that table. Exactly how much data needs to be added depends on the size of the table. Apparently this algorithm is an internal one, because as of this writing, we don't know of a configuration parameter you can use to adjust this trigger point. One thing we do know: adding 10,000 rows to a 50,000-row table will probably cause the statistics to be auto-revised, but adding that same number of rows to a 1,000,000-row table will not.

As a developer, you will want to work with the database administrator to make sure indexes are maintained (rebuilt) at regular intervals. Rebuilding an index not only restores the fill factor, but it also causes the statistics to be updated. Although, technically, database maintenance is the database administrator's realm, the physical database designer needs to plan for the growth and maintenance of the database. If nothing else, poor maintenance will lead to poor performance, which might then be attributed to a nonscalable design.

Generating Index Fragmentation Reports

SQL Server provides tools to check indexes and show whether they are fragmented and, if so, how badly. If you suspect your database is not running well because of page splitting and index fragmentation, these utilities will check to see whether your suspicions are correct. The command to use, from the Query Analyzer, is DBCC SHOWCONTIG. In prior versions of SQL Server, you had to supply the table ID or index ID—not the table or index name. In SQL Server 2000, you can use the actual table or index name, or even the name of an indexed view. The output from this utility is concise, but you might be able to use a little explanation to interpret what it is telling you. We ran it on the Northwind database, because on our system the Order Details table was fairly fragmented. The syntax for DBCC SHOWCONTIG is simply this:

```
use Northwind
DBCC SHOWCONTIG ([Order Details])
```

In the results, shown in Figure 16-2, the pages' scanned value is 9. That means the data in this table occupies nine pages, or we have to read in nine pages to retrieve the whole table. We know that an extent is composed of eight pages, so this table should, if optimized, fit on two extents with some space left over. To read the whole table, we should have to read two extents. Reading two extents would require one "extent switch" as we move from extent one to extent two. That's the best possible case, and for this table, the lowest numbers we could ever expect to be possible.

Now take a look at the numbers brought back by DBCC SHOWCONTIG. The output actually shows that we read six extents, which means that SQL Server had to do five extent switches in the course of reading this table. Don't assume that the rows of the table are spread out over six extents—that is not what this report is saying. We know that the data in the table occupies nine pages; the report says so. But because of pages being split, added, and released, the pages are scattered over multiple extents. Here's a possible scenario whereby this report could be referencing two physical extents. Pages one and two are on the first extent, E1. Because page two had split, page three is on the second extent, E2. Pages four and five are on E1, but again, page five had split so page six is on E2. Pages seven and eight are located on E1; page nine is located on E2 because of a page split in seven or eight. The data is still in order on each page and is in order based on the logical sequencing of the pages—although this might not synchronize with the physical page

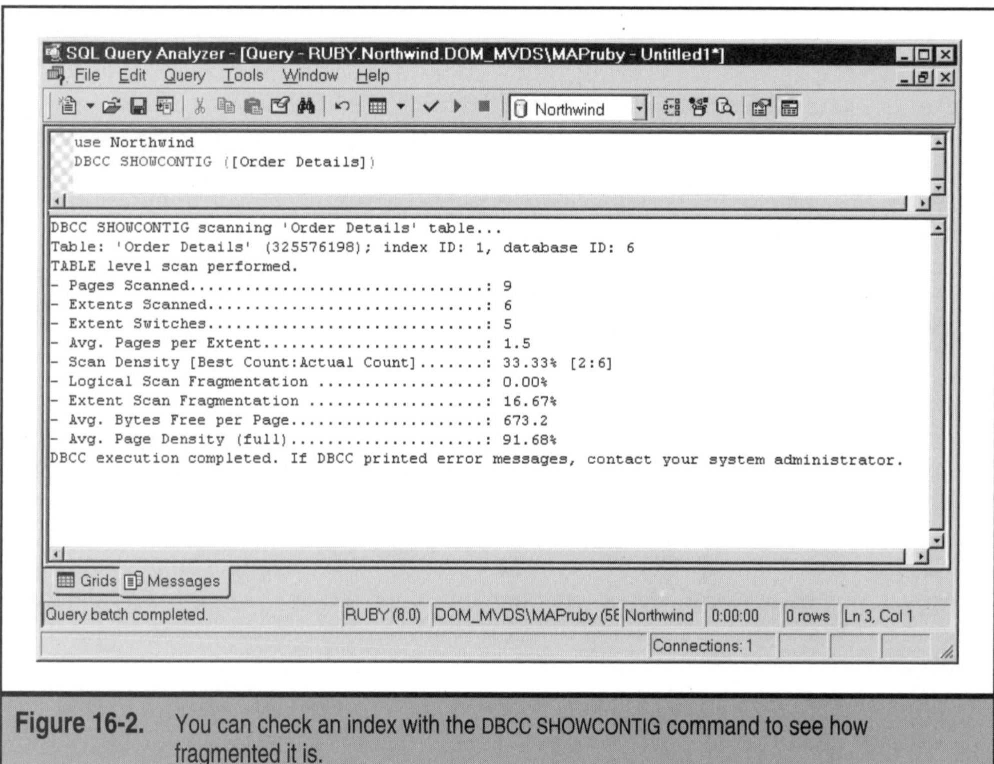

Figure 16-2. You can check an index with the DBCC SHOWCONTIG command to see how fragmented it is.

numbers. To read the data pages in their logical order would mean reading extents in the order E1, E2, E1, E2, E1, E2, for a total of six extent reads.

The most important value in this report is the Scan Density, which is the best count (the ideal number of extents that would have to be read if everything was contiguously linked) versus the actual count (the number of extents read). This is expressed as a 2:6 ratio, or 33 percent. If there were no fragmentation, and if the pages were stored in optimal order, the Scan Density would be a 2:2 ratio, or 100 percent. Also listed in Figure 16-2 are the Logical Scan Fragmentation, a measure of the out-of-order leaf pages of the index (not relevant for heaps), and the Extent Scan Fragmentation, which shows the percentage of out-of-order extents (again, relates to leaf pages/extents, not relevant for heap structures). Ideally, both of these values should be zero.

Dropping Indexes

Dropping an index is as simple as saying the following:

```
DROP INDEX tblEmployee.idx_Emp_jobtitle
```

Note that the index references the *tablename.indexname* in the DROP INDEX command, which is a little different from the CREATE INDEX command. We've already mentioned that you cannot drop an index that was created by a primary key or a unique constraint. If you drop a clustered index and there are nonclustered indexes on the same table, all of the nonclustered indexes will be rebuilt and row pointers will replace the clustered index key values in the leaf level of the index tree. So, to avoid overstressing your production system, if you really need to remove all the indexes on a table, you would first remove all nonclustered indexes and then drop the clustered index.

Index Rebuild Commands

If you drop an index and re-create it, you can restore the fill factor and update the statistics at the same time. Rebuilding also defragments the index and restores good performance. But not all indexes can be simply dropped and re-created at will, nor is dropping and re-creating an index something you can do without thought of the consequences. You cannot drop an index that was created by a constraint—as a result of a primary key declaration or a unique declaration when you created or altered a table. If you drop a clustered index, all the nonclustered indexes associated with it also get rebuilt, substituting row pointers for the index key values in the index leaf pages. Then when you re-create the clustered index, all these nonclustered indexes are rebuilt a second time, substituting the index key values for the row pointers. That's a lot of work! What you need is a way to rebuild a clustered index in place, without having to drop and re-create it. Fortunately, SQL Server has some commands that do just that.

Create Index with DROP_EXISTING

You can re-create an index in place by using a CREATE INDEX statement with the DROP_EXISTING clause. The CREATE INDEX with DROP_EXISTING is used in lieu of a DROP INDEX followed by a CREATE INDEX statement. The CREATE INDEX must reference an index that's already in the database or the command will fail. The DROP_EXISTING clause tells SQL Server that the index being referenced is consistent and that no corruption exists in the index key value set, so it can go ahead and rebuild the index using the existing key values. The rebuilt index will be defragmented, and the rebuild process can skip the sort step normally associated with building a clustered index, because the data is already sorted.

The CREATE INDEX with DROP_EXISTING really does drop the referenced index, which means it cannot be used with any indexes created by a primary key or unique constraint. These indexes—clustered or nonclustered—cannot be dropped, even though SQL Server Books Online suggests that DROP_EXISTING should work with indexes automatically created by these constraints.

In SQL 7.0, you could rebuild a constraint-created, nonclustered index by using the DROP_EXISTING option. However, that feature has been removed in SQL 2000. Now you cannot rebuild either clustered or nonclustered indexes if they were created as a result of a constraint. You have to use a different command to rebuild these indexes, the DBCC DBREINDEX command. This command rebuilds indexes dynamically, including any indexes created by primary key or unique constraints, without having to drop and re-create them. The DBCC DBREINDEX command can rebuild all the indexes on a table at once—just give it the table name and leave the index field blank, as follows:

```
DBCC DBREINDEX (tblEmployee)
```

To rebuild a single index, even one that was created as part of a primary key or unique constraint, use the following:

```
DBCC DBREINDEX (tblEmployee, tblEmployee_PK)
```

NEW IN 2000: INDEXING ON MATERIALIZED VIEWS

As we mentioned in Chapter 12, one of the great new features in SQL Server 2000 is the indexed view. This is the ability to keep views available for many users, instead of re-creating the view in memory whenever it is accessed. You can do this by creating a clustered index on the view, which causes the view to be stored rather than discarded. You can even create additional nonclustered indexes on the view, the same way you would create indexes on a table. The Query Optimizer then has the option to consider these indexed views when deciding how to evaluate a query; it may use the view even when it is not specifically mentioned in the query.

INDEX OPTIMIZATION

In addition to keeping the index keys short and maintaining the index by periodic rebuilding to reduce fragmentation, there are some other strategies for optimizing the performance of your indexes. One approach is to place the nonclustered indexes on a separate filegroup, which is located on a different physical disk from the device containing the tables. This will allow one set of disk heads to read the index and return a list of pointers, while another set of disk heads is reading the data rows that correspond to the pointers. The first rows of data will reach the user very quickly. As the user scrolls down through the data or as the front-end application processes the rows, more rows are being retrieved and delivered. The perceived response time is good, and the retrieval task is split between two sets of read/write heads, so everyone is happy.

The Index Tuning Wizard

Many factors influence how many and what kind of indexes should be built in a database: the volume of data, the number and type of users, the type of queries, the size of the columns, and even the speed of the hard disk and controller. There's a trade-off between storing extra indexes and having to do more table scans to retrieve the data. Do you use a fill factor to optimize inserts at the expense of having to read in more pages to resolve a query? Performance may vary over time and change as you upgrade the server. It is quite a challenge to balance all the possibilities, which is why selecting the right set of indexes is as much an art as it is a science. But if you want to inject a little more science into the process, SQL Server provides an Index Tuning Wizard.

The Index Tuning Wizard will analyze a typical workload on the server, looking at which queries are run and how often, which tables are accessed, and which indexes are used in a real production environment. It will then analyze the workload and recommend the best combination of indexes, based on the workload and the information in the Query Optimizer. It will offer suggestions about the effects of the proposed changes. Then it will generate a set of SQL statements to implement the proposed changes. The changes can be applied immediately, scheduled to run later, or saved to a file and run when the administrator decides the time is right, such as when the server is not being heavily used.

The Index Tuning Wizard can make recommendations. If it determines that some indexes are not optimized or are not being used, it will suggest that you drop them. You can also ask the Index Tuning Wizard to leave all current indexes in place and just make suggestions for additional indexes. Typically, you would use this option if you were having problems with a few queries and you were looking for some assistance in performance tuning.

The Index Tuning Wizard requires a typical workload to do its analysis. One way to supply this workload is to capture it with the SQL Profiler tool. You can try to simulate a workload using SQL scripts, but the Profiler trace will probably be more representative of the way your database responds when placed under load by the users.

CHAPTER 17

Stored Procedures

Converting T-SQL queries to stored procedures is one of the easiest and best ways to see performance gains in SQL Server. Stored procedures offer many benefits over interactive queries, including easier programming of client interfaces, enforcement of code logic standards across all applications, and enhanced security. In a client/server environment, stored procedures allow for a reduction in overall network traffic.

Stored procedures change the role of the database server from a general data store, whose function is to pass large volumes of data across the network to a calling program, to that of a true database server that does enhanced query resolution and conditional logic application, and that will return only the final result set to the calling program.

WHAT IS A STORED PROCEDURE?

A stored procedure, according to SQL Server 2000 Books Online, is "a group of Transact-SQL statements compiled into a single execution plan." Stored procedures are the meat and potatoes of writing database code. They can be the body of code that makes up any application that is underlain by a database and can be called from any of these applications. Stored procedures are a way of standardizing code and business logic throughout all applications that access a database, and a way of abstracting the table details from the end-user.

Stored procedures can be run from the Query Analyzer window. They can be called from within batch files or from user interfaces written in Access, Visual Basic, or any other programming language. You can pass parameters to a stored procedure, just like any other programming subroutine. The stored procedure will return data values, status codes, and error messages so you can respond appropriately. Stored procedures can call other stored procedures. Stored procedures can be run locally or on a remote server. You can instruct SQL Server to run certain stored procedures automatically at startup to perform system housekeeping tasks. By including the request to execute one or more stored procedures in a T-SQL script, you can schedule the procedures to run at regular intervals in the Enterprise Manager job queue.

CREATING STORED PROCEDURES

A stored procedure is just a compiled T-SQL script, so the first step in creating a stored procedure is to create and test the SQL script by running it from the Query Analyzer. Once you are satisfied that the script does what you want it to do, you can then turn it into a stored procedure. A stored procedure is specific to the database in which it is created. If you want the same stored procedure to appear in all databases, create it in the model database before you start creating the other user databases. Alternatively, if you already have user databases in production, you can create the stored procedure in one database, generate a T-SQL script of the stored procedure, and run the script in each of the other databases in which you want this stored procedure. As usual, the database owner and members of the ddl_admin role can create objects, and the database owner can grant permission to others to create stored procedures.

Microsoft "strongly recommends" that you do not use the prefix sp_ for the stored procedures you create. Microsoft has supplied hundreds of system-stored procedures, which are stored in the Master database and are available from anywhere in any database, and they all begin with sp_. If you run a stored procedure beginning with sp_, SQL Server will always look in the Master database first. If it doesn't find the procedure in the Master database, it will then look in the local database. Not only does this take longer, but there's always the risk that there will be a system stored procedure in the Master database with the same name. Should this happen, SQL Server will run the Master database version of the stored procedure, and your procedure will never get executed. The other side of this argument is that you can build a stored procedure in the Master database, call it sp_whatever, and then it will appear to SQL Server as a system-stored procedure. You'll be able to call this "stealth system-stored procedure" from anywhere on the server, without supplying the *full database_name.owner_name.object_name.*

Most programming languages have a process that goes like this: write code, save code, compile code, link, and run. T-SQL stored procedures operate just a little differently. You first write the code—create a procedure in the Query Analyzer. When you save the code, SQL Server will parse it, checking only the syntax of the stored procedure. It will make an entry of the stored procedure name in sysobjects, and it will write the text of the stored procedure into the syscomments table. Code compilation is done at runtime—it's not until the stored procedure is run for the first time that a check is done to make sure all the objects referenced in the stored procedure actually exist. At this time, SQL Server also determines an optimal access plan to retrieve the data. This *delayed name resolution* process is new to SQL 7.0 and 2000. This scheme allows you to create stored procedures that reference objects that don't yet exist. You can create objects in any order, although in our experience it's much easier to code from the top down. You can call a procedure that doesn't exist from within another procedure and then create the called procedure. You can also reference a table in another stored procedure that a coworker is still developing. The limitation of this technique means that if all referenced objects—stored procedures, tables, and so on—are not in place when you run your stored procedure, your stored procedure will fail. So, as a final check before releasing your stored procedure to production, you should run it to confirm that all pieces of the puzzle have been assembled and are ready to go.

Prior to version 7.0 of SQL Server, all objects, such as tables that were referenced by a stored procedure, had to be in existence when a stored procedure was created. The only exception to this rule was a second stored procedure that might be referenced by the stored procedure being created. If you happen to be working with a database whose compatibility level is set to 65, you will get an error message for any object that is referenced but does not yet exist when you create your stored procedure.

Once the object references have been verified, the Query Optimizer analyzes the steps in the procedure and creates an optimized execution plan. This execution plan is loaded into memory and used to run the procedure. It will then stay in memory until the

SQL Server is restarted or until SQL Server removes it from memory to reuse the space. If the stored procedure's execution plan is not found in memory, a new execution plan will be created. Re-creating the new execution plan will reoptimize the execution plan for the stored procedure.

When you create a stored procedure, the best approach—as with any other object in the database—is to create it with the owner as dbo (database owner). If you reference an object inside a stored procedure with a statement such as a SELECT or INSERT, and fail to reference the owner of the object, the owner of the object is assumed to be the owner of the stored procedure. Creating all database objects with owner dbo simplifies the ownership structure of your database objects and will simplify object troubleshooting when something goes wrong.

The following example creates a stored procedure in the Strawberry database. You're using your stored procedure naming convention, so the stored procedure name is prefixed with usp_ for user stored procedure. This stored procedure will generate a list of employees, including person identifiers, last and first names, and job titles.

```
CREATE PROCEDURE usp_employeelist AS
SELECT P.PersonID, LastName, FirstName, JobTitle
FROM tblPerson P JOIN tblEmployee E ON p.PersonID = E.PersonID
GO
GRANT EXECUTE ON usp_employeelist TO PUBLIC
GO
EXEC usp_employeelist
```

The SELECT statement is the same one you used when you built a view on the join of the Person and the Employee tables. You GRANT permission on the stored procedure to everyone who is a member of the public role for this database. Finally, you run the stored procedure to make sure it's working as planned.

Creating Stored Procedures Through the Graphical Tools

You can create a stored procedure by using the graphical interface, although you still have to know how to write the code. Open the database hierarchy in Enterprise Manager and select the Strawberry database. Right-click Stored Procedures and select New Stored Procedure. This opens a window in which you can type the code, as shown in Figure 17-1. You can even do a syntax check from this window, but there is no wizard to prompt you through creating the stored procedure code.

A more helpful graphical environment might be the Query Analyzer.

1. Open a Query Analyzer window.
2. From the top toolbar, click the arrow on the leftmost icon and it will drop down a list of options, one of which is Create Procedure.
3. Select this option, and the list expands to show more options, including Create Basic Procedure Template and Create Procedure With Output Parameters.

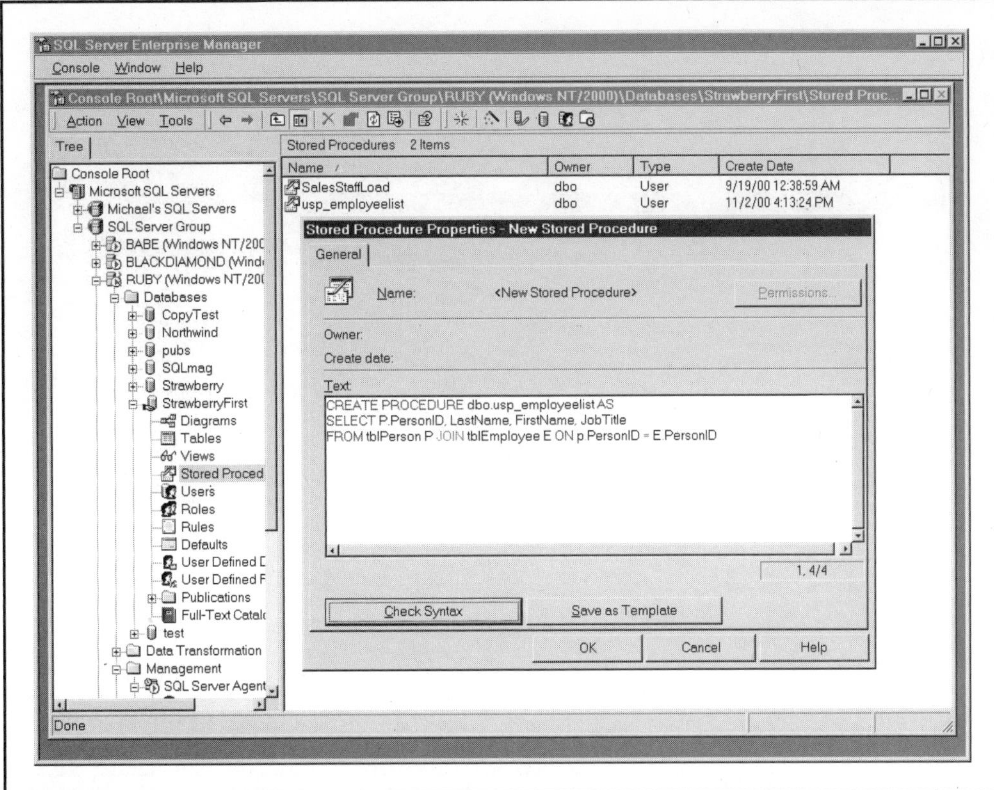

Figure 17-1. You can create stored procedures in Enterprise Manager; you must write the code yourself.

4. Select any of these options to open a new window with a template for the procedure laid out, as shown in Figure 17-2. Now all you have to do is substitute the names of the various objects for your procedure, the datatypes, and defaults, and of course, add the code for the procedure to run.

Temporary Stored Procedures

You can create a temporary stored procedure by starting the procedure name with the # or ## (pound or double-pound) symbol. Temporary stored procedures, like all temporary objects, are created in the tempdb database. A single # symbol means the procedure should be created as a local or private temporary stored procedure. Only the session that created the procedure can see it and run it, and only for the duration of the session the stored procedure was created in. A double # symbol will cause SQL Server to create a

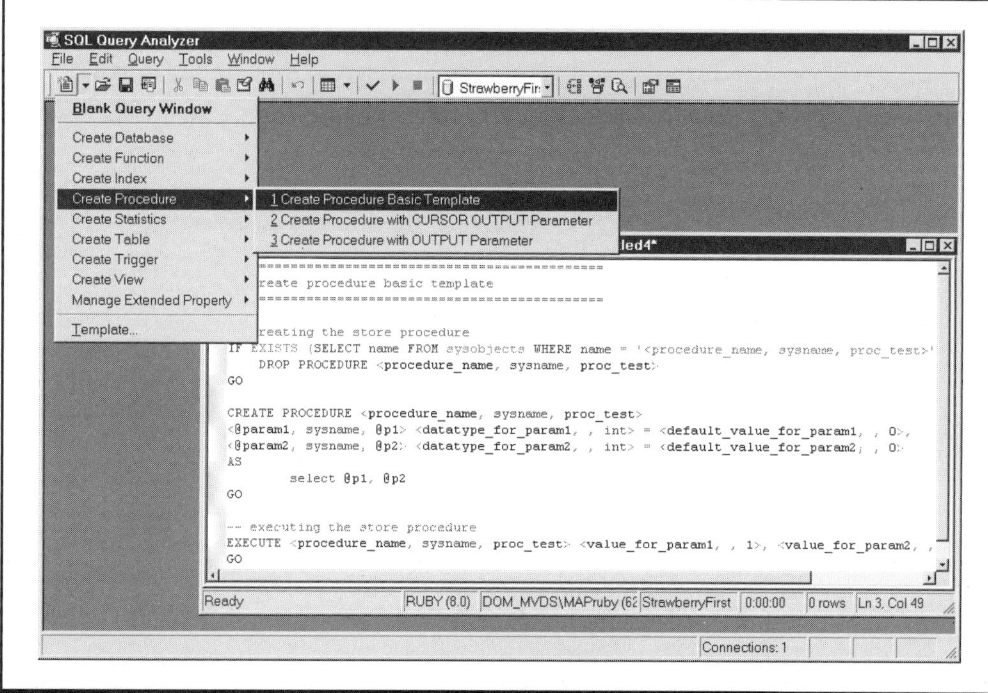

Figure 17-2. The Query Analyzer has a template to get you started on writing stored procedures.

global procedure that is visible to other users. You can GRANT permission to other users to run the temporary procedure. When the connection that created the procedure is terminated and the session is ended, nobody else can execute the procedure. Existing connections currently running the procedure can complete, but they cannot reconnect. The global temporary stored procedure is gone.

Temporary stored procedures created in tempdb are supported for backward compatibility with earlier versions of SQL Server. Execution plan reuse in versions of SQL Server prior to 7.0 was not highly evolved; practically the only way to reuse a query execution plan was to create a stored procedure out of the query.

If you want to create a "temporary" stored procedure that will persist after the session in which it was created, you can create the procedure directly in tempdb. Don't use the ## symbol, though. These persistent temporary stored procedures will hang around after the connections that created them have disconnected. However, they are deleted whenever the SQL Server service restarts, along with everything else in tempdb. There's an extra level of complexity involved in remembering to call the procedure in another database, as in the following:

```
Exec tempdb.dbo.usp_tempproc
```

If you really need to use a stored procedure, but you don't want to leave it behind in the database after you've used it, you can create it as a regular stored procedure, use it, and then immediately drop it, all from within a controlling T-SQL batch script. This approach has an additional benefit: you are using space in your own database rather than competing with other users for space and resources in tempdb.

PROCEDURE CACHING

One reason that stored procedures perform so well is that once a procedure has been run, it is retained in the *procedure cache* (a section of memory that is controlled by SQL Server) for the next time it is needed. SQL Server uses some sophisticated algorithms to decide which procedures are retained in cache, so that the least-frequently-used procedures are most likely to be discarded if processing activity outpaces the memory limitations. Supplementing the least-frequently-used algorithm, SQL Server also tends to retain procedures that take more work to compile, at the expense of procedures that can be recompiled quickly. From version 7.0 onward, SQL Server has the ability to vary the amount of memory allocated to the procedure cache dynamically, balancing it against the demands of the data cache. Also added in version 7.0 is the ability to allow multiple user connections to use the same copy of a procedure, even though each connection has a different set of input parameters. (In previous versions, if two connections called for the same stored procedure, you'd have two copies of the procedure in memory.) There are some restrictions about the environment settings having to be the same (ANSI null settings and so on); but if the two connections are consistent regarding these settings, SQL Server will keep only a single copy of each procedure in memory.

Temporary Stored Procedures vs. Cached Queries

Creating temporary stored procedures in tempdb was standard operating procedure in earlier versions of SQL Server, but you should consider a different approach in SQL Server 7.0 and later. SQL Server can now reuse execution plans generated by both online queries and stored procedures—it stores the execution plan in the procedure cache. If a user runs the same query twice, SQL Server knows it can use the same execution plan for both queries. If a query is the same except for some parameter, such as a query to look up customer data that varies only in the customer number, SQL Server performs a process known as *auto-parameterization*. It still knows that it can use the same execution plan for the two queries, but it substitutes a different value each time for the customer number. You have the option of telling SQL Server that you intend to run the same query repeatedly, using the SP_EXECUTESQL stored procedure.

Now that a query execution plan is stored in the procedure cache, what is the difference between a cached query and a temporary stored procedure (#proc_name) that's created in tempdb? The answer is, not that much, except that again the cached query uses resources and space in the local database, and the temporary stored procedure uses equivalent resources and space in tempdb. This is why Microsoft recommends the use of cached queries rather than temporary stored procedures. MS suggests that you use the temporary stored procedures only for backward compatibility when connecting to older versions of SQL Server.

PARAMETERIZATION OF STORED PROCEDURES

As we mentioned at the start of this chapter, you can pass parameters into a stored procedure—up to 1,024 of them—making the stored procedure very flexible. You have to define the parameters when you create the stored procedure and include a datatype for the parameter. When you run the procedure, SQL Server checks to make sure that the data assigned to the input parameters matches the datatype specified for that parameter. If you need to have a parameter value returned from the stored procedure, you have to say so, and you must explicitly make it an output parameter. You also have the option of specifying a default value for any of the parameters.

Passing Parameters

Passing parameters to a stored procedure works the same way as passing values to an INSERT statement. You can pass the parameters based on position, specifying parameter values in the order in which they are listed in the stored procedure; or you can list the parameters one by one, with their corresponding values, in any order. Almost every stored procedure will have some parameters that are always required and others that are optional. List the required parameters first when you create the procedure, and then add the optional parameters. That way, when you run the stored procedure, you can specify the required parameters by position and leave off the optional parameters if they are not needed.

If you have parameters for which you want to define default values, list those at the end of the parameters list and don't reference them if you want to use the default value when you run the procedure.

The following procedure can be used to add a new employee. It is updating both the Person table and the Employee table with the most critical information, some of which is supplied by default values. Optional information can be added later, using UPDATE statements.

```
CREATE PROCEDURE usp_AddNewEmployee
-- declare variables for tblPerson
@LastName varchar(20),
@FirstName varchar (20),
@MailingAddress varchar (40),
@City varchar (20),
@State char (2),
@Zip char (10),
-- declare variables for tblEmployee
```

```
@JobTitle varchar (20),
@SSN char (12),
@PayAmount money,
@PayPeriod varchar(10),
-- declare default values for tblPerson fields
@PersonType char(1) = 'e',
-- declare default values for tblEmployee fields
@I9OnFile char(3)= 'Yes',
@W4OnFile char (3) = 'Yes'
AS
BEGIN TRAN
INSERT INTO [tblPerson]
VALUES(@LastName, @FirstName, @MailingAddress, @City,
       @State, @Zip, @PersonType, DEFAULT)
declare @personID int
SELECT @personID = @@identity
INSERT INTO [tblEmployee]
VALUES(@PersonID, @JobTitle, @SSN, @I9onFile, @W4OnFile,
       @PayAmount, @Payperiod, DEFAULT)
COMMIT
GO
```

Notice that the parameters in the procedure do not quite follow the same order as the columns in the table. We put the I9OnFile, W4OnFile, and PersonType at the end. For most employees, you will have I-9 and W-4 forms; and, of course, you're talking about employees, so the default person type will be "e." For that reason, we also provided defaults of "yes" for the two forms. When entering data through this stored procedure, the user can simply leave off the last two values if the paperwork is in order.

The next step is to input some data. You can then use the stored procedure usp_employeelist you created earlier to check that the data was entered correctly.

```
exec usp_AddNewEmployee 'Khan', 'Genghis', '1201 Steppe Way',
'Ulan Bator', 'MN', '12345', 'e', 'Enforcer', '000-00-0000',
600.00, 'Daily'
GO
exec usp_employeelist
```

In this example, you entered the data by position. Data can also be entered by listing the parameters and values, in which case the order does not matter, as in the following example:

```
exec usp_AddNewEmployee
@FirstName  = 'Kublai',
@LastName = 'Khan',
@SSN = '000-00-0002',
```

```
@JobTitle = 'SubEnforcer',
@MailingAddress = '1205 Yurt Street',
@City = 'Ulan Bator',
@State = 'MN',
@Zip = '12345',
@PayAmount = 500,
@PayPeriod = 'daily'
```

Returning Parameters

If you want a parameter returned so you can use the value in subsequent T-SQL statements, you have to do a couple of extra steps. First, define the parameter as an output parameter when you create the procedure, by adding the word OUTPUT to the definition of the parameter. When you call the procedure, include OUTPUT in the call for that parameter. If you forget to define the parameter as an output parameter and then request it as an output, SQL Server returns an error message. But if you define it as an output parameter and then forget to ask for it as an output, you will not get an error message. SQL Server just assumes you did not want that parameter returned this time. For example, you might have a procedure for computing sales totals that can return weekly, monthly, or quarterly totals, but you might run it with a request for only the monthly totals to be output.

The following example demonstrates the need for declaring a parameter as an output parameter in both the stored procedure definition and the execution of the stored procedure. First, you'll create and run a stored procedure that returns a value. Then you'll remove the OUTPUT keyword in the execution call and see what happens. Finally, you'll create the stored procedure again with the OUTPUT in the execution call but not in the procedure definition.

```
-- #1, The following example returns the pay amount for any employee,
-- using the employee number as an input.
CREATE PROCEDURE usp_GetSalary
@employeeid int,
-- declare the next parameter as an output parameter
@salary money output
AS
Select @salary = PayAmount FROM tblEmployee
WHERE PersonId = @employeeID
GO
-- execute the procedure, using emp# 15 as the input
declare @salary money
exec usp_GetSalary 15, @salary output
```

```
select @salary

-- #2, create a new copy of the stored procedure,
-- then execute it without the OUTPUT keyword in the execution call
CREATE PROCEDURE usp_GetSalary2
@employeeid int,
-- declare the next parameter as an output parameter
@salary money output
AS
Select @salary = PayAmount FROM tblEmployee
WHERE PersonId = @employeeID
GO
-- execute the procedure, using emp# 15 as the input
declare @salary money
exec usp_GetSalary2 15, @salary
select @salary

-- #3, create a third copy of the stored procedure without the
-- OUTPUT in the procedure definition,
-- then execute it with the OUTPUT keyword in the execution call
CREATE PROCEDURE usp_GetSalary3
@employeeid int,
-- declare the next parameter as an output parameter
@salary money
AS
Select @salary = PayAmount FROM tblEmployee
WHERE PersonId = @employeeID
GO
-- execute the procedure, using emp# 15 as the input
declare @salary money
exec usp_GetSalary3 15, @salary output
select @salary
```

The results of the execution of these three stored procedures are shown in Figure 17-3. The first stored procedure (upper left) was created with an output parameter in the definition and executed with a declared output variable. The result returned is the correct salary for employee 15. The second stored procedure (middle right) was created the same way as the first procedure, but it's executed without benefit of the output variable. The result set is NULL. The third stored procedure (lower center) was created without an output parameter and executed as though it did have the output parameter. This is the option that will return an error message.

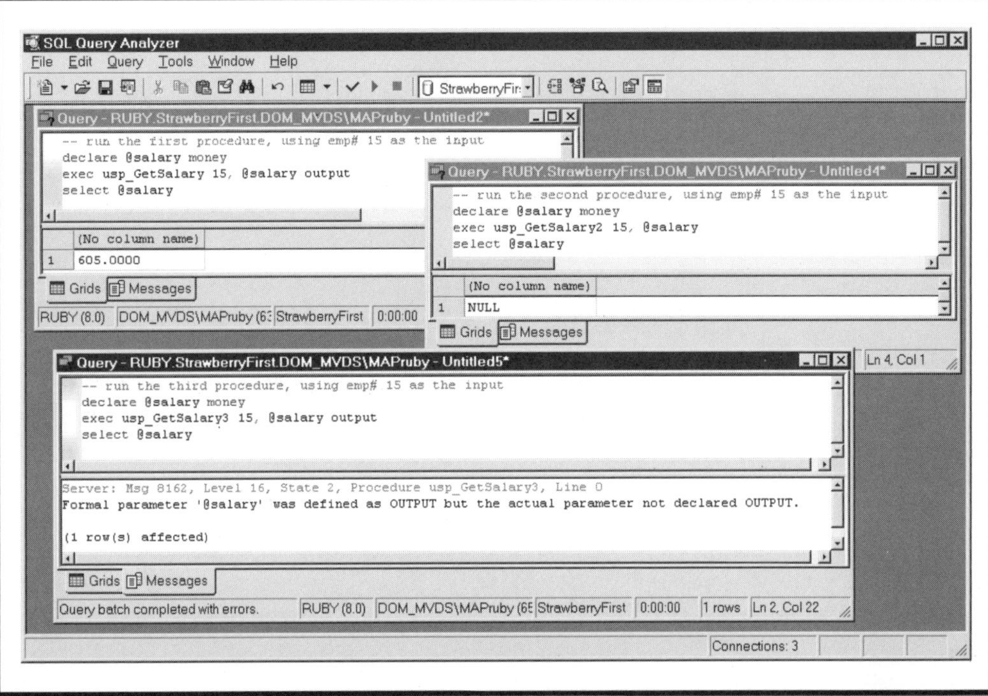

Figure 17-3. A stored procedure can return data to the calling program if the parameters are specifically described as output parameters.

ALTERING AND DROPPING STORED PROCEDURES

The ANSI SQL standard says that to change the definition of a stored procedure you have to drop the procedure and re-create it. But just as with views, stored procedures have associated permissions, and those permissions will vanish when the procedure is dropped. You have to grant the permissions all over again when you re-create the procedure. That's not too inconvenient if you have a record of the stored procedure and accompanying permissions stored in a T-SQL script outside the database, but it's a pain if you or your DBA assigns permissions through the graphical interface. So Microsoft has added a command to ALTER a stored procedure, allowing you to change the definition without actually having to drop the stored procedure, so the permissions remain intact. The ALTER PROCEDURE statement also will modify a stored procedure without affecting any dependent procedures or triggers. To run the ALTER PROCEDURE command, you must be the owner of the procedure or a member of the sysadmin, db_owner, or db_ddladmin role. The following is an example of how to use the ALTER PROCEDURE statement. First create a new procedure that brings back a person's name and job title in response to an employee identifier.

```
CREATE PROCEDURE usp_ShowEmployee
@empno int
AS
SELECT FirstName + ' ' + LastName, JobTitle
FROM tblPerson p INNER JOIN tblEmployee e ON p.PersonID = e.PersonID
WHERE p.PersonID = @empno
GO
-- run the stored procedure
exec usp_ShowEmployee 12
```

Now modify the stored procedure without dropping and re-creating. Add PayAmount and a column heading to the person's name.

```
ALTER PROCEDURE usp_ShowEmployee
@empno int
AS
SELECT FirstName + ' ' + LastName AS 'Person Name', JobTitle, PayAmount
FROM tblPerson p INNER JOIN tblEmployee e ON p.PersonID = e.PersonID
WHERE p.PersonID = @empno
GO
-- run the stored procedure
exec usp_ShowEmployee 12
```

The output is shown in Figure 17-4. The upper-left frame is the CREATE PROCEDURE code. It returns a name and a job title. The frame in the lower right is the ALTER PROCEDURE code, which has modified the procedure without requiring a drop and re-create.

The DROP PROCEDURE statement removes the stored procedure from the database, taking it out of the procedure cache, and removing the entries from the sysobjects and syscomments tables. To drop a stored procedure, you must either own the procedure or be part of the sysadmin, db_ddladmin, or db_owner role; you must also include the owner name when specifying the procedure to be dropped.

To drop the extra copies of usp_GetSalary, use the following:

```
DROP PROCEDURE usp_GetSalary2
DROP PROCEDURE usp_GetSalary3
```

RECOMPILE OPTIONS

Stored procedures are popular with developers because they are efficient and they are already compiled and in memory when clients use them. Because these objects are so powerful, you want to keep them optimized, so occasionally you might need to recompile a stored procedure. You might have a stored procedure that is run infrequently—perhaps

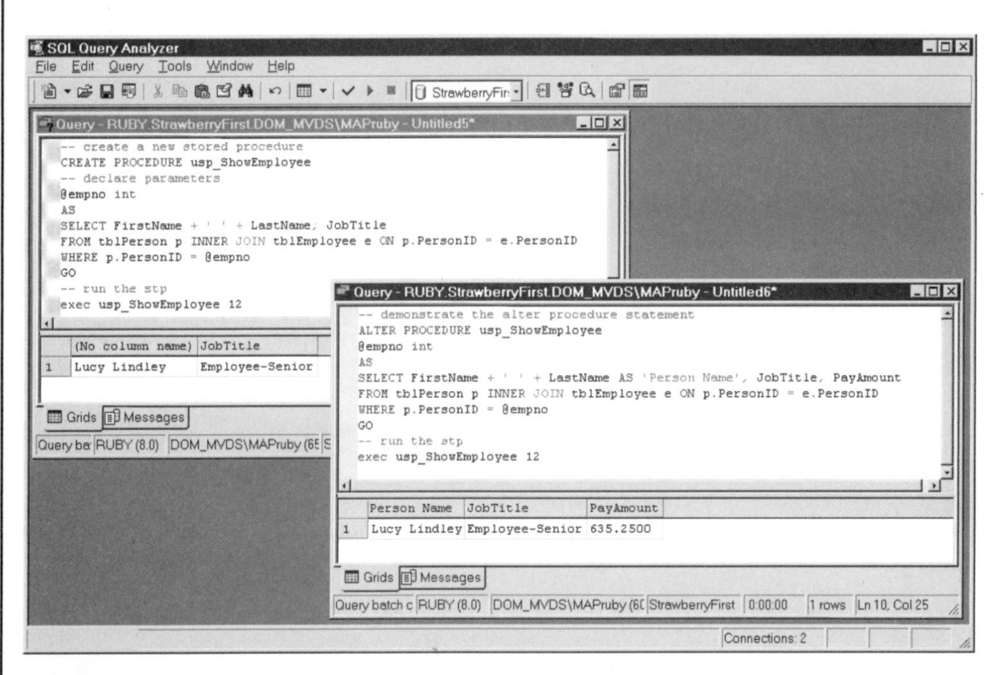

Figure 17-4. The ALTER PROCEDURE statement allows you to modify a procedure in place, without having to drop and re-create.

to generate a quarterly sales report. As we mentioned earlier in this chapter, every time the SQL Server starts up, there are no stored procedures in memory. As each procedure is run, SQL Server loads the stored procedure into memory and computes an execution plan for each one. Have you heard of 7-by-24 operations? If your SQL Server has not been cycled (brought down and brought back up again) for some time, or if the table statistics have changed during this period of time that the server has been operational, there's a chance that the current execution plan for your stored procedure is out of date. It may be worth a few CPU cycles to make sure that your infrequently run complex stored procedures are optimized each time they run. You might include a WITH RECOMPILE option in the procedure code when you create these stored procedures.

It is quite possible that SQL Server will have to recompile your procedures, even without the RECOMPILE option encoding. If you have a stored procedure that you run only once every three months, it is highly possible that your procedure will not still be in the procedure cache. If you recall, the least-frequently-used algorithm will more than likely have commandeered the pages your stored procedure occupied and used them for other procedures. However, the more memory you have on your server, the less frequent these mandated recompiles will be.

The WITH RECOMPILE option in the stored procedure definition causes the procedure to be dropped from the procedure cache immediately after it completes, thus freeing up the memory it had occupied. If you are memory constrained on your server, it might be worth the trade-off—spending more CPU cycles to constantly recompile the stored procedure—to have fewer memory resources tied up in the procedure cache.

If you want to run a stored procedure with a nontypical set of parameters, where you suspect that the optimization on the execution plan currently in cache might not be ideal, you can do a one-time WITH RECOMPILE declaration in the execution statement. This will dynamically recompile the stored procedure to optimize it for your nontypical parameters—but what about the typical parameter set? How will execution of a typical parameter set be affected? The stored procedure will now be less than optimized for a typical parameter set, so the neighborly thing to do would be to run the stored procedure a second time, this time on a typical dataset, again using WITH RECOMPILE.

You should recompile the stored procedures after you run some maintenance tasks, such as rebuilding indexes; this will recompute the statistics. Your best bet is to run the SP_RECOMPILE stored procedure, which causes each database object specified to be recompiled the next time it is run. We suspect that all SP_RECOMPILE does is flush any stored procedures out of the current cache. SP_RECOMPILE will take the name of a procedure as an argument, but a much more efficient approach is to use the name of the table on which you built the stored procedures as the argument. Then every procedure that references that table will be recompiled.

Books Online states that "SQL Server automatically recompiles stored procedures and triggers when it is advantageous to do so" Although no more detail is supplied, the same logic applies as for the automatic rebuilding of statistical information, when large amounts of data have been added to the tables, for example. In SQL Server versions prior to 7.0, the compiled procedure was stored in a table called sysprocedures and retrieved if the execution plan was not found in cache. This table no longer exists, so SQL Server has to go back to the original definition in syscomments and recompile the stored procedure from scratch. The procedures will be recompiled more often in versions 7.0 and 2000, trading a few seconds of recompile time for more highly optimized procedures.

HANDLING ERROR MESSAGES

You can write a stored procedure so that it returns a status code to indicate whether or not it ran correctly. You can also write it to raise error messages, and you can even cause the error message to be written to the Windows NT/2000 event log. The default return code of 0 indicates that all is well and the procedure completed without any errors. SQL Server has reserved codes –1 through –99 for its own use and currently is using –1 through –15. When you write a stored procedure, you can have it return status codes for various situations and even have your calling application check for these codes, with appropriate responses.

In the previous example, you asked for an employee's salary by inputting the employee number. But what should happen if you input an employee number and that number isn't in the employee table? You could check for the value of salary returned being NULL, but that still leaves a big unanswered question—is the salary truly NULL, or is there no employee with that employee identifier? There's a big difference between these two conditions. Actually, you should have the stored procedure check to make sure the input value is valid before letting it handle the query. In this example, check the employee number, and if it is not correct, return an error code of 2 (a positive 2, so that you're not trying to use one of SQL Server's reserved error codes). The calling application then checks the return code. If it is 2, the calling application sends a message to the user. If the return code is 0, the application returns the result set to the user.

```
CREATE PROCEDURE usp_SalaryReturn
@employeeid int, @salary money output
AS
IF NOT EXISTS (SELECT * FROM  tblEmployee WHERE PersonId = @employeeID)
 Return 2
ELSE Select @salary = PayAmount FROM tblEmployee
WHERE PersonId = @employeeID
GO
-- Execute the procedure
-- Declare @retcode as variable for return code,
-- @salary as variable to hold returned value
-- execute procedure to return @retcode, request
-- @salary as an output to be returned;
-- look for employee #15, who exists in the Employee table
declare @retcode int
declare @salary money
exec @retcode = usp_SalaryReturn 15, @salary output
IF @retcode =2  PRINT 'No such employee number in the Employee table'
ELSE select @salary
GO
--  Now run the procedure with an employee number (#3)
-- who is not in the Employee table
declare @retcode int
declare @salary money
exec @retcode = usp_SalaryReturn 3, @salary output
IF @retcode =2  PRINT 'No such employee number in the Employee table'
ELSE select @salary
GO
```

Adding Custom Error Messages

If you want to return more detailed information about the error, you can invoke or raise an error message that has been created and stored in SQL Server. Many system error messages are available, but these are going to be triggered by system events rather than by something happening within your application. For a more flexible error messaging approach, you can define your own custom error messages and then call them from within your stored procedures.

All error messages for SQL Server are stored in the sysmessages table in the Master database. Creating custom error messages is a two-step process. First you define your custom messages by adding them to the sysmessages table, and then you call the custom messages you've created.

Microsoft has reserved numbers up to 50,000 for SQL Server error messages (now there's a scary thought!), but most of them are assigned by block and are not used yet. Start numbering your custom error messages at 50,001. Because the error messages are all stored centrally in the Master database, rather than in individual databases, they can be called from any database on the server. If you have several development teams, you might want to follow Microsoft's example and allocate blocks of error message numbers, one block to each of the different databases.

To create a custom error message, you can use Enterprise Manager or a system-stored procedure, SP_ADDMESSAGE. Enterprise Manager is a good place to start because you can see the system error messages, which may provide some hints on how to write your own.

1. In Enterprise Manager, select your server.
2. From the Management Console top menu, choose Tools | Manage SQL Server Messages. The Manage SQL Server Messages – *your_server_name* dialog box opens. (Alternatively, you can right-click the server name, and then click All Tasks | Manage SQL Server Messages.) This dialog box lets you search for existing error messages. When it first opens, the search boxes are empty, as shown in Figure 17-5. Note the severity levels assigned to the error messages that are listed in the largest window of the dialog box. You can scroll down and see the various levels. The severity level is an integer between 0 and 25. Zero is just for informational messages, 1 through 6 are reserved, and 19 through 25 can only be assigned by a system administrator. Nineteen and above are fatal errors that will cause the process to terminate. Typically, you want to assign a severity level between 7 and 18 to your custom error messages.
3. If you click the Messages tab at this point, the Messages window is blank. That's only because you need to set up a search. This window holds the result set.
4. Return to the Search tab, and type the word **deadlock** into the Message Text Contains box.
5. Make sure that you do not have any of the severity levels highlighted before you click Find. The result set is returned in the Messages tab, and you should see several messages, as shown in Figure 17-6, including the infamous 1205 listed at severity 13. Note that none of these messages is logged in the Windows event log, but that's okay, because you really don't want to fill up the NT/2000 event log with deadlock messages.

6. Click the Edit button to see the entire text of the error message, and from here you can send the message to the Windows NT event log.

To create your own error message, start from this same Messages window.

1. Click the New button.
2. In the New SQL Server Message dialog box, fill in the error number, the severity, and the error message. Select the language and whether you want this posted to the event log.
3. Click OK.

These are pretty much the same parameters you would supply if you used the Query Analyzer, SP_ADDMESSAGE stored procedure, to create your custom error message. We'll discuss the parameters as they apply to either the GUI or the SP_ADDMESSAGE stored procedure.

The syntax of the SP_ADDMESSAGE stored procedure is as follows:

```
SP_ADDMESSAGE message_number, severity, 'message text',  'language', 'true|false', 'replace'
```

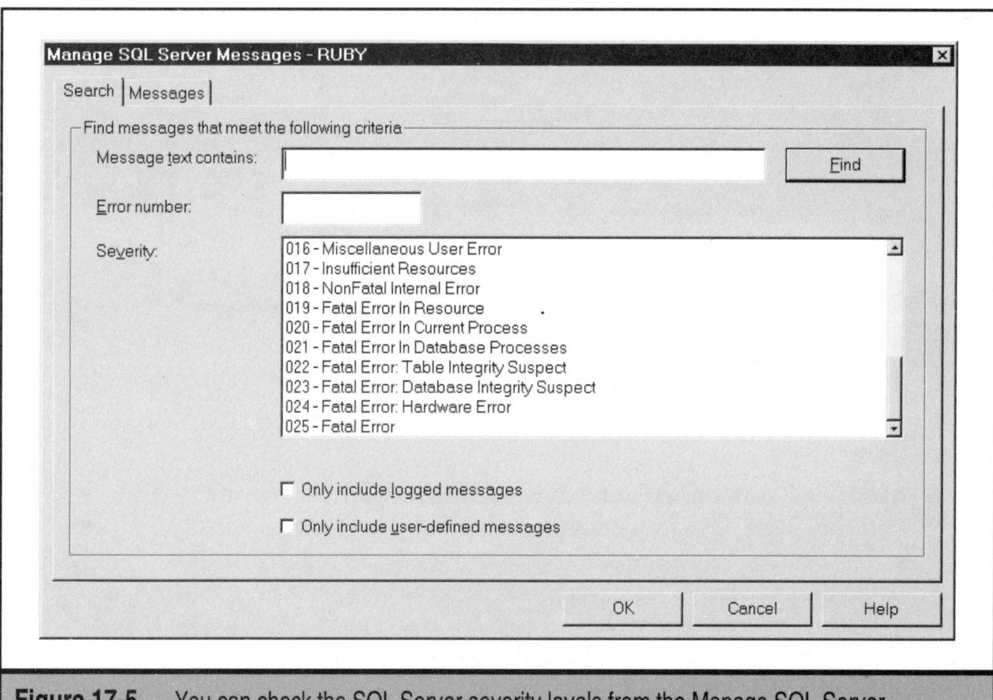

Figure 17-5. You can check the SQL Server severity levels from the Manage SQL Server Messages dialog box.

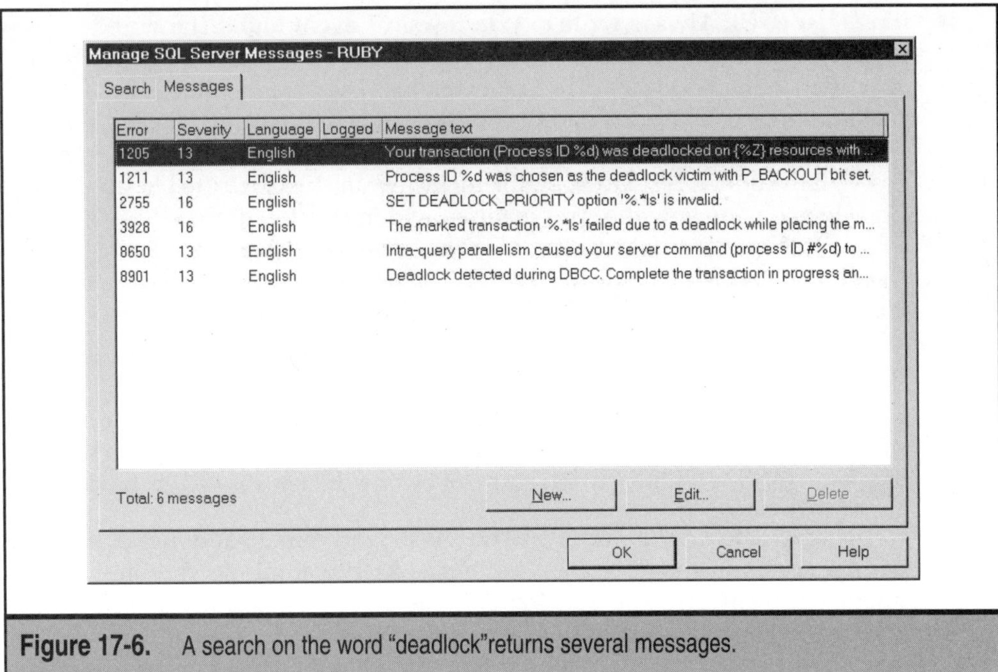

Figure 17-6. A search on the word "deadlock"returns several messages.

- ***message_number*** **(GUI: Error Number)** You need to assign an error message number to your error message. Remember that it must be greater than 50,000 and less than or equal to 99,999.
- ***severity*** **(GUI: Severity)** The severity level is your call, depending on how serious you consider the problem.
- ***message text*** **(GUI: Message Text)** When you create an error message, make sure the message text is descriptive of the problem and understandable by the end-user, if that's who will be reading your error message. The error message can be up to 255 characters long, including spaces, but don't feel that you have to use every space! If you can get your message across concisely, be succinct, and still transfer to the reader what the problem is, do so. Your error message may be more efficient than some long-winded explanation, and it may be usable in more than one situation.
- ***language*** **(GUI: Language)** You can specify a language for the message. This indicator records which language the message is written in. You can have multiple languages installed on a single server, so it is possible to deliver a custom error message in more than one language. The combination of message number plus language has to be unique, so the same message number can be assigned to many messages, each in a different language.

- *true | false* **(GUI: Always write to Windows NT event log)** The stored procedure offers a true/false option. True says that you want this message to be written to the Windows NT/2000 event log. The default value is false. The GUI is a check box; check it and the option will be set to true. If the option is set to true, the message is always written to the log file whenever the error is raised. If the option is set to false, the message can still be written to the event log, depending on how the error is raised within the stored procedure. If you want the procedure to write out to the event log, you need to have sysadmin privileges when you create it. The person or process running the stored procedure that evokes the custom error message doesn't need sysadmin privileges, because the user runs the procedure with the permissions of the owner.
- *replace* **(no comparable GUI)** The replace option will overwrite any existing error message with this number. An attempt to insert a message with a number already in use would otherwise return an error, which is the GUI behavior.

The only people who can run the SP_ADDMESSAGE procedure to add messages to the Master database are the members of the sysadmin and serveradmin server roles. This restriction might help maintain some consistency in the assignment and use of the blocks of numbers that are assigned to various development groups.

A corresponding SP_DROPMESSAGE stored procedure has the same limitations on who can run it: sysadmins or serveradmins. You have to supply only the message number and (if there is more than one message with that same number) the language. On the GUI, clicking the Delete button removes whichever error message you have highlighted in the window, as long as you have the authority to do so.

To add an error message for the scenario in which someone has input a nonexistent employee number, using the SP_ADDMESSAGE procedure, you would use something like this:

```
Exec sp_addmessage 50102,11, 'You input employee number %d but no such employee
number was found in the table', 'english',  'false', 'replace'
```

The %d is a placeholder so the employee number that's causing a problem can be returned in the error message.

Using Error Messages

Now that you have defined your first error message, you can start to use it in the stored procedures you create. You do this with the RAISERROR function. Normally, you'd put a test in your code, to see whether the previous step ran as expected, or a check for some other error condition. If the check returns false, the procedure continues on to the next step. But if it returns true, a RAISERROR invokes the appropriate error message. The

RAISERROR is usually accompanied by a RETURN command to exit out of the procedure at that point. There may also be a ROLLBACK if a transaction was involved.

Here's an example of how the RAISERROR function works. In the preceding code, where someone does input the wrong employee number to the stored procedure, modify the code to include a RAISERROR, as shown here:

```
ALTER PROCEDURE usp_SalaryReturn
@employeeid int, @salary money output
AS
IF NOT EXISTS (SELECT * FROM  tblEmployee WHERE PersonId = @employeeID)
 BEGIN
 RAISERROR (50102, 11, 1, @employeeid)
 RETURN
 END
ELSE
Select @salary = PayAmount FROM tblEmployee WHERE PersonId = @employeeID
GO
```

In the RAISERROR statement, you supply the error number, severity, state, and variables. The @employeeid variable is plugged into the error message in place of the %d placeholder. The state is used as an additional indicator as to where the error came from. If the error can be called from more than one place in the code, the state can be set to different values, so the returned message will indicate exactly where the RAISERROR was activated. Now run the procedure, with one employee number that does exist and one that doesn't, as shown here:

```
-- this employee number does exist in the Employee table
DECLARE @salary MONEY
EXEC usp_SalaryRaise 12, @salary OUTPUT
-- this employee number does not exist in the Employee table
DECLARE @salary MONEY
EXEC usp_SalaryRaise 3, @salary OUTPUT
```

On the nonexistent employee number, you should see the following error message returned:

```
Server: Msg 50102, Level 11, State 1, Procedure usp_SalaryRaise, Line 6
You input employee number 3 but no such employee number was found in the Employee table
```

If you run a SELECT @@ERROR immediately after the error message that was returned, it will return an error code 50102.

The error message can be written to the Windows event log. It can cause an alert to fire and corrective action to be taken. But if you are programming the user interface in Access or Visual Basic, the error code number, 50102, may be of more value than the text of the message. From a calling application, it's a lot easier to check for a numeric error code and respond to it than it is to look for text error messages.

Ad Hoc Error Messages

When you are first developing and testing code, you may not be ready to add messages to the Master database sysmessages table. You can do something temporary: you can use an ad hoc message in place of an error number. Modify the stored procedure usp_SalaryReturn, replacing the number with the text of the message, as shown here:

```
ALTER PROCEDURE usp_SalaryReturn
@employeeid int, @salary money output
AS
IF NOT EXISTS (SELECT * FROM  tblEmployee WHERE PersonId = @employeeID)
 BEGIN
 RAISERROR ('Test message. Employee number %d was not found', 11, 1, @employeeid)
 RETURN
 END
ELSE
Select @salary = PayAmount FROM tblEmployee WHERE PersonId = @employeeID
GO
-- now run the code, using an employee number that does not exist
-- in the Employee table
DECLARE @salary MONEY
EXEC usp_SalaryReturn 3, @salary OUTPUT
```

You should see the following error message returned:

```
Server: Msg 50000, Level 11, State 1, Procedure usp_SalaryReturn, Line 6
Test message. Employee number 3 was not found
```

Because you used a text expression in lieu of an error number with this message, if you run a SELECT @@ERROR, the result set will return a value of 50000, as will any other ad hoc message. That's why we suggest that this is a useful technique during the development phase, but you will eventually want to return a specific error number and have the client interfaces respond to that number in case of an error.

EXTENDED STORED PROCEDURES

One of the benefits of having SQL Server so tightly integrated with the operating system is that you can have extended stored procedures. A normal stored procedure is compiled T-SQL code. An extended stored procedure is not written in T-SQL. Usually it is written in C or C++, and is compiled as a dynamic-link library (DLL). Running an extended stored procedure allows SQL Server to work outside of the normal boundaries of database programming. Just about anything you can code in a DLL you can do with an extended stored procedure. You can find out more about how to create your own extended stored procedures by searching MSDN, using the keywords "extended stored procedure, creating," or by studying the installed code examples in the installation folder Microsoft SQL Server\80\

Tools\Devtools\Samples\ODS. The code samples are packaged as compressed, self-extracting files.

Microsoft supplies quite a few of these extended stored procedures with each release of SQL Server. An extended stored procedure will start with either sp_ or xp_ and is registered in the Master database. From Enterprise Manager, if you expand the Master database hierarchy, you will see an entry for extended stored procedures. Click that object to show a list of the extended stored procedures in the right pane of the Management Console. If you right-click one of these procedures and select Properties, you can get the name of the DLL. Unfortunately, there's no space here for a comment line, so you are left wondering what the procedure does. Some of them are explained in Books Online, and some are undocumented.

When you add your own extended stored procedure to SQL Server, you can use the Enterprise Manager interface. Right-click on Extended Stored Procedures and select New Extended Stored Procedure. All you have to do is supply a name for the procedure and the name of the corresponding DLL file, which should be in the DLL directory. By default, that would be DRIVELETTER:\MSSQL\BINN\DLL. You can also set permissions from this extended stored procedure dialog box. And, of course, you can do all this by using a stored procedure: SP_ADDEXTENDEDPROC takes the name of the procedure and the name of the DLL as arguments. You have to be a system administrator to add these extended stored procedures to the Master database.

Running an extended stored procedure is no different from any other stored procedure, in that it can be called when needed and you can supply parameters for it. The rules about specifying a parameter as an output apply—if you want a parameter to be retained for use in subsequent statements, you must say so when you call the procedure. Extended stored procedures can return status codes and result sets. You will find that to run an extended stored procedure, because they are all in the Master database, you will have to address them with the master.dbo prefix if you call them from within any other database.

The topic of how to program extended stored procedures is beyond the scope of this book, but if you want to experiment with them, you'll find some sample stored procedures included with all the C source code and other files you will need to create one. Search in SQL Server Books Online, typing **extended stored procedures, sample** for the exact location and contents of these files.

SECURITY ISSUES WITH STORED PROCEDURES

The code for a stored procedure is inserted into the syscomments table when you create the stored procedure. If you need to hide the details of your code, as you might when developing software applications for public sale, all you have to do is include the keywords WITH ENCRYPTION when you create the procedure. SQL Server can recompile the code when the source is encrypted, but there is no way to decrypt it. If you need to encrypt the source code for your stored procedures, make sure you keep a copy of the code in a safe place.

Before encryption was introduced in SQL Server 6.0, some programmers would run the procedure once to compile it. Because the compiled code was stored in the sysprocedures table in these early versions, the programmers would then delete the code from syscomments. Invariably, the procedures never got recompiled until it came time to upgrade the SQL Server. So if you have upgraded an older version database to SQL Server 2000 and the stored procedure code is nowhere to be found, this is what may have happened.

The other side of stored procedure security is client access—allowing users to execute the stored procedures. A stored procedure is just another database object on which permissions can be granted, revoked, or denied. Normally, the average end-user is not allowed any direct access to the tables in the database. They can see and modify the data only through views and stored procedures. End-users are given execute permission on a stored procedure. When they execute the procedure, they execute it with the permissions of whoever owns the procedure. Therefore, whoever owns the procedure needs to have all the necessary permissions to select or modify any objects referenced by that procedure. If all the objects—including the stored procedure—are owned by a dbo, there will be no unexpected rejections of client requests to execute the procedure.

REMOTE STORED PROCEDURES

Remote stored procedures are simply stored procedures that originate on a remote server. There's nothing magic about them. Every stored procedure is a local procedure to the server on which it was created. However, before you can start calling stored procedures on other servers, the servers have to be set up to recognize each other. This is done by configuring the Linked Server properties. From Enterprise Manager, expand the server hierarchy and select Security | Linked Servers. To run a remote stored procedure, you must supply the four-part name, in the format *server.database.owner.procname*. The remote stored procedure will run on the remote server and will return the results to your calling application.

Setting Up Linked Servers

Setting up a linked server is not that complex. Most problems with linked servers are associated with the usual security issues you encounter when trying to spread the workload over multiple computers. From Enterprise Manager, expand the server hierarchy, and select Security | Linked Servers. Right-click Linked Servers and select New Linked Server. This action opens a dialog box, as shown in Figure 17-7. Notice that you have to type the name of the server you're linking to. There's no drop-down box to show a list of available servers—that's a security feature (or a program development oversight!). Also notice that you have a choice of saying whether the linked server is a SQL Server or some other data source, including any OLE DB–compliant data source, such as Oracle, or ODBC data source, including Microsoft Access. You can execute stored procedures or queries on database platforms other than SQL Server from a SQL Server. If this is SQL Server that you're linking to, check the SQL Server box and all the other options will no longer be available—SQL Server knows how to connect to another SQL Server. It's a little more complex if the other server is not a SQL Server, because then you have to supply additional information. Because the additional information varies according to the type of server, we are not going to list all the options here. Instead, we refer you to SQL Server Books Online for the specifics for each type of connection.

The second tab in the Linked Server dialog box is Security, as shown in Figure 17-8. When a user runs a stored procedure on a remote server, what really happens is that the local server takes the request and passes it to the linked server, along with some security information. The linked server then assesses the security credentials and decides whether it can proceed to run the stored procedure.

Several options are available for passing security credentials. You can specify a local login and allow it to connect to the remote server. If the local login exactly matches a login with the right permissions on the remote server, you can check the Impersonate box, as shown in Figure 17-8 with the login DOM_MVDS\sqlexec. When the servers are part of the same Windows NT domain, or the appropriate trust relationships have been established between domains, all you need to do is add the same Windows NT/2000 users or groups to both servers. The list of local logins who have access to the linked server should

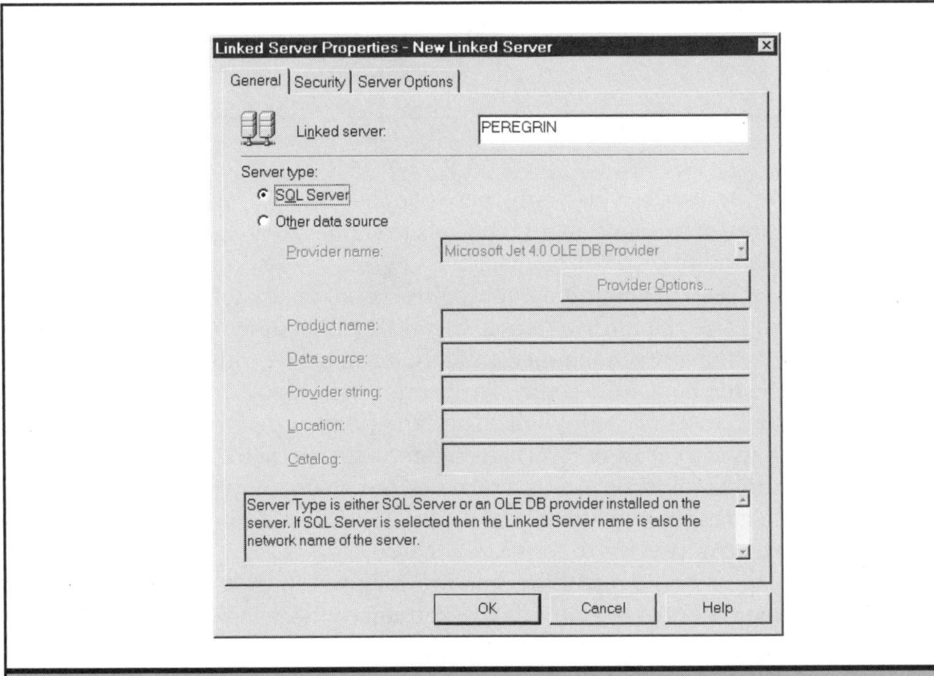

Figure 17-7. The Linked Server dialog box is under the Security menu, because connecting to other servers involves many security issues.

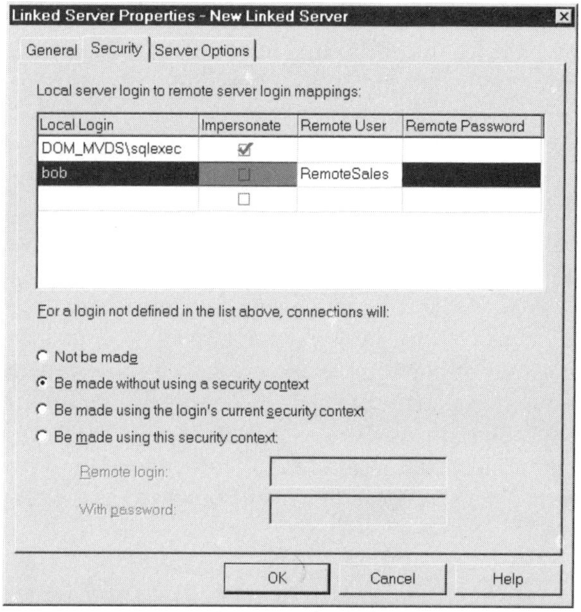

Figure 17-8. Local user Bob is mapped to a special remote user account, RemoteSales, on the target linked server.

be kept to a minimum and restricted to only those people who really need to access the remote server. If you are not cautious about who gets to connect, you may be opening up a back door into an otherwise secure system.

If the linked server does not have the same login accounts as the local server, you have the option of mapping a local login to a remote user account, as shown in Figure 17-8 with the local login Bob, who has been mapped to RemoteSales. You must supply the name and password for the remote user account. The drop-down box on the left allows you to select the local user, but you have to type the name and password of the remote user. This is almost certainly a security feature. You can map more than one local login to the same remote user. By mapping multiple local users to one remote login, you lose the ability to track who is making changes in the remote database. The drop-down list of local logins shows only users, not groups.

You can block logins not explicitly defined or mapped to the remote server from getting access. For logins not defined in the list, you can connect using one of three security contexts:

- You can specify that they connect without any security context. This is something you would not do for another SQL Server, but you would do it for some other data source that doesn't have the security of a SQL Server.

- You can specify that they use the current security context of the login, which works when the logins exist on both servers.
- You can map all logins in the list to a single account on the linked server, which means giving up the ability to distinguish individual user actions on the remote server, but simplifying the administration of the accounts on each server.

The third tab in the New Linked Server dialog box is the Server Options tab. Here you can set the collation properties. If the two servers are "collation compatible" (as shown in Figure 17-9), it would not matter where you ran a query, as you would get back the same results. But if they are not compatible, it might make a difference in the result set, depending on where it was run. Note that the term is "compatible," not necessarily identical. It also makes a difference to performance, because if the servers are not collation compatible, SQL Server has to bring the remote data set to the local server and do string comparisons locally. This is something you want to be aware of when setting up linked servers in other countries. If the collations are compatible but different, you have the option of using the local or the remote collation for query resolution. Again, the local collation would imply that string comparisons are done at the calling server and not on the remote server.

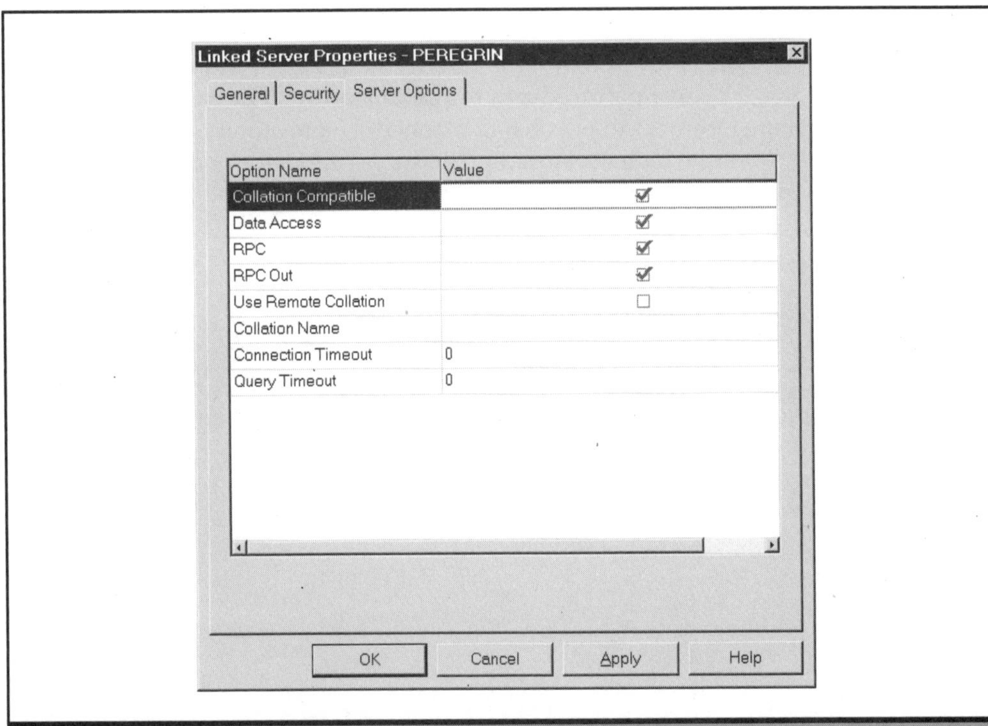

Figure 17-9. Collation-compatible servers are the most efficient when dealing with linked servers and calls to remote stored procedures.

If you are more comfortable administering your linked servers from the Query Analyzer, you can add and configure linked servers with the SP_ADDLINKEDSERVER, SP_ADDLINKEDSRVLOGIN, and SP_SERVEROPTION stored procedures. The three stored procedures correspond to the three tabs in the New Linked Server Properties dialog box.

Once your linked servers are configured, you can run the stored procedures using the syntax mentioned at the beginning of this section, *server.database.owner.procname*. If you're having problems running remote procedures, the first thing you do is check to make sure you can run the stored procedure on its local server. Once you've confirmed that local execution of a stored procedure works fine, then and only then do you begin unraveling the complexity of cross-database security issues.

AUTOMATIC STORED PROCEDURES

We mentioned at the start of this chapter that you can have stored procedures run automatically at startup. You might want to generate reports about the state of your databases or perform some maintenance task. Any procedure can be set to run on startup, using the (what else?) SP_PROCOPTION stored procedure. The syntax for this procedure is

```
sp_procoption 'proc-name', 'startup', 'true|false'
```

You want to be careful how and in what order you designate stored procedures at server startup. If you set several procedures to run at startup, they may all start at the same time, using more resources than you had planned. To prevent this from happening and to control the order in which the stored procedures run, make one controlling procedure that calls each of the others in turn and then set only the one to autostart with the server.

CHAPTER 18

Triggers

In Chapter 17, we discussed stored procedures. Now we are going to look at triggers, which are a special type of stored procedure. Triggers are run automatically when a user modifies the data or inserts or deletes a row in a table. Triggers are very powerful and have many uses in SQL Server. We will look at some of those uses in this chapter, but we are sure you will find many more uses for triggers as you develop your own applications.

INTRODUCTION TO TRIGGERS

A trigger is a set of T-SQL statements, just like a stored procedure. The major difference between triggers and stored procedures is that, unlike a stored procedure, a trigger cannot be executed directly. Instead, a trigger is created as part of a table definition. When a change is made to that table, the trigger fires and the code in the trigger runs. The user doesn't have to do anything special to activate the trigger—it's automatically activated by the data changes made to the table by the user's query. In a like manner, the user cannot prevent a trigger from firing. Starting with SQL Server 7.0, you can disasble a trigger, but you must have administrative privileges to do so. For the average end-user, a trigger is something that just happens behind the scenes; most users don't even know when and if triggers are firing.

Triggers are very powerful. They were used in the beginning of SQL Server to guarantee data integrity, in the days before declarative integrities were part of the SQL Server database management system. With triggers, you can compare before and after versions of data, you can read from and update data in other tables and even other databases, and you can execute both local and remote stored procedures. You can use triggers to enforce complex default and check constraints—those that extend beyond a single column definition. You can write a trigger for any rule or regulation that you can express in code.

Triggers are commonly used to make changes in one table based on changes made to another table. For example, a salesperson adds an item to an order. The trigger in the order items table then updates the quantity in stock in the inventory table, decreasing it by the quantity ordered.

If you have a computed value in a table, such as the year-to-date salary for employees, you could use a trigger to keep this up to date. Whenever someone makes a change or addition to the payroll table, as would happen each pay period as the paychecks are entered, the trigger would update the year-to-date salary. Throughout this book, we have discussed the pros and cons of storing computed values and maintaining derived data in tables; the final decision is up to you. If you decide that a column of computed values will help your database performance, a trigger is an extremely efficient and effective way to keep the computed column synchronized with the base data it's derived from.

SQL Server has had a basic set of triggers since its inception: INSERT, UPDATE, and DELETE. A new type of trigger, the INSTEAD OF trigger, was introduced in SQL Server 2000. A traditional trigger (INSERT, UPDATE, or DELETE) fires after an action or event, and it's now classified by Microsoft as an AFTER trigger. The INSTEAD OF trigger fires instead of the action that triggered it. AFTER triggers can be created only on tables; INSTEAD OF triggers can be created on tables or on indexed views. INSTEAD OF triggers do have some limitations, however. If a table is modified as a result of a cascading update or delete—a row in a master table is deleted and that delete cascades to the rows in an associated child table—any AFTER trigger on the child table would fire, but an INSTEAD OF trigger on the same table would be ignored.

A key point about triggers, which you should keep in mind when designing a flow of events, is that a trigger is part of a transaction. If a data modification occurs and causes a trigger to fire that causes changes to data in another table, and if the first modification is rolled back, all the subsequent changes (including those invoked by the trigger) must also be rolled back. If the first trigger firing were to initiate additional trigger firings with associated changes to still other tables, the entire sequence of data modifications would have to be rolled back, regardless of the number of tables or levels of trigger firings involved.

As an example, let's suppose that a customer service representative places an order for ten widgets on behalf of a customer. This entry in the order details table fires a trigger that updates the inventory table, diminishing the widget quantity-on-hand value by the number ordered. With each update to the inventory table, a trigger on the table looks to see whether the quantity of widgets has fallen below the critical limit for placing a new order. At this point, you might find it tempting to code a trigger on the inventory table that would send an email to the supplier to request another truckload of widgets if the quantity-on-hand were to fall below the reorder point. (If this is beginning to sound familiar, we discussed a very similar situation in Chapter 14, on locking.) But hold on now—until the customer service representative commits the order, you have an uncommitted dependency. So what could happen to torpedo the sale? What if the order details trigger was capable of going to the customer table and reading the customer credit limit? And what if the trigger also popped out to the accounts receivable table, searching for an overdue, blocked, or limited status for this customer number? If it turns out that the customer doesn't have enough available credit to buy ten widgets or that this customer account is blocked, the original order has to be rolled back or undone. This means that the trigger-initiated change to the inventory table is also rolled back. However, if you had coded that email trigger on the inventory table, your email would already be gone.

SQL Server does have protections built in that will prevent you from doing things with triggers that you cannot roll back. You cannot, for example, create or drop database objects (tables, views, or indexes) from within a trigger. But email is an exception—you can't roll back an email (and is there anyone reading this who has not sent an email and then wished they could issue a rollback?). One way to handle this is to code the trigger so that you check the customer credit and status before you update the inventory. Then you know that this customer is qualified to buy before you begin to decrement inventory and trigger reorder emails. Triggers are written to enforce business rules, and business logic governs the order in which checks are done within a trigger.

An alternative to sending an email from within a trigger would be to have a shopping list table, a concept similar to the shopping cart when you're ordering from an Internet store. When an inventory item reaches its reorder point, it's added to the shopping list by inserting a row into the table. If the customer's order is rolled back, so is the entry in the shopping list table. If the customer's order commits, so does the entry in the shopping list table. You can then create a scheduled task that checks the shopping list, perhaps once a day or once an hour; notifies the suppliers; and updates the inventory table to show that the item is on order. This task sees only committed transactions in the shopping list table, so there is no risk of an uncommitted dependency in this scenario.

It's not a good idea to return data from a trigger. This is not to say you would ban all SELECT statements from triggers, although a SELECT statement in a trigger will cause locks to be retained longer and could possibly impact performance. You might have a SELECT statement inside a trigger that checks the inventory table to make sure an item is in stock, but you wouldn't return the quantity on hand to the calling application. This would really impact performance by more than doubling the network traffic between a calling application and SQL Server, and it would increase the amount of comparison and processing needed by the calling application. Typically, the calling application is making a modification to a table; it does not expect to have to handle results returned from the server. Triggers are not for retrieving data in normal operations. For that task, use a stored procedure.

Prior to SQL Server 7.0, you could define at most three triggers on a table—one for UPDATE, one for INSERT, and one for DELETE. Now you can have multiple AFTER triggers on a table. For the previous inventory example, you could have a trigger that checks for available inventory and another that checks the customer credit rating. Then you could have a third trigger that updates the inventory quantity on hand for each item ordered, and a fourth that updates the last-ordered date in the customer table.

The disadvantage of multiple triggers is that you have little control over the order in which they run. You can specify which trigger is to be executed first and which is to run last, using the SP_SETTRIGGERORDER stored procedure, but everything in between will run in some undefined order. If you have merge replication enabled on your database, it insists that its trigger be the first to run, thus removing the first-executed option from any other trigger on the table. Therefore, if you program all of the required actions into a single trigger, obviously you control the sequence of these actions.

Inside Triggers: The INSERTED and DELETED Virtual Tables

One of the very powerful features of trigger code is its ability to compare the new version of a record with an old version. You can then make conditional decisions in your code based on what has changed in the record. Knowing how this is done also gives you insight into how transaction rollbacks can happen. The key to it all lies in the two virtual tables called INSERTED and DELETED. When you insert a row, the INSERTED table contains a copy of the new row. When you delete a row, the DELETED table contains a copy of the row that was deleted. When you update a row, both the INSERTED and DELETED tables are available to you, containing the old and the new versions of a record. What you're really talking about when you refer to these virtual tables is an entry in the transaction log. The transaction log captures after-images of inserted records, before-images of deleted records, and both before- and after-images of updated records. You can refer to these images in your trigger code by calling for the INSERTED and DELETED tables. Then you can compare values in the columns of these virtual tables with the corresponding values in the actual tables. We'll see some examples of how these tables are used later in this chapter.

CREATING TRIGGERS

When you create a trigger, you have to supply a name for it. A trigger is an object in the database; therefore, each trigger name must be unique throughout the entire database. A trigger is part of a table definition, so you have to say which table it belongs to. Triggers can be added to a table at any time, and dropped, without affecting the table or the data it contains. If you drop the table, the triggers are dropped also and must be rebuilt if you rebuild the table. You can specify a trigger as being for an INSERT, UPDATE, or DELETE action, or any combination of the three.

The syntax of the code to create a trigger using the Query Analyzer and T-SQL, as taken from SQL Server Books Online and abbreviated, is shown here:

```
CREATE TRIGGER trigger_name ON { table | view }
[ WITH ENCRYPTION ]
{   { { FOR | AFTER | INSTEAD OF }
    { [ DELETE ] [ , ] [ INSERT ] [ , ] [ UPDATE ] }
          [ WITH APPEND ]
          [ NOT FOR REPLICATION ]
          AS
          sql_statement goes here [ ...n ] }
```

As always, you can also create a trigger from Enterprise Manager. Select the database, expand the database hierarchy, select the table on which you want to create the trigger, right-click, and choose All Tasks | Manage Triggers. From the dialog box, you can add a new trigger or modify an existing one. You can also get to this dialog box from the Table Design window, by clicking on the triggers icon, as shown in Figure 18-1. Just as with stored procedures, you have to supply the code for the trigger.

You might find it easier to use the Query Analyzer, which has some templates for building triggers. In the Query Analyzer window, click the icon on the left end of the toolbar and you will see four CREATE TRIGGER options—one for the INSTEAD OF trigger and three for the AFTER trigger, as shown in Figure 18-2. Notice when you look at the code

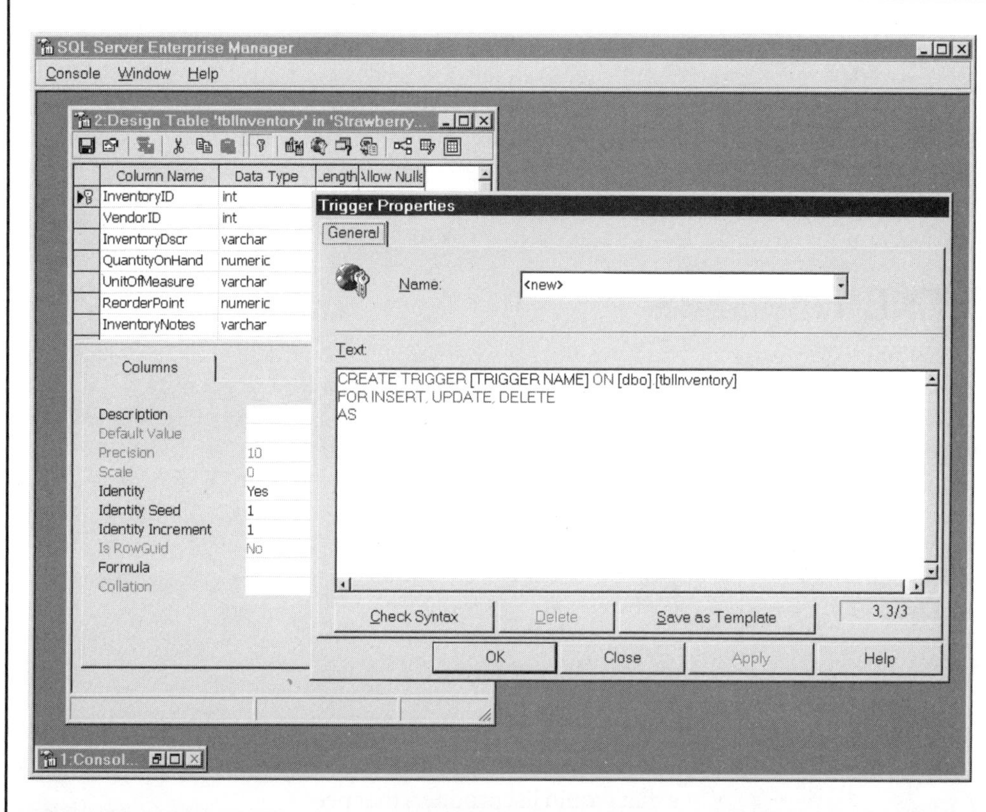

Figure 18-1. You can create a trigger from Enterprise Manager, but you still have to know how to write the code.

generated by these templates, they all contain a RAISERROR statement. Figure 18-3 is the simplest template, an AFTER trigger. The RAISERROR is there because a rollback can be initiated from anywhere in a sequence of cascading triggers. Therefore, it is a good idea to provide some feedback about where the problem has occurred.

As an example, let's create a trigger on the Inventory table. When the QuantityOnHand is updated, the trigger compares the new value with the ReorderPoint. If the number in the QuantityOnHand column has dropped below the value of ReorderPoint, the trigger will make a note in the InventoryNotes column that the product should be reordered. You could

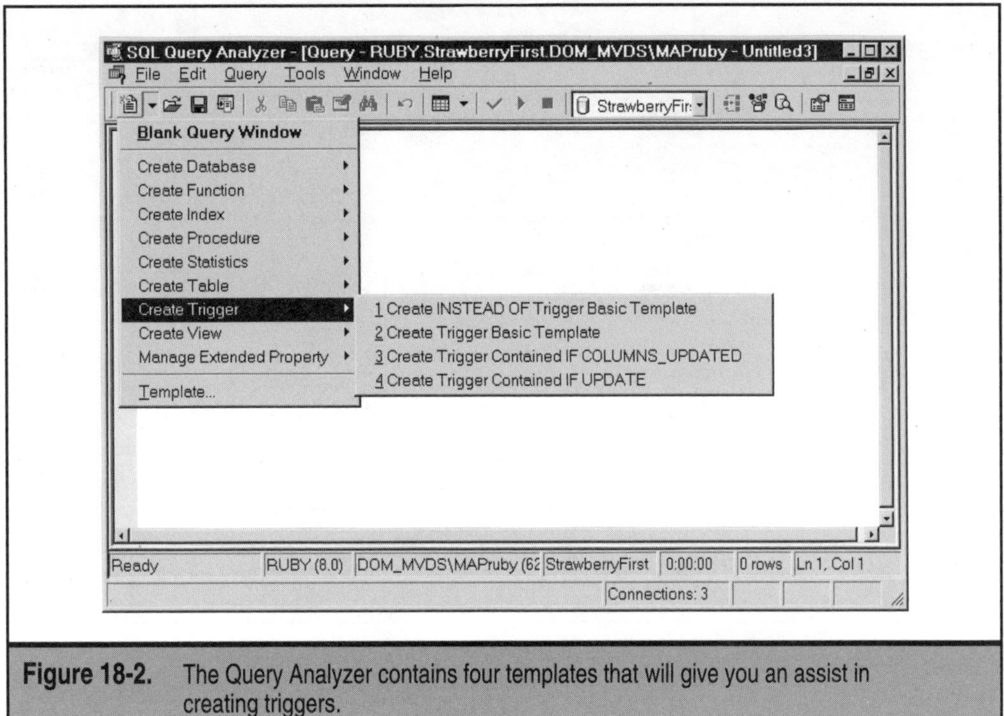

Figure 18-2. The Query Analyzer contains four templates that will give you an assist in creating triggers.

also write a stored procedure that would list products that need to be reordered, by comparing the values of QuantityOnHand and ReorderPoint. In a small database like this, there's not much difference between a stored procedure and a trigger doing this job. But in a large database, the stored procedure could take quite a bit of time to run, it might create some lock contention with other applications, and it would have to be executed often enough so that you didn't run out of inventory. Because you know the Strawberry Smooches Company will grow, you're going to design this correctly from the beginning.

You want to put a notation in InventoryNotes, so that initially someone can scan through the records in this table and make note of the products that should be reordered. As the company grows and the inventory table increases in size, and as you develop more triggers on this table, you'll build a stored procedure that executes daily, checks the InventoryNotes for the word "reorder," and places the appropriate order with the item supplier.

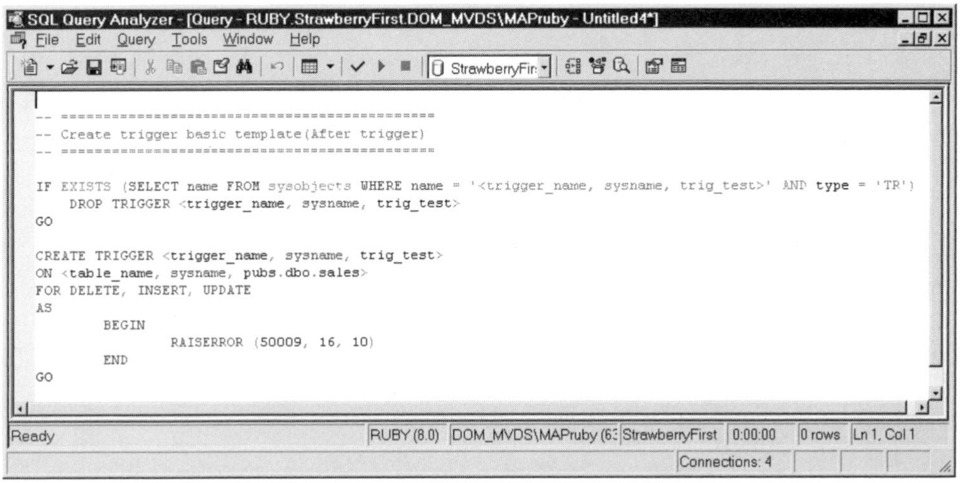

```
-- =============================================
-- Create trigger basic template(After trigger)
-- =============================================

IF EXISTS (SELECT name FROM sysobjects WHERE name = '<trigger_name, sysname, trig_test>' AND type = 'TR')
    DROP TRIGGER <trigger_name, sysname, trig_test>
GO

CREATE TRIGGER <trigger_name, sysname, trig_test>
ON <table_name, sysname, pubs.dbo.sales>
FOR DELETE, INSERT, UPDATE
AS
        BEGIN
                RAISERROR (50009, 16, 10)
        END
GO
```

Figure 18-3. The basic trigger template contains a RAISERROR, to help you pinpoint trouble spots in trigger execution.

```
-- Create trigger to check quantity on hand against
-- reorder point if quantity on hand is below reorder point
-- change inventory notes. Only modify inventory notes if it is null
IF EXISTS (SELECT name FROM sysobjects
   WHERE name = 'ut_InventoryUpdate' AND type = 'TR')
   DROP TRIGGER ut_InventoryUpdate
GO
CREATE TRIGGER ut_InventoryUpdate ON tblInventory
FOR UPDATE AS
IF (((SELECT (QuantityOnHand - ReorderPoint) FROM inserted) <=  0)
AND ((SELECT tblinventory.InventoryNotes
      FROM tblInventory join inserted ON
       tblInventory.InventoryID = inserted.InventoryID  )  IS NULL ) )
-- update the Inventory table, add a note to reorder the item
UPDATE tblInventory
SET InventoryNotes  = 'Reorder this item'
WHERE tblInventory.InventoryID =  (SELECT InventoryID FROM inserted)
GO
--  Check the current inventory table
SELECT * FROM tblInventory
-- for ID 1, drop the quantity to 1,
-- which is below the reorder point of 2
```

```
UPDATE tblInventory
SET QuantityOnHand = 1 WHERE InventoryID = 1
-- Check the inventory table again
SELECT * FROM tblInventory
-- reset for id = 1
UPDATE tblInventory
SET QuantityOnHand = 3 , InventoryNotes = NULL WHERE InventoryID = 1
GO
SELECT * FROM tblInventory
-- now change reorder point, this also updates InventoryNotes
UPDATE tblInventory
SET reorderpoint = 3 WHERE InventoryID = 1
GO
SELECT * FROM tblInventory
--reset the reorder point
UPDATE tblInventory
SET reorderpoint = 1, InventoryNotes = NULL WHERE InventoryID = 1
SELECT * FROM tblInventory
--  Clean up by dropping the trigger
DROP TRIGGER ut_InventoryUpdate
```

Normally, the trigger for the QuantityOnHand would be activated by an INSERT to the Sale table, which would ripple through the SaleItem table, the Product table, and the Manufacturing table into the Inventory table. A Strawberry Smooochie is composed of many components, so with every sale there will be multiple changes to the Inventory table, and any one of several items could hit its reorder point. When you have an UPDATE trigger on a table, it will fire no matter how the table is updated—whether it's from a direct entry from the Query Analyzer window, a stored procedure called from an application, or a client/server application using ODBC or OLE DB. From the preceding code, it doesn't matter whether you update the QuantityOnHand value or the ReorderPoint value—the effect is the same: the trigger fires.

To see the trigger on this table, open Enterprise Manager and expand the database hierarchy, select Strawberry, and then select Tables. Right-click the Inventory table and select All Tasks | Manage Triggers. The Trigger Properties dialog box opens to show the trigger code, as shown in Figure 18-4.

Permissions

Because the trigger is going to fire automatically, you don't have to give users permission on a trigger. If the user can modify a table, the trigger fires automatically in response to the UPDATE, INSERT, or DELETE. The important point about permissions is that triggers often perform operations on other tables, either a SELECT or a data modification operation. The trigger works like a stored procedure, in that the trigger can perform actions using

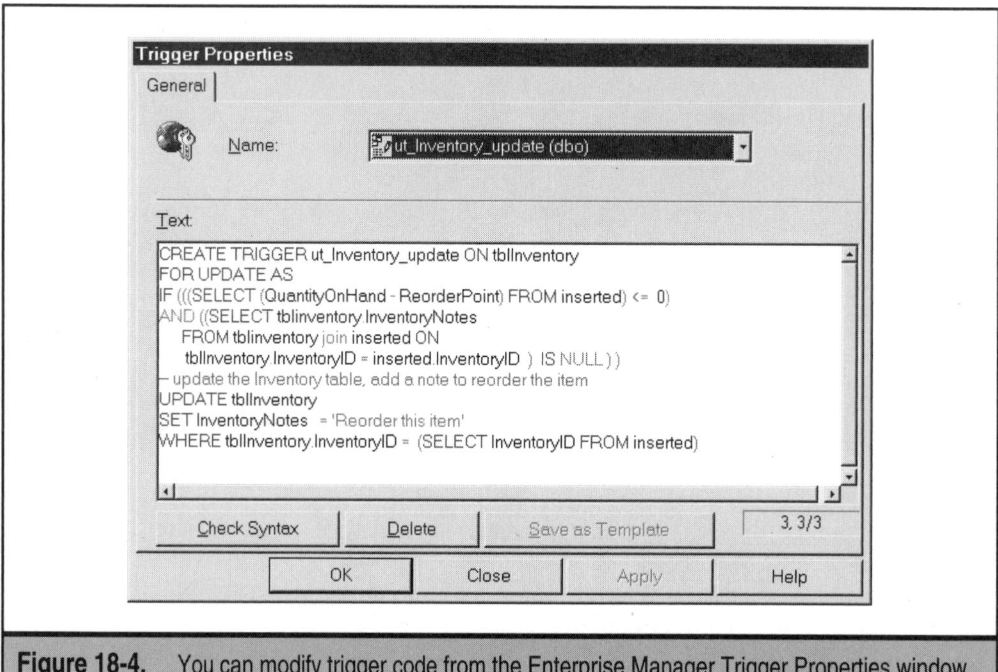

Figure 18-4. You can modify trigger code from the Enterprise Manager Trigger Properties window.

the owner's own security context, even though the user updating the table would normally be denied permissions to perform these actions.

In a mail-order operation, the data entry staff who take customer orders would not have permission to update the inventory table directly. In the following example, you create two tables containing only an integer and date-time column. You add a trigger so that updating table CheckPerms will update the timestamp in the second table, CheckPerms2. You have a user called Bob, who is given permission to run updates on CheckPerms, but he is specifically denied permission to update CheckPerms2. Once the tables and trigger are in place with the correct permissions, you need to bring up the Query Analyzer window and log on as Bob, using SQL Server authentication. If your SQL Server is not set up to use mixed mode security, you'll need to do a few extra things to make this exercise work. If you don't already have a test NT/Windows 2000 account called Bob, you'll have to create one. From an NT Server/Windows 2000 computer, create a new account called Bob, password Bob, in User Manager for Domains. Make Bob a member of Domain Users. Then you'll be ready to execute the SELECT and UPDATE statements that are listed next.

```
-- as DBO, create and load the test tables CheckPerms and CheckPerms2
CREATE TABLE CheckPerms (Num int, LastUpdate datetime)
GO
```

```
INSERT CheckPerms VALUES (1, getdate())
GO
CREATE TABLE CheckPerms2 (Num int, LastUpdate datetime)
GO
INSERT CheckPerms2 VALUES (1, getdate())
GO
-- create the trigger that will check permissions
-- if the user can update table CheckPerms then this
-- trigger will cause the LastUpdate field of
-- CheckPerms2 to be updated
CREATE TRIGGER ust_lastupdateperm ON CheckPerms FOR UPDATE AS
UPDATE CheckPerms2
SET LastUpdate = getdate()
GO
-- create login bob, password bob, default database is Strawberry
EXEC sp_addlogin 'bob','bob', 'Strawberry'
-- create user bob in the Strawberry database
EXEC sp_adduser 'bob', 'bob'
-- grant permissions to bob
GRANT SELECT, UPDATE ON CheckPerms to bob
GRANT SELECT, UPDATE ON CheckPerms2 to bob
-- logged in as bob, select from the two tables
SELECT * FROM CheckPerms
SELECT * FROM CheckPerms2
-- logged in as bob, update table CheckPerms
UPDATE CheckPerms
SET Num = 2
-- logged in as bob, redo the select and see the change
SELECT * FROM CheckPerms
SELECT * FROM CheckPerms2
-- however, bob cannot update table CheckPerms2 directly
UPDATE CheckPerms2
SET Num = 2                    -- update attempt fails
-- log in as dbo and clean up the database
DROP TABLE CheckPerms
DROP TABLE CheckPerms2
DROP TRIGGER ust_lastupdateperm
sp_dropuser bob
sp_droplogin bob
```

Notice that when Bob updates CheckPerms, the trigger changes the timestamp in CheckPerms2, just the way the trigger said it would. However, Bob cannot directly update CheckPerms2 because of the DENY issued to him on that table. This is one way you can restrict access to tables in your database, yet allow users to get the work done.

Trigger source code can be encrypted, just like stored procedure source code. The text of the trigger is placed in the syscomments table when you create the trigger, so if you want to prevent users or others from reading the code, use the WITH ENCRYPTION option when you create the trigger. Just as with stored procedures, there is no way to decrypt a trigger once it's been encrypted, so make sure you maintain a copy of the trigger source code in a safe place.

ALTERING AND DROPPING TRIGGERS

We have mentioned before that dropping an object also drops all the permissions on that object, but—as you saw in the previous section—permissions are not an issue with triggers. Nonetheless, in version 7.0, Microsoft added an ALTER TRIGGER command to SQL Server. The syntax of the ALTER TRIGGER statement is similar to the CREATE TRIGGER statement (from SQL Server Books Online):

```
ALTER TRIGGER trigger_name
ON ( table | view ) [ WITH ENCRYPTION ]
{ ( FOR | AFTER | INSTEAD OF )
   {[ DELETE ] [ , ] [ INSERT ] [ , ] [ UPDATE ] }
        [ NOT FOR REPLICATION ]
        AS
        sql_statement goes here[ ...n ] }
```

Previous versions of SQL Server had an interesting "feature": they did not warn you when you overwrote an existing trigger. As only one trigger of each type (INSERT, UPDATE, or DELETE) was allowed on a table, an older trigger already on a table could be overwritten by any new trigger that you might create on that table, and you'd never know about it until some processing or performance problem arose. Now, you can have multiple AFTER triggers on a table. You get an error message only if you try to create a trigger that has the exact same name as an existing trigger.

Dropping a trigger is easy. From Enterprise Manager, select the database, expand the database hierarchy, select the table that has the trigger you want to remove, right-click, and choose All Tasks | Manage Triggers. When the Manage Triggers window opens, select the correct trigger from the list box, and click Delete.

If you prefer the T-SQL approach to removing a trigger, first make sure that you're in the correct database and then use the following command:

```
DROP TRIGGER trigger_name
```

Remember, because a trigger is considered a database object, each trigger name is unique throughout a database, so you don't even have to reference the database name in the DROP TRIGGER command. You can list more than one trigger to be dropped in the same command.

Disable/Enable Triggers

Another new feature introduced in SQL Server 7.0 is the ability to disable a trigger. When a trigger is disabled, the trigger definition is still in place, but the trigger actions do not happen. In previous versions, the only way to prevent a trigger from firing was to drop the trigger. If the database administrator had to run some operation, such as loading a large data set, where he didn't want the trigger to fire for each time a record was loaded, he had to drop the trigger. Usually, the database administrator would have a T-SQL script that contained code to drop any triggers on the table, a bcp load template to help load the data, and code to re-create the triggers.

Such a script nowadays would contain code to disable the trigger, bcp load the data, and enable the trigger. So what's the difference? To enable a trigger, all the database administrator needs is an ENABLE TRIGGER command. To re-create the trigger, the database administrator needs to have access to the source code, which may not be possible because of security or licensing issues. Plus, when using source code to re-create a trigger, there is always the possibility of a coding error creeping into the trigger code.

Enabling a trigger does not recompile it, which might be exactly what you want to do after a large data load operation. Add an EXEC SP_RECOMPILE command to the end of the T-SQL script mentioned previously.

The syntax for disabling and enabling triggers uses the ALTER TABLE command:

```
ALTER TABLE table_name
DISABLE TRIGGER trigger_name
--OR
ALTER TABLE table_name
ENABLE TRIGGER trigger_name
```

If you have multiple triggers on a table, and you want to disable and then enable all of them, simply code as follows:

```
ALTER TABLE table_name
DISABLE TRIGGER ALL
-- followed by
ALTER TABLE table_name
ENABLE TRIGGER ALL
```

All the triggers on that table will be first disabled, and then enabled.

IF UPDATE()

The CREATE TRIGGER statement has another option: IF UPDATE(). This can be used as a shortcut for comparing the old and new versions of a record. You can quickly check to see whether a value in a particular column has changed, and if it has, you can take some action. The syntax of the CREATE TRIGGER IF UPDATE() option is as follows:

```
CREATE TRIGGER trigger_name
ON { table | view }
[ WITH ENCRYPTION ]
    { ( FOR | AFTER | INSTEAD OF ) { [ INSERT ] [ , ] [ UPDATE ] }
        [ WITH APPEND ]
        [ NOT FOR REPLICATION ]
        AS
        { IF UPDATE ( column )
            [ { AND | OR } UPDATE ( column ) ]
                [ ...n ]
        sql_statement goes here  [ ...n ]      }
```

How do you use this? Let's say you want to prevent changes to a column that is part of a foreign key relationship, and for whatever reason, you don't want to use foreign key constraints. You can issue an error message and a rollback if the before and after values of the column, as specified in the IF UPDATE (*column*) section of the trigger, are different. The IF UPDATE() function compares the values in the INSERTED and DELETED tables for the named column. You could, of course, add a query to your transaction code to do exactly that, but the IF UPDATE() function is faster to code and executes faster than a query.

Here's an example: Suppose you wanted the inventory reorder trigger to fire only if the QuantityOnHand changed, but not when you change the ReorderPoint of the Inventory table. There are several ways you can code this. One would be to use IF UPDATE() on the QuantityOnHand column, as shown here:

```
-- check to see if the trigger exists and if it does, delete it
IF EXISTS (SELECT name FROM sysobjects
          WHERE name = 'ut_InventoryUpdate' AND type = 'TR')
    DROP TRIGGER ut_InventoryUpdate
GO
-- create the trigger
CREATE TRIGGER ut_InventoryUpdate ON tblInventory
FOR UPDATE
AS
IF UPDATE (QuantityOnhand)
BEGIN
IF (((select (QuantityOnHand - ReorderPoint) from  inserted) <=  0)
AND ((select tblInventory.InventoryNotes FROM tblInventory JOIN inserted
      ON tblInventory.InventoryID = inserted.InventoryID  )  IS NULL ) )
UPDATE tblInventory
SET InventoryNotes  = 'Reorder this item'
```

```
where tblInventory.InventoryID =  (SELECT InventoryID  from inserted)
END
GO
--  Now test the trigger
-- Check the current inventory table
SELECT * FROM tblInventory
-- for ID#1, drop QuantityOnHand below the value of ReorderPoint
UPDATE tblInventory
SET QuantityOnHand = 1   WHERE InventoryID = 1
-- Check the inventory table again
SELECT * FROM tblInventory
-- reset values for ID#1
UPDATE tblInventory
SET QuantityOnHand = 3 , InventoryNotes  = NULL WHERE InventoryID = 1
GO
SELECT * FROM tblInventory
-- change reorder point and test to see if the trigger fires
UPDATE tblInventory
SET ReorderPoint  = 3 WHERE InventoryID = 1
GO
SELECT * FROM tblInventory
--reset the reorder point value
UPDATE tblInventory
SET ReorderPoint = 1, InventoryNotes = NULL WHERE InventoryID = 1
SELECT * FROM tblInventory
```

Changing the value of QuantityOnHand in the Inventory table did cause the trigger to fire and insert the note "reorder this item" into the InventoryNotes column for record ID#1. However, changing the value of ReorderPoint did not cause this trigger to fire.

INSTEAD OF TRIGGERS

Yet another new feature in SQL Server 2000 is the INSTEAD OF trigger. This new trigger differs in many ways from the AFTER trigger. Only one INSTEAD OF trigger of each type (INSERT, UPDATE, and DELETE) is allowed per database object (table or indexed view). This type of trigger, in a complete and radical departure from the usual way a trigger operates, does not activate after the change has already been made to the table. What it does is take the request to modify the data and modify it to do other processes. This may initially seem like an odd thing to do, but in fact, the INSTEAD OF trigger does have a place in SQL Server 2000. It complements another new feature, the indexed view.

We mentioned in Chapter 12 that you are restricted in how you can update using a view. In particular, updating a view based on a join of two or more base tables can be problematic. The INSTEAD OF trigger takes care of this situation and allows you to update the base tables by using an indexed view that's created from the join of these base tables. This is very useful, especially from a security standpoint, because now all users can be restricted from modifying the base tables directly. You can insist that they access and update the data only through the views you have defined for them.

In the last chapter, you created a stored procedure that added a new employee to the Person table and to the Employee table, in one process. Now you're going to do the same thing, but you're going to use an updateable indexed view.

First define the view. The view has to be created from a join of two tables, so you know it's not possible to use this view directly to insert a record. Then create an index on the view, as shown here:

```
CREATE VIEW _NewEmployee WITH SCHEMABINDING
AS
SELECT dbo.tblPerson.PersonID, LastName, FirstName, MailingAddr,
       City, State, Zip, JobTitle, SSN, I9onFile, W4onFile,
       PayAmount, PayPeriod
FROM dbo.tblPerson JOIN dbo.tblEmployee
                   ON tblPerson.PersonID = tblEmployee.PersonID
GO
-- check to make sure the view works
SELECT * FROM _NewEmployee
-- index the view on the PersonID column
CREATE UNIQUE CLUSTERED INDEX ind_NewEmp
 ON _NewEmployee (PersonID)
GO
```

To confirm that this view is indeed indexed, Figure 18-5 is a display of the SP_HELP command. The type of object is indeed a view; the index name is ind_NewEmp.

Trying to insert a record using this view is really very problematic. Any INSERT statement on the view will fail unless the number of values supplied in the INSERT exactly matches the number of columns in the view. That means you have to supply a value for the PersonID column—yet you know that the values of that column in the Person table are automatically generated. You can't input values directly into PersonID without turning off the automatic identity insert property. Also, there's no column in the view that represents the PersonType. In and of itself this will not cause an insert to fail, because the PersonType column is nullable. But because this is a view of employees, the PersonType code value should be set to "e." If you're going to be inserting records using this view, you need some way to supply that value.

INSTEAD OF trigger to the rescue. The INSTEAD OF trigger will intercept the INSERT instruction and modify it to compensate for these problems. You still have the inserted table

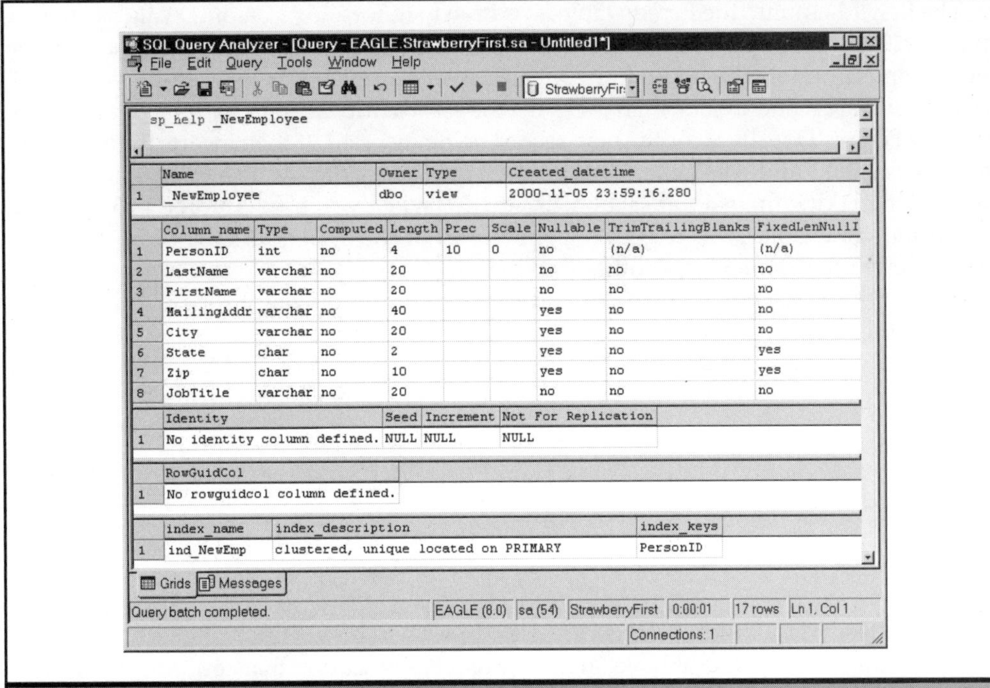

Figure 18-5. The SP_HELP stored procedure confirms that this object is a view, and the view has an index built on it.

to which you can refer—if you recall, this virtual table contains the row as it was initially inserted into the view. The trigger definition looks like this:

```
CREATE TRIGGER ust_NewEmpTrig ON _NewEmployee
INSTEAD OF INSERT
AS
  BEGIN
  INSERT INTO tblPerson
  SELECT LastName, FirstName, MailingAddr, City, State, Zip, 'e',
         NEWID() FROM inserted
  INSERT INTO tblEmployee
  SELECT @@identity , JobTitle, SSN, I9onFile, W4onFile, PayAmount,
         PayPeriod, NEWID() FROM inserted
END
GO
```

The first INSERT into the Person table is written to ignore any PersonID value specified in an INSERT statement written against the view. It also provides a value for the PersonType column, which you know must be "e," because this is an employee INSERT operation. The second INSERT then picks up the @@identity system variable, so it knows what the PersonID really is for the new record being inserted. It then inserts the appropriate data into the Employee table. You grouped the two INSERTs with a BEGIN and an END, rather than making them a transaction, as you did when you used a stored procedure to update the same tables. The trigger is already part of a transaction, so you would not be gaining anything by creating another transaction.

Now that the trigger is in place, you can add an employee through this view, as shown in the following example:

```
INSERT INTO _NewEmployee
VALUES ('0', 'Khan', 'Shere', '25 Bangalore Blvd', 'Minnetonka',
        'MN', '45678', 'Public Relations', '010-01-0101', 'yes',
        'yes', 100, 'weekly')
-- Check the insert to make sure it worked
select * from _NewEmployee
where PersonID = @@identity
```

In practice, you wouldn't expect your end-users to be writing T-SQL INSERT statements like this, but you might have an Access or VB application that connects to the view and uses it as the basis of a data entry screen.

What happens if you want to remove this employee from the database? Normally, because of referential integrity constraints, you would have to drop this employee record first from the Employee table and then from the Person table. However, your users can only see the data through this view, so what are they supposed to do? Right now, they can't directly delete a record from a table.

To prove this to yourself, try to run this DELETE statement. To make sure you get the correct record, use SSN for the WHERE condition.

```
DELETE FROM _NewEmployee WHERE SSN = '010-01-0101'
```

You'll find that this DELETE is rejected because it would affect multiple base tables. It's time for another trigger, this time an INSTEAD OF() trigger for the DELETE query:

```
CREATE TRIGGER ust_DelNewEmpTrig ON _NewEmployee
INSTEAD OF DELETE AS
BEGIN
DELETE  FROM  tblEmployee
WHERE tblEmployee.PersonID IN (SELECT PersonID FROM deleted)
DELETE  FROM  tblPerson
WHERE tblPerson.PersonID  IN (SELECT PersonID FROM deleted)
END
GO
```

You have to write this trigger so that the first deleted record is from the Employee table. Then you can delete from the Person table. This is because of the referential integrity constraint that exists between the two tables—the Person table is parent, the Employee table is child. In the query, each DELETE clause uses a subquery with an IN operator to check for the matching PersonIDs from the deleted table. That's because it's possible that more than one record could be deleted in the same operation. The deleted table can contain multiple rows, depending on how you write the DELETE query that causes this trigger to fire. You have to account for any eventuality.

You cannot define an INSTEAD OF trigger on a table that has a foreign key with a cascade delete constraint on it. Granted, all these new features contained within SQL Server 2000 are a little tough to keep straight, but once you get used to them, you'll wonder how you lived without them.

Let's remove the Khan clan from our list of employees, using this view. If you still have Kubla and Genghis from the last chapter, you can delete them and Shere Khan all at the same time. Instead of limiting the DELETE query by Social Security number, you will use last name:

```
DELETE FROM _NewEmployee WHERE LastName = 'Khan'
```

This time, the DELETE operation works. You should see two messages stating "one row(s) affected"—one for each of the two tables as the employee record is deleted—or "three row(s) affected" if all three of the Khan clan are still in the employee list.

If you want to remove the objects created in this chapter, drop the view. All associated indexes and triggers will automatically be dropped.

```
DROP VIEW _NewEmployee
```

All these new features are neat, but there are one or two rather puzzling things that might happen when you're using them. This suggests that either there are rough edges in the SQL Server code or we need better explanations from SQL Server Books Online.

For instance, when you connect to SQL Server with MS Access or MS Query, you'll have no problem inserting and deleting records using this indexed view. It won't matter whether you use Windows NT or Windows 2000, Access 97/Access 2000, or Excel 97/Excel 2000—we tested them all. However, when we tried to use Enterprise Manager, to select the view, and chose Open View | Return All Rows, we were unable to insert a record. The error message returned said that SQL Server could not insert NULL into the PersonID column in the Employee table. This is the second table—the child table—and it would have data inserted into it only after the INSERT on the Person table. For some reason, the INSTEAD OF INSERT trigger did not work when using this interface.

On the other hand, a DELETE operation will work just fine from Enterprise Manager. Additional checking reveals that, in the absence of the INSTEAD OF DELETE trigger, it is still possible to delete a row from the view using Enterprise Manager. However, trying to run a DELETE query from the Query Analyzer caused the aforementioned error message, and attempted delete operations from Access and MS Query also resulted in error messages. The implication is that in Enterprise Manager table datasheet mode, some code behind the scenes recognizes how to handle cross-table, hierarchically dependent record deletes, even without the aid of an INSTEAD OF DELETE trigger, and this logic is missing everywhere else. What you see in Enterprise Manager is not quite the same thing as what you get when you connect through the Query Analyzer or from a client (ODBC/OLE DB) application.

TRIGGERS AND CONSTRAINTS

Part of the reason for using triggers is being supplanted by new SQL Server features and constraints. Triggers were once used to enforce referential integrity, a function that has been taken over by the foreign key constraint (also called declarative referential integrity or DRI). Triggers were used to handle cascading changes from primary keys to all associated foreign key values, propagating these changes through the tables of a database. This function is also being taken over by the cascading update and delete built into the foreign key constraints, as of SQL Server 2000. For now and for the foreseeable future, you can use triggers for any of these functions, if you prefer.

If you've upgraded an older database, a SQL Server 6.5 database to SQL Server 2000, it's probably worth the investment to make some changes in the way things work. The first thing you'll want to do is replace the triggers that enforce referential integrity and instead create comparable foreign key constraints, because of the way the constraints work. (We'll explain in more detail about how much more efficient constraints are later in this chapter.) At the same time, you might want to leave cascading updates and cascading deletes under trigger control. The basic difference is that referential constraints prevent bad things from happening, such as records being orphaned, while triggered cascade operations help events happen, such as deleting records that otherwise would be orphaned. Constraints are better at preventing; triggers are good for making things happen.

One important thing to remember is that if you have a constraint and a trigger, both of which respond to the same condition, the trigger will never fire. For example, a foreign key constraint that could prevent a record from being deleted would prevent the DELETE from taking place, so the ON DELETE trigger would never fire.

Triggers for Referential Integrity

Until SQL Server 6.0, triggers were the only way to enforce referential integrity between tables. Now you can use foreign key constraints to enforce these relationships. However, there is still one situation in which triggers have to be used and in which you can't use constraints. A foreign key constraint cannot reference a table outside of its own database; a trigger can.

In the previous example, you added a new employee to the Person table and to the Employee table, and for the sake of illustration let's imagine that these tables are part of a Personnel database. Now you want to take some of that information and insert a record into the Payroll database to make sure this employee gets paid. You can create an AFTER INSERT trigger on the Employee table to ensure that the record is also added to the Payroll database. Then you could add an AFTER UPDATE trigger, so that if any information changed, such as salary level, address, or eligibility for benefits, the change would be reflected automatically in the Payroll database.

It is unlikely that you would want to delete any information about an employee or about his payroll records. Even when a person leaves the company, his records will have to be kept for many reasons, not least of which is the IRS. Rather than relying on the database administrator to program security settings that allow INSERT and UPDATE actions but disallow DELETE operations, you may want to put in a trigger for attempted DELETE actions. The trigger might just generate an error message and then roll back the DELETE, making sure that no application can delete an employee record. It could take even more complex action, such as copying the employee record into an Employee Archive table, and then removing all but the NOT NULL data from the Employee table and setting a flag to indicate that this is an ex-employee. To do so, the trigger could get the record from the deleted virtual table and insert it into the Employee Archive table. Either the AFTER DELETE trigger on the Employee table or an AFTER INSERT trigger on the Employee Archive table could then modify the Payroll database to make sure that paychecks are not issued from this point on.

Triggers for Cascade Deletes and Updates

Now that you can implement cascading updates and cascading deletes as constraints, there's less reason to use a trigger for these operations. However, if you need to cascade a change from one database to another, you'll have to use triggers rather than constraints.

Let's say you've decided to allow DELETE operations on the Employee table, employing a trigger to move the deleted record to the Employee Archive table. With some additional code in the trigger, you can cascade the DELETE to the Payroll database and DELETE the employee from the appropriate tables in that database. Again, a trigger on the affected tables in the Payroll database could move the deleted row into an archive table, so the records would not be lost.

If you ever had to change an employee's identifier, you could use a trigger to cascade the update to all associated tables. The update would be made to the Employee table by the Personnel staff and the change automatically propagated to the Payroll database through an AFTER UPDATE trigger.

There are, of course, many other ways to achieve the same cascading results, including replication of the Employee and Employee Archive tables from the Personnel database to the Payroll database. Or Payroll might decide to run a stored procedure that queries the Personnel database and retrieves changes (based on a date-of-last-update column) from the Employee and Employee Archive tables. This last approach works for INSERT and UPDATE operations, but it raises questions about how to identify records that have been deleted.

Triggers may be the better of the two approaches if the databases are on the same SQL Server. But when databases are on different servers, you have set up a *distributed transaction*, in which the Personnel database and the Payroll database have to be updated by their respective SQL Servers. A distributed transaction means that your network has to be reliable, and both servers have to be operational. The people in the Personnel department will not be too happy if they cannot delete an employee's records just because of some network problems! For multiple servers, you might give some serious consideration to a replication scenario with a short latency (delay period). SQL Server replication has some fault tolerance built into it. We'll talk more about replication in the next chapter.

Nesting or Non-Nesting Triggers

We have talked about how a trigger can update a table, which has a trigger that causes another modification on a third table, and so on. There's a limit to how far this process of cascading triggers can go. SQL Server places a limit of 32 levels deep on nesting triggers. The intent of this limit is to stop a trigger from modifying a table that fires a second trigger, which modifies the original table that fires the first trigger…this could be an infinite loop, unless something stops it. You probably will not need to set up triggers that go anything like 32 levels deep. Just think of how long a rollback on a 32-level nested trigger would take!

There is an option to turn off nesting altogether. This is a server-level option. When you activate this option, the trigger on your original table can modify another table, but the triggers on that table will not fire, thereby limiting trigger firing to one level. You might consider doing this if SQL Server has to function in a heterogeneous distributed environment—that is, in a mixed database platform group with database servers that don't support nested triggers. Otherwise, we suggest leaving this option at the default setting, allowing nesting of triggers.

To set the nesting option, right-click the server name in Enterprise Manager and select Properties. Go to the Server Settings tab, and in the middle of the box you'll see the check box for allowing or disallowing nested triggers. Notice that this setting applies to the server and therefore to all the databases on this instance of SQL Server. To set this option using T-SQL, you would run the following code:

```
EXEC SP_CONFIGURE  'Nested Triggers', 1
GO
RECONFIGURE  WITH OVERRIDE
GO
```

The reconfigure with override forces the change to take place immediately, rather than waiting for the next time the SQL Server service is restarted. A value of 1, the default, turns nesting on, and 0 turns it off.

Recursive Triggers

Recursive triggers are more of a critical decision than nesting triggers. When recursive triggers were introduced in SQL Server 7.0, the implementation was half-baked at best, and it contained some major flaws in the implementation. SQL Server recursive triggers have the appearance of a feature that was added simply because some other RDBMS had this feature, but it was not thought out thoroughly nor was it implemented correctly.

The default behavior of SQL Server is designed to avoid the situation in which a trigger makes an update to its own table, which then fires the trigger again, which would update the table, which would fire the trigger again, and so on, in an endless loop. An example of this would be a trigger that updates the LastModifiedBy and UserName columns for a table, so you can track who makes changes to the table. Suppose that someone in Personnel finally gets around to updating your salary. The update triggers a change to these two columns, and if you coded the triggers wrong, this could mean that the update trigger might fire again, updating the same two columns over and over, until it hit the 32-level restriction. SQL Server will not normally allow a trigger to activate itself. Triggers by default are nonrecursive. It is still possible to have a change on table 1 that causes a change to table 2, which that causes a change to table 1 that causes a change to table 2, and on and on. This is most likely poor programming, but it can happen.

If your boss is too cheap to buy you a copy of some project management software, you could use SQL Server to build a Gantt chart to keep track of your software development projects. Suppose your latest software project has ten steps, and the start of each is dependent on the completion of the previous step. When you enter the start time and date of the project, and time estimates for each step, with some slick programming, you can produce a Gantt chart. But what happens when the start of the project is delayed three days because your lead programmer overdosed on junk food and had to be rushed to the emergency room? You have to update the start date of the first step of the project. You have an AFTER UPDATE trigger that updates other dependent records in the table if the start date is modified. The trigger first updates the end date of step 1. You would need to have the trigger fire again, to update the start date of step 2, and fire again to update the end date of step 2, and so on all the way through to the end of the project. In this case, you need a recursive trigger, one where the trigger update activity causes the same trigger to activate again and again, all within the same table.

With SQL Server 2000, you can have these recursive triggers. Unfortunately, if you turn on the recursion property, *all the triggers in the database become recursive*, because recursion is a database property, not a trigger property. So one unwitting programmer turns on recursive triggers, and immediately all sorts of weird things start happening on other tables. Had any thought gone into this new recursive trigger feature, recursion would have been implemented as a trigger property, so you could make the decision as to whether it would be recursive trigger by trigger.

A second problem in the implementation of recursion is that recursive triggers are also subject to the 32-level limit. This is an absurd limitation. Someone has confused nesting and recursion. With recursive triggers, there's no reason for the 32-level limit. If your Gantt chart is working fine with 30 steps in your project schedule, and you have to add three more steps, it won't work anymore. Does this make sense?

SQL Server Books Online doesn't contain much good information on this topic. In fact, it is quite confused, again not making the proper distinction between nesting and recursion. It talks about "direct recursion," which is recursion as you have always known it (a trigger changes its own table and activates itself over and over again). It also talks about "indirect recursion," which is nonsense. There is no such thing as "indirect recursion." According to Books Online, indirect recursion is supposedly when table A changes and its trigger causes a change in table B, which has a trigger that causes a change in table A that sets off a loop. This is more accurately known as a *circular reference* or, in many cases, a programming error. At one point, Books Online does say that only direct recursion is prevented when recursive triggers are set off. Then it goes on to say that to prevent indirect recursion, you have to turn off nesting also. Of course you do. Turning off nesting would prevent the looping that Books Online calls indirect recursion. Actually, turning off nesting turns off recursion as well.

To make sense of all of this, let's define the terms properly. *Nesting* is the capability for a change to one table to fire a trigger that causes a change to another table, which fires another trigger. *Recursion* is a special case in which the trigger updates its own table, thus firing the same trigger. Because recursion depends on triggers activating triggers, it depends on nesting being turned on.

If you really feel that you must turn on recursive triggers, you can do so from Enterprise Manager by selecting a database, right-clicking, and selecting Properties. Choose the Options tab. Check the box to turn on recursive triggers, but don't do this on a production database or anything other than a small personal test database to test how they work. We suggest that you wait until recursive triggers are properly implemented before using them in your production applications.

You can also turn recursive triggers on and off with the SP_DBOPTION stored procedure, if you want to do so in a script. The syntax is shown here:

```
EXEC SP_DBOPTION Strawberry , 'Recursive_Triggers', TRUE | FALSE
```

True turns on recursive triggers for the entire database; false turns them off. The following examples of recursive triggers and nesting triggers involve changing the behavior of your database and of your server. *Do not* try this code on a production system.

The following code builds a table with a last_update column and then creates a trigger to insert the current date and time into that column when the table is updated. Normally, that works just fine, until you turn on recursive triggers, and then it fails as it hits that 32-level limit—because there's no check to stop the recursion.

```
-- Make sure that nesting is on (server properties)
-- and recursive triggers are off (database properties)
-- create a table with a LastUpdate column, insert a row
CREATE TABLE tblCheckTriggers
 (   Num int,
     LastUpdate datetime)
GO
INSERT INTO tblCheckTriggers VALUES (1, getdate())
GO
SELECT * FROM tblCheckTriggers
GO
--create a trigger to modify the LastUpdate column
CREATE TRIGGER ut_LastUpdate ON tblCheckTriggers
FOR UPDATE AS
UPDATE tblCheckTriggers SET LastUpdate = getdate()
```

```
GO
--  check the current values, update, check values again
--  LastUpdate column should change
SELECT * FROM tblCheckTriggers
GO
UPDATE tblCheckTriggers
SET Num = 2
GO
SELECT * FROM tblCheckTriggers
GO
-- now set recursive triggers on
SP_DBOPTION Strawberry, 'recursive_triggers', true
GO
-- the update causes a loop and stops when it hits the 32 level limit
UPDATE tblCheckTriggers
SET Num = 3
GO
SELECT * FROM tblCheckTriggers
GO
-- set recursive triggers off, drop the table
SP_DBOPTION Strawberry, 'recursive_triggers', FALSE
GO
DROP TABLE tblCheckTriggers
GO
```

Now let's set up a circular reference to see what effect nesting has on triggers. Create two tables, each with a LastUpdate column. The trigger works so that when one table is updated, it changes the last-update column in the other table.

```
--  create two tables with a LastUpdate column
--  add a row to each
CREATE TABLE tblCheckTriggers
 (   Num int,
     LastUpdate datetime)
GO
CREATE TABLE tblCheckTriggers2
 (   Num2 int,
     LastUpdate2 datetime)
GO
INSERT INTO tblCheckTriggers
VALUES (1, getdate())
GO
INSERT INTO tblCheckTriggers2
VALUES (1, getdate())
```

```
GO
-- create a trigger on each table that updates the other table
-- setting up a circular reference
CREATE TRIGGER ut_tblCheckTriggersUpdate ON tblCheckTriggers
FOR UPDATE AS
   UPDATE tblCheckTriggers2
   SET LastUpdate2 = getdate()
GO
CREATE TRIGGER ut_tblCheckTriggers_update2 ON tblCheckTriggers2
FOR UPDATE AS
   UPDATE tblCheckTriggers
   SET LastUpdate = getdate()
GO
-- now try an update, don't worry about the cross join
-- only the first select will work
-- with the circular reference you will hit the 32 level limit
SELECT * FROM tblCheckTriggers, tblCheckTriggers2
GO
UPDATE tblCheckTriggers
SET Num = 2
GO
SELECT * FROM tblCheckTriggers, tblChecktriggers2
GO
SELECT * FROM tblCheckTriggers   -- update did not succeed
GO
--  turn off nested triggers. without nesting, the 32 level cut off
--  will not be reached
EXEC SP_CONFIGURE 'NESTED TRIGGERS', 0
GO
RECONFIGURE WITH OVERRIDE
-- now do the update again
-- notice that when you update the Num column in table 1
-- the trigger updates the LastUpdate column in table 2
-- and that is as far as it can get
-- the trigger on table 2 does not fire
SELECT * FROM tblCheckTriggers, tblCheckTriggers2
GO
UPDATE tblCheckTriggers
SET Num = 2
GO
SELECT * FROM tblCheckTriggers, tblCheckTriggers2
GO
```

```
-- cleanup
DROP TABLE tblCheckTriggers
DROP TABLE tblCheckTriggers2
GO
EXEC SP_CONFIGURE 'nested triggers', 1
GO
RECONFIGURE WITH OVERRIDE
EXEC SP_DBOPTION Strawberry, 'recursive_triggers', FALSE
GO
```

PERFORMANCE ISSUES

Triggers are compiled code, so they are relatively efficient. Triggers are generally slower than constraints created for the same task. This is because a constraint is, to use a word made popular a few years ago, "proactive." They prevent things from happening. A trigger of the AFTER type is activated only when something has already happened; so if there's a problem, the trigger has to undo—rollback—whatever changes were made. You could describe a trigger as "reactive." Inevitably, reacting to a condition will take longer than never allowing the problem to occur in the first place. So when a constraint can be used, it should be used instead of a trigger. However, when you hit the limits of what a constraint can do, you have to revert to triggers.

Typically, the code in a trigger is more complex than you would find in a constraint, so the complexity of what a trigger does adds to the perception of slowness. Trigger performance is really impacted when it has to access another table—especially if that table is not already in cache—or when it has to access another database or even another server. An entry in the Order table, as we have discussed, can result in SELECT operations against the Customer table, the Product table, and the Accounts Receivable table, and UPDATE operations to the Inventory and Shipping tables. This is not a situation of the trigger itself taking that long to run, it's the amount of work the trigger has to do and the number of objects it has to reference.

If trigger performance is an issue in your database, consider the following troubleshooting tips to see if you can optimize the performance. First, try to use constraints instead of triggers whenever possible.

You can also try to minimize the impact of a rollback. With both triggers and stored procedures, it's a good idea to do all your checking first, before you start making changes to tables. The less you have to roll back, the better. Rollbacks are time-consuming and resource-intensive, and they can impact other users. Do everything possible to avoid having to invoke a rollback.

The performance impact of a trigger is not measured by simply timing how the trigger itself runs. You also have to consider the impact on other users of the database. If your trigger executes a whole series of updates on multiple tables, all of those tables will have locks set, with the potential for conflict with other users. The longer the trigger actions take to complete, the greater the possibility of conflict.

Consider whether all of the actions coded into the trigger really have to be done as part of the trigger. Could some or all of these actions be achieved by some less intensive approach? Just because two events happen together does not mean that a trigger is the only way to program them. For example, a salesperson enters an order in a form built in Access or VB. When the salesperson clicks the GO button on the form, that activates a stored procedure. The stored procedure inserts the order into the Order and Order Details tables. Would you code a trigger on the Order Details table to update the Inventory table? You certainly could, but you could also add another line to the stored procedure to directly update the Inventory table.

Using a trigger to update the Inventory table ensures that any change to Order Details is always reflected in Inventory, even if the change is because the store manager had to manually change some Order Details records to fix errors initiated by the data entry staff. Conversely, if the stored procedure is the only way possible for all users to manage orders, you might prefer to code all the UPDATE steps as part of the stored procedure. Someone looking at the code a year from now would find it easier to follow if all the UPDATE actions are listed in one stored procedure. With the trigger approach, it's not obvious that the stored procedure will cause an UPDATE to the Inventory table via a trigger. Either approach will involve the same amount of work to update the tables and will hold the same locks until the end of the transaction, although the timing of the lock requests and grants may differ. Performance gains may be minimal between these two options.

In previous sections of this chapter, we mentioned that placing an order involves updating the Inventory table, which then might fire another trigger that checks to see whether the reorder point has been reached. The people who run the physical inventory warehouse send out orders once a day. They deal with hundreds of products from six different suppliers. Rather than send out many orders throughout the day as each item hits its reorder point, they want to consolidate the orders to each vendor and send out only six purchase orders a day, at most. So perhaps you don't need that trigger—the one that runs during an order entry—on the Inventory table. You could, instead, have a stored procedure that runs every day at the close of business, checking the quantity of each item against its reorder point. Now you have one stored procedure that runs once a day, rather than a trigger that fires thousands of times each day, once for every order placed. Now each order operation runs just a little bit faster. As long as the reorder point is high enough, you shouldn't run out of any item. However, if your business runs on just-in-time inventory, you might be safer with the trigger.

Try to avoid distributed transactions in triggers. They add a lot of system overhead and require a very robust network. A minor network outage could turn into a major issue for the users and the company. If the Order table in a retail store has a trigger on it that causes an UPDATE operation to the local Inventory table, that's reasonable. If it also updates the inventory at a central warehouse, that's probably overkill, especially if it would involve a distributed transaction. A much better solution would be to set up replication of the local inventory table to the central warehouse database, so the warehouse will know within minutes if an item is in short supply. The warehouse table could then have UPDATE triggers that ship more stock to the store if the inventory at the store is low, and that place resupply orders with the vendors if the total quantity in the warehouse falls below some set reorder point. Programming the triggers on the central warehouse server takes some of the load off the local server in the store, giving the store staff better response time when they're dealing directly with customers.

Remember also that SQL Server will recompile stored procedures and triggers "when it is advantageous to do so," so your trigger code will usually be optimized. If you have any doubts about this, add the SP_RECOMPILE stored procedure to your daily or weekly database maintenance plans.

Error Handling

The ability to provide customized, application-specific error messages is one advantage triggers have over constraints. Constraints simply return a system message about a constraint violation. Constraints name the table and columns involved, but the error number, as found in the @@error variable, will be the number for a constraint violation. That's not very helpful to client applications, which find it easier to deal with a numeric error code than having to parse an error message. With triggers, just as with stored procedures, you can use the RAISERROR function to send back custom error message values.

One of the surprising things about triggers is that if the actions specified by the trigger fail, no error message is returned to the user. For instance, if a trigger attempts to update a record in another table and that record does not exist, the trigger doesn't return an error code. It's up to you to add whatever level of checking you feel is appropriate to handle these situations. You might decide to return an error message if the trigger cannot find the objects it needs to access or modify, or if for some reason it invokes a rollback of the transaction.

Let's illustrate this by an example. You create a trigger on the Payroll table. When you insert a paycheck record, the trigger automatically updates the Employee table, adding the amount of the paycheck to the year-to-date salary for the employee. Would you first check to see whether the employee record you were updating actually existed? Probably not, because the employee record in the Payroll database was inserted by a trigger on the Employee table. Therefore, there shouldn't be a record in the Payroll table that does not have an entry in the Employee table. As you have referential integrity constraints set up between the tables, there's no way the record in the Employee table could have been deleted while leaving a record in the Payroll table. So in this case, you decide it really is not necessary to perform this check. Even if the two tables were on separate servers, you would still have your referential integrity in place, but this time it would be enforced by triggers. Still, there's no need to check for the employee record, as you know it has to be there.

In your Inventory UPDATE trigger, you might decide to use a RAISERROR when the trigger updates the reorder message. If you chose to log this message to the Windows NT/2000 event log, the DBA could set up an alert to notify someone when the stock fell below the reorder point. The following example shows an ad hoc RAISERROR, but you would probably add a custom error message to the sysmessages table, as we described in the last chapter in the discussion about stored procedure error handling.

```
CREATE TRIGGER ut_InventoryUpdate ON tblInventory
FOR UPDATE AS
IF (((SELECT (QuantityOnHand - ReorderPoint) FROM inserted) <= 0)
AND ((SELECT tblinventory.InventoryNotes
      FROM tblinventory JOIN inserted
      ON tblInventory.InventoryID = inserted.inventoryID) IS NULL ))
BEGIN
UPDATE tblInventory
SET InventoryNotes  = 'Reorder this item'
WHERE tblInventory.InventoryID =  (SELECT InventoryID  FROM inserted)
DECLARE @inventnum int
SELECT  @inventnum = InventoryID  FROM inserted
PRINT  'inventory number' + CONVERT(char(4), @inventnum)
RAISERROR ('Reorder point reached on product %d ' , 11, 1, @inventnum)
END
GO
-- drop the quantity for id = 1 to 1
-- which is below reorder point of 2
UPDATE tblInventory
SET QuantityOnHand = 1  WHERE InventoryID = 1
GO
SELECT * FROM tblInventory    -- message appears on row #1
GO
-- cleanup, reset the table, and drop the trigger
UPDATE tblInventory
SET QuantityOnHand = 3 , InventoryNotes = NULL WHERE InventoryID = 1
GO
DROP TRIGGER ut_InventoryUpdate
GO
```

Figure 18-6 shows the results of the UPDATE operation, which returns the expanded error message. Triggers definitely have an advantage over constraints in creating informative error messages.

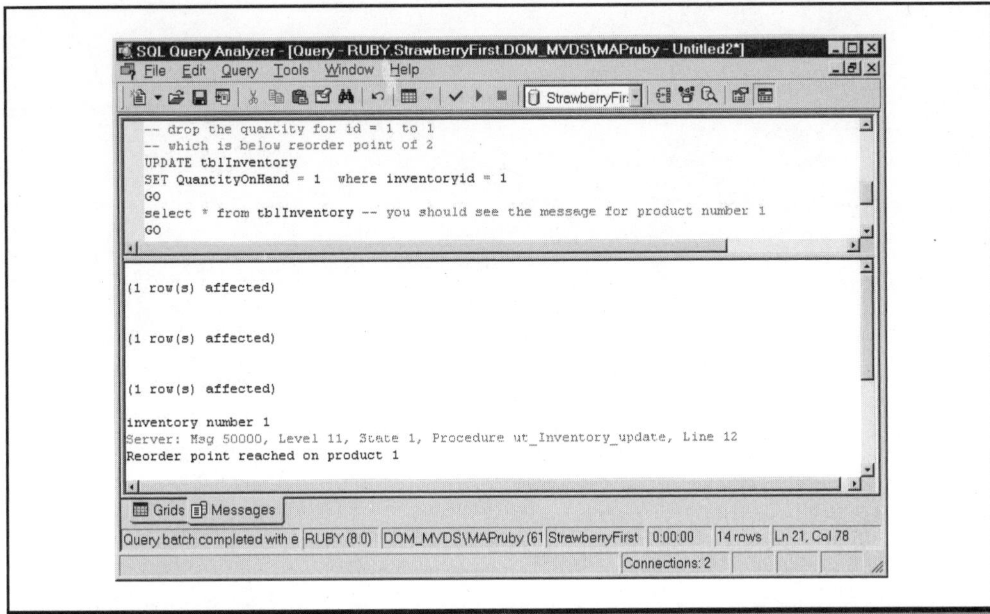

Figure 18-6. Trigger code can return custom error messages.

CHAPTER 19

Distributed Data and Replication

Distributed data and replicated data are not the same thing. Distribution implies that a single set of data is divided and parts of the data set are physically located in two or more places. The data set is disjointed—some of it is here, some of it is there. Replicated data implies multiple copies of a single data set. It implies that these copies are located physically apart from each other, and that some mechanism is in place to keep the copies synchronized.

Distributed databases and replicated databases are also different. A distributed database is one in which a single database is spread across multiple servers, each of which operates under the control of its own CPU and system clock. Keeping the data synchronized—for instance, enforcing referential integrity constraints—must be done either by user program control or by some distributed database management system synchronization mechanism.

A replicated database is composed of multiple copies of a single database, each copy of which can be located on its own servers. Changes to one copy of the data must be reflected in all other copies. This can be in real time, in near-real time, or on a scheduled basis (hourly, daily, or weekly). Synchronizing these changes is the task of the replication monitor and administration software. You can distribute copies of all or part of your database by using replication; hence, the confusion in terminology.

In this chapter, we'll look at both distribution and replication, investigate some of the features of each, and then weight the pros and cons to see which would work best for you.

WHY DISTRIBUTE DATA?

The definition of distributed data, in the world of SQL Server, is when the data that is being accessed resides on different SQL Servers. One SQL Server can support multiple databases, so you could not consider cross-database operations on the same SQL Server to be truly distributed, because one set of SQL Server services is taking care of the coordination between databases. For instance, locks are all stored on the same server in the Master database.

Once you move one of the databases to a different SQL Server, however, you're involving multiple servers and now you have a distributed database situation. Locking and transaction control become significantly more complex. Collation schemes from server to server can have an impact on operations. A distributed database environment can even involve different vendor products (SQL Server, Oracle, and Access, for example).

With SQL Server 2000, it is possible for multiple instances of SQL Server to reside on the same physical computer. Such a configuration would be treated as a multi-server setup, the same as if an installation of SQL Server and an installation of Oracle resided on the same server. Actually, Microsoft handles interdatabase operations on the same SQL Server as multi-server operations. However, all this happens internally behind the scenes, with no intervention needed by the user or the database programmer.

You can distribute data many ways within the SQL Server environment. We've already looked at some of these techniques, including distributed transactions, the use of remote stored procedures, and running queries and stored procedures on linked servers.

In this chapter, we will recap some of these approaches and introduce a related scheme that we have mentioned frequently throughout the book: replication.

The first questions you need to ask when you start thinking about distributing data are these: Why are you doing this? What's the purpose behind it? What do you hope to gain from it? Are you aware of the costs in addition to the benefits of distributed data? There are a lot of reasons for distributing data, including but not limited to these:

- Keeping a copy of the data for archival and backup purposes
- Making a copy of the data available to data analysts and program developers
- Making the data more available to remote locations
- Splitting the data storage load across multiple servers
- Splitting the data processing load across multiple servers

You can probably add other reasons for distributing data—reasons that are specific to your organization. If you think you will need to distribute your data, here are some questions that might help you decide which approach will work best for your situation:

- Will you need to keep full copies of all the data at each location in the distributed data network, or do you plan to partition it—have some of the data here, some there?
- Who is allowed to update the data? Who uses it for read-only data analysis and informational purposes?
- How important is it that the data be up to date everywhere? Can you live with a bit of latency at some, if not all, locations?
- How reliable is your network? How often does it go down? How long does it stay down?

Log Shipping

If you need a "warm site" backup server that will be available for emergencies if the primary server fails, *log shipping* may be what you need. This warm site server would also be available for data readers—data analysts and report writers—to work from. Log shipping automates the process of backing up the transaction log on the primary server (most likely your production server), moving the backup file to another server (the destination server), and restoring the log to a copy of the database on the destination server. In the past, this process was performed manually, often aided by custom-crafted T-SQL scripts. Now it has been automated as part of the Database Maintenance Wizard, but unfortunately, it's available only in the Enterprise edition of SQL Server 2000.

SQL Server Books Online references to log shipping are fairly incoherent in this first release version of the product. In Books Online's description of log shipping, it's not clear what you can and cannot do. Log shipping is not true hot-site failover, as the latency (time between when a change to data at the source is seen at the destination) is significant.

In addition, the flow of data changes is one way. All data changes are made to the primary server; the destination servers are for reading only. Any change made to data on a destination server would be overwritten by the next restore of a transaction log from the primary server. There is no way to update data from the destination to the primary server.

If you can live with those limitations, log shipping can be an effective solution when up-to-the-minute consistency with the primary database is not essential. Most of the time, the data analysts will be looking for long-term trends and the report writers can function well with data that's a few hours old.

Data Transformation Services

With the power of Data Transformation Services (DTS), you can set up tasks that not only move data from one server to another, but also transform the data as it is being moved. DTS was added to SQL Server in version 7.0. It was initially meant to be used as a tool when moving transactional data into data warehouses, cleaning and reorganizing it in the process. But DTS has many other uses—in fact, you could write a whole book about DTS.

DTS can copy entire databases from one server to another, and it can copy selected objects from one database to another. You can copy the tables, views, and user-defined datatypes; indexes; triggers and stored procedures; and even logins and permissions from the source database to the target database if you are planning to set up a complete simulation.

If your plan is to create a read-only version of the source database for your data readers, you should leave off copying over the indexes, triggers, stored procedures, logins, and permissions, because you will be setting up totally different schemes of indexing and permissions. The logins may be very different from those on the source database; you may have a totally different population of users accessing this version. There's no point in copying over the triggers and stored procedures, because there shouldn't be a need to modify the data on the target server—after all, it's supposed to be a read-only copy. Chances are, you wouldn't want the triggers firing again on the destination server, especially if they were to generate resupply orders to your vendors.

Although setting up and scheduling DTS tasks may be seen as the responsibility of the database administrator, the database designer should also be involved in planning DTS strategy. For example, if you have a read-only copy of your transactional database for your data readers to use for analyzing and reporting, the indexing strategy can and should be optimized for each database. It's not unusual to find that read-only databases have three or four times the number of indexes as their transactional counterparts. Even though the data is the same, the constraints, triggers, stored procedures, and other functions will probably be very different between these two databases.

In SQL Server 2000, there's a new feature that allows for a combination of replication and DTS, so you can transform the data while it is being replicated. If you activate this option, it will slow down the replication process, but it's a very powerful option and may be worthy of consideration. We'll talk more about replication further on in this chapter.

Remote Queries and Stored Procedures

In Chapter 17, we talked about linked servers and stored procedures, and some of the possibilities for remote access offered by this scheme. Once you've set up the linked servers and identified permissions for the user community, your users can launch queries against the remote servers. If your situation is one in which remote queries are the exception rather than the rule, this approach may have more merit than any of those we've discussed up to this point. Rather than moving the data from server to server or database to database, simply give your users the wherewithal to query remote servers.

Distributed Transactions

Of all the ways to query distributed data, distributed transactions are the most resource intensive. They are also the best way to ensure that all of your data is consistent and synchronized in real time. But unless this is an absolute requirement, distributed transactions impose terrible restrictions, including the need for the network to be 100-percent reliable all the time.

A SQL Server distributed transaction is one that spans two or more databases. Like all transactions, it must be fully completed or—if interrupted before the COMMIT operation is completed—fully undone. SQL Server manages the distributed transaction internally; to the end-user, it looks like a local transaction.

On each of the servers involved in a distributed transaction is a software component called a *resource manager*. These resource managers have to cooperate with each other to make sure that a distributed transaction can successfully complete. Resource managers are coordinated by a transaction manager, such as the Microsoft Distributed Transaction Coordinator (DTC). Transaction COMMITs are not just local. In a distributed transaction, the COMMIT has a distributed component handled by the transaction manager, to ensure that some of the resource managers aren't committing a transaction while others are rolling back the same transaction.

The scheme used to COMMIT a distributed transaction is called a *two-phase commit*, and it works something like this:

1. A user starts a transaction (BEGIN TRANSACTION) from the local database (this is the controlling resource manager).
2. The local transaction is escalated to a distributed transaction if one of two actions happens before the transaction commits or is rolled back:
   - An INSERT, DELETE, or UPDATE statement is executed that references a table on a remote database.
   - The transaction issues a stored procedure call to a remote database. The remote component of the transaction is handled by the resource manager of the remote database.

3. Microsoft DTC becomes part of the operation. It registers (enlists, in Microsoft-speak) all resource managers of the databases that will be participating in the distributed transaction.
4. The controlling resource manager issues a COMMIT statement.
5. Control passes to DTC for the distributed COMMIT operation. Phase 1: DTC sends a "prepare to commit" request to each resource manager. Each resource manager then does what it needs to do to get ready to commit, including flushing buffers and releasing extraneous locks. Then each resource manager sends back to DTC a success status message.
6. DTC collects the success messages. If any messages are missing, DTC issues a ROLLBACK command to each resource manager, and the distributed transaction is rolled back.
7. If all resource managers report success, DTC initiates phase 2 of the two-phase commit by sending COMMIT commands to each resource manager. Each resource manager immediately commits its portion of the transaction and frees any resources being held. Should the network connection fail between DTC and a resource manager before the resource manager gets the COMMIT command, the resource manager has no option but to maintain its resource locks, and for all intents and purposes, that database is on hold until the network comes back up.

Now you can see why distributed transactions are the most resource intensive. Without an extremely robust network, the potential for chaos and blocked transactions is very high. If you absolutely need the immediacy of two-phase commit processing and totally synchronized data, you must ensure that your hardware layer can support this scheme.

REPLICATION

Replication is a truly elegant solution that provides 90 percent of the capability of a distributed transaction at a fraction of the cost. Replication has limitations, but as long as you can live within these limitations, you will have an extremely powerful tool to use.

The concept of replication is quite simple: Changes made to a primary database can be applied to a copy of the database within some small time delay (latency). The time delay can range from seconds to days, depending on your needs. Replication is another topic worthy of a book on its own, so we will concentrate on the design issues that surround setting up a replication solution. We'll cover how to plan for replication in your database design, even if you don't intend to implement it immediately. And we'll discuss how replication works, the different replication modes, and the various physical replication models.

Replication Terminology

First we need to define some terms as they are used in Microsoft SQL Server replication. The server where the data originates and which is responsible for updating the data is known as the *publisher*. The server where the copy of the data resides and which is updated with the changes from the publisher is known as the *subscriber*. It's possible to replicate data from one database to another on the same server or even between tables in the same database, so the publisher and the subscriber can be the same computer. One publisher can support many subscribers. A subscriber can accept data from more than one publisher.

The third component is the *distributor*. The distributor is a SQL Server database that stores the changes from the publisher and passes them along to the subscriber. Its exact role varies depending on the type of replication you use. The distributor can be a separate SQL Server, or the publisher can also serve as the distributor. It is less common, although theoretically possible, to have the distributor and subscriber components on the same system. SQL Server Books Online further defines distributors as "local" or "remote," a poor choice of terms (in our estimation) that has caused unnecessary confusion.

Within the limits of this terminology, a distributor is local when the publisher and the distributor are on the same SQL Server. It is remote when they are on different SQL Servers. In SQL Server Books Online 2000, the definition has been enhanced to include the use of "remote" when the distributor is on a different instance of SQL Server on the same computer. There is no such thing as a remote distributor. The distributor should either be on the same SQL Server as the publisher or no more than 6 feet away, preferably with its own dedicated fiber-optic network connection to the publishing database. Unfortunately, the use of the word "remote" has led some people to think that you can have the publishing database located in New York and the distribution database located in London, which is total nonsense.

Putting the distributor on its own SQL Server does make sense if you have a heavily loaded publishing server—for example, in a telephone order processing center. Using a dedicated distributor will take the load off the publisher, thus enhancing the response time seen by the customer service operators. One distributor can serve multiple publishers.

A *publication* is data that has been designated for replication. A publication is composed of *articles*. An article is a table or a subset of a table, and in SQL Server 2000, an article can be created from an indexed view. An article can also be a database object such as a stored procedure. A publication is a group of articles that, generally, are related to each other. In earlier versions of SQL Server, subscribers could subscribe to one article of a publication, but there was no guarantee that referential integrity would be maintained unless they subscribed to the entire publication. Now, in SQL Server 2000, a subscriber must subscribe to the entire publication.

A database may have many publications, each with a customized set of articles intended for different subscribers. Security options control who can subscribe to a publication, so even though an article is published, it may not be available to everyone on the network.

A *push subscription* is one that is set up at the publisher, and that pushes the data out to the subscriber via the distribution database. A *pull subscription* is initiated at the subscriber and pulls the data from the distribution database to the subscriber. In a push subscription, the work of making sure that the updates happen is handled by the distribution agent running on the distributor. In a pull subscription, the distribution agent runs on the subscriber, and it does the work of moving the data. If you have only one or two subscribers, the additional load of push subscriptions may not be a performance issue; but if you have ten or twenty (or more) subscribers, you might want to plan on pull subscriptions rather than risk overloading the distributor.

For either a push or a pull subscription, the database administrator can set up the subscription without ever leaving his chair, no matter where the servers are physically located. First, you need to have all the servers involved already registered with your copy of Enterprise Manager. Next, you need to have all the publications defined. Then, for a push subscription, just connect to the publishing database and set up the push subscriptions, one or many. You can see all the subscribers from one window, so you can set up more than one subscription at the same time.

To create a pull subscription, connect to the subscriber with Enterprise Manager and set up the subscription, one server at a time. The only exception to this rule that we know about is pull replication subscribers in Hawaii or the Bahamas—for whatever reason, these cannot be set up remotely. Each requires a visit in person by the database administrator, and it usually takes at least two weeks of on-site work to make sure that the pull replication is working smoothly. We have no explanation to offer for this phenomenon, although it might have something to do with the difference in temperature or the pressure of the water on undersea cables.

Partitioning Data for Replication

When you publish data for replication, you can choose exactly what gets published. You can SELECT columns from a table that will be published, and you can include a WHERE clause to restrict the rows that appear in a published article. There are many reasons why you'd want to limit the type and amount of data you're publishing, including security and sensitivity, reduction in network traffic, and lower storage requirements on the subscriber. You can choose not to replicate columns in which the data might be considered sensitive, private, or unnecessary. A good example of this would be the replication of your sales database that you built for your marketing team. In the customer table of the sales database, you replicated only the columns for customer ID, city, state, and zip code—you didn't replicate the name, street address, or telephone number. The analysts can examine purchasing trends by city or by zip code, but they cannot access any personal information about the customer.

Replication allows you to separate the data entry staff (the data writers) on the publisher from the data analysts (the data readers) on the subscribers, and finally resolve their conflicting demands. Plus, you can optimize the design and performance for each system, which you could never do when the data readers and data writers were sharing a single database. Couple this with the new DTS features that combine with replication, and you have a very powerful solution.

In SQL Server 2000, you can transform the data with DTS while it's being replicated. If, for example, you wanted to replicate data from your highly normalized transactional database to a moderately denormalized data mart, in past versions of SQL Server you had to do it with a two-step process. First, you had to replicate the table structures precisely, and then you created a sequence of views that gave end-users the appearance of denormalized data. With SQL Server 2000, you can use data mappings and column manipulations on string functions to modify the data that arrives at the subscriber. You can even join publisher tables and produce a single combined table at the subscriber. In essence, you're publishing a DTS package. In a simple example, the publishing database contains customer data with separate columns for first and last name. You want to present this same customer name in the subscribing database as a single column. Therefore, you can combine the text strings for first name and for last name, and output a single full-name text string as you replicate with a DTS package.

Replication Schemes

There are four logical schemes for replicating data in SQL Server 2000—the three standard techniques: snapshot replication, transactional replication, and merge replication; and then there is a hybrid of replication and distributed database called "replication with immediate update subscribers."

Snapshot Replication

The first, and most basic, replication scheme is snapshot replication. Data is copied from the publisher onto the subscriber. Periodically, the entire dataset is copied over to the subscriber, overwriting whatever is already there, as illustrated in Figure 19-1. Data flows from the publisher to a snapshot folder on the distributor. It's then rerouted to the subscribers for snapshot replication and synchronizing other types of replication. This works well for small databases, but the amount of data transferred may make it prohibitive for larger databases or shops with limited bandwidth networks.

Under certain circumstances, it may not be necessary to keep the subscriber synchronized with the publisher all the time. For example, if the financial wizards in your company are constantly modifying the corporate budget predictions for the next five years, you might choose to inject a little stability into your day-to-day operations. Therefore, you might copy a snapshot of the budget database only once a month. In this case, snapshot replication works really well. By synchronizing on a monthly basis, you insulate your staff from the uncertainty of dynamic financial predictions.

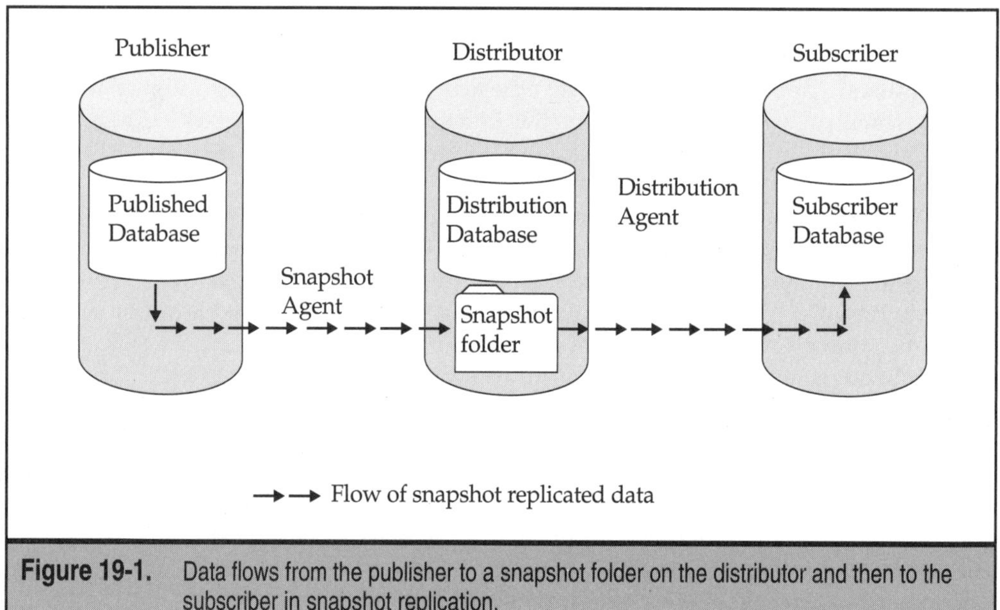

Figure 19-1. Data flows from the publisher to a snapshot folder on the distributor and then to the subscriber in snapshot replication.

Typically, snapshot replication is used when the amount of data is not large and the frequency of replication is low. Often, snapshot replication will happen once a week, usually at a time when the systems are not otherwise busy. Except when synchronization is happening, the subscriber doesn't have any impact on the day-to-day operations of the publisher.

In practice, there is little difference in the end result if you use either snapshot replication or a DTS scheduled task to copy the data from one server to another. The decision is more a question of which approach you are most comfortable with.

Transactional Replication

Most people who have been using SQL Server for a while tend to think of replication as the transaction log–based replication, which has been available for many years and many versions of SQL Server, and which improves with each version. The concept behind transaction log–based replication is that you start with two identical copies of the database (snapshot synchronization). Then the changes in the publisher's transaction log are copied over to the subscriber and applied to that database within a minute or more of the change happening. Thus, the two databases stay synchronized.

In transactional replication, the distributor is keeping track of all the changes to tables that are part of publications. These changes are stored in a distribution database. This is a database just like any other, with its own transaction log. The Log Reader Agent runs on the distributor and is continuously connected to the publisher to monitor the transaction log for changes to published data. Then, as shown in Figure 19-2, the Log Reader Agent copies any committed transaction that is marked for replication from the publisher to the distributor. Each database that is participating in replication will have one active Log Reader Agent. This close linking of the distributor and publisher is why you don't want the two located very far apart physically. The data is retained in the distribution database until all the subscribers have been updated. It can be retained for some period of time, usually hours or days, based on a user-settable configuration parameter, in case a subscriber has to restore from an earlier backup and reapply the transactions from the publisher. Then it's removed.

There will be some impact on the publishing database with transaction log–based replication because of the constantly running Log Reader Agent. You can minimize the impact by moving the distributor to another server computer, but the Log Reader Agent is still copying transactions from the production server. The impact is going to be small, however, compared to the potential conflict you would have with data readers and data writers locking horns over long-running, complex queries blocking update transactions.

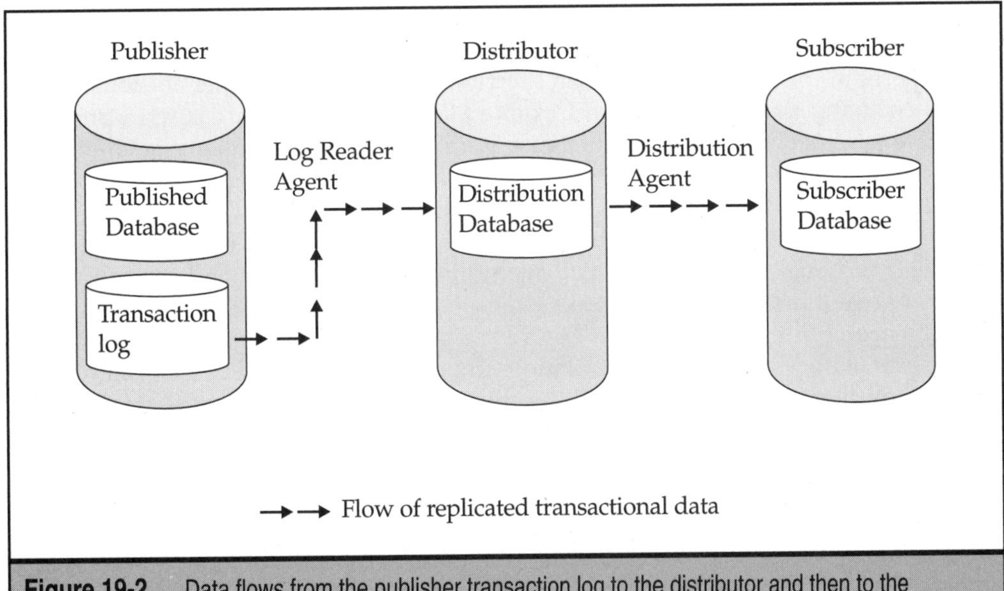

Figure 19-2. Data flows from the publisher transaction log to the distributor and then to the subscriber in transaction replication.

Merge Replication

Merge replication is the third type of standard replication. Merge replication was first introduced in SQL Server 7.0. It was intended to combine the benefits of replication with the capability to update the data from anywhere. As the name implies, you can make changes to the data at both the publisher and the subscriber. When the two connect, they exchange information about the data that was changed and merge the results. If the changed data records from the publisher and the subscriber have no overlap, the result is that the changes are merged and both servers are resynchronized. However, if the changed data records from the publisher overlap with records from the subscriber, there is trouble. This is a conflict situation, and the conflict has to be resolved. You can configure rules for conflict resolution so the conflicts are handled automatically, perhaps giving one site priority over another so the first site's changes are always accepted in a conflict situation.

Merge replication works best when conflicts can be kept to a minimum and if the rules for conflict resolution are simple and straightforward. For example, if you have a centralized home office and many small branch offices, you might set up a replication scheme to send data to them, and then allow them to make changes to the data and have the changes returned to the home office. To reduce the possibility of multiple changes to the same data record, each office subscribes only to the data set that affects its operations directly. That means that only one subscriber branch office and home office can see and modify a single data set.

To resolve conflicts, you may elect to impose some simple rules, such as "home office is always right," or "it's the salesperson's territory, and they know their customers best, so let their changes take precedence." If you're a C programmer, you can write programs to resolve complex conflicts. The worst case is a situation in which many different users can make changes to the same data. Conflict resolution becomes much more complex in this case, and if any of the subscribers tend to be disconnected from the main network for periods of time, some of them might be working with data that is not correct. It's even possible that changes to the data can be overwritten and lost if the conflict resolution algorithms are not carefully constructed.

You need to think very carefully before you implement merge replication. While it might seem like a way around the limitations imposed by the snapshot and transactional replication schemes, you may be adding more complexity to your replication model than you can handle, and you may be risking data integrity in the process. In most companies, a data set is "owned" by an organizational unit. The concept of "a single point of data entry" can do much to protect data integrity and provide data consistency. Does the home office really need to overwrite changes to data originating at a branch office? Is this a control issue? We're not talking about the database administrator fixing the occasional bit of corrupted data; we're talking about a home office that continually second-guesses and superimposes its will on its own branch offices. Don't set up merge replication to try to compensate for a politically flawed organization—it won't work. Instead, consider a scheme in which each branch publishes its data to the home office at a certain time of the day, using snapshot replication or transactional replication. Then have a stored procedure you can execute immediately following the synchronization that will fix any errant or problem records from the branch office, and that will notify someone at the branch office about which records have been corrected and how.

Remember that conflict resolution often means nothing more than deciding whose changes get discarded. If one group of users' changes are frequently overwritten, it is going to be hard to convince them that the database is reliable and accurate.

SQL Server Books Online recommends merge replications for applications in which you expect conflicts to occur. We recommend getting to the bottom of why the conflicts are occurring. If the data conflicts are a result of political tension or discord, it is not the job of the database administrator to resolve the conflicts. That's what management is for. If conflicts are occurring consistently, you're looking at an organizational problem. There's something wrong with the way the workflow is being implemented. You cannot fix processes that are fundamentally flawed by computerizing them. It's much harder to fix the underlying problem once it's been institutionalized in the database. This is why we are enthusiastic about snapshot and transactional replication but reluctant to recommend that anyone use merge replication.

Despite our advice, if you must implement merge replication, you should know a few things about how it works. In merge replication, the changes are not stored on the distribution database, as illustrated in Figure 19-3. The distributor actually plays less of a role in this type of replication than in transaction replication. When you configure merge replication, SQL Server adds several new tables to your database. If the configuration process finds a column with the ROWGUIDCOL property (the global unique identifier), it will use that column for its designated row identifier. Otherwise, it will add a GUID column and an associated index to ensure that it has a globally unique identifier for each row. This can add substantial size to the publishing database. It also adds triggers to the replicated tables, so that whenever a record is modified, the trigger adds information about the change to the merge system tables. Now that SQL Server supports multiple triggers on a table, these merge triggers can coexist with other triggers you might have already defined on the table.

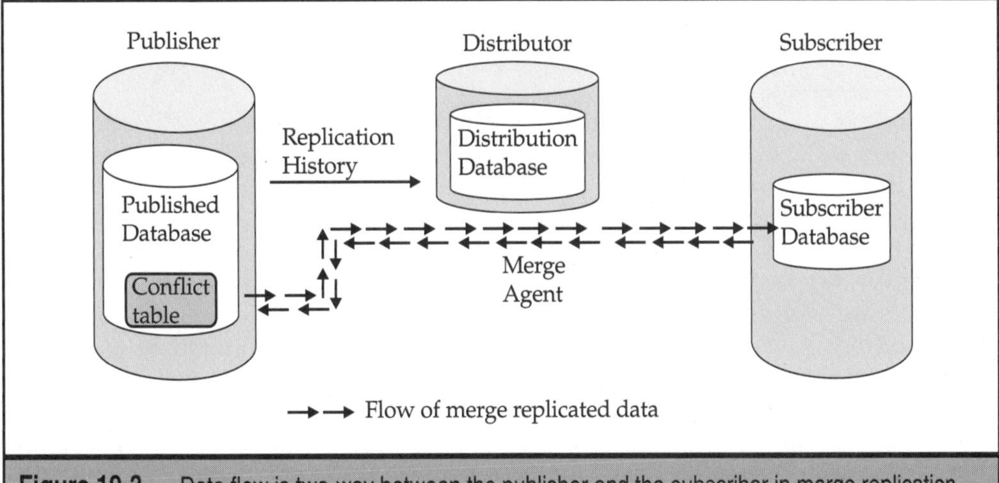

Figure 19-3. Data flow is two-way between the publisher and the subscriber in merge replication.

Merge replication adds more overhead to production operations than do either of the replication techniques we've discussed so far. The increased size of the publisher database, the additional trigger firings on data modifications, the additional writes to the replication system tables, and the occasional conflict resolution (or lack thereof) with the potential for loss of data integrity because of ill-designed conflict resolution rules, add up to more risk than you should be willing to take with your databases.

Replication with Immediate Updating Subscribers

This option is a hybrid technique that combines distributed transactions and either snapshot or transactional replication (usually the latter). You can update data on the subscriber. Those updates are then distributed to the publisher, using two-phase commit technology. The updated publisher then replicates the change to all other subscribers. We'll look at an example of replication with immediate updating subscribers in just a moment, after we introduce the physical topologies for replication.

Replication Topology

When you design a replication scenario, you must understand how the data needs to flow and what each of the various servers' primary roles should be. There are several different physical topologies (architectures) for replication, and any of them can be implemented using transactional, snapshot, or merge replication. These topologies vary from the simple (central publisher/subscriber) to the complex (multiple publisher/subscriber). Your replication environment will most likely be a variation of one of these models, based on your specific needs.

Central Publisher

The central publisher model works well in situations in which data is published at one location and then must be distributed to multiple subscribers. Subscribers treat the data as read-only. Figure 19-4 is an illustration of the central publisher model. The publisher in the middle of the figure is pushing data out to each of the subscribers in the array around the publisher server.

A good example of a central publisher would be a local business that sells many different products, each of which has a service manual, parts list, and price list. This information needs to be kept up to date at the company's retail outlets, repair depots, and customer service centers. The publisher and distributor would be physically located at the same site, probably at the company's home office. They might share a server or they each might reside on their own dedicated servers, linked by a very fast, wide-bandwidth connection. You could use either push or pull subscriptions, depending on the relative power of the distributor server and the subscriber servers. You could mix the subscriptions, pushing to the less powerful, older model subscriber computers on the network, and allow the newer, more powerful subscriber servers to pull their subscriptions. If the data being published is relatively static, you could use snapshot replication to update the subscribers over the weekends. On the other hand, if the data is dynamic, you'd want to use transactional replication. If your subscriber offices don't need minute-by-minute changes sent to them, and if

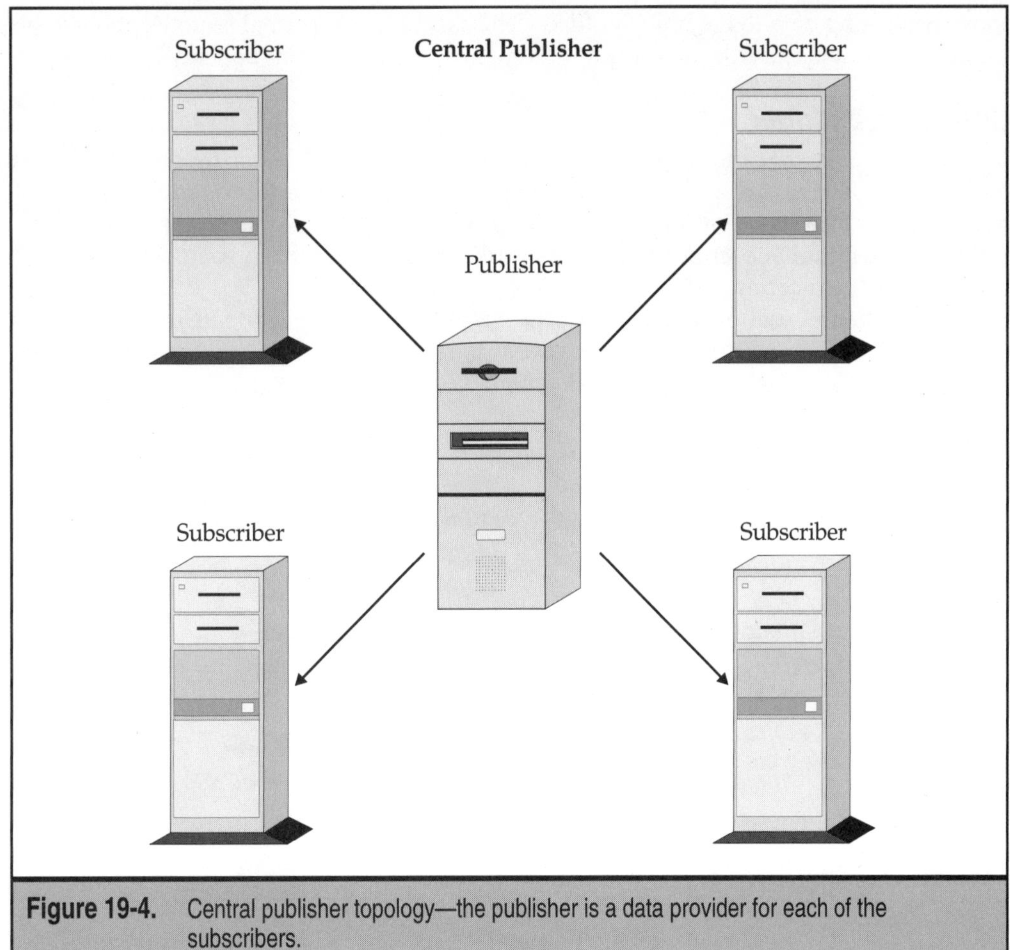

Figure 19-4. Central publisher topology—the publisher is a data provider for each of the subscribers.

transactional replication is putting too much of a load on the subscriber servers during business hours, you could schedule replication to happen when the subscriber offices are closed.

This model can be extended to incorporate multiple publishers, all of which can be handled by one distributor, as illustrated in Figure 19-5. In this model, the engineering department could publish the parts lists and service manuals from its departmental server. The accounting department could publish price lists from a different server. Both engineering and accounting publications are serviced by a single corporate distributor. The model is essentially the same, with one minor exception. Now you have two publications, so each subscriber has to subscribe to both. Timing the delivery of two publications is an inexact science. Replication cannot keep data from separate databases synchronized. You could occasionally have a price for a nonexistent part or a part without a price. This issue has to be resolved at the home office—in other words, the engineering database needs to be synchronized with the accounting department database before it starts replicating data to the branch offices. This is an organizational issue. A publication cannot span databases nor can replication repair broken company policies.

Central Subscriber

The central subscriber model is the inverse of the central publisher model. It contains multiple publishers, each of which has its own distributor. Figure 19-6 is an illustration of this model, which has multiple publishers all rolling up their data to the central subscriber. The central subscriber subscribes to the publications from each publisher and consolidates the incoming data.

A good example of how this could be used is retail stores reporting in to a central supply warehouse. This could be incorporated as part of the hot-to-inventory scheme from the point-of-sale stations at each retail outlet. You want to identify the origin of each

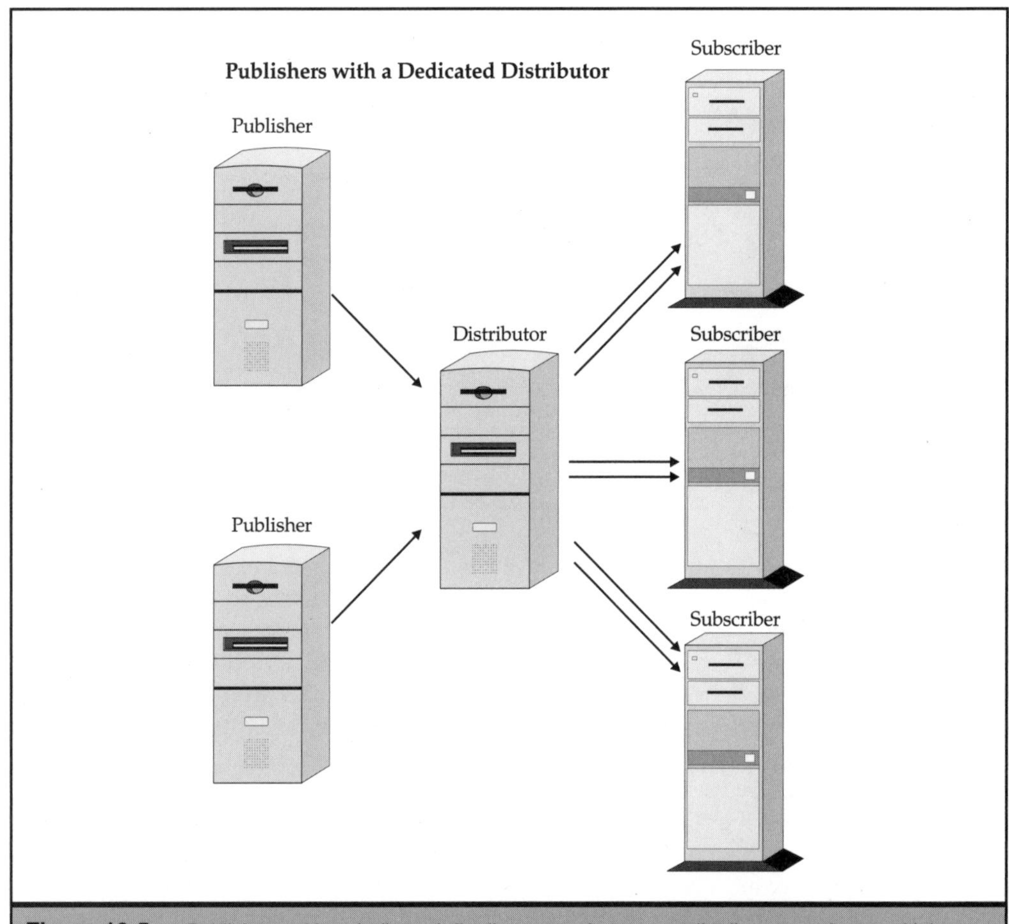

Figure 19-5. Publishers with a dedicated distributor topology—one distributor services multiple publishers and is the data provider for many subscribers.

transaction, so that as item sales are rung up and the decremented amounts are replicated from the retail stores to the central warehouse, you can identify which retail outlet needs reorders on which products. Not only do you get speedy information about reorders, but now you can combine reorders for like products from separate stores so you can maximize the quantity discounts your vendors offer. It is possible that your SQL Server installation could in time pay for itself if you exploit just this one feature.

Obviously, transactional replication is your best choice for this scenario. You wouldn't want to use distributed transactions here because you don't want to limit the ability of the stores to perform an update simply because the network connection to the central warehouse is down. If this happens and you have transactional replication in place, when the network comes back up, the replication publisher will simply update the central warehouse with all the changes since the last time replication occurred.

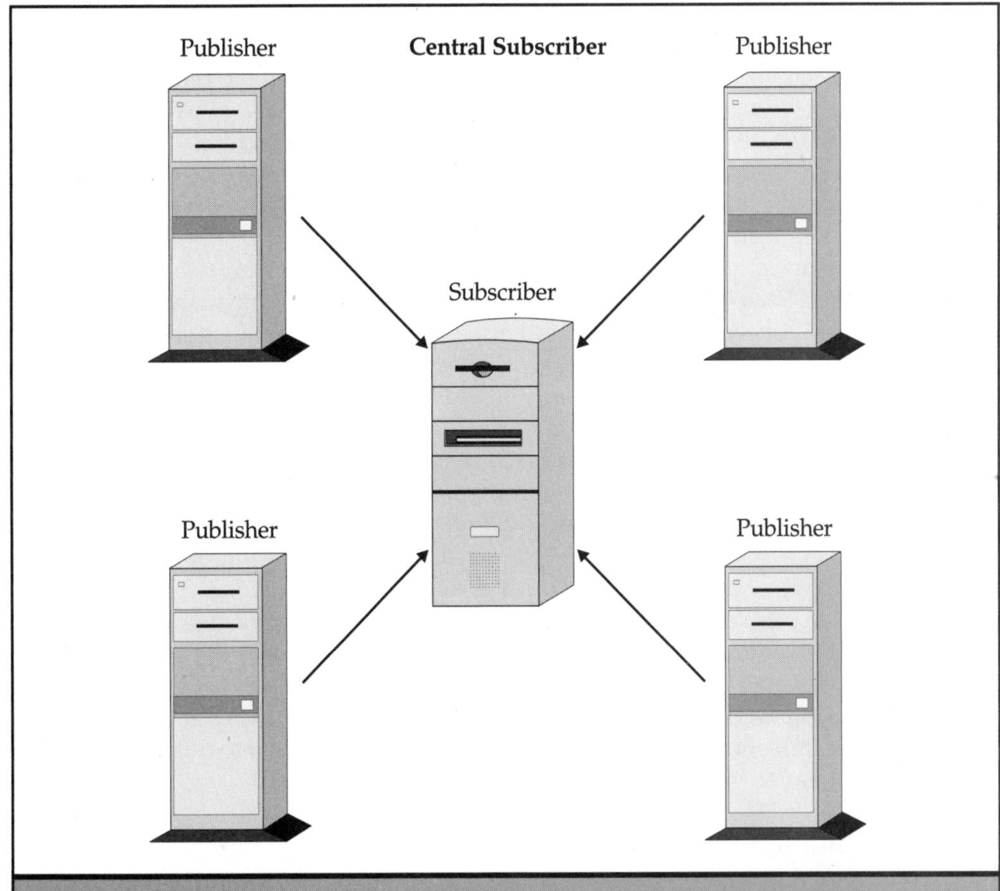

Figure 19-6. Central subscriber topology—data is rolled up from each of the publishers to be coalesced at a central subscriber.

If you decide to implement this kind of replication, you need to make some adjustments to the design of your database at the central warehouse. The official Microsoft documentation on the central subscriber model is overly simplistic. It shows an ideal solution—three or four publishers all sending their data to the same table on a central subscriber. However, life is rarely ideal, and the central subscriber model doesn't work that way. Transactional replication has to have the data synchronized on both publisher and subscriber, as a starting point. Synchronization is usually done as a one-time snapshot replication task when replication is first initiated. Envision this scenario: Publisher A sends its snapshot to the central subscriber, which loads publisher A data into the target table. Publisher A is now ready to start transactional replication. Publisher B sends its snapshot to the central subscriber. Snapshot replication, by definition, simply truncates and reloads the target table, without regard to what is already there. When publisher B synchronizes, it wipes out the data that publisher A had just loaded. So when publisher A tries to do transactional replication, it gets an error message because it cannot find its data on the target table of the central subscriber.

There are workarounds for this problem, such as using a DTS package that combines the data from each publisher and copies it into the target table on the central subscriber. Any solution other than a snapshot synchronization means you are now doing a manual synchronization. That's a lot of work and requires too much intervention by the database administrator. Occasionally, replication will fail, for any number of reasons. You can set parameters that will enable automatic recovery, but once in a while you have to manually intervene. When this happens, you must resynchronize.

A more elegant solution to this scenario is to set up the subscriber so that it has one table per publisher. Each publisher can then synchronize and replicate to its own target table without any concerns over what is happening with the other publishers. If one publisher gets out of sync, you can quickly resynchronize with it, and not disrupt all the other publishers. This totally circumvents the problem discussed in the preceding paragraphs by isolating each publisher from its counterparts.

But, you say, my users need to be able to query the central warehouse inventory and get a list of products that need to be reordered. They're not programmers, they don't want to be writing complex join queries, and if they query each table one at a time, what if they forget to query one? Does that mean one retail outlet will be without inventory the next day? That's why Microsoft introduced indexed views into SQL Server 2000, to alleviate these kinds of problem situations. Build an indexed view. With a view, you can make all the separate inventory tables appear as one table to the people at the warehouse who are in charge of managing inventory. You can even create a trigger on the indexed view that would tell you the total quantity of an item across all stores has fallen below the reorder point. Alternatively, you can create a stored procedure and set it to run as a timed task once or twice a day to generate your "shopping list."

Publisher/Subscriber and Subscriber/Publisher

In practice, your replication scenario may be some combination of the central publisher and central subscriber models, as illustrated in Figure 19-7. The home office usually wants to keep track of what is happening at branch offices with the central subscriber model, so data from the branch offices is rolling up to the home office. But the home office also has control over corporate policies and may want to send out data using the central publisher model, thereby rolling data out to the branch offices. This data from the home office may be summary data derived from the data collected from the branches, or it may be data originating at the home office, such as a list of approved vendors.

In other cases, the home office may want to collect data from each of its branch offices, and then turn it around and replicate the same data to the other branches. For example, when you go into a store looking for the latest hot item, like a Furby or a Tickle Me Elmo (readers with young children will understand), and they are out of stock, the sales staff can often check the inventory at neighboring stores for you because they have the other stores' inventory counts stored on their local computers.

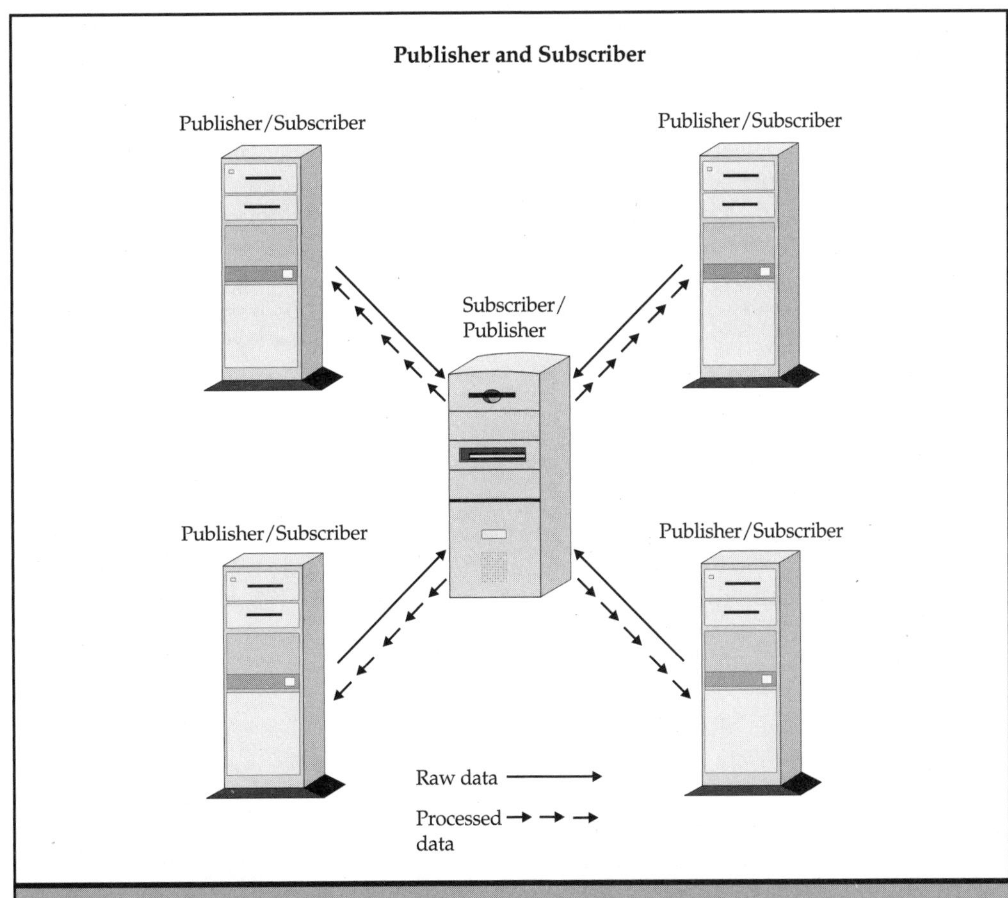

Figure 19-7. Publisher/subscriber and subscriber/publisher topology—each server is both a publisher and a subscriber, and data flow is two-way.

Before you jump into implementing this latter kind of replication scenario, you need to ask some tough questions. Realistically, how often does one retail outlet need to know what is in stock at another retail outlet? If checking another retail outlet's inventory happens only once or twice a day, does that justify replicating data between ten retail outlets and the home office? The storage requirements for all the databases will jump dramatically. If you determine that you must have all the inventory from all the retail outlets stored locally at each retail outlet, give serious thought to how it will be stored. If it's all in one big table, a clerk at any given retail outlet would have to read a huge number of database pages to list the data for their store. You can circumvent this somewhat by creating a clustered index on the data that starts with the value of the store identifiers, but you're still looking at range of value processing on a huge table. If you have to implement this scenario, use a separate table per retail outlet inventory.

Another benefit to the multi-table solution is security administration. Security is much easier to set up, administer, and enforce if it is by table rather than by content. You can allow updates on the local retail outlet's inventory table but permit only reads on the replicated tables from other retail outlets. If all the data is in one table, security enforcement becomes tremendously complex. While you can control permissions on specific columns in a table, there is no equivalent security setting for rows. You'd have to write a trigger that checked every modification to the inventory table, permitting updates to the data for the local branch inventory while rolling back update attempts to the replicated data. This trigger would have to run for every update, adding yet more overhead to an already overloaded database.

All in all, we would recommend that you not replicate the data collected at the home office back out to all the branch retail outlets. If retail outlet A needs to know if an item is in stock at any other retail outlet, have the clerk from retail outlet A run a remote stored procedure that accesses the inventory table at the home office warehouse server. If that search returns what the clerk was looking for, have him run another remote procedure on the server at the retail outlet where the item is in stock (retail outlet B). This second procedure will verify that the item is indeed still in stock—that it hasn't just been sold and the result not yet reported to the central warehouse. If the customer so chooses, the clerk at retail outlet A can also place the item on reserve, and most importantly, notify someone at retail outlet B to take the item off the shelf. If this scheme sounds too complex, revert to the old-fashioned method: call retail outlet B on the telephone, speak to a real person, wait while they take Elmo off the shelf and hide him behind the counter, and then give the customer directions to retail outlet B.

Multiple Publisher–Multiple Subscriber

The concept of multiple publisher–multiple subscriber replication has been superceded in many cases by merge replication. But multiple publisher–multiple subscriber replication can be employed effectively if it is set up correctly. The idea, as illustrated in Figure 19-8, is that there is no central authority. Each server is responsible for maintaining and publishing its own data. Each server wears two hats: it is a publisher and a distributor of its own data, and it is a subscriber of data from other servers. Each server is allowed to modify only its own local data and must treat the subscribed data as if it is read-only. If that rule is followed, there should be no conflicts and, therefore, no need to have conflict resolution and mediation.

As an example, suppose you have three retail outlets. Each retail outlet wants to share its inventory information with the other two. You've decided against distributed transactions because of the cost of the two-phase commit and the potential for putting the whole operation at risk in the event of a network outage. Replication sounds like a good way to go. You have rules in place that each retail outlet can update only its own data, and updates should be propagated within a few minutes. You've determined that transactional replication is your best option, organized into a multiple publisher–multiple subscriber topology. Each retail outlet publishes its own inventory data and subscribes to the publications from the other two retail outlets.

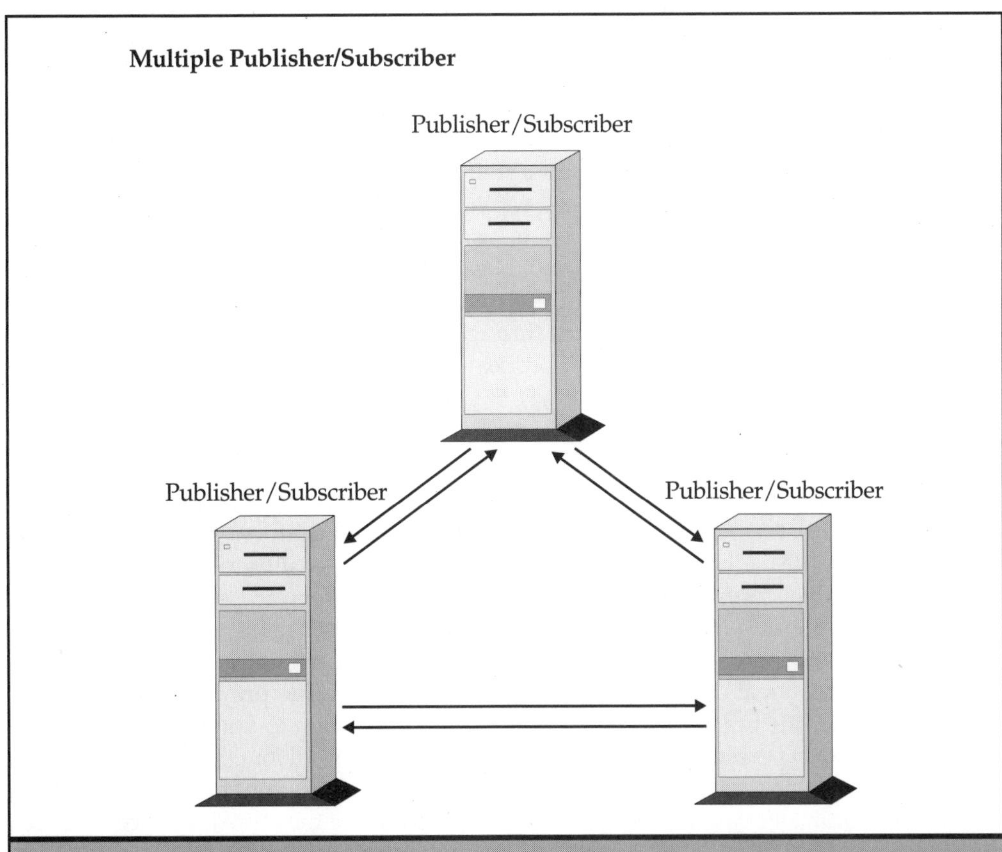

Figure 19-8. Multiple publisher–multiple subscriber topology—each server publishes to every other server, and every server is a subscriber.

The big design decision is whether to keep all the inventory data from all retail outlets in one big table or to separate the inventories into three tables, one for each retail outlet. If you want all the data in one table, there is the question of how to set it up initially. We've been over the problem of more than one publisher synchronizing into a single subscriber, which you'd have to address if you decided on a single large table. You decide to separate the tables, one for each retail outlet's inventory, and then create an indexed view, using a UNION operator to virtually combine all inventory into a single virtual table. What is the only downside to this decision? When you add a fourth retail outlet, you'll have to modify the indexed view to include the inventory from the fourth store.

One additional modification you might think about is something that will minimize the amount of data you have to include in your nightly backups. If you create the tables to hold the replicated data in the same filegroup as your local data, your scheduled backups will be backing up the replicated data as well, and this is totally unnecessary. If you instead create the tables for the replicated data in a different filegroup and use a filegroup backup strategy, back up only your own local data, and you'll save time and storage space. You could even consider keeping the replicated data in a separate database on each server. The UNION operation can work across databases to combine the replicated inventory to the local inventory whenever needed.

You realize now that security will be simpler to manage and maintain with separate tables, just as in the central subscriber model. If all the data were in a single table, you'd need a trigger to check for users updating replicated data. With separate tables, you give read-only permission on the replicated data—so much simpler! The replication setup itself is simpler with multiple tables than with a simple table. You just build a publication out of the entire inventory table and publish that. The Log Reader Agent even has an easier time because it doesn't have to work through the extra rules you'd have to set up to figure out which transactions should be replicated. All transactions affecting the local inventory table are replicated.

Publisher with Republisher

When you have a complex replication scenario, you can often simplify it, and perhaps reduce your network traffic, by having a server act as a store-and-forward system, as illustrated in Figure 19-9. This store-and-forward server will be a subscriber to the primary publisher. You then configure replication on the store-and-forward subscriber so that it publishes the replicated data again, to a different set of subscribers.

For example, suppose your organization has its main office in Langley, Virginia, and you have many international offices, including several in Europe. The principal publisher and distributor servers are in Langley. You need to set up replication to London, Paris, Dublin, and Munich. Ninety percent of the replicated data is common to all four subscribers, so if you set up a central publisher topology you'd be moving nearly four times as much data across the transatlantic link as you needed to. Fortunately, because of the time differences between Europe and North America, all the replication activity happens at night.

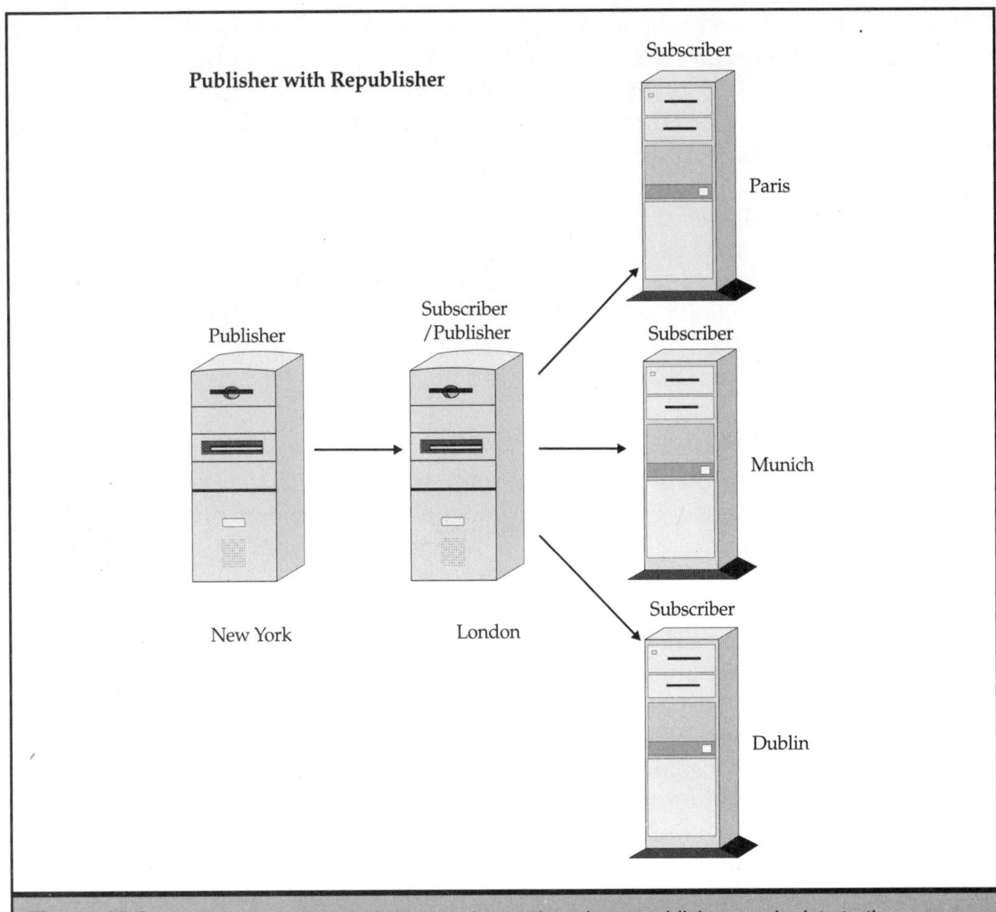

Figure 19-9. Publisher with republisher topology—the primary publisher sends data to the republisher, which then distributes to the subscribers.

There is a way to optimize the network traffic and reduce the amount of data going across the transatlantic link. Langley publishes 100 percent of the data that needs to be transmitted to Europe to London. That makes London a subscriber to Langley. You then configure the SQL Server in London to republish portions of the data, as needed, to Paris, Dublin, and Munich. These servers then become subscribers to the London publisher. All the data is transferred once across the transatlantic link, instead of four times. The distributor in Langley is handling only one subscription to Europe, freeing it to replicate to South America and Asia, where you also have set up store-and-forward servers in Lima and Singapore.

In this scenario, you can take advantage of the time differences between the primary publisher in Langley and the store-and-forward subscribers in the rest of the world to schedule replication at convenient times. If the published data takes two hours to transfer, you can start the replication to London at 7:00 P.M. eastern standard time, which is 12:00 midnight in London. The task should be completed by 2:00 A.M. in London. At 2:30 A.M., republishing starts to Paris (3:30 A.M.), Dublin (2:30 A.M.), and Munich (3:30 A.M.). By 5:30 A.M., Munich has all the previous day's data from Langley, ready for when they get to work at 9:00 A.M.

Don't confuse this scenario with the "remote distributor" mentioned earlier in this chapter. Microsoft documents even make this mistake. London is not acting as a distributor for Langley. London is a subscriber to Langley. Both Langley and London have their own distributor, which is either the publisher or another server sitting next to it. If you need a term for the London server, other than store-and-forward publisher, we refer to it as a "redistribution server" and Microsoft uses the term "republisher."

Central Publisher with Immediate Updating Subscribers

We mentioned the immediate updating subscriber earlier in this chapter. We said that this technique combines two-phase commit and replication. It would normally be used in a central publisher topology. The scenario is the one of the central inventory warehouse that is publishing the inventory data to all the retail outlets.

Each retail outlet starts by receiving a snapshot of its own local data. The data is then replicated, using the immediate updating subscriber option, to the central inventory warehouse, which also replicates the data to the other retail outlets. Whenever a change is made at retail outlet A, the change is also made as a distributed transaction from the central inventory warehouse. Within a few minutes, transactional replication propagates the changes to retail outlets B, C, and D. So each retail outlet has its own data, plus subscriptions to the data from all the other retail outlets.

This approach means you don't have to set up a publishing server at each retail outlet. The only publisher is at the warehouse. Everyone else is a subscriber. Your replication scenario is simpler, but at the expense of having introduced the complexity of distributed transactions. If the network between the retail outlet and the warehouse is down, the retail outlet may be unable to record a sale into its server. Replication with immediate updating subscribers may be feasible on a corporate or academic campus where the network is part of your own infrastructure, but you want to think twice before implementing it for a retail operation in which you have to rely on a third party to provide the network component.

Security Issues in Replication

The database administrator needs to be aware of some security issues, including the accounts under which the various SQL Server agents run and the permissions they require. For example, in a push subscription, the distribution agent has to be able to write files to the subscriber for the synchronization to work. That's an operating system–level write permission. Conversely, in a pull subscription, the distribution agent must have read permission on the directory on the distributor's disk where the synchronization files are stored.

But beyond the permissions needed for replication to work is a larger issue of data security. The more places the data is stored, the more chance of a break-in going undetected or of data being made available to someone who should not have access to it. Security at the home office may be strong, but what about security procedures at the smaller branch offices? There may be less emphasis on both physical and network security in a smaller office. Some recent high-profile security breaches have centered around credit card data someone has downloaded to a desktop computer during stress testing, and then the desktop computer has either been hacked into electronically or just physically disappeared from the building. Corporate laptops are stolen at airports every day, and no one has any idea of how much proprietary, sensitive, or even secret information is breached.

Preparing for Replication

Even if you are not implementing replication any time soon, you might consider adding a column to any table that might be replicated. This column is used to identify the origin of the data. Imagine looking at a view built on inventory data from four retail outlets. You have four rows for product number 1838, and four quantities—but which one comes from which retail outlet? If you add a retail outlet number or code column to the inventory table, it may appear redundant. At each retail outlet, this column will contain all the same values. But once you start coalescing the data at the central inventory warehouse, its use will be obvious and invaluable. For the same reason, if you plan to add merge replication, you need to add a column with the ROWGUIDCOL property. It's always better to plan ahead than to try to fix things later.

Guidelines for Distributing Data

There are so many replication and distribution options and features in SQL Server 2000 that it's hard to keep track of them. There's almost always more than one way to address any situation. In Table 19-1, you'll find suggestions as to when each of the techniques for handling distributed data might be appropriate. Ultimately, there's no '"right" way to do something; there's only better or worse. Every solution has some trade-off. The decision about which technique you choose depends on many factors, including ease of programming, ease of maintenance, time constraints, and political factors. One thing is sure: when you start dealing with distributed data, you will find yourself applying everything you know about SQL Server and hitting the books to find out even more.

As we said at the beginning of this chapter, we can only introduce you to the complex topic of replication. Replication really deserves a book of its own. But for now, we need to recover from writing this one. Hope you got something out of it.

	Backup and Restore	Log Shipping	Partitioned Database	DTS	Remote Queries	Distributed Transactions	Snapshot Replication	Transactional Replication	Merge Replication	Snapshot Replication Updating Subscribers	Transactional Replication Updating Subscribers
Copy for archive	X	X		X							
Copy for analysts	X	X		X			X	X			
Copy to data warehouse	X	X		X				X			
Remote locations							X	X			
Split storage load across servers			X								
Split processing load across servers			X			X					
Data is partitioned			X								
Data is same at all locations	X	X					X	X		X	X
Data must be always synchronized			X			X				X	X

Table 19-1. Suggestions About When Each of the Techniques for Handling Distributed Data Might Be Appropriate

	Backup and Restore	Log Shipping	Partitioned Database	DTS	Remote Queries	Distributed Transactions	Snapshot Replication	Transactional Replication	Merge Replication	Snapshot Replication Updating Subscribers	Transactional Replication Updating Subscribers
Network is reliable			X		X	X				X	X
Network is not reliable							X	X			
Subscribers connected all the time	X	X	X		X	X	X	X		X	X
Subscribers connected some of the time	X			X				X	X		
Subscribers connected infrequently								X	X		
Subscribers need to make changes									X	X	X
Subscribers cannot make changes	X	X					X	X			

Table 19-1. Suggestions About When Each of the Techniques for Handling Distributed Data Might Be Appropriate *(continued)*

	Backup and Restore	Log Shipping	Partitioned Database	DTS	Remote Queries	Distributed Transactions	Snapshot Replication	Transactional Replication	Merge Replication	Snapshot Replication Updating Subscribers	Transactional Replication Updating Subscribers
Data is transformed between servers				X	X	X	X	X	X	X	X
Data integrity must be maintained	X	X	X	X	X	X	X	X		X	X

Table 19-1. Suggestions About When Each of the Techniques for Handling Distributed Data Might Be Appropriate *(continued)*

PART V

Data Models and Recommended Readings

APPENDIX A

A Recipe for Strawberry Smoooches

By Beverly Diederich
Owner and president of the Strawberry Smoooches Company

8 oz. water

5 Tbsp. sugar

7 whole strawberries (fresh or frozen)

1-1/3 cups ice cubes

2 whole fresh strawberries, cleaned but with green bits left in place, for garnish

Add the first four ingredients to a blender in the order listed above. Blend at high speed. Pour into two tall glasses (you can chill or frost the glasses first, if you like). With a sharp knife cut half-way through the whole garnish strawberries. Position one on the rim of each glass. Serve with a straw, napkin, and long-handled spoon. Makes two 8-oz. servings.

APPENDIX B

The Strawberry Smoooches Company Conceptual Data Model

Here is the conceptual data model for the Strawberry Smooooches Company as created with Microsoft Visio 2000. A conceptual model represents the concepts, foundations, and business rules of a company. This model contains entities that cover person management, events management, inventory management, and manufacturing.

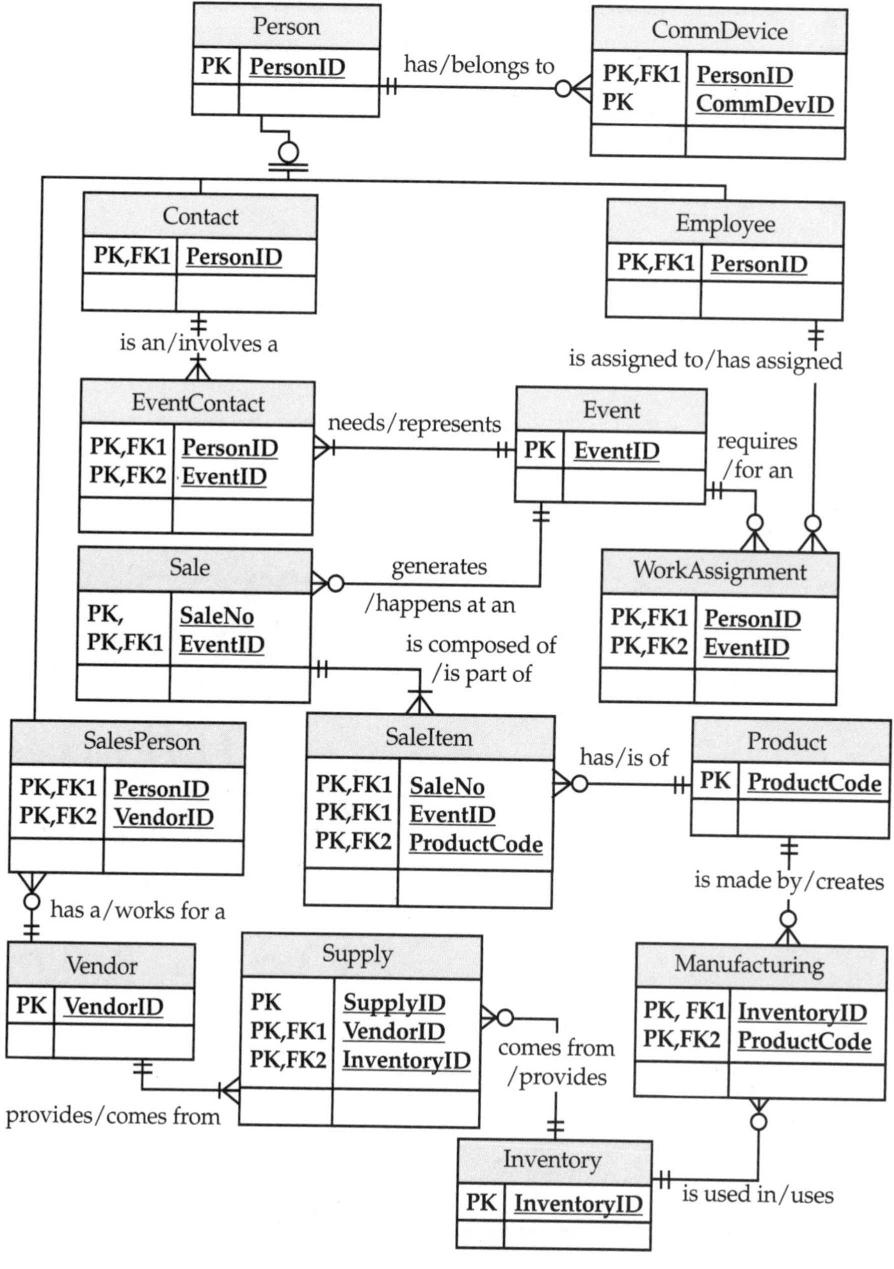

APPENDIX C

The Strawberry Smoooches Company Logical Data Model

The logical data model of the Strawberry Smooooches Company is a detailed representation of the reality of the business requirements, and like the entity model, it is vendor-neutral. The entities and relationships are more completely defined in this logical model than in the conceptual model. The attribute list for each entity is expanded, and each attribute is more completely defined, with datatypes and lengths, potential for nullability, and suitability for indexing. Rules are defined for each of the relationships that govern the behavior of data when changes to data values occur.

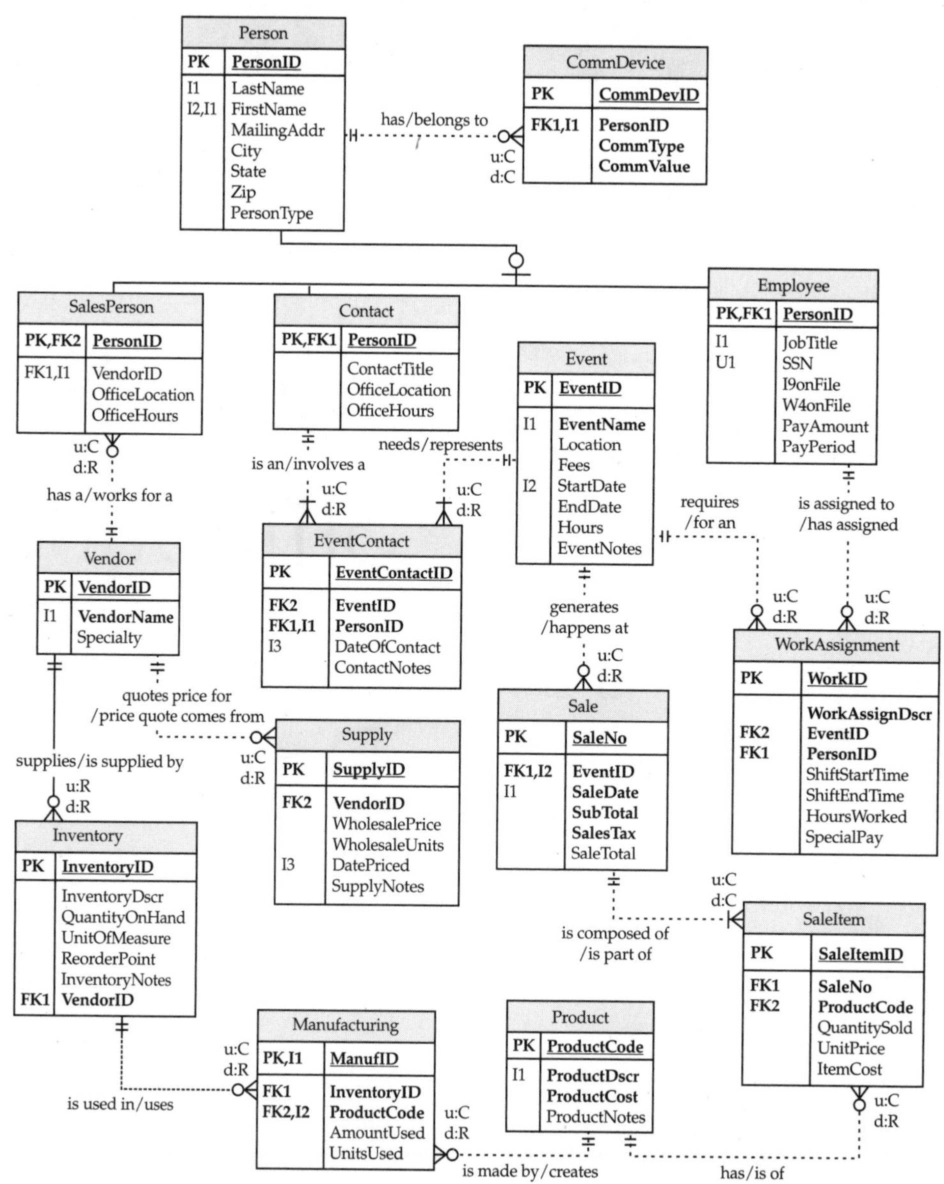

APPENDIX D

The Strawberry Smoooches Company Physical Data Model

This physical model of the Strawberry Smooooches Company is the representation of the real business. It's also a specification for implementing the Strawberry database, and it is associated with a specific vendor's database product (SQL Server 2000). The physical data model should take advantage of the strengths and compensate for the weaknesses of a specific vendor product.

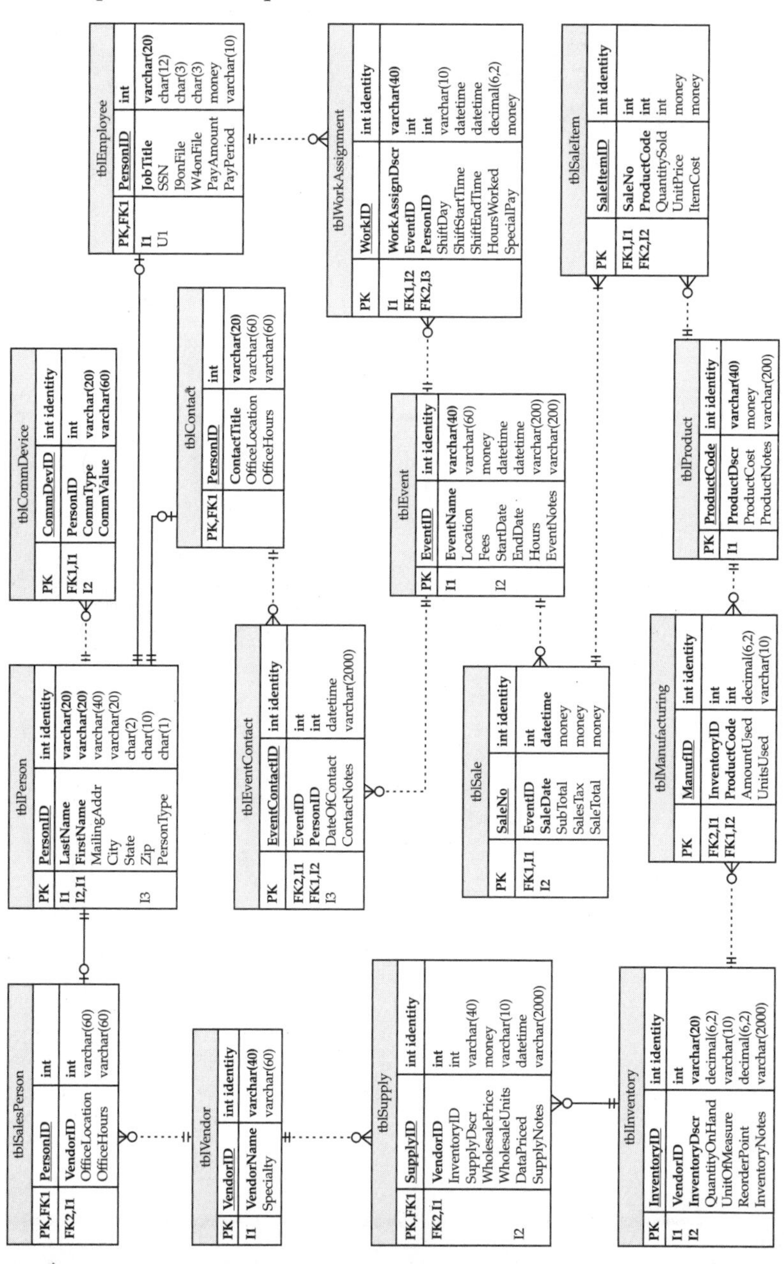

APPENDIX E

The Strawberry Smoooches Company Database: DDL and Data

Following is a SQL script to create the Strawberry database. It was generated directly from SQL Server 2000. You can find an electronic copy of this code on the Osborne Web site located at **www.Osborne.com**.

DATA DEFINITION LANGUAGE

Create the Strawberry Database

```
/****** Object: Database Strawberry Script Date: 11/9/00 ******/

IF EXISTS (SELECT name FROM master.dbo.sysdatabases
WHERE name = N'Strawberry')
 DROP DATABASE [Strawberry]
GO

CREATE DATABASE [Strawberry]  ON (NAME = N'Strawberry_Data',
FILENAME = N'd:\sql2000data\Strawberry.mdf' , SIZE = 50,
  MAXSIZE = 200, FILEGROWTH = 10)
LOG ON (NAME = N'Strawberry_log',
  FILENAME = N'd:\sql2000data\Strawberry.ldf' ,
  SIZE = 10, MAXSIZE = 20, FILEGROWTH = 5)
 COLLATE SQL_Latin1_General_CP1_CI_AS
GO

exec sp_dboption N'Strawberry', N'autoclose', N'false'
GO

exec sp_dboption N'Strawberry', N'bulkcopy', N'false'
GO

exec sp_dboption N'Strawberry', N'trunc. log', N'false'
GO

exec sp_dboption N'Strawberry', N'torn page detection', N'true'
GO

exec sp_dboption N'Strawberry', N'read only', N'false'
GO

exec sp_dboption N'Strawberry', N'dbo use', N'false'
GO

exec sp_dboption N'Strawberry', N'single', N'false'
GO

exec sp_dboption N'Strawberry', N'autoshrink', N'false'
```

```
GO

exec sp_dboption N'Strawberry', N'ANSI null default', N'false'
GO

exec sp_dboption N'Strawberry', N'recursive triggers', N'false'
GO

exec sp_dboption N'Strawberry', N'ANSI nulls', N'false'
GO

exec sp_dboption N'Strawberry', N'concat null yields null', N'false'
GO

exec sp_dboption N'Strawberry', N'cursor close on commit', N'false'
GO

exec sp_dboption N'Strawberry', N'default to local cursor', N'false'
GO

exec sp_dboption N'Strawberry', N'quoted identifier', N'false'
GO

exec sp_dboption N'Strawberry', N'ANSI warnings', N'false'
GO

exec sp_dboption N'Strawberry', N'auto create statistics', N'true'
GO

exec sp_dboption N'Strawberry', N'auto update statistics', N'true'
GO
```

Create the Tables

```
/****** Object:  Table [dbo].[tblEvent]    Script Date: 11/9/00 ******/
CREATE TABLE [dbo].[tblEvent] (
 [EventID] [int] IDENTITY (1, 1) NOT NULL ,
 [EventName] [varchar] (40)  NOT NULL ,
 [Location] [varchar] (60)  NULL ,
 [Fees] [money] NULL ,
 [StartDate] [datetime] NULL ,
 [EndDate] [datetime] NULL ,
 [Hours] [varchar] (200)  NULL ,
 [EventNotes] [varchar] (200)  NULL
) ON [PRIMARY]
GO

/****** Object:  Table [dbo].[tblInventory]    Script Date: 11/9/00 ******/
CREATE TABLE [dbo].[tblInventory] (
```

```
 [InventoryID] [int] IDENTITY (1, 1) NOT NULL ,
 [VendorID] [int] NULL ,
 [InventoryDscr] [varchar] (40)  NOT NULL ,
 [QuantityOnHand] [numeric](6, 2) NULL ,
 [UnitOfMeasure] [varchar] (10)  NULL ,
 [ReorderPoint] [numeric](6, 2) NULL ,
 [InventoryNotes] [varchar] (2000)  NULL
) ON [PRIMARY]
GO

/****** Object:  Table [dbo].[tblPerson]    Script Date: 11/9/00 ******/
CREATE TABLE [dbo].[tblPerson] (
 [PersonID] [int] IDENTITY (1, 1) NOT NULL ,
 [LastName] [varchar] (20)  NOT NULL ,
 [FirstName] [varchar] (20)  NOT NULL ,
 [MailingAddr] [varchar] (40)  NULL ,
 [City] [varchar] (20)  NULL ,
 [State] [char] (2)  NULL ,
 [Zip] [char] (10)  NULL ,
 [PersonType] [char] (1)  NULL
) ON [PRIMARY]
GO

/****** Object:  Table [dbo].[tblProduct]    Script Date: 11/9/00 ******/
CREATE TABLE [dbo].[tblProduct] (
 [ProductCode] [int] IDENTITY (1, 1) NOT NULL ,
 [ProductDscr] [varchar] (40)  NOT NULL ,
 [ProductCost] [money] NULL ,
 [ProductNotes] [varchar] (200)  NULL
) ON [PRIMARY]
GO

/****** Object:  Table [dbo].[tblVendor]    Script Date: 11/9/00  ******/
CREATE TABLE [dbo].[tblVendor] (
 [VendorID] [int] IDENTITY (1, 1) NOT NULL ,
 [VendorName] [varchar] (40)  NOT NULL ,
 [Specialty] [varchar] (60)  NULL
) ON [PRIMARY]
GO

/****** Object:  Table [dbo].[tblCommDevice]    Script Date: 11/9/00 ******/
CREATE TABLE [dbo].[tblCommDevice] (
 [CommDevID] [int] IDENTITY (1, 1) NOT NULL ,
 [PersonID] [int] NOT NULL ,
 [CommType] [varchar] (20)  NULL ,
 [CommValue] [varchar] (60)  NOT NULL
) ON [PRIMARY]
GO
```

```
/****** Object:  Table [dbo].[tblContact]    Script Date: 11/9/00 ******/
CREATE TABLE [dbo].[tblContact] (
 [PersonID] [int] NOT NULL ,
 [ContactTitle] [varchar] (20)  NOT NULL ,
 [OfficeLocation] [varchar] (60)  NULL ,
 [OfficeHours] [varchar] (60)  NULL
) ON [PRIMARY]
GO

/****** Object:  Table [dbo].[tblEmployee]    Script Date: 11/9/00 ******/
CREATE TABLE [dbo].[tblEmployee] (
 [PersonID] [int] NOT NULL ,
 [JobTitle] [varchar] (20)  NOT NULL ,
 [SSN] [char] (12)  NULL ,
 [I9onFile] [char] (3)  NULL ,
 [W4onFile] [char] (3)  NULL ,
 [PayAmount] [money] NULL ,
 [PayPeriod] [varchar] (10)  NULL
) ON [PRIMARY]
GO

/****** Object:  Table [dbo].[tblManufacturing]  Script Date: 11/9/00 ******/
CREATE TABLE [dbo].[tblManufacturing] (
 [ManufID] [int] IDENTITY (1, 1) NOT NULL ,
 [InventoryID] [int] NOT NULL ,
 [ProductCode] [int] NOT NULL ,
 [AmountUsed] [numeric](6, 2) NULL ,
 [UnitUsed] [varchar] (10)  NULL
) ON [PRIMARY]
GO

/****** Object:  Table [dbo].[tblSale]    Script Date: 11/9/00 ******/
CREATE TABLE [dbo].[tblSale] (
 [SaleNo] [int] IDENTITY (1, 1) NOT NULL ,
 [EventID] [int] NOT NULL ,
 [SaleDate] [datetime] NOT NULL ,
 [SubTotal] [money] NULL ,
 [SalesTax] [money] NULL ,
 [SaleTotal] [money] NULL
) ON [PRIMARY]
GO

/****** Object:  Table [dbo].[tblSalesPerson]    Script Date: 11/9/00 ******/
CREATE TABLE [dbo].[tblSalesPerson] (
 [PersonID] [int] NOT NULL ,
 [VendorID] [int] NOT NULL ,
 [OfficeLocation] [varchar] (60)  NULL ,
 [OfficeHours] [varchar] (60)  NULL
) ON [PRIMARY]
```

```
GO

/****** Object:  Table [dbo].[tblSupply]    Script Date: 11/9/00 ******/
CREATE TABLE [dbo].[tblSupply] (
 [SupplyID] [int] IDENTITY (1, 1) NOT NULL ,
 [VendorID] [int] NOT NULL ,
 [InventoryID] [int] NULL ,
 [SupplyDscr] [nvarchar] (40)  NULL ,
 [WholesalePrice] [money] NULL ,
 [WholesaleUnits] [varchar] (10)  NULL ,
 [DatePriced] [datetime] NULL ,
 [SupplyNotes] [varchar] (2000)  NULL
) ON [PRIMARY]
GO

/**** Object:  Table [dbo].[tblEventContact]    Script Date: 11/9/00 ****/
CREATE TABLE [dbo].[tblEventContact] (
 [EventContactID] [int] IDENTITY (1, 1) NOT NULL ,
 [EventID] [int] NOT NULL ,
 [PersonID] [int] NOT NULL ,
 [DateOfContact] [datetime] NULL ,
 [ContactNotes] [varchar] (2000)  NULL
) ON [PRIMARY]
GO

/****** Object:  Table [dbo].[tblSaleItem]    Script Date: 11/9/00 ******/
CREATE TABLE [dbo].[tblSaleItem] (
 [SaleItemID] [int] IDENTITY (1, 1) NOT NULL ,
 [SaleNo] [int] NOT NULL ,
 [ProductCode] [int] NOT NULL ,
 [QuantitySold] [int] NULL ,
 [UnitPrice] [money] NULL ,
 [ItemCost] [money] NULL
) ON [PRIMARY]
GO

/**** Object:  Table [dbo].[tblWorkAssignment]    Script Date: 11/9/00 ****/
CREATE TABLE [dbo].[tblWorkAssignment] (
 [WorkID] [int] IDENTITY (1, 1) NOT NULL ,
 [WorkAssignmentDscr] [varchar] (40)  NOT NULL ,
 [EventID] [int] NOT NULL ,
 [PersonID] [int] NOT NULL ,
 [ShiftDay] [varchar] (10)  NULL ,
 [ShiftStartTime] [datetime] NULL ,
 [ShiftEndTime] [datetime] NULL ,
 [HoursWorked] [numeric](6, 2) NULL ,
 [SpecialPay] [money] NULL
) ON [PRIMARY]
GO
```

Create Primary Key Constraints

```
ALTER TABLE [dbo].[tblEvent] WITH NOCHECK ADD
CONSTRAINT [tblEvent_PK] PRIMARY KEY  CLUSTERED
 (
  [EventID]
 )  ON [PRIMARY]
GO

ALTER TABLE [dbo].[tblInventory] WITH NOCHECK ADD
 CONSTRAINT [tblInventory_PK] PRIMARY KEY  CLUSTERED
 (
  [InventoryID]
 )  ON [PRIMARY]
GO

ALTER TABLE [dbo].[tblPerson] WITH NOCHECK ADD
 CONSTRAINT [tblPerson_PK] PRIMARY KEY  CLUSTERED
 (
  [PersonID]
 )  ON [PRIMARY]
GO

ALTER TABLE [dbo].[tblProduct] WITH NOCHECK ADD
 CONSTRAINT [tblProduct_PK] PRIMARY KEY  CLUSTERED
 (
  [ProductCode]
 )  ON [PRIMARY]
GO

ALTER TABLE [dbo].[tblVendor] WITH NOCHECK ADD
 CONSTRAINT [tblVendor_PK] PRIMARY KEY  CLUSTERED
 (
  [VendorID]
 )  ON [PRIMARY]
GO

ALTER TABLE [dbo].[tblCommDevice] WITH NOCHECK ADD
 CONSTRAINT [tblCommDevice_PK] PRIMARY KEY  CLUSTERED
 (
  [CommDevID]
 )  ON [PRIMARY]
GO

ALTER TABLE [dbo].[tblContact] WITH NOCHECK ADD
 CONSTRAINT [tblContact_PK] PRIMARY KEY  CLUSTERED
 (
  [PersonID]
 )  ON [PRIMARY]
```

```
GO

ALTER TABLE [dbo].[tblEmployee] WITH NOCHECK ADD
 CONSTRAINT [tblEmployee_PK] PRIMARY KEY  CLUSTERED
 (
  [PersonID]
 )  ON [PRIMARY]
GO

ALTER TABLE [dbo].[tblManufacturing] WITH NOCHECK ADD
 CONSTRAINT [tblManufacturing_PK] PRIMARY KEY  CLUSTERED
 (
  [ManufID]
 )  ON [PRIMARY]
GO

ALTER TABLE [dbo].[tblSale] WITH NOCHECK ADD
 CONSTRAINT [tblSale_PK] PRIMARY KEY  CLUSTERED
 (
  [SaleNo]
 )  ON [PRIMARY]
GO

ALTER TABLE [dbo].[tblSalesPerson] WITH NOCHECK ADD
 CONSTRAINT [tblSalesPerson_PK] PRIMARY KEY  CLUSTERED
 (
  [PersonID]
 )  ON [PRIMARY]
GO

ALTER TABLE [dbo].[tblSupply] WITH NOCHECK ADD
 CONSTRAINT [tblSupply_PK] PRIMARY KEY  CLUSTERED
 (
  [SupplyID]
 )  ON [PRIMARY]
GO

ALTER TABLE [dbo].[tblEventContact] WITH NOCHECK ADD
 CONSTRAINT [tblEventContact_PK] PRIMARY KEY  CLUSTERED
 (
  [EventContactID]
 )  ON [PRIMARY]
GO

ALTER TABLE [dbo].[tblSaleItem] WITH NOCHECK ADD
 CONSTRAINT [tblSaleItem_PK] PRIMARY KEY  CLUSTERED
 (
  [SaleItemID]
 )  ON [PRIMARY]
```

```
GO

ALTER TABLE [dbo].[tblWorkAssignment] WITH NOCHECK ADD
 CONSTRAINT [tblWorkAssignment_PK] PRIMARY KEY  CLUSTERED
 (
  [WorkID]
 )  ON [PRIMARY]
GO
```

Create Foreign Key Constraints

```
ALTER TABLE [dbo].[tblCommDevice] ADD
CONSTRAINT [tblPerson_tblCommDevice_FK1] FOREIGN KEY
 (
  [PersonID]
 ) REFERENCES [dbo].[tblPerson] (
  [PersonID]
 ) NOT FOR REPLICATION
GO

ALTER TABLE [dbo].[tblContact] ADD
 CONSTRAINT [tblPerson_tblContact_FK1] FOREIGN KEY
 (
  [PersonID]
 ) REFERENCES [dbo].[tblPerson] (
  [PersonID]
 ) NOT FOR REPLICATION
GO

ALTER TABLE [dbo].[tblEmployee] ADD
 CONSTRAINT [tblPerson_tblEmployee_FK1] FOREIGN KEY
 (
  [PersonID]
 ) REFERENCES [dbo].[tblPerson] (
  [PersonID]
 ) NOT FOR REPLICATION
GO

ALTER TABLE [dbo].[tblManufacturing] ADD
 CONSTRAINT [tblInventory_tblManufacturing_FK1] FOREIGN KEY
 (
  [InventoryID]
 ) REFERENCES [dbo].[tblInventory] (
  [InventoryID]
 ) NOT FOR REPLICATION ,
 CONSTRAINT [tblProduct_tblManufacturing_FK1] FOREIGN KEY
 (
  [ProductCode]
 ) REFERENCES [dbo].[tblProduct] (
```

```
    [ProductCode]
  ) NOT FOR REPLICATION
GO

ALTER TABLE [dbo].[tblSale] ADD
  CONSTRAINT [tblEvent_tblSale_FK1] FOREIGN KEY
  (
    [EventID]
  ) REFERENCES [dbo].[tblEvent] (
    [EventID]
  ) NOT FOR REPLICATION
GO

ALTER TABLE [dbo].[tblSalesPerson] ADD
  CONSTRAINT [tblPerson_tblSalesPerson_FK1] FOREIGN KEY
  (
    [PersonID]
  ) REFERENCES [dbo].[tblPerson] (
    [PersonID]
  ) NOT FOR REPLICATION ,
  CONSTRAINT [tblVendor_tblSalesPerson_FK1] FOREIGN KEY
  (
    [VendorID]
  ) REFERENCES [dbo].[tblVendor] (
    [VendorID]
  ) NOT FOR REPLICATION
GO

ALTER TABLE [dbo].[tblSupply] ADD
  CONSTRAINT [FK_tblSupply_tblInventory] FOREIGN KEY
  (
    [InventoryID]
  ) REFERENCES [dbo].[tblInventory] (
    [InventoryID]
  ) ON UPDATE CASCADE  NOT FOR REPLICATION ,
  CONSTRAINT [FK_tblSupply_tblVendor] FOREIGN KEY
  (
    [VendorID]
  ) REFERENCES [dbo].[tblVendor] (
    [VendorID]
  ) ON UPDATE CASCADE  NOT FOR REPLICATION
GO

ALTER TABLE [dbo].[tblEventContact] ADD
  CONSTRAINT [tblContact_tblEventContact_FK1] FOREIGN KEY
  (
    [PersonID]
  ) REFERENCES [dbo].[tblContact] (
    [PersonID]
```

```
 ) NOT FOR REPLICATION ,
 CONSTRAINT [tblEvent_tblEventContact_FK1] FOREIGN KEY
 (
  [EventID]
 ) REFERENCES [dbo].[tblEvent] (
  [EventID]
 ) NOT FOR REPLICATION
GO

ALTER TABLE [dbo].[tblSaleItem] ADD
 CONSTRAINT [tblProduct_tblSaleItem_FK1] FOREIGN KEY
 (
  [ProductCode]
 ) REFERENCES [dbo].[tblProduct] (
  [ProductCode]
 ) NOT FOR REPLICATION ,
 CONSTRAINT [tblSale_tblSaleItem_FK1] FOREIGN KEY
 (
  [SaleNo]
 ) REFERENCES [dbo].[tblSale] (
  [SaleNo]
 ) NOT FOR REPLICATION
GO

ALTER TABLE [dbo].[tblWorkAssignment] ADD
 CONSTRAINT [tblEmployee_tblWorkAssignment_FK1] FOREIGN KEY
 (
  [PersonID]
 ) REFERENCES [dbo].[tblEmployee] (
  [PersonID]
 ) NOT FOR REPLICATION ,
 CONSTRAINT [tblEvent_tblWorkAssignment_FK1] FOREIGN KEY
 (
  [EventID]
 ) REFERENCES [dbo].[tblEvent] (
  [EventID]
 ) NOT FOR REPLICATION
GO
```

Create Indexes

```
CREATE  UNIQUE INDEX [idu_tblEmployee_SSNckey] ON [dbo].[tblEmployee]([SSN])
ON [PRIMARY]
GO

CREATE  INDEX [idx_tblPerson_FullName] ON [dbo].[tblPerson]([LastName],
[FirstName]) ON [PRIMARY]
GO

CREATE  INDEX [idx_tblPerson_FirstName] ON [dbo].[tblPerson]([FirstName])
```

```
ON [PRIMARY]
GO

CREATE  INDEX [idx_tblPerson_Zip] ON [dbo].[tblPerson]([Zip])
ON [PRIMARY]
GO

CREATE  INDEX [idx_tblSalesPerson_VendorID] ON
[dbo].[tblSalesPerson]([VendorID]) ON [PRIMARY]
GO

CREATE  INDEX [idx_tblVendor_Name] ON [dbo].[tblVendor]([VendorName])
ON [PRIMARY]
GO

CREATE  INDEX [idx_tblSupply_VendorID] ON [dbo].[tblSupply]([VendorID])
ON [PRIMARY]
GO

CREATE  INDEX [idx_tblSupply_InventoryID]
ON [dbo].[tblSupply]([InventoryID]) ON [PRIMARY]
GO

CREATE  INDEX [idx_tblInventory_VendorID] ON [dbo].[tblInventory]([VendorID]) ON [PRIMARY]
GO

CREATE  INDEX [idx_tblInventory_VendorDscr]
ON [dbo].[tblInventory]([InventoryDscr]) ON [PRIMARY]
GO

CREATE  INDEX [idx_tblCommDevice_PersonID]
ON [dbo].[tblCommDevice]([PersonID]) ON [PRIMARY]
GO

CREATE  INDEX [idx_tblCommDevice_CommType]
ON [dbo].[tblCommDevice]([CommType]) ON [PRIMARY]
GO

CREATE  INDEX [idx_tblEventContact_EventID]
ON [dbo].[tblEventContact]([EventID]) ON [PRIMARY]
GO

CREATE  INDEX [idx_tblEventContact_PersonID]
ON [dbo].[tblEventContact]([PersonID]) ON [PRIMARY]
GO
```

```
CREATE  INDEX [idx_tblEvent_EventName] ON [dbo].[tblEvent]([EventName])
ON [PRIMARY]
GO

CREATE  INDEX [idx_tblEvent_StartDate] ON [dbo].[tblEvent]([StartDate])
ON [PRIMARY]
GO

CREATE  INDEX [idx_tblSale_EventID] ON [dbo].[tblSale]([EventID])
ON [PRIMARY]
GO

CREATE  INDEX [idx_tblSale_SaleDate] ON [dbo].[tblSale]([SaleDate])
ON [PRIMARY]
GO

CREATE  INDEX [idx_tblSaleItem_SaleNo] ON [dbo].[tblSaleItem]([SaleNo])
ON [PRIMARY]
GO

CREATE  INDEX [idx_tblSaleItem_ProductCode]
ON [dbo].[tblSaleItem]([ProductCode]) ON [PRIMARY]
GO

CREATE  INDEX [idx_tblEmployee_JobTitle] ON [dbo].[tblEmployee]([JobTitle]) ON [PRIMARY]
GO

CREATE  INDEX [idx_tblWorkAssign_WorkDscr]
ON [dbo].[tblWorkAssignment]([WorkAssignmentDscr]) ON [PRIMARY]
GO

CREATE  INDEX [idx_tblWorkAssign_EventID]
ON [dbo].[tblWorkAssignment]([EventID]) ON [PRIMARY]
GO

CREATE  INDEX [idx_tblWorkAssign_PersonID]
ON [dbo].[tblWorkAssignment]([PersonID]) ON [PRIMARY]
GO

CREATE  INDEX [idx_tblProduct_ProdDscr] ON [dbo].[tblProduct]([ProductDscr]) ON [PRIMARY]
GO

CREATE  INDEX [idx_tblManuf_InvID]
ON [dbo].[tblManufacturing]([InventoryID]) ON [PRIMARY]
GO

CREATE  INDEX [idx_tblManuf_ProdCode]
ON [dbo].[tblManufacturing]([ProductCode]) ON [PRIMARY]
GO
```

STRAWBERRY DATA

Following are copies of the data contained within the tables of the Strawberry database. It was exported from the Strawberry SQL Server. You can find an electronic copy of this data on the Osborne Web site located at **www.Osborne.com**.

The Person Table

The Person table contains data about all the different kinds of people who are part of the Strawberry Smooches Company.

Person ID	LastName	FirstName	Mailing Add	City	State	Zip	Person Type
1	Adams	Albert	111 Abbey Lane	McLeod	MN	03499	c
2	Baker	Beverly	222 Boots Boulevard	Litchfield	MN	03423	s
3	Connors	Charlie	333 Charring Cross	Meeker	MN	03456	c
4	Diederich	Debra	444 Domino Lane	New London	MN	03459	e
5	Embers	Emory	555 Elm Avenue	Wayzata	MN	03442	s
6	Forrest	Frieda	666 Forest Parkway	McGregor	MN	03501	c
7	Gannet	George	777 Gilmore Street	New Ulm	MN	03455	s
8	Holmes	Harriette	888 Herring Way	Meeker	MN	03456	c
9	Iverson	Iggy	999 Isoceles Triangle	Wayzata	MN	03442	s
10	Jackson	Jane	111 Jacobs Corner	New Ulm	MN	03455	c
11	Kenmore	Kenny	222 Kilkenny Lane	New London	MN	03459	e
12	Lindley	Lucy	333 Locust Avenue	Wayzata	MN	03442	e
13	Moore	Mike	444 Maple Street	New London	MN	03459	c
14	Noxon	Nancy	555 Nitley Way	McLeod	MN	03499	s

Person ID	LastName	FirstName	Mailing Add	City	State	Zip	Person Type
15	Orson	Ollie	666 Oak Avenue	New Ulm	MN	03455	e
16	Poolet	Paula	777 Paupers Lane	McGregor	MN	03501	e
17	Quigley	Quentin	888 Q Street West	Wayzata	MN	03442	c
18	Reilly	Ruth	999 Robbers Lane	McLeod	MN	03499	e
19	Samuels	Sam	111 Sedentary Street	Hutchinson	MN	03433	c
20	Thompson	Tina	222 Tee Corner	Wayzata	MN	03442	s
21	Ulysses	Ullie	333 Umpah Street	New London	MN	03459	e
22	VanHusen	Vicky	444 Viceroy Avenue	Hutchinson	MN	03433	s
23	Waterson	Wally	555 Wall Street	Litchfield	MN	03423	s
24	Xenon	Xena	666 Xenobia Court	Hutchinson	MN	03433	c
25	Yates	Yvon	777 Yankton Lane	McGregor	MN	03501	s
26	Zenobia	ZaZa	888 Z Street East	New Ulm	MN	03455	e

The CommDevice Table

The CommDevice table holds phone numbers, email addresses, and even Web site addresses for each person in the Person table—as few or as many as necessary for each person. It's linked back to the Person table by PersonID.

CommDevID	PersonID	CommType	CommValue
1	1	office	415-111-1111
2	2	office	415-222-2222
3	3	office	415-333-3333
4	4	home	415-444-4441
5	4	work	415-444-4442

CommDevID	PersonID	CommType	CommValue
6	4	cell	415-444-4443
7	5	office	415-555-5555
8	6	office	415-666-6666
9	7	office	415-777-7777
10	8	office	415-888-8888
11	9	office	415-999-9999
12	10	office	415-010-1010
13	11	office	415-011-1111
14	12	home	415-012-1212
15	12	work	415-444-4442
16	13	home	415-013-1313
17	13	work	415-444-4442
18	14	office	415-014-1414
19	15	office	415-015-1515
20	16	home	415-016-1616
21	16	work	415-444-4442
22	17	home	415-017-1717
23	17	work	415-444-4442
24	18	office	415-018-1818
25	19	home	415-019-1919
26	19	work	415-444-4442
27	20	office	415-020-2020
28	21	office	415-021-2121
29	22	home	415-022-2222
30	22	work	415-444-4442
31	23	office	415-023-2323
32	24	office	415-024-2424
33	25	office	415-025-2525
34	26	home	415-026-2626
35	26	work	415-444-4442

The Employee Table

The Employee table contains data about employees of the Strawberry Smooooches Company and is linked back to the Person table by the PersonID.

PersonID	JobTitle	SSN	I9on File	W4on File	PayAmount	PayPeriod
4	employee-owner	111-11-1111	yes	yes	$1,250.00	bi-monthly
11	employee	222-22-2222	yes	yes	$605.00	weekly
12	Employee-Senior	333-33-3333	yes	yes	$635.25	weekly
15	Employee-Senior	444-44-4444	yes	yes	$605.00	weekly
16	employee	777-77-7777	yes	yes	$665.50	weekly
18	employee	888-88-8888	yes	yes	$605.00	weekly
21	employee	555-55-5555	yes	yes	$635.25	weekly
26	employee	666-66-6666	yes	yes	$605.00	Weekly
48	employee	987-65-4321	yes	yes	$550.00	Weekly

The SalesPerson Table

The SalesPerson table contains data about salespeople who work for the Strawberry Smooooches Company vendors. It is linked back to the Person table by the PersonID, and it's linked to the Vendor table by VendorID.

PersonID	VendorID	OfficeLocation	OfficeHours
2	1	Wayzata	M-F, 8A.M.-5P.M.
5	4	McGregor	M-F, 8A.M.-5P.M.
7	4	New Ulm	M-F, 8A.M.-5P.M.
9	2	McGregor	M-F, 8A.M.-5P.M.
14	1	New London	M-F, 8A.M.-5P.M.
20	3	Litchfield	M-F, 8A.M.-5P.M.
22	5	Litchfield	M-F, 8A.M.-5P.M.
23	2	Hutchinson	M-F, 8A.M.-5P.M.
25	3	New London	M-F, 8A.M.-5P.M.

The Contact Table

The Contact table contains data about people who are contacts for each of the events that the Strawberry Smooches Company will be part of. It is linked back to the Person table by the PersonID.

PersonID	ContactTitle	OfficeLocation	OfficeHours
1	fair coordinator	McLeod	M-F, 8A.M.-5P.M.
3	fair coordinator	Meeker	M-F, 8A.M.-5P.M.
6	fair coordinator	McGregor	M-F, 8A.M.-5P.M.
8	town supervisor	Meeker	M-F, 8A.M.-5P.M.
10	town supervisor	New Ulm	M-F, 8A.M.-5P.M.
13	town supervisor	New London	M-F, 8A.M.-5P.M.
17	town supervisor	Wayzata	M-F, 8A.M.-5P.M.
19	town supervisor	Hutchinson	M-F, 8A.M.-5P.M.
24	festival coordinator	Hutchinson	M-F, 8A.M.-5P.M.

The EventContact Table

The EventContact table contains data about notes and the date the note was made regarding an event—past, current, or future. It's linked to the Contact table by PersonID and to the Event table by EventID.

Event ContactID	EventID	PersonID	Date of Contact	ContactNotes
10	1	1	5/1/00	may be able to get a spot on the main fairway
11	2	3	5/2/00	need to get special license
12	3	6	5/15/00	arrange for drainage (ice chests)
13	4	8	5/15/00	special passes needed for emps
14	5	10	5/20/00	main fairway
15	6	13	5/20/00	limited to one stand
16	7	17	6/1/00	special passes needed for emps
17	8	19	6/2/00	just off main fairway
18	9	24	6/5/00	costumes for emps
10	1	1	5/1/00	may be able to get a spot on the main fairway

Event ContactID	EventID	PersonID	Date of Contact	ContactNotes
11	2	3	5/2/00	need to get special license
12	3	6	5/15/00	arrange for drainage (ice chests)
13	4	8	5/15/00	special passes needed for emps
14	5	10	5/20/00	main fairway
15	6	13	5/20/00	limited to one stand
16	7	17	6/1/00	special passes needed for emps
17	8	19	6/2/00	just off main fairway
18	9	24	6/5/00	costumes for emps
19	1	1	5/2/00	confirmed, got a spot on the main fairway
20	1	1	5/3/00	finalized space rental
21	2	3	5/5/00	Got special license
22	3	6	5/19/00	Confirmed, drainage area will work with our ice chests
23	3	6	5/20/00	Finalized arrangements for ice deliveries during fete
24	4	8	5/16/00	Applied for special passes
25	4	8	5/20/00	Got special passes
26	5	10	5/22/00	Finalized arrangements for supplies delivery
27	6	13	5/25/00	Negotiated a second stand at far end of fairway

The Event Table

The Event table is a listing of events that the Strawberry Smoooches Company may have or might be part of. It's used for historical reference, planning, and scheduling.

EventID	EventName	Location	Fees
1	McLeod County Ag Festival	McLeod County Fairgrounds	$50.00
2	Meeker County Ag Festival	Meeker County Fairgrounds	$50.00
3	Warren Cranberry Festival	Warren County Fairgrounds	$60.00
4	Litchfield Watercade	Litchfield Public Beach	$100.00
5	New London Waterdays	New London Town Beach	$50.00

EventID	EventName	Location	Fees
6	Wild Rice Days	Hutchinson Picnic Grounds	$50.00
7	Greater Wayzata Festival	Wayzata Town Square	$100.00
8	Market Platz Daze	New Ulm Town Green	$50.00
9	Renaissance Festival	McGregor Park	$75.00

EventID	StartDate	EndDate	Hours	EventNotes
1	6/23/00	6/25/00	Fri 12-7P.M., Sat 10A.M.-7P.M., Sun 10A.M.-5P.M.	
2	6/30/00	7/4/00	Fri 12-7P.M., Sat, Sun, Mon 10A.M.-7P.M., Tues 10A.M.-5P.M.	
3	7/7/00	7/9/00	Fri, Sat, Sun 12-9P.M.	
4	7/14/00	7/16/00	Fri, Sat, 12-8P.M., Sun 12-5P.M.	
5	7/21/00	7/23/00	Fri 12-7P.M., Sat, Sun 10A.M.-7P.M.	
6	7/28/00	7/3/00	Fri 12-7P.M., Sat 10A.M.-7P.M., Sun 10A.M.-5P.M.	
7	8/4/00	8/6/00	Fri, Sat, Sun 12-9P.M.	
8	8/11/00	8/13/00	Fri, Sat, 12-8P.M., Sun 12-5P.M.	
9	8/19/00	8/20/00	Sat, Sun 10A.M.-7P.M.	

The Product Table

The Product table contains a list of products that the Strawberry Smoooches Company has for sale.

ProductCode	ProductDscr	ProductCost	ProductNotes
1	Artesian Water, Still, 12-0z	$1.50	
2	Artesian Water, Still, 16-oz	$2.00	
3	Artesian Water, Carbonated, 12-oz	$1.50	
4	Artesian Water, Carbonated, 16-oz	$2.00	

ProductCode	ProductDscr	ProductCost	ProductNotes
5	Strawberry Smoooches, 8-oz	$2.00	best-seller
6	Strawberry Smoooches, 16-oz	$3.00	

The Vendor Table

The Vendor table contains a list of vendors who do business with the Strawberry Smoooches Company.

VendorID	VendorName	Specialty
1	Filo Bros. Fresh Foods, Inc.	strawberries
2	Ramsey Restaurant Supplies, Inc.	equipment
3	Peterson Paper Products, Inc.	paper
4	Walmart	misc
5	Nobel-Sysco Foodstuff, Inc.	bottled water
6	Gallo Bros Fresh Produce	fruit

The Supply Table

The Supply table is a list of products and prices from the vendors, which is used to control pricing and do comparison shopping. It's linked to the Vendor table by VendorID.

Supply ID	Vendor ID	Wholesale Price	Wholesale Units	Date Priced	Supply Notes
1	4	$25.00	100-lb	2000-06-01	
2	5	$22.50	100-lb	2000-06-01	
3	4	$30.00	100-lb	2000-06-12	Seems to impart a sweeter taste.
4	5	$28.00	100-lb	2000-06-12	Best price around.
5	3	$2.98	1000-ct	2000-06-22	
6	2	$2.79	1000-ct	2000-06-22	
7	4	$2.65	1000-ct	2000-06-22	

The Inventory Table

The Inventory table contains a listing of the materials that the Strawberry Smooooches Company has in inventory. Because some of the products that the company sells needs to be assembled at the point of sale, it's necessary to have the required ingredients in stock. This table is used to maintain inventory supplies. It's linked to the Vendor table by VendorID.

Inventory ID	Vendor ID	InventoryDscr	Quantity on Hand	Unit of Measure	Reorder Point	Inventory Notes
1	5	Artesian Water, Still, 12-oz	3	case	1	
2	5	Artesian Water, Still, 16-oz	2	case	1	
3	5	Artesian Water, Carbonated, 12-oz	3	case	1	
4	5	Artesian Water, Carbonated, 16-oz	2	case	1	
5	1	Strawberries, frozen	20	16-oz pkg	5	
6	1	Strawberries, fresh	3	4-pt flat	1	
7	5	Sugar	10	10-lb sack	2	
8	2	Plastic Water Glass 8-oz	200	count	50	
9	2	Plastic Water Glass 16-oz	300	count	75	
10	4	Plastic Straws				
11	4	Napkins	20	200-ct pkg	5	
12	4	Plastic Long-handled Spoons	30	25-ct pkg	5	
13		Ice Cubes				
14		Water for Smooooches	5	20-gal	2	

The Manufacturing Table

The Manufacturing table contains the recipes used to make the product out of materials in inventory. It's linked to the Inventory table by InventoryID and to the Product table by ProductCode.

ManufID	InventoryID	ProductCode	AmountUsed	UnitUsed
1	5	5	7	count
2	7	5	5	Tbsp
3	14	5	8	ounce
4	13	5	1	cup
5	6	5	1	count
6	5	6	14	count
7	7	6	10	Tbsp
8	14	6	16	ounce
9	13	6	2.67	cup
10	6	6	2	count

The WorkAssignment Table

The WorkAssignment table is used to schedule employees who will be working events. It's linked to the Employee table by PersonID and to the Event table by EventID.

Work ID	Work Assignment Dscr	Event ID	Person ID	ShiftDay	ShiftStart Time	ShiftEnd Time	Hours Worked	Special Pay
2	booth	1	4	Friday	11:30:00 AM	7:30:00 PM	8	
3	booth	1	18	Friday	12:00:00 PM	7:30:00 PM	7.5	20
4	booth	1	16	Saturday	9:30:00 AM	3:00:00 PM	5.5	
5	booth	1	18	Saturday	2:00:00 PM	7:30:00 PM	5.5	
6	booth	1	4	Saturday	10:00:00 AM	6:00:00 PM	8	
7	booth	1	16	Sunday	9:30:00 AM	2:00:00 PM	4.5	20

Work ID	Work Assignment Dscr	Event ID	Person ID	ShiftDay	ShiftStart Time	ShiftEnd Time	Hours Worked	Special Pay
8	booth	1	18	Sunday	1:00:00 PM	5:30:00 PM	4.5	
9	booth	1	4	Sunday	10:00:00 AM	5:30:00 PM	7.5	
10	office	1	4	Monday	8:00:00 AM	5:00:00 PM	8	
11	office	1	15	Monday	8:00:00 AM	5:00:00 PM	8	20
12	booth	2	4	Friday	11:30:00 AM	7:30:00 PM	8	
13	booth	2	11	Friday	12:00:00 AM	7:30:00 PM	7.5	
14	booth	2	11	Saturday	9:30:00 AM	3:00:00 PM	5.5	
15	booth	2	12	Saturday	2:00:00 PM	7:30:00 PM	5.5	
16	booth	2	4	Saturday	10:00:00 AM	6:00:00 PM	8	
17	booth	2	12	Sunday	9:30:00 AM	3:00:00 PM	5.5	
18	booth	2	11	Sunday	2:00:00 PM	7:30:00 PM	5.5	
19	booth	2	4	Sunday	10:00:00 AM	6:00:00 PM	8	
20	booth	2	21	Monday	9:30:00 AM	3:00:00 PM	5.5	
21	booth	2	26	Monday	2:00:00 PM	7:30:00 PM	5.5	
22	booth	2	4	Monday	9:30:00 AM	4:30:00 PM	7	
23	booth	2	21	Tues	9:30:00 AM	2:30:00 PM	5	
24	booth	2	26	Tues	1:00:00 PM	5:30:00 PM	4.5	
25	booth	2	4	Tues	12:00:00 PM	5:30:00 PM	5.5	
26	office	2	4	Wednesday	8:00:00 AM	5:00:00 PM	8	

Work ID	Work Assignment Dscr	Event ID	Person ID	ShiftDay	ShiftStart Time	ShiftEnd Time	Hours Worked	Special Pay
27	office	2	15	Wednesday	8:00:00 AM	5:00:00 PM	8	
28	office	2	15	Wednesday	8:00:00 AM	5:00:00 PM	8	
29	booth	3	4	Friday	11:30:00 AM	7:30:00 PM	8	
30	booth	3	18	Friday	12:00:00 PM	5:30:00 PM	5.5	
31	booth	3	16	Friday	4:00:00 PM	9:30:00 PM	5.5	
32	booth	3	16	Saturday	11:30:00 AM	7:30:00 PM	8	
33	booth	3	18	Saturday	12:00:00 PM	5:30:00 PM	5.5	
34	booth	3	4	Saturday	4:00:00 PM	9:30:00 PM	5.5	
35	booth	3	16	Sunday	11:30:00 AM	7:30:00 PM	8	
36	booth	3	18	Sunday	12:00:00 PM	5:30:00 PM	5.5	
37	booth	3	4	Sunday	4:00:00 PM	9:30:00 PM	5.5	
38	office	3	4	Monday	8:00:00 AM	5:00:00 PM	8	
39	office	3	15	Monday	8:00:00 AM	5:00:00 PM	8	
40	booth	4	4	Friday	11:30:00 AM	7:30:00 PM	8	
41	booth	4	11	Friday	12:00:00 PM	5:00:00 PM	5	
42	booth	4	12	Friday	2:30:00 AM	7:30:00 AM	5	
43	booth	4	11	Saturday	11:30:00 AM	3:30:00 PM	5	
44	booth	4	12	Saturday	3:30:00 PM	8:30:00 PM	5	
45	booth	4	4	Saturday	12:30:00 PM	8:30:00 PM	8	

Work ID	Work Assignment Dscr	Event ID	Person ID	ShiftDay	ShiftStart Time	ShiftEnd Time	Hours Worked	Special Pay
46	booth	4	12	Sunday	11:30:00 AM	5:30:00 PM	6	
47	booth	4	4	Sunday	12:00:00 PM	5:30:00 PM	5.5	
48	office	4	4	Monday	8:00:00 AM	5:00:00 PM	8	
49	office	4	15	Monday	8:00:00 AM	5:00:00 PM	8	
50	booth	5	4	Friday	11:30:00 AM	7:30:00 PM	8	
51	booth	5	21	Friday	12:00:00 PM	5:00:00 PM	5	
52	booth	5	26	Friday	2:30:00 PM	7:30:00 PM	5	
53	booth	5	21	Saturday	9:30:00 AM	2:30:00 AM	5	
54	booth	5	26	Saturday	2:30:00 AM	7:30:00 PM	5	
55	booth	5	4	Saturday	11:00:00 AM	7:00:00 PM	8	
56	booth	5	21	Sunday	9:30:00 AM	2:30:00 PM	6	
57	booth	5	26	Sunday	11:30:00 AM	7:30:00 PM	8	
58	booth	5	4	Sunday	11:30:00 AM	7:30:00 PM	8	
59	office	5	4	Monday	8:00:00 AM	5:00:00 PM	8	
60	office	5	15	Monday	8:00:00 AM	5:00:00 PM	8	
61	booth	6	4	Friday	11:30:00 AM	7:30:00 PM	8	
62	booth	6	16	Friday	12:00:00 PM	5:00:00 PM	5	
63	booth	6	18	Friday	2:30:00 AM	7:30:00 AM	5	
64	booth	6	16	Saturday	9:30:00 AM	3:30:00 PM	6	

Work ID	Work Assignment Dscr	Event ID	Person ID	ShiftDay	ShiftStart Time	ShiftEnd Time	Hours Worked	Special Pay
65	booth	6	18	Saturday	1:30:00 PM	7:30:00 PM	6	
66	booth	6	4	Saturday	12:30:00 PM	7:30:00 PM	7	
67	booth	6	16	Sunday	9:30:00 AM	2:30:00 PM	5	
68	booth	6	18	Sunday	1:30:00 PM	5:30:00 PM	5	
69	booth	6	4	Sunday	11:30:00 AM	5:30:00 PM	6	
70	office	6	4	Monday	8:00:00 AM	5:00:00 PM	8	
71	office	6	15	Monday	8:00:00 AM	5:00:00 PM	8	
72	booth	7	4	Friday	11:30:00 AM	7:30:00 PM	8	
73	booth	7	11	Friday	12:00:00 PM	5:30:00 PM	5.5	
74	booth	7	12	Friday	4:00:00 PM	9:30:00 PM	5.5	
75	booth	7	11	Saturday	11:30:00 AM	5:30:00 PM	6	
76	booth	7	12	Saturday	3:30:00 PM	9:30:00 AM	6	
77	booth	7	4	Saturday	4:00:00 PM	9:30:00 PM	5.5	
78	booth	7	11	Sunday	11:30:00 AM	7:30:00 PM	8	
79	booth	7	12	Sunday	12:00:00 PM	5:30:00 PM	5.5	
80	booth	7	4	Sunday	4:00:00 PM	9:30:00 PM	5.5	
81	office	7	4	Monday	8:00:00 AM	5:00:00 PM	8	
82	office	7	15	Monday	8:00:00 AM	5:00:00 PM	8	
83	backup	1	15	Saturday	8:00:00 AM	12:00:0 0 PM	4	15

The Sale Table

The Sale table contains a record of sales made at each Event. It's linked to the Event table by EventID.

SaleNo	EventID	SaleDate	SubTotal	SalesTax	SaleTotal
1	1	06/23/2000	$ 10.00	$ 0.30	$ 10.30
2	1	06/23/2000	$ 5.00	$ 0.15	$ 5.15
3	1	06/23/2000	$ 15.00	$ 0.45	$ 15.45
4	1	06/23/2000	$ 10.50	$ 0.32	$ 10.82
5	1	06/23/2000	$ 6.00	$ 0.18	$ 6.18
6	1	06/23/2000	$ 10.00	$ 0.30	$ 10.30
7	1	06/23/2000	$ 6.00	$ 0.18	$ 6.18
8	1	06/24/2000	$ 5.00	$ 0.15	$ 5.15
9	1	06/24/2000	$ 10.00	$ 0.30	$ 10.30
10	1	06/24/2000	$ 5.00	$ 0.15	$ 5.15
11	1	06/24/2000	$ 15.00	$ 0.45	$ 15.45
12	1	06/24/2000	$ 10.50	$ 0.32	$ 10.82
13	1	06/24/2000	$ 6.00	$ 0.18	$ 6.18
14	1	06/24/2000	$ 10.00	$ 0.30	$ 10.30
15	1	06/24/2000	$ 6.00	$ 0.18	$ 6.18
16	1	06/24/2000	$ 5.00	$ 0.15	$ 5.15
17	1	06/24/2000	$ 10.00	$ 0.30	$ 10.30
18	1	06/25/2000	$ 5.00	$ 0.15	$ 5.15
19	1	06/25/2000	$ 15.00	$ 0.45	$ 15.45
20	1	06/25/2000	$ 10.50	$ 0.32	$ 10.82
21	1	06/25/2000	$ 6.00	$ 0.18	$ 6.18
22	1	06/25/2000	$ 10.00	$ 0.30	$ 10.30
23	1	06/25/2000	$ 6.00	$ 0.18	$ 6.18
24	1	06/25/2000	$ 5.00	$ 0.15	$ 5.15
25	1	06/25/2000	$ 10.00	$ 0.30	$ 10.30
26	1	06/25/2000	$ 5.00	$ 0.15	$ 5.15
27	1	06/25/2000	$ 15.00	$ 0.45	$ 15.45
28	1	06/25/2000	$ 10.50	$ 0.32	$ 10.82
29	1	06/25/2000	$ 6.00	$ 0.18	$ 6.18

SaleNo	EventID	SaleDate	SubTotal	SalesTax	SaleTotal
30	1	06/25/2000	$ 10.00	$ 0.30	$ 10.30
31	1	06/25/2000	$ 6.00	$ 0.18	$ 6.18
32	1	06/25/2000	$ 5.00	$ 0.15	$ 5.15
33	1	06/25/2000	$ 10.00	$ 0.30	$ 10.30
34	2	06/30/2000	$ 5.00	$ 0.15	$ 5.15
35	2	06/30/2000	$ 15.00	$ 0.45	$ 15.45
36	2	06/30/2000	$ 10.50	$ 0.32	$ 10.82
37	2	06/30/2000	$ 6.00	$ 0.18	$ 6.18
38	2	06/30/2000	$ 10.00	$ 0.30	$ 10.30
39	2	06/30/2000	$ 6.00	$ 0.18	$ 6.18
40	2	06/30/2000	$ 5.00	$ 0.15	$ 5.15
41	2	07/01/2000	$ 10.00	$ 0.30	$ 10.30
42	2	07/01/2000	$ 5.00	$ 0.15	$ 5.15
43	2	07/01/2000	$ 15.00	$ 0.45	$ 15.45
44	2	07/01/2000	$ 10.50	$ 0.32	$ 10.82
45	2	07/01/2000	$ 6.00	$ 0.18	$ 6.18
46	2	07/01/2000	$ 10.00	$ 0.30	$ 10.30
47	2	07/01/2000	$ 6.00	$ 0.18	$ 6.18
48	2	07/01/2000	$ 5.00	$ 0.15	$ 5.15
49	2	07/02/2000	$ 10.00	$ 0.30	$ 10.30
50	2	07/02/2000	$ 5.00	$ 0.15	$ 5.15
51	2	07/02/2000	$ 15.00	$ 0.45	$ 15.45
52	2	07/02/2000	$ 10.50	$ 0.32	$ 10.82
53	2	07/02/2000	$ 6.00	$ 0.18	$ 6.18
54	2	07/02/2000	$ 10.00	$ 0.30	$ 10.30
55	2	07/02/2000	$ 6.00	$ 0.18	$ 6.18
56	2	07/02/2000	$ 5.00	$ 0.15	$ 5.15
57	2	07/03/2000	$ 10.00	$ 0.30	$ 10.30
58	2	07/03/2000	$ 5.00	$ 0.15	$ 5.15
59	2	07/03/2000	$ 15.00	$ 0.45	$ 15.45
60	2	07/03/2000	$ 10.50	$ 0.32	$ 10.82
61	2	07/03/2000	$ 6.00	$ 0.18	$ 6.18

SaleNo	EventID	SaleDate	SubTotal	SalesTax	SaleTotal
62	2	07/03/2000	$ 10.00	$ 0.30	$ 10.30
63	2	07/03/2000	$ 6.00	$ 0.18	$ 6.18
64	2	07/03/2000	$ 5.00	$ 0.15	$ 5.15
65	2	07/04/2000	$ 10.00	$ 0.30	$ 10.30
66	2	07/04/2000	$ 5.00	$ 0.15	$ 5.15
67	2	07/04/2000	$ 15.00	$ 0.45	$ 15.45
68	2	07/04/2000	$ 10.50	$ 0.32	$ 10.82
69	2	07/04/2000	$ 6.00	$ 0.18	$ 6.18
70	2	07/04/2000	$ 10.00	$ 0.30	$ 10.30
71	2	07/04/2000	$ 6.00	$ 0.18	$ 6.18
72	2	07/04/2000	$ 5.00	$ 0.15	$ 5.15
73	2	07/04/2000	$ 10.00	$ 0.30	$ 10.30
74	2	07/04/2000	$ 5.00	$ 0.15	$ 5.15
75	2	07/04/2000	$ 15.00	$ 0.45	$ 15.45
76	2	07/04/2000	$ 10.50	$ 0.32	$ 10.82
77	2	07/04/2000	$ 6.00	$ 0.18	$ 6.18
78	2	07/04/2000	$ 10.00	$ 0.30	$ 10.30
79	2	07/04/2000	$ 6.00	$ 0.18	$ 6.18
80	2	07/04/2000	$ 5.00	$ 0.15	$ 5.15
81	3	07/07/2000	$ 10.00	$ 0.30	$ 10.30
82	3	07/07/2000	$ 5.00	$ 0.15	$ 5.15
83	3	07/07/2000	$ 15.00	$ 0.45	$ 15.45
84	3	07/07/2000	$ 10.50	$ 0.32	$ 10.82
85	3	07/07/2000	$ 6.00	$ 0.18	$ 6.18
86	3	07/07/2000	$ 10.00	$ 0.30	$ 10.30
87	3	07/07/2000	$ 6.00	$ 0.18	$ 6.18
88	3	07/07/2000	$ 5.00	$ 0.15	$ 5.15
89	3	07/07/2000	$ 10.00	$ 0.30	$ 10.30
90	3	07/07/2000	$ 5.00	$ 0.15	$ 5.15
91	3	07/07/2000	$ 15.00	$ 0.45	$ 15.45
92	3	07/07/2000	$ 10.50	$ 0.32	$ 10.82
93	3	07/07/2000	$ 6.00	$ 0.18	$ 6.18

SaleNo	EventID	SaleDate	SubTotal	SalesTax	SaleTotal
94	3	07/07/2000	$ 10.00	$ 0.30	$ 10.30
95	3	07/07/2000	$ 6.00	$ 0.18	$ 6.18
96	3	07/08/2000	$ 5.00	$ 0.15	$ 5.15
97	3	07/08/2000	$ 10.00	$ 0.30	$ 10.30
98	3	07/08/2000	$ 5.00	$ 0.15	$ 5.15
99	3	07/08/2000	$ 15.00	$ 0.45	$ 15.45
100	3	07/08/2000	$ 10.50	$ 0.32	$ 10.82
101	3	07/08/2000	$ 6.00	$ 0.18	$ 6.18
102	3	07/08/2000	$ 10.00	$ 0.30	$ 10.30
103	3	07/08/2000	$ 6.00	$ 0.18	$ 6.18
104	3	07/08/2000	$ 5.00	$ 0.15	$ 5.15
105	3	07/08/2000	$ 10.00	$ 0.30	$ 10.30
106	3	07/08/2000	$ 5.00	$ 0.15	$ 5.15
107	3	07/08/2000	$ 15.00	$ 0.45	$ 15.45
108	3	07/08/2000	$ 10.50	$ 0.32	$ 10.82
109	3	07/08/2000	$ 6.00	$ 0.18	$ 6.18
110	3	07/08/2000	$ 10.00	$ 0.30	$ 10.30
111	3	07/08/2000	$ 6.00	$ 0.18	$ 6.18
112	3	07/08/2000	$ 5.00	$ 0.15	$ 5.15
113	3	07/09/2000	$ 10.00	$ 0.30	$ 10.30
114	3	07/09/2000	$ 5.00	$ 0.15	$ 5.15
115	3	07/09/2000	$ 15.00	$ 0.45	$ 15.45
116	3	07/09/2000	$ 10.50	$ 0.32	$ 10.82
117	3	07/09/2000	$ 6.00	$ 0.18	$ 6.18
118	3	07/09/2000	$ 10.00	$ 0.30	$ 10.30
119	3	07/09/2000	$ 6.00	$ 0.18	$ 6.18
120	3	07/09/2000	$ 5.00	$ 0.15	$ 5.15
121	3	07/09/2000	$ 10.00	$ 0.30	$ 10.30
122	3	07/09/2000	$ 5.00	$ 0.15	$ 5.15
123	3	07/09/2000	$ 15.00	$ 0.45	$ 15.45
124	3	07/09/2000	$ 10.50	$ 0.32	$ 10.82
125	3	07/09/2000	$ 6.00	$ 0.18	$ 6.18

SaleNo	EventID	SaleDate	SubTotal	SalesTax	SaleTotal
126	3	07/09/2000	$ 10.00	$ 0.30	$ 10.30
127	3	07/09/2000	$ 6.00	$ 0.18	$ 6.18
128	3	07/09/2000	$ 5.00	$ 0.15	$ 5.15
129	3	07/09/2000	$ 10.00	$ 0.30	$ 10.30
130	3	07/09/2000	$ 5.00	$ 0.15	$ 5.15
131	4	07/14/2000	$ 15.00	$ 0.45	$ 15.45
132	4	07/14/2000	$ 10.50	$ 0.32	$ 10.82
133	4	07/14/2000	$ 6.00	$ 0.18	$ 6.18
134	4	07/14/2000	$ 10.00	$ 0.30	$ 10.30
135	4	07/14/2000	$ 6.00	$ 0.18	$ 6.18
136	4	07/14/2000	$ 5.00	$ 0.15	$ 5.15
137	4	07/14/2000	$ 10.00	$ 0.30	$ 10.30
138	4	07/14/2000	$ 5.00	$ 0.15	$ 5.15
139	4	07/14/2000	$ 15.00	$ 0.45	$ 15.45
140	4	07/14/2000	$ 10.50	$ 0.32	$ 10.82
141	4	07/14/2000	$ 6.00	$ 0.18	$ 6.18
142	4	07/14/2000	$ 10.00	$ 0.30	$ 10.30
143	4	07/14/2000	$ 6.00	$ 0.18	$ 6.18
144	4	07/14/2000	$ 5.00	$ 0.15	$ 5.15
145	4	07/15/2000	$ 10.00	$ 0.30	$ 10.30
146	4	07/15/2000	$ 5.00	$ 0.15	$ 5.15
147	4	07/15/2000	$ 15.00	$ 0.45	$ 15.45
148	4	07/15/2000	$ 10.50	$ 0.32	$ 10.82
149	4	07/15/2000	$ 6.00	$ 0.18	$ 6.18
150	4	07/15/2000	$ 10.00	$ 0.30	$ 10.30
151	4	07/15/2000	$ 6.00	$ 0.18	$ 6.18
152	4	07/15/2000	$ 5.00	$ 0.15	$ 5.15
153	4	07/15/2000	$ 10.00	$ 0.30	$ 10.30
154	4	07/15/2000	$ 5.00	$ 0.15	$ 5.15
155	4	07/15/2000	$ 15.00	$ 0.45	$ 15.45
156	4	07/15/2000	$ 10.50	$ 0.32	$ 10.82
157	4	07/15/2000	$ 6.00	$ 0.18	$ 6.18

SaleNo	EventID	SaleDate	SubTotal	SalesTax	SaleTotal
158	4	07/15/2000	$ 10.00	$ 0.30	$ 10.30
159	4	07/15/2000	$ 6.00	$ 0.18	$ 6.18
160	4	07/15/2000	$ 5.00	$ 0.15	$ 5.15
161	4	07/15/2000	$ 10.00	$ 0.30	$ 10.30
162	4	07/15/2000	$ 5.00	$ 0.15	$ 5.15
163	4	07/15/2000	$ 15.00	$ 0.45	$ 15.45
164	4	07/16/2000	$ 10.50	$ 0.32	$ 10.82
165	4	07/16/2000	$ 6.00	$ 0.18	$ 6.18
166	4	07/16/2000	$ 10.00	$ 0.30	$ 10.30
167	4	07/16/2000	$ 6.00	$ 0.18	$ 6.18
168	4	07/16/2000	$ 5.00	$ 0.15	$ 5.15
169	4	07/16/2000	$ 10.00	$ 0.30	$ 10.30
170	4	07/16/2000	$ 5.00	$ 0.15	$ 5.15
171	4	07/16/2000	$ 15.00	$ 0.45	$ 15.45
172	4	07/16/2000	$ 10.50	$ 0.32	$ 10.82
173	4	07/16/2000	$ 6.00	$ 0.18	$ 6.18
174	4	07/16/2000	$ 10.00	$ 0.30	$ 10.30
175	4	07/16/2000	$ 6.00	$ 0.18	$ 6.18
176	4	07/16/2000	$ 5.00	$ 0.15	$ 5.15
177	4	07/16/2000	$ 10.00	$ 0.30	$ 10.30
178	4	07/16/2000	$ 5.00	$ 0.15	$ 5.15
179	4	07/16/2000	$ 15.00	$ 0.45	$ 15.45
180	4	07/16/2000	$ 10.50	$ 0.32	$ 10.82
181	4	07/16/2000	$ 6.00	$ 0.18	$ 6.18
182	4	07/16/2000	$ 10.00	$ 0.30	$ 10.30
183	4	07/16/2000	$ 6.00	$ 0.18	$ 6.18
184	4	07/16/2000	$ 5.00	$ 0.15	$ 5.15
185	4	07/16/2000	$ 10.00	$ 0.30	$ 10.30
186	4	07/16/2000	$ 5.00	$ 0.15	$ 5.15
187	5	07/21/2000	$ 15.00	$ 0.45	$ 15.45
188	5	07/21/2000	$ 10.50	$ 0.32	$ 10.82
189	5	07/21/2000	$ 6.00	$ 0.18	$ 6.18

SaleNo	EventID	SaleDate	SubTotal	SalesTax	SaleTotal
190	5	07/21/2000	$ 10.00	$ 0.30	$ 10.30
191	5	07/21/2000	$ 6.00	$ 0.18	$ 6.18
192	5	07/21/2000	$ 5.00	$ 0.15	$ 5.15
193	5	07/21/2000	$ 10.00	$ 0.30	$ 10.30
194	5	07/21/2000	$ 5.00	$ 0.15	$ 5.15
195	5	07/21/2000	$ 15.00	$ 0.45	$ 15.45
196	5	07/21/2000	$ 10.50	$ 0.32	$ 10.82
197	5	07/21/2000	$ 6.00	$ 0.18	$ 6.18
198	5	07/21/2000	$ 10.00	$ 0.30	$ 10.30
199	5	07/21/2000	$ 6.00	$ 0.18	$ 6.18
200	5	07/21/2000	$ 5.00	$ 0.15	$ 5.15
201	5	07/21/2000	$ 10.00	$ 0.30	$ 10.30
202	5	07/21/2000	$ 5.00	$ 0.15	$ 5.15
203	5	07/21/2000	$ 15.00	$ 0.45	$ 15.45
204	5	07/21/2000	$ 10.50	$ 0.32	$ 10.82
205	5	07/21/2000	$ 6.00	$ 0.18	$ 6.18
206	5	07/22/2000	$ 10.00	$ 0.30	$ 10.30
207	5	07/22/2000	$ 6.00	$ 0.18	$ 6.18
208	5	07/22/2000	$ 5.00	$ 0.15	$ 5.15
209	5	07/22/2000	$ 10.00	$ 0.30	$ 10.30
210	5	07/22/2000	$ 5.00	$ 0.15	$ 5.15
211	5	07/22/2000	$ 15.00	$ 0.45	$ 15.45
212	5	07/22/2000	$ 10.50	$ 0.32	$ 10.82
213	5	07/22/2000	$ 6.00	$ 0.18	$ 6.18
214	5	07/22/2000	$ 10.00	$ 0.30	$ 10.30
215	5	07/22/2000	$ 6.00	$ 0.18	$ 6.18
216	5	07/22/2000	$ 5.00	$ 0.15	$ 5.15
217	5	07/22/2000	$ 10.00	$ 0.30	$ 10.30
218	5	07/22/2000	$ 5.00	$ 0.15	$ 5.15
219	5	07/22/2000	$ 15.00	$ 0.45	$ 15.45
220	5	07/22/2000	$ 10.50	$ 0.32	$ 10.82
221	5	07/22/2000	$ 6.00	$ 0.18	$ 6.18

SaleNo	EventID	SaleDate	SubTotal	SalesTax	SaleTotal
222	5	07/22/2000	$ 10.00	$ 0.30	$ 10.30
223	5	07/22/2000	$ 6.00	$ 0.18	$ 6.18
224	5	07/22/2000	$ 5.00	$ 0.15	$ 5.15
225	5	07/22/2000	$ 10.00	$ 0.30	$ 10.30
226	5	07/22/2000	$ 5.00	$ 0.15	$ 5.15
227	5	07/22/2000	$ 15.00	$ 0.45	$ 15.45
228	5	07/22/2000	$ 10.50	$ 0.32	$ 10.82
229	5	07/22/2000	$ 6.00	$ 0.18	$ 6.18
230	5	07/22/2000	$ 10.00	$ 0.30	$ 10.30
231	5	07/22/2000	$ 6.00	$ 0.18	$ 6.18
232	5	07/22/2000	$ 5.00	$ 0.15	$ 5.15
233	5	07/22/2000	$ 10.00	$ 0.30	$ 10.30
234	5	07/22/2000	$ 5.00	$ 0.15	$ 5.15
235	5	07/22/2000	$ 15.00	$ 0.45	$ 15.45
236	5	07/22/2000	$ 10.50	$ 0.32	$ 10.82
237	5	07/23/2000	$ 6.00	$ 0.18	$ 6.18
238	5	07/23/2000	$ 10.00	$ 0.30	$ 10.30
239	5	07/23/2000	$ 6.00	$ 0.18	$ 6.18
240	5	07/23/2000	$ 5.00	$ 0.15	$ 5.15
241	5	07/23/2000	$ 10.00	$ 0.30	$ 10.30
242	5	07/23/2000	$ 5.00	$ 0.15	$ 5.15
243	5	07/23/2000	$ 15.00	$ 0.45	$ 15.45
244	5	07/23/2000	$ 10.50	$ 0.32	$ 10.82
245	5	07/23/2000	$ 6.00	$ 0.18	$ 6.18
246	5	07/23/2000	$ 10.00	$ 0.30	$ 10.30
247	5	07/23/2000	$ 6.00	$ 0.18	$ 6.18
248	5	07/23/2000	$ 5.00	$ 0.15	$ 5.15
249	5	07/23/2000	$ 10.00	$ 0.30	$ 10.30
250	5	07/23/2000	$ 5.00	$ 0.15	$ 5.15
251	5	07/23/2000	$ 15.00	$ 0.45	$ 15.45
252	5	07/23/2000	$ 10.50	$ 0.32	$ 10.82
253	5	07/23/2000	$ 6.00	$ 0.18	$ 6.18

SaleNo	EventID	SaleDate	SubTotal	SalesTax	SaleTotal
254	5	07/23/2000	$ 10.00	$ 0.30	$ 10.30
255	5	07/23/2000	$ 6.00	$ 0.18	$ 6.18
256	5	07/23/2000	$ 5.00	$ 0.15	$ 5.15
257	5	07/23/2000	$ 10.00	$ 0.30	$ 10.30
258	5	07/23/2000	$ 5.00	$ 0.15	$ 5.15
259	5	07/23/2000	$ 15.00	$ 0.45	$ 15.45
260	5	07/23/2000	$ 10.50	$ 0.32	$ 10.82
261	5	07/23/2000	$ 6.00	$ 0.18	$ 6.18
262	5	07/23/2000	$ 10.00	$ 0.30	$ 10.30
263	5	07/23/2000	$ 6.00	$ 0.18	$ 6.18
264	5	07/23/2000	$ 5.00	$ 0.15	$ 5.15
265	6	07/28/2000	$ 10.00	$ 0.30	$ 10.30
266	6	07/28/2000	$ 5.00	$ 0.15	$ 5.15
267	6	07/28/2000	$ 15.00	$ 0.45	$ 15.45
268	6	07/28/2000	$ 10.50	$ 0.32	$ 10.82
269	6	07/28/2000	$ 6.00	$ 0.18	$ 6.18
270	6	07/28/2000	$ 10.00	$ 0.30	$ 10.30
271	6	07/28/2000	$ 6.00	$ 0.18	$ 6.18
272	6	07/28/2000	$ 5.00	$ 0.15	$ 5.15
273	6	07/28/2000	$ 10.00	$ 0.30	$ 10.30
274	6	07/28/2000	$ 5.00	$ 0.15	$ 5.15
275	6	07/28/2000	$ 15.00	$ 0.45	$ 15.45
276	6	07/28/2000	$ 10.50	$ 0.32	$ 10.82
277	6	07/28/2000	$ 6.00	$ 0.18	$ 6.18
278	6	07/28/2000	$ 10.00	$ 0.30	$ 10.30
279	6	07/28/2000	$ 6.00	$ 0.18	$ 6.18
280	6	07/28/2000	$ 5.00	$ 0.15	$ 5.15
281	6	07/28/2000	$ 10.00	$ 0.30	$ 10.30
282	6	07/28/2000	$ 5.00	$ 0.15	$ 5.15
283	6	07/28/2000	$ 15.00	$ 0.45	$ 15.45
284	6	07/28/2000	$ 10.50	$ 0.32	$ 10.82
285	6	07/28/2000	$ 6.00	$ 0.18	$ 6.18

SaleNo	EventID	SaleDate	SubTotal	SalesTax	SaleTotal
286	6	07/28/2000	$ 10.00	$ 0.30	$ 10.30
287	6	07/28/2000	$ 6.00	$ 0.18	$ 6.18
288	6	07/28/2000	$ 5.00	$ 0.15	$ 5.15
289	6	07/29/2000	$ 10.00	$ 0.30	$ 10.30
290	6	07/29/2000	$ 5.00	$ 0.15	$ 5.15
291	6	07/29/2000	$ 15.00	$ 0.45	$ 15.45
292	6	07/29/2000	$ 10.50	$ 0.32	$ 10.82
293	6	07/29/2000	$ 6.00	$ 0.18	$ 6.18
294	6	07/29/2000	$ 10.00	$ 0.30	$ 10.30
295	6	07/29/2000	$ 6.00	$ 0.18	$ 6.18
296	6	07/29/2000	$ 5.00	$ 0.15	$ 5.15
297	6	07/29/2000	$ 10.00	$ 0.30	$ 10.30
298	6	07/29/2000	$ 5.00	$ 0.15	$ 5.15
299	6	07/29/2000	$ 15.00	$ 0.45	$ 15.45
300	6	07/29/2000	$ 10.50	$ 0.32	$ 10.82
301	6	07/29/2000	$ 6.00	$ 0.18	$ 6.18
302	6	07/29/2000	$ 10.00	$ 0.30	$ 10.30
303	6	07/29/2000	$ 6.00	$ 0.18	$ 6.18
304	6	07/29/2000	$ 5.00	$ 0.15	$ 5.15
305	6	07/29/2000	$ 10.00	$ 0.30	$ 10.30
306	6	07/29/2000	$ 5.00	$ 0.15	$ 5.15
307	6	07/29/2000	$ 15.00	$ 0.45	$ 15.45
308	6	07/29/2000	$ 10.50	$ 0.32	$ 10.82
309	6	07/29/2000	$ 6.00	$ 0.18	$ 6.18
310	6	07/29/2000	$ 10.00	$ 0.30	$ 10.30
311	6	07/29/2000	$ 6.00	$ 0.18	$ 6.18
312	6	07/29/2000	$ 5.00	$ 0.15	$ 5.15
313	6	07/29/2000	$ 10.00	$ 0.30	$ 10.30
314	6	07/29/2000	$ 5.00	$ 0.15	$ 5.15
315	6	07/29/2000	$ 15.00	$ 0.45	$ 15.45
316	6	07/30/2000	$ 10.50	$ 0.32	$ 10.82
317	6	07/30/2000	$ 6.00	$ 0.18	$ 6.18

SaleNo	EventID	SaleDate	SubTotal	SalesTax	SaleTotal
318	6	07/30/2000	$ 10.00	$ 0.30	$ 10.30
319	6	07/30/2000	$ 6.00	$ 0.18	$ 6.18
320	6	07/30/2000	$ 5.00	$ 0.15	$ 5.15
321	6	07/30/2000	$ 10.00	$ 0.30	$ 10.30
322	6	07/30/2000	$ 5.00	$ 0.15	$ 5.15
323	6	07/30/2000	$ 15.00	$ 0.45	$ 15.45
324	6	07/30/2000	$ 10.50	$ 0.32	$ 10.82
325	6	07/30/2000	$ 6.00	$ 0.18	$ 6.18
326	6	07/30/2000	$ 10.00	$ 0.30	$ 10.30
327	6	07/30/2000	$ 6.00	$ 0.18	$ 6.18
328	6	07/30/2000	$ 5.00	$ 0.15	$ 5.15
329	6	07/30/2000	$ 10.00	$ 0.30	$ 10.30
330	6	07/30/2000	$ 5.00	$ 0.15	$ 5.15
331	6	07/30/2000	$ 15.00	$ 0.45	$ 15.45
332	6	07/30/2000	$ 10.50	$ 0.32	$ 10.82
333	6	07/30/2000	$ 6.00	$ 0.18	$ 6.18
334	6	07/30/2000	$ 10.00	$ 0.30	$ 10.30
335	6	07/30/2000	$ 6.00	$ 0.18	$ 6.18
336	6	07/30/2000	$ 5.00	$ 0.15	$ 5.15
337	6	07/30/2000	$ 10.00	$ 0.30	$ 10.30
338	6	07/30/2000	$ 5.00	$ 0.15	$ 5.15
339	6	07/30/2000	$ 15.00	$ 0.45	$ 15.45
340	6	07/30/2000	$ 10.50	$ 0.32	$ 10.82
341	6	07/30/2000	$ 6.00	$ 0.18	$ 6.18
342	6	07/30/2000	$ 10.00	$ 0.30	$ 10.30
343	6	07/30/2000	$ 6.00	$ 0.18	$ 6.18
344	6	07/30/2000	$ 5.00	$ 0.15	$ 5.15
345	6	07/30/2000	$ 10.00	$ 0.30	$ 10.30
346	6	07/30/2000	$ 5.00	$ 0.15	$ 5.15
347	6	07/30/2000	$ 15.00	$ 0.45	$ 15.45
348	6	07/30/2000	$ 10.50	$ 0.32	$ 10.82
349	6	07/30/2000	$ 6.00	$ 0.18	$ 6.18

SaleNo	EventID	SaleDate	SubTotal	SalesTax	SaleTotal
350	6	07/30/2000	$ 10.00	$ 0.30	$ 10.30
351	6	07/30/2000	$ 6.00	$ 0.18	$ 6.18
352	6	07/30/2000	$ 5.00	$ 0.15	$ 5.15
353	6	07/30/2000	$ 10.00	$ 0.30	$ 10.30
354	6	07/30/2000	$ 5.00	$ 0.15	$ 5.15
355	6	07/30/2000	$ 15.00	$ 0.45	$ 15.45
356	6	07/30/2000	$ 10.50	$ 0.32	$ 10.82
357	6	07/30/2000	$ 6.00	$ 0.18	$ 6.18
358	6	07/30/2000	$ 10.00	$ 0.30	$ 10.30
359	6	07/30/2000	$ 6.00	$ 0.18	$ 6.18
360	6	07/30/2000	$ 5.00	$ 0.15	$ 5.15
361	6	07/30/2000	$ 10.00	$ 0.30	$ 10.30
362	6	07/30/2000	$ 5.00	$ 0.15	$ 5.15
363	6	07/30/2000	$ 15.00	$ 0.45	$ 15.45
364	6	07/30/2000	$ 10.50	$ 0.32	$ 10.82
365	6	07/30/2000	$ 6.00	$ 0.18	$ 6.18
366	6	07/30/2000	$ 10.00	$ 0.30	$ 10.30
367	6	07/30/2000	$ 6.00	$ 0.18	$ 6.18
368	6	07/30/2000	$ 5.00	$ 0.15	$ 5.15
369	6	07/30/2000	$ 10.00	$ 0.30	$ 10.30
370	6	07/30/2000	$ 5.00	$ 0.15	$ 5.15
371	6	07/30/2000	$ 15.00	$ 0.45	$ 15.45
372	6	07/30/2000	$ 10.50	$ 0.32	$ 10.82
373	6	07/30/2000	$ 6.00	$ 0.18	$ 6.18
374	6	07/30/2000	$ 10.00	$ 0.30	$ 10.30
375	6	07/30/2000	$ 6.00	$ 0.18	$ 6.18
376	6	07/30/2000	$ 5.00	$ 0.15	$ 5.15
377	6	07/30/2000	$ 10.00	$ 0.30	$ 10.30
378	6	07/30/2000	$ 5.00	$ 0.15	$ 5.15
379	6	07/30/2000	$ 15.00	$ 0.45	$ 15.45
380	6	07/30/2000	$ 10.50	$ 0.32	$ 10.82
381	6	07/30/2000	$ 6.00	$ 0.18	$ 6.18

SaleNo	EventID	SaleDate	SubTotal	SalesTax	SaleTotal
382	6	07/30/2000	$ 10.00	$ 0.30	$ 10.30
383	6	07/30/2000	$ 6.00	$ 0.18	$ 6.18
384	6	07/30/2000	$ 5.00	$ 0.15	$ 5.15
385	6	07/30/2000	$ 10.00	$ 0.30	$ 10.30
386	6	07/30/2000	$ 5.00	$ 0.15	$ 5.15
387	6	07/30/2000	$ 15.00	$ 0.45	$ 15.45
388	6	07/30/2000	$ 10.50	$ 0.32	$ 10.82
389	6	07/30/2000	$ 6.00	$ 0.18	$ 6.18
390	6	07/30/2000	$ 10.00	$ 0.30	$ 10.30
391	7	08/04/2000	$ 6.00	$ 0.18	$ 6.18
392	7	08/04/2000	$ 5.00	$ 0.15	$ 5.15
393	7	08/04/2000	$ 10.00	$ 0.30	$ 10.30
394	7	08/04/2000	$ 5.00	$ 0.15	$ 5.15
395	7	08/04/2000	$ 15.00	$ 0.45	$ 15.45
396	7	08/04/2000	$ 10.50	$ 0.32	$ 10.82
397	7	08/04/2000	$ 6.00	$ 0.18	$ 6.18
398	7	08/04/2000	$ 10.00	$ 0.30	$ 10.30
399	7	08/04/2000	$ 6.00	$ 0.18	$ 6.18
400	7	08/04/2000	$ 5.00	$ 0.15	$ 5.15
401	7	08/04/2000	$ 10.00	$ 0.30	$ 10.30
402	7	08/04/2000	$ 5.00	$ 0.15	$ 5.15
403	7	08/04/2000	$ 15.00	$ 0.45	$ 15.45
404	7	08/04/2000	$ 10.50	$ 0.32	$ 10.82
405	7	08/04/2000	$ 6.00	$ 0.18	$ 6.18
406	7	08/04/2000	$ 10.00	$ 0.30	$ 10.30
407	7	08/04/2000	$ 6.00	$ 0.18	$ 6.18
408	7	08/04/2000	$ 5.00	$ 0.15	$ 5.15
409	7	08/04/2000	$ 10.00	$ 0.30	$ 10.30
410	7	08/04/2000	$ 5.00	$ 0.15	$ 5.15
411	7	08/04/2000	$ 15.00	$ 0.45	$ 15.45
412	7	08/04/2000	$ 10.50	$ 0.32	$ 10.82
413	7	08/04/2000	$ 6.00	$ 0.18	$ 6.18

SaleNo	EventID	SaleDate	SubTotal	SalesTax	SaleTotal
414	7	08/04/2000	$ 10.00	$ 0.30	$ 10.30
415	7	08/04/2000	$ 6.00	$ 0.18	$ 6.18
416	7	08/04/2000	$ 5.00	$ 0.15	$ 5.15
417	7	08/05/2000	$ 10.00	$ 0.30	$ 10.30
418	7	08/05/2000	$ 5.00	$ 0.15	$ 5.15
419	7	08/05/2000	$ 15.00	$ 0.45	$ 15.45
420	7	08/05/2000	$ 10.50	$ 0.32	$ 10.82
421	7	08/05/2000	$ 6.00	$ 0.18	$ 6.18
422	7	08/05/2000	$ 10.00	$ 0.30	$ 10.30
423	7	08/05/2000	$ 6.00	$ 0.18	$ 6.18
424	7	08/05/2000	$ 5.00	$ 0.15	$ 5.15
425	7	08/05/2000	$ 10.00	$ 0.30	$ 10.30
426	7	08/05/2000	$ 5.00	$ 0.15	$ 5.15
427	7	08/05/2000	$ 15.00	$ 0.45	$ 15.45
428	7	08/05/2000	$ 10.50	$ 0.32	$ 10.82
429	7	08/05/2000	$ 6.00	$ 0.18	$ 6.18
430	7	08/05/2000	$ 10.00	$ 0.30	$ 10.30
431	7	08/05/2000	$ 6.00	$ 0.18	$ 6.18
432	7	08/05/2000	$ 5.00	$ 0.15	$ 5.15
433	7	08/05/2000	$ 10.00	$ 0.30	$ 10.30
434	7	08/05/2000	$ 5.00	$ 0.15	$ 5.15
435	7	08/05/2000	$ 15.00	$ 0.45	$ 15.45
436	7	08/05/2000	$ 10.50	$ 0.32	$ 10.82
437	7	08/05/2000	$ 6.00	$ 0.18	$ 6.18
438	7	08/05/2000	$ 10.00	$ 0.30	$ 10.30
439	7	08/05/2000	$ 6.00	$ 0.18	$ 6.18
440	7	08/05/2000	$ 5.00	$ 0.15	$ 5.15
441	7	08/05/2000	$ 10.00	$ 0.30	$ 10.30
442	7	08/05/2000	$ 5.00	$ 0.15	$ 5.15
443	7	08/06/2000	$ 15.00	$ 0.45	$ 15.45
444	7	08/06/2000	$ 10.50	$ 0.32	$ 10.82
445	7	08/06/2000	$ 6.00	$ 0.18	$ 6.18

SaleNo	EventID	SaleDate	SubTotal	SalesTax	SaleTotal
446	7	08/06/2000	$ 10.00	$ 0.30	$ 10.30
447	7	08/06/2000	$ 6.00	$ 0.18	$ 6.18
448	7	08/06/2000	$ 5.00	$ 0.15	$ 5.15
449	7	08/06/2000	$ 10.00	$ 0.30	$ 10.30
450	7	08/06/2000	$ 5.00	$ 0.15	$ 5.15
451	7	08/06/2000	$ 15.00	$ 0.45	$ 15.45
452	7	08/06/2000	$ 10.50	$ 0.32	$ 10.82
453	7	08/06/2000	$ 6.00	$ 0.18	$ 6.18
454	7	08/06/2000	$ 10.00	$ 0.30	$ 10.30
455	7	08/06/2000	$ 6.00	$ 0.18	$ 6.18
456	7	08/06/2000	$ 5.00	$ 0.15	$ 5.15
457	7	08/06/2000	$ 10.00	$ 0.30	$ 10.30
458	7	08/06/2000	$ 5.00	$ 0.15	$ 5.15
459	7	08/06/2000	$ 15.00	$ 0.45	$ 15.45
460	7	08/06/2000	$ 10.50	$ 0.32	$ 10.82
461	7	08/06/2000	$ 6.00	$ 0.18	$ 6.18
462	7	08/06/2000	$ 10.00	$ 0.30	$ 10.30
463	7	08/06/2000	$ 6.00	$ 0.18	$ 6.18
464	7	08/06/2000	$ 5.00	$ 0.15	$ 5.15
465	7	08/06/2000	$ 10.00	$ 0.30	$ 10.30
466	7	08/06/2000	$ 5.00	$ 0.15	$ 5.15
467	7	08/06/2000	$ 15.00	$ 0.45	$ 15.45
468	7	08/06/2000	$ 10.50	$ 0.32	$ 10.82
469	7	08/06/2000	$ 6.00	$ 0.18	$ 6.18
470	7	08/06/2000	$ 10.00	$ 0.30	$ 10.30
471	7	08/06/2000	$ 6.00	$ 0.18	$ 6.18
472	7	08/06/2000	$ 5.00	$ 0.15	$ 5.15
473	7	08/06/2000	$ 10.00	$ 0.30	$ 10.30
474	7	08/06/2000	$ 5.00	$ 0.15	$ 5.15
475	7	08/06/2000	$ 15.00	$ 0.45	$ 15.45
476	7	08/06/2000	$ 10.50	$ 0.32	$ 10.82
477	7	08/06/2000	$ 6.00	$ 0.18	$ 6.18

SaleNo	EventID	SaleDate	SubTotal	SalesTax	SaleTotal
478	8	08/11/2000	$ 10.00	$ 0.30	$ 10.30
479	8	08/11/2000	$ 6.00	$ 0.18	$ 6.18
480	8	08/11/2000	$ 5.00	$ 0.15	$ 5.15
481	8	08/11/2000	$ 10.00	$ 0.30	$ 10.30
482	8	08/11/2000	$ 5.00	$ 0.15	$ 5.15
483	8	08/11/2000	$ 15.00	$ 0.45	$ 15.45
484	8	08/11/2000	$ 10.50	$ 0.32	$ 10.82
485	8	08/11/2000	$ 6.00	$ 0.18	$ 6.18
486	8	08/11/2000	$ 10.00	$ 0.30	$ 10.30
487	8	08/11/2000	$ 6.00	$ 0.18	$ 6.18
488	8	08/11/2000	$ 5.00	$ 0.15	$ 5.15
489	8	08/11/2000	$ 10.00	$ 0.30	$ 10.30
490	8	08/11/2000	$ 5.00	$ 0.15	$ 5.15
491	8	08/11/2000	$ 15.00	$ 0.45	$ 15.45
492	8	08/11/2000	$ 10.50	$ 0.32	$ 10.82
493	8	08/11/2000	$ 6.00	$ 0.18	$ 6.18
494	8	08/11/2000	$ 10.00	$ 0.30	$ 10.30
495	8	08/11/2000	$ 6.00	$ 0.18	$ 6.18
496	8	08/11/2000	$ 5.00	$ 0.15	$ 5.15
497	8	08/11/2000	$ 10.00	$ 0.30	$ 10.30
498	8	08/11/2000	$ 5.00	$ 0.15	$ 5.15
499	8	08/11/2000	$ 15.00	$ 0.45	$ 15.45
500	8	08/11/2000	$ 10.50	$ 0.32	$ 10.82
501	8	08/11/2000	$ 6.00	$ 0.18	$ 6.18
502	8	08/11/2000	$ 10.00	$ 0.30	$ 10.30
503	8	08/11/2000	$ 6.00	$ 0.18	$ 6.18
504	8	08/11/2000	$ 5.00	$ 0.15	$ 5.15
505	8	08/11/2000	$ 10.00	$ 0.30	$ 10.30
506	8	08/11/2000	$ 5.00	$ 0.15	$ 5.15
507	8	08/11/2000	$ 15.00	$ 0.45	$ 15.45
508	8	08/12/2000	$ 10.50	$ 0.32	$ 10.82
509	8	08/12/2000	$ 6.00	$ 0.18	$ 6.18

SaleNo	EventID	SaleDate	SubTotal	SalesTax	SaleTotal
510	8	08/12/2000	$ 10.00	$ 0.30	$ 10.30
511	8	08/12/2000	$ 6.00	$ 0.18	$ 6.18
512	8	08/12/2000	$ 5.00	$ 0.15	$ 5.15
513	8	08/12/2000	$ 10.00	$ 0.30	$ 10.30
514	8	08/12/2000	$ 5.00	$ 0.15	$ 5.15
515	8	08/12/2000	$ 15.00	$ 0.45	$ 15.45
516	8	08/12/2000	$ 10.50	$ 0.32	$ 10.82
517	8	08/12/2000	$ 6.00	$ 0.18	$ 6.18
518	8	08/12/2000	$ 10.00	$ 0.30	$ 10.30
519	8	08/12/2000	$ 6.00	$ 0.18	$ 6.18
520	8	08/12/2000	$ 5.00	$ 0.15	$ 5.15
521	8	08/12/2000	$ 10.00	$ 0.30	$ 10.30
522	8	08/12/2000	$ 5.00	$ 0.15	$ 5.15
523	8	08/12/2000	$ 15.00	$ 0.45	$ 15.45
524	8	08/12/2000	$ 10.50	$ 0.32	$ 10.82
525	8	08/12/2000	$ 6.00	$ 0.18	$ 6.18
526	8	08/12/2000	$ 10.00	$ 0.30	$ 10.30
527	8	08/12/2000	$ 6.00	$ 0.18	$ 6.18
528	8	08/12/2000	$ 5.00	$ 0.15	$ 5.15
529	8	08/12/2000	$ 10.00	$ 0.30	$ 10.30
530	8	08/12/2000	$ 5.00	$ 0.15	$ 5.15
531	8	08/12/2000	$ 15.00	$ 0.45	$ 15.45
532	8	08/12/2000	$ 10.50	$ 0.32	$ 10.82
533	8	08/12/2000	$ 6.00	$ 0.18	$ 6.18
534	8	08/12/2000	$ 10.00	$ 0.30	$ 10.30
535	8	08/12/2000	$ 6.00	$ 0.18	$ 6.18
536	8	08/12/2000	$ 5.00	$ 0.15	$ 5.15
537	8	08/12/2000	$ 10.00	$ 0.30	$ 10.30
538	8	08/12/2000	$ 5.00	$ 0.15	$ 5.15
539	8	08/12/2000	$ 15.00	$ 0.45	$ 15.45
540	8	08/12/2000	$ 10.50	$ 0.32	$ 10.82
541	8	08/13/2000	$ 6.00	$ 0.18	$ 6.18

SaleNo	EventID	SaleDate	SubTotal	SalesTax	SaleTotal
542	8	08/13/2000	$ 10.00	$ 0.30	$ 10.30
543	8	08/13/2000	$ 6.00	$ 0.18	$ 6.18
544	8	08/13/2000	$ 5.00	$ 0.15	$ 5.15
545	8	08/13/2000	$ 10.00	$ 0.30	$ 10.30
546	8	08/13/2000	$ 5.00	$ 0.15	$ 5.15
547	8	08/13/2000	$ 15.00	$ 0.45	$ 15.45
548	8	08/13/2000	$ 10.50	$ 0.32	$ 10.82
549	8	08/13/2000	$ 6.00	$ 0.18	$ 6.18
550	8	08/13/2000	$ 10.00	$ 0.30	$ 10.30
551	8	08/13/2000	$ 6.00	$ 0.18	$ 6.18
552	8	08/13/2000	$ 5.00	$ 0.15	$ 5.15
553	8	08/13/2000	$ 10.00	$ 0.30	$ 10.30
554	8	08/13/2000	$ 5.00	$ 0.15	$ 5.15
555	8	08/13/2000	$ 15.00	$ 0.45	$ 15.45
556	8	08/13/2000	$ 10.50	$ 0.32	$ 10.82
557	8	08/13/2000	$ 6.00	$ 0.18	$ 6.18
558	8	08/13/2000	$ 10.00	$ 0.30	$ 10.30
559	8	08/13/2000	$ 6.00	$ 0.18	$ 6.18
560	8	08/13/2000	$ 5.00	$ 0.15	$ 5.15
561	8	08/13/2000	$ 10.00	$ 0.30	$ 10.30
562	8	08/13/2000	$ 5.00	$ 0.15	$ 5.15
563	8	08/13/2000	$ 15.00	$ 0.45	$ 15.45
564	8	08/13/2000	$ 10.50	$ 0.32	$ 10.82
565	8	08/13/2000	$ 6.00	$ 0.18	$ 6.18
566	8	08/13/2000	$ 10.00	$ 0.30	$ 10.30
567	8	08/13/2000	$ 6.00	$ 0.18	$ 6.18
568	8	08/13/2000	$ 5.00	$ 0.15	$ 5.15
569	8	08/13/2000	$ 10.00	$ 0.30	$ 10.30
570	8	08/13/2000	$ 5.00	$ 0.15	$ 5.15
571	8	08/13/2000	$ 15.00	$ 0.45	$ 15.45
572	9	08/19/2000	$ 10.50	$ 0.32	$ 10.82
573	9	08/19/2000	$ 6.00	$ 0.18	$ 6.18

SaleNo	EventID	SaleDate	SubTotal	SalesTax	SaleTotal
574	9	08/19/2000	$ 10.00	$ 0.30	$ 10.30
575	9	08/19/2000	$ 6.00	$ 0.18	$ 6.18
576	9	08/19/2000	$ 5.00	$ 0.15	$ 5.15
577	9	08/19/2000	$ 10.00	$ 0.30	$ 10.30
578	9	08/19/2000	$ 5.00	$ 0.15	$ 5.15
579	9	08/19/2000	$ 15.00	$ 0.45	$ 15.45
580	9	08/19/2000	$ 10.50	$ 0.32	$ 10.82
581	9	08/19/2000	$ 6.00	$ 0.18	$ 6.18
582	9	08/19/2000	$ 10.00	$ 0.30	$ 10.30
583	9	08/19/2000	$ 6.00	$ 0.18	$ 6.18
584	9	08/19/2000	$ 5.00	$ 0.15	$ 5.15
585	9	08/19/2000	$ 10.00	$ 0.30	$ 10.30
586	9	08/19/2000	$ 5.00	$ 0.15	$ 5.15
587	9	08/19/2000	$ 15.00	$ 0.45	$ 15.45
588	9	08/19/2000	$ 10.50	$ 0.32	$ 10.82
589	9	08/19/2000	$ 6.00	$ 0.18	$ 6.18
590	9	08/19/2000	$ 10.00	$ 0.30	$ 10.30
591	9	08/19/2000	$ 6.00	$ 0.18	$ 6.18
592	9	08/19/2000	$ 5.00	$ 0.15	$ 5.15
593	9	08/19/2000	$ 10.00	$ 0.30	$ 10.30
594	9	08/19/2000	$ 5.00	$ 0.15	$ 5.15
595	9	08/19/2000	$ 15.00	$ 0.45	$ 15.45
596	9	08/19/2000	$ 10.50	$ 0.32	$ 10.82
597	9	08/19/2000	$ 6.00	$ 0.18	$ 6.18
598	9	08/20/2000	$ 10.00	$ 0.30	$ 10.30
599	9	08/20/2000	$ 6.00	$ 0.18	$ 6.18
600	9	08/20/2000	$ 5.00	$ 0.15	$ 5.15
601	9	08/20/2000	$ 10.00	$ 0.30	$ 10.30
602	9	08/20/2000	$ 5.00	$ 0.15	$ 5.15
603	9	08/20/2000	$ 15.00	$ 0.45	$ 15.45
604	9	08/20/2000	$ 10.50	$ 0.32	$ 10.82
605	9	08/20/2000	$ 6.00	$ 0.18	$ 6.18

SaleNo	EventID	SaleDate	SubTotal	SalesTax	SaleTotal
606	9	08/20/2000	$ 10.00	$ 0.30	$ 10.30
607	9	08/20/2000	$ 6.00	$ 0.18	$ 6.18
608	9	08/20/2000	$ 5.00	$ 0.15	$ 5.15
609	9	08/20/2000	$ 10.00	$ 0.30	$ 10.30
610	9	08/20/2000	$ 5.00	$ 0.15	$ 5.15
611	9	08/20/2000	$ 15.00	$ 0.45	$ 15.45
612	9	08/20/2000	$ 10.50	$ 0.32	$ 10.82
613	9	08/20/2000	$ 6.00	$ 0.18	$ 6.18
614	9	08/20/2000	$ 10.00	$ 0.30	$ 10.30
615	9	08/20/2000	$ 6.00	$ 0.18	$ 6.18
616	9	08/20/2000	$ 5.00	$ 0.15	$ 5.15
617	9	08/20/2000	$ 10.00	$ 0.30	$ 10.30
618	9	08/20/2000	$ 5.00	$ 0.15	$ 5.15
619	9	08/20/2000	$ 15.00	$ 0.45	$ 15.45
620	9	08/20/2000	$ 10.50	$ 0.32	$ 10.82
621	9	08/20/2000	$ 6.00	$ 0.18	$ 6.18
622	9	08/20/2000	$ 10.00	$ 0.30	$ 10.30
623	9	08/20/2000	$ 6.00	$ 0.18	$ 6.18
624	9	08/20/2000	$ 5.00	$ 0.15	$ 5.15
625	9	08/20/2000	$ 10.00	$ 0.30	$ 10.30
626	9	08/20/2000	$ 5.00	$ 0.15	$ 5.15
627	9	08/20/2000	$ 15.00	$ 0.45	$ 15.45
628	9	08/20/2000	$ 10.50	$ 0.32	$ 10.82
629	9	08/20/2000	$ 6.00	$ 0.18	$ 6.18
630	9	08/20/2000	$ 10.00	$ 0.30	$ 10.30
631	9	08/20/2000	$ 6.00	$ 0.18	$ 6.18
632	9	08/20/2000	$ 5.00	$ 0.15	$ 5.15
633	9	08/20/2000	$ 10.00	$ 0.30	$ 10.30
634	9	08/20/2000	$ 5.00	$ 0.15	$ 5.15
635	9	08/20/2000	$ 15.00	$ 0.45	$ 15.45
636	9	08/20/2000	$ 10.50	$ 0.32	$ 10.82
637	9	08/20/2000	$ 6.00	$ 0.18	$ 6.18

SaleNo	EventID	SaleDate	SubTotal	SalesTax	SaleTotal
638	9	08/20/2000	$ 10.00	$ 0.30	$ 10.30
639	9	08/20/2000	$ 6.00	$ 0.18	$ 6.18
640	9	08/20/2000	$ 5.00	$ 0.15	$ 5.15

The SaleItem Table

The SaleItem table contains the details of each sale, what kind and how many of each product has been sold. It's linked to the Sale table by SaleNoID and to the Product table by ProductCode.

SaleItemID	SaleNo	ProductCode	QuantitySold	UnitPrice	ItemCost
1	1	5	2	$ 2.00	$ 4.00
2	1	1	2	$ 3.00	$ 6.00
3	2	6	1	$ 3.00	$ 3.00
4	2	2	1	$ 2.00	$ 2.00
5	3	6	3	$ 3.00	$ 9.00
6	3	2	3	$ 2.00	$ 6.00
7	4	1	3	$ 1.50	$ 4.50
8	4	6	2	$ 3.00	$ 6.00
9	5	1	2	$ 1.50	$ 3.00
10	5	6	1	$ 3.00	$ 3.00
11	6	4	4	$ 2.00	$ 8.00
12	6	1	5	$ 2.00	$ 2.00
13	7	3	2	$ 1.50	$ 3.00
14	7	6	1	$ 3.00	$ 3.00
15	8	5	1	$ 2.00	$ 2.00
16	8	6	1	$ 3.00	$ 3.00
17	9	5	2	$ 2.00	$ 4.00
18	9	1	2	$ 3.00	$ 6.00
19	10	6	1	$ 3.00	$ 3.00
20	10	2	1	$ 2.00	$ 2.00
21	11	5	2	$ 2.00	$ 4.00
22	11	1	2	$ 3.00	$ 6.00
23	12	6	1	$ 3.00	$ 3.00

SaleItemID	SaleNo	ProductCode	QuantitySold	UnitPrice	ItemCost
24	12	2	1	$ 2.00	$ 2.00
25	13	6	3	$ 3.00	$ 9.00
26	13	2	3	$ 2.00	$ 6.00
27	14	1	3	$ 1.50	$ 4.50
28	14	6	2	$ 3.00	$ 6.00
29	15	1	2	$ 1.50	$ 3.00
30	15	6	1	$ 3.00	$ 3.00
31	16	4	4	$ 2.00	$ 8.00
32	16	1	5	$ 2.00	$ 2.00
33	17	3	2	$ 1.50	$ 3.00
34	17	6	1	$ 3.00	$ 3.00
35	18	5	1	$ 2.00	$ 2.00
36	18	6	1	$ 3.00	$ 3.00
37	19	5	2	$ 2.00	$ 4.00
38	19	1	2	$ 3.00	$ 6.00
39	20	6	1	$ 3.00	$ 3.00
40	20	2	1	$ 2.00	$ 2.00
41	21	5	2	$ 2.00	$ 4.00
42	21	1	2	$ 3.00	$ 6.00
43	22	6	1	$ 3.00	$ 3.00
44	22	2	1	$ 2.00	$ 2.00
45	23	6	3	$ 3.00	$ 9.00
46	23	2	3	$ 2.00	$ 6.00
47	24	1	3	$ 1.50	$ 4.50
48	24	6	2	$ 3.00	$ 6.00
49	25	1	2	$ 1.50	$ 3.00
50	25	6	1	$ 3.00	$ 3.00
51	26	4	4	$ 2.00	$ 8.00
52	26	1	5	$ 2.00	$ 2.00
53	27	3	2	$ 1.50	$ 3.00
54	27	6	1	$ 3.00	$ 3.00
55	28	5	1	$ 2.00	$ 2.00

SaleItemID	SaleNo	ProductCode	QuantitySold	UnitPrice	ItemCost
56	28	6	1	$ 3.00	$ 3.00
57	29	5	2	$ 2.00	$ 4.00
58	29	1	2	$ 3.00	$ 6.00
59	30	6	1	$ 3.00	$ 3.00
60	30	2	1	$ 2.00	$ 2.00
61	31	5	2	$ 2.00	$ 4.00
62	31	1	2	$ 3.00	$ 6.00
63	32	6	1	$ 3.00	$ 3.00
64	32	2	1	$ 2.00	$ 2.00
65	33	6	3	$ 3.00	$ 9.00
66	33	2	3	$ 2.00	$ 6.00
67	34	1	3	$ 1.50	$ 4.50
68	34	6	2	$ 3.00	$ 6.00
69	35	1	2	$ 1.50	$ 3.00
70	35	6	1	$ 3.00	$ 3.00
71	36	4	4	$ 2.00	$ 8.00
72	36	1	5	$ 2.00	$ 2.00
73	37	3	2	$ 1.50	$ 3.00
74	37	6	1	$ 3.00	$ 3.00
75	38	5	1	$ 2.00	$ 2.00
76	38	6	1	$ 3.00	$ 3.00
77	39	5	2	$ 2.00	$ 4.00
78	39	1	2	$ 3.00	$ 6.00
79	40	6	1	$ 3.00	$ 3.00
80	40	2	1	$ 2.00	$ 2.00
81	41	5	2	$ 2.00	$ 4.00
82	41	1	2	$ 3.00	$ 6.00
83	42	6	1	$ 3.00	$ 3.00
84	42	2	1	$ 2.00	$ 2.00
85	43	6	3	$ 3.00	$ 9.00
86	43	2	3	$ 2.00	$ 6.00
87	44	1	3	$ 1.50	$ 4.50

SaleItemID	SaleNo	ProductCode	QuantitySold	UnitPrice	ItemCost
88	44	6	2	$ 3.00	$ 6.00
89	45	1	2	$ 1.50	$ 3.00
90	45	6	1	$ 3.00	$ 3.00
91	46	4	4	$ 2.00	$ 8.00
92	46	1	5	$ 2.00	$ 2.00
93	47	3	2	$ 1.50	$ 3.00
94	47	6	1	$ 3.00	$ 3.00
95	48	5	1	$ 2.00	$ 2.00
96	48	6	1	$ 3.00	$ 3.00
97	49	5	2	$ 2.00	$ 4.00
98	49	1	2	$ 3.00	$ 6.00
99	50	6	1	$ 3.00	$ 3.00
100	50	2	1	$ 2.00	$ 2.00
101	51	5	2	$ 2.00	$ 4.00
102	51	1	2	$ 3.00	$ 6.00
103	52	6	1	$ 3.00	$ 3.00
104	52	2	1	$ 2.00	$ 2.00
105	53	6	3	$ 3.00	$ 9.00
106	53	2	3	$ 2.00	$ 6.00
107	54	1	3	$ 1.50	$ 4.50
108	54	6	2	$ 3.00	$ 6.00
109	55	1	2	$ 1.50	$ 3.00
110	55	6	1	$ 3.00	$ 3.00
111	56	4	4	$ 2.00	$ 8.00
112	56	1	5	$ 2.00	$ 2.00
113	57	3	2	$ 1.50	$ 3.00
114	57	6	1	$ 3.00	$ 3.00
115	58	5	1	$ 2.00	$ 2.00
116	58	6	1	$ 3.00	$ 3.00
117	59	5	2	$ 2.00	$ 4.00
118	59	1	2	$ 3.00	$ 6.00
119	60	6	1	$ 3.00	$ 3.00

SaleItemID	SaleNo	ProductCode	QuantitySold	UnitPrice	ItemCost
120	60	2	1	$ 2.00	$ 2.00
121	61	5	2	$ 2.00	$ 4.00
122	61	1	2	$ 3.00	$ 6.00
123	62	6	1	$ 3.00	$ 3.00
124	62	2	1	$ 2.00	$ 2.00
125	63	6	3	$ 3.00	$ 9.00
126	63	2	3	$ 2.00	$ 6.00
127	64	1	3	$ 1.50	$ 4.50
128	64	6	2	$ 3.00	$ 6.00
129	65	1	2	$ 1.50	$ 3.00
130	65	6	1	$ 3.00	$ 3.00
131	66	4	4	$ 2.00	$ 8.00
132	66	1	5	$ 2.00	$ 2.00
133	67	3	2	$ 1.50	$ 3.00
134	67	6	1	$ 3.00	$ 3.00
135	68	5	1	$ 2.00	$ 2.00
136	68	6	1	$ 3.00	$ 3.00
137	69	5	2	$ 2.00	$ 4.00
138	69	1	2	$ 3.00	$ 6.00
139	70	6	1	$ 3.00	$ 3.00
140	70	2	1	$ 2.00	$ 2.00
141	71	5	2	$ 2.00	$ 4.00
142	71	1	2	$ 3.00	$ 6.00
143	72	6	1	$ 3.00	$ 3.00
144	72	2	1	$ 2.00	$ 2.00
145	73	6	3	$ 3.00	$ 9.00
146	73	2	3	$ 2.00	$ 6.00
147	74	1	3	$ 1.50	$ 4.50
148	74	6	2	$ 3.00	$ 6.00
149	75	1	2	$ 1.50	$ 3.00
150	75	6	1	$ 3.00	$ 3.00
151	76	4	4	$ 2.00	$ 8.00

SaleItemID	SaleNo	ProductCode	QuantitySold	UnitPrice	ItemCost
152	76	1	5	$ 2.00	$ 2.00
153	77	3	2	$ 1.50	$ 3.00
154	77	6	1	$ 3.00	$ 3.00
155	78	5	1	$ 2.00	$ 2.00
156	78	6	1	$ 3.00	$ 3.00
157	79	5	2	$ 2.00	$ 4.00
158	79	1	2	$ 3.00	$ 6.00
159	80	6	1	$ 3.00	$ 3.00
160	80	2	1	$ 2.00	$ 2.00
161	81	5	2	$ 2.00	$ 4.00
162	81	1	2	$ 3.00	$ 6.00
163	82	6	1	$ 3.00	$ 3.00
164	82	2	1	$ 2.00	$ 2.00
165	83	6	3	$ 3.00	$ 9.00
166	83	2	3	$ 2.00	$ 6.00
167	84	1	3	$ 1.50	$ 4.50
168	84	6	2	$ 3.00	$ 6.00
169	85	1	2	$ 1.50	$ 3.00
170	85	6	1	$ 3.00	$ 3.00
171	86	4	4	$ 2.00	$ 8.00
172	86	1	5	$ 2.00	$ 2.00
173	87	3	2	$ 1.50	$ 3.00
174	87	6	1	$ 3.00	$ 3.00
175	88	5	1	$ 2.00	$ 2.00
176	88	6	1	$ 3.00	$ 3.00
177	89	5	2	$ 2.00	$ 4.00
178	89	1	2	$ 3.00	$ 6.00
179	90	6	1	$ 3.00	$ 3.00
180	90	2	1	$ 2.00	$ 2.00
181	91	5	2	$ 2.00	$ 4.00
182	91	1	2	$ 3.00	$ 6.00
183	92	6	1	$ 3.00	$ 3.00

SaleItemID	SaleNo	ProductCode	QuantitySold	UnitPrice	ItemCost
184	92	2	1	$ 2.00	$ 2.00
185	93	6	3	$ 3.00	$ 9.00
186	93	2	3	$ 2.00	$ 6.00
187	94	1	3	$ 1.50	$ 4.50
188	94	6	2	$ 3.00	$ 6.00
189	95	1	2	$ 1.50	$ 3.00
190	95	6	1	$ 3.00	$ 3.00
191	96	4	4	$ 2.00	$ 8.00
192	96	1	5	$ 2.00	$ 2.00
193	97	3	2	$ 1.50	$ 3.00
194	97	6	1	$ 3.00	$ 3.00
195	98	5	1	$ 2.00	$ 2.00
196	98	6	1	$ 3.00	$ 3.00
197	99	5	2	$ 2.00	$ 4.00
198	99	1	2	$ 3.00	$ 6.00
199	100	6	1	$ 3.00	$ 3.00
200	100	2	1	$ 2.00	$ 2.00
201	101	5	2	$ 2.00	$ 4.00
202	101	1	2	$ 3.00	$ 6.00
203	102	6	1	$ 3.00	$ 3.00
204	102	2	1	$ 2.00	$ 2.00
205	103	6	3	$ 3.00	$ 9.00
206	103	2	3	$ 2.00	$ 6.00
207	104	1	3	$ 1.50	$ 4.50
208	104	6	2	$ 3.00	$ 6.00
209	105	1	2	$ 1.50	$ 3.00
210	105	6	1	$ 3.00	$ 3.00
211	106	4	4	$ 2.00	$ 8.00
212	106	1	5	$ 2.00	$ 2.00
213	107	3	2	$ 1.50	$ 3.00
214	107	6	1	$ 3.00	$ 3.00
215	108	5	1	$ 2.00	$ 2.00

SaleItemID	SaleNo	ProductCode	QuantitySold	UnitPrice	ItemCost
216	108	6	1	$ 3.00	$ 3.00
217	109	5	2	$ 2.00	$ 4.00
218	109	1	2	$ 3.00	$ 6.00
219	110	6	1	$ 3.00	$ 3.00
220	110	2	1	$ 2.00	$ 2.00
221	111	5	2	$ 2.00	$ 4.00
222	111	1	2	$ 3.00	$ 6.00
223	112	6	1	$ 3.00	$ 3.00
224	112	2	1	$ 2.00	$ 2.00
225	113	6	3	$ 3.00	$ 9.00
226	113	2	3	$ 2.00	$ 6.00
227	114	1	3	$ 1.50	$ 4.50
228	114	6	2	$ 3.00	$ 6.00
229	115	1	2	$ 1.50	$ 3.00
230	115	6	1	$ 3.00	$ 3.00
231	116	4	4	$ 2.00	$ 8.00
232	116	1	5	$ 2.00	$ 2.00
233	117	3	2	$ 1.50	$ 3.00
234	117	6	1	$ 3.00	$ 3.00
235	118	5	1	$ 2.00	$ 2.00
236	118	6	1	$ 3.00	$ 3.00
237	119	5	2	$ 2.00	$ 4.00
238	119	1	2	$ 3.00	$ 6.00
239	120	6	1	$ 3.00	$ 3.00
240	120	2	1	$ 2.00	$ 2.00
241	121	5	2	$ 2.00	$ 4.00
242	121	1	2	$ 3.00	$ 6.00
243	122	6	1	$ 3.00	$ 3.00
244	122	2	1	$ 2.00	$ 2.00
245	123	6	3	$ 3.00	$ 9.00
246	123	2	3	$ 2.00	$ 6.00
247	124	1	3	$ 1.50	$ 4.50

SaleItemID	SaleNo	ProductCode	QuantitySold	UnitPrice	ItemCost
248	124	6	2	$ 3.00	$ 6.00
249	125	1	2	$ 1.50	$ 3.00
250	125	6	1	$ 3.00	$ 3.00
251	126	4	4	$ 2.00	$ 8.00
252	126	1	5	$ 2.00	$ 2.00
253	127	3	2	$ 1.50	$ 3.00
254	127	6	1	$ 3.00	$ 3.00
255	128	5	1	$ 2.00	$ 2.00
256	128	6	1	$ 3.00	$ 3.00
257	129	5	2	$ 2.00	$ 4.00
258	129	1	2	$ 3.00	$ 6.00
259	130	6	1	$ 3.00	$ 3.00
260	130	2	1	$ 2.00	$ 2.00
261	131	5	2	$ 2.00	$ 4.00
262	131	1	2	$ 3.00	$ 6.00
263	132	6	1	$ 3.00	$ 3.00
264	132	2	1	$ 2.00	$ 2.00
265	133	6	3	$ 3.00	$ 9.00
266	133	2	3	$ 2.00	$ 6.00
267	134	1	3	$ 1.50	$ 4.50
268	134	6	2	$ 3.00	$ 6.00
269	135	1	2	$ 1.50	$ 3.00
270	135	6	1	$ 3.00	$ 3.00
271	136	4	4	$ 2.00	$ 8.00
272	136	1	5	$ 2.00	$ 2.00
273	137	3	2	$ 1.50	$ 3.00
274	137	6	1	$ 3.00	$ 3.00
275	138	5	1	$ 2.00	$ 2.00
276	138	6	1	$ 3.00	$ 3.00
277	139	5	2	$ 2.00	$ 4.00
278	139	1	2	$ 3.00	$ 6.00
279	140	6	1	$ 3.00	$ 3.00

SaleItemID	SaleNo	ProductCode	QuantitySold	UnitPrice	ItemCost
280	140	2	1	$ 2.00	$ 2.00
281	141	5	2	$ 2.00	$ 4.00
282	141	1	2	$ 3.00	$ 6.00
283	142	6	1	$ 3.00	$ 3.00
284	142	2	1	$ 2.00	$ 2.00
285	143	6	3	$ 3.00	$ 9.00
286	143	2	3	$ 2.00	$ 6.00
287	144	1	3	$ 1.50	$ 4.50
288	144	6	2	$ 3.00	$ 6.00
289	145	1	2	$ 1.50	$ 3.00
290	145	6	1	$ 3.00	$ 3.00
291	146	4	4	$ 2.00	$ 8.00
292	146	1	5	$ 2.00	$ 2.00
293	147	3	2	$ 1.50	$ 3.00
294	147	6	1	$ 3.00	$ 3.00
295	148	5	1	$ 2.00	$ 2.00
296	148	6	1	$ 3.00	$ 3.00
297	149	5	2	$ 2.00	$ 4.00
298	149	1	2	$ 3.00	$ 6.00
299	150	6	1	$ 3.00	$ 3.00
300	150	2	1	$ 2.00	$ 2.00
301	151	5	2	$ 2.00	$ 4.00
302	151	1	2	$ 3.00	$ 6.00
303	152	6	1	$ 3.00	$ 3.00
304	152	2	1	$ 2.00	$ 2.00
305	153	6	3	$ 3.00	$ 9.00
306	153	2	3	$ 2.00	$ 6.00
307	154	1	3	$ 1.50	$ 4.50
308	154	6	2	$ 3.00	$ 6.00
309	155	1	2	$ 1.50	$ 3.00
310	155	6	1	$ 3.00	$ 3.00
311	156	4	4	$ 2.00	$ 8.00

SaleItemID	SaleNo	ProductCode	QuantitySold	UnitPrice	ItemCost
312	156	1	5	$ 2.00	$ 2.00
313	157	3	2	$ 1.50	$ 3.00
314	157	6	1	$ 3.00	$ 3.00
315	158	5	1	$ 2.00	$ 2.00
316	158	6	1	$ 3.00	$ 3.00
317	159	5	2	$ 2.00	$ 4.00
318	159	1	2	$ 3.00	$ 6.00
319	160	6	1	$ 3.00	$ 3.00
320	160	2	1	$ 2.00	$ 2.00
321	161	5	2	$ 2.00	$ 4.00
322	161	1	2	$ 3.00	$ 6.00
323	162	6	1	$ 3.00	$ 3.00
324	162	2	1	$ 2.00	$ 2.00
325	163	6	3	$ 3.00	$ 9.00
326	163	2	3	$ 2.00	$ 6.00
327	164	1	3	$ 1.50	$ 4.50
328	164	6	2	$ 3.00	$ 6.00
329	165	1	2	$ 1.50	$ 3.00
330	165	6	1	$ 3.00	$ 3.00
331	166	4	4	$ 2.00	$ 8.00
332	166	1	5	$ 2.00	$ 2.00
333	167	3	2	$ 1.50	$ 3.00
334	167	6	1	$ 3.00	$ 3.00
335	168	5	1	$ 2.00	$ 2.00
336	168	6	1	$ 3.00	$ 3.00
337	169	5	2	$ 2.00	$ 4.00
338	169	1	2	$ 3.00	$ 6.00
339	170	6	1	$ 3.00	$ 3.00
340	170	2	1	$ 2.00	$ 2.00
341	171	5	2	$ 2.00	$ 4.00
342	171	1	2	$ 3.00	$ 6.00
343	172	6	1	$ 3.00	$ 3.00

SaleItemID	SaleNo	ProductCode	QuantitySold	UnitPrice	ItemCost
344	172	2	1	$ 2.00	$ 2.00
345	173	6	3	$ 3.00	$ 9.00
346	173	2	3	$ 2.00	$ 6.00
347	174	1	3	$ 1.50	$ 4.50
348	174	6	2	$ 3.00	$ 6.00
349	175	1	2	$ 1.50	$ 3.00
350	175	6	1	$ 3.00	$ 3.00
351	176	4	4	$ 2.00	$ 8.00
352	176	1	5	$ 2.00	$ 2.00
353	177	3	2	$ 1.50	$ 3.00
354	177	6	1	$ 3.00	$ 3.00
355	178	5	1	$ 2.00	$ 2.00
356	178	6	1	$ 3.00	$ 3.00
357	179	5	2	$ 2.00	$ 4.00
358	179	1	2	$ 3.00	$ 6.00
359	180	6	1	$ 3.00	$ 3.00
360	180	2	1	$ 2.00	$ 2.00
361	181	5	2	$ 2.00	$ 4.00
362	181	1	2	$ 3.00	$ 6.00
363	182	6	1	$ 3.00	$ 3.00
364	182	2	1	$ 2.00	$ 2.00
365	183	6	3	$ 3.00	$ 9.00
366	183	2	3	$ 2.00	$ 6.00
367	184	1	3	$ 1.50	$ 4.50
368	184	6	2	$ 3.00	$ 6.00
369	185	1	2	$ 1.50	$ 3.00
370	185	6	1	$ 3.00	$ 3.00
371	186	4	4	$ 2.00	$ 8.00
372	186	1	5	$ 2.00	$ 2.00
373	187	3	2	$ 1.50	$ 3.00
374	187	6	1	$ 3.00	$ 3.00
375	188	5	1	$ 2.00	$ 2.00

SaleItemID	SaleNo	ProductCode	QuantitySold	UnitPrice	ItemCost
376	188	6	1	$ 3.00	$ 3.00
377	189	5	2	$ 2.00	$ 4.00
378	189	1	2	$ 3.00	$ 6.00
379	190	6	1	$ 3.00	$ 3.00
380	190	2	1	$ 2.00	$ 2.00
381	191	5	2	$ 2.00	$ 4.00
382	191	1	2	$ 3.00	$ 6.00
383	192	6	1	$ 3.00	$ 3.00
384	192	2	1	$ 2.00	$ 2.00
385	193	6	3	$ 3.00	$ 9.00
386	193	2	3	$ 2.00	$ 6.00
387	194	1	3	$ 1.50	$ 4.50
388	194	6	2	$ 3.00	$ 6.00
389	195	1	2	$ 1.50	$ 3.00
390	195	6	1	$ 3.00	$ 3.00
391	196	4	4	$ 2.00	$ 8.00
392	196	1	5	$ 2.00	$ 2.00
393	197	3	2	$ 1.50	$ 3.00
394	197	6	1	$ 3.00	$ 3.00
395	198	5	1	$ 2.00	$ 2.00
396	198	6	1	$ 3.00	$ 3.00
397	199	5	2	$ 2.00	$ 4.00
398	199	1	2	$ 3.00	$ 6.00
399	200	6	1	$ 3.00	$ 3.00
400	200	2	1	$ 2.00	$ 2.00
401	201	5	2	$ 2.00	$ 4.00
402	201	1	2	$ 3.00	$ 6.00
403	202	6	1	$ 3.00	$ 3.00
404	202	2	1	$ 2.00	$ 2.00
405	203	6	3	$ 3.00	$ 9.00
406	203	2	3	$ 2.00	$ 6.00
407	204	1	3	$ 1.50	$ 4.50

SaleItemID	SaleNo	ProductCode	QuantitySold	UnitPrice	ItemCost
408	204	6	2	$ 3.00	$ 6.00
409	205	1	2	$ 1.50	$ 3.00
410	205	6	1	$ 3.00	$ 3.00
411	206	4	4	$ 2.00	$ 8.00
412	206	1	5	$ 2.00	$ 2.00
413	207	3	2	$ 1.50	$ 3.00
414	207	6	1	$ 3.00	$ 3.00
415	208	5	1	$ 2.00	$ 2.00
416	208	6	1	$ 3.00	$ 3.00
417	209	5	2	$ 2.00	$ 4.00
418	209	1	2	$ 3.00	$ 6.00
419	210	6	1	$ 3.00	$ 3.00
420	210	2	1	$ 2.00	$ 2.00
421	211	5	2	$ 2.00	$ 4.00
422	211	1	2	$ 3.00	$ 6.00
423	212	6	1	$ 3.00	$ 3.00
424	212	2	1	$ 2.00	$ 2.00
425	213	6	3	$ 3.00	$ 9.00
426	213	2	3	$ 2.00	$ 6.00
427	214	1	3	$ 1.50	$ 4.50
428	214	6	2	$ 3.00	$ 6.00
429	215	1	2	$ 1.50	$ 3.00
430	215	6	1	$ 3.00	$ 3.00
431	216	4	4	$ 2.00	$ 8.00
432	216	1	5	$ 2.00	$ 2.00
433	217	3	2	$ 1.50	$ 3.00
434	217	6	1	$ 3.00	$ 3.00
435	218	5	1	$ 2.00	$ 2.00
436	218	6	1	$ 3.00	$ 3.00
437	219	5	2	$ 2.00	$ 4.00
438	219	1	2	$ 3.00	$ 6.00
439	220	6	1	$ 3.00	$ 3.00

SaleItemID	SaleNo	ProductCode	QuantitySold	UnitPrice	ItemCost
440	220	2	1	$ 2.00	$ 2.00
441	221	5	2	$ 2.00	$ 4.00
442	221	1	2	$ 3.00	$ 6.00
443	222	6	1	$ 3.00	$ 3.00
444	222	2	1	$ 2.00	$ 2.00
445	223	6	3	$ 3.00	$ 9.00
446	223	2	3	$ 2.00	$ 6.00
447	224	1	3	$ 1.50	$ 4.50
448	224	6	2	$ 3.00	$ 6.00
449	225	1	2	$ 1.50	$ 3.00
450	225	6	1	$ 3.00	$ 3.00
451	226	4	4	$ 2.00	$ 8.00
452	226	1	5	$ 2.00	$ 2.00
453	227	3	2	$ 1.50	$ 3.00
454	227	6	1	$ 3.00	$ 3.00
455	228	5	1	$ 2.00	$ 2.00
456	228	6	1	$ 3.00	$ 3.00
457	229	5	2	$ 2.00	$ 4.00
458	229	1	2	$ 3.00	$ 6.00
459	230	6	1	$ 3.00	$ 3.00
460	230	2	1	$ 2.00	$ 2.00
461	231	5	2	$ 2.00	$ 4.00
462	231	1	2	$ 3.00	$ 6.00
463	232	6	1	$ 3.00	$ 3.00
464	232	2	1	$ 2.00	$ 2.00
465	233	6	3	$ 3.00	$ 9.00
466	233	2	3	$ 2.00	$ 6.00
467	234	1	3	$ 1.50	$ 4.50
468	234	6	2	$ 3.00	$ 6.00
469	235	1	2	$ 1.50	$ 3.00
470	235	6	1	$ 3.00	$ 3.00
471	236	4	4	$ 2.00	$ 8.00

SaleItemID	SaleNo	ProductCode	QuantitySold	UnitPrice	ItemCost
472	236	1	5	$ 2.00	$ 2.00
473	237	3	2	$ 1.50	$ 3.00
474	237	6	1	$ 3.00	$ 3.00
475	238	5	1	$ 2.00	$ 2.00
476	238	6	1	$ 3.00	$ 3.00
477	239	5	2	$ 2.00	$ 4.00
478	239	1	2	$ 3.00	$ 6.00
479	240	6	1	$ 3.00	$ 3.00
480	240	2	1	$ 2.00	$ 2.00
481	241	5	2	$ 2.00	$ 4.00
482	241	1	2	$ 3.00	$ 6.00
483	242	6	1	$ 3.00	$ 3.00
484	242	2	1	$ 2.00	$ 2.00
485	243	6	3	$ 3.00	$ 9.00
486	243	2	3	$ 2.00	$ 6.00
487	244	1	3	$ 1.50	$ 4.50
488	244	6	2	$ 3.00	$ 6.00
489	245	1	2	$ 1.50	$ 3.00
490	245	6	1	$ 3.00	$ 3.00
491	246	4	4	$ 2.00	$ 8.00
492	246	1	5	$ 2.00	$ 2.00
493	247	3	2	$ 1.50	$ 3.00
494	247	6	1	$ 3.00	$ 3.00
495	248	5	1	$ 2.00	$ 2.00
496	248	6	1	$ 3.00	$ 3.00
497	249	5	2	$ 2.00	$ 4.00
498	249	1	2	$ 3.00	$ 6.00
499	250	6	1	$ 3.00	$ 3.00
500	250	2	1	$ 2.00	$ 2.00
501	251	5	2	$ 2.00	$ 4.00
502	251	1	2	$ 3.00	$ 6.00
503	252	6	1	$ 3.00	$ 3.00

SaleItemID	SaleNo	ProductCode	QuantitySold	UnitPrice	ItemCost
504	252	2	1	$ 2.00	$ 2.00
505	253	6	3	$ 3.00	$ 9.00
506	253	2	3	$ 2.00	$ 6.00
507	254	1	3	$ 1.50	$ 4.50
508	254	6	2	$ 3.00	$ 6.00
509	255	1	2	$ 1.50	$ 3.00
510	255	6	1	$ 3.00	$ 3.00
511	256	4	4	$ 2.00	$ 8.00
512	256	1	5	$ 2.00	$ 2.00
513	257	3	2	$ 1.50	$ 3.00
514	257	6	1	$ 3.00	$ 3.00
515	258	5	1	$ 2.00	$ 2.00
516	258	6	1	$ 3.00	$ 3.00
517	259	5	2	$ 2.00	$ 4.00
518	259	1	2	$ 3.00	$ 6.00
519	260	6	1	$ 3.00	$ 3.00
520	260	2	1	$ 2.00	$ 2.00
521	261	5	2	$ 2.00	$ 4.00
522	261	1	2	$ 3.00	$ 6.00
523	262	6	1	$ 3.00	$ 3.00
524	262	2	1	$ 2.00	$ 2.00
525	263	6	3	$ 3.00	$ 9.00
526	263	2	3	$ 2.00	$ 6.00
527	264	1	3	$ 1.50	$ 4.50
528	264	6	2	$ 3.00	$ 6.00
529	265	1	2	$ 1.50	$ 3.00
530	265	6	1	$ 3.00	$ 3.00
531	266	4	4	$ 2.00	$ 8.00
532	266	1	5	$ 2.00	$ 2.00
533	267	3	2	$ 1.50	$ 3.00
534	267	6	1	$ 3.00	$ 3.00
535	268	5	1	$ 2.00	$ 2.00

SaleItemID	SaleNo	ProductCode	QuantitySold	UnitPrice	ItemCost
536	268	6	1	$ 3.00	$ 3.00
537	269	5	2	$ 2.00	$ 4.00
538	269	1	2	$ 3.00	$ 6.00
539	270	6	1	$ 3.00	$ 3.00
540	270	2	1	$ 2.00	$ 2.00
541	271	5	2	$ 2.00	$ 4.00
542	271	1	2	$ 3.00	$ 6.00
543	272	6	1	$ 3.00	$ 3.00
544	272	2	1	$ 2.00	$ 2.00
545	273	6	3	$ 3.00	$ 9.00
546	273	2	3	$ 2.00	$ 6.00
547	274	1	3	$ 1.50	$ 4.50
548	274	6	2	$ 3.00	$ 6.00
549	275	1	2	$ 1.50	$ 3.00
550	275	6	1	$ 3.00	$ 3.00
551	276	4	4	$ 2.00	$ 8.00
552	276	1	5	$ 2.00	$ 2.00
553	277	3	2	$ 1.50	$ 3.00
554	277	6	1	$ 3.00	$ 3.00
555	278	5	1	$ 2.00	$ 2.00
556	278	6	1	$ 3.00	$ 3.00
557	279	5	2	$ 2.00	$ 4.00
558	279	1	2	$ 3.00	$ 6.00
559	280	6	1	$ 3.00	$ 3.00
560	280	2	1	$ 2.00	$ 2.00
561	281	5	2	$ 2.00	$ 4.00
562	281	1	2	$ 3.00	$ 6.00
563	282	6	1	$ 3.00	$ 3.00
564	282	2	1	$ 2.00	$ 2.00
565	283	6	3	$ 3.00	$ 9.00
566	283	2	3	$ 2.00	$ 6.00
567	284	1	3	$ 1.50	$ 4.50

SaleItemID	SaleNo	ProductCode	QuantitySold	UnitPrice	ItemCost
568	284	6	2	$ 3.00	$ 6.00
569	285	1	2	$ 1.50	$ 3.00
570	285	6	1	$ 3.00	$ 3.00
571	286	4	4	$ 2.00	$ 8.00
572	286	1	5	$ 2.00	$ 2.00
573	287	3	2	$ 1.50	$ 3.00
574	287	6	1	$ 3.00	$ 3.00
575	288	5	1	$ 2.00	$ 2.00
576	288	6	1	$ 3.00	$ 3.00
577	289	5	2	$ 2.00	$ 4.00
578	289	1	2	$ 3.00	$ 6.00
579	290	6	1	$ 3.00	$ 3.00
580	290	2	1	$ 2.00	$ 2.00
581	291	5	2	$ 2.00	$ 4.00
582	291	1	2	$ 3.00	$ 6.00
583	292	6	1	$ 3.00	$ 3.00
584	292	2	1	$ 2.00	$ 2.00
585	293	6	3	$ 3.00	$ 9.00
586	293	2	3	$ 2.00	$ 6.00
587	294	1	3	$ 1.50	$ 4.50
588	294	6	2	$ 3.00	$ 6.00
589	295	1	2	$ 1.50	$ 3.00
590	295	6	1	$ 3.00	$ 3.00
591	296	4	4	$ 2.00	$ 8.00
592	296	1	5	$ 2.00	$ 2.00
593	297	3	2	$ 1.50	$ 3.00
594	297	6	1	$ 3.00	$ 3.00
595	298	5	1	$ 2.00	$ 2.00
596	298	6	1	$ 3.00	$ 3.00
597	299	5	2	$ 2.00	$ 4.00
598	299	1	2	$ 3.00	$ 6.00
599	300	6	1	$ 3.00	$ 3.00

SaleItemID	SaleNo	ProductCode	QuantitySold	UnitPrice	ItemCost
600	300	2	1	$ 2.00	$ 2.00
601	301	5	2	$ 2.00	$ 4.00
602	301	1	2	$ 3.00	$ 6.00
603	302	6	1	$ 3.00	$ 3.00
604	302	2	1	$ 2.00	$ 2.00
605	303	6	3	$ 3.00	$ 9.00
606	303	2	3	$ 2.00	$ 6.00
607	304	1	3	$ 1.50	$ 4.50
608	304	6	2	$ 3.00	$ 6.00
609	305	1	2	$ 1.50	$ 3.00
610	305	6	1	$ 3.00	$ 3.00
611	306	4	4	$ 2.00	$ 8.00
612	306	1	5	$ 2.00	$ 2.00
613	307	3	2	$ 1.50	$ 3.00
614	307	6	1	$ 3.00	$ 3.00
615	308	5	1	$ 2.00	$ 2.00
616	308	6	1	$ 3.00	$ 3.00
617	309	5	2	$ 2.00	$ 4.00
618	309	1	2	$ 3.00	$ 6.00
619	310	6	1	$ 3.00	$ 3.00
620	310	2	1	$ 2.00	$ 2.00
621	311	5	2	$ 2.00	$ 4.00
622	311	1	2	$ 3.00	$ 6.00
623	312	6	1	$ 3.00	$ 3.00
624	312	2	1	$ 2.00	$ 2.00
625	313	6	3	$ 3.00	$ 9.00
626	313	2	3	$ 2.00	$ 6.00
627	314	1	3	$ 1.50	$ 4.50
628	314	6	2	$ 3.00	$ 6.00
629	315	1	2	$ 1.50	$ 3.00
630	315	6	1	$ 3.00	$ 3.00
631	316	4	4	$ 2.00	$ 8.00

SaleItemID	SaleNo	ProductCode	QuantitySold	UnitPrice	ItemCost
632	316	1	5	$ 2.00	$ 2.00
633	317	3	2	$ 1.50	$ 3.00
634	317	6	1	$ 3.00	$ 3.00
635	318	5	1	$ 2.00	$ 2.00
636	318	6	1	$ 3.00	$ 3.00
637	319	5	2	$ 2.00	$ 4.00
638	319	1	2	$ 3.00	$ 6.00
639	320	6	1	$ 3.00	$ 3.00
640	320	2	1	$ 2.00	$ 2.00
641	321	5	2	$ 2.00	$ 4.00
642	321	1	2	$ 3.00	$ 6.00
643	322	6	1	$ 3.00	$ 3.00
644	322	2	1	$ 2.00	$ 2.00
645	323	6	3	$ 3.00	$ 9.00
646	323	2	3	$ 2.00	$ 6.00
647	324	1	3	$ 1.50	$ 4.50
648	324	6	2	$ 3.00	$ 6.00
649	325	1	2	$ 1.50	$ 3.00
650	325	6	1	$ 3.00	$ 3.00
651	326	4	4	$ 2.00	$ 8.00
652	326	1	5	$ 2.00	$ 2.00
653	327	3	2	$ 1.50	$ 3.00
654	327	6	1	$ 3.00	$ 3.00
655	328	5	1	$ 2.00	$ 2.00
656	328	6	1	$ 3.00	$ 3.00
657	329	5	2	$ 2.00	$ 4.00
658	329	1	2	$ 3.00	$ 6.00
659	330	6	1	$ 3.00	$ 3.00
660	330	2	1	$ 2.00	$ 2.00
661	331	5	2	$ 2.00	$ 4.00
662	331	1	2	$ 3.00	$ 6.00
663	332	6	1	$ 3.00	$ 3.00

SaleItemID	SaleNo	ProductCode	QuantitySold	UnitPrice	ItemCost
664	332	2	1	$ 2.00	$ 2.00
665	333	6	3	$ 3.00	$ 9.00
666	333	2	3	$ 2.00	$ 6.00
667	334	1	3	$ 1.50	$ 4.50
668	334	6	2	$ 3.00	$ 6.00
669	335	1	2	$ 1.50	$ 3.00
670	335	6	1	$ 3.00	$ 3.00
671	336	4	4	$ 2.00	$ 8.00
672	336	1	5	$ 2.00	$ 2.00
673	337	3	2	$ 1.50	$ 3.00
674	337	6	1	$ 3.00	$ 3.00
675	338	5	1	$ 2.00	$ 2.00
676	338	6	1	$ 3.00	$ 3.00
677	339	5	2	$ 2.00	$ 4.00
678	339	1	2	$ 3.00	$ 6.00
679	340	6	1	$ 3.00	$ 3.00
680	340	2	1	$ 2.00	$ 2.00
681	341	5	2	$ 2.00	$ 4.00
682	341	1	2	$ 3.00	$ 6.00
683	342	6	1	$ 3.00	$ 3.00
684	342	2	1	$ 2.00	$ 2.00
685	343	6	3	$ 3.00	$ 9.00
686	343	2	3	$ 2.00	$ 6.00
687	344	1	3	$ 1.50	$ 4.50
688	344	6	2	$ 3.00	$ 6.00
689	345	1	2	$ 1.50	$ 3.00
690	345	6	1	$ 3.00	$ 3.00
691	346	4	4	$ 2.00	$ 8.00
692	346	1	5	$ 2.00	$ 2.00
693	347	3	2	$ 1.50	$ 3.00
694	347	6	1	$ 3.00	$ 3.00
695	348	5	1	$ 2.00	$ 2.00

SaleItemID	SaleNo	ProductCode	QuantitySold	UnitPrice	ItemCost
696	348	6	1	$ 3.00	$ 3.00
697	349	5	2	$ 2.00	$ 4.00
698	349	1	2	$ 3.00	$ 6.00
699	350	6	1	$ 3.00	$ 3.00
700	350	2	1	$ 2.00	$ 2.00
701	351	5	2	$ 2.00	$ 4.00
702	351	1	2	$ 3.00	$ 6.00
703	352	6	1	$ 3.00	$ 3.00
704	352	2	1	$ 2.00	$ 2.00
705	353	6	3	$ 3.00	$ 9.00
706	353	2	3	$ 2.00	$ 6.00
707	354	1	3	$ 1.50	$ 4.50
708	354	6	2	$ 3.00	$ 6.00
709	355	1	2	$ 1.50	$ 3.00
710	355	6	1	$ 3.00	$ 3.00
711	356	4	4	$ 2.00	$ 8.00
712	356	1	5	$ 2.00	$ 2.00
713	357	3	2	$ 1.50	$ 3.00
714	357	6	1	$ 3.00	$ 3.00
715	358	5	1	$ 2.00	$ 2.00
716	358	6	1	$ 3.00	$ 3.00
717	359	5	2	$ 2.00	$ 4.00
718	359	1	2	$ 3.00	$ 6.00
719	360	6	1	$ 3.00	$ 3.00
720	360	2	1	$ 2.00	$ 2.00
721	361	5	2	$ 2.00	$ 4.00
722	361	1	2	$ 3.00	$ 6.00
723	362	6	1	$ 3.00	$ 3.00
724	362	2	1	$ 2.00	$ 2.00
725	363	6	3	$ 3.00	$ 9.00
726	363	2	3	$ 2.00	$ 6.00
727	364	1	3	$ 1.50	$ 4.50

SaleItemID	SaleNo	ProductCode	QuantitySold	UnitPrice	ItemCost
728	364	6	2	$ 3.00	$ 6.00
729	365	1	2	$ 1.50	$ 3.00
730	365	6	1	$ 3.00	$ 3.00
731	366	4	4	$ 2.00	$ 8.00
732	366	1	5	$ 2.00	$ 2.00
733	367	3	2	$ 1.50	$ 3.00
734	367	6	1	$ 3.00	$ 3.00
735	368	5	1	$ 2.00	$ 2.00
736	368	6	1	$ 3.00	$ 3.00
737	369	5	2	$ 2.00	$ 4.00
738	369	1	2	$ 3.00	$ 6.00
739	370	6	1	$ 3.00	$ 3.00
740	370	2	1	$ 2.00	$ 2.00
741	371	5	2	$ 2.00	$ 4.00
742	371	1	2	$ 3.00	$ 6.00
743	372	6	1	$ 3.00	$ 3.00
744	372	2	1	$ 2.00	$ 2.00
745	373	6	3	$ 3.00	$ 9.00
746	373	2	3	$ 2.00	$ 6.00
747	374	1	3	$ 1.50	$ 4.50
748	374	6	2	$ 3.00	$ 6.00
749	375	1	2	$ 1.50	$ 3.00
750	375	6	1	$ 3.00	$ 3.00
751	376	4	4	$ 2.00	$ 8.00
752	376	1	5	$ 2.00	$ 2.00
753	377	3	2	$ 1.50	$ 3.00
754	377	6	1	$ 3.00	$ 3.00
755	378	5	1	$ 2.00	$ 2.00
756	378	6	1	$ 3.00	$ 3.00
757	379	5	2	$ 2.00	$ 4.00
758	379	1	2	$ 3.00	$ 6.00
759	380	6	1	$ 3.00	$ 3.00

SaleItemID	SaleNo	ProductCode	QuantitySold	UnitPrice	ItemCost
760	380	2	1	$ 2.00	$ 2.00
761	381	5	2	$ 2.00	$ 4.00
762	381	1	2	$ 3.00	$ 6.00
763	382	6	1	$ 3.00	$ 3.00
764	382	2	1	$ 2.00	$ 2.00
765	383	6	3	$ 3.00	$ 9.00
766	383	2	3	$ 2.00	$ 6.00
767	384	1	3	$ 1.50	$ 4.50
768	384	6	2	$ 3.00	$ 6.00
769	385	1	2	$ 1.50	$ 3.00
770	385	6	1	$ 3.00	$ 3.00
771	386	4	4	$ 2.00	$ 8.00
772	386	1	5	$ 2.00	$ 2.00
773	387	3	2	$ 1.50	$ 3.00
774	387	6	1	$ 3.00	$ 3.00
775	388	5	1	$ 2.00	$ 2.00
776	388	6	1	$ 3.00	$ 3.00
777	389	5	2	$ 2.00	$ 4.00
778	389	1	2	$ 3.00	$ 6.00
779	390	6	1	$ 3.00	$ 3.00
780	390	2	1	$ 2.00	$ 2.00
781	391	5	2	$ 2.00	$ 4.00
782	391	1	2	$ 3.00	$ 6.00
783	392	6	1	$ 3.00	$ 3.00
784	392	2	1	$ 2.00	$ 2.00
785	393	6	3	$ 3.00	$ 9.00
786	393	2	3	$ 2.00	$ 6.00
787	394	1	3	$ 1.50	$ 4.50
788	394	6	2	$ 3.00	$ 6.00
789	395	1	2	$ 1.50	$ 3.00
790	395	6	1	$ 3.00	$ 3.00
791	396	4	4	$ 2.00	$ 8.00

SaleItemID	SaleNo	ProductCode	QuantitySold	UnitPrice	ItemCost
792	396	1	5	$ 2.00	$ 2.00
793	397	3	2	$ 1.50	$ 3.00
794	397	6	1	$ 3.00	$ 3.00
795	398	5	1	$ 2.00	$ 2.00
796	398	6	1	$ 3.00	$ 3.00
797	399	5	2	$ 2.00	$ 4.00
798	399	1	2	$ 3.00	$ 6.00
799	400	6	1	$ 3.00	$ 3.00
800	400	2	1	$ 2.00	$ 2.00
801	401	5	2	$ 2.00	$ 4.00
802	401	1	2	$ 3.00	$ 6.00
803	402	6	1	$ 3.00	$ 3.00
804	402	2	1	$ 2.00	$ 2.00
805	403	6	3	$ 3.00	$ 9.00
806	403	2	3	$ 2.00	$ 6.00
807	404	1	3	$ 1.50	$ 4.50
808	404	6	2	$ 3.00	$ 6.00
809	405	1	2	$ 1.50	$ 3.00
810	405	6	1	$ 3.00	$ 3.00
811	406	4	4	$ 2.00	$ 8.00
812	406	1	5	$ 2.00	$ 2.00
813	407	3	2	$ 1.50	$ 3.00
814	407	6	1	$ 3.00	$ 3.00
815	408	5	1	$ 2.00	$ 2.00
816	408	6	1	$ 3.00	$ 3.00
817	409	5	2	$ 2.00	$ 4.00
818	409	1	2	$ 3.00	$ 6.00
819	410	6	1	$ 3.00	$ 3.00
820	410	2	1	$ 2.00	$ 2.00
821	411	5	2	$ 2.00	$ 4.00
822	411	1	2	$ 3.00	$ 6.00
823	412	6	1	$ 3.00	$ 3.00

SaleItemID	SaleNo	ProductCode	QuantitySold	UnitPrice	ItemCost
824	412	2	1	$ 2.00	$ 2.00
825	413	6	3	$ 3.00	$ 9.00
826	413	2	3	$ 2.00	$ 6.00
827	414	1	3	$ 1.50	$ 4.50
828	414	6	2	$ 3.00	$ 6.00
829	415	1	2	$ 1.50	$ 3.00
830	415	6	1	$ 3.00	$ 3.00
831	416	4	4	$ 2.00	$ 8.00
832	416	1	5	$ 2.00	$ 2.00
833	417	3	2	$ 1.50	$ 3.00
834	417	6	1	$ 3.00	$ 3.00
835	418	5	1	$ 2.00	$ 2.00
836	418	6	1	$ 3.00	$ 3.00
837	419	5	2	$ 2.00	$ 4.00
838	419	1	2	$ 3.00	$ 6.00
839	420	6	1	$ 3.00	$ 3.00
840	420	2	1	$ 2.00	$ 2.00
841	421	5	2	$ 2.00	$ 4.00
842	421	1	2	$ 3.00	$ 6.00
843	422	6	1	$ 3.00	$ 3.00
844	422	2	1	$ 2.00	$ 2.00
845	423	6	3	$ 3.00	$ 9.00
846	423	2	3	$ 2.00	$ 6.00
847	424	1	3	$ 1.50	$ 4.50
848	424	6	2	$ 3.00	$ 6.00
849	425	1	2	$ 1.50	$ 3.00
850	425	6	1	$ 3.00	$ 3.00
851	426	4	4	$ 2.00	$ 8.00
852	426	1	5	$ 2.00	$ 2.00
853	427	3	2	$ 1.50	$ 3.00
854	427	6	1	$ 3.00	$ 3.00
855	428	5	1	$ 2.00	$ 2.00

SaleItemID	SaleNo	ProductCode	QuantitySold	UnitPrice	ItemCost
856	428	6	1	$ 3.00	$ 3.00
857	429	5	2	$ 2.00	$ 4.00
858	429	1	2	$ 3.00	$ 6.00
859	430	6	1	$ 3.00	$ 3.00
860	430	2	1	$ 2.00	$ 2.00
861	431	5	2	$ 2.00	$ 4.00
862	431	1	2	$ 3.00	$ 6.00
863	432	6	1	$ 3.00	$ 3.00
864	432	2	1	$ 2.00	$ 2.00
865	433	6	3	$ 3.00	$ 9.00
866	433	2	3	$ 2.00	$ 6.00
867	434	1	3	$ 1.50	$ 4.50
868	434	6	2	$ 3.00	$ 6.00
869	435	1	2	$ 1.50	$ 3.00
870	435	6	1	$ 3.00	$ 3.00
871	436	4	4	$ 2.00	$ 8.00
872	436	1	5	$ 2.00	$ 2.00
873	437	3	2	$ 1.50	$ 3.00
874	437	6	1	$ 3.00	$ 3.00
875	438	5	1	$ 2.00	$ 2.00
876	438	6	1	$ 3.00	$ 3.00
877	439	5	2	$ 2.00	$ 4.00
878	439	1	2	$ 3.00	$ 6.00
879	440	6	1	$ 3.00	$ 3.00
880	440	2	1	$ 2.00	$ 2.00
881	441	5	2	$ 2.00	$ 4.00
882	441	1	2	$ 3.00	$ 6.00
883	442	6	1	$ 3.00	$ 3.00
884	442	2	1	$ 2.00	$ 2.00
885	443	6	3	$ 3.00	$ 9.00
886	443	2	3	$ 2.00	$ 6.00
887	444	1	3	$ 1.50	$ 4.50

SaleItemID	SaleNo	ProductCode	QuantitySold	UnitPrice	ItemCost
888	444	6	2	$ 3.00	$ 6.00
889	445	1	2	$ 1.50	$ 3.00
890	445	6	1	$ 3.00	$ 3.00
891	446	4	4	$ 2.00	$ 8.00
892	446	1	5	$ 2.00	$ 2.00
893	447	3	2	$ 1.50	$ 3.00
894	447	6	1	$ 3.00	$ 3.00
895	448	5	1	$ 2.00	$ 2.00
896	448	6	1	$ 3.00	$ 3.00
897	449	5	2	$ 2.00	$ 4.00
898	449	1	2	$ 3.00	$ 6.00
899	450	6	1	$ 3.00	$ 3.00
900	450	2	1	$ 2.00	$ 2.00
901	451	5	2	$ 2.00	$ 4.00
902	451	1	2	$ 3.00	$ 6.00
903	452	6	1	$ 3.00	$ 3.00
904	452	2	1	$ 2.00	$ 2.00
905	453	6	3	$ 3.00	$ 9.00
906	453	2	3	$ 2.00	$ 6.00
907	454	1	3	$ 1.50	$ 4.50
908	454	6	2	$ 3.00	$ 6.00
909	455	1	2	$ 1.50	$ 3.00
910	455	6	1	$ 3.00	$ 3.00
911	456	4	4	$ 2.00	$ 8.00
912	456	1	5	$ 2.00	$ 2.00
913	457	3	2	$ 1.50	$ 3.00
914	457	6	1	$ 3.00	$ 3.00
915	458	5	1	$ 2.00	$ 2.00
916	458	6	1	$ 3.00	$ 3.00
917	459	5	2	$ 2.00	$ 4.00
918	459	1	2	$ 3.00	$ 6.00
919	460	6	1	$ 3.00	$ 3.00

SaleItemID	SaleNo	ProductCode	QuantitySold	UnitPrice	ItemCost
920	460	2	1	$ 2.00	$ 2.00
921	461	5	2	$ 2.00	$ 4.00
922	461	1	2	$ 3.00	$ 6.00
923	462	6	1	$ 3.00	$ 3.00
924	462	2	1	$ 2.00	$ 2.00
925	463	6	3	$ 3.00	$ 9.00
926	463	2	3	$ 2.00	$ 6.00
927	464	1	3	$ 1.50	$ 4.50
928	464	6	2	$ 3.00	$ 6.00
929	465	1	2	$ 1.50	$ 3.00
930	465	6	1	$ 3.00	$ 3.00
931	466	4	4	$ 2.00	$ 8.00
932	466	1	5	$ 2.00	$ 2.00
933	467	3	2	$ 1.50	$ 3.00
934	467	6	1	$ 3.00	$ 3.00
935	468	5	1	$ 2.00	$ 2.00
936	468	6	1	$ 3.00	$ 3.00
937	469	5	2	$ 2.00	$ 4.00
938	469	1	2	$ 3.00	$ 6.00
939	470	6	1	$ 3.00	$ 3.00
940	470	2	1	$ 2.00	$ 2.00
941	471	5	2	$ 2.00	$ 4.00
942	471	1	2	$ 3.00	$ 6.00
943	472	6	1	$ 3.00	$ 3.00
944	472	2	1	$ 2.00	$ 2.00
945	473	6	3	$ 3.00	$ 9.00
946	473	2	3	$ 2.00	$ 6.00
947	474	1	3	$ 1.50	$ 4.50
948	474	6	2	$ 3.00	$ 6.00
949	475	1	2	$ 1.50	$ 3.00
950	475	6	1	$ 3.00	$ 3.00
951	476	4	4	$ 2.00	$ 8.00

SaleItemID	SaleNo	ProductCode	QuantitySold	UnitPrice	ItemCost
952	476	1	5	$ 2.00	$ 2.00
953	477	3	2	$ 1.50	$ 3.00
954	477	6	1	$ 3.00	$ 3.00
955	478	5	1	$ 2.00	$ 2.00
956	478	6	1	$ 3.00	$ 3.00
957	479	5	2	$ 2.00	$ 4.00
958	479	1	2	$ 3.00	$ 6.00
959	480	6	1	$ 3.00	$ 3.00
960	480	2	1	$ 2.00	$ 2.00
961	481	5	2	$ 2.00	$ 4.00
962	481	1	2	$ 3.00	$ 6.00
963	482	6	1	$ 3.00	$ 3.00
964	482	2	1	$ 2.00	$ 2.00
965	483	6	3	$ 3.00	$ 9.00
966	483	2	3	$ 2.00	$ 6.00
967	484	1	3	$ 1.50	$ 4.50
968	484	6	2	$ 3.00	$ 6.00
969	485	1	2	$ 1.50	$ 3.00
970	485	6	1	$ 3.00	$ 3.00
971	486	4	4	$ 2.00	$ 8.00
972	486	1	5	$ 2.00	$ 2.00
973	487	3	2	$ 1.50	$ 3.00
974	487	6	1	$ 3.00	$ 3.00
975	488	5	1	$ 2.00	$ 2.00
976	488	6	1	$ 3.00	$ 3.00
977	489	5	2	$ 2.00	$ 4.00
978	489	1	2	$ 3.00	$ 6.00
979	490	6	1	$ 3.00	$ 3.00
980	490	2	1	$ 2.00	$ 2.00
981	491	5	2	$ 2.00	$ 4.00
982	491	1	2	$ 3.00	$ 6.00
983	492	6	1	$ 3.00	$ 3.00

SaleItemID	SaleNo	ProductCode	QuantitySold	UnitPrice	ItemCost
984	492	2	1	$ 2.00	$ 2.00
985	493	6	3	$ 3.00	$ 9.00
986	493	2	3	$ 2.00	$ 6.00
987	494	1	3	$ 1.50	$ 4.50
988	494	6	2	$ 3.00	$ 6.00
989	495	1	2	$ 1.50	$ 3.00
990	495	6	1	$ 3.00	$ 3.00
991	496	4	4	$ 2.00	$ 8.00
992	496	1	5	$ 2.00	$ 2.00
993	497	3	2	$ 1.50	$ 3.00
994	497	6	1	$ 3.00	$ 3.00
995	498	5	1	$ 2.00	$ 2.00
996	498	6	1	$ 3.00	$ 3.00
997	499	5	2	$ 2.00	$ 4.00
998	499	1	2	$ 3.00	$ 6.00

NOTE: This table contains 1,280 records, but because of space constraints, we've shown only 998 here. You can see the remaining records on the Osborne Web site at **www.osborne.com**.

APPENDIX F

Bibliography and Recommended Readings

DATA MODELING

Database Design for Mere Mortals, by Michael J. Hernandez. Addison-Wesley, 1997. ISBN 0-20-169471-9.

Database Modeling & Design, Third Edition, by Toby J. Teorey. Morgan Kaufmann Publishers, Inc., 1999. ISBN 1-55-860500-2.

The Data Model Resource Book: A Library of Logical Data Models and Data Warehouse Designs, by Len Silverston, William H. Inmon, and Kent Graziano. Wiley Computer Publishing, 1997. ISBN 0-47-115364-8.

The Data Warehouse Lifecycle Toolkit, by Ralph Kimball, Laura Reeves, Margy Ross, and Warren Thornthwaite. Wiley Computer Publishing, 1998. ISBN 0-47-125547-5.

DATABASE AND SYSTEMS FOUNDATIONS

Client/Server Survival Guide, Third Edition, by Robert Orfali, Dan Harkey and Jeri Edwards. Wiley Computer Publishing, 1999. ISBN 0-47-131615-6.

Database System Concepts, by Abraham Silberschatz, Henry F. Korth, and S. Sudarshan. WCB/McGraw-Hill, 1999. ISBN 0-07-031086-6.

Modern Database Management, Fifth Edition, by Fred R. McFadden, Jeffrey A. Hoffer, and Mary B. Prescott. Addison-Wesley, 1999. ISBN 0-80-536054-9.

SQL Server 7 Books Online, Microsoft Corporation, 1998.

SQL Server 2000 Books Online, Microsoft Corporation, 2000.

Systems Analysis and Design Methods, Fourth Edition, by Jeffrey L. Whitten, Lonnie D. Bentley, and Kevin C. Dittman. Irwin/McGraw-Hill, 1998. ISBN 0-25-619906-X.

PRIVACY AND SECURITY

Database Nation: The Death of Privacy in the 21st Century, by Simson Garfinkel. O'Reilly & Associates, 2000. ISBN 1-56592-653-6.

Our Vanishing Privacy, by Robert Ellis Smith. Breakout Productions, 1993. ISBN 1-89-362601-6.

The End of Privacy, by Charles J. Sykes. St. Martin's Press, 1999. ISBN 0-31-220350-0.

SQL PROGRAMMING

SQL 3: Implementing the SQL Foundation Standard, by Paul J. Fortier. Osborne/McGraw-Hill, 1999. ISBN 0-07-022062-X.

SQL Instant Reference, by Martin Gruber. Sybex, Inc., 1993. ISBN 0-78-211148-3.

SQL Server 2000 Stored Procedure Programming (Database Pro Library), by Dejan Sunderic and Tom Woodhead. Osborne/McGraw-Hill, 2000. ISBN 0-07-212566-7

SQL SERVER INTERNALS AND ADMINISTRATION

Inside Microsoft SQL Server 7.0, by Ron Soukup and Kalen Delaney. Microsoft Press, 1999. ISBN 0-73-560517-3.

SQL Server 6.5 Unleashed, Second Edition, by David Solomon, Ray Rankins, et al. SAMs Publishing, 1996. ISBN 0-67-230956-4.

BOOKS IN THE OSBORNE/MCGRAW-HILL SQL SERVER 2000 SERIES

SQL Server 2000: A Beginner's Guide, by Dusan Petrovic. ISBN 0-07-212587-X.

SQL Server 2000 Administration, by Mark Linsenbardt and Shane Stigler. ISBN 0-07-212618-3.

SQL Server 2000 Backup and Recovery, by Anil Desai. ISBN 0-07-213027-X.

SQL Server 2000 Design and T-SQL Programming, by Michael Reilly and Michelle Poolet. ISBN 0-07-212375-3.

SQL Server 2000 Developer's Guide, by Michael Otey and Paul Conte. ISBN 0-07-212569-1.

SQL Server 2000 Stored Procedure Programming, by Dejan Sunderic and Tom Woodhead. ISBN 0-07-212566-7.

SQL Server 2000: The Complete Reference, by Jeffrey Shapiro. ISBN 0-07-212588-8.

SQL Server 2000 Web Application Developer's Guide, by Craig Utley. ISBN 0-07-212610-1.

AUTHOR LISTING

Microsoft Corporation, *SQL Server 7 Books Online*, 1998.

Microsoft Corporation, *SQL Server 2000 Books Online*, 2000.

Desai, Anil. *SQL Server 2000 Backup and Recovery*, Osborne/McGraw-Hill, 2000.

Fortier, Paul. *SQL 3: Implementing the SQL Foundation Standard*, McGraw-Hill, 1999.

Garfinkel, Simson. *Database Nation: The Death of Privacy in the 21st Century*, O'Reilly & Associates, 2000.

Gruber, Martin. *SQL Instant Reference*, Sybex, Inc., 1993.

Hernandez, Michael J. *Database Design for Mere Mortals*, Addison-Wesley, 1997.

Kimball, Ralph, Laura Reeves, Margy Ross, and Warren Thornthwaite. *The Data Warehouse Lifecycle Toolkit*, Wiley Computer Publishing, 1998.

Linsenbardt, Mark, and Shane Stigler. (2000) *SQL Server 2000 Administration*, Osborne/McGraw-Hill.

McFadden, Fred R., Jeffrey A. Hoffer, and Mary B. Prescott. *Modern Database Management, Fifth Edition*, Addison-Wesley, 1999.

Orfali, Robert, Dan Harkey, and Jeri Edwards. *Client/Server Survival Guide, Third Edition*, Wiley Computer Publishing, 1999.

Otey, Michael, and Paul Conte. *SQL Server 2000 Developer's Guide*, Osborne/McGraw-Hill, 2001.

Petrovic, Dusan. *SQL Server 2000: A Beginner's Guide*, Osborne/McGraw-Hill, 2000.

Reilly, Michael, and Michelle Poolet. *SQL Server 2000 Design and T-SQL Programming*, Osborne/McGraw-Hill, 2001.

Shapiro, Jeffrey. *SQL Server 2000: The Complete Reference*, Osborne/McGraw-Hill, 2000.

Silberschatz, Abraham, Henry F. Korth, and S. Sudarshan. *Database System Concepts*, WCB/McGraw-Hill, 1999.

Silverston, Len, William H. Inmon, and Kent Graziano. *The Data Model Resource Book: A Library of Logical Data Models and Data Warehouse Designs*, Wiley Computer Publishing, 1997.

Smith, Robert Ellis. *Our Vanishing Privacy*, Breakout Productions, 1993.

Solomon, David, Ray Rankins, et al. *SQL Server 6.5 Unleashed, Second Edition*, SAMs Publishing, 1996.

Soukup, Ron, and Kalen Delaney. *Inside Microsoft SQL Server 7.0*, Microsoft Press, 1999.

Sunderic, Dejan, and Tom Woodhead. *SQL Server 2000 Stored Procedure Programming (Database Pro Library)*, Osborne/McGraw-Hill, 2000.

Sykes, Charles J. *The End of Privacy*, St. Martin's Press, 1999.

Teorey, Toby J. *Database Modeling and Design, Third Edition*, Morgan Kaufmann Publishers, Inc., 1999

Utley, Craig. *SQL Server 2000 Web Application Developer's Guide*, Osborne/McGraw-Hill, 2000.

Whitten, Jeffrey L., Lonnie D. Bentley, and Kevin C. Dittman. *Systems Analysis and Design Methods, Fourth Edition*, Irwin/McGraw-Hill, 1998.

Index

Symbols

A

B

C

D

E

F

G

H

I

J

L

M

N

O

P

Q

R

S

T

U

V

W

X

Z